iOS 7 Development Recipes

A Problem-Solution Approach

Joseph Hoffman
Hans-Eric Grönlund
Colin Francis
Shawn Grimes

Apress·

iOS 7 Development Recipes: A Problem-Solution Approach

ISBN-13 (pbk): 978-1-4302-5959-6

ISBN-13 (electronic): 978-1-4302-5960-2

President and Publisher: Paul Manning
Lead Editor: Barbara McGuire
Technical Reviewer: Matthew Knott
Editorial Board: Steve Anglin, Mark Beckner, Ewan Buckingham, Gary Cornell, Louise Corrigan, Morgan Ertel, Jonathan Gennick, Jonathan Hassell, Robert Hutchinson, Michelle Lowman, James Markham, Matthew Moodie, Jeff Olson, Jeffrey Pepper, Douglas Pundick, Ben Renow-Clarke, Dominic Shakeshaft, Gwenan Spearing, Matt Wade, Tom Welsh
Coordinating Editors: Katie Sullivan and Kevin Shea
Copy Editors: April Rondeau and Kim Wimpsett
Compositor: SPi Global
Indexer: SPi Global
Artist: SPi Global
Cover Designer: Anna Ishchenko

Distributed to the book trade worldwide by Springer Science+Business Media New York, 233 Spring Street, 6th Floor, New York, NY 10013. Phone 1-800-SPRINGER, fax (201) 348-4505, e-mail orders-ny@springer-sbm.com, or visit www.springeronline.com. Apress Media, LLC is a California LLC and the sole member (owner) is Springer Science + Business Media Finance Inc (SSBM Finance Inc). SSBM Finance Inc is a Delaware corporation.

For information on translations, please e-mail rights@apress.com, or visit www.apress.com.

Apress and friends of ED books may be purchased in bulk for academic, corporate, or promotional use. eBook versions and licenses are also available for most titles. For more information, reference our Special Bulk Sales–eBook Licensing web page at www.apress.com/bulk-sales.

Any source code or other supplementary materials referenced by the author in this text is available to readers at www.apress.com. For detailed information about how to locate your book's source code, go to www.apress.com/source-code/.

I dedicate this book to Amanda, my friends, and my family.

—Joe Hoffman

Contents at a Glance

Contents

About the Authors

Joseph Hoffman is an electrical engineer who does freelance web and iOS development in his spare time. In 2012 he started NSCookbook.com, which is an iOS programming tutorial site that provides tutorials in recipe format.

Hans-Eric Grönlund has developed software professionally since 1990. He's currently an employee at Knowit, a leading Scandinavian IT consultancy company, where he helps teams develop software with agile methods.

Software development is not only Hans-Eric's profession; it's also his hobby. In his spare time, he has taught himself how to write programs in many different languages on various platforms. His latest passion, obviously, is Objective-C on iOS. Hans-Eric's Twitter ID is @hansEricG.

Colin Francis is an iOS developer originally from Maryland. After studying iOS development with the assistance of Shawn Grimes, the two of them authored iOS 5 Recipes (Apress). He currently lives in Miami, where he works primarily on music-based applications for iOS.

Shawn Grimes and his wife, Stephanie, run Campfire Apps, LLC, a mobile app development company focused on apps for children and families. Together, they have started the APPlied Club program, which teaches mobile app development to high school students. Shawn is active in the Baltimore, Maryland, development scene and co-runs the Baltimore Mobile Developers group with Chris Stone.

About the Technical Reviewer

Matthew Knott has over 15 years of experience in software development and now leads a team of developers building ground-breaking software for the education sector. He is a lover of all things C-based and is an experienced C, C#, and Objective-C programmer.

Matthew took his passion for developing software that makes life easier and applied it to making iOS apps about four years ago, going on to release a number of apps. A real iOS development enthusiast and lover of all things Xcode, Matthew can regularly be found evangelizing about its virtues on Twitter or on his blog at www.mattknott.com.

More than anything else, he enjoys spending time with his wife and two children in a beautiful part of Wales, United Kingdom.

Acknowledgments

First, I'd like to thank the authors of the previous edition—Hans-Eric Grönlund, Colin Francis, and Shawn Grimes—for providing a great foundation to build on. Not only did it help me write this book, it taught me a ton as well.

I'd like to thank my buddy, Mike, for inspiring me to learn iOS and for helping me learn and sort out the tough problems.

The Apress team has been awesome throughout this project. Big thanks to Katie Sullivan and Kevin Shea for curbing my procrastination; Barbara McGuire, for her encouragement and amazing feedback; Matthew Knott, for all the time spent reviewing code and keeping me honest; and finally, April Rondeau and Kim Wimpsett for correcting my countless capitalization and grammar errors.

I'd like to thank Amanda, my friends, and my family for their understanding and support along the way. I know I've been a hermit; I'll make it up to you all.

—Joe Hoffman

Introduction

The easy part of software development is knowing how to write code in the programming language at hand. The tougher part is mastering the programming interfaces of the platform and getting to the level where you can effectively turn ideas into working features with real values. iOS 7, although extremely powerful and easy to use, is no exception to this. Objective-C, considered by many to be a somewhat "funky" programming language, is a language you can get your head around quickly and even learn to appreciate. However, you're likely to spend a lot of time learning the various APIs and frameworks.

We believe the best way to acquire the necessary knowledge and reach a plateau of high productivity is through hands-on experience. We think the best way to learn is to follow step-by-step procedures, creating small projects in which you can test and tweak the features and get a feel for them before you implement them in your real projects.

With this idea in mind, we created *iOS 7 Development Recipes*. This book contains over 600 pages of sample code accompanied by instructions about how to create small test apps that allow you to run the code on your iOS 7 device or in the iOS simulator.

We have tried to cover as many topics as possible based on the features of iOS 7. We hope this book provides the fundamentals you need to start converting your great ideas into fantastic apps.

Who This Book Is For

When you read this book, it will help if you have a basic knowledge of Objective-C, have taken your first steps in Xcode, and have written a couple of Hello World apps. If you haven't, don't worry; simply pay extra attention to the first eight recipes of Chapter 1. They should provide most of the basics you will need in order to follow along with the recipes in the rest of the book.

How This Book Is Structured

For the most part, the example-based chapters of this book do not build on one another; that is, you do not have to read the chapters sequentially. You should be able to read the chapters and build your apps in any order you want, depending on your specific interests. Whenever we do build on an example from a different chapter, we will let you know.

However, we recommend that you at least skim Chapter 1, "Application Recipes," then Chapter 2, "Storyboard Recipes," and finally Chapter 3, "Layout Recipes," before moving on.

The first chapter contains recipes for common tasks, such as creating outlets and actions, which are referenced throughout the book and should be fully understood before you move ahead.

The second chapter covers storyboards. Storyboards are an alternative way of building user interfaces. Storyboards show both the individual screens (single view controllers) and the connections (segues) between them. Before the introduction of storyboards in iOS 5, .xib files were typically used to build the interface. The .xib files were individual scenes; that is, one .xib file per scene. The connections between .xib files were handled in code. While you still have the ability to use .xib files, it is clear that Apple is pushing developers more and more to use storyboards instead.

The third chapter provides basic knowledge of the layout tools for iOS 7. Reading that chapter might be helpful when you create the user interfaces of the recipes later, especially if you want your scenes to look good on multiple devices.

This book uses a mix of programmatic interface building, storyboards, and .xib files. For the most part, you will start every application with a single view application template for the iPhone that will include a storyboard. We will instruct you otherwise if this is not the case.

Throughout this book, we assume you are developing in the latest versions of iOS and Xcode, which at the time of writing are iOS 7.0 and Xcode 5.0.

Many of the recipes in this book cannot be fully tested on the iOS simulator, and as such will require both an iOS device and a provisioning profile, which you can acquire when you subscribe to the iOS Developer Program. At the time of this writing, the developer program costs $99.00 USD. We've pointed out each recipe that cannot be tested in the iOS simulator.

Note   Since the introduction of iPhone 5, there are two screen sizes to account for: the 3.5" screen and the 4" screen. The width in both screens is the same, but the 4" screen is taller. Most of the interfaces in this book are laid out to look good on a 3.5" screen and will have unused space if run on a 4" screen. Feel free to modify the interface to better fit a 4" screen if that is what you want. Chapter 3 discusses Auto Layout, which will give you the tools to make an interface look good on either size screen.

What's New in This Edition

By now you undoubtedly have seen the fresh look of iOS 7. Because of the new software, we've made numerous changes to the images and code we provided in the previous edition of this book, *iOS 6 Recipes: A Problem-Solution Approach*. While we couldn't address everything iOS 7 has to offer in this new edition, we tried to add some topics we found very useful to the average developer.

Because iOS 7 is a major overhaul in design, all the images and figures have been updated to reflect the new design. Apple has made numerous minor changes to existing APIs for iOS 7. We updated the code in this book to reflect those changes.

Due to Apple's added emphasis on storyboards, we have changed the examples in this book to take advantage of storyboards rather than .xib files. Previous editions of this book were largely based on .xib files. In addition, we created a new chapter for storyboards (Chapter 2), which now includes instructions for creating tab view controllers.

Auto Layout has changed with iOS 7, so we have updated Chapter 3 to reflect these changes. Auto Layout constraints no longer exist for the developer. This greatly increases developer freedom and flexibility.

Apple added nice features to the Map Kit framework, which allow you to get directions from Apple as well as take full advantage of 3-D map support. We have included recipes that show you how to use both of these new features in Chapter 7.

iOS 7 gives us the ability to detect and read QR codes with the camera natively. We added a new recipe to Chapter 9, "Camera Recipes," that shows how to read QR codes.

We also added Chapter 12, which focuses on Core Graphics. While the previous edition touched on Core Graphics, we have expanded the content in its own chapter.

The most exciting contribution to this new edition is a new chapter on animation (Chapter 13). This chapter introduces some UIView animation basics and then moves on to the new UIKit Dynamics framework. This framework allows for realistic, physics-inspired animation.

Downloading the Code

The code for the examples included in this book is available on the Apress web site at www.apress.com. You can find a link on the book's information page under the Source Code/Downloads tab. This tab is located under the Related Titles section of the page.

Contacting the Author

If you have any questions or comments regarding this book, I would be happy to hear them. Contact me at NSCookbook@gmail.com and include "iOS 7 Recipes" in the subject line, or write a comment on my blog at http://www.NSCookbook.com.

Chapter 1

Application Recipes

This chapter serves as both a refresher for creating apps for iOS and a foundation for completing the basic tasks that are repeated throughout this book. The first eight recipes walk you through fundamental tasks such as setting up an application, connecting and referencing user interface elements in your code, and adding images and sound files to your project. The knowledge you will acquire from the recipes in this chapter is necessary to complete many of the tasks in the other chapters of this book.

The last four recipes in this chapter deal with select, useful tasks such as setting up simple APIs for default error and exception handling, including a "lite" version of your app in your projects, and making an app launch seem quick and easy in the eyes of the user. For the most part, these tasks won't be repeated in the remainder of this book; however, we feel they are essential knowledge for any developer.

Recipe 1-1: Setting Up a Single View Application

Many of the recipes in this book are implemented in a test application with a single view. Such a project is easy to set up in Xcode using the Single View Application template. This template enables you to use storyboards.

A storyboard is a way to build interfaces consisting of multiple scenes and their connections. Before the introduction of storyboards in iOS 5, .xib files were typically used to build the interface for individual scenes; in other words, there was one .xib file per scene. The connections between .xib files were handled in code. While you still have the ability to use .xib files, Apple is pushing developers to use storyboards instead. As such, you will be using storyboards for most of this book.

To create a new single view application, go to the main menu and select File ➤ New ➤ Project. This brings up the dialog box with available project templates (see Figure 1-1). The template you want is located on the Application page under the iOS section. Choose "Single View Application" and click "Next."

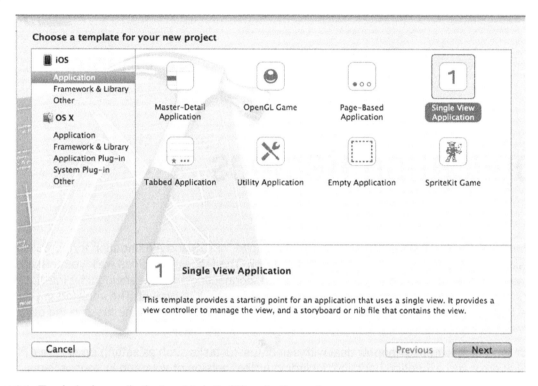

Figure 1-1. The single view application template in the iOS application section

Enter a few properties for your Application recipes:

■   A *Product Name*, such as **My Test App**

■   An *Organization Name*, which can be your name, unless you already have an organization name

■   A *Company Identifier*, which preferably is your Internet domain, if you have one

If you like, you can also enter a class prefix that will be applied to all classes you create using the Objective-C file template. This can be a good idea if you want to avoid future name conflicts with third-party code; however, if this app is meant only for testing a feature, you can leave the class prefix item blank.

You also need to specify which device type your application is for: iPad, iPhone, or both (Universal). Choose iPhone or iPad if you are testing. You can also pick Universal, but then the template will generate more code, which you probably don't need if your only purpose is trying a new feature. Figure 1-2 shows the properties you need to fill out in the project options window.

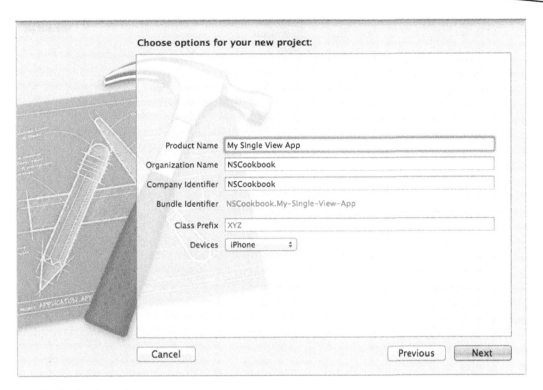

Figure 1-2. Configuring the project

Click the "Next" button and then select a folder where the project will be stored. Bear in mind that Xcode creates a new folder for the project within the folder you pick, so select the root folder for your projects.

There's often a good reason to place the project under *version control*. It allows you to check changes to the code so you can go back to a previous version if something goes wrong or if you simply want to see the history of changes to the application. Xcode comes with Git, a feature-rich, open-source version-control system that allows multiple developers to work on a project simultaneously with ease. To initialize it for your project, check the "Create local git repository for this project" checkbox, as in Figure 1-3. As of Xcode 5, you can specify a server as well as your Mac for this repository.

Figure 1-3. Selecting the parent folder for the project

Now click the "Create" button. An application with an app delegate, a storyboard, and a view controller class will be generated for you (see Figure 1-4).

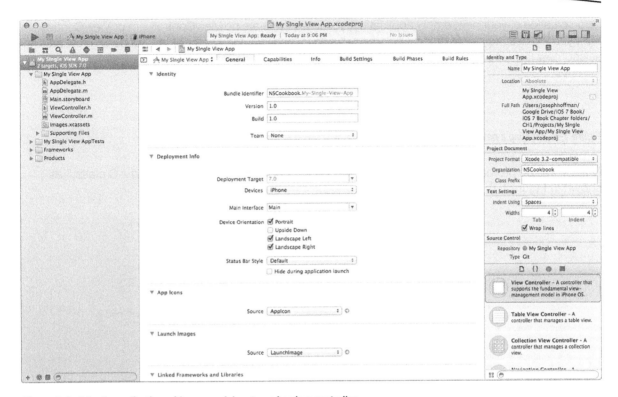

Figure 1-4. A basic application with an app delegate and a view controller

The setup is now complete, and you can build and run the application (which at this point shows only a blank screen).

At this point, you have a good foundation on which you can build for the next seven recipes.

An Alternate Way

Whether or not to use storyboards is a topic of debate among developers. Some developers love storyboards, while others dislike them. As a developer, it is likely you will work on projects that don't use storyboards or that use a mix of .xib files and storyboards. We won't argue for or against storyboards, but many developers tend to agree that storyboards can present difficulties when using version control and when multiple developers need to work on the same storyboard. With this in mind, it might be beneficial to learn the .xib approach. Learning this approach is entirely optional, so you can move on to Recipe 1-2 if you choose.

To create an empty application and add a ViewController class with an accompanying .xib file, you first need to create a new project. Choose "Empty Application" instead of "Single View Application" (refer to Figure 1-1) and then click "Next."

The next screen will look almost the same as Figure 1-2. This time, there will be a new check box called "Use Core Data." Leave it cleared and click "Next." Again, you'll be prompted for a save location. Find a suitable location to save and click "Create."

Upon creation of your new, empty application, you'll see there are no ViewController.m or ViewController.h files; you will need to create those. Click the "+" sign in the lower-left corner of the Xcode window and select "new file" (see Figure 1-5). You can also press Cmd + N.

Figure 1-5. *Creating a new file in Xcode*

Next, you'll be prompted to choose a template for your new file. Choose "Objective-C class," as shown in Figure 1-6.

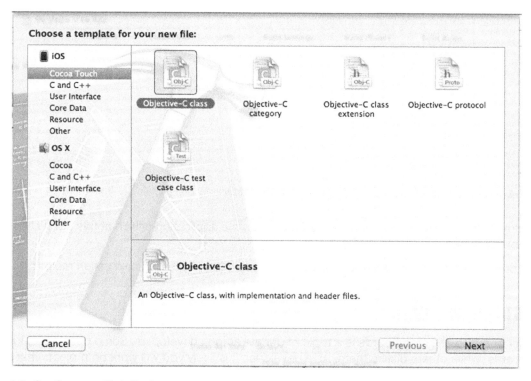

Figure 1-6. *Creating a new file in Xcode*

You will be prompted for file options. Give your new class the name of "ViewController" and choose "UIViewController" from the drop-down box (see Figure 1-7). Make sure you select the "With XIB for user interface" check box. Click "Next."

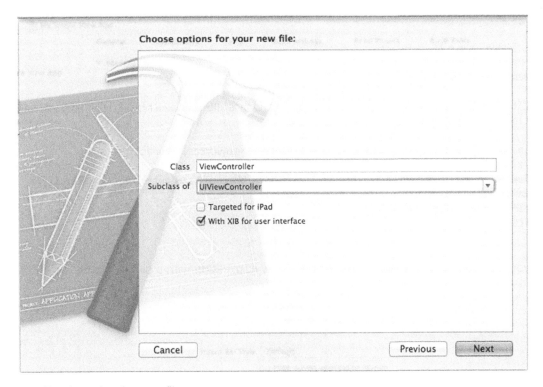

Figure 1-7. Choosing options for a new file

Now that you have created the class, you will need to select the AppDelegate.m and AppDelegate.h files from the Project Navigator on the left and then modify the code, as shown in Listing 1-1.

Listing 1-1. Adding properties to the single view AppDelegate.h file

AppDelegate.h

```
#import <UIKit/UIKit.h>

@class ViewController;
#import "ViewController.h"

@interface AppDelegate : UIResponder<UIApplicationDelegate>

@property (strong, nonatomic) UIWindow *window;
@property (strong, nonatomic) ViewController *viewController;

@end
```

AppDelegate.m

```
#import "AppDelegate.h"

@implementation AppDelegate

- (BOOL)Application recipes:(UIApplication *)application didFinishLaunchingWithOptions:
(NSDictionary *)launchOptions
{
self.window = [[UIWindowalloc] initWithFrame:[[UIScreenmainScreen] bounds]];
// Override point for customization after application launch.
self.viewController = [[ViewControlleralloc] initWithNibName:@"ViewController" bundle:nil];
self.window.rootViewController = self.viewController;
    [self.windowmakeKeyAndVisible];
returnYES;
}
```

Once you are finished, you should have a single view application with a single .xib file, as shown in Figure 1-8.

Figure 1-8. A single view application with the .xib approach

Recipe 1-2: Linking a Framework

The iOS operating system is organized into *frameworks*. A framework is a directory of code libraries and resources that are needed to support the library. To use the functionalities of a framework, you need to link the corresponding binary to your project. For UIKit, Foundation, and CoreGraphics frameworks, Xcode does this automatically when you create a new project. However, many important features and functions reside in frameworks such as CoreMotion, CoreData, MapKit, and so on. For these types of frameworks, you need to follow the following steps to add them:

1. Select the project node (the root node) in the project navigator panel on the left of the Xcode project window (Figure 1-4). This brings up the project editor panel.

2. Select the target in the Targets dock, as shown on the left of Figure 1-9. If you have more than one target, such as a unit test target, you need to perform these steps for each of them.

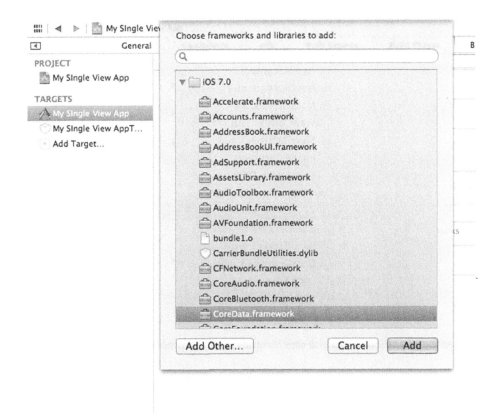

Figure 1-9. Adding the Core Data framework

3. Navigate to the Build Phases tab and expand the Link Binary with Libraries section. There you will see a list of the currently linked frameworks. Alternatively, you can scroll to the bottom of the page under the General tab.

4. Click the "Add items (+)" button at the bottom of the list. This brings up a list of available frameworks.

5. Select the framework you want to link and use the "Add" button to include it (see Figure 1-9).

Tip   To make it easier to find a particular framework, you can use the search field to filter the list.

When you add a framework to your project, a corresponding framework reference node is placed in your project tree (see Figure 1-10).

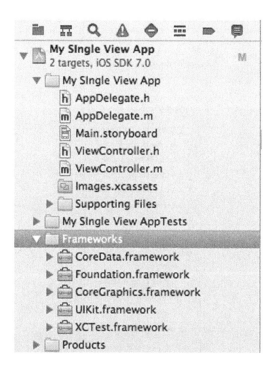

Figure 1-10. When adding a framework, a reference node is created inside the framework group of your process tree

Now, to use the functions and classes from within your code, you only need to import the framework. This is normally done in a header file (.h) within your project, as shown in Listing 1-2, where we import CoreData in the ViewController.h file.

Listing 1-2. Importing the CoreData framework

```
//
//  ViewController.h
//  My Single View App
//
```

```
#import <UIKit/UIKit.h>
#import <CoreData/CoreData.h>

@interface ViewController : UIViewController

@end
```

> **Note**   If you don't know the header file for a framework, don't worry. All framework APIs follow the same pattern, namely #import <FrameworkName/FrameworkName.h>.

With the framework binary linked and the API imported, you can start using its functions and classes in your code.

Recipe 1-3: Adding a User Interface Control View

iOS provides a number of built-in control views, such as buttons, labels, text fields, and so on, that you can use to compose your user interface. Xcode makes designing user interfaces easy with a built-in editor, Interface Builder. Interface Builder is a graphical editor, which allows you to edit both .xib files and storyboards by dragging and dropping components. All you need to do is to drag the controls you want from the object library and position them the way you want in your view. The editor helps you make a pleasing user interface by snapping to standard spaces.

In this recipe, we'll show you how to add a system button to your view. A system button is a button with default iOS styling. We'll assume you've already created a single view application in which to try this.

To create a new button, select the Main.storyboard file to bring up storyboard. Be sure the Utilities View (the panel on the right) is visible. If it isn't, select the corresponding button in the toolbar (see Figure 1-11).

Figure 1-11. The button to hide or show the Utilities View is located in the upper-right corner of Xcode

Make sure the object library is visible in the Utilities View (lower-right corner of Xcode). Click the "Show the Object Library" button (see Figure 1-12) if it isn't.

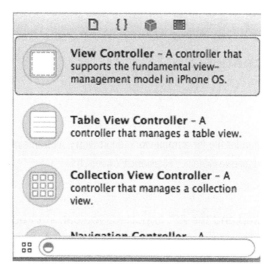

Figure 1-12. *The object library contains the built-in user interface controls*

Now locate the button in the Object Library and drag it onto the view. Blue guidelines will help you center it, as shown in Figure 1-13.

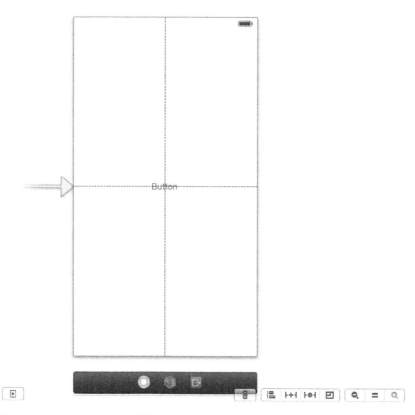

Figure 1-13. *Dragging a system button from the Object Library*

Change the text either by double-clicking the button or by setting the corresponding attribute in the attributes inspector, as shown in Figure 1-14. In the attributes inspector, you can also change other attributes, such as color or font. In previous versions of iOS, a button has a border. The new design philosophy set forth by Apple in iOS 7 embraces borderless buttons.

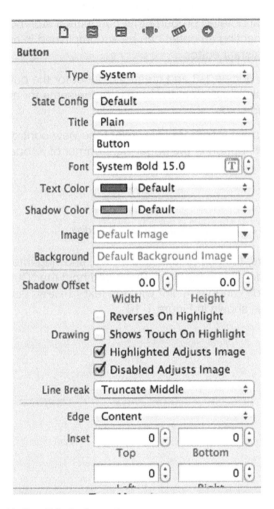

Figure 1-14. Setting the button text in the attributes inspector

You can now build and run your application. Your button shows, but it won't respond if you tap it. For that, you need to connect it to your code by means of outlets and actions, which are the topics of the next two recipes.

Recipe 1-4: Creating an Outlet

iOS is built on the Model-View-Controller design pattern. One effect of this is that the views are completely separated from the code that operates on the views (the so-called controllers). To reference a view from a view controller, you need to create an *outlet* in your controller and hook it up with the view. An outlet is an annotated property that connects a storyboard object to a class so you can reference it in code. Connecting an outlet can be accomplished in many different ways, but the simplest is to use Xcode's assistant editor.

We'll build on what you did in Recipe 1-3 and create an outlet for the button. Although the referenced view in this example is a button, the steps are the same for any other type of view, be it a label, text field, table view, and so on.

To create an outlet, open the main.storyboard file, select the view controller that contains the button, and click the "Assistant Editor" button in the upper-right corner of Xcode (see Figure 1-15.)

Figure 1-15. *The center button in the editor group activates the assistant editor*

With the assistant editor active, the edit area is split in two, showing Interface Builder on the left and the view controller's header file on the right. Press and hold the "Ctrl" key while dragging a blue line from the button to the code window. A hint with the text "Insert Outlet, Action, or Outlet Collection" should appear, as shown in Figure 1-16.

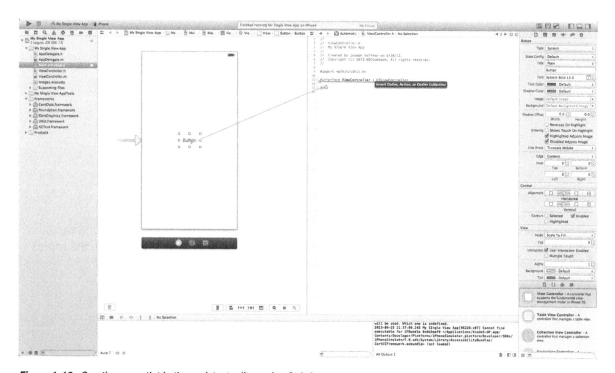

Figure 1-16. *Creating an outlet in the assistant editor using Ctrl-drag*

> **Note**   Because an outlet is really only a special kind of an Objective-C property, you need to drag the blue line to somewhere it can be declared in code; that is, somewhere between the @interface and @end declarations.

In the dialog box that appears (shown in Figure 1-17), give the outlet a name. This will be the name of the property that you'll use to reference the button later from your code, so name it accordingly. Be sure that Connection is set to "Outlet" and that the type is correct (it should be UIButton for system buttons). Also, because you are using ARC (Automatic Reference Counting for memory management) by default, outlets should always use the Weak storage type.

Figure 1-17. *Configuring an outlet*

> **Note**   Although Objective-C properties should generally use the Strong storage type, outlets are an exception. The details are beyond the scope of this book, but briefly the reason has to do with internal memory management; using Weak spares you from writing certain cleanup code that you would otherwise have to write. Throughout this book, we assume that you're creating your outlets using Weak storage.

Click the "Connect" button. By doing this, Xcode creates a property and hooks it up with the button. Your view controller's header file should now look similar to Figure 1-18; the little dot next to the property indicates that it is connected to a view in the storyboard or .xib file.

```
 5   //  Created by joseph hoffman on 6/20/13.
 6   //  Copyright (c) 2013 NSCookbook. All rights reserved.
 7   //
 8
 9   #import <UIKit/UIKit.h>
10
11   @interface ViewController : UIViewController
12
13   @property (weak, nonatomic) IBOutlet UIButton *myButton;
14
15   @end
16
```

Figure 1-18. *An outlet property connected to a button in the storyboard*

The outlet is now ready, and you can reference the button from your code using the property. To demonstrate that, add the code in Listing 1-3 to the viewDidLoad method in the ViewController.m file.

Listing 1-3. Demonstrating a referenced outlet

```
- (void)viewDidLoad
{
    [super viewDidLoad];
// Do any additional setup after loading the view, typically from a nib.
[self.myButton setTitle:@"Outlet1!" forState:UIControlStateNormal];
}
```

If you build and run your application, as Figure 1-19 shows, the button's title should now be "Outlet1!" instead of "Click Me!"

Figure 1-19. The button title changed from code using an outlet reference

The next step is to make something happen when the button is tapped. This is what actions are for, which is the topic of the next recipe.

Recipe 1-5: Creating an Action

Actions are the way in which user interface controls notify your code (usually the view controller) that a user event has occurred; for example, when a button has been tapped or a value has been changed. The control responds to such an event by calling the action method you've provided.

In this recipe you will continue to build on what you've done in Recipes 1-3 and 1-4. The next few pages will help you create and connect an action method to receive "Touch Up Inside" events from the button. You then add code that displays an alert when the user taps the button.

To create an action, your Xcode should still be in assistant-editor mode with both the user interface and the header file showing. If not, press the button shown in Figure 1-15 to make it display.

Ctrl-click and drag the line from the button to the view controller's @interface section, exactly as you did when you created the outlet earlier. Only this time, change the connection type to `Action`, as in Figure 1-20.

Figure 1-20. Configuring an action method

When you set the connection type to `Action`, you'll notice that the dialog box changes to show a different set of attributes. These attributes are different from the outlet connection type. (Compare Figure 1-20 to Figure 1-17.)The new attributes are `Type`, `Event`, and `Arguments`. Usually, the default values provided by Xcode are fine, but there might be situations where you would want to change them. The three attributes can be briefly described as follows:

- Type: The type of the sender argument; that is, the parameter input type for the action. This can be either the generic type ID or the specific type, which in this case is `UIButton`. It's usually a good idea to use the generic type so you can invoke the action method in other situations and not be forced to provide a `UIButton` (in this case).

■ Event: This is the event type you want the action method to respond to. The most common events are touch events and events that indicate a value has changed. There are numerous kinds of touch events you can choose from.

■ Arguments: This attribute dictates what arguments the action method will have. Possible values are the following:

■ None, which is no argument

■ Sender, which has the type you entered in the Type attribute

■ Sender and Event, which is an object holding additional information about the event that occurred

For the sake of this recipe, leave the attributes at id, Touch Up Inside, and Sender, respectively, but enter showAlert as the name.

> **Note** The convention in iOS is to name actions according to what will happen when an event gets triggered rather than a name that conveys the event type. Pick names such as showAlert, playCurrentTrack, and shareImage over names such as buttonClicked or textChanged.

Finalize the creation of the action by clicking the "Connect" button in the dialog box. Xcode then creates an action method in the view controller's class and hooks it up with the button. Your ViewController.h file should now look like Figure 1-21.

```
5   //  Created by joseph hoffman on 6/20/13.
6   //  Copyright (c) 2013 NSCookbook. All rights reserved.
7   //
8
9   #import <UIKit/UIKit.h>
10
11  @interface ViewController : UIViewController
12
13  @property (weak, nonatomic) IBOutlet UIButton *myButton;
14
15  - (IBAction)showAlert:(id)sender;
16  @end
17
```

Figure 1-21. An outlet and an action connected to an object in the storyboard

Now you're ready to implement the behavior you want when the user taps the button. In this case, you show an alert view that says "Hello Brother!" Add the code in Listing 1-4 to your ViewController.h file.

Listing1-4. Implementing the alert behavior

```
@implementation ViewController

// ...

- (IBAction)showAlert:(id)sender
{
    UIAlertView *alert = [[UIAlertView alloc] initWithTitle:@"Testing Actions"
                                                    message:@"Hello Brother!"
                                                   delegate:nil
                                          cancelButtonTitle:@"Dismiss"
                                          otherButtonTitles:nil];
    [alert show];
}

@end
```

You can now build and run the application. When you tap the button, you should see your greeting alert, as in Figure 1-22.

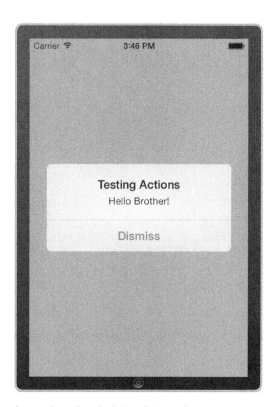

Figure 1-22. An action method showing an alert when the button is tapped

Sometimes it happens that the code and the `storyboard` files get out of sync with connected outlets and actions. Usually this happens when you remove an action method or an outlet property in your code and replace it with a new one. In those cases, you get a runtime error. To fix this, remove the connection from Interface Builder in the connections inspector. The connections inspector can be found in the same pane as the attributes inspector under the circle with the arrow. Figure 1-23 shows two connected action methods for the same event inside the connections inspector. You can remove the lingering action method by clicking the "×" icon next to it.

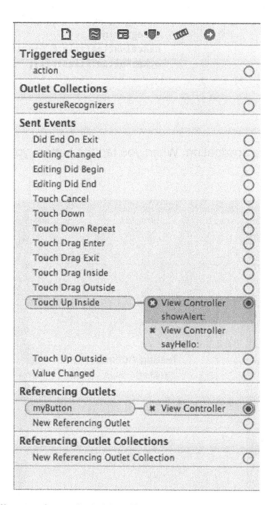

***Figure 1-23.** A button with two different action methods (showAlert: and sayHello:) connected to the same event*

Recipe 1-6: Creating a Class

A common task in iOS programming is to create new classes. Whether your aim is to subclass an existing class or create a new domain-model class to hold your data, you can use the Objective-C class template to generate the necessary files.

In this recipe, we'll show you how to create and add a new class to your project. If you don't have a suitable project to try this in, create a new single view application.

For a new class, go to the project navigator and select the group folder in which you want to store the files for your new class. Normally, this is the group folder with the same name as your project, but as your application grows you may want to organize your files into subfolders.

Go to the main menu and select File ➤ New ➤ File (or simply use the keyboard shortcut command [⌘]+ N). Then select the Objective-C class template in the iOS Cocoa Touch section (see Figure 1-24).

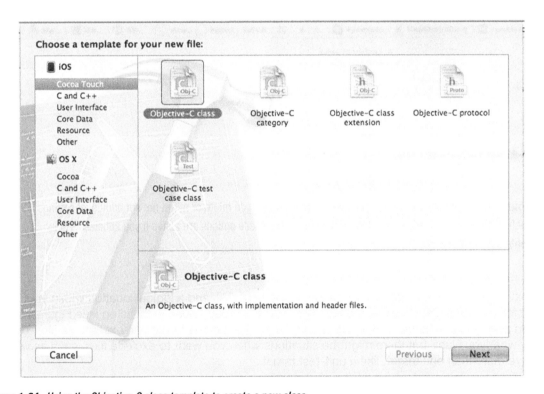

Figure 1-24. Using the Objective-C class template to create a new class

On the following page, enter "MyClass" in the class field and choose "NSObject" from the subclass of the drop-down list. The convention in Objective-C is to name classes using the PascalCase style.

Here you are creating a new class called "MyClass," and you are making "NSObject" the parent class. An NSObject class is the best selection for a general class, but you might want to select a parent class of a different type, according to your needs. For example, if you want to create a new view controller, the parent class would be UIViewController.

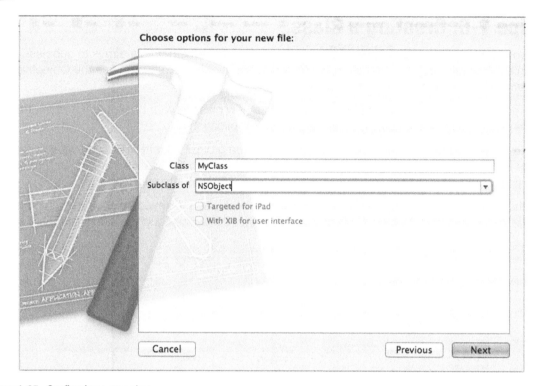

Figure 1-25. Configuring a new class

> **Note**   Depending on which class you select as the parent, you might or might not set additional settings
> such as Targeted for iPad, or With XIB for user interface. These options are active if you subclass a view
> controller of some kind.

The next step is to select a physical location on the hard disk and a logical location within your
project for your new class; that is, the file folder and the group folder. In this step (see Figure 1-26),
you can also decide whether your class should be included in the target (the executable file). This is
usually what you want, but there might be situations when you want to exclude files, such as when
you have more than one target, like a unit-test target.

Figure 1-26. Selecting the physical (file folder) and logical (group folder) places for a class

Most of the time you can just accept the default values for the locations, so go ahead and click "Create."
Xcode then generates two new files for your project: MyClass.h and MyClass.m. They contain the code
of an empty class, as in the header and implementation files shown in Listing 1-5 and Listing 1-6.

Listing 1-5. A new class header file

```
//
//  MyClass.h
//  My App
//

#import <Foundation/Foundation.h>

@interface MyClass : NSObject

@end
```

Listing 1-6. A new class implementation file

```
//
//  MyClass.m
//  My App
//

#import "MyClass.h"

@implementation MyClass

@end
```

Recipe 1-7: Adding an Info.plist Property

The iOS platform uses a special file called `Info.plist` to store application-wide properties. The file resides in the Supporting Files folder of your project and is named after your project with "-Info.plist" as a suffix. The format of the file is XML, but you can more conveniently edit the values in Xcode's property list editor, as shown in Figure 1-27.

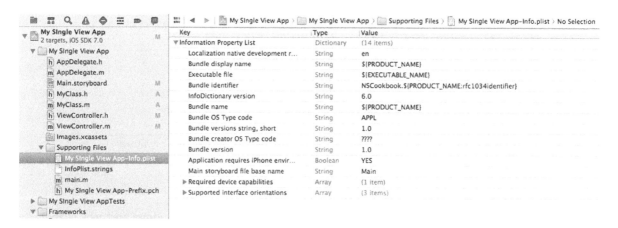

Figure 1-27. The .plist editor in Xcode

The structure of a property list file is that the root element is a dictionary that contains values identified by string keys. The values are often a string but can be other types, such as Booleans, dates, arrays of values, or even dictionaries.

If you select the `Info.plist` in the project navigator, you see that it already contains several items. These are the most commonly used keys. However, sometimes you need to add a value that isn't contained by default, such as if your app is using location services and you want to set the `NSLocationUsageDescription` property.

Follow these steps to add a new application property key and value:

1. Expand the Supporting Files folder in the project navigator.

2. Select the file `<Application Name>-Info.plist`. This brings up the property list editor.

3. Select the root item, which is called Information Property List.

4. Press the "Return" key. Xcode adds a new row to the dictionary.

5. Type the property's key identifier or select one from the list that is presented to you. Note that if you enter an identifier and Xcode recognizes it as a standard property, it displays a more descriptive key. For example, `NSLocationUsageDescription` changes into `Privacy - Location Usage Description` after pressing "Return." Behind the scenes, though, it's the identifier you typed in that's stored.

6. If the property key isn't defined within iOS (for example, your own custom key), you are allowed to change the property type. Simply click the type in the Type column and a list of possible values will be displayed.

7. Enter a value for the key by double-clicking the value column of the new row and typing the new value.

Recipe 1-8: Adding a Resource File

Most apps need to access resource files, such as images or sound files. You enable that by adding them to your project and then referencing them through their names. In this recipe, you add an image file to your project and then use it to populate an image view. Although you use an image file in this example, the process is the same for any other type of file.

As usual, you need a single view project to try this in, so go ahead and create one if you don't have a suitable one already.

The best way to import a file is to simply drag it from Finder, iPhoto, or any other application that supports the dragging of files. Drag an image file of your liking into the project navigator in Xcode. A good place to put resource files is in the Supporting Files group folder, but you can add it to any group folder within your project.

> **Note**   You can also use the File ➤ Add Files to My App menu item to add resource files to your project.

In the dialog box that appears, be sure to select the "Copy items into destination group's folder (if needed)" check box, as shown in Figure 1-28.This ensures that your image stays with the project even if you move it to a different location.

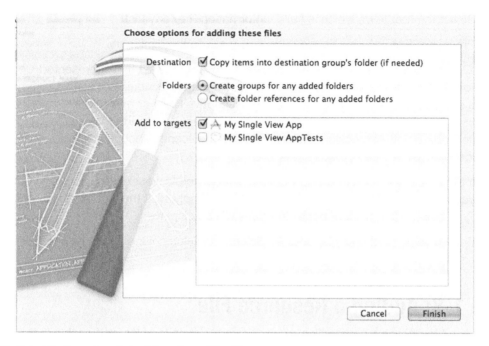

Figure 1-28. Select the "copy items" check box when adding files

Your image, as Figure 1-29 shows, is now part of your project and can be referenced through its filename.

Figure 1-29. An application with an embedded image file

To see how you can reference the image within your application, add an image view to your user interface and make it fill the entire view. Be sure the image view is selected, and then go to the attributes inspector to connect it to your image file by selecting your file from the image attribute's drop-down menu. You probably should also change the Mode attribute to Aspect Fill or your image might look stretched. If you have been following along since Recipe 1-1, your button created earlier might now be covered up by the image view. To send the image view to the back, select the image view and choose editor ➤ arrange ➤ send to back from the file menu. If necessary, move the button to a lighter area of the photo where it is easier to read.

Your app should now resemble the one in Figure 1-30.

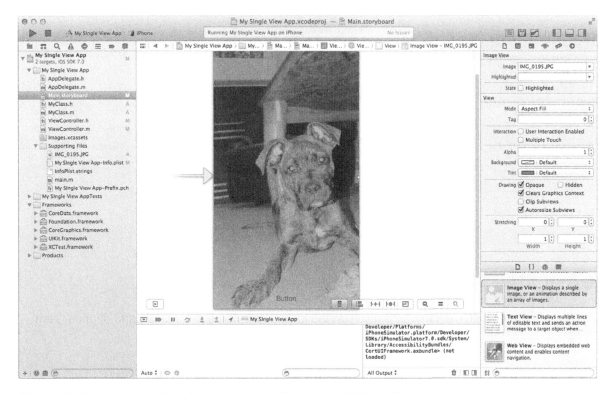

Figure 1-30. A user interface with an image view referencing an embedded image file

Using the Asset Catalog

A good way to handle icons and buttons is by using the new Xcode asset catalog feature. The problem with dealing with multiple devices is that screen resolutions might change, as they do for a retina versus non-retina iPhone. For an app to look good on both devices, each piece of artwork needs to have a 1x and 2x resolution copy. The asset catalog organizes these various resolution copies for you, so you need to refer to it by only one name.

In your project navigator, you will see a file called "images.xcassets." Select this file; you should see an interface in the editor window of Xcode, as shown in Figure 1-31. Here you will see two image sets, one for the app icon and one for the launch image.

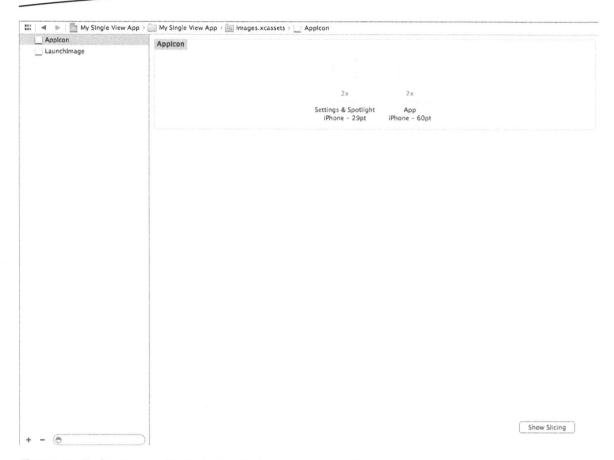

Figure 1-31. The image assets file seen by selecting image.xcassets from the project navigator

To create an image set, click the "+" button on the lower left of the editor screen and choose "New Image Set," as shown in Figure 1-32.

Figure 1-32. Creating a new image set

Once a new image set is created with a generic name, rename the image set by double-clicking the name. You now will notice that you have a place to put both a 1x and a 2x resolution image into the image set, as shown in Figure 1-33.

Figure 1-33. A newly created image set

Add images by simply dragging from your finder into either the 1x or 2x image placeholder box. These images need to be .PNG files or you will not be able to add them to the asset catalog. Select "Done," and your image set should show the images instead of a placeholder.

Recipe 1-9: Handling Errors

How well your application is handling errors might very well be the difference between success and failure in terms of user experience. Nevertheless, error handling is an oft-neglected part of software development, and iOS apps are no exception. Apps that crash without explanation or fail silently with all sorts of weird behavior are not uncommon.

You should spend a little extra time with handling errors to get them right. Like all things boring, you're better off dealing with them straight away. One thing you can do to make the effort easier is to create a default error handler—a single piece of code that can handle most of your errors.

This recipe shows you how to set up a simple error handler that, based on the error object you provide, alerts the user and even provides recovery options for the user when available.

Setting Up a Framework for Error Handling

By convention in iOS, fatal, non-recoverable errors are implemented using exceptions. For potentially recoverable errors, however, the course of action is to use a more traditional method with a Boolean return value and an output parameter containing the error details. Listing 1-7 shows an example of this pattern with Core Data's `NSManagedObjectContext:save:` method.

Listing 1-7. A pattern for handling potentially recoverable errors

```
NSError *error = nil;
if ([managedObjectContext save:&error] == NO)
{
    NSLog(@"Unhandled error:\n%@, %@", error, [error userInfo]);
}
```

The error handling in the preceding example dumps the error details to the standard output and then silently carries on as if nothing happened. Obviously, this approach is rather poor and is not the best strategy from a usability perspective.

For this recipe, we'll build a small framework that helps you handle errors with the same ease as in the code above, but with a much better user experience. When we're done, your error-handling code will look like Listing 1-8.

Listing 1-8. A better way of handling potentially recoverable errors with a framework

```
NSError *error = nil;
if ([managedObjectContext save:&error] == NO)
{
[ErrorHandler handleError:error fatal:NO];
}
```

Let's set up the scaffolding for the internal error-handling framework. Start by creating a new single view application project. In this new project, create a new class file that subclasses NSObject. Give the new class the name "ErrorHandler." Open ErrorHandler.h and add the declaration shown in Listing 1-9.

Listing 1-9. Adding a declaration for the handleErrors: fatal: class method

```
//
//  ErrorHandler.h
// Default Error Handling
//

#import <Foundation/Foundation.h>

@interface ErrorHandler : NSObject

+(void)handleError:(NSError *)error fatal:(BOOL)fatalError;

@end
```

The "+" next to the handleError: fatal: method in Listing 1-9 denotes a class method. This means you do not need to create an instance of a class to call it.

For now, just add an empty stub, a blank method implementation, of this class method in the ErrorHandler.m file. This unfinished method is shown in Listing 1-10. Without this stub, Xcode will give you a warning for incomplete implementation.

Listing 1-10. Creating a stub for the handleErrors: fatal: class method

```
//
//  ErrorHandler.m
// Default Error Handling
//

#import "ErrorHandler.h"

@implementation ErrorHandler
```

```
+(void)handleError:(NSError *)error fatal:(BOOL)fatalError
{
    // TODO: Handle the error
}
```

@end

Before implementing the method shown in Listing 1-10, you need to set up code that will test it. You will create a simple user interface with two buttons that fake a non-fatal and a fatal error, respectively. Once completed, you will return and finish this method.

Open Main.storyboard and select the main view. Drag out two buttons from the object library and make them resemble the ones in Figure 1-34.

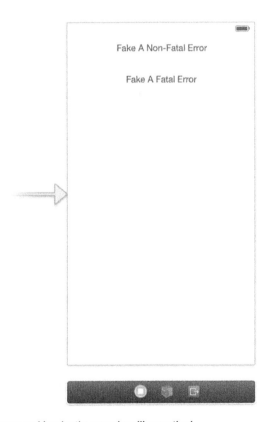

Figure 1-34. *Buttons that fake an error and invoke the error-handling method*

Create actions for the two buttons, "Fake A Non-Fatal Error" and "Fake A Fatal Error," as you did in Recipe 1-5. Use the following respective names:

- fakeNonFatalError
- fakeFatalError

Make sure you import ErrorHandler.h in the view controller's header file. ViewController.h should now resemble the code in Listing 1-11.

Listing 1-11. The ViewController.h file with the import statement and the two actions

```
//
//  ViewController.h
//  Recipe 1-10: Default Error Handling
//

#import <UIKit/UIKit.h>
#import "ErrorHandler.h"

@interface ViewController : UIViewController

- (IBAction)fakeNonFatalError:(id)sender;
- (IBAction)fakeFatalError:(id)sender;

@end
```

Now, switch to ViewController.m and add the implementation for the fakeNonFatalError: action method shown in Listing 1-12. It simply creates a fake NSError object with a single recovery option (Retry). The error object is then handed over to the error-handler class, with a flag saying it's not a fatal error (meaning it shouldn't cause the app to shut itself down).

Listing 1-12. Implementing the fakeNonFatalError: action method

```
- (IBAction)fakeNonFatalError:(id)sender
{
    NSString *description = @"Connection Error";
    NSString *failureReason = @"Can't seem to get a connection.";
    NSArray *recoveryOptions = @[@"Retry"];
    NSString *recoverySuggestion = @"Check your wifi settings and retry.";

    NSDictionary *userInfo =
[NSDictionary dictionaryWithObjects:
@[description, failureReason, recoveryOptions, recoverySuggestion, self]
        forKeys:
@[NSLocalizedDescriptionKey,NSLocalizedFailureReasonErrorKey,
NSLocalizedRecoveryOptionsErrorKey, NSLocalizedRecoverySuggestionErrorKey,
NSRecoveryAttempterErrorKey]];

    NSError *error = [[NSError alloc] initWithDomain:@"NSCookbook.iOS7recipesbook"code:42
userInfo:userInfo];

    [ErrorHandler handleError:error fatal:NO];
}
```

We won't explain everything, but the userInfo dictionary that you've built for this fake error contains the key NSRecoveryAttempterErrorKey, with the value set to self. What this means is that the view controller acts as the recovery-attempter object for this error. For reasons that will become clear later, you need to implement one method from the NSRecoveryAttempting protocol, namely attemptRecoveryFromError:optionIndex:. This method is invoked on the recovery attempts that you implement later. For the purpose of this recipe, you simply fake a failed recovery attempt by returning NO, as shown in Listing 1-13.

Listing 1-13. Faking a failed recovery attempt by returning "NO" in the attemptRecoveryFromError method

```
- (BOOL)attemptRecoveryFromError:(NSError *)error optionIndex:(NSUInteger)recoveryOptionIndex
{
    return NO;
}
```

Next, implement the `fakeFatalError:` action method. It creates a simpler error without recovery options, but flags the error as fatal in the error-handling method. The implementation is shown in Listing 1-14.

Listing 1-14. Implementing the fakeFatalError action method

```
- (IBAction)fakeFatalError:(id)sender
{
    NSString *description = @"Data Error";
    NSString *failureReason = @"Data is corrupt. The app must shut down.";
    NSString *recoverySuggestion = @"Contact support!";

    NSDictionary *userInfo = [NSDictionary dictionaryWithObjects:
@[description, failureReason,recoverySuggestion]
forKeys:
@[NSLocalizedDescriptionKey,
NSLocalizedFailureReasonErrorKey,NSLocalizedRecoverySuggestionErrorKey]];

    NSError *error = [[NSError alloc] initWithDomain:@"NSCookbook.iOS7recipesbook"
                                       code:22 userInfo:userInfo];

    [ErrorHandler handleError:error fatal:YES];
}
```

Now that you have the interface of the default error-handling API set up and know the ways to test it, you can start implementing the actual error handling.

Notifying the User

The very least a decent default error-handling method should do is notify the user that an error has occurred. Switch back to the `ErrorHandler.m` file and add the code in Listing 1-15 to the `handleError:fatal:`method stub you created in Listing 1-10.

Listing 1-15. Adding a notification to the handleError: fatal method to alert the user of an error

```
+(void)handleError:(NSError *)error fatal:(BOOL)fatalError
{
    NSString *localizedCancelTitle = NSLocalizedString(@"Dismiss", nil);
    if (fatalError)
        localizedCancelTitle = NSLocalizedString(@"Shut Down", nil);
```

```
// Notify the user
UIAlertView *alert = [[UIAlertView alloc] initWithTitle:[error localizedDescription]
                                                message:[error localizedFailureReason]
                                               delegate:nil
                                      cancelButtonTitle:localizedCancelTitle
                                      otherButtonTitles:nil];

[alert show];
// Log to standard out
NSLog(@"Unhandled error:\n%@, %@", error, [error userInfo]);
}
```

You can now build and run the application to see how this will look. Try tapping the non-fatal error button first, which should display an alert like the one in Figure 1-35.

Figure 1-35. An error alert with a fake error

If you tap the button that fakes a fatal error, you'll get a similar alert. However, for errors flagged as fatal, you want the app to shut down automatically after the user has been notified. Let's implement that now.

To get started, we're going to provide the alert view with a delegate. *Delegation* is a pattern in which one object (the delegate) acts on behalf of another (the delegating object). The object that acts on behalf of another can then send a message back to the delegating object so the delegating object can act accordingly.

With delegation, you can intercept when the user dismisses the alert view. In this way, you can abort the execution there. Add the code to the handleError:fatal: method, as shown in Listing 1-16. At this point your code will not compile, but don't worry—we will sort it out soon.

Listing 1-16. Adding a delegate to intercept an alert-view dismissal

```
+(void)handleError:(NSError *)error fatal:(BOOL)fatalError
{
    NSString *localizedCancelTitle = NSLocalizedString(@"Dismiss", nil);
    if (fatalError)
        localizedCancelTitle = NSLocalizedString(@"Shut Down", nil);

    // Notify the user
    ErrorHandler *delegate = [[ErrorHandler alloc] initWithError:error fatal:fatalError];
    if (!retainedDelegates) {
        retainedDelegates = [[NSMutableArray alloc] init];
    }
    [retainedDelegates addObject:delegate];

    UIAlertView *alert = [[UIAlertView alloc] initWithTitle:[error localizedDescription]
                                                    message:[error localizedFailureReason]
                                                   delegate:delegate
                                          cancelButtonTitle:localizedCancelTitle
                                          otherButtonTitles:nil];

    [alert show];
    // Log to standard out
    NSLog(@"Unhandled error:\n%@, %@", error, [error userInfo]);
}
```

The retainedDelegates hack deserves some explanation. The delegate property of an alert view is a so-called weak reference. What this means is that it will not keep the delegate from deallocating if all other references to it are released.

To keep the delegate from being prematurely deallocated (by ARC), you'll use a static array. As long as a delegate is a member of the retainedDelegates array, a strong reference is kept that will keep the delegate alive. As you'll see later, once the delegate's job is finished it will remove itself from the array, which will allow it to become deallocated.

Add the declaration of the retainedDelegates array at the top of the @implementation block of the ErrorHandler class, as shown in Listing 1-17.

Listing 1-17. Adding a retainedDelegates declaration to the @implementation block of ErrorHandler.m

```
//
//  ErrorHandler.m
//  Recipe 1-10 Default Error Handling
//

#import "ErrorHandler.h"

@implementation ErrorHandler
```

```
static NSMutableArray *retainedDelegates = nil;

// ...

@end
```

Now, go to the ErrorHandler.h file again, and add the code shown in Listing 1-18.

Listing 1-18. Declaring the UIAlertView delegate

```
//
//  ErrorHandler.h
//  Recipe 1-10: Default Error Handling
//

#import <Foundation/Foundation.h>

@interface ErrorHandler : NSObject<UIAlertViewDelegate>

@property (strong, nonatomic)NSError *error;
@property (nonatomic)BOOL fatalError;

-(id)initWithError:(NSError *)error fatal:(BOOL)fatalError;

+(void)handleError:(NSError *)error fatal:(BOOL)fatalError;

@end
```

Listing 1-18 turns the ErrorHandler class into an alert-view delegate. Of course, you could have created a new class for this purpose, but this way is a bit easier.

Now, switch to ErrorHandler.m and implement the initWithError: method, as shown in Listing 1-19.

Listing 1-19. Adding the initWithError: method to the ErrorHandler.m file

```
-(id)initWithError:(NSError *)error fatal:(BOOL)fatalError
{
    self = [super init];
    if (self) {
        self.error = error;
        self.fatalError = fatalError;
    }
    return self;
}
```

Finally, implement the clickedButtonAtIndex: delegate method so as to abort in case of a fatal error. As you can see from the code that follows, you also release the delegate by removing it from the retainedDelegates array, as shown in Listing 1-20.

Listing 1-20. Implementing the clickedButtonAtIndex: delegate method

```
-(void)alertView:(UIAlertView *)alertView clickedButtonAtIndex:(NSInteger)buttonIndex
{
if (self.fatalError) {
// In case of a fatal error, abort execution
        abort();
}
// Job is finished, release this delegate
    [retainedDelegates removeObject:self];
}
```

If you rerun the app now and tap the "Fake a Fatal Error" button, the app will abort execution right after you've dismissed the error message if you tap the "Shut Down" button (see Figure 1-36).

Figure 1-36. An alert view displaying a fake fatal error

Notifying the user and logging the error is the least we should do when handling an unexpected error, so the code you've implemented so far is a good candidate for a default error-handling method. However, there is one more feature of the NSError class that you should support: recovery options.

Implementing Recovery Options

NSError offers a way for the notifying method to provide custom recovery options. For example, a method that is called upon to establish a connection of some kind might provide a "Retry" option in case of a timeout failure.

The localizedRecoveryOptions array of an NSObject holds the titles of available recovery options as defined by the caller method. Additionally, the localizedRecoverySuggestion property can be used to give the user an idea of how to handle the error. The option titles as well as the recovery suggestions are suitable for communicating directly with the user, such as in an alert view.

The last piece of the NSError recovery functionality is the recoveryAttempter property. This references an object that conforms to the NSErrorRecoveryAttempting informal protocol, which is what you will use to invoke a particular recovery action.

Let's integrate this information in the handleError:fatalError: method, as shown in Listing 1-21.

Listing 1-21. Adding recovery options to the handleError: fatal method

```objc
+(void)handleError:(NSError *)error fatal:(BOOL)fatalError
{
    NSString *localizedCancelTitle = NSLocalizedString(@"Dismiss", nil);
    if (fatalError)
        localizedCancelTitle = NSLocalizedString(@"Shut Down", nil);

    // Notify the user
    ErrorHandler *delegate = [[ErrorHandler alloc] initWithError:error fatal:fatalError];
    if (!retainedDelegates) {
        retainedDelegates = [[NSMutableArray alloc] init];
    }
    [retainedDelegates addObject:delegate];

    UIAlertView *alert = [[UIAlertView alloc] initWithTitle:[error localizedDescription]
                                            message:[error localizedFailureReason]
                                            delegate:delegate
                                    cancelButtonTitle:localizedCancelTitle
                                    otherButtonTitles:nil];

    if ([error recoveryAttempter])
    {
        // Append the recovery suggestion to the error message
        alert.message = [NSString stringWithFormat:@"%@\n%@", alert.message,
        error.localizedRecoverySuggestion];
        // Add buttons for the recovery options
        for (NSString * option in error.localizedRecoveryOptions)
        {
            [alert addButtonWithTitle:option];
        }
    }

    [alert show];
    // Log to standard out
    NSLog(@"Unhandled error:\n%@, %@", error, [error userInfo]);
}
```

The code added in Listing 1-21 checks to see if there is a recoveryAttempter object. If there is one, it adds recovery suggestions and the accompanying buttons to go with those suggestions.

Implement the actual recovery attempts in the alertView:clickedButtonAtIndex: method by making the changes shown in Listing 1-22.

Listing 1-22. Handling the alert button clicks

```
-(void)alertView:(UIAlertView *)alertView clickedButtonAtIndex:(NSInteger)buttonIndex
{
    if (buttonIndex != [alertView cancelButtonIndex])
    {
        NSString *buttonTitle = [alertView buttonTitleAtIndex:buttonIndex];
        NSInteger recoveryIndex = [[self.error localizedRecoveryOptions]
                                    indexOfObject:buttonTitle];
        if (recoveryIndex != NSNotFound)
        {
            if ([[self.error recoveryAttempter] attemptRecoveryFromError:self.error
                                                    optionIndex:recoveryIndex] == NO)
            {
                // Redisplay alert since recovery attempt failed
                [ErrorHandler handleError:self.error fatal:self.fatalError];
            }
        }
    }
    else
    {
        // Cancel button clicked

        if (self.fatalError)
        {
            // In case of a fatal error, abort execution
            abort();
        }
    }

    // Job is finished, release this delegate
    [retainedDelegates removeObject:self];
}
```

In Listing 1-22, you handle the instance in which a user clicks the "Retry" button. If this button is clicked, it will retry the task and redisplay the alert if it fails again. Of course, because you created the error, it will always fail, but in a real application this error might be cleared. For example, in a scenario such as getting a connection, the error might be cleared once the connection is established.

You are now finished with the default error-handling method. To test this last feature, build and run the app and tap the "Fake a Non-Fatal Error" button again. This time the error alert should resemble the one in Figure 1-37.

Figure 1-37. An error alert with a "Retry" option

Now you have a convenient default error-handling method that extracts information from an NSError object and does the following:

1. Alerts the user

2. If available, provides the user with recovery options

3. Logs the error to the standard error output

In the next recipe we show you how you can handle exceptions with the same ease.

Recipe 1-10: Handling Exceptions

Exceptions in iOS are by convention reserved for unrecoverable errors. When an exception is raised, it should ultimately result in program termination. For that reason, iOS apps rarely catch exceptions internally, but rather let the default exception-handling method deal with them.

The default exception-handling method catches any uncaught exceptions, writes some debug information to the console, and then terminates the program. Although this is the safe way to deal with iOS exceptions, there is a severe usability problem associated with this approach. Because the console can't be seen from a real device, the app just disappears in the hands of the user, with no explanation whatsoever.

This recipe shows you how you can make the user experience a little better while keeping a reasonably safe exception-handling approach that will work in most situations.

A Strategy for Handling Exceptions

As a general strategy, terminating the app upon uncaught exceptions is a good solution because it's safe and will prevent bad things, like data corruption, from happening. However, we'd like to make a couple of improvements to iOS's default exception handling.

The first thing we want to do is notify the user about the uncaught exception. From a user's point of view, this is best done at the time of the exception, just before the program terminates. However, the program might then be operating in a hostile environment due to fatal errors, such as out-of-memory or pointer errors. In those situations, complex things like user interface programming should be avoided.

A good compromise is to log the error and alert the user on the next app launch. To accomplish this, you need to intercept uncaught exceptions and set a flag that persists between the two sessions.

Setting Up a Test Application

As you did in the preceding recipe, you will set up a test application to try this out. Start by creating a new single view application. Then add a button to the main view to make it look similar to Figure 1-38.

Figure 1-38. *A button to throw a fake exception*

Add an action for the button called throwFakeException and implement it, as shown in Listing 1-23.

Listing 1-23. Implementing the throwFakeException: method

```
- (IBAction)throwFakeException:(id)sender
{
    NSException *e = [[NSException alloc] initWithName:@"FakeException"
reason:@"The developer sucks!" userInfo:[NSDictionary dictionaryWithObject:@"Extra info"
forKey:@"Key"]];
    [e raise];
}
```

With the test code in place, you can move on to the implementation of the handling of exceptions.

Intercepting Uncaught Exceptions

The way to intercept uncaught exceptions in iOS is to register a handler with the NSSetUncaughtException function. The handler is a void function with an NSException reference as the only parameter, such as the one in Listing 1-24.

Listing 1-24. An example exception handler

```
void myExceptionHandler(NSException *exception)
{
    // Handle Exceptions
}
```

The exception handler you will implement should set a flag that informs the app that an exception occurred on the last run. For that you'll use NSUserDefaults, which is designed for persisting settings between sessions. Now, in the AppDelegate.m file, add the method shown in Listing 1-25.

Listing 1-25. Adding a method to set a flag in NSUserDefaults when an error occurred on the last run

```
void exceptionHandler(NSException *exception)
{
    //Set flag
    NSUserDefaults *settings = [NSUserDefaults standardUserDefaults];

[settings setBool:YES forKey:@"ExceptionOccurredOnLastRun"];
    [settings synchronize];
}
```

Next, register the exception handler in the Application recipes:didFinishLaunchingWithOptions: method, as shown in Listing 1-26.

Listing 1-26. Registering an exception

```
-(BOOL)Application recipes:(UIApplication *)application
didFinishLaunchingWithOptions:(NSDictionary *)launchOptions
{
NSSetUncaughtExceptionHandler(&exceptionHandler);

    // Normal Setup Code
    // ...
}
```

The next thing you'll do is add a self-check in `Application recipes:didFinishLaunchingWithOptions:` to see if the previous session ended in an exception. If that's the case, your app should reset the flag and notify the user with an alert view. Add this code before the line where you register, as shown in Listing 1-27.

Listing 1-27. Check if an exception flag is set and handle it with an alert view

```
- (BOOL)Application recipes:(UIApplication *)application didFinishLaunchingWithOptions:(NSDictionary
*)launchOptions
{
    // Default exception handling code
    NSUserDefaults *settings = [NSUserDefaults standardUserDefaults];

    if ([settings boolForKey:@"ExceptionOccurredOnLastRun"])
    {
        // Reset exception occurred flag
        [settings setBool:NO forKey:@"ExceptionOccurredOnLastRunKey"];
        [settings synchronize];

        // Notify the user
        UIAlertView *alert = [[UIAlertView alloc] initWithTitle:@"We're sorry"
message:@"An error occurred on the previous run." delegate:nil
cancelButtonTitle:@"Dismiss" otherButtonTitles:nil];
        [alert show];
    }

    NSSetUncaughtExceptionHandler(&exceptionHandler);

    // ...
}
```

Now you have the basic structure of your improved default-handling method in place. If you run the app now and tap the button to raise the fake exception, your app will terminate. However, if you start it up again, you'll get an alert, such as the one in Figure 1-39, notifying you of the error that occurred earlier.

Figure 1-39. An error message notifying the user of an error that caused the app to close down on the previous run

That's great, but let's make this feature a bit more useful.

Reporting Errors

Many uncaught exceptions in iOS apps are pure programming errors—bugs that you can fix if you only get proper information about them. For this reason, iOS creates a crash report when an app has terminated due to an uncaught exception.

However, even though a developer can extract the information about crashes, she needs to connect the device to a computer to do so. If your app is out there in the hands of real users, retrieving the crash report might be impossible or inconvenient at best.

As an alternative, we'd like users to be able to send these error reports directly to us. You can make this possible by adding an "Email Report" button to the error alert.

First you need to store information about the exception so you can retrieve it on the next run if the user decides to send the error report. A good way to do this is to use the natural source of error logging, the stderr stream.

The stderr stream is the channel to which NSLog sends the log messages. By default, this is the console, but it's possible to redirect the stderr stream to a file by using the freopen function. To do that, add the code in Listing 1-28 to the Application recipes:didFinishLaunchingWithOptions: method.

Listing 1-28. Redirecting the stderr error stream to a file

```
- (BOOL)Application recipes:(UIApplication *)application didFinishLaunchingWithOptions:(NSDictionary
*)launchOptions
{
    // Default exception handling code
    NSUserDefaults *settings = [NSUserDefaults standardUserDefaults];

    if ([settings boolForKey:@"ExceptionOccurredOnLastRun"])
    {
        // Reset exception occurred flag
        [settings setBool:NO forKey:@"ExceptionOccurredOnLastRunKey"];
        [settings synchronize];

        // Notify the user
        UIAlertView *alert = [[UIAlertView alloc] initWithTitle:@"We're sorry" message:@"An error
occurred on the previous run." delegate:nil cancelButtonTitle:@"Dismiss" otherButtonTitles:nil];
        [alert show];
    }

    NSSetUncaughtExceptionHandler(&exceptionHandler);

    // Redirect stderr output stream to file
    NSArray *paths = NSSearchPathForDirectoriesInDomains(NSDocumentDirectory,
                                                NSUserDomainMask, YES);
    NSString *documentsPath = [paths objectAtIndex:0];
    NSString *stderrPath = [documentsPath stringByAppendingPathComponent:@"stderr.log"];

    freopen([stderrPath cStringUsingEncoding:NSASCIIStringEncoding], "w", stderr);

    // ...
}
```

Listing 1-28 makes it so that all entries to NSLog are written to a file named stderr.log in the app's documents directory on the device. The file is recreated (thanks to the **"w"** argument) for each new session, so the file only contains information and error logs from the previous run, which is what you want for the error report.

On uncaught exceptions, iOS writes some basic information about the crash and sends it to stderr (and thus your file). However, two important pieces of information are not logged; namely, the exception's userInfo dictionary and a symbolized (that is, readable) call stack. Fortunately, you can add that information from your exception-handling function, as shown in Listing 1-29.

Listing 1-29. Modifying the exception handler to the exception's userInfo and symbolized call stack to the file

```
void exceptionHandler(NSException *exception)
{
    NSLog(@"Uncaught exception: %@\nReason: %@\nUser Info: %@\nCall Stack: %@",
        exception.name, exception.reason, exception.userInfo, exception.callStackSymbols);

    //Set flag
    NSUserDefaults *settings = [NSUserDefaults standardUserDefaults];
```

```
[settings setBool:YES forKey:@"ExceptionOccurredOnLastRun"];
    [settings synchronize];
}
```

Now that you have the exception data persisted, you can move on to add the button with which the user can send the information to you.

Adding the Button

To add an "Email Report" button, you must make two small changes to the code that creates the alert view in Listing 1-30.

Listing 1-30. Adding an "Email Report" button to the alert view

```
UIAlertView *alert = [[UIAlertView alloc] initWithTitle:@"We're sorry"
message:@"An error occurred on the previous run." delegate:self
cancelButtonTitle:@"Dismiss" otherButtonTitles:nil];
[alert addButtonWithTitle:@"Email  Report"];
[alert show];
```

You added a button to the alert view and told it to send all events to the AppDelegate object (by declaring self as the delegate). To avoid the compiler warning, you also need to make the AppDelegate an alert-view delegate by declaring the UIAlertViewDelegate protocol. To do that, open AppDelegate.h and make the following change:

```
@interface AppDelegate : UIResponder <UIApplicationDelegate, UIAlertViewDelegate>

//...

@end
```

Now you can add the alertView:didDismissWithButtonIndex: alert-view delegate method, which will intercept when a user taps the "Email Report" button. Go back to AppDelegate.m and add the code in Listing 1-31.

Listing 1-31. Adding a delegate method to intercept an "Email Report" button-pressed event

```
-(void)alertView:(UIAlertView *)alertView didDismissWithButtonIndex:(NSInteger)buttonIndex
{
    if (buttonIndex == 1)
    {
        //todo: Email a report here
    }
}
```

Before you write the code for the email report, you need to fix a problem with the current code. Because alert views in iOS are displayed asynchronously, the code for redirecting the stderr output is run before Application recipes:didDismissWithButtonIndex: is invoked. This erases the content of the file prematurely. To fix this, you have to make two changes. First, in Application recipes:didFinishLaunchingWithOptions:, be sure the exception-handling setup code is run only if there has been no exception by adding the code in Listing 1-32.

Listing 1-32. Adding code to check if there has been no exception before handling setup

```
- (BOOL)Application recipes:(UIApplication *)application didFinishLaunchingWithOptions:(NSDictionary
*)launchOptions
{
    // Default exception handling code
    NSUserDefaults *settings = [NSUserDefaults standardUserDefaults];

    if ([settings boolForKey:@"ExceptionOccurredOnLastRun"])
    {
        // Reset exception occurred flag
        [settings setBool:NO forKey:@"ExceptionOccurredOnLastRunKey"];
        [settings synchronize];

        // Notify the user
        UIAlertView *alert = [[UIAlertView alloc] initWithTitle:@"We're sorry" message:@"An error
occurred on the previous run." delegate:self cancelButtonTitle:@"Dismiss" otherButtonTitles:nil];
        [alert addButtonWithTitle:@"Email a Report"];
        [alert show];
    }
    else
    {

        NSSetUncaughtExceptionHandler(&exceptionHandler);

        // Redirect stderr output stream to file
        NSArray *paths = NSSearchPathForDirectoriesInDomains(NSDocumentDirectory,
                                            NSUserDomainMask, YES);
        NSString *documentsPath = [paths objectAtIndex:0];
        NSString *stderrPath = [documentsPath stringByAppendingPathComponent:@"stderr.log"];

        freopen([stderrPath cStringUsingEncoding:NSASCIIStringEncoding], "w", stderr);
    }

    // ...
}
```

The second task you need to perform is to add the setup code to
alertView:didDismissWithButtonIndex: so that it sets up the exception handling for the case in
which there *has* been an exception. The necessary changes have been shown in Listing 1-33.

Listing 1-33. Adding code to handle the case when there is an exception

```
-(void)alertView:(UIAlertView *)alertView didDismissWithButtonIndex:(NSInteger)buttonIndex
{
    NSArray *paths = NSSearchPathForDirectoriesInDomains(NSDocumentDirectory,
                                            NSUserDomainMask, YES);
NSString *documentsPath = [paths objectAtIndex:0];
NSString *stderrPath = [documentsPath stringByAppendingPathComponent:@"stderr.log"];
```

```
    if (buttonIndex == 1)
    {
        //todo: Email a report here
    }

NSSetUncaughtExceptionHandler(&exceptionHandler);

    // Redirect stderr output stream to file
    freopen([stderrPath cStringUsingEncoding:NSASCIIStringEncoding], "w", stderr);
}
```

Now you're ready for the final step: composing an error-report email.

Emailing the Report

When the user presses the "Email Report" button, you'll use the MFMailComposeViewController class to handle the email. This class is part of the MessageUI framework, so go ahead and link it to the project. (Details about how to link framework binaries can be found in Recipe 1-2).

Next, you need to import MessageUI.h and MFMailComposeViewController.h to your AppDelegate.h file. Also, because you'll need to respond to events from the mail view controller, add MFMailComposeViewControllerDelegate to the list of supported protocols. The AppDelegate.h file should now look like the code in Listing 1-34.

Listing 1-34. Importing frameworks and adding the MFMailComposeViewController delegate

```
#import <UIKit/UIKit.h>
#import <MessageUI/MessageUI.h>
#import <MessageUI/MFMailComposeViewController.h>

@interface AppDelegate : UIResponder <UIApplicationDelegate, UIAlertViewDelegate,
MFMailComposeViewControllerDelegate>

// ...

@end
```

Now you can create and present MFMailComposeViewController with the error report. Add the code in Listing 1-35 to the alertView:didDismissWithButtonIndex: method.

Listing 1-35. Code necessary for creating and presenting MFMailComposeViewController with the error report

```
-(void)alertView:(UIAlertView *)alertView didDismissWithButtonIndex:(NSInteger)buttonIndex
{
    NSArray *paths = NSSearchPathForDirectoriesInDomains(NSDocumentDirectory,
                                                NSUserDomainMask, YES);
    NSString *documentsPath = [paths objectAtIndex:0];
    NSString *stderrPath = [documentsPath stringByAppendingPathComponent:@"stderr.log"];
```

```
    if (buttonIndex == 1)
    {
        // Email a report
        MFMailComposeViewController *mailComposer = [[MFMailComposeViewController alloc] init];
        mailComposer.mailComposeDelegate = self;
        [mailComposer setSubject:@"Error Report"];
        [mailComposer setToRecipients:[NSArray arrayWithObject:@"support@mycompany.com"]];
        // Attach log file
        NSArray *paths = NSSearchPathForDirectoriesInDomains(NSDocumentDirectory,
                                                   NSUserDomainMask, YES);
        NSString *documentsPath = [paths objectAtIndex:0];
        NSString *stderrPath = [documentsPath stringByAppendingPathComponent:@"stderr.log"];

        NSData *data = [NSData dataWithContentsOfFile:stderrPath];

        [mailComposer addAttachmentData:data mimeType:@"Text/XML" fileName:@"stderr.log"];
        UIDevice *device = [UIDevice currentDevice];
        NSString *emailBody =
[NSString stringWithFormat:@"My Model: %@\nMy OS: %@\nMy Version: %@",
[device model], [device systemName], [device systemVersion]];
        [mailComposer setMessageBody:emailBody isHTML:NO];
        [self.window.rootViewController presentViewController:mailComposer animated:YES
                                                  completion:nil];
    }

    NSSetUncaughtExceptionHandler(&exceptionHandler);

    // Redirect stderr output stream to file
    freopen([stderrPath cStringUsingEncoding:NSASCIIStringEncoding], "w", stderr);
}
```

To dismiss the mail compose controller, you also need to respond to the
mailComposeController:didFinishWithResult:error: message, which is sent by the controller
upon send or cancel events. Add the code in Listing 1-36 to your AppDelegate.m file.

Listing 1-36. Adding a method to respond to a mailComposeController error message

```
-(void)mailComposeController:(MFMailComposeViewController *)controller
didFinishWithResult:(MFMailComposeResult)result error:(NSError *)error
{
    [self.window.rootViewController dismissViewControllerAnimated:YES completion:nil];
}
```

Your app now has a good default exception handler that is user friendly, useful, and safe. When you
test it now, you'll see that the alert view has an additional button that allows you to send the report
through email. Figure 1-40 shows you an example of this.

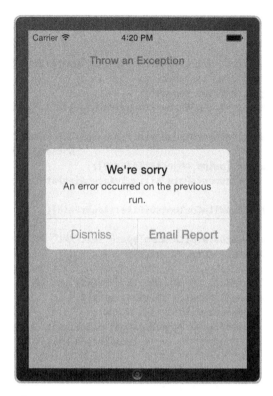

Figure 1-40. *An error alert with an option to send an error report by email*

A Final Touch

There is one more thing you might want to consider when implementing this recipe. Because you redirect stderr to a file, no error logging is displayed in the output console. This might be a problem during development when you conduct most of your testing in the simulator. During that time, you probably want the error messages to show in the console rather than being stored in a file.

Fortunately, there is a simple solution. You can use the predefined conditional TARGET_IPHONE_SIMULATOR to allow your exception-handling code to work only when the app is run on a real device. This will allow you to log errors to the console. The code in Listing 1-37 shows how to achieve this.

Listing 1-37. *Adding a conditional to handle exceptions only when running on a real device*

```
- (BOOL)Application recipes:(UIApplication *)application didFinishLaunchingWithOptions:(NSDictionary
*)launchOptions
{
    #if !TARGET_IPHONE_SIMULATOR
    // Default exception handling code

    // ...

    #endif

returnYES;
}
```

This concludes our default exception-handling recipe. By having a well-considered strategy for handling errors, you not only save yourself time, but you also give the users the respect they deserve. We hope that with the help of these two recipes you have seen the value of good exception handling, and that it's really not that difficult to achieve. You've probably already seen ways in which these simple examples can be improved. Why not venture into that? After all, the sooner you build these features into your app, the more use you'll have for them.

Recipe 1-11: Adding a Lite Version

Offering a lite version of your app is a great way to give customers a chance to try your app before buying it. Maintaining two code bases, however, can be quite tiresome and can get out of hand as you incorporate new features into your app. This recipe shows you how you can set up the project to include both versions in one code base.

Adding a Build Target

For this recipe, we have created a new single view application with the name "Recipe 1-11: Adding A Lite Version."

Select your project file in the project and targets lists and then select the build target for your project, as shown in Figure 1-41.Now press ⌘+D to duplicate the target. You are prompted to "Duplicate Only" or "Duplicate and Transition to iPad," as shown in Figure 1-42. Click "Duplicate Only" to create a new target that you will use for your lite build. This results in a separate build target with which you can implement a second version.

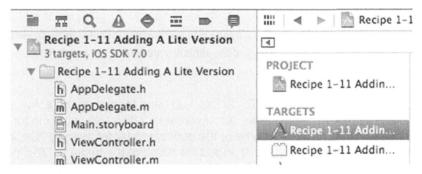

Figure 1-41. Selecting a build target for a project

Figure 1-42. Project duplication options

Rename the new target by appending "Lite" to the title, which is done by double-clicking the target name. You also should change the new target's `Product Name` attribute to signal that it's a lite version. You'll find the `Product Name` attribute in the Build Settings tab under the Packaging heading (see Figure 1-43**)**.

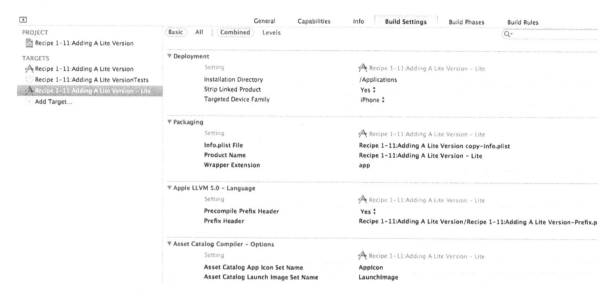

Figure 1-43. *Appending "Lite" to the target's name and the Product Name build setting*

Tip   The easiest way to find a particular build attribute is to use the search field in the upper-left corner of the Build Settings tab. Just type *Product Name* and the attributes are filtered out as you type.

You can now build and run the lite version. To do this, you need to change the active scheme. When you duplicated the regular target earlier, Xcode created a new build scheme for you. This new scheme is named identically to the initial name of the duplicated target, namely "Recipe1-11: Adding a Lite Version copy." Even though you have changed the name of the target to "Recipe 1-11: Adding a Lite Version–Lite", Xcode doesn't change the scheme name accordingly. If this bothers you, you can rename it in the Manage Schemes window, which you can reach from the "Active Scheme" button located just right of the stop button (see Figure 1-44). To rename it, highlight the copy and click the name once.

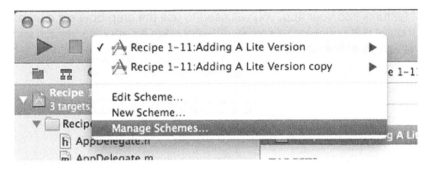

Figure 1-44. *Go to Manage Schemes if you want to change the name of the lite build scheme*

Note   Keep in mind that the two targets must have separate bundle identifiers to show up as separate apps when you install and run them on your device (or simulator). Xcode sets up different bundle identifiers by default, but be careful when making changes.

Coding for a Specific Version

Now you need a way to differentiate between the two builds in your source code. For instance, you might want to limit some features in the lite version or show ads to the non-paying users. Some code in the lite version should not be compiled into the full version and vice versa. This is where preprocessor macros come in handy.

What you want to do is add a preprocessing macro named LITE_VERSION to the lite version target. Again, this is done in the Build Settings tab, under the compiler's preprocessing header. You'll need to expand the Build Settings tab to view all build settings, done by pressing the "All" button in the top-left corner of the window. Hover over the Debug macro, click the add icon (+) that appears next to it, and enter LITE_VERSION in the edit field. Be sure to do the same for the release macro as well. Figure 1-45 shows an example of these changes.

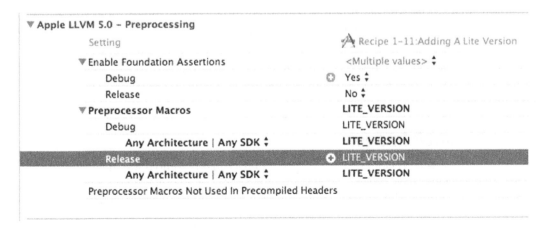

Figure 1-45. *Defining the LITE_VERSION conditional in the preprocessor macros*

To build different features into your app, you will need to use the preprocessor macro you created. Anywhere in your code that you want to specify different code for your lite version versus the full version, use the following #ifdef directive:

```
#ifdef LITE_VERSION
// Stuff for Lite version
#else
// Stuff for Full version
#endif
```

Alternatively, you can use the negated form if that's more convenient:

```
#ifndef LITE_VERSION
// Code exclusively for Full version
#endif
```

> **Note**   You can also control which files are included in each build. For example, you might not need to include the full version artwork in the lite version. Click your lite project target and go to the Build Phases tab. Expand the Copy Bundle Resources ribbon and remove or add any files that are specific to the lite version.

Recipe 1-12: Adding Launch Images

For the sake of the user experience, it is generally considered bad practice to show a so-called "splash screen" at application startup. The user is normally eager to start playing with your app and is not interested in your branding information. Nor are they particularly eager to watch your cool video, regardless of how much time and money you spent on it.

The extra few seconds it takes for the user to view and/or dismiss the splash screen can be quite annoying and might be unfavorable to the overall experience.

There is an exception to the rule, however. Many apps take a little while to load, a few seconds during which it remains unresponsive and uninteresting. Because this could be as bad as a splash screen in terms of user experience, your app should do what it can to mitigate the effect. One way of doing this is to display an image that is removed as soon as the launch is finished and the app is ready to take on user actions.

These images are called *launch images* and are really easy to implement in iOS. The function of displaying an image while the app is loading is already built-in. All you have to do is to provide the appropriate images.

Designing Launch Images

Apple's philosophy regarding launch images is that they should resemble the main view of the app as much as possible. This makes the loading time seem a little quicker and therefore more responsive. This is a better alternative to an image with a branded, splash-like design.

For example, if your app's main view consists of a table view, your launch image could look something like Figure 1-46.

Figure 1-46. *A launch image should resemble the main view of your app*

Also, it's recommended that launch images don't contain elements that might need to be translated or changed during localization. For example, the launch image in Figure 1-46 doesn't contain any navigation bar buttons. These have been edited out, as have the elements in the status bar.

Even though there is support for language-specific versions of the launch images, it's suggested you don't use it due to the increased amount of space the additional launch images will require.

Launch Image Files

Depending on the nature of your app and which devices it supports, you'll need to create one or more launch images. Including a launch image in your app is just a matter of adding it to the project. In the past, simple naming conventions told iOS how to categorize images and their appropriate sizes depending on which device is used.

A launch image can be created by first selecting the Images.xcassets file, which should be included in a new single view application by default.

You'll see that two image sets have been created already. One set is for the app icon and the other is for the launch image. Select the "LaunchImage" image set, and you will see the interface shown in Figure 1-47.

Figure 1-47. Asset catalog image-set view

If you click one of these image placeholder squares, you will see the type of image expected in the attributes inspector, as well as which versions of iOS you are supporting. For our 2x image, you'll see that it is expecting a size of 640 x 960 pixels, as shown in Figure 1-48.

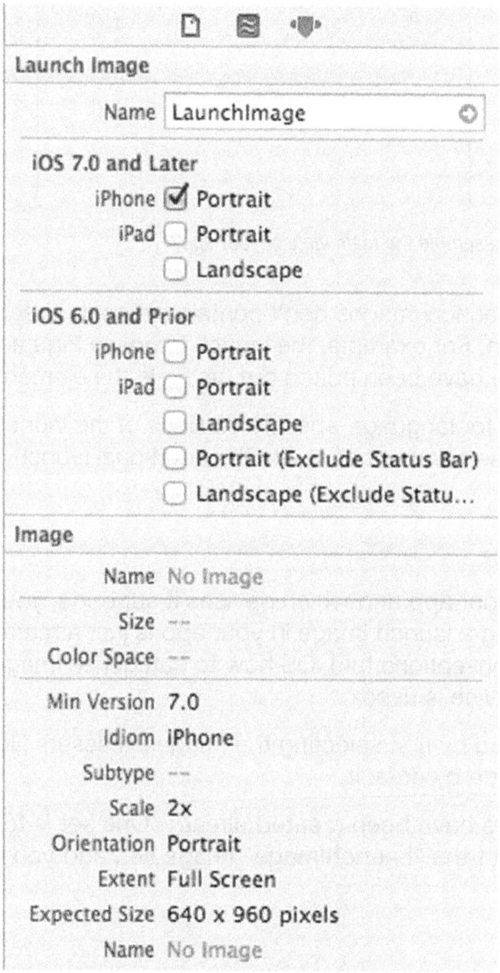

Figure 1-48. Asset catalog attributes inspector view, which shows expected size

Once you have created an image of the expected size, you can add it to the project by simply dragging and dropping it onto the image placeholder box shown in Figure 1-49. Just be aware that your launch image has to be of type .PNG or it will not work. Also, if you try to add an incorrectly sized image to the box, you'll get a compiler warning.

iPhone Portrait

Figure 1-49. *Asset catalog image drag and drop*

After dragging and dropping, the image gets saved to the images.xcassets ➤ LaunchImage. launchimage folder. You will also need to create an image for the R4 image space in Figure 1-49, just as you did for the 2x image.

If you happen to have multiple launch images, you can choose which launch-image set you would like to use by selecting the root project node from the project navigator and changing the launch-image source, which is located under the General tab in the editor window, as shown in Figure 1-50.

Figure 1-50. *Selecting an image set to use for the launch image*

Summary

In this chapter, you've acquired (or refreshed) some fundamental knowledge you need to follow the remaining recipes within this book. You've seen how to set up a basic application, how to build user interfaces, and how to control them with your code. Additionally, you've learned the difference between errors and exceptions in iOS, and you've seen how you can implement a strategy to handle them.

Chapter 2

Storyboard Recipes

In the beginning of mobile development, paper and pen were used to sketch out design flows for applications. Then came flowcharting software, in which you could digitally record your workflows and processes. Now developers have an Xcode tool called "Storyboards" that offers a visual representation of an app's workflow, which can produce a working framework for your app.

In the first two recipes of this chapter, you will use storyboards to build a simple, multipage application in iOS 7 that contains information about a fictional app-making company. The last recipe of the chapter will show you how to create a tab-bar application using storyboards.

So, What's in a Story (board)?

A storyboard is a collection of `.xib` files packaged together along with some metadata about the views and their relationships to each other. It is the ultimate separation of views from models and controllers that was intended since the early days of Model-View-Controller (MVC) programming. A storyboard provides a way for you to easily create multiple scenes and the connections between them by simply dragging and dropping components. The benefit to using storyboards is that you can do all of this with very little code.

The storyboard has two main components: scenes and segues.

Scenes

A scene is any view that fills the screen of a device. Scenes contain user interface (UI) objects and are controlled by view controllers. Figure 2-1 displays five different scenes in the storyboard that you will soon build.

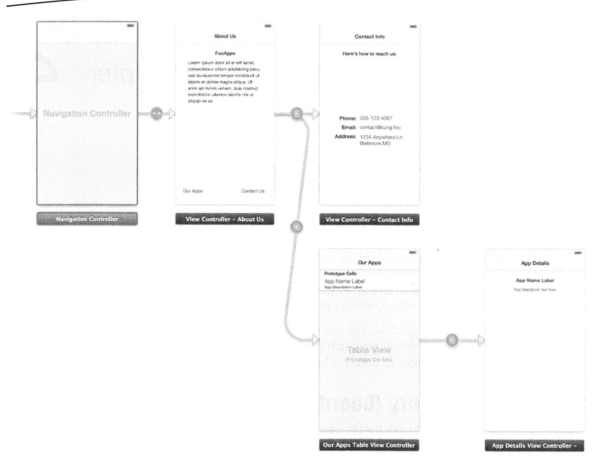

Figure 2-1. A storyboard with five scenes

Segues

A segue is basically a connection between two scenes that allows one scene to lead to another scene. When one scene leads to another, we say that the first scene is presenting the second. Likewise, the second scene is the presented scene.

There are several types of segues you can create:

- *Push segue* – A push segue requires a navigation controller or a tab-bar controller in order to operate. When moving from one view controller to another, you are pushing a new view controller on to that navigation or tab-bar controller's stack. The benefit is that the navigation or tab-bar controller can keep track of other view controllers on the stack and automatically provide navigation between them. Whenever you use a navigation controller or tab-bar controller, you should use this type of segue.

- *Modal segue* – A modal segue does not need a navigation controller to perform the segue. The caveat is that you lose the functionality of the automatic navigation because a modal segue is simply one view controller presenting another view controller.

- *Pop-over segue* – A pop-over segue is like a modal segue except it creates a small window that is presented over the top of the current scene. A pop-over is available only in iPad apps.

- *Custom segue* – A custom segue is used for coding custom transitions between scenes.

A segue is of the class UIStoryboardSegue and contains three properties: sourceViewController, destinationViewController, and identifier. The identifier is an NSString that can be used to identify specific segues from your code.

The app would normally initiate a segue based on an action from the user. This can be the touching of a button or table view cell, or it could be the result of a gesture recognizer. Segues are represented on the storyboard by a line connecting two scenes, as shown in Figure 2-2.

Figure 2-2. *A segue connecting two scenes*

Multiple scenes can be tied to a single scene through segues, as you will see in later in this chapter. Depending on how you organize your storyboard, segues can go from right to left or from left to right.

Recipe 2-1: Implementing a Navigation Controller

In this example, you will build a simple project that displays information about a company. It uses a navigation bar to display the title of the current page.

Storyboards are available in all the application templates in Xcode except the empty project template. For this recipe you'll use the Single View Application template. Name the project "Recipe 2-1 to 2-2: About Us," as demonstrated in Figure 2-3.

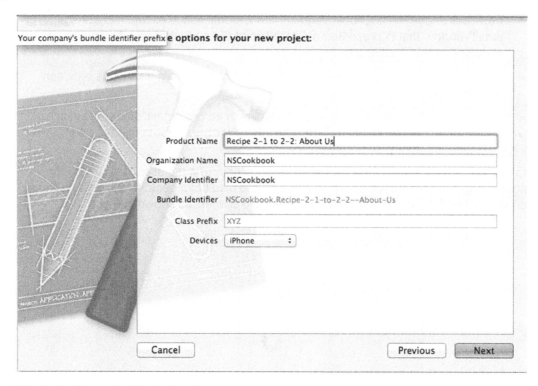

Figure 2-3. Configuring a project for storyboard use

After you've created your project, you'll see in the project navigator, as Figure 2-4 demonstrates, that your project contains a file named "`Main.storyboard`." Click this file to load it into Interface Builder and start building your storyboard.

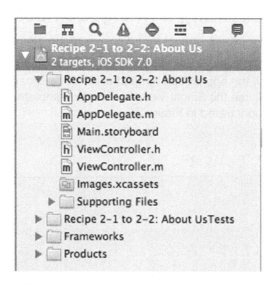

Figure 2-4. A project with a storyboard file

The first thing you're going to do is embed the main view in a navigation controller. Do this by selecting the view and then selecting Editor ➤ Embed In ➤ Navigation Controller in the main menu. This creates a navigation controller and connects it to your existing storyboard view. Figure 2-5 shows an example.

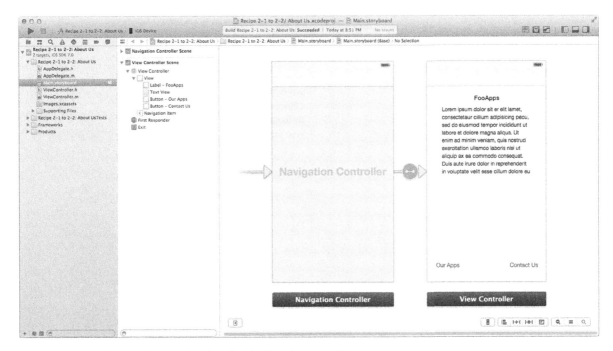

Figure 2-5. *The main view in a storyboard, embedded in a view controller*

Finally, create the user interface of the main view. Add a label, a text view, and two buttons to it and make it resemble Figure 2-6. To save space, the view controller in the example has been moved to overlap the navigation controller.

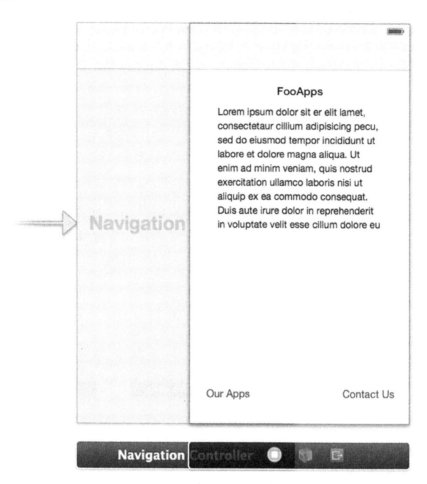

Figure 2-6. *A simple user interface to display company information*

> **Note**   Typically, navigation controllers are tied directly to a table-view controller when you drag them from
> the object library. This is the default configuration for the navigation controller seen in the object library.
> Because we do not want to get into the intricacies of a table view controller quite yet, we opted to connect a
> navigation controller to a view instead.

When you run this application on a 3.5" display, the two buttons will be cut off. To fix this, select
both buttons and, from the lower-right corner of the editor, press the button shown in Figure 2-7 and
choose "reset to suggested constraints." This is an AutoLayout feature that we'll talk about in detail
in Chapter 3.

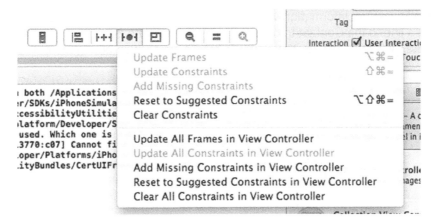

Figure 2-7. Applying suggested constraints so buttons show up on a 3.5" display

Adding a New Scene to the Storyboard

The next step is to add a new scene that displays the company contact information when the "Contact Us" button is tapped. Do this by dragging a view controller from the object library onto the storyboard.

To start, set up the user interface of the new scene so that it resembles the view on the right in Figure 2-8.

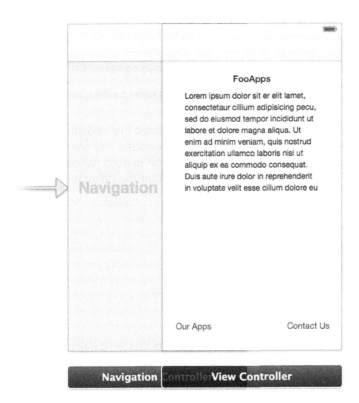

Figure 2-8. The storyboard with a new scene for contact information

To connect the new contact information view to the About Us view, Ctrl-click the "Contact Us" button and drag a line to the Contact Info view, as shown in Figure 2-9. This is the same action used to connect outlets, only this time you're using it to create a transition or segue between two scenes.

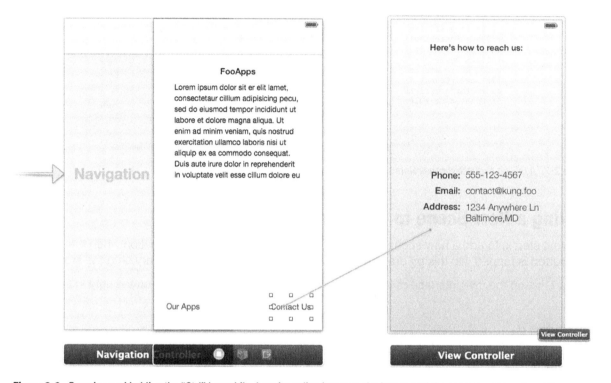

Figure 2-9. Pressing and holding the "Ctrl" key while dragging a line between the button and the scene creates a transition

When you release the mouse button a pop-up will display, asking how you want the transition to be performed. You can choose between **push**, **modal**, and **custom seques**. Because you are using a navigation controller, select "**push**" (as in Figure 2-10) so that a "Back" button is automatically set up for you in the navigation bar. After the connection is made, you'll notice that the navigation bar is automatically added to the new view.

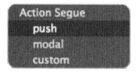

Figure 2-10. Selecting the "push" action segue

Make the navigation bar display the title of the current scene. One way to do that is to select "Navigation Item" in the view controller navigator (see Figure 2-11). Another way is to simply click the navigation bar.

Figure 2-11. Selecting the navigation item of a storyboard view controller

Set the Title attribute in the attribute inspector with the view selected, as shown in Figure 2-12. Set the title of the main view controller to "About Us." Then select the view containing the contact information and set its navigation item's title to "Contact Info."

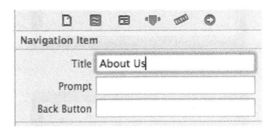

Figure 2-12. Setting the title of a navigation item

You set the identifier of a segue by selecting it in the storyboard and viewing its properties in the attributes inspector, as shown in Figure 2-13.

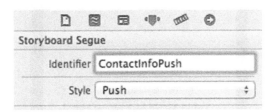

Figure 2-13. Setting a segue identifier in the attributes inspector

One habit to get into is providing your segues with an identifier. This helps future-proof your apps if you end up connecting multiple segues to one view. You can check the identifier of the calling segue to see the path the user is using to reach the presented scene. Typically you would take advantage of the prepareForSegue method to obtain the identifier.

If you run this app now, as shown by Figures 2-14 and 2-15, the "Contact Us" button will work and will display the Contact Info view. Note that this works without having to write a single line of code!

Figure 2-14. Main simulated view

Figure 2-15. The resulting view when the "Contact Us" button has been tapped

Recipe 2-2: Implementing a UITableViewController

Now let's expand upon the example from Recipe 2-1 and implement a UITableViewController, a class that manages a table view. This recipe will show you how to create a detail view that dynamically changes based on the cell selected in a table view. The first item that should come to mind when thinking about lists in iOS is UITableViewController. Storyboarding takes UITableViewController to a whole new level of convenience (refer to Chapter 4 for an extensive introduction to table views as they are used outside storyboards).

First, drag a UITableViewController to the storyboard from the object library, creating an Apps Table view.

In a table view scene there is a section called "Prototype Cells" at the top (see Figure 2-16). With storyboards, you can customize the layout and objects of a UITableViewCell with something called a prototype. We'll go into this further later in this recipe.

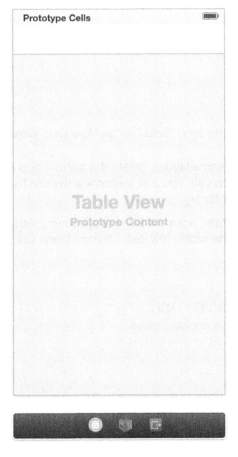

Figure 2-16. *A table view controller scene*

Select the table view and, in the attributes inspector, change the table view's Content attribute from Dynamic Prototypes to "Static Cells." Also, change the Style attribute to "Grouped," which gives a good separation between groups. Figure 2-17 shows these settings and the resulting table view.

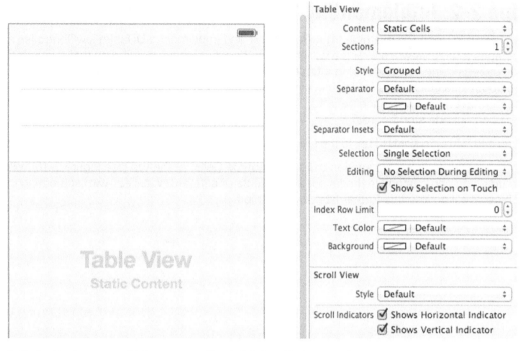

Figure 2-17. *A table view scene with Content set to "Static Cells" and Style set to "Grouped"*

Because every cell will have the same layout, delete the bottom two cells so you can customize and then quickly duplicate the top cell. You can customize the cell like any other container view by dragging objects from the object library.

Select the cell and choose "Subtitle" from the Style drop-down menu in the attributes inspector. This creates a title and a subtitle on the table view cell. Change these values, as shown in Figure 2-18, by double-clicking each one.

Figure 2-18. *A customized table view cell*

Now you'll duplicate the cell to create three instances of it. Do that by clicking and holding the "Alt" key (⌥), while dragging the cell downward. Repeat again to add a third row to the table view. Now you can customize the two new cells so they contain unique information, resembling Figure 2-19.

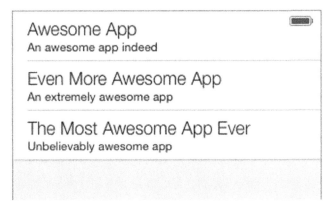

Figure 2-19. A table view with three customized cells

All that is left is to connect the "Our Apps" button to this new view. Select the button in the About Us view and Ctrl-click-drag to the table view scene you just created. Then set up a push segue between the "Our Apps" button and the table view scene. Your storyboard should look similar to Figure 2-20.

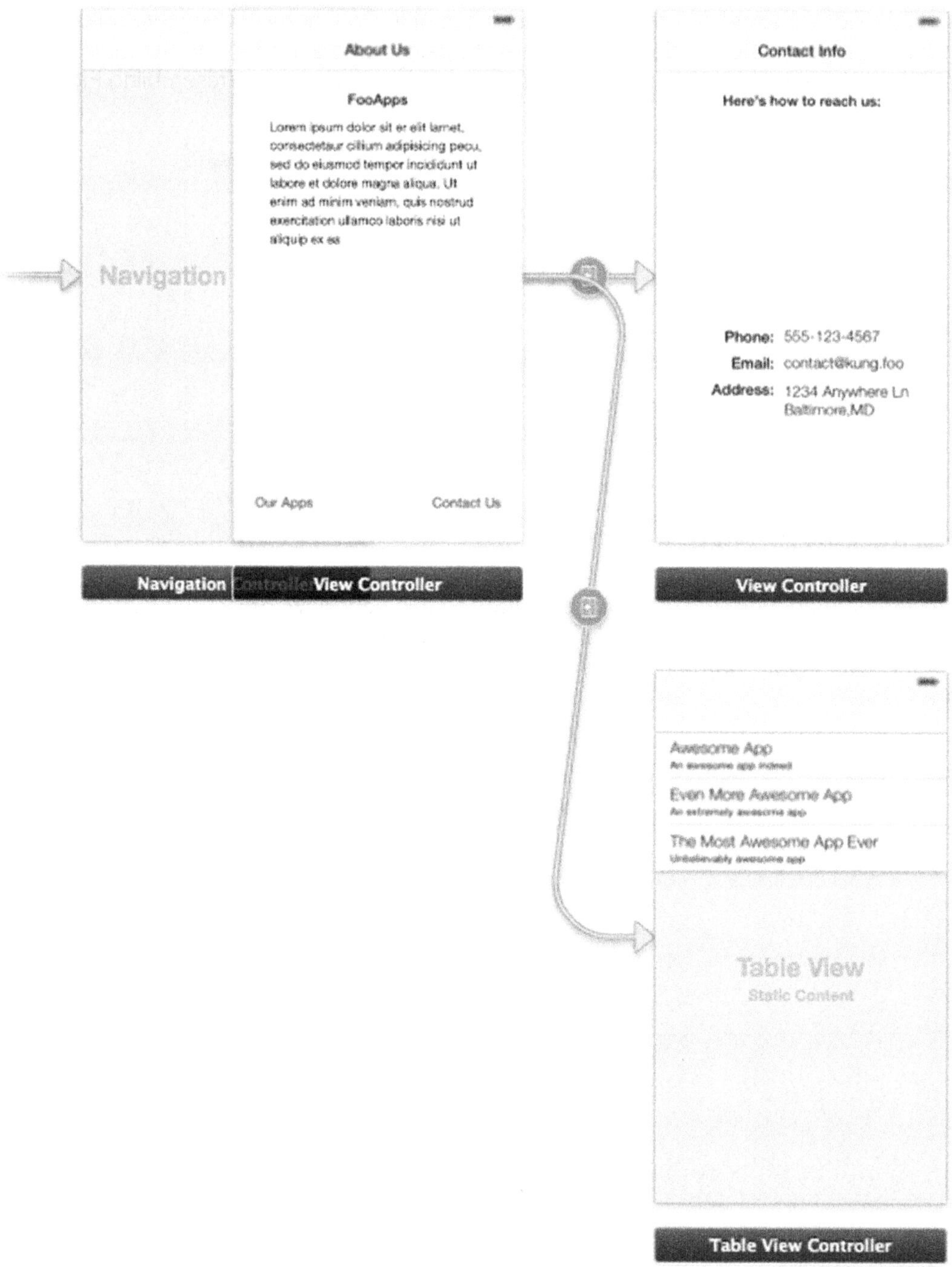

Figure 2-20. *A storyboard with three scenes*

> **Note**   What you may discern from Figure 2-20 is that storyboards require a lot of screen space. As your app grows, it can get quite difficult to work effectively with the user interface, especially for iPad apps. This is one of the reasons why some developers, despite all the advantages that come with storyboards, prefer to stick with `.xib` files and keep designing the user interfaces individually.

Now when you run the application, you can tap the "Our Apps" button, and the table view scene will show as in Figure 2-21. You've accomplished all this without writing any code. Amazing!

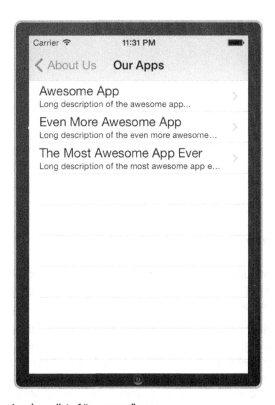

Figure 2-21. *The table view scene showing a list of "awesome" apps*

Adding a Detail View

The preceding app segment works well enough without any code, but by adding just a little bit of code behind the scenes you can create an even more powerful interface in a very short period of time. Before you start coding, you will need to set up the interface. When you see a table view, you instinctively know that there is likely to be a detail view waiting for you when you touch one of the cells. Let's add that detail view now.

To create a detail view, you'll first drag and drop a new view controller onto the storyboard. Make it look like Figure 2-22 by adding a label for the title and a text view for the description text.

Figure 2-22. A detail view user interface

In a real scenario, this page would likely contain additional information, such as a link to a web page where you can purchase the app in question. However, we're going to keep this example as simple as possible and just show the name and the description.

You want each of the table view cells to segue to this view when touched, so Ctrl-drag the line from each of the three cells to the detail view. This time when you release the mouse button, you'll notice that you can choose between setting up a selection segue or an accessory action. (see Figure 2-23). For the purpose of this recipe, though, create push selection segues that will trigger a transition when the cell is selected (as opposed to when its accessory button is tapped).

Figure 2-23. A pop-up with options to create either a selection segue or an accessory button action for a table view cell

Again, once you've connected the cells to the detail view using the push method, the view will display the navigator bar. In the same way you did earlier, set the title in the corresponding navigator item to "App Details."

As Figure 2-24 shows, there should now be three segues connecting the table view to the app details scene.

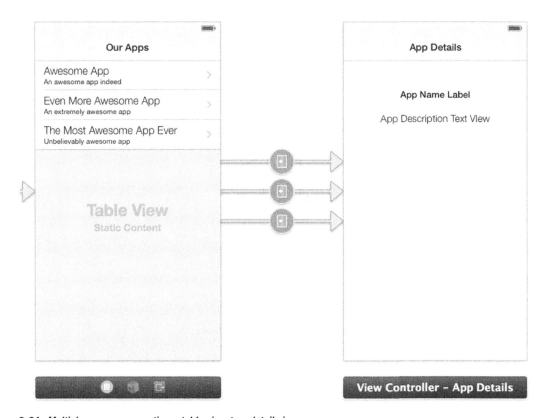

Figure 2-24. Multiple segues connecting a table view to a detail view

Select the first segue and enter an identifier for it in the attributes inspector. Set it to "PushAppDetailsFromCell1," as shown in Figure 2-25.

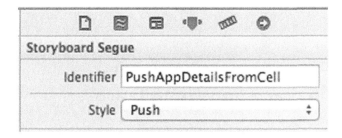

Figure 2-25. Setting an identifier for a segue that's pushing a detail view

Repeat the process for the other two segues and set their identifier to "PushAppDetailsFromCell2" and "PushAppDetailsFromCell3," respectively. You'll use these identifiers later to identify which segue triggered a transition to the app details scene.

You've gotten this far without using any code, but that convenience is about to end. You need to start generating some dynamic content on the app details view controller, and you are going to need to dive into some code for that.

Create a model class to hold information about your apps. Create a new class (CMD + N), a subclass of NSObject, with the name "AppDetails." (Refer to Recipe 1-6 for information about creating a new class.)

Add the following properties and init method declarations to the header file of the new class, as shown in Listing 2-1.

Listing 2-1. Adding a custom initializer method declaration and accompanying properties

```
//
//  AppDetails.h
//  Recipe 2-1 to 2-2: About Us
//

#import <Foundation/Foundation.h>

@interface AppDetails : NSObject

@property(strong, nonatomic) NSString *name;
@property(strong, nonatomic) NSString *description;

-(id)initWithName:(NSString *)name description:(NSString *)descr;

@end
```

The implementation of the initWithName:description: method goes into the AppDetails.m file, as shown in Listing 2-2.

Listing 2-2. Implementing the custom initializer method

```
//
//  AppDetails.m
//  Recipe 2-1 to 2-2: About Us
//

#import "AppDetails.h"

@implementation AppDetails

-(id)initWithName:(NSString *)name description:(NSString *)descr
{
self = [superinit];
if (self)
```

```
    {
self.name = name;
self.description = descr;
    }
returnself;
}

@end
```

In the preceding bit of code, you are simply creating a custom initializer that sets the name and description of the detail view controller when a new instance of the class is created.

Setting Up a Custom View Controller

With the data object in place, you can make the detail view controller display the attributes of an AppDetails object. For that, you need to attach a custom view controller class to the detail view.

To do this, create a new Objective-C class with the name "AppDetailsViewController" and make it a subclass of UIViewController. Make sure the "With XIB for user interface" checkbox is cleared. Refer to Figure 1-25 for the location of this checkbox.

Now attach the new view controller class to the app details scene. Go back to the storyboard editor and select the view controller object at the bottom of the app details scene (see Figure 2-26).

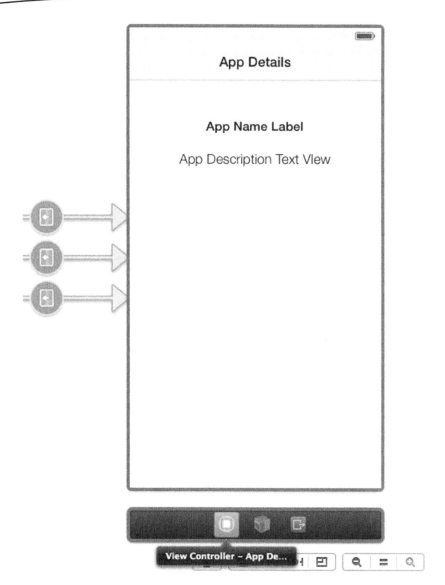

Figure 2-26. *Selecting the view controller object of a scene*

With the view controller object selected, go to the identity inspector and set the Class attribute to "AppDetailsViewController," as shown in Figure 2-27.

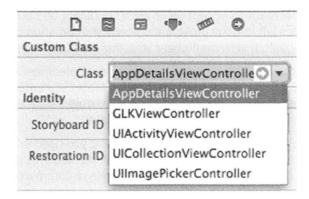

Figure 2-27. Attaching a custom view controller class to a scene

Create outlets for the name label and the description text view. Do this by using the assistant editor (see Recipe 1-4). Use the following respective outlet names:

- nameLabel
- descriptionTextView

You also need a property to hold the current app details object. Add the code in Listing 2-3 to your AppDetailsViewController.h file.

Listing 2-3. Importing the AppDetails class and creating a property for it

```
//
//  AppDetailsViewController.h
//  About Us
//

#import <UIKit/UIKit.h>
#import "AppDetails.h"

@interface AppDetailsViewController : UIViewController

@property (weak, nonatomic) IBOutlet UILabel *nameLabel;
@property (weak, nonatomic) IBOutlet UITextView *descriptionTextView;
@property (strong, nonatomic) AppDetails *appDetails;

@end
```

In AppDetailsViewController.m, add the code in Listing 2-4 to the viewDidLoad method.

Listing 2-4. Setting the name label and description text outlets from the AppDetails class

```
- (void)viewDidLoad
{
    [super viewDidLoad];
    // Do any additional setup after loading the view.
    self.nameLabel.text = self.appDetails.name;
    self.descriptionTextView.text = self.appDetails.description;
}
```

The app details scene is now ready to accept an `AppDetails` object and populate its label and text view with data from it. What's left to do is provide the scene with an appropriate object. For this, you need to create yet another custom view controller class, this time for the table view scene.

So, as you did before with the app details scene, create a new Objective-C class. This time make it a subclass of `UITableViewController` and name it "OurAppsTableViewController." Attach the new class to the "Our Apps" scene by selecting its view controller object from the storyboard. In the identity inspector, set `OurAppsTableViewController` as its class.

Open the new `OurAppsTableViewController.m` file. The first thing you need to do is get rid of the existing table view datasource and delegate methods that are there by default. This is because you're using a static table view content, as defined in your storyboard. So delete or comment out the following methods:

- `numberOfSectionsInTableView:`

- `tableView:numberOfRowsInSection:`

- `tableView:cellForRowAtIndexPath:`

- `tableView:didSelectRowAtIndexPath:`

Now you need to tie one of the three segues to the app details scene. You will need to know which segue is called upon by determining which table view cell was selected. This can be done by overriding the prepareForSegue:sender: method.

> **Note**   In our example, we are simply determining which segue triggered which transition, but the prepareForSeque:sender: method is also useful for passing data from one view controller to the next.

Add the code in Listing 2-5 to the `OurAppsTableViewController.m` file.

Listing 2-5. Implementing the "prepare for segue" method

```
//
//  OurAppsTableViewController.m
//  Recipe 2-1 to 2-2: About Us
//
#import "OurAppsTableViewController.h"
#import "AppDetailsViewController.h"
#import "AppDetails.h"

@implementation OurAppsTableViewController

- (void)prepareForSegue:(UIStoryboardSegue *)segue sender:(id)sender
{
NSString *name;
NSString *description;
if ([segue.identierisEqualToString:@"PushAppDetailsFromCell1"])
    {
        name = @"Awesome App";
        description = @"Long description of the awesome app...";
    }
```

```
elseif ([segue.identifierisEqualToString:@"PushAppDetailsFromCell2"])
    {
        name = @"Even More Awesome App";
        description = @"Long description of the even more awesome app...";
    }
elseif ([segue.identifierisEqualToString:@"PushAppDetailsFromCell3"])
    {
        name = @"The Most Awesome App Ever";
        description = @"Long description of the most awesome app ever seen...";
    }
else
    {
return;
    }

AppDetailsViewController *appDetailsViewController = segue.destinationViewController;
    appDetailsViewController.appDetails =
    [[AppDetailsalloc] initWithName:name description:description];
}
// ...

@end
```

As you can see from the code, you are identifying each segue by its identifier and creating an AppDetails object with information about the corresponding app. You then hand over the object to the view controller for the app details scene.

If you run your app now, you'll see that each of the table view cells will show different information in the app details scene. Figure 2-28 demonstrates a simulated result of this application.

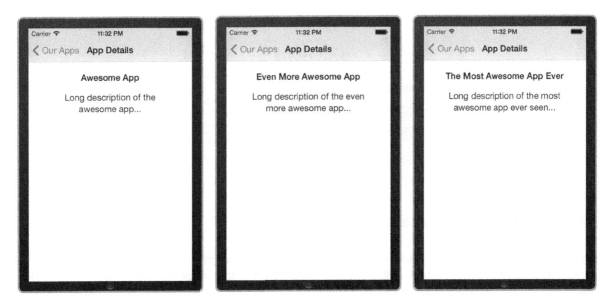

Figure 2-28. Three app details scenes with information about three apps

Using Cell Prototypes

The app is working as intended up to this point, but what if you add new apps to your inventory? With the current implementation, you would have to update the table view with new cells for each new app item. In this section, we show you how you can update the table view dynamically instead, using cell prototypes instead of static cells.

Start by changing the table view from static to dynamic. To do this, return to the "Our Apps" scene and delete the three rows. This also removes the three connected segues. Now select the table view and, in the attributes inspector, change the Content attribute from "Static Cells" to "Dynamic Prototypes," as shown in Figure 2-29. Make sure the Prototype Cells field is set to "1" as well.

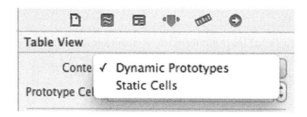

Figure 2-29. *Changing table view content from "Static Cells" to "Dynamic Prototypes"*

Next, you need to modify the prototype cell that will be the template for the cells you'll later add dynamically. You can design the cell the same way you did with the static cells; however, you'll make one change by adding a disclosure indicator icon to it. Do this with the Accessory attribute for the cell. Figure 2-30 shows the prototype cell with the gray disclosure indicator icon, which looks like an arrow pointing to the right.

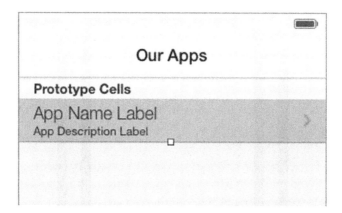

Figure 2-30. *A table view cell prototype with two labels and a disclosure indicator*

Next, you need to set a reuse identifier, which will be used later to retrieve instances based on the prototype cell. With the prototype cell selected, go to the attributes inspector and enter "AppCell" for the Identifier attribute, as shown in Figure 2-31.

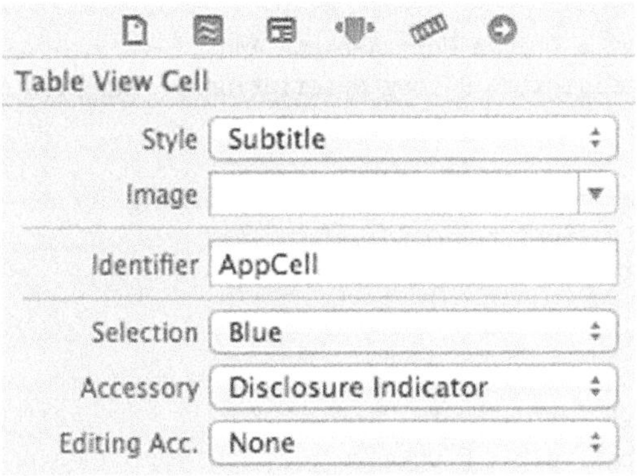

Figure 2-31. *Setting a reuse identifier for a cell prototype*

Now create a segue for the transition to the app details scene. Ctrl-drag a line from the prototype cell to the app details scene. As you did with the static cells, use the "push" selection segue type.

Select the segue you just created and set its Identifier attribute to "PushAppDetails."

You are now finished with the setup of the prototype cell. The remaining task is to write the code for the dynamic displaying of the table view content. Switch to OurAppsTableViewController.m and add the code shown in Listing 2-6.

Listing 2-6. *Adding table view delegate methods*

```
- (NSInteger)numberOfSectionsInTableView:(UITableView *)tableView
{
return1;
}

- (NSInteger)tableView:(UITableView *)tableView numberOfRowsInSection:(NSInteger)section
{
return3;
}

- (UITableViewCell *)tableView:(UITableView *)tableView cellForRowAtIndexPath:(NSIndexPath *)
indexPath
{
//Set the CellIdentifier that you set in the storyboard
static NSString *CellIdentifier = @"AppCell";

    UITableViewCell *cell = [tableView dequeueReusableCellWithIdentifier:CellIdentifier];

switch (indexPath.row)
    {
case0:
            cell.textLabel.text = @"Awesome App";
            cell.detailTextLabel.text = @"Long description of the awesome app...";
break;
```

```
case1:
            cell.textLabel.text = @"Even More Awesome App";
            cell.detailTextLabel.text = @"Long description of the even more awesome app...";
break;
case2:
            cell.textLabel.text = @"The Most Awesome App Ever";
            cell.detailTextLabel.text =
@"Long description of the most awesome app ever seen...";
break;

default:
            cell.textLabel.text = @"Unkown";
            cell.detailTextLabel.text = @"Unknown";
break;
    }

return cell;
}
```

You can now make the prepareForSegue:sender: method a lot simpler by utilizing the information stored in the cells. Update the prepareForSegue:sender: method's implementation, as shown in Listing 2-7.

Listing 2-7. Simplifying the prepareForSegue method

```
- (void)prepareForSegue:(UIStoryboardSegue *)segue sender:(id)sender
{
if ([segue.identifierisEqualToString:@"PushAppDetails"])
    {
AppDetailsViewController *appDetailsViewController = segue.destinationViewController;
UITableViewCell *cell = sender;
        appDetailsViewController.appDetails =
        [[AppDetailsalloc] initWithName:cell.textLabel.text
description:cell.detailTextLabel.text];
    }
}
```

Now when you run the app, the table view loads as before using the one prototype cell and the datasource. Figure 2-32 shows the simulated result of your newest updates to your application. In this example, you are still using static data for the AppDetails class, but this app could easily be extended to use a core data object model or even to pull a list of apps from a remote file on your server. Those features will be covered in more detail in Chapter 14.

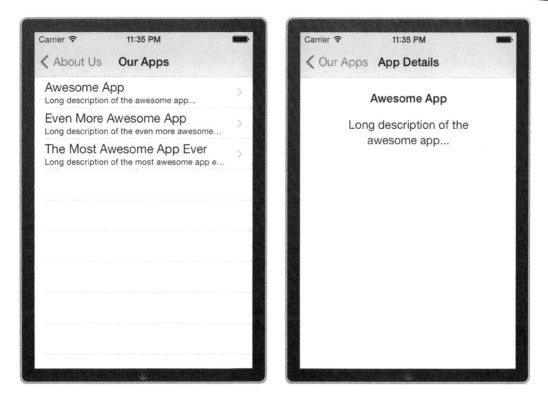

Figure 2-32. The same table view loading its content through its view controller using a prototype cell

Recipe 2-3: Implementing a UITabBarController

A tab bar controller is another handy controller for segmenting your application into multiple sections. Ideally, these sections would contain a series of views that are related to each other. A good example of a UITabViewController is the one currently used by the iTunes app. At the bottom of the app you'll see tabs for Music, Movies, TV Shows, and so on. This recipe demonstrates the creation of a tab bar controller app that will display some news categories.

To begin, we'll need to create a new single view application project. Yes, we could create a tabbed application, but that takes the fun out of it. Title the new project "Recipe 2-3: News App." When the new single view project opens, select the Main.storyboard file from the project navigator and delete the view that is already created for you. With the Main.storyboard file still open, drag a tab bar controller object into the storyboard from the object library. Your storyboard should now resemble Figure 2-33.

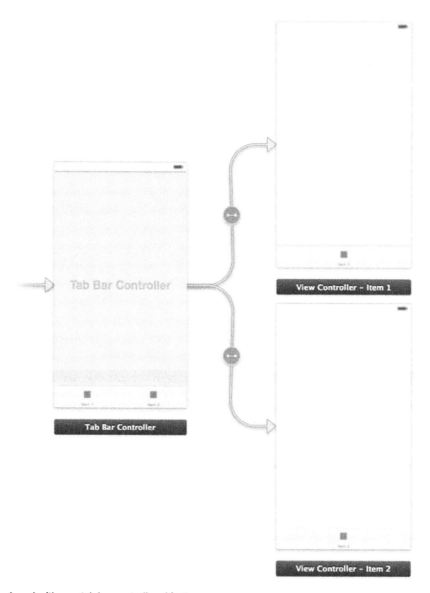

Figure 2-33. Storyboard with new tab bar controller object

The first two scenes have already been created for you, so drag two more view controllers onto the screen so as to have four scenes.

Once the two new view controllers are on the storyboard, while holding the control button, click and drag from the tab bar controller to one of the new view controllers. When prompted for the segue type, choose Relationship Segue ➤ view controllers from the dialog box, as shown in Figure 2-34. Repeat for the other view controller you added to the screen.

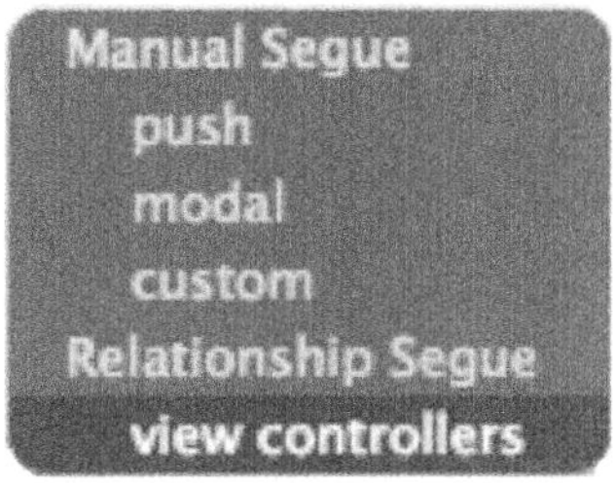

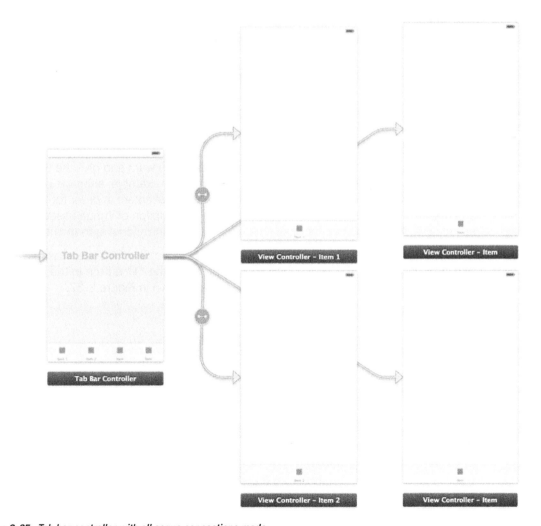

Figure 2-34. *Selecting the correct segue type for a tab bar controller*

At this point, all the segue connections should be made between the view controllers and the tab bar controllers. If you have done everything correctly, you should see segue connections, as shown in Figure 2-35.

Figure 2-35. *Tab bar controller with all segue connections made*

If you look at the bottom of the tab bar controller in Figure 2-36, you'll see that the tabs have updated accordingly. You will also notice that all the icons are the same and that the labels are not very descriptive. We'll fix these next.

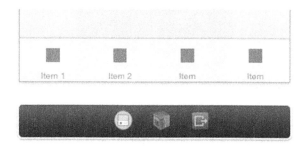

Figure 2-36. *Updated icons that appear as a result of connecting a view controller*

For this app we're going to create four new categories: Headlines, Sports, Tech, and Politics. To change these icons and labels, we simply need to change the individual view icon properties.

To change the image icon, we'll first need to add images to the project. The iOS Human Interface Guidelines from Apple specify that tab bar icons should be 60 x 60 pixels for retina devices and 30 x 30 pixels for non-retina devices. Both sizes will be needed for any project that needs to maintain compatibility with non-retina devices. Files need to be in PNG format and work best when they are black and white. You can find the iOS Human Interface Guidelines at `https://developer.apple.com/library/ios/documentation/userexperience/conceptual/mobilehig/`.

If you create your own images, title the 30 x 30 pixel icon whatever you want and give the 60 x 60 pixel icon the same name but add @2x to the end of the file name. For example: anImage.png and anImage@2x.png. Prior to Xcode 5, this naming convention was a requirement in order for the compiler to choose the appropriate size for retina devices. Now, with the introduction of image assets, this is no longer a requirement. Still, it's a good naming convention from an organizational standpoint.

Because we'll be creating four categories, we'll need four icons. Select the "images.xcassets" file in the project navigator and create four new image sets by pressing the "+" button in the lower-left corner of the editor window and choosing "New Image Set," as shown in Figure 2-37.

Figure 2-37. *Creating a new image set*

Name the image sets "headlinesIcon," "politicsIcon," "sportsIcon," and "techIcon" by double-clicking each image set in the left pane of the editor window (Figure 2-38).

Figure 2-38. Creating a new image set

Once the images are created, drag and drop the .png icon file from your finder onto one of the boxes provided in the image set, as shown in Figure 2-39. The 1x box corresponds to the 30 x 30 pixel image, and the 2x box corresponds to the 60 x 60 pixel image. Do this for each of the image sets.

Figure 2-39. Dragging and dropping a 30 x 30 pixel image to a 1x location

Now that we have all our images sets, we can start editing the icon attributes on the view controllers. Select the Main.storyboard file and then select the icon on the first view item (Item 1) by clicking it, as shown in Figure 2-40.

Figure 2-40. Selecting a tab bar icon for editing

From the attributes inspector you can change the title, image, badge, identifier, and tag. For this example, you'll set only the title and image. Give the first view icon a title of "Headlines" and change the image title to "headlinesIcon" (Figure 2-41). Repeat this process for the tab bar icons of the other three views.

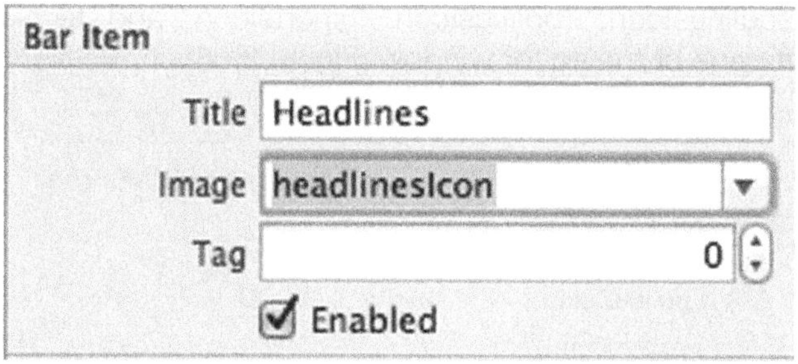

Figure 2-41. *Changing icon attributes*

Next, you should add a label to each of the view controllers so you know for sure that the view has changed. Add labels and title them, as shown in Figure 2-42.

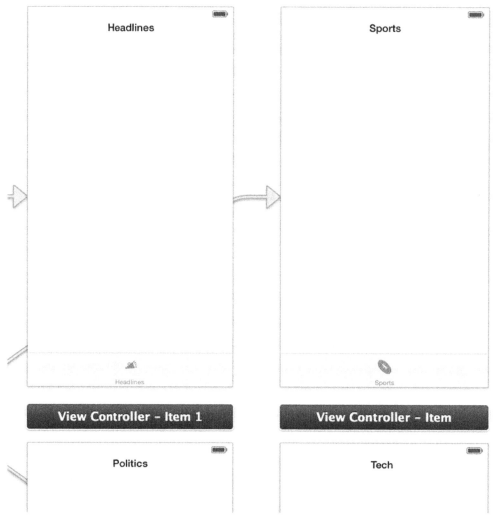

Figure 2-42. *Changing icon attributes*

Now you are ready to run the application. You'll notice at the bottom of the screen in Figure 2-43 that the four icons are there with the images we specified. The selected icon gets highlighted by default when that view controller is active.

Figure 2-43. *The final tab bar controller app*

Summary

In this chapter, we have covered navigation controllers, table view controllers, and tab view controllers. By now you should have a pretty good grasp of how to navigate and utilize storyboards. In the next chapter, we will demonstrate auto layout, a subject we briefly touched on in this chapter. Auto layout can help you position objects in a view so that they display correctly on all screen sizes and in various orientations.

Chapter 3

Chapter **3**

Layout Recipes

The user interface and its layout are essential to most applications, especially in iOS with its orientation-sensitive devices. Users expect apps to support both portrait and landscape orientation in most cases. They also expect apps to run on both the iPhone and iPad. In other words, they expect your apps to have dynamic layouts.

This chapter shows you how to use Auto Layout, a great way to build dynamic user interfaces in iOS 7. Auto Layout is a feature first introduced in Xcode 4, and it provides a way to handle view layouts in iOS apps via the interface builder as well as programmatically. Auto Layout offers a very powerful model with which you can build layouts that scale and adapt to screen rotations in a way that was not possible without reverting to complicated code. Auto Layout also makes tasks such as supporting multiple languages, which might read right-to-left, a breeze.

Xcode 5 introduces many capabilities that make the process of creating layouts more flexible and less error prone. The developer now has more control over layouts; however, with more control comes more ways to create errors.

In this chapter, you will learn how to create flexible interfaces using Auto Layout. We will cover creating these interfaces using the interface builder and also using the programmatic method. Lastly, we will cover the types of errors incurred and how to troubleshoot them.

Recipe 3-1: Using Auto Layout

In this recipe, we show you how Auto Layout works. You will learn how to add constraints, which are relationships between views, in various ways. You will also learn how to disable auto constraints as well as how to take advantage of the preview tool. The preview tool allows you to render your layout in real time without simulating.

Auto Layout Constraints

Auto Layout, in its essence, consists of "constraints" dictating the relationship between user interface elements as well as a layout engine that enforces the constraints. A *constraint* is a rule that dictates how elements should behave when other elements near them, such as the containing view, change. By this definition, the layout engine enforces these rules.

In Chapter 1, we used a handy Xcode 5 feature to set the suggested constraints on some buttons. Auto Layout, which is turned on by default, allows you to set up constraints to make your application look good in various sizes and orientations. To see how Auto Layout works, you will create an application with a simple user interface that automatically adapts to both portrait and landscape orientations.

Start by creating a new single view application and then build a user interface in the provided view controller, such as the one in Figure 3-1, using labels, a text field, and a text view. To make the boundary lines more clear, give your view controller a gray background color. You can do this by selecting your view controller in the storyboard and changing the background property in the attributes inspector.

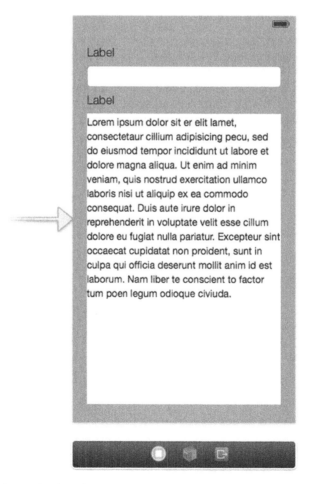

Figure 3-1. The user interface in portrait orientation

When you position and size the elements, be sure to use the default spacing between those elements and the main view's boundaries, as well as between those elements and the subviews; in other words, where Interface Builder snaps during dragging, as shown in Figure 3-2.

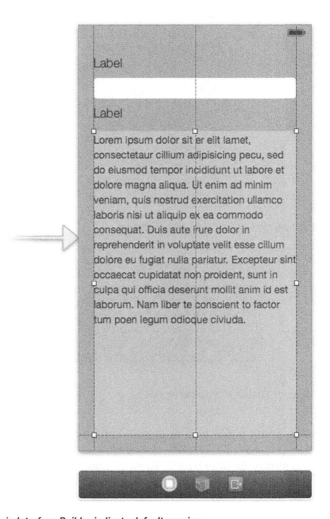

Figure 3-2. The dashed lines in Interface Builder indicate default spacing

Unlike Xcode 4, Xcode 5 does not add constraints to your layout until you are ready for them. Instead, if you have not specified any constraints, Xcode will add fixed position and size constraints at build time. This will ensure your interface looks exactly as it does in the Interface Builder window. This is handy for when you are prototyping and you don't really care what it does in a different screen resolution or rotation.

When you are ready to add constraints, there are several ways to do so. We'll demonstrate three different approaches in the following sections.

Adding Constraints Using the Control-Click and Drag Method

Starting with the text field, control-click and drag from the left side of the text field to the view controller and choose "Leading Space to Container" from the popup, as shown in Figure 3-3 and Figure 3-4.

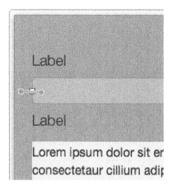

Figure 3-3. Control-click and drag from the text field to the view controller

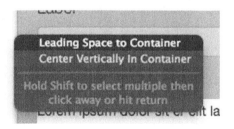

Figure 3-4. Choosing "Leading Space to Container" from the popup

Now you should see that the constraint was successfully added to the text field, as indicated by the orange line that appears (Figure 3-5). The line is orange instead of blue because we have a problem, as indicated in the status window by the warning icon. Without getting into too much detail, this orange line is telling us we don't have enough constraints.

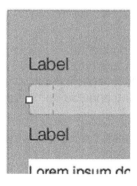

Figure 3-5. Choosing "Leading Space to Container" from the popup

Note   Orange lines are an addition in Xcode 5; previously, constraints were added for you. Because you now have more flexibility, you can create these types of errors. We'll cover errors in more depth in Recipe 3-3.

If you control-click and drag from one object to another, say between the label and the text field, you'll see that the popup will have different options, as shown in Figure 3-6.

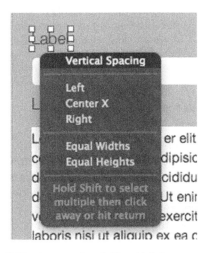

Figure 3-6. *Options shown when control-clicking between text field and label*

Now, we could go through and control-click from each item and add constraints manually, or we could use some more new features in Xcode 5 to speed up the process.

Adding Constraints Using the Auto Layout Issue-Resolving Menu

Apple has added a new menu to Xcode 5 that helps us add constraints quickly. By using the Auto Layout issue-resolving menu, we have access to a number of tools that can suggest constraints for us. Select all the objects and choose the "Reset to Suggested Constraints" option from the issue-resolving menu, as shown in Figure 3-7.

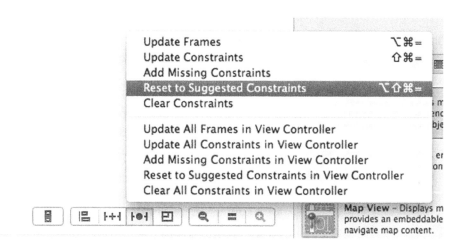

Figure 3-7. Resetting to suggested constraints from the issue-resolving menu

The view controller should now have a number of new constraints, as shown in Figure 3-8. You will also see that there are no more issues showing up in the status bar. Notice that none of these objects have specified height and width constraints. This is because of a nifty little feature called *intrinsic content size*. Intrinsic content size will determine the height and width based on the content contained within it. Normally, you would not want to add explicit width or height constraints because if the size of the content changes, you might have clipped text or other bizarre results.

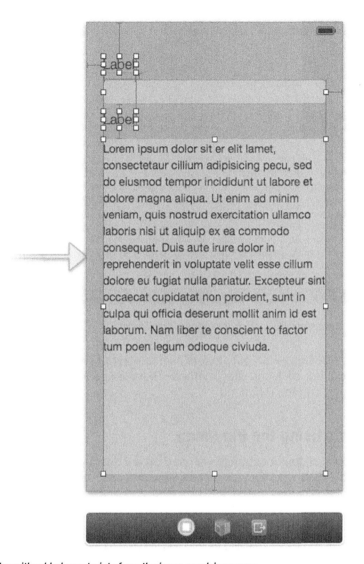

Figure 3-8. *View controller with added constraints from the issue-resolving menu*

Now that the issues have all been cleared, you can build and run the application to see how it is affected in both portrait and landscape modes (Figure 3-9). To change the simulator to landscape view, select hardware ➤ rotate right from the simulator file menu.

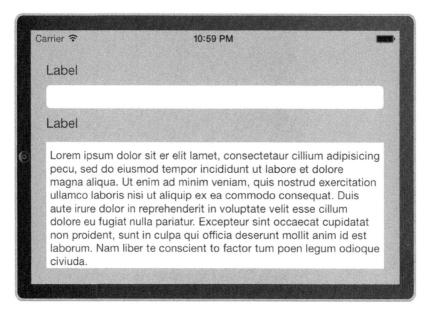

Figure 3-9. Simulated app in landscape view taking advantage of Auto Layout

You now know how to use suggested constraints as a starting point, and you also know how to add constraints using the control-click and drag method. There is one more way to add and manipulate constraints, which is by using the Pin menu.

Adding Constraints Using the Pin Menu

Because we already have all the constraints we need on our scene, we'll want to delete some before we can demonstrate the Pin menu. Select the text view and choose "clear constraints" from the issue-resolving menu.

> **Note** You can delete constraints individually by selecting the constraint line and pressing the "delete" key.

With all the constraints removed from the text view, select the text view (if it is not already selected) and press the "Pin" button to bring up its menu, as shown in Figure 3-10. Fill in the values for the top, right, left, and bottom distance to the nearest neighbor. If there is no neighbor, then the distance to the nearest neighbor becomes the distance to the edge of the superview. That is, if a label does not have anything between it and the edge of the screen (superview), then the closest neighbor becomes the edge of the screen.

Figure 3-10. Adding missing constraints to the text view using the Pin menu

Notice that there are suggested values already provided. Despite this, you actually have to type them in to take effect. So type the following values and click "Add constraints:"

- Top: 13
- Left: 20
- Right: 20
- Bottom: 20

Now select the text view again and take a look at the constraints that were added. You should now see four new constraints, as shown in Figure 3-11.

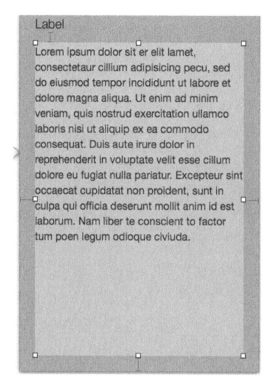

Figure 3-11. *Constraints added from the Pin menu*

Constraint Priorities

These new Auto Layout changes in Xcode 5 are a huge time saver compared with the Xcode 4 version of Auto Layout. However, what if you wanted a slightly different layout behavior for the Name text field, for example? What if you didn't want it to grow beyond a certain width when switching between device orientations? (It's a common principle in human computer interaction that the size of input fields should reflect the size of expected content). Let's say you want the Name text field to grow when the screen rotates, but only up to 350 pixels. This is where Auto Layout starts to shine.

Translated into the language of constraints, you want to add a constraint that states that the text field's width must be no more than 350 pixels. Adding this constraint yields a logical problem, though. When the screen rotates, the system can't satisfy both the constraints. The constraint that pins the right edge of the text field conflicts with the one that dictates its maximum width.

What can you do about that? One idea is to remove the constraint inserted by Interface Builder. However, it doesn't take much thought to realize that it would leave you with a constraint that's true for many values, but not decisive enough to settle for one value. No, you need both constraints: you want the right edge of the text field to pin to the right edge of the screen *unless that makes the width larger than 350 pixels*. The solution is *constraint priorities*.

Auto Layout offers the possibility to set a priority value between 0 and 1000 on individual constraints. A value of 1000 means the constraint is required, but for any other value the constraint with the higher priority takes precedence. In this case, it means you can make the width constraint required but set a lower priority for the "pin to the right edge" constraint. Then, when the screen rotates, the width constraint will "win" over the other and you will get the effect you seek.

Start by adding the width constraint. Select the text field and click the "Pin" button in the Auto Layout bar located in the lower-right corner of Interface Builder. Then select the width constraint, as shown in Figure 3-12. For now, you can leave the width value the same. Click the "Add Constraints" button.

Figure 3-12. *The Auto Layout bar in Interface Builder allows you to add your own constraints*

Now select the newly added width constraint by clicking it. In the attributes inspector for the new width constraint, set the relation to "Less Than or Equal" and the constant to "350." Leave the priority at 1,000 (required), as shown in Figure 3-13.

Figure 3-13. *Setting a width constraint to "Less Than or Equal" to "350"*

What's left to do now is to lower the priority of the "trailing space to superview" constraint. Make sure the text field is selected and then select the right constraint, the one between the edge of the text field and the view controller edge. Change the value of the property to "500," as shown in Figure 3-14.

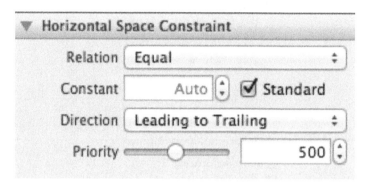

Figure 3-14. *Lowering the priority of a constraint to 500*

If you have done this last step correctly, your new constraints should resemble Figure 3-15. A circle indicating a "less than or equal" size is on the width constraint, and the lower priority constraint is now dashed.

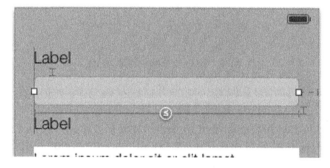

Figure 3-15. *Constraints indicating a "less than or equal" size, with a lower priority right-hand constraint*

If you build and run your application now, you will see that when you rotate the device, the text field grows but stays at the maximum width of 350, as shown in Figure 3-16.

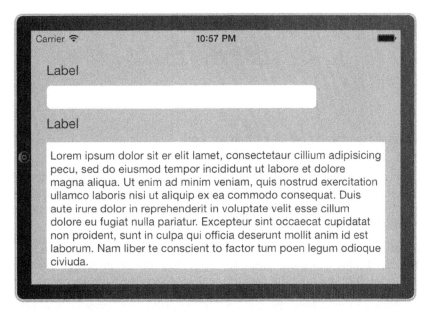

Figure 3-16. A user interface with a text field that has a width constraint of 350 pixels

Adding a Trailing Button

Let's make things a little more complicated. What if you want to add a button on the right side of the text field while still keeping the current width constraint? You can accomplish this using Auto Layout. In this section, we'll create a trailing button, which is a button that will stay pinned to the trailing (in this case, right) edge of the text field.

Before jumping in and adding constraints, it's a good idea to stop and think about the layout in terms of constraints. You should do the following:

1. Allow the width of the text field to be less than or equal to 350.

2. Pin the trailing edge of the text field to the leading edge of the button.

3. Pin the trailing edge of the button to the trailing edge of the screen, unless the first constraint is violated.

> **Note** The reason we're using the terms *leading* and *trailing* instead of left and right (which are also valid attributes) is that trailing and leading are defined as adapting to changes of text directions in, for example, the Hebrew language, which is read right to left. In such an instance, *leading* becomes right and *trailing* becomes left, and the user interface adapts accordingly. This is yet another reason to use Auto Layout.

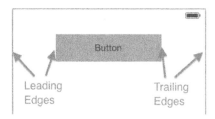

Figure 3-17. *Leading and trailing edges in a left-to-right language locale*

Before you add the button to the user interface, delete the trailing edge constraint on the text field and resize the text field to a width of 199 points. You can easily change this value in the size inspector found in the utilities pane. For the time being, don't worry about the issue warning you get by removing this constraint.

Now add a new button to the right of the text field and snap it to the default snap line on the right. You could add the constraints using the "reset to suggested" constraints and it will work fine, but for the sake of better understanding, use the control-click method using the following steps:

1. Control-click and drag from the text field to the button and choose "Center Y" from the pop up.

2. Control-click and drag from the button to the edge of the view controller and choose "Trailing Space to Container."

3. Control-click and drag from the trailing edge of the text field to the leading edge of the button and choose "Horizontal Spacing."

4. Select the button and choose "add a width and height" from the Pin menu. You don't need to put in values; just use the ones that are there.

5. Select the constraint that is created between the trailing edge of the button and the right-side container and change the priority to 500.

If you have done everything correctly, your constraints should resemble Figure 3-18.

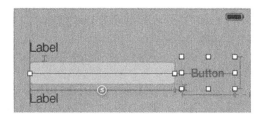

Figure 3-18. *Correct trailing-edge button constraints*

Note   Although you typically should not add fixed widths to any objects that can have variable content size, we had to add fixed widths in this example. This is because without a fixed width on either the text field or the button, Auto Layout would not know which one to stretch.

Once all the constraints are in place, build and run your application. When rotated, the user interface should adapt nicely and keep the text field at the maximum width while the button stays pinned to its right, as shown in Figure 3-19.

Figure 3-19. A user interface with a text field that has a width constraint of 350 pixels and a button trailing to its right

Disabling Auto Layout

In contrast, let's look at how the app behaves with Auto Layout turned off. Select the entire view controller and go to the file inspector, located in Xcode's right Utilities View panel. In the Interface Builder Document section (see Figure 3-20), deselect "Use Auto Layout."

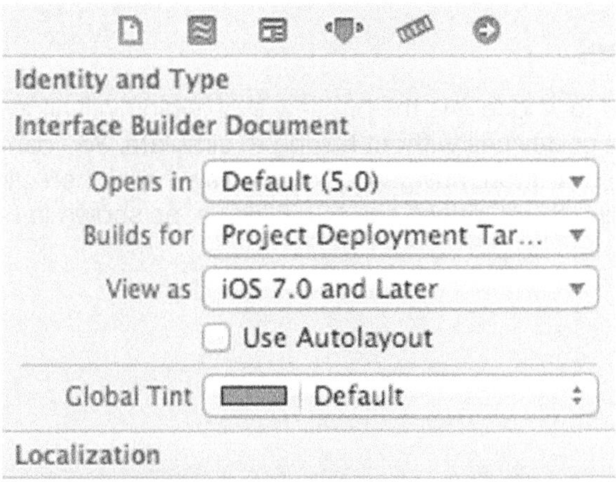

Figure 3-20. Auto Layout is turned on by default for new projects

> **Note**   It is not normally recommended to disable Auto Layout and then re-enable it, as it will wipe out all your constraints.

Now build and run the app again. As you can see in Figure 3-21, rotating the device results in a significantly worse user experience.

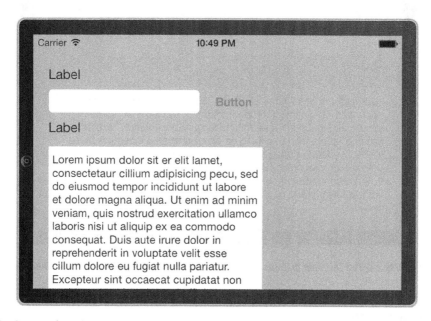

Figure 3-21. A landscape orientation user interface without Auto Layout enabled

> **Note**   This behavior is exactly what you would see if you never added any constraints to begin with.

Using the Preview Tool

A new handy feature added to Xcode 5 is the preview tool, which will allow you to preview Auto Layout in other orientations or devices without having to simulate. You can get to the preview tool by clicking the "Related Files" button, navigating to "Preview," and then clicking "Main.storyboard" while simultaneously pressing the "Option" and "Shift" keys, as shown in Figure 3-22.

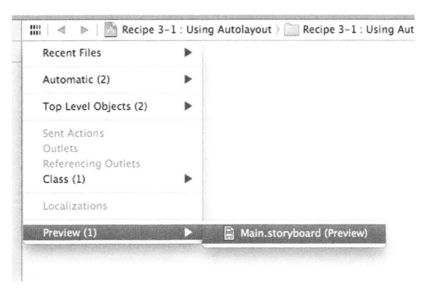

Figure 3-22. *Getting to the preview tool*

Next, you'll see a popup dialog box. Click the "+" button, which is shown highlighted in Figure 3-23, and press "Enter." This will split your storyboard editor window with a preview window.

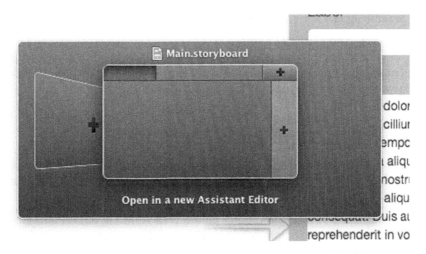

Figure 3-23. *Getting to the preview tool*

You can select the orientation and device from the lower-right corner of the new preview window, as shown in Figure 3-24. You'll notice that the constraints have been re-added by us.

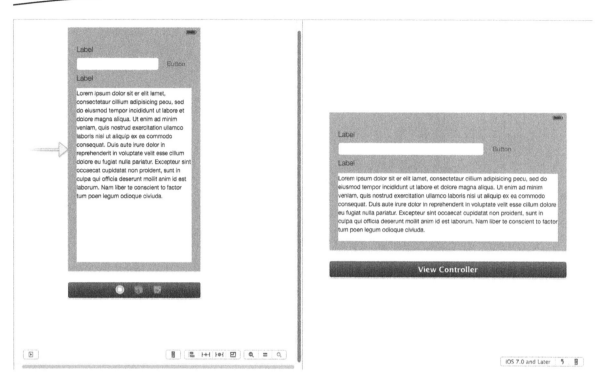

Figure 3-24. *Storyboard editor window with a landscape layout preview on the right*

Although simple, we hope that the preceding example has opened your eyes to the possibilities of Auto Layout. The next recipe takes it to the next level, where you'll create constraints from code, thus constructing a truly dynamic layout.

Recipe 3-2: Programming Auto Layout

The preferred way to set up Auto Layout constraints is to use Interface Builder, as shown in Recipe 3.2. The main reason is that Interface Builder makes it easier to diagnose bad constraints, plus it's much faster.

However, there are situations in which you can't define your Auto Layout constraints in Interface Builder, such as if you create the user interface components dynamically in code. For these situations, you need to revert to code for setting up the constraints. In this recipe, we'll show you how.

Setting Up the Application

For this recipe, you will build a simple app that has three buttons: one for adding a new image view to the screen, one for removing the last image view added, and one for removing all added image views. You will use Auto Layout to position the buttons in a row at the top of your screen. You also will use Auto Layout to position the image views so they overlap each other, with the last-added image view on top and with each image view having a 10 percent increase in size compared to the previous.

Start by creating a new single view application and then add the following properties to its view controller, as shown in Listing 3-1.

Listing 3-1. Adding interface properties to ViewController.h

```
//
//  ViewController.h
//  Recipe 2.2 Coding Auto Layout
//

#import <UIKit/UIKit.h>

@interface ViewController : UIViewController

@property (strong, nonatomic) UIButton *addButton;
@property (strong, nonatomic) UIButton *removeButton;
@property (strong, nonatomic) UIButton *clearButton;
@property (strong, nonatomic) NSMutableArray *imageViews;
@property (strong, nonatomic) NSMutableArray *imageViewConstraints;

@end
```

Create the three buttons directly in code using a `helper` method to reduce code duplication. Switch to `ViewController.m` and add the code shown in Listing 3-2.

Listing 3-2. Adding a helper method to create three buttons in the ViewController.m file

```
- (UIButton *)addButtonWithTitle:(NSString *)title action:(SEL)selector
{
    UIButton *button = [UIButton buttonWithType:UIButtonTypeSystem];
    [button setTitle:title forState:UIControlStateNormal];
    [button addTarget:self action:selector forControlEvents:UIControlEventTouchUpInside];
    button.translatesAutoresizingMaskIntoConstraints = NO;
    [self.view addSubview:button];
    return button;
}
```

Listing 3-2 creates a new button with the provided title and action method. What's notable here is the setting of the `translatesAutoresizingMaskIntoConstraints` property of the button to NO. This is important to do if you're defining your own Auto Layout constraints; otherwise, you're likely to end up with conflicting constraints. Recipe 3-3 has more to say on this subject.

> **Note**   You don't explicitly set view frames when using Auto Layout. Instead, a view's position and size are dictated by the constraints you define.

With the `helper` method in place, you can turn to the `viewDidLoad` method and add code to create the buttons, as shown in Listing 3-3.

Listing 3-3. Calling the helper method to create the three buttons

```
- (void)viewDidLoad
{
    [super viewDidLoad];
    self.addButton = [self addButtonWithTitle:@"Add" action:@selector(addImageView)];
    self.removeButton = [self addButtonWithTitle:@"Remove" action:@selector(removeImageView)];
    self.clearButton = [self addButtonWithTitle:@"Clear" action:@selector(clearImageViews)];
}
```

Next, add stubs, as shown in Listing 3-4, for the three action methods for each of the three buttons. You'll implement these methods later, but leave them empty for now.

Listing 3-4. Adding placeholder stubs for the button actions

```
- (void)addImageView
{
}

- (void)removeImageView
{
}

- (void)clearImageViews
{
}
```

If you run your application now, you would see nothing but a white screen. The buttons wouldn't show because you haven't defined any Auto Layout constraints to dictate their positions and sizes. So let's go ahead and do that.

There are two principal ways to create constraints from code. You can either use Visual Format Language, a visually descriptive syntax for defining Auto Layout constraints, or you can use the `constraintWithItem:attribute:relatedBy:toItem:attribute:multiplier:constant:` method. The former has the advantage in that it provides better visualization of the constraints created; the latter, on the other hand, provides completeness (not all constraints can be expressed using Visual Format Language).

Often you'll mix the two ways to create your constraints. In this case, use the format language for positioning the buttons and a mix of the two for placing the image views.

Visual Format Language

Before moving on and creating the constraints, let's take a quick look at Visual Format Language. For example, this string defines constraints that position button2 right next to button1 with a spacing of 20 pixels between the two:

```
[button1]-20-[button2]
```

A single hyphen indicates default spacing:

```
[button1]-[button2]
```

Here are same constraints but for vertical layout:

```
V:[button1]-[button2]
```

Although horizontal is the default, you can explicitly state it:

```
H:[button1]-[button2]
```

The spacing toward the superview is indicated with a | character. The following example states that textField should be pinned to both leading and trailing ends of the superview, with default spacing:

```
|-[textField]-|
```

You can also define a component size. This example specifies that button1 is 50 pixels wide and button2 has the same width as button1:

```
[button1(50)]-[button2(==button1)]
```

You also can have inequalities, as in the following example, which specifies that button1 is at least 50 pixels wide:

```
[button1(>=50)]
```

You can set both a minimum and a maximum width at the same time:

```
[button1(>=50, <=100)]
```

You also can set priorities on the size constraints. For example, button1 is at least 50 pixels wide, but with a priority at 500, which makes it non-required but desirable:

```
[button1(>=50@500)
```

Table 3-1 shows the syntax elements and some additional examples of Visual Format Language.

Table 3-1. *Visual Format Language Syntax Elements*

Syntax Elements	Examples	Description
H:, V:	H:|-[statusLabel]-| V:|[textView]|	Horizontal or vertial orientation. Default orientation is horizontal, so the H: can therefore be omitted.
|	|[textView]|	Indicates the superview; its leading end if on the left side and trailing on the right
-	[button1]-[button2]	Standard space
-N-	|-20-[view]	An N-sized spacing
[view]		Indicates a subview
==, >=, <=	[view1(==view2)] [view(>=30, <=100)]	Relation operators. Can only be used in size constraints
@N	[view(==50@500)] [view1(==view2@500, >=30)]	Constraint priority. Can only be used in size constraints. Default priority is 1000 (i.e., a required constraint)

Now, let's add constraints that position the three buttons in a row at the top of the screen. Because these constraints are always the same, you add them directly in the viewDidLoad method. Start by creating a dictionary that contains the buttons, with identifying keys, as shown in Listing 3-5. Auto Layout uses the dictionary to map identifiers in the format language strings to the corresponding views (buttons in this case).

Listing 3-5. *Creating a dictionary for buttons and their identifying keys*

```
NSDictionary *viewsDictionary =
[[NSDictionary alloc] initWithObjectsAndKeys:
self.addButton, @"addButton",
self.removeButton, @"removeButton",
self.clearButton, @"clearButton", nil];
```

Then you add the constraints that pin the buttons to each other in a row. Do this by calling the ad dConstraints:constraintsWithVisualFormat:options:metrics:views: method of the main view, providing the visual format string (marked in bold), as shown in Listing 3-6.

Listing 3-6. *Adding constraints to pin buttons to each other*

```
[self.view addConstraints:[NSLayoutConstraint
    constraintsWithVisualFormat:@"H:|-[addButton]-[removeButton]-[clearButton]"
    options:0 metrics:nil views:viewsDictionary]];
```

Next, pin the buttons to the top of the screen, as shown in Listing 3-7.

Listing 3-7. Pinning buttons to the top of the screen

```
[self.view addConstraints:[NSLayoutConstraint
    constraintsWithVisualFormat:@"V:|-[addButton]"
    options:0 metrics:nil views:viewsDictionary]];
[self.view addConstraints:[NSLayoutConstraint
    constraintsWithVisualFormat:@"V:|-[removeButton]"
    options:0 metrics:nil views:viewsDictionary]];
[self.view addConstraints:[NSLayoutConstraint
    constraintsWithVisualFormat:@"V:|-[clearButton]"
    options:0 metrics:nil views:viewsDictionary]];
```

The viewDidLoad method should look like Listing 3-8 at this point.

Listing 3-8. The viewDidLoad method with Listings 3-5 to 3-7 added to it

```
- (void)viewDidLoad
{
    [super viewDidLoad];
    self.addButton = [self addButtonWithTitle:@"Add" action:@selector(addImageView)];
    self.removeButton = [self addButtonWithTitle:@"Remove" action:@selector(removeImageView)];
    self.clearButton = [self addButtonWithTitle:@"Clear" action:@selector(clearImageViews)];

    NSDictionary *viewsDictionary =
[[NSDictionary alloc] initWithObjectsAndKeys:
self.addButton, @"addButton",
self.removeButton, @"removeButton",
self.clearButton, @"clearButton", nil];

    [self.view addConstraints:[NSLayoutConstraint
constraintsWithVisualFormat:@"H:|-[addButton]-[removeButton]-[clearButton]"
options:0 metrics:nil views:viewsDictionary]];

    [self.view addConstraints:[NSLayoutConstraint
constraintsWithVisualFormat:@"V:|-[addButton]"
options:0 metrics:nil views:viewsDictionary]];
    [self.view addConstraints:[NSLayoutConstraint
constraintsWithVisualFormat:@"V:|-[removeButton]"
options:0 metrics:nil views:viewsDictionary]];
    [self.view addConstraints:[NSLayoutConstraint
constraintsWithVisualFormat:@"V:|-[clearButton]"
options:0 metrics:nil views:viewsDictionary]];
}
```

You now can build and run your application. Your screen should look like the one in Figure 3-25.

Figure 3-25. A row of buttons positioned using Auto Layout

Now that you've verified that the layout is as expected, it's time to implement the respective button's action method. We'll start with the adding of image views.

Adding Image Views

Before you move on and start implementing the addImageView action method, you need to do a little more setup and initialization. First, you need an image that you're going to populate the image views with. (For simplicity, we use the same image for all image views.) Using a finder window, drag an image of your liking, which is in the PNG format, to the Supporting Files folder of your project. (Chapter 1 contains a detailed description about how to add resource files, such as images, to an Xcode project.) In the following code, be sure to replace the name "sweflag," which is the name of the image we chose, to the name of your image file.

Next, initialize the two array properties that you added to the view controller's header file in the beginning of this recipe. Add the code in Listing 3-9 to the viewDidLoad method. The code for creating the three buttons and their constraints has been removed for brevity.

Listing 3-9. Initializing the two array properties for holding image views and their constraints

```
- (void)viewDidLoad
{
    [super viewDidLoad];

    // ...

    self.imageViews = [[NSMutableArray alloc]initWithCapacity:10];
    self.imageViewConstraints = [[NSMutableArray alloc]initWithCapacity:10];
}
```

Now implement the addImageView action method, as shown in Listing 3-10.

Listing 3-10. Implementing the addImageView action

```
- (void)addImageView
{
    UIImage *image = [UIImage imageNamed:@"sweflag"];
    UIImageView *imageView = [[UIImageView alloc] initWithImage:image];
    [self.view addSubview:imageView];
    imageView.translatesAutoresizingMaskIntoConstraints = NO;
    [self.imageViews addObject:imageView];

    [self rebuildImageViewsConstraints];
}
```

The implementation in Listing 3-10 is straightforward. It creates and adds an image view to the main view, sets its translatesAutoresizingMaskIntoConstraints property to NO so as not to conflict with the custom constraints you'll set up in a minute, adds itself to the imageViews array for later reference, and finally orders a rebuild of all the image views' constraints.

Defining the Image Views' Constraints

The rebuildImageViewsConstraints helper method removes all previous image view constraints and recreates them. The basic structure, without the actual creating of the constraints, is shown in Listing 3-11.

Listing 3-11. Starting point for the rebuildImageViewsConstraints method

```
- (void)rebuildImageViewsConstraints
{
    [self.view removeConstraints:self.imageViewConstraints];
    [self.imageViewConstraints removeAllObjects];

    if (self.imageViews.count == 0)
        return;

    // TODO: Build the imageViewConstraints array

    [self.view addConstraints:self.imageViewConstraints];
}
```

To build the `imageViewConstraints` array (beginning at the code comment shown in Listing 3-11), start with the constraints that pin the first image view to the left side of the screen and immediately below the row of buttons. At the same time, set the first image view's size to 50x50 points. Listing 3-12 shows this code.

Listing 3-12. Building the imageViewConstraints array

```
UIImageView *firstImageView = [self.imageViews objectAtIndex:0];

NSDictionary *viewsDictionary = [[NSDictionary alloc]
    initWithObjectsAndKeys:self.addButton, @"firstButton", firstImageView, @"firstImageView", nil];

// Pin first view to the top left corner
[self.imageViewConstraints addObjectsFromArray:[NSLayoutConstraint
    constraintsWithVisualFormat:@"H:|-[firstImageView(50)]"
    options:0 metrics:nil views:viewsDictionary]];

[self.imageViewConstraints addObjectsFromArray:[NSLayoutConstraint
    constraintsWithVisualFormat:@"V:[firstButton]-[firstImageView(50)]"
    options:0 metrics:nil views:viewsDictionary]];
```

Each of the remaining image views (if any) overlap the previous one with an offset of 10 pixels to the right and down. Additionally, for effect, each image is 10 percent bigger than the previous. In pseudo code, what you should do is something like this:

```
imageView(N).X = imageView(N-1).X + 10;
imageView(N).Y = imageView(N-1).Y + 10;
imageView(N).Width = imageView(N-1).Width * 1.1;
imageView(N).Height = imageView(N-1).Height * 1.1;
```

Unfortunately, you cannot translate to Auto Layout constraints using the visual format notation. Instead, you must create the corresponding constraints explicitly, as shown in Listing 3-13.

Listing 3-13. Creating constraints explicitly for overlapping and offsetting images

```
if (self.imageViews.count > 1)
{
    UIImageView *previousImageView = firstImageView;

    for (int i=1; i < self.imageViews.count; i++)
    {
        UIImageView *imageView = [self.imageViews objectAtIndex:i];

        [self.imageViewConstraints addObject:[NSLayoutConstraint
            constraintWithItem:imageView attribute:NSLayoutAttributeLeading
            relatedBy:NSLayoutRelationEqual
            toItem:previousImageView attribute:NSLayoutAttributeLeading
            multiplier:1 constant:10]];

        [self.imageViewConstraints addObject:[NSLayoutConstraint
            constraintWithItem:imageView attribute:NSLayoutAttributeTop
            relatedBy:NSLayoutRelationEqual
```

```
            toItem:previousImageView attribute:NSLayoutAttributeTop
            multiplier:1 constant:10]];

    [self.imageViewConstraints addObject:[NSLayoutConstraint
        constraintWithItem:imageView attribute:NSLayoutAttributeWidth
        relatedBy:NSLayoutRelationEqual
        toItem:previousImageView attribute:NSLayoutAttributeWidth
        multiplier:1.1 constant:0]];

    [self.imageViewConstraints addObject:[NSLayoutConstraint
        constraintWithItem:imageView attribute:NSLayoutAttributeHeight
        relatedBy:NSLayoutRelationEqual
        toItem:previousImageView attribute:NSLayoutAttributeHeight
        multiplier:1.1 constant:0]];

    previousImageView = imageView;
    }
}
```

> **Note** The Visual Format Language of Auto Layout was designed for readability over completeness.
> Therefore, you cannot use it to express special cases such as overlaps and multiplied-property references.
> For these cases, you have to create the constraints explicitly using the `constraintWithItem:attribute`
> `:relatedBy:toItem:attribute:multiplier:constant:` method.

The complete `rebuildImageViewsConstraints` method, once complete, should look like Listing 3-14.

Listing 3-14. The complete rebuildImageViewsConstraints method

```
- (void)rebuildImageViewsConstraints
{
    [self.view removeConstraints:self.imageViewConstraints];
    [self.imageViewConstraints removeAllObjects];

    if (self.imageViews.count == 0)
        return;

    UIImageView *firstImageView = [self.imageViews objectAtIndex:0];

    // Pin first view to the top left corner
    NSDictionary *viewsDictionary =
        [[NSDictionary alloc] initWithObjectsAndKeys:
            self.addButton, @"firstButton",
            firstImageView, @"firstImageView", nil];

    [self.imageViewConstraints addObjectsFromArray:[NSLayoutConstraint
        constraintsWithVisualFormat:@"H:|-[firstImageView(50)]"
        options:0 metrics:nil views:viewsDictionary]];
```

```
    [self.imageViewConstraints addObjectsFromArray:[NSLayoutConstraint
        constraintsWithVisualFormat:@"V:[firstButton]-[firstImageView(50)]"
        options:0 metrics:nil views:viewsDictionary]];

    if (self.imageViews.count > 1)
    {
        UIImageView *previousImageView = firstImageView;

        for (int i=1; i < self.imageViews.count; i++)
        {
            UIImageView *imageView = [self.imageViews objectAtIndex:i];

            [self.imageViewConstraints addObject:[NSLayoutConstraint
                constraintWithItem:imageView attribute:NSLayoutAttributeLeading
                relatedBy:NSLayoutRelationEqual
                toItem:previousImageView attribute:NSLayoutAttributeLeading
                multiplier:1 constant:10]];

            [self.imageViewConstraints addObject:[NSLayoutConstraint
                constraintWithItem:imageView attribute:NSLayoutAttributeTop
                relatedBy:NSLayoutRelationEqual
                toItem:previousImageView attribute:NSLayoutAttributeTop
                multiplier:1 constant:10]];

            [self.imageViewConstraints addObject:[NSLayoutConstraint
                constraintWithItem:imageView attribute:NSLayoutAttributeWidth
                relatedBy:NSLayoutRelationEqual
                toItem:previousImageView attribute:NSLayoutAttributeWidth
                multiplier:1.1 constant:0]];

            [self.imageViewConstraints addObject:[NSLayoutConstraint
                constraintWithItem:imageView attribute:NSLayoutAttributeHeight
                relatedBy:NSLayoutRelationEqual
                toItem:previousImageView attribute:NSLayoutAttributeHeight
                multiplier:1.1 constant:0]];

            previousImageView = imageView;
        }

    }

    [self.view addConstraints:self.imageViewConstraints];
}
```

The only task remaining now is to implement the action methods for removing the last image view and removing all image views. This implementation is shown in Listing 3-15.

Listing 3-15. Action method implementation to remove and clear image views

```
- (void)removeImageView
{
    if (self.imageViews.count > 0)
    {
        [self.imageViews.lastObject removeFromSuperview];
        [self.imageViews removeLastObject];
        [self rebuildImageViewsConstraints];
    }
}

- (void)clearImageViews
{
    if (self.imageViews.count > 0)
    {
        for (int i=self.imageViews.count - 1; i >= 0; i--)
        {
            UIImageView *imageView = [self.imageViews objectAtIndex:i];
            [imageView removeFromSuperview];
            [self.imageViews removeObjectAtIndex:i];
        }

        [self rebuildImageViewsConstraints];
    }
}
```

The methods in Listing 3-15 are fairly straightforward. In the removeImageView action, check to see if there are any image views. If there are image views, remove that object from the view and then remove it from the array that contains it. The clearImageViews does the same thing the removeImageView action does, except it steps through every image view in the array and removes them one at a time. Both methods rebuild the constraints once they are finished removing image views.

Your app is now finished. If you build and run it, you should be able to repeatedly add and remove image views using the three buttons. Figure 3-26 shows an example in which we've added several image views.

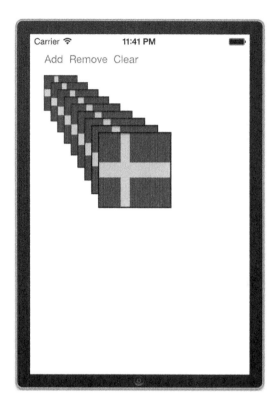

Figure 3-26. *Overlapping image views positioned using Auto Layout*

As Figure 3-27 shows, thanks to Auto Layout, the app works equally well in landscape orientation.

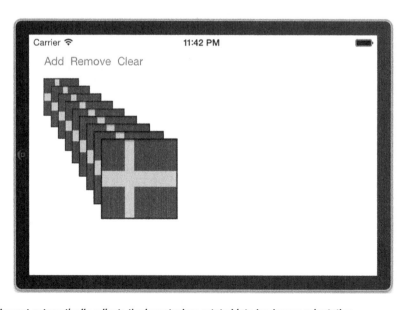

Figure 3-27. *Auto Layout automatically adjusts the layout when rotated into landscape orientation*

Recipe 3-3: Debugging Auto Layout Code

Auto Layout errors in code can be quite difficult to work out because you can't visually see the errors like you can in Interface Builder. The general advice is to think carefully about the constraints before you start coding them. However, to minimize the time spent in trial-and-error mode, it's important to know what's actually wrong with a problematic layout. In other words, you need to know how to debug it.

Besides syntax errors in Visual Format strings, there are two major ways in which an Auto Layout code might fail. The first is *unsatisfiability*, which means there are two or more constraints conflicting with each other in such a way that the layout engine can't simultaneously satisfy them. The second way is caused by *ambiguity*. That happens when the defined constraints aren't specific enough, leaving the layout engine with several possible values for a property.

> **Note**   When you do autolayout programmatically, errors fall under the category of unsatisfiability (conflicting constraints) or ambiguity when creating layouts visually in the interface builder. There is a third type of error called misplaced views, which indicates mismatched position or size. The orange lines in the visual editor indicate all these errors.

In this recipe, we show you examples of both unsatisfiable and ambiguous constraints. We'll show you how to identify and tackle them.

Dealing with Ambiguous Layouts

To get started, you need a new project, so create one using the single view application template. We'll begin with a simple example of an ambiguous layout. Let's say you want to programmatically add three buttons of equal size to the top of the screen. In the view controller's `viewDidLoad` method, add the code in Listing 3-16 to create the buttons and add them to the main view.

Listing 3-16. Creating buttons and adding them to the main view

```
- (void)viewDidLoad
{

    [superviewDidLoad];
UIButton *button1 = [UIButtonbuttonWithType:UIButtonTypeSystem];
    [button1 setTitle:@"Button 1"forState:UIControlStateNormal];
    button1.translatesAutoresizingMaskIntoConstraints = NO;
    [self.viewaddSubview:button1];

UIButton *button2 = [UIButtonbuttonWithType:UIButtonTypeSystem];
    [button2 setTitle:@"Button 2"forState:UIControlStateNormal];
    button2.translatesAutoresizingMaskIntoConstraints = NO;
    [self.viewaddSubview:button2];
```

```
UIButton *button3 = [UIButtonbuttonWithType:UIButtonTypeSystem];
    [button3 setTitle:@"Button 3"forState:UIControlStateNormal];
    button3.translatesAutoresizingMaskIntoConstraints = NO;
    [self.viewaddSubview:button3];
}
```

Then add constraints to pin the buttons to the top of the screen, as shown in Listing 3-17.

Listing 3-17. Adding constraints to pin buttons to the top of the screen

```
- (void)viewDidLoad
{
    [super viewDidLoad];

    // ...

    NSDictionary *viewsDictionary = NSDictionaryOfVariableBindings(button1, button2, button3);

    [self.view addConstraints:[NSLayoutConstraint constraintsWithVisualFormat:@"V:|-[button1]"
        options:0 metrics:nil views:viewsDictionary]];
    [self.view addConstraints:[NSLayoutConstraint constraintsWithVisualFormat:@"V:|-[button2]"
        options:0 metrics:nil views:viewsDictionary]];
    [self.view addConstraints:[NSLayoutConstraint constraintsWithVisualFormat:@"V:|-[button3]"
        options:0 metrics:nil views:viewsDictionary]];
}
```

> **Note** NSDictionaryOfVariableBindings() is a convenience function that creates the dictionary
> needed by NSLayoutConstraint to map identifiers in your visual format strings to the views. It creates
> entries for the provided views using the variable names as keys.

Finally, add constraints for the horizontal layout, pinning the buttons to each other and to the bounds
of the screen, as shown in Listing 3-18.

Listing 3-18. Adding constraints for pinning buttons to each other and screen bounds horizontally

```
- (void)viewDidLoad
{
    [super viewDidLoad];

    // ...

    [self.view addConstraints:[NSLayoutConstraint
        constraintsWithVisualFormat:@"|-[button1]-[button2]-[button3]-|"
        options:0 metrics:nil views:viewsDictionary]];
}
```

Build and run the app, expecting to see your buttons in a nice row at the top of the screen. The
buttons show up, but when you rotate the screen, as shown in Figure 3-28, one of the buttons gets
significantly wider than the other two.

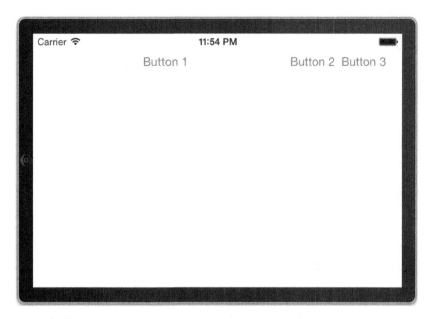

Figure 3-28. Due to ambiguous constraints, one of the buttons is wider than the other two

What's going on here? Your first thought when something like this happens might be that you have ambiguous constraints. To verify if that's the case, leave the app running but go back to Xcode and click the "Pause Program Execution" button (see Figure 3-29) in the Debug Area toolbar.

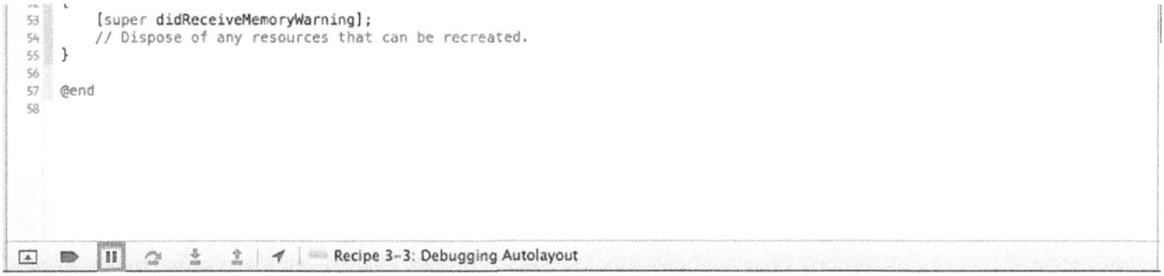

```
53        [super didReceiveMemoryWarning];
54        // Dispose of any resources that can be recreated.
55    }
56
57    @end
58
```

Figure 3-29. The "Pause Program Execution" button in Xcode

With the program paused, you can then use the (lldb) prompt to enter the following command:

po [[UIWindow keyWindow] _Auto LayoutTrace]

You then get a trace showing that the three buttons indeed have ambiguous layouts (see Figure 3-30.)

```
(lldb) po [[UIWindow keyWindow] _autolayoutTrace]

*<UIWindow:0x8a67f70>
|   *<UIView:0x8d784e0>
|   |   *<UIButton:0x8d78620> - AMBIGUOUS LAYOUT
|   |   |   <UIButtonLabel:0x8d78d80>
|   |   *<UIButton:0x8d79c70> - AMBIGUOUS LAYOUT
|   |   |   <UIButtonLabel:0x8d79db0>
|   |   *<UIButton:0x8d7add0> - AMBIGUOUS LAYOUT
|   |   |   <UIButtonLabel:0x8d7af10>
(lldb)

All Output ⇕                                    🗑  ▯▯ ▯▯
```

Figure 3-30. *An Auto Layout trace indicating ambiguous layouts*

> **Note**   po (or *print-object*) is a debugger command that prints out the description text of an object. It can be a very useful tool when debugging your application.

So what's the problem? Usually, when it comes to ambiguous layouts the problem is a sign that you're missing one or more constraints. The problem in this case is that you haven't specified the widths of the buttons specifically enough. All you've said is that the buttons should be pinned to each other and to the edges of the screen, so when the size of the screen increases, the layout engine has several options: it can increase the width of the first button, it can increase the width of the second button, and so on.

What you want, though, is to have buttons of equal widths. To solve the problem, simply add constraints specifying that button2 and button3 are the same width as button1, as shown in Listing 3-19.

Listing 3-19. *Setting button2 and button3 to equal widths*

```
- (void)viewDidLoad
{
    [super viewDidLoad];

    // ...

    NSDictionary *viewsDictionary = NSDictionaryOfVariableBindings(button1, button2, button3);

    [self.view addConstraints:[NSLayoutConstraint constraintsWithVisualFormat:@"V:|-[button1]"
        options:0 metrics:nil views:viewsDictionary]];
    [self.view addConstraints:[NSLayoutConstraint constraintsWithVisualFormat:@"V:|-[button2]"
        options:0 metrics:nil views:viewsDictionary]];
    [self.view addConstraints:[NSLayoutConstraint constraintsWithVisualFormat:@"V:|-[button3]"
        options:0 metrics:nil views:viewsDictionary]];

    [self.view addConstraints:[NSLayoutConstraint
        constraintsWithVisualFormat:@"|-[button1]-[button2(==button1)]-[button3(==button1)]-|"
        options:0 metrics:nil views:viewsDictionary]];
}
```

This leaves the layout engine with only one option: to increase the widths equally for all three buttons. Now when you build and run, you'll get the expected result, as in Figure 3-31.

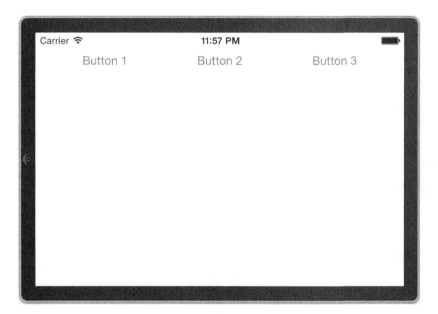

Figure 3-31. A user interface with constraints specifying the buttons to be of equal width

Handling Unsatisfiability

The opposite of ambiguous constraints is unsatisfiable constraints. In those cases, the probable cause is not too few, but rather too many constraints, or that two constraints conflict. This can be a little trickier to solve because you've added those constraints for a purpose. Therefore, the unsatisfiability might be a sign you've made logical errors and need to rethink the entire layout.

However, let's start with a simple yet common mistake that occurs in unsatisfiable constraints. Let's say you forgot to set `translatesAutoresizingMaskIntoConstraints` to `NO` for one of your buttons. That usually results in conflicting constraints between the ones the framework adds (for the autoresizing mask) and your own.

To see what happens, comment out the row in Listing 3-20 that sets the `translatesAutoresizingMaskIntoConstraints` property of your third button.

Listing 3-20. Commenting out the translatesAutoresizingMaskIntonContraints property for button3

```
- (void)viewDidLoad
{
    [super viewDidLoad];

    // ...

    UIButton *button3 = [UIButton buttonWithType:UIButtonTypeRoundedRect];
    [button3 setTitle:@"Button 3" forState:UIControlStateNormal];
// button3.translatesAutoresizingMaskIntoConstraints = NO;
    [self.view addSubview:button3];

    // ...
}
```

If you build and run now, you'll see that the buttons seem to have disappeared from the screen, as in Figure 3-32.

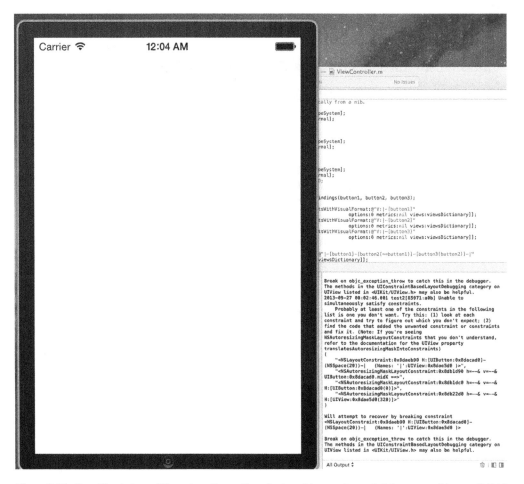

Figure 3-32. Forgetting to turn off the automatic creation of autoresizing mask constraints can result in unsatisfiable constraints errors

If you look in the error log, you'll see a long error text starting with the reason for the failure:

```
2013-07-05 17:15:53.268 Recipe 3-3: Debugging Auto Layout[40301:c07] Unable to simultaneously
satisfy constraints.
```

Probably at least one of the constraints in the list in the log is one you don't want. Try this: (1) look at each constraint and try to figure out which one you don't expect; (2) find the code that added the unwanted constraint or constraints and fix it.

> **Note** If you're seeing NSAutoresizingMaskLayoutConstraints that you don't understand, refer to the documentation for the UIView property translatesAutoresizingMaskIntoConstraints.

```
(
    "<NSLayoutConstraint:0x8ded860 H:|-(NSSpace(20))-[UIButton:0x8df8070]    (Names:
'|':UIView:0x8df7ee0 )>",
    "<NSLayoutConstraint:0x8ded8b0 H:[UIButton:0x8df8070]-(NSSpace(8))-[UIButton:0x8d75230]>",
    "<NSLayoutConstraint:0x8def8a0 UIButton:0x8d75230.width == UIButton:0x8df8070.width>",
    "<NSLayoutConstraint:0x8def8d0 H:[UIButton:0x8d75230]-(NSSpace(8))-[UIButton:0x8ddf420]>",
    "<NSLayoutConstraint:0x8def910 UIButton:0x8ddf420.width == UIButton:0x8df8070.width>",
    "<NSAutoresizingMaskLayoutConstraint:0x8d6f390 h=--& v=--& UIButton:0x8ddf420.midX ==>"
)
```

Indeed, you seem to have NSAutoresizingMaskLayoutConstraints associated with one of your buttons. So there's your problem. Uncomment the row you previously commented out and rerun your application. It should now work as previously.

Now, let's create another example of an unsatisfiable layout. Let's say you want to change the layout from the preceding section (the one with three buttons) so that the button widths don't grow beyond 100 points wide when the screen rotates. Add the width constraint shown in Listing 3-21.

Listing 3-21. Creating a constraint on all the buttons to limit their growth to 100 points

```
[self.view addConstraints:[NSLayoutConstraint
    constraintsWithVisualFormat:@"|-[button1(<=100)]-[button2(==button1)]-[button3(==button1)]-|"
    options:0 metrics:nil views:viewsDictionary]];
```

If you build and run this, the buttons look great in portrait mode, but when you rotate the screen a strange thing happens. As Figure 3-33 shows, the first two buttons get aligned to the left, while the third button is pinned to the right side of the screen.

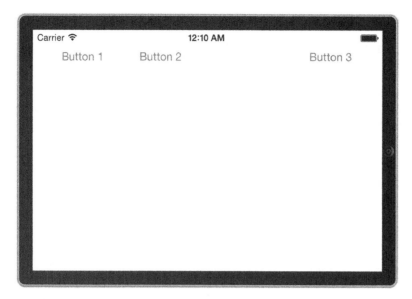

Figure 3-33. *Casually adding a width constraint can have unexpected results*

Again, the error log indicates that you are dealing with unsatisfiable constraints. Let's take a closer look at the involved constraints:

```
(
    "<NSLayoutConstraint:0x8da7220 H:|-(NSSpace(20))-[UIButton:0x8da3bd0]    (Names:
'|':UIView:0x8da3a40 )>",
    "<NSLayoutConstraint:0x8da7370 H:[UIButton:0x8da3bd0(<=100)]>",
    "<NSLayoutConstraint:0x8da73b0 H:[UIButton:0x8da3bd0]-(NSSpace(8))-[UIButton:0x8d38fd0]>",
    "<NSLayoutConstraint:0x8da73e0 UIButton:0x8d38fd0.width == UIButton:0x8da3bd0.width>",
    "<NSLayoutConstraint:0x8da7410 H:[UIButton:0x8d38fd0]-(NSSpace(8))-[UIButton:0x8d3e3f0]>",
    "<NSLayoutConstraint:0x8da7440 UIButton:0x8d3e3f0.width == UIButton:0x8da3bd0.width>",
    "<NSLayoutConstraint:0x8da7470 H:[UIButton:0x8d3e3f0]-(NSSpace(20))-|    (Names:
'|':UIView:0x8da3a40 )>",
    "<NSAutoresizingMaskLayoutConstraint:0x8da7160 h=--& v=--& V:[UIView:0x8da3a40(480)]>"
)
```

The two NSAutoresizingMaskLayoutConstraint entries are associated with the main view and are fine (you shouldn't turn the translatesAutoresizingMaskIntoConstraints on for root views). But the others give clues about what's going wrong. The problem here is that you have pinned the group of buttons to the screen edges. So when the screen rotates, the button widths will grow beyond 100 pixels and the layout engine can't satisfy the width constraint you added.

What you need to do here is to rethink the layout. What do you want?

- Buttons of equal widths?

- Buttons positioned next to each other, with the default spacing?

- The left and right buttons pinned to the respective screen edges, unless that causes the button widths to grow beyond 100 pixels? In that case, do you want the group of buttons to stay centered in the screen?

The key here is in the third point where "unless" indicates that you should use non-required constraints; however, let's start with the first two points. They can be expressed in the same visual format string, as shown in bold in Listing 3-22.

Listing 3-22. The new visual format string

```
[self.view addConstraints:[NSLayoutConstraint
    constraintsWithVisualFormat:@"[button1(<=100)]-[button2(==button1)]-[button3(==button1)]"
    options:0 metrics:nil views:viewsDictionary]];
```

You might be wondering what exactly we did here that changed from Listing 3-21. Look carefully and you will see that the left and right screen edge constraints have been removed (designated by "|-" and "-|").

> **Note** You might be wondering why we didn't also pin `button1` to the left edge of the screen and `button3` to the right in the preceding format string. The reason is that those constraints should be non-required, but in Visual Format Language you can only set priorities (for example, making them non-required) for size constraints. It's not possible to set priorities for constraints that operate on properties such as leading and trailing edges.

Next, you need to loosely pin the group of buttons to the screen edges (with a 20-point spacing), as shown in Listing 3-23.

Listing 3-23. Adding loose constraints to the screen edges with 20-point spacing

```
NSLayoutConstraint *pinToLeft =
    [NSLayoutConstraint
        constraintWithItem:button1 attribute:NSLayoutAttributeLeading
        relatedBy:NSLayoutRelationEqual
        toItem:self.view attribute:NSLayoutAttributeLeading
        multiplier:1 constant:20];
pinToLeft.priority = 500;
[self.view addConstraint:pinToLeft];

NSLayoutConstraint *pinToRight =
    [NSLayoutConstraint
        constraintWithItem:button3 attribute:NSLayoutAttributeTrailing
        relatedBy:NSLayoutRelationEqual
        toItem:self.view attribute:NSLayoutAttributeTrailing
        multiplier:1 constant:20];
pinToRight.priority = 500;
[self.view addConstraint:pinToRight];
```

Finally, you need the rule that tells the group to center in the screen. This can be a required constraint because it is true even if the group is pinned to the screen edges. Add the code shown in Listing 3-24.

Listing 3-24. Creating a center constraint for the group

```
NSLayoutConstraint *center =
    [NSLayoutConstraint
        constraintWithItem:button2 attribute:NSLayoutAttributeCenterX
        relatedBy:NSLayoutRelationEqual toItem:self.view attribute:NSLayoutAttributeCenterX
         multiplier:1 constant:0];
[self.view addConstraint:center];
```

Here's the resulting viewDidLoad method, with changes marked in bold:

```
- (void)viewDidLoad
{
    [super viewDidLoad];

    UIButton *button1 = [UIButton buttonWithType:UIButtonTypeRoundedRect];
    [button1 setTitle:@"Button 1" forState:UIControlStateNormal];
    button1.translatesAutoresizingMaskIntoConstraints = NO;
    [self.view addSubview:button1];

    UIButton *button2 = [UIButton buttonWithType:UIButtonTypeRoundedRect];
    [button2 setTitle:@"Button 2" forState:UIControlStateNormal];
    button2.translatesAutoresizingMaskIntoConstraints = NO;
    [self.view addSubview:button2];

    UIButton *button3 = [UIButton buttonWithType:UIButtonTypeRoundedRect];
    [button3 setTitle:@"Button 3" forState:UIControlStateNormal];
    button3.translatesAutoresizingMaskIntoConstraints = NO;
    [self.view addSubview:button3];

    NSDictionary *viewsDictionary = NSDictionaryOfVariableBindings(button1, button2, button3);

    [self.view addConstraints:
      [NSLayoutConstraint constraintsWithVisualFormat:@"V:|-[button1]" options:0 metrics:nil
views:viewsDictionary]];
    [self.view addConstraints:
      [NSLayoutConstraint constraintsWithVisualFormat:@"V:|-[button2]" options:0 metrics:nil
views:viewsDictionary]];
    [self.view addConstraints:
      [NSLayoutConstraint constraintsWithVisualFormat:@"V:|-[button3]" options:0 metrics:nil
views:viewsDictionary]];

    [self.view addConstraints:[NSLayoutConstraint
        constraintsWithVisualFormat:@"[button1(<=100)]-[button2(==button1)]-[button3(==button1)]"
        options:0 metrics:nil views:viewsDictionary]];
```

```
NSLayoutConstraint *pinToLeft = [NSLayoutConstraint
    constraintWithItem:button1 attribute:NSLayoutAttributeLeading
    relatedBy:NSLayoutRelationEqual
    toItem:self.view attribute:NSLayoutAttributeLeading
    multiplier:1 constant:20];
pinToLeft.priority = 500;
[self.view addConstraint:pinToLeft];

NSLayoutConstraint *pinToRight = [NSLayoutConstraint
    constraintWithItem:button3 attribute:NSLayoutAttributeTrailing
    relatedBy:NSLayoutRelationEqual
    toItem:self.view attribute:NSLayoutAttributeTrailing
    multiplier:1 constant:20];
pinToRight.priority = 500;
[self.view addConstraint:pinToRight];

NSLayoutConstraint *center = [NSLayoutConstraint
    constraintWithItem:button2 attribute:NSLayoutAttributeCenterX
    relatedBy:NSLayoutRelationEqual
    toItem:self.view attribute:NSLayoutAttributeCenterX
    multiplier:1 constant:0];
[self.view addConstraint:center];
}
```

Now you can build and run your application again. When rotated to landscape orientation, it should look as it did in portrait orientation, and there should be no errors in the error log. The user interface should resemble Figure 3-34.

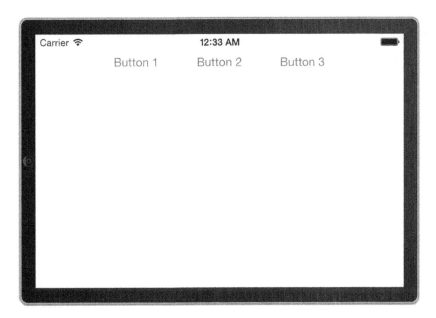

Figure 3-34. *A layout with maximum button widths correctly set*

Summary

In this chapter, you learned the basics of Auto Layout and how to use it to build dynamic user interfaces that adapt to changes in screen size and orientation. You set up constraints in Interface Builder as well as in code. You also looked at the two error states, ambiguous constraints and unsatisfiable constraints, and how to debug them.

Chapter 4

Table and Collection View Recipes

All day, every single day, we receive information. Whether in the form of video, radio, music, emails, 140-character messages, or even sights and sounds, there is always new data to acquire and process. As developers, we work to create and manage the medium between this information and end users through data organization and display. We must be able to take the immense stream of information available and process it down to simple, concise pieces that our specific audience will be interested in. On top of this, we also have to make our data look visually appealing, while still maintaining efficiency and organization.

In iOS development, there are two great tools for achieving these goals: `UITableView`, with its well-known user interface that has pretty much become what users expect from data-based apps, and `UICollectionView`, which brings multicolumn support to the table.

The UITableView, or simply table view, is the most common way of displaying a list of information. As an example, a music app uses a table view to display the songs in a user's library. A table view comprises configurable cells that make up the individual rows in the table view.

The UICollectionView, or simply collection view, is similar to a UITableView; however, it has columns as well as rows. The grid structure of a collection view makes it more suitable for displaying photos and items of that nature. For example, the content of a photo album in a photo app is an example of a collection view. Collection views also comprise configurable cells, with each cell having a column and a row.

Throughout this chapter, we focus on the step-by-step methodology for creating, implementing, and customizing both types of views.

Recipe 4-1: Creating an Ungrouped Table

You can use two kinds of UITableViews in iOS: the grouped table and the ungrouped table. Your use of one or the other will depend on the requirements of your application, but we start here by focusing on an ungrouped table due to its ease of implementation.

Setting Up the Application

To build a fully functional and customizable UITableView-based application, we start from the ground up with an empty application and end with a useful table for displaying information about various countries. Instead of using the storyboard approach as we did in Chapter 2, we'll be using .xib files to illustrate multiscene development.

In Xcode, create a new project and select the Empty Application template. This gives you only an application delegate, from which you can build all your view controllers. You will be using a single project throughout most of this chapter, so give your project whatever name you prefer. Also, be sure to deselect the "Use Core Data" option because we won't be using it in this chapter. Figure 4-1 shows these options.

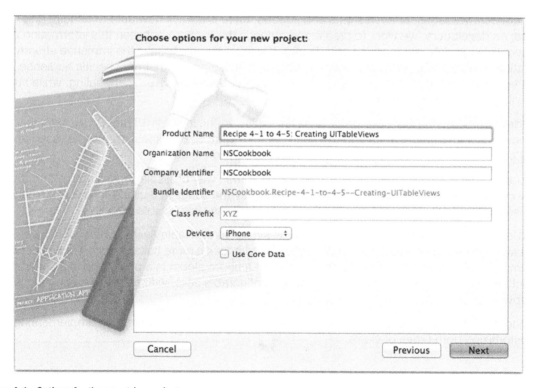

Figure 4-1. *Options for the countries project*

Because you started with an empty application, you begin by making your main view controller, which contains your table view.

Create a new file using the Objective-C class template. On the next screen, enter
"MainTableViewController" as the class name and select "UIViewController" as the subclass.
It's important that you also select "With XIB for user interface" option so that Xcode creates a
user interface file for your view controller. Refer to Recipe 1-6 for more in-depth instructions about
creating a class.

> **Note**   Some might find it more convenient to create a subclass of UITableViewController, as you are
> immediately given a UITableView as well as some of the methods required to use it. The downside of this
> approach is that the UITableView given in the controller's .xib file is more difficult to configure and reframe.
> For this reason, in this recipe you are using a UIViewController subclass, and you will simply add in your
> UITableView and its methods yourself.

Now, select the MainTableViewController.xib file to bring up Interface Builder. Continue by
dragging a table view from the object library into your view and resize it so it fits beneath the status
bar. This results in the display shown in Figure 4-2.

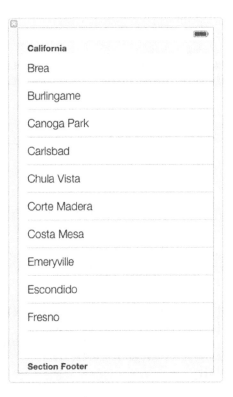

Figure 4-2. A table view with a 20-point padding around it

Now, switch to the MainViewController.m file and set the title in the viewDidLoad method, as shown
in Listing 4-1.

Listing 4-1. Setting the title in MainViewController.m

```
- (void)viewDidLoad
{
    [super viewDidLoad];
    // Do any additional setup after loading the view from its nib.
    self.title = @"Countries";
}
```

The title appears in the navigation bar, which you set up next. This is done in the application delegate, so switch to your AppDelegate.h file and add the code shown in Listing 4-2.

Listing 4-2. Adding properties to AppDelegate.h

```
//
//  AppDelegate.h
//  Recipe 4-1 to 4-5 Creating UITableViews
//

#import <UIKit/UIKit.h>
#import "MainTableViewController.h"

@interface AppDelegate : UIResponder <UIApplicationDelegate>

@property (strong, nonatomic) UIWindow *window;
@property (nonatomic, strong) UINavigationController *navigationController;
@property (nonatomic, strong) MainTableViewController *tableViewController;

@end
```

Now, switch to AppDelegate.m and add the code in Listing 4-3 to the application:didFinishLaunchingWithOptions: method.

Listing 4-3. Setting up necessary code for the UINavigationController

```
- (BOOL)application:(UIApplication *)application didFinishLaunchingWithOptions:(NSDictionary *)
launchOptions
{
    self.window = [[UIWindow alloc] initWithFrame:[[UIScreen mainScreen] bounds]];
    // Override point for customization after application launch.
    self.window.backgroundColor = [UIColor whiteColor];

    self.tableViewController = [[MainTableViewController alloc] init];
    self.navigationController = [[UINavigationController alloc]
                            initWithRootViewController:self.tableViewController];
    self.window.rootViewController = self.navigationController;
    [self.window makeKeyAndVisible];
    return YES;
}
```

The code in Listing 4-3 simply creates an instance for the MainTableViewController and the UINavigationController. The UINavigationController is set up with the MainTableViewController as its root view controller. Then you simply set the window root view controller to the UINavigationController.

The application skeleton is now complete. It has a navigation controller with your MainTableViewController as the root view controller. When running the project in the iOS simulator, you should see a screen like the one in Figure 4-3.

Figure 4-3. *Basic application with an empty UITableView*

Adding a Model for Countries

Next, you will use an array to store the information called upon in order to display your table's information. Declare it as a property of your view controller, with the type NSMutableArray, and the name "countries," as shown in the code in Listing 4-4.

Listing 4-4. *Creating an NSMutableArray property for countries*

```
//
//  Country.h
//  Recipe 4-1 to 4-5 Creating UITableViews
//

#import <UIKit/UIKit.h>
```

```
@interface MainTableViewController : UIViewController
```

@property (strong, nonatomic) NSMutableArray *countries;

```
@end
```

In the array you will store objects representing countries, so let's create a model for that. Create a new file as before by using the Objective-C class template. Name your new class "Country," and make sure it is a subclass of NSObject.

You'll store four pieces of information in your Country class: name, capital city, motto, and a UIImage that contains the country's flag. Define these properties in your Country.h class, as shown in Listing 4-5.

Listing 4-5. Setting country information properties in the new Country.h class

```
//
//  Country.h
//  Recipe 4-1 to 4-5 Creating UITableViews
//

#import <Foundation/Foundation.h>

@interface Country : NSObject
```

@property (nonatomic, strong) NSString *name;
@property (nonatomic, strong) NSString *capital;
@property (nonatomic, strong) NSString *motto;
@property (nonatomic, strong) UIImage *flag;

```
@end
```

Now that your model is set up, you can return to your view controller. The compiler needs to access the methods of the new Country class that you have just set up, so add the following import statement to MainTableViewController.h:

```
#import "Country.h"
```

Before you proceed to creating the test data, make sure you have downloaded the image files for the flags you will be using for the countries you add. In this recipe, you use flags of the United States, England (as opposed to the United Kingdom), Scotland, France, and Spain. We downloaded some public domain flag images from Wikipedia: the United States, France, and Spain from http://en.wikipedia.org/wiki/Gallery_of_sovereign-state_flags, and England and Scotland from http://commons.wikimedia.org/wiki/Flags_of_formerly_independent_states. An image size of around 200 pixels is good enough for your purposes.

Caution   Whenever you are working with images, watch carefully for any and all copyright issues. Public domain images, such as those used here from Wikipedia, are free to use and fairly easy to find.

After you have all the files downloaded and visible in the finder, select and drag them into your project in Xcode under Supporting Files. A dialog box appears with options for adding the files to your project. Make sure the option labeled "Copy items into destination group's folder (if needed)" is checked, as in Figure 4-4.

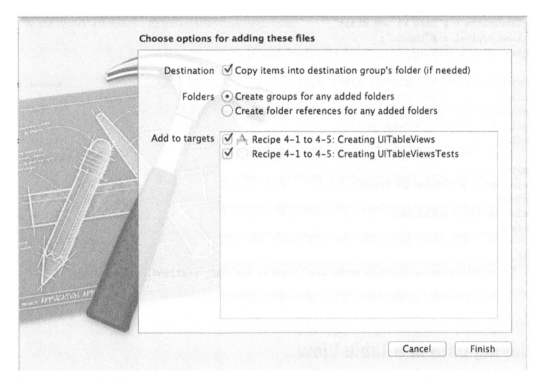

Figure 4-4. *Dialog box for adding files; make sure the first option is checked*

Set up your test data—the five countries mentioned earlier—in the viewDidLoad method of the MainTableViewController.m file, as shown in Listing 4-6.

Listing 4-6. Setting country properties and adding them to the countries array

```
- (void)viewDidLoad
{
    [super viewDidLoad];

    self.title = @"Countries";

    Country *usa = [[Country alloc] init];
    usa.name = @"United States of America";
    usa.motto = @"E Pluribus Unum";
    usa.capital = @"Washington, D.C.";
    usa.flag = [UIImage imageNamed:@"usa.png"];

    Country *france = [[Country alloc] init];
    france.name = @"French Republic";
```

```
    france.motto = @"Liberté, Égalité, Fraternité";
    france.capital = @"Paris";
    france.flag = [UIImage imageNamed:@"france.png"];

    Country *england = [[Country alloc] init];
    england.name = @"England";
    england.motto = @"Dieu et mon droit";
    england.capital = @"London";
    england.flag = [UIImage imageNamed:@"england.png"];

    Country *scotland = [[Country alloc] init];
    scotland.name = @"Scotland";
    scotland.motto = @"In My Defens God Me Defend";
    scotland.capital = @"Edinburgh";
    scotland.flag = [UIImage imageNamed:@"scotland.png"];

    Country *spain = [[Country alloc] init];
    spain.name = @"Kingdom of Spain";
    spain.motto = @"Plus Ultra";
    spain.capital = @"Madrid";
    spain.flag = [UIImage imageNamed:@"spain.png"];

    self.countries =
        [NSMutableArray arrayWithObjects:usa, france, england, scotland, spain, nil];

}
```

Displaying Data in a Table View

To display your test data in your table view, you need a way to reference it from your code. So you'll need to add an outlet named "countriesTableView." Open the .xib file and control-click and drag from the table view to the interface file, just as you would for a button outlet.

For the sake of organization, all the methods that a UITableView can call are split into two groups: delegate methods and datasource methods. Delegate methods, on the one hand, are used to handle any kind of visual elements of the UITableView, such as the row height of cells. Datasource methods, on the other hand, deal with the information displayed in the UITableView, such as the configuration of any given cell's information.

Your table view communicates with your program through two protocols: UITableViewDelegate and UITableViewDataSource. You'll need to add a little bit of code to the interface line to let the class know it's conforming to these protocols, so add them to its header, as shown in Listing 4-7.

Listing 4-7. Declaring the use of protocols

```
//
//  MainTableViewController.h
//  Recipe 4-1 to 4-5: Creating UITableViews
//

#import <UIKit/UIKit.h>
#import "Country.h"

@interface MainTableViewController : UIViewController <UITableViewDelegate, UITableViewDataSource>

@property (weak, nonatomic) IBOutlet UITableView *countriesTableView;
@property (strong, nonatomic) NSMutableArray *countries;

@end
```

The next step is to connect your view controller to the table view. Switch to MainTableViewController.m and set the table view's delegate and dataSource properties in the viewDidLoad method, as shown in Listing 4-8. Setting these properties lets the table view know that the data population and handling of interactions will take place in the MainTableViewController.

Listing 4-8. Setting the table view delegate and datasource as "self" in MainTableViewController.m

```
- (void)viewDidLoad
{
    [super viewDidLoad];
    // Do any additional setup after loading the view from its nib.
    self.title = @"Countries";
    self.countriesTableView.delegate = self;
    self.countriesTableView.dataSource = self;

    Country *usa = [[Country alloc] init];
    usa.name = @"United States of America";
    usa.motto = @"E Pluribus Unum";
    usa.capital = @"Washington, D.C.";
    usa.flag = [UIImage imageNamed:@"usa.png"];

    // ...
}
```

> **Note**   With the table view selected, you can also set up delegate and datasource by dragging from the circles in the connections inspector to "File's Owner" in the document outline under Placeholders, as shown in Figure 4-5. When working with storyboards, "File's Owner" becomes the name of the view controller.

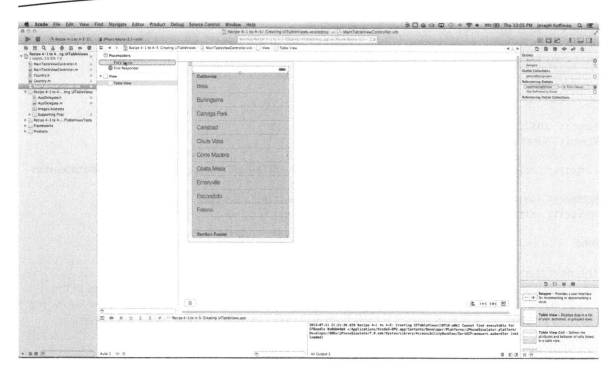

Figure 4-5. Alternative way of connecting delegate and datasources

To create an ungrouped UITableView, you must correctly implement two main methods.

First, you need to specify how many rows will be displayed in the table view. This is done through the tableView:numberOfRowsInSection: method. Your table view has only one section because it's ungrouped, so there is no need to consult the section parameter. All you need to do is return the number of countries in your array, as shown in Listing 4-9.

Listing 4-9. Implementing the tableView:numberOfRowsInSection: method

```
-(NSInteger)tableView:(UITableView *)tableView numberOfRowsInSection:(NSInteger)section
{
    return [self.countries count];
}
```

Second, you must create a method to specify how the UITableView's cells are configured, using the tableView:cellForRowAtIndexPath: method. Listing 4-10 is a generic implementation of this method, which you can modify for your data.

Listing 4-10. Generic implementation of the tableView:cellForRowAtIndexPath: method

```
- (UITableViewCell *)tableView:(UITableView *)tableView cellForRowAtIndexPath:(NSIndexPath *)
indexPath
{
    static NSString *CellIdentifier = @"Cell";

    UITableViewCell *cell =
```

```
        [tableView dequeueReusableCellWithIdentifier:CellIdentifier];
    if (cell == nil)
    {
        cell = [[UITableViewCell alloc] initWithStyle:UITableViewCellStyleDefault
                reuseIdentifier:CellIdentifier];
        cell.accessoryType = UITableViewCellAccessoryDisclosureIndicator;
        cell.textLabel.font = [UIFont systemFontOfSize:19.0];
        cell.detailTextLabel.font = [UIFont systemFontOfSize:12];
    }

    cell.textLabel.text = [NSString stringWithFormat:@"Cell %i", indexPath.row];

    return cell;
}
```

If you run your application now, you will see that your table view has five cells, one for each entry in your countries array. Each cell, as Figure 4-6 shows, has a generic title (Cell 0, Cell 1, Cell 2, and so on) and a disclosure accessory indicator. The disclosure accessory indicator is the little gray arrow on the right of the cell that lets the user know that tapping the cell will display details about that cell.

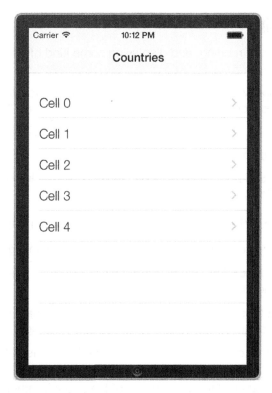

Figure 4-6. Your app displaying five cells with generic text and a disclosure accessory indicator

Because you haven't implemented any functionality for the accessory views yet, nothing happens when you tap the cells. You will take care of that, as well as customize the look and content of the cells, in a moment, but first we'll discuss cell reuse.

Considerations for Cached Cells and Reuse

The preceding code deserves some explanation. A table view in iOS tries to save memory and time by reusing cells that are currently not in view of the user. It takes a cell that has been scrolled out of sight and reuses it to display another cell that has become visible.

However, it's up to you to make the reuse scheme work. First, you must define the different types of cells your table view supports (that is, cells that share the same look and components). Each such cell type is identified by a reuse identifier of your choice.

The second thing your app must do is call the dequeueReusableCellWithIdentifier: method to see whether there is a free cell to reuse before you allocate a new one. In the preceding example, you can see that you first attempt to dequeue a reusable cell. If none are available (that is, if the cell is nil), then you create a new cell and give it a generic setup that can be reused for all your cells. Then, no matter whether the cell was dequeued or created, you update the text to the appropriate value.

Configuring the Cells

Now that your application is up, running, and displaying some kind of information, you can work on your specific implementation.

To configure your cells to properly fit your data, the first thing you have to do is change the display style of your rows. Change the allocation/initialization line in your tableView:cellForRowAtIndexPath: method, as shown in Listing 4-11.

Listing 4-11. Updating the display style of the rows

```
cell = [[UITableViewCell alloc] initWithStyle:UITableViewCellStyleSubtitle
reuseIdentifier:CellIdentifier];
```

There are four different UITableViewCell styles that you can use, each with a slightly different display:

- UITableViewCellStyleDefault: Only one label, as shown in Figure 4-5.
- UITableViewCellStyleSubtitle: Just like the Default style, but with a subtitle line underneath the main text.
- UITableViewCellStyleValue1: Two text lines, with the primary line on the left side of the cell and the secondary detail text label on the right.
- UITableViewCellStyleValue2: Two text lines with the focus put on the detail text label.

Next, you can set the cell's text label to be the name of the country rather than simply the count of the cell. Adjust the setting of the cell.textLabel.text property, as shown in Listing in 4-12.

Listing 4-12. Setting the cell text label

```
Country *item = [self.countries objectAtIndex:indexPath.row];
cell.textLabel.text = item.name;
```

You can set the subtitle of the text very similarly using the detailTextLabel property of the cell. Set it to the capital of the country, as shown in Listing 4-13.

Listing 4-13. Setting the cell subtitle label

```
cell.detailTextLabel.text = item.capital;
```

The UITableViewCell class also has a property called imageView, which, when given an image, places it to the left of the title label. Implement this action by adding Listing 4-14 to your cell configuration.

Listing 4-14. Generic implementation of the tableView:cellForRowAtIndexPath: method

```
cell.imageView.image = item.flag;
```

You'll probably notice that if you run your program now, all your flags will appear, but with varying aspect ratios, making your view look less professional. Setting the frame of the cell's imageView will not fix this problem, so here is a quick solution.

First, in your view controller implementation file, define a class method that draws a UIImage in a given size, as shown in Listing 4-15.

Listing 4-15. Creating a class method to draw UIImage in a given size

```
+ (UIImage *)scale:(UIImage *)image toSize:(CGSize)size
{
    UIGraphicsBeginImageContext(size);
    [image drawInRect:CGRectMake(0, 0, size.width, size.height)];
    UIImage *scaledImage = UIGraphicsGetImageFromCurrentImageContext();
    UIGraphicsEndImageContext();
    return scaledImage;
}
```

Place this method's handler in your view controller's private @interface declaration to avoid any potential compiler problems. The private @interface declaration is where you put your private method declarations; it resides at the top of your view controller's implementation file, as shown in Listing 4-16.

Listing 4-16. Creating a private method handler for scale: image: toSize: method

```
//
//  MainTableViewController.h
//  Recipe 4-1 to 4-5 Creating UITableViews
//

#import "MainTableViewController.h"

@interface MainTableViewController ()
```

```objc
+ (UIImage *)scale:(UIImage *)image toSize:(CGSize)size;
```

```objc
@end
```

```objc
@implementation MainTableViewController
```

```objc
// ...
```

```objc
// Implementation of the scale method goes here
+ (UIImage *)scale:(UIImage *)image toSize:(CGSize)size
{
    // ...
}
```

```objc
@end
```

Then you can adjust the image-setting lines of code to utilize this method, as shown in Listing 4-17.

Listing 4-17. Utilizing the scale: image: toSize: method to adjust image size

```objc
cell.imageView.image =
    [MainTableViewController scale: item.flag toSize:CGSizeMake(115, 75)];
```

After all these configurations, the resulting tableView:cellForRowAtIndexPath: method should look like Listing 4-18.

Listing 4-18. Completed tableView:cellForRowAtIndexPath: method

```objc
- (UITableViewCell *)tableView:(UITableView *)tableView cellForRowAtIndexPath:(NSIndexPath *)
indexPath
{
    static NSString *CellIdentifier = @"Cell";

    UITableViewCell *cell = [tableView dequeueReusableCellWithIdentifier:CellIdentifier];
    if (cell == nil)
    {
        cell = [[UITableViewCell alloc] initWithStyle:UITableViewCellStyleSubtitle reuseIdentifier:
CellIdentifier];
        cell.accessoryType = UITableViewCellAccessoryDisclosureIndicator;
        cell.textLabel.font = [UIFont systemFontOfSize:19.0];
        cell.detailTextLabel.font = [UIFont systemFontOfSize:12];
    }

    Country *item = [self.countries objectAtIndex:indexPath.row];
    cell.textLabel.text = item.name;
    cell.detailTextLabel.text = item.capital;
    cell.imageView.image =
        [MainTableViewController scale: item.flag toSize:CGSizeMake(115, 75)];

    return cell;
}
```

Build and run your application; it should resemble Figure 4-7, complete with country information and flag images.

Figure 4-7. *Your table populated with country information*

Implementing the Accessory Views

Now that you have a nice-looking table with your five countries, you can work on extending beyond the basic functionality of the table view. First, you'll focus on the most straightforward ability, which is to act upon the selection of a specific row.

For the purpose of this recipe, you will build your application in such a way that upon the selection of a row, a separate view controller will appear that displays all the known information about the selected country.

Start by creating a new view controller like the one at the beginning of this recipe by using the Objective-C class template and UIViewController as the parent class. Name the new class "CountryDetailsViewController" and make sure the "With XIB for user interface" option is selected.

Construct this controller's view in its .xib file so that it resembles the one shown in Figure 4-8 by using a combination of labels, text fields, and an image view. For this example, we sized the UIImage view to 111 points wide by 68 points high. You can do this easily from the size inspector, with the UIImage view selected.

Figure 4-8. CountryDetailsViewController's .xib file and configuration

Create outlets for the components you'll be changing dynamically (that is, the country label, the image view, and the two text fields). Use the following respective property names:

- `nameLabel`
- `capitalTextField`
- `mottoTextField`
- `flagImageView`

You need to be able to manipulate the behavior of the two text fields. To allow your view controller to respond to events from these text fields, add the `UITextFieldDelegate` protocol declaration to its header, as shown in Listing 4-19.

Listing 4-19. Adding UITextFieldDelegate to the view controller header file

```
@interface CountryDetailsViewController : UIViewController<UITextFieldDelegate>
```

To make your view controller as generic as possible, give it a property of your `Country` class to hold the currently displayed data. This way, you simply populate your view with the necessary data, and, if desired, you could even make it possible to easily repopulate with different data without changing views. Add an import statement for the `Country` class, as shown in Listing 4-20.

Listing 4-20. Importing a country class

```
#import "Country.h"
```

Declare the property, as shown in Listing 4-21.

Listing 4-21. Declaring currentCountry property

```
@property (strong, nonatomic) Country *currentCountry;
```

Your detailed view controller needs a way to tell whoever invoked it that it's finished and should be removed from view. The convention in iOS is to set up a custom protocol and a delegate property for that purpose. So make additions to your CountryDetailsViewController.h file, as shown in Listing 4-21.

Listing 4-21. Setting up custom protocol and delegate properties in CountryDetailsViewController.h

```
//
//  CountryDetailsViewsController.h
//  Recipe 4-1 to 4-5 Creating UITableViews
//

#import <UIKit/UIKit.h>
#import "Country.h"

/* Forward declaration needed for the protocol to use
 the CountryDetailsViewController type */
@class CountryDetailsViewController;

@protocol CountryDetailsViewControllerDelegate <NSObject>
-(void)countryDetailsViewControllerDidFinish:(CountryDetailsViewController *)sender;
@end

@interface CountryDetailsViewController : UIViewController<UITextFieldDelegate>
//...
```

Create a property for the delegate, as shown in Listing 4-22, so you can later set the owner of the delegate.

Listing 4-22. Creating a delegate property CountryDetailsViewController.h

```
#import <UIKit/UIKit.h>
#import "Country.h
//...

@property (weak, nonatomic) IBOutlet UILabel *nameLabel;
@property (weak, nonatomic) IBOutlet UIImageView *flagImageView;
@property (weak, nonatomic) IBOutlet UITextField *capitalTextField;
@property (weak, nonatomic) IBOutlet UITextField *mottoTextField;

@property (strong, nonatomic) Country *currentCountry;
@property (strong, nonatomic) id<CountryDetailsViewControllerDelegate> delegate;

@end
```

Now, switch your focus to the implementation file of your details view controller. There's plenty to be done there, so let's start by adding a method to populate the view, as shown in Listing 4-23.

Listing 4-23. Implementing populateViewWithCountry: method

```
-(void)populateViewWithCountry:(Country *)country
{
    self.currentCountry = country;

    self.flagImageView.image = country.flag;
    self.nameLabel.text = country.name;
    self.capitalTextField.text = country.capital;
    self.mottoTextField.text = country.motto;
}
```

You will want this method to be called after your view is loaded, but right before your view is displayed, which is when viewWillAppear:animated: is invoked. So add the call to the new delegate method to your detailed view controller, as shown in Listing 4-24.

Listing 4-24. Calling the populateViewWithCountry: delegate from within the viewWillAppear method

```
-(void)viewWillAppear:(BOOL)animated
{

    [self populateViewWithCountry:self.currentCountry];
}
```

Next, let's consider the text fields. You should dismiss the keyboard when the user is done editing, so implement the textFieldShouldReturn: delegate method, as shown in Listing 4-25.

Listing 4-25. Implementing the textFieldShouldReturn: method

```
-(BOOL)textFieldShouldReturn:(UITextField *)textField
{
    [textField resignFirstResponder];
    return NO;
}
```

For the foregoing delegate method to be called, you need to connect your view controller to the delegate properties of the text fields. Do this in the viewDidLoad method, as shown in Listing 4-26.

Listing 4-26. Setting the delegates in the viewDidLoad method

```
self.mottoTextField.delegate = self;
self.capitalTextField.delegate = self;
```

Because you are allowing the user to make changes to your data, you should include a button to revert to the original data to cancel edits. Add this to the right side of your navigation bar by adding the code in Listing 4-27 to the viewDidLoad method.

Listing 4-27. Creating a navigation bar button for reverting to original data

```
- (void)viewDidLoad
{
    [super viewDidLoad];
    // Do any additional setup after loading the view from its nib.
    self.mottoTextField.delegate = self;
    self.capitalTextField.delegate = self;

    UIBarButtonItem *revertButton =
        [[UIBarButtonItem alloc] initWithTitle:@"Revert"
                                         style:UIBarButtonItemStyleBordered
                                        target:self
                                        action:@selector(revert)];

    self.navigationItem.rightBarButtonItems =
        [NSArray arrayWithObject:revertButton];
}
```

The revert selector that you specified as the revertButton action is easily implemented. It should merely repopulate the view with the data from the currentCountry property. Add the implementation shown in Listing 4-28 to your CountryDetailsViewController.m file.

Listing 4-28. Implementing the revert method

```
-(void)revert
{
    [self populateViewWithCountry:self.currentCountry];
}
```

The last thing you need to do is implement functionality to save any changes to the given Country upon returning to your MainTableViewController. You implement the method viewWillDisappear:animated: to do this. Add the code in Listing 4-29 to the CountryDetailsViewController.m file.

Listing 4-29. Adding a viewWillDisappear method override

```
-(void)viewWillDisappear:(BOOL)animated
{
    // End any editing that might be in progress at this point
    [self.view.window endEditing: YES];

    // Update the country object with the new values
    self.currentCountry.capital = self.capitalTextField.text;
    self.currentCountry.motto = self.mottoTextField.text;
    [self.delegate countryDetailsViewControllerDidFinish:self];
}
```

The detailed view controller is finished for now; switch back to the header file of your MainTableViewController and add to the header the CountryDetailsViewControllerDelegate protocol that you created. You need to import the class you created first.

```
#import "CountryDetailsViewController.h"
```

To make your implementation of the CountryDetailsViewController delegate method easier, you should create an instance variable that refers to the index path of whichever row was selected so that you can save processing power by refreshing only that row. After you add the variable of type NSIndexPath, called selectedIndexPath, your header file should now look like Listing 4-30, with recent changes marked in bold.

Listing 4-30. Adding a delegate declaration and an instance variable to MainTableViewController.h

```
//
//  MainTableViewController.h
//  Recipe 4-1 to 4-5 Creating UITableViews
//

#import <UIKit/UIKit.h>
#import "Country.h"
#import "CountryDetailsViewController.h"

@interface MainTableViewController : UIViewController<UITableViewDelegate,
    UITableViewDataSource, CountryDetailsViewControllerDelegate>
{
    NSIndexPath *selectedIndexPath;
}

@property (weak, nonatomic) IBOutlet UITableView *countriesTableView;
@property (strong, nonatomic) NSMutableArray *countries;

@end
```

You can now implement the CountryDetailsViewController's delegate. Switch to MainTableViewController.m and add the delegate method, as shown in Listing 4-31.

Listing 4-31. Adding the countryDetailsViewControllerDidFinish: delegate method

```
-(void)countryDetailsViewControllerDidFinish:(CountryDetailsViewController *)sender
{
    if (selectedIndexPath)
    {
        [self.countriesTableView beginUpdates];
        [self.countriesTableView reloadRowsAtIndexPaths:
[NSArray arrayWithObject:selectedIndexPath] withRowAnimation:UITableViewRowAnimationNone];
        [self.countriesTableView endUpdates];
    }
    selectedIndexPath = nil;
}
```

The beginUpdates and endUpdates methods, though somewhat unnecessary here, are very useful for reloading data in a table view. They specify that any calls to reload data in between begin and end update calls should be animated. Because all your reloading of data occurs while the UITableView is offscreen, it is not quite necessary, but it does not harm your application.

Finally, to actually act on the selection of a given row in a UITableView, all you need to do is implement the UITableView's delegate method tableView:didSelectRowAtIndexPath, as shown in Listing 4-32.

Listing 4-32. Implementing the tableView: didSelectRowAtIndexPath: method

```
-(void)tableView:(UITableView *)tableView
didSelectRowAtIndexPath:(NSIndexPath *)indexPath
{
    [tableView deselectRowAtIndexPath:indexPath animated:YES];

    selectedIndexPath = indexPath;

    Country *chosenCountry = [self.countries objectAtIndex:indexPath.row];
    CountryDetailsViewController *detailedViewController =
        [[CountryDetailsViewController alloc] init];
    detailedViewController.delegate = self;
    detailedViewController.currentCountry = chosenCountry;

    [self.navigationController pushViewController:detailedViewController animated:YES];
}
```

The UITableView class also has a multitude of other delegate methods for dealing with the selection or deselection of a row, which include the following:

- tableView:willSelectRowAtIndexPath: Lets the delegate know that a row is about to be selected

- tableView:didSelectRowAtIndexPath: Lets the delegate know that a row was selected

- tableView:willDeselectRowAtIndexPath: Lets the delegate know that a row is about to be deselected

- tableView:didDeselectRowAtIndexPath: Lets the delegate know that a row was deselected

Using these four delegate methods, you can fully customize the behavior of a UITableView to fit any application.

When running this project now, you can view and edit country information, as shown in Figure 4-9.

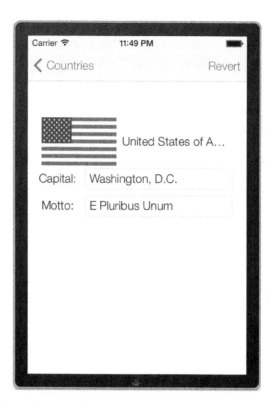

Figure 4-9. The resulting display of your CountryDetailsViewController

Enhanced User Interaction

When you're dealing with applications that focus on UITableViews, you often want to allow the user to access multiple views from the same table. For example, the phone application on an iPhone has a voicemail tab, which displays a UITableView containing the various voicemails left on the phone. The user can then either play the voicemail by selecting a row from the table or view the contact information of the original caller by selecting a smaller info icon on the right side of the row. You can implement a similar behavior by implementing another UITableView delegate method.

First, you must change the type of "accessory" of the cells in your UITableView. This refers to the icon displayed on the far right side of any given row. In your tableView:cellForRowAtIndexPath: method, find the following line:

```
cell.accessoryType = UITableViewCellAccessoryDisclosureIndicator;
```

Change this value to UITableViewCellAccessoryDetailDisclosureButton. This gives you the info icon that can respond to touches. The four possible values for this property are as follows:

- UITableViewCellAccessoryNone: Specifies a lack of accessory.

- UITableViewCellAccessoryDisclosureIndicator: Adds a gray arrow on the right side of a row, as you have been using until now.

▓ UITableViewCellAccessoryDetailDisclosureButton: Your most recent choice, which specifies an interaction-enabled button.

▓ UITableViewCellAccessoryCheckmark: Adds a checkmark to a given row; this is especially useful in conjunction with the tableView:didSelectRowAtIndexPath: method to make it possible to add and remove check marks from a list as necessary.

Note   Whereas these four available accessory types are pretty useful and cover almost any generic use, it's certainly easy to think of a reason to want something entirely different over on the right side of your row. You can easily customize a UITableViewCell accessory through the accessoryView property to be any other UIView subclass.

Now that you turned your accessory into a button, it is incredibly easy to implement an action to handle this interaction. Implement another UITableView delegate method, tableView:accessoryButtonTappedForRowWithIndexPath:. For your testing purposes, make this action exactly the same as that of a row selection, with an extra NSLog(), as shown in Listing 4-33, although it should be very easy to see how you could implement different actions.

Listing 4-33. Implementing the tableView: accessoryButtonTappedForRowWithIndexPath: method

```
-(void)tableView:(UITableView *)tableView accessoryButtonTappedForRowWithIndexPath:(NSIndexPath *)
indexPath
{
    [tableView deselectRowAtIndexPath:indexPath animated:YES];

    selectedIndexPath = indexPath;

    Country *chosenCountry = [self.countries objectAtIndex:indexPath.row];
    CountryDetailsViewController *detailedViewController =
        [[CountryDetailsViewController alloc] init];
    detailedViewController.delegate = self;
    detailedViewController.currentCountry = chosenCountry;

    NSLog(@"Accessory Button Tapped");
    [self.navigationController pushViewController:detailedViewController animated:YES];
}
```

When you run this app, tapping the accessory buttons should run your newest functionalities, as shown in Figure 4-10.

Figure 4-10. *Your UITableView with detail-disclosure buttons responding to events*

Considerations for Cell View Customization

Just as with the accessory view, several other parts of a UITableViewCell are customizable by way of their views. The UITableViewCell class includes several properties for other views you can edit, including the following:

- imageView: The UIImageView to the left of the textLabel in a cell, as shown by your flags in the previous example; if no image is given to this view, then the cell will appear as if the UIImageView did not exist (as opposed to a blank UIImageView taking up space).

- contentView: The main UIView of the UITableViewCell, which includes all the text; you might want to customize this to implement a more powerful or versatile UITableViewCell.

- backgroundView: A UIView set to nil in plain-style tables (like you have used so far), and otherwise for grouped tables; this view appears behind all other views in the table, so it is great for specifically customizing the visual display of the cell.

▤ selectedBackgroundView: This `UIView` is inserted above the `backgroundView` but behind all other views when a cell is selected. It can also be easily given an alpha animation (fading opacity in or out) by use of the `-setSelected:animated:` action.

▤ multipleSelectionBackgroundView: This `UIView` acts just like the `selectedBackgroundView` but is used when a `UITableView` is enabled so as to allow the selection of multiple rows.

▤ accessoryView: As discussed earlier, this allows you to create entirely different views for a row's accessory, so you could implement your own custom display and behavior beyond the preset values.

▤ editingAccessoryView: This is similar to the `accessoryView` property but specifically for when a `UITableView` is in "editing" mode, which you will see in more detail soon.

Although most developers stick to the generic `UITableView` because it fits well with the iOS design theme, if you look around the app store you can find some creative implementations using custom views. All this extra customization might add a lot of development time to your project, but a high-quality, custom `UITableView` certainly stands out in an application for its uniqueness. See cocoacontrols.com or search `github.com` for code examples of custom table view implementations. When creating custom UITableViews, be sure to be mindful of the impact it might have on the performance of your app.

Recipe 4-2: Editing a UITableView

If you look at almost any `UITableView` in an application you commonly use, such as your device's music player, you'll probably notice that you can edit the table in some way. In your music application, you can swipe across a row to reveal a "Delete" button, which when tapped will remove the item in question. In your email application, you can press the "Edit" button in the upper-right corner to allow the selection of multiple messages for deletion, movement, and other functions. Both of these functionalities are based on the concept of editing a `UITableView`.

The first thing you should consider is putting your `UITableView` into editing mode, because in order for your users to use your editing functionality, they need to be able to access it. Do this by adding an "Edit" button to the top-right corner of your view. This is surprisingly easy to do by adding the line shown in Listing 4-34 to the `viewDidLoad` method of your main table view controller.

Listing 4-34. Adding an edit button to the navigation bar

```
- (void)viewDidLoad
{
    [super viewDidLoad];
    // Do any additional setup after loading the view from its nib.
    self.title = @"Countries";
    self.countriesTableView.delegate = self;
    self.countriesTableView.dataSource = self;
    self.navigationItem.rightBarButtonItem = self.editButtonItem;

    // ...
}
```

This editButtonItem property is not actually a property that you need to define, as it is preset for all UIViewController subclasses. The great thing about this button is that it is programmed not only to call a specific method, but also to toggle its text between "Edit" and "Done."

The editButtonItem by default is set to call the method setEditing:animated:, for which you create a simple implementation, as shown in Listing 4-35.

Listing 4-35. Implementing the setEditing:animated: override method

```
-(void)setEditing:(BOOL)editing animated:(BOOL)animated
{
    [super setEditing:editing animated:animated];
    [self.countriesTableView setEditing:editing animated:animated];
}
```

The main concepts of this method are simple: first you call the super method, which handles the toggling of the button's text, and then you set the editing mode of your UITableView according to the parameters given.

At this point, your application's "Edit" button triggers the editing mode of the UITableView, allowing you to reveal "Delete" buttons for any given row. However, because you haven't actually implemented any behavior for these buttons, you can't delete any rows from your table yet. To do this, you must first implement one more delegate method, tableView:commitEditingStyle:forRowAt IndexPath:.

Listing 4-36 is a basic implementation of the method that you'll start with.

Listing 4-36. Implementing the tableView:commitEditingStyle:editingStyle:forRowAtIndexPath: method

```
-(void)tableView:(UITableView *)tableView commitEditingStyle:(UITableViewCellEditingStyle)
editingStyle forRowAtIndexPath:(NSIndexPath *)indexPath
{
    if (editingStyle == UITableViewCellEditingStyleDelete)
    {
        Country *deletedCountry = [self.countries objectAtIndex:indexPath.row];
        [self.countries removeObject:deletedCountry];

        [self.countriesTableView
            deleteRowsAtIndexPaths:[NSArray arrayWithObject:indexPath]
            withRowAnimation:UITableViewRowAnimationAutomatic];
    }
}
```

It is important that you delete the actual piece of data from your model before removing the row(s) from your UITableView, similar to how in the preceding recipe you first deleted a country from the array and then removed its table view row. If you don't do it in that order, your application might throw an exception.

Now when you run your app you can tap the "Edit" button to put your UITableView into editing mode, which will resemble Figure 4-11.

Figure 4-11. Your UITableView in editing mode, with functionality for removing rows

UITableView Row Animations

In the method you just added, you specified an animation type to be performed on the deletion of a row, called UITableViewRowAnimationAutomatic. The parameter that accepts this value has various other preset values with which you can customize the visual behavior of your rows, including the following:

- UITableViewRowAnimationBottom
- UITableViewRowAnimationFade
- UITableViewRowAnimationLeft
- UITableViewRowAnimationMiddle
- UITableViewRowAnimationNone
- UITableViewRowAnimationRight
- UITableViewRowAnimationTop

The animation type that you choose won't result in any significant difference in how your application performs, but it can certainly change how an application looks and feels to the user. It's best to play around with these to determine which animation looks best in your application.

At this point, your method should now be able to handle the deletion of rows from your table. Because you wrote your program to recreate your data every time the application runs, it should be relatively easy to test this. When you are about to delete a row from a table, your table should resemble Figure 4-12.

Figure 4-12. *Deleting a row from a table*

But Wait, There's More!

Deletion is not the only kind of editing that can occur in a UITableView. Although not used quite as often, iOS includes functionality to allow rows to be created and inserted with the same method with which they were deleted.

The default editing style for any row in a UITableView is UITableViewCellEditingStyleDelete, so to implement row insertion, you need to change this. For fun, you will give every other row an "insertion" editing style by implementing the tableView:editingStyleForRowAtIndexPath: method, as shown in Listing 4-37.

Listing 4-37. *Modifying tableView:editingStyleForRowAtIndexPath: to add insertion*

```
-(UITableViewCellEditingStyle)tableView:(UITableView *)tableView editingStyleForRowAtIndexPath:(NSI
ndexPath *)indexPath
{
    if ((indexPath.row % 2) == 1)
```

```
    {
        return UITableViewCellEditingStyleInsert;
    }
    return UITableViewCellEditingStyleDelete;
}
```

Just as before, you need to specify the behavior to be followed upon the selection of an "Insertion" button. Add a case to your tableView:commitEditingStyle:forRowAtIndexPath: so the method looks like Listing 4-38.

Listing 4-38. Adding behavior to handle an "Insertion" button

```
-(void)tableView:(UITableView *)tableView commitEditingStyle:(UITableViewCellEditingStyle)
editingStyle forRowAtIndexPath:(NSIndexPath *)indexPath
{
    if (editingStyle == UITableViewCellEditingStyleDelete)
    {
        Country *deletedCountry = [self.countries objectAtIndex:indexPath.row];
        [self.countries removeObject:deletedCountry];

        [countriesTableView
            deleteRowsAtIndexPaths:[NSArray arrayWithObject:indexPath]
            withRowAnimation:UITableViewRowAnimationAutomatic];
    }
    else if (editingStyle == UITableViewCellEditingStyleInsert)
    {
        Country *copiedCountry = [self.countries objectAtIndex:indexPath.row];
        Country *newCountry = [[Country alloc] init];
        newCountry.name = copiedCountry.name;
        newCountry.flag = copiedCountry.flag;
        newCountry.capital = copiedCountry.capital;
        newCountry.motto = copiedCountry.motto;

        [self.countries insertObject:newCountry atIndex:indexPath.row+1];

        [self.countriesTableView insertRowsAtIndexPaths:
                [NSArray arrayWithObject:[NSIndexPath indexPathForRow:indexPath.row+1
                                            inSection:indexPath.section]]
                withRowAnimation:UITableViewRowAnimationRight];
    }
}
```

You can see that you have chosen an easy implementation for insertion. All you have done is to insert a copy of the selected row. You should note that by changing the index values in this method, you could easily insert objects into nearly any row in the table; it is not necessary to insert into only the following row.

As with the deletion, you must make sure that your data model is updated before your table view is, so you add the new Country to your array before you insert the new row into your UITableView.

When running your app and editing your table, you can see both deletion and insertion buttons, as in Figure 4-13.

Figure 4-13. Editing a UITableView via insertion or deletion

You can use two other `UITableView` delegate methods in combination with editing to further customize your application's behavior. We'll just mention them quickly here before closing this recipe and going on with reordering table views.

- The `tableView:willBeginEditingRowAtIndexPath:` method allows you to get a kind of "first look" at whichever row was selected for editing and act accordingly.

- The `tableView:didEndEditingRowAtIndexPath:` method can be used as a completion block, in that you can specify any actions you deem necessary to be performed on a row, but only after you have completed a row's editing.

Recipe 4-3: Reordering a UITableView

Now that we have covered deletion and insertion of rows, the next logical step in terms of functionality of a table is to make it so you can move your rows around. This is pretty simple to incorporate, given how you have set up your application.

First, you have to specify which of your rows are allowed to move. Do this by implementing the `tableView:canMoveRowAtIndexPath:` delegate method, as shown in Listing 4-39.

Listing 4-39. Implementing the tableView:canMoveRowAtIndexPath: method

```
-(BOOL)tableView:(UITableView *)tableView canMoveRowAtIndexPath:(NSIndexPath *)indexPath
{
    return YES;
}
```

We took the easy way out of this by simply making all the rows editable, but you can of course change this depending on your application.

Now, you simply need to implement a delegate to update your data model on the successful movement of a row, as shown in Listing 4-40.

Listing 4-40. Implementing the tableView:moveRowAtIndexPath:toIndexPath: method

```
-(void)tableView:(UITableView *)tableView moveRowAtIndexPath:
(NSIndexPath *)sourceIndexPath toIndexPath:(NSIndexPath *)destinationIndexPath
{
    [self.countries exchangeObjectAtIndex:sourceIndexPath.row
        withObjectAtIndex:destinationIndexPath.row];
    [self.countriesTableView reloadData];
}
```

Just as with insertion, you must make sure to correct your array to match the reordering, but the UITableView handles the actual swapping of rows automatically.

For extra control over the reordering of the table, you can implement an extra method called tableView:targetIndexPathForMoveFromRowAtIndexPath:. This delegate method is called every time a cell is dragged over another cell as a possible movement, and its normal use is for "retargeting" a destination row. In this way, you can check the proposed destination and either confirm the proposed move or reject it and return a different destination.

Although you haven't implemented functionality to confirm or reject your proposed movements, your application now successfully allows you to move and reorder your rows, in addition to the previous deletion and copying functionalities, as in Figure 4-14.

Figure 4-14. *Your table with a reordering of cells feature*

Recipe 4-4: Creating a Grouped UITableView

Now that you have almost completed all the basics of using an ungrouped UITableView, you can adjust your application to consider a "grouped" approach. All the functionalities you implemented with an ungrouped table also apply to a grouped one, so you will not have to make a great number of changes.

The absolute first thing you need to do to use a grouped table is to switch the "style" of the UITableView from "plain" to "grouped." The easiest way to do this is in your view controller's .xib file by selecting your UITableView and changing the style in the attribute inspector, which results in a display similar to the one in Figure 4-15.

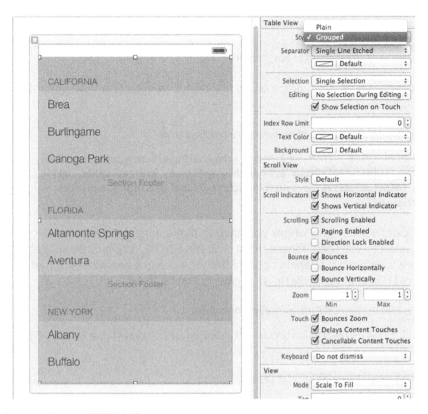

Figure 4-15. Configuring a "grouped" UITableView

While this is the only action necessary to change the style of your table, the problem is that until now your data model has been formatted for an ungrouped style. You don't have your data grouped at all. To remedy this problem, you will change the organization method by which your data is stored.

Rather than having one array containing all five of your countries, you will separate your countries into their groups, with each group being an NSMutableArray, and then put these arrays into a larger NSMutableArray.

For your application, you will divide your five Country objects into two categories: one for countries in the United Kingdom and one for all the others.

First, you need to create two more NSMutableArrays to be your subarrays, so add these two properties to MainTableViewController.h, as shown in Listing 4-41. You will end up with a total of three NSMutableArray properties.

Listing 4-41. Adding NSMutableArray properties to contain country groups

```
@property (strong, nonatomic) NSMutableArray *countries;
@property (strong, nonatomic) NSMutableArray *unitedKingdomCountries;
@property (strong, nonatomic) NSMutableArray *nonUKCountries;
```

Now, change your viewDidLoad method to accommodate this change. Delete the line shown in Listing 4-42.

Listing 4-42. Line that needs to be removed from the viewDidLoad method

```
self.countries =
    [NSMutableArray arrayWithObjects:usa, france, england, scotland, spain, nil];
```

Now, add the line in Listing 4-43 in place of the line removed in Listing 4-42 in order to properly organize your countries.

Listing 4-43. Creating country groups and adding them to the countries array

```
self.unitedKingdomCountries = [NSMutableArray arrayWithObjects:england, scotland, nil];
self.nonUKCountries = [NSMutableArray arrayWithObjects:usa, france, spain, nil];
self.countries = [NSMutableArray arrayWithObjects:self.unitedKingdomCountries,
self.nonUKCountries, nil];
```

Now comes the slightly tricky part where you have to make sure all your datasource and delegate methods are adjusted to your new format. First, you have to include a retrieval of the group's array, and then you have to retrieve a specific country from the group's array in each method. First, change your tableView:cellForRowAtIndexPath, as shown in Listing 4-44.

Listing 4-44. Updating the tableView:cellForRowAtIndexPath: method

```
- (UITableViewCell *)tableView:(UITableView *)tableView cellForRowAtIndexPath:(NSIndexPath *)
indexPath
{
    static NSString *CellIdentifier = @"Cell";

    UITableViewCell *cell = [tableView dequeueReusableCellWithIdentifier:CellIdentifier];
    if (cell == nil)
    {
        cell = [[UITableViewCell alloc] initWithStyle:UITableViewCellStyleSubtitle
                reuseIdentifier:CellIdentifier];
        cell.accessoryType = UITableViewCellAccessoryDetailDisclosureButton;
        cell.textLabel.font = [UIFont systemFontOfSize:19.0];
        cell.detailTextLabel.font = [UIFont systemFontOfSize:12];
    }

    NSArray *group = [self.countries objectAtIndex:indexPath.section];
    Country *item = [group objectAtIndex:indexPath.row];
    cell.textLabel.text = item.name;
    cell.detailTextLabel.text = item.capital;
    cell.imageView.image =
        [MainTableViewController scale: item.flag toSize:CGSizeMake(115, 75)];

    return cell;
}
```

Next, change the tableView:numberOfRowsInSection:, as shown in Listing 4-45.

Listing 4-45. Updating the tableView:numberOfRowsInSection: method

```
-(NSInteger)tableView:(UITableView *)tableView numberOfRowsInSection:(NSInteger)section
{
    NSArray *group = [self.countries objectAtIndex:section];
    return [group count];
}
```

Listing 4-46 shows the update to tableView:didSelectRowAtIndexPath.

Listing 4-46. Updating the tableView:didSelectRowAtIndexPath: method

```
-(void)tableView:(UITableView *)tableView didSelectRowAtIndexPath:(NSIndexPath *)indexPath
{
    [tableView deselectRowAtIndexPath:indexPath animated:YES];

    selectedIndexPath = indexPath;

    NSArray *group = [self.countries objectAtIndex:indexPath.section];
    Country *chosenCountry = [group objectAtIndex:indexPath.row];
    CountryDetailsViewController *detailedViewController =
        [[CountryDetailsViewController alloc] init];
    detailedViewController.delegate = self;
    detailedViewController.currentCountry = chosenCountry;

    [self.navigationController pushViewController:detailedViewController animated:YES];
}
```

See the same change in tableView:accessoryButtonTappedForRowWithIndexPath:, shown in
Listing 4-47.

Listing 4-47. Updating the tableView:accessoryButtonTappedForRowWithIndexpath: method

```
-(void)tableView:(UITableView *)tableView accessoryButtonTappedForRowWithIndexPath:(NSIndexPath *)
indexPath
{
    [tableView deselectRowAtIndexPath:indexPath animated:YES];

    selectedIndexPath = indexPath;

    NSArray *group = [self.countries objectAtIndex:indexPath.section];
    Country *chosenCountry = [group objectAtIndex:indexPath.row];
    CountryDetailsViewController *detailedViewController =
        [[CountryDetailsViewController alloc] init];
    detailedViewController.delegate = self;
    detailedViewController.currentCountry = chosenCountry;

    NSLog(@"Accessory Button Tapped");
    [self.navigationController pushViewController:detailedViewController animated:YES];
}
```

For the `tableView:moveRowAtIndexPath:toIndexPath:` method, you can make a quick assumption that you are moving only rows that are in the same section, to make your coding easier. Notice when you run the application later that this actually works well. As with your current implementation, the `UITableView` does not allow a `Country` to switch groups, as expected in this particular application. For an application where it might be reasonable to have objects change groups, include code to do so accordingly.

Update the code for the `tableView:moveRowAtIndexPath:toIndexpath:` method, as shown in Listing 4-48.

Listing 4-48. Updating the tableView:moveRowAtIndexPath:toIndexPath: method

```
-(void)tableView:(UITableView *)tableView moveRowAtIndexPath:
(NSIndexPath *)sourceIndexPath toIndexPath:(NSIndexPath *)destinationIndexPath
{
    //Assume same Section
    NSMutableArray *group = [self.countries objectAtIndex:sourceIndexPath.section];
    if (destinationIndexPath.row < [group count])
    {
        [group exchangeObjectAtIndex:sourceIndexPath.row
            withObjectAtIndex:destinationIndexPath.row];
    }
    [self.countriesTableView reloadData];
}
```

The last method you must fix is `tableView:commitEditingStyle:forRowAtIndexPath:`, which looks like Listing 4-49.

Listing 4-49. Updating the tableView:commitEditingStyle:forRowAtIndexPath

```
-(void)tableView:(UITableView *)tableView commitEditingStyle:(UITableViewCellEditingStyle)
editingStyle forRowAtIndexPath:(NSIndexPath *)indexPath
{
    if (editingStyle == UITableViewCellEditingStyleDelete)
    {
        NSMutableArray *group = [self.countries objectAtIndex:indexPath.section];
        Country *deletedCountry = [group objectAtIndex:indexPath.row];
        [group removeObject:deletedCountry];

        [self.countriesTableView deleteRowsAtIndexPaths:[NSArray arrayWithObject:indexPath] withRowA
nimation:UITableViewRowAnimationAutomatic];
    }
    else if (editingStyle == UITableViewCellEditingStyleInsert)
    {
        NSMutableArray *group = [self.countries objectAtIndex:indexPath.section];
        Country *copiedCountry = [group objectAtIndex:indexPath.row];
        Country *newCountry = [[Country alloc] init];
        newCountry.name = copiedCountry.name;
        newCountry.flag = copiedCountry.flag;
        newCountry.capital = copiedCountry.capital;
        newCountry.motto = copiedCountry.motto;
```

```
        [group insertObject:newCountry atIndex:indexPath.row+1];

        [self.countriesTableView insertRowsAtIndexPaths:
            [NSArray arrayWithObject:[NSIndexPath indexPathForRow:indexPath.row+1
              inSection:indexPath.section]]
            withRowAnimation:UITableViewRowAnimationRight];
    }
}
```

Finally, because you *did* switch your UITableView over to a grouped style, you need to implement just two extra methods to ensure correct functionality.

First, you need to specify how many sections your UITableView will have, using the method shown in Listing 4-50.

Listing 4-50. Implementing the numberOfSectionsInTableView: method

```
-(NSInteger)numberOfSectionsInTableView:(UITableView *)tableView
{
    return [self.countries count];
}
```

Second, you should specify headers for each section, which will basically be the titles for your groups. Because you already know how your data is formatted, this is pretty easy to do. Add the implementation shown in Listing 4-51.

Listing 4-51. Implementing the tableView:titleForHeaderInSection: method

```
-(NSString *)tableView:(UITableView *)tableView titleForHeaderInSection:(NSInteger)section
{
    if (section == 0)
    {
        return @"United Kingdom Countries";
    }
    return @"Non-United Kingdom Countries";
}
```

If your data model were more complicated, you would probably want to have the names of your groups stored somewhere with the groups themselves. A good way to achieve this would be with an NSDictionary, where you would store the names of the groups as the dictionary keys, and the group items would be the dictionary objects.

The UITableViewDelegate protocol also includes a method that allows the developer to customize the text displayed in a "Delete" button when editing a UITableView. This method (Listing 4-52) is entirely optional and varies in its use based on the needs of any given application.

Listing 4-52. Optional method to change the delete button text

```
-(NSString *)tableView:(UITableView *)tableView titleForDeleteConfirmationButtonForRowAtIndexPath:
(NSIndexPath *)indexPath
{
    return NSLocalizedString(@"Remove", @"Delete");
}
```

After making all these changes, running your app should result in a view similar to the one in Figure 4-16.

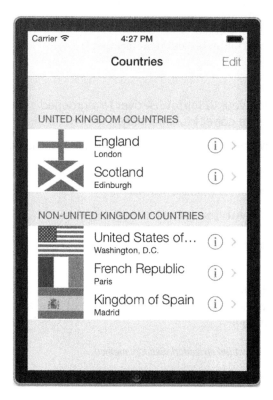

***Figure 4-16.** Your application with grouped items and section headers*

As a final embellishment for your table, you can also add footers to your sections. These work just like headers, but, as you might guess, they appear at the bottom of your groups. Listing 4-53 shows a quick method to add footers to your UITableView.

Listing 4-53. A method implementation for adding footers to the groups

```
-(NSString *)tableView:(UITableView *)tableView titleForFooterInSection:(NSInteger)section
{
    if (section == 0)
        return @"United Kingdom Countries";
    return @"Non-United Kingdom Countries";
}
```

In keeping with all the other customizable parts of a UITableView, these headers and footers are also easily customized beyond a simple NSString. If you use the methods tableView:viewForHeaderInSection: and tableView:viewForFooterInSection:, you can programmatically create your own subview to be used as a header or footer, allowing for full control over your UITableView's display.

At this point, you now have a fully functional grouped UITableView, complete with all the same abilities as your ungrouped one! Figure 4-17 shows the final result of your setup.

Figure 4-17. Your completed grouped UITableView with both headers and footers

Recipe 4-5: Registering a Custom Cell Class

For a moment, let's return to the method that's responsible for creating and initializing a given table view cell. For reference, Listing 4-54 shows the implementation from the previous recipes.

Listing 4-54. Repeated implementation for initializing a table view cell

```
- (UITableViewCell *)tableView:(UITableView *)tableView cellForRowAtIndexPath:(NSIndexPath *)
indexPath
{
    static NSString *CellIdentifier = @"Cell";

    UITableViewCell *cell =
        [tableView dequeueReusableCellWithIdentifier:CellIdentifier];
    if (cell == nil)
    {
        cell = [[UITableViewCell alloc] initWithStyle:UITableViewCellStyleSubtitle
                                reuseIdentifier:CellIdentifier];
        cell.accessoryType = UITableViewCellAccessoryDetailDisclosureButton;
        cell.textLabel.font = [UIFont systemFontOfSize:19.0];
        cell.detailTextLabel.font = [UIFont systemFontOfSize:12];
    }
```

```
        NSArray *group = [self.countries objectAtIndex:indexPath.section];
        Country *item = [group objectAtIndex:indexPath.row];
        cell.textLabel.text = item.name;
        cell.detailTextLabel.text = item.capital;
        cell.imageView.image =
            [MainTableViewController scale: item.flag toSize:CGSizeMake(115, 75)];

        return cell;
}
```

The code follows a common implementation pattern of the `tableView:cellForRowAtIndexPath:` method, and it does its job well. However, there are a couple of problems with it. For one thing, it's quite long, and it's not obvious from a quick glance what it does. A more serious problem is that it's not particularly reusable; if you create another application and want similar-looking table view cells, your only option is to copy and paste the preceding code into the other project.

A better solution would be to make a custom table view cell class of your own so you can reuse it between projects, or even within one project if it contains several table views. A custom class could also make the setup code significantly simpler and more self-explanatory. Recipe 4-5 shows you how to change the Country project's current implementation of the `tableView:cellForRowAtIndexPath:` method into one that utilizes a custom table view cell class.

Creating a Custom Table View Cell Class

Start by creating a new class using the `Objective-C` class template. Name the new class "CountryCell" and make it a subclass of `UITableViewCell`. Open `CountryCell.h` and add a country property to the class, as shown in Listing 4-55.

Listing 4-55. Adding a country property to the new CountryCell.m interface

```
//
//  CountryCell.m
//  Recipe 4-1 to 4-5 Creating UITableViews
//

#import <UIKit/UIKit.h>
#import "Country.h"

@interface CountryCell : UITableViewCell

@property (strong, nonatomic) Country *country;

@end
```

Now, switch to the `CountryCell.m` file. The designated initializer of table view cells is the `initWithStyle:reuseIdentifier:` method. Override this method and provide the initialization that is common for all country cells—that is, cell style, accessory type, and the fonts of the two labels, as shown in Listing 4-56.

Listing 4-56. Overriding the initializer to set up common properties

```
- (id)initWithStyle:(UITableViewCellStyle)style reuseIdentifier:(NSString *)reuseIdentifier
{
    self = [super initWithStyle:UITableViewCellStyleSubtitle
            reuseIdentifier:reuseIdentifier];
    if (self)
    {
        // Initialization code
        self.accessoryType = UITableViewCellAccessoryDetailDisclosureButton;
        self.textLabel.font = [UIFont systemFontOfSize:19.0];
        self.detailTextLabel.font = [UIFont systemFontOfSize:12];
    }
    return self;
}
```

Next, we're going to implement a special setter method—a method that controls how a property is set—for the country property. This method updates the parts of the cell that are different for each country. These are the text label, the detailed text label, and the flag image. Implement the setter as shown in Listing 4-57.

Listing 4-57. Implementing the custom country property setter method

```
- (void)setCountry:(Country *)country
{
    if (country != _country)
    {
        _country = country;
        self.textLabel.text = _country.name;
        self.detailTextLabel.text = _country.capital;
        self.imageView.image =
            [CountryCell scale: _country.flag toSize:CGSizeMake(115, 75)];
    }
}
```

If you try to compile the code now it will fail because it doesn't recognize the scale:toSize: class method, which is currently declared in MainTableViewController. In a real scenario, you'd probably want to move the method to some kind of helper class that is shared throughout your application, but for the purpose of this recipe it's sufficient to move it from MainTableViewController into your CountryCell class. Make sure you remove the method declaration in the @interface section of your MainTableViewController as well as the method.

Your complete implementation file should now resemble the code shown in Listing 4-58.

Listing 4-58. The complete CountryCell.m implementation

```
//
//  CountryCell.m
//  Recipe 4-1 to 4-5 Creating UITableViews
//

#import "CountryCell.h"
```

```objc
@implementation CountryCell

- (id)initWithStyle:(UITableViewCellStyle)style reuseIdentifier:(NSString *)reuseIdentifier
{
    self = [super initWithStyle:UITableViewCellStyleSubtitle reuseIdentifier:reuseIdentifier];
    if (self)
    {
        // Initialization code
        self.accessoryType = UITableViewCellAccessoryDetailDisclosureButton;
        self.textLabel.font = [UIFont systemFontOfSize:19.0];
        self.detailTextLabel.font = [UIFont systemFontOfSize:12];
    }
    return self;
}

+ (UIImage *)scale:(UIImage *)image toSize:(CGSize)size
{
    UIGraphicsBeginImageContext(size);
    [image drawInRect:CGRectMake(0, 0, size.width, size.height)];
    UIImage *scaledImage = UIGraphicsGetImageFromCurrentImageContext();
    UIGraphicsEndImageContext();
    return scaledImage;
}

- (void)setCountry:(Country *)country
{
    if (country != _country)
    {
        _country = country;
        self.textLabel.text = _country.name;
        self.detailTextLabel.text = _country.capital;
        self.imageView.image =
            [CountryCell scale: _country.flag toSize:CGSizeMake(115, 75)];
    }
}

@end
```

Your custom table view cell class is now ready to be used from your table view controller.

Registering Your Cell Class

To register your cell class, switch to MainTableViewController.m and add the line in Listing 4-59 to its viewDidLoad method. To make it compile, you also need to import CountryCell.h.

Listing 4-59. Importing the CountryCell class into the MainTableViewController.m file

```objc
#import "MainTableViewController.h"
#import "CountryCell.h"

@implementation MainTableViewController
```

```
// ...

- (void)viewDidLoad
{
    [super viewDidLoad];
    // Do any additional setup after loading the view from its nib.
    self.title = @"Countries";
    self.countriesTableView.delegate = self;
    self.countriesTableView.dataSource = self;
    self.countriesTableView.layer.cornerRadius = 8.0;
    self.navigationItem.rightBarButtonItem = self.editButtonItem;

    [self.countriesTableView registerClass:CountryCell.class
        forCellReuseIdentifier:@"CountryCell"];

    // ...
}
```

The preceding code registers your CountryCell class with the table view. This uses a feature of iOS 7 that changes the semantics of the dequeueReusableCellWithIdentifier: method a little. The new behavior of that method is that if a suitable cached cell object cannot be found, a new cell is created as long as a registered class with the given identifier exists.

It's now time to reap the benefits of your changes and implement the tableView:cellForRowAtIndexP ath: method, which at this point can be shrunk into only four lines of code, as shown in Listing 4-60.

Listing 4-60. Updating the tableView:cellForRowAtIndexPath: method to take advantage of the new class

```
- (UITableViewCell *)tableView:(UITableView *)tableView cellForRowAtIndexPath:(NSIndexPath *)
indexPath
{
    CountryCell *cell = [tableView dequeueReusableCellWithIdentifier:@"CountryCell"];
    NSArray *group = [self.countries objectAtIndex:indexPath.section];
    cell.country = [group objectAtIndex:indexPath.row];
    return cell;
}
```

If you build and run your code now, it should work just like before. But now your code is a bit better encapsulated and better prepared for reuse.

Recipe 4-6: Creating a Flag Picker Collection View

One great feature that was added in iOS 6 and remains nearly unchanged in iOS 7 is the collection view. It has evolved from the good old table view, not to be its replacement, but rather to be a natural complement. Unlike table views, which display data in a single column and have a lot of built-in functionality based on that layout, collection views provide total control of how items are laid out, but offer fewer built-in functions. Collection views offer more possibilities but at the price of more work on the part of the developer.

The exceptional flexibility of the collection view comes from a total separation between the view and its layout. What this means is that you can get full control of the layout of items by providing a custom layout object. However, Apple provides a ready-to-use Layout class that will work in most situations. This class provides a basic multicolumn layout that expands in one direction (that is, supports either horizontal or vertical scrolling).

In this recipe, we'll show you how to set up a collection view with this built-in layout class, called `UICollectionViewFlowLayout`. You'll use it to create a picker view, in which a user can browse a collection of flags and select one of them.

Setting Up the Application

Because this app displays a collection of flags, you should start by gathering some flag images for your test data. Download as many flag images as you like from `http://en.wikipedia.org/wiki/Gallery_of_sovereign-state_flags`, but to make sense there should be at least 15 of them from several continents. As a reference, we downloaded the following flags:

- African flags: Ghana, Kenya, Morocco, Mozambique, Rwanda, and South Africa

- Asian flags: China, India, Japan, Mongolia, Russia, and Turkey

- Australasian flags: Australia and New Zealand

- European flags: France, Germany, Iceland, Ireland, Italy, Malta, Poland, Spain, Sweden, and the United Kingdom

- North American flags: Canada, Mexico, and the United States

- South American flags: Argentina, Brazil, and Chile

Tip   To keep the app size down, download the 200-pixel PNG format of the flags. This format and size is found by clicking the flag image on the Wikipedia flag gallery, which takes you to a page with links to the available sizes and formats for the flag image. It's also recommended that you change their file names to contain only the name of the country, such as France.png.

Now, create a new single view application and add the flag images to the project. An easy way to do this is to gather the flag images in a folder and drag it onto the project navigator. It might be a good idea to create a new group folder to host the files, preferably in the Supporting Files folder, as shown in Figure 4-18.

Figure 4-18. An application with flag resource images in a group folder of their own

The next task you need to perform is to set up a simple user interface that displays a big flag and the name of the country it belongs to. A button below the flag will allow the user to select a different flag using the Flag Picker that you'll soon build. Select the `Main.storyboard` file to edit the single view controller and add a label, an image view, and a button to the view in such a way that it resembles Figure 4-19. Initialize the image view with one of your flag images by setting the image view's image attribute in the attribute inspector.

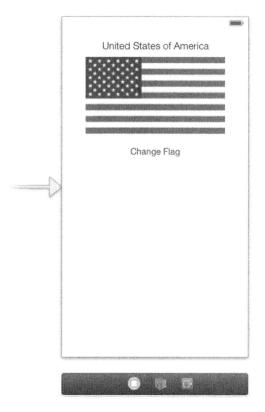

Figure 4-19. A simple user interface that displays a country name and its flag

Because you'll change the content of both the label and the image view at runtime, you need outlets to reference them from your code. Create these outlets and name them "countryLabel" and "flagImageView," respectively. Similarly, create an action named "pickFlag" for when the user taps the button.

Your ViewController.h file should now resemble Listing 4-61.

Listing 4-61. The starting ViewController.h file

```
//
//  ViewController.h
//  Recipe 4-6 Creating a flag picker collection view
//

#import <UIKit/UIKit.h>

@interface ViewController : UIViewController

@property (weak, nonatomic) IBOutlet UILabel *countryLabel;
@property (weak, nonatomic) IBOutlet UIImageView *flagImageView;

- (IBAction)pickFlag:(id)sender;

@end
```

You're now going to leave the main user interface for a while and instead turn to implementing the Flag Picker view controller that will be displayed from the pickFlag: action method. But before you can do that you need to create a simple data model that you can use to transfer data between the picker and the main view.

Creating a Data Model

In this recipe, you will set up a simple model to hold the data. You will create a class that holds an image of a flag and the name of the country it belongs to. Create a new Objective-C class named "Flag" with NSObject as its parent. Then, in Flag.h, add the code in Listing 4-62 to declare properties and an initialization method for the class.

Listing 4-62. Declaring properties and an initialization method for the Flag class

```
//
//  Flag.h
//  Recipe 4-6 Creating a flag picker collection view
//

#import <Foundation/Foundation.h>

@interface Flag : NSObject

@property (strong, nonatomic)NSString *name;
@property (strong, nonatomic)UIImage *image;
```

```
- (id)initWithName:(NSString *)name imageName:(NSString *)imageName;
```

`@end`

Now, switch to `Flag.m` to add implementation of the initialization method, as shown in Listing 4-63.

Listing 4-63. Implementing the custom initialization method in Flag.m

```
//
//  Flag.m
//  Recipe 4-6 Creating a flag picker collection view
//

#import "Flag.h"

@implementation Flag

- (id)initWithName:(NSString *)name imageName:(NSString *)imageName
{
    self = [super init];
    if (self) {
        self.name = name;
        NSString *imageFile = [[NSBundle mainBundle] pathForResource:imageName ofType:@"png"];
        self.image = [[UIImage alloc] initWithContentsOfFile:imageFile];
    }
    return self;
}

@end
```

> **Note** The `initWithName:imageName:` method loads the image resource file into memory. In a real scenario, you'd probably want to use lazy initialization in a custom property getter. This allows you to initialize the image resource when you access the property with the custom getter. By doing this, you defer the loading until the image is actually requested. But for this recipe, loading the flag file on creation is fine.

You're now ready to move on and start implementing the Flag Picker.

Building the Flag Picker

When the user taps the "Change Flag" button of the user interface, the app will display a collection of flags for the user to choose from. This is the perfect job for a collection view, so let's set one up.

First, you need a new view controller to handle the collection view, so create a new subclass of `UICollectionViewController`. Name the new class "FlagPickerViewController." You do not need an `.xib` file to handle its user interface, so make sure the option "With XIB for user interface" is deselected.

With the new class in place, set up the delegation pattern to use for notifying the main view that a flag has been picked. Go to the header file of the new class and add the code in Listing 4-64.

Listing 4-64. Setting up the delegation pattern for the FlagPickerViewController

```
//
//  FlagPickerViewController.h
//  Recipe 4-6 Creating a flag picker collection view
//

#import <UIKit/UIKit.h>
#import "Flag.h"

@class FlagPickerViewController;

@protocol FlagPickerViewControllerDelegate <NSObject>

-(void)flagPicker:(FlagPickerViewController *)flagPicker didPickFlag:(Flag *)flag;

@end

@interface FlagPickerViewController : UICollectionViewController

- (id)initWithDelegate:(id<FlagPickerViewControllerDelegate>)delegate;

@property (weak, nonatomic)id<FlagPickerViewControllerDelegate>delegate;

@end
```

You also need some instance variables to hold the available flags. Because you are going to group the flags according to which continent they originate from, you need six arrays, as shown in Listing 4-65.

Listing 4-65. Creating instance arrays to hold the flags of each group

```
//
//  FlagPickerViewController.h
//  Recipe 4-6 Creating a flag picker collection view
//

// ...

@interface FlagPickerViewController : UICollectionViewController
{
@private
    NSArray *africanFlags;
    NSArray *asianFlags;
    NSArray *australasianFlags;
    NSArray *europeanFlags;
    NSArray *northAmericanFlags;
    NSArray *southAmericanFlags;
}
```

```
- (id)initWithDelegate:(id<FlagPickerViewControllerDelegate>)delegate;

@property (weak, nonatomic)id<FlagPickerViewControllerDelegate>delegate;

@end
```

Now, switch to the FlagPickerViewController.m file and add the implementation for the initialization method, as shown in Listing 4-66.

Listing 4-66. Adding a custom initialization to the FlagPickerViewController.m file

```
//
//  FlagPickerViewController.m
//  Recipe 4-6 Creating a flag picker collection view
//

#import "FlagPickerViewController.h"

@implementation FlagPickerViewController

- (id)initWithDelegate:(id<FlagPickerViewControllerDelegate>)delegate
{
    UICollectionViewFlowLayout *layout =
        [[UICollectionViewFlowLayout alloc] init];
    self = [super initWithCollectionViewLayout:layout];
    if (self)
    {
        self.delegate = delegate;
    }
    return self;
}

// ...

@end
```

As you can see from the preceding code, the method creates a layout object to handle the positioning of the items. We're using the built-in UICollectionViewFlowLayout, which provides a simple multicolumn layout that flows in one direction (horizontally by default). The method also sets the delegate property that you will use later to notify the invoker that a selection has been made.

Next, create the collection of available flags. Find the viewDidLoad method and add the code in Listing 4-67. Note that you should adjust the code according to which flags you actually downloaded and imported into your project.

Listing 4-67. Adding and initializing flags in their respective groups

```
- (void)viewDidLoad
{
    [super viewDidLoad];
    // Do any additional setup after loading the view from its nib.
```

```
    africanFlags = [NSArray arrayWithObjects:
        [[Flag alloc] initWithName:@"Ghana" imageName:@"Ghana"],
        [[Flag alloc] initWithName:@"Kenya" imageName:@"Kenya"],
        [[Flag alloc] initWithName:@"Morocco" imageName:@"Morocco"],
        [[Flag alloc] initWithName:@"Mozambique" imageName:@"Mozambique"],
        [[Flag alloc] initWithName:@"Rwanda" imageName:@"Rwanda"],
        [[Flag alloc] initWithName:@"South Africa" imageName:@"South_Africa"],
        nil];

    asianFlags = [NSArray arrayWithObjects:
        [[Flag alloc] initWithName:@"China" imageName:@"China"],
        [[Flag alloc] initWithName:@"India" imageName:@"India"],
        [[Flag alloc] initWithName:@"Japan" imageName:@"Japan"],
        [[Flag alloc] initWithName:@"Mongolia" imageName:@"Mongolia"],
        [[Flag alloc] initWithName:@"Russia" imageName:@"Russia"],
        [[Flag alloc] initWithName:@"Turkey" imageName:@"Turkey"],
        nil];

    australasianFlags = [NSArray arrayWithObjects:
        [[Flag alloc] initWithName:@"Australia" imageName:@"Australia"],
        [[Flag alloc] initWithName:@"New Zealand" imageName:@"New_Zealand"],
        nil];

    europeanFlags = [NSArray arrayWithObjects:
        [[Flag alloc] initWithName:@"France" imageName:@"France"],
        [[Flag alloc] initWithName:@"Germany" imageName:@"Germany"],
        [[Flag alloc] initWithName:@"Iceland" imageName:@"Iceland"],
        [[Flag alloc] initWithName:@"Ireland" imageName:@"Ireland"],
        [[Flag alloc] initWithName:@"Italy" imageName:@"Italy"],
        [[Flag alloc] initWithName:@"Poland" imageName:@"Poland"],
        [[Flag alloc] initWithName:@"Russia" imageName:@"Russia"],
        [[Flag alloc] initWithName:@"Spain" imageName:@"Spain"],
        [[Flag alloc] initWithName:@"Sweden" imageName:@"Sweden"],
        [[Flag alloc] initWithName:@"Turkey" imageName:@"Turkey"],
        [[Flag alloc] initWithName:@"United Kingdom" imageName:@"United_Kingdom"],
        nil];

    northAmericanFlags = [NSArray arrayWithObjects:
        [[Flag alloc] initWithName:@"Canada" imageName:@"Canada"],
        [[Flag alloc] initWithName:@"Mexico" imageName:@"Mexico"],
        [[Flag alloc] initWithName:@"United States" imageName:@"United_States"],
        nil];

    southAmericanFlags = [NSArray arrayWithObjects:
        [[Flag alloc] initWithName:@"Argentina" imageName:@"Argentina"],
        [[Flag alloc] initWithName:@"Brazil" imageName:@"Brazil"],
        [[Flag alloc] initWithName:@"Chile" imageName:@"Chile"],
        nil];
}
```

Collection views follow the same data pattern as table views, meaning that they allow data to be grouped into sections. As you'll see, the datasource methods to notify the collection view regarding how many sections there are and how many items they contain are very similar to the ones used for table views. Add the following two methods shown in Listing 4-68 to provide that data.

Listing 4-68. Adding datasource methods to set the number of sections and items

```objc
//
//  FlagPickerViewController.m
//  Recipe 4-6 Creating a flag picker collection view
//

// ...

@implementation FlagPickerViewController

// ...

-(NSInteger)numberOfSectionsInCollectionView:(UICollectionView *)collectionView
{
    return 6;
}

-(NSInteger)collectionView:(UICollectionView *)collectionView numberOfItemsInSection:(NSInteger)
section
{
    switch (section) {
        case 0:
            return africanFlags.count;
        case 1:
            return asianFlags.count;
        case 2:
            return australasianFlags.count;
        case 3:
            return europeanFlags.count;
        case 4:
            return northAmericanFlags.count;
        case 5:
            return southAmericanFlags.count;

        default:
            return 0;
    }
}

@end
```

> **Note**   As you might have noticed, we did not explicitly assign a datasource delegate for the collection view. The collection view controller class handles this automatically; if you don't provide a specific delegate object it will assign itself to the task. This is true for both the `UICollectionViewDelegate` and the `UICollectionViewDataSource` properties of the collection view.

Now you have set up the collection view so that it knows how many sections and how many items it should display. The next step is to let the collection view know how to display the items. This is done by creating and registering cell views and a so-called supplementary view.

Defining the Collection View Interface

A collection view delegates the actual displaying of items and section-specific details to views provided by you. These views are called cell views and supplementary views. *Supplementary views* are things such as section headers and footers, while *cell views* are the individual items. It's your job to define these views and register them with the collection view.

You will set up these cells programmatically, and you'll start with the cell view. It should contain a thumbnail image of a flag and a small label displaying the country name. Start by creating a new `UICollectionViewCell` subclass with the name "FlagCell." Then add the property declarations to the header file of the new class, as shown in Listing 4-69.

Listing 4-69. Adding property declarations to the FlagCell.h file

```
//
//  FlagCell.h
//  Recipe 4-6 Creating a flag picker collection view
//

#import <UIKit/UIKit.h>

@interface FlagCell : UICollectionViewCell

@property (strong, nonatomic) UILabel *nameLabel;
@property (strong, nonatomic) UIImageView *flagImageView;

@end
```

In the implementation file, add the initialization code to the `initWithFrame:` method, as shown in Listing 4-70. The code basically does two things: it creates and adds a label and an image view to the content view of the cell, and it changes the color of the background view that's displayed when the cell is highlighted.

Listing 4-70. Adding code to FlagCell.m to create and add labels and images, as well to as change the background color

```
//
//  FlagCell.m
//  Recipe 4-6 Creating a flag picker collection view
//
```

```
#import "FlagCell.h"

@implementation FlagCell

- (id)initWithFrame:(CGRect)frame
{
    self = [super initWithFrame:frame];
    if (self) {
        // Initialization code
        self.nameLabel =
            [[UILabel alloc] initWithFrame:CGRectMake(0, 56, 100, 19)];
        self.nameLabel.textAlignment = NSTextAlignmentCenter;
        self.nameLabel.backgroundColor = [UIColor clearColor];
        self.nameLabel.textColor = [UIColor whiteColor];
        self.nameLabel.font = [UIFont systemFontOfSize:12.0];
        [self.contentView addSubview:self.nameLabel];

        self.flagImageView =
            [[UIImageView alloc] initWithFrame:CGRectMake(6, 6, 88, 49)];
        [self.contentView addSubview:self.flagImageView];

        self.selectedBackgroundView = [[UIView alloc] initWithFrame:frame];
        self.selectedBackgroundView.backgroundColor = [UIColor grayColor];
    }
    return self;
}

@end
```

Now, you're going to repeat the process for the header supplementary view. It'll simply contain a label to display the name of the continent in the header of the respective section. Create a new class, this time as a subclass of UICollectionReusableView and with the name "ContinentHeader." Then add the property declaration to its header file, as shown in Listing 4-71.

Listing 4-71. Adding a label property to the ContinentHeader.h file

```
//
//  ContinentHeader.h
//  Recipe 4-6 Creating a flag picker collection view
//

#import <UIKit/UIKit.h>

@interface ContinentHeader : UICollectionReusableView

@property (strong, nonatomic) UILabel *label;

@end
```

Next, add the initialization code to the implementation file, as shown in Listing 4-72.

Listing 4-72. Adding initialization code to ContinentHeader.m

```
//
//  ContinentHeader.m
//  Recipe 4-6 Creating a flag picker collection view
//

#import "ContinentHeader.h"

@implementation ContinentHeader

- (id)initWithFrame:(CGRect)frame
{
    self = [super initWithFrame:frame];
    if (self) {
        // Initialization code
        self.label = [[UILabel alloc] initWithFrame:
            CGRectMake(0, 0, frame.size.width, frame.size.height)];
        self.label.font = [UIFont systemFontOfSize:20];
        self.label.textColor = [UIColor whiteColor];
        self.label.backgroundColor = [UIColor clearColor];
        self.label.textAlignment = NSTextAlignmentCenter;
        [self addSubview:self.label];
    }
    return self;
}

@end
```

To use these two views to display the content, you need to register them with the collection view. Return to the FlagPickerViewController.m file and add the code in Listing 4-73 to the viewDidLoad method (note that the code to set up the flag data has been removed for brevity).

Listing 4-73. Registering the FlagCell and ContinentHeader views in FlagPickerViewController.m

```
//
//  FlagPickerViewController.m
//  Recipe 4-6 Creating a flag picker collection view
//

#import "FlagPickerViewController.h"
#import "FlagCell.h"
#import "ContinentHeader.h"

@implementation FlagPickerViewController

// ...

- (void)viewDidLoad
{
    [super viewDidLoad];
    // Do any additional setup after loading the view from its nib.
```

```
// ...

[self.collectionView registerClass:FlagCell.class
    forCellWithReuseIdentifier:@"FlagCell"];
[self.collectionView registerClass:ContinentHeader.class
    forSupplementaryViewOfKind:UICollectionElementKindSectionHeader
    withReuseIdentifier:@"ContinentHeader"];
}

// ...

@end
```

With the cell and supplementary views registered, you can implement the datasource and delegate methods that will create and set them up. Still in the FlagPickerViewController.m file, add the delegate method shown in Listing 4-74.

Listing 4-74. Implementing the collectionView:cellForItemAtIndexPath: method

```
-(UICollectionViewCell*)collectionView:(UICollectionView *)collectionView cellForItemAtIndexPath:(NS
IndexPath *)indexPath
{
FlagCell *cell =
        [collectionView dequeueReusableCellWithReuseIdentifier:@ "FlagCell"
        forIndexPath:indexPath];
    Flag *flag = [self flagForIndexPath:indexPath];
    cell.nameLabel.text = flag.name;
    cell.flagImageView.image = flag.image;
    return cell;
}
```

The dequeueReusableCellWithReuseIdentifier: method looks to see whether it can reuse an already created cell or whether it must create a new one if there's none. No matter what, you can rely on receiving an allocated instance of a cell that you then just update with the current data before you return it to the collection view.

Also, the method uses a helper method, flagForIndexPath:, to get the corresponding flag instance from the data model. The implementation of that helper method is given in Listing 4-75.

Listing 4-75. Implementing the flagForIndexpath: helper method

```
-(Flag *)flagForIndexPath:(NSIndexPath *)indexPath
{
    switch (indexPath.section) {
        case 0:
            return [africanFlags objectAtIndex:indexPath.row];
        case 1:
            return [asianFlags objectAtIndex:indexPath.row];
        case 2:
            return [australasianFlags objectAtIndex:indexPath.row];
        case 3:
            return [europeanFlags objectAtIndex:indexPath.row];
```

```
        case 4:
            return [northAmericanFlags objectAtIndex:indexPath.row];
        case 5:
            return [southAmericanFlags objectAtIndex:indexPath.row];

        default:
            return nil;
    }
}
```

Now, the corresponding datasource method for the supplementary view (the section header) looks like the code that follows. Add it to the FlagPickerViewController class as well:

```
- (UICollectionReusableView *)collectionView:(UICollectionView *)collectionView viewForSupplementary
ElementOfKind:(NSString *)kind atIndexPath:(NSIndexPath *)indexPath
{
    ContinentHeader *headerView = [collectionView
dequeueReusableSupplementaryViewOfKind:UICollectionElementKindSectionHeader withReuseIdentifier:@"Co
ntinentHeader" forIndexPath:indexPath];

    headerView.label.text = [self nameForSection:indexPath.section];

    return headerView;
}
```

Again, you are using a helper method to get data from your data model. This time you query the name of a section using the implementation shown in Listing 4-76.

Listing 4-76. Implementing the nameForSection: method

```
- (NSString *)nameForSection:(NSInteger)index
{
    switch (index)
    {
        case 0:
            return @"African Flags";
        case 1:
            return @"Asian Flags";
        case 2:
            return @"Australasian Flags";
        case 3:
            return @"European Flags";
        case 4:
            return @"North American Flags";
        case 5:
            return @"South American Flags";
        default:
            return @"Unknown";
    }
}
```

At this point, what's remaining before the defining of the collection view user interface is complete is to set the sizes of the cells and supplementary views. Do that in the collectionView:collectionViewLayout:sizeForItemAtPath: and the collectionView:collectionViewLayout:referenceSizeForHeaderInSection: datasource methods, as shown in Listing 4-77.

Listing 4-77. Implementing delegates for setting the size and supplementary views of cells

```
- (CGSize)collectionView:(UICollectionView *)collectionView layout:(UICollectionViewLayout*)
collectionViewLayout sizeForItemAtIndexPath:(NSIndexPath *)indexPath
{
    return CGSizeMake(100, 75);
}

- (CGSize)collectionView:(UICollectionView *)collectionView layout:(UICollectionViewLayout*)
collectionViewLayout referenceSizeForHeaderInSection:(NSInteger)section
{
    return CGSizeMake(50, 50);
}
```

> **Note**   When you set the size of a header or footer in a collection view flow layout, only one dimension is considered. For example, if the flow is vertical, only the height component of the CGSize is used to determine the actual size of the supplementary view. The width is instead inferred by the width of the collection view. The converse is true for horizontal flows, which only consider the width you provide.

The last task you need to complete in the Flag Picker is to add code that notifies the main view when a flag has been picked. This is easy now that the infrastructure is in place. Add the delegate method to FlagPickerViewController, as shown in Listing 4-78.

Listing 4-78. Adding the collectionView:didSelectItemAtIndexPath: method

```
-(void)collectionView:(UICollectionView *)collectionView didSelectItemAtIndexPath:(NSIndexPath *)
indexPath
{
    Flag *selectedFlag = [self flagForIndexPath:indexPath];
    [self.delegate flagPicker:self didPickFlag:selectedFlag];
}
```

You're done with the implementation of the Flag Picker. Now it's time to turn your focus back to the main view.

Displaying the Flag Picker

To use the Flag Picker you just built, you first need to prepare the main view controller to be a Flag Picker delegate. Making it conform to the FlagPickerViewControllerDelegate protocol you defined earlier does this. Switch to ViewController.h and add the code in Listing 4-79.

Listing 4-79. Making the main view controller conform to the FlagPickerViewControllerDelegate protocol

```
//
//  ViewController.h
//  Recipe 4-6 Creating a flag picker collection view
//

#import <UIKit/UIKit.h>
#import "FlagPickerViewController.h"

@interface ViewController : UIViewController<FlagPickerViewControllerDelegate>

@property (weak, nonatomic) IBOutlet UILabel *countryLabel;
@property (weak, nonatomic) IBOutlet UIImageView *flagImageView;

- (IBAction)pickFlag:(id)sender;

@end
```

Finally, you can now implement the pickFlag: action method. Go to ViewController.m and add the implementation, as shown in Listing 4-80.

Listing 4-80. Implementing the pickFlag action method in ViewController.m

```
- (IBAction)pickFlag:(id)sender
{
    UICollectionViewController *flagPicker =
        [[FlagPickerViewController alloc] initWithDelegate:self];

    [self presentViewController:flagPicker animated:YES completion:NULL];
}
```

In Listing 4-80, you first create a new UICollectionViewController instance and initialize it with the ViewController class as the delegate. Then you present the new UICollectionViewController as the current view.

Finally, add the method that responds to a selection event from the Flag Picker (Listing 4-81). It simply dismisses the Flag Picker and updates the image view and the label with the new information.

Listing 4-81. Implementing the flagPicker: didPickFlag: delegate method

```
-(void)flagPicker:(FlagPickerViewController *)flagPicker didPickFlag:(Flag *)flag
{
    self.flagImageView.image = flag.image;
    self.countryLabel.text = flag.name;
    [self dismissViewControllerAnimated:YES completion:NULL];
}
```

You now can build and run your application. When you tap the "Change Flag" button, you should be presented with a view resembling the one in Figure 4-20.

Figure 4-20. *A collection view displaying a set of flags*

You can scroll among the flags and select one that will then be used to update the main view, such as in Figure 4-21.

Figure 4-21. *An updated main view after a flag has been selected in the Flag Picker*

However, there is one small problem you'll notice if you rotate the device (by pressing ■ + →) and activate the Flag Picker. As Figure 4-22 shows, the section headers are no longer centered.

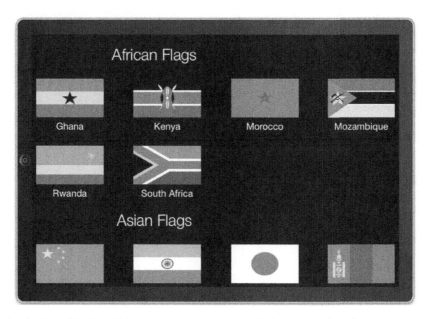

Figure 4-22. *The header files of the Flag Picker are not properly centered in landscape orientation*

Using Auto Layout to Center the Headers

The reason the header labels don't stay centered is that they are created with a fixed size. This works as long as the app stays in portrait mode, but when the screen rotates, the static-sized labels don't follow, causing the effect you see in Figure 4-22.

To fix that problem, you can use a little Auto Layout magic. Go to `ContinentHeader.m` and add the code in Listing 4-82 to the `initWithFrame:` method. What this code does is add an Auto Layout constraint that instructs the label to expand to the width of its parent (the header view) and stay that way even if the parent's frame changes.

Listing 4-82. *Adding Auto Layout constraints to fix a rotation problem (additions are in bold)*

```
//
//  ContinentHeader.m
//  Recipe 4-6 Creating a flag picker collection view
//

#import "ContinentHeader.h"

@implementation ContinentHeader

- (id)initWithFrame:(CGRect)frame
{
    self = [super initWithFrame:frame];
    if (self) {
        // Initialization code
```

```
        self.label = [[UILabel alloc] initWithFrame:
            CGRectMake(0, 0, frame.size.width, frame.size.height)];
        self.label.font = [UIFont systemFontOfSize:20];
        self.label.textColor = [UIColor whiteColor];
        self.label.backgroundColor = [UIColor clearColor];
        self.label.textAlignment = NSTextAlignmentCenter;
        [self addSubview:self.label];

        self.label.translatesAutoresizingMaskIntoConstraints = NO;

        NSDictionary *viewsDictionary =
            [[NSDictionary alloc] initWithObjectsAndKeys:
             self.label, @"label", nil];
        [self addConstraints:
            [NSLayoutConstraint constraintsWithVisualFormat:@"H:|[label]|"
            options:0 metrics:nil views:viewsDictionary]];
    }
    return self;
}

@end
```

If you run the app now, you'll see that this edit has the desired effect on the headers. They are now centered, even in landscape orientation, as shown in Figure 4-23.

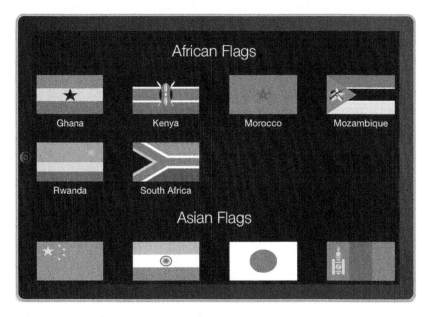

Figure 4-23. *The continent labels in this app are centered using Auto Layout*

Summary

In this chapter, we have shown you two of the core components of the iOS 7 platform: the table view and the collection view. We have shown you how to set them up and use them within your app. We have also given you a glimpse of the level of customization control the developer has over these views, though the full Apple documentation has a great deal more to say on the subject.

However, the key to table views and collection views is not how they work, but the data they present. It is up to you as a developer to find the information that users want or need and present it to them in the most efficient and flexible way possible. Table views and collection views are fantastic tools, but the purpose they serve is far more important, and this is what ultimately will be the final product you deliver to your customers.

Chapter 5

Location Recipes

Knowing a device's correct location and heading has enabled developers to take apps to a whole new level. Apps that utilize location services in new ways keep showing up, and the potential uses seem endless. You can build entire apps around these features, such as routing or fitness tracking apps, or you can use location services to enhance the user's experience in more traditional apps. A good example of the latter is the built-in Reminders app, which can remind you of certain tasks when you reach a certain location, such as calling a friend when you get home.

Apple has been paying a lot of attention to this field lately, and iOS 7 offers better accuracy and better availability than its predecessor, as well as some new default behaviors that will improve battery life. With iOS 7, you are better equipped than ever to make your apps location-aware. This chapter shows you how to get started.

About Core Location

The Core Location framework has everything you need to implement location awareness into your app. In particular, it supports the following:

- Location tracking
- Monitoring significant location changes
- Monitoring entrances or exits of custom regions
- Getting the current heading
- Translating coordinates into addresses (forward geocoding)
- Translating addresses into coordinates (reverse geocoding)

To do its job, Core Location utilizes data from several sources, including cellular masts, nearby wi-fi networks, GPS, and the magnetometer. There is some really complex stuff going on inside that we don't have to care about because the framework encapsulates it into an easy-to-use, all-in-one-place API.

Standard and Significant Change Services

There are two primary methods for finding the location of a device: *the standard location service* and *the significant location change service*. Which one you use depends on how accurate you need that information to be and how often you need to be notified that a device's location has changed.

The standard location service provides more accurate location information and invokes the GPS if the requested accuracy requires it. This greater accuracy comes at a cost in terms of a longer time to get a location and an increased drain of the battery. If you are going to use the standard location service, you should use it with precision and only when necessary.

The significant location change service provides some flexibility and is recommended for most applications that don't need highly accurate location information. For instance, if you need to know the town or city where someone is located, the significant location change service is perfectly acceptable. You get a fast response without using a lot of battery power because it uses the cellular signal to determine the device's location. Another benefit of the significant location change service is it runs in the background on the device. Your app does not have to be running in the foreground to receive location updates from this service, unlike the standard location service.

Recipe 5-1: Getting Basic Location Information

This recipe shows you how to use the standard location service to give you some basic information about the device's current location, course, and speed.

Setting Up the Application

Start by creating a new single view application and add the Core Location framework to the project. (See Chapter 1 for instructions about how to create the project and link the framework library).

You will use a very simple user interface with a title label, a text view to display location information, and a switch control to let the user turn location updates on and off. Bring up the storyboard by selecting the Main.storyboard file in the project navigator. Add the label and the switch to your single view by dragging them from the object library. Make the text view big enough to contain four rows. Likewise, make sure the initial state of the switch is set to "Off."

Your user interface should now resemble the one in Figure 5-1.

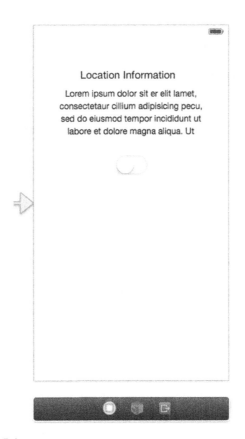

Figure 5-1. User interface for Recipe 5-1

Now create outlet properties for the text view and the switch. Name them "locationInformationView" and "locationUpdatesSwitch." You also need to know when the user taps on the switch control, so go ahead and create an action for the switch. Name it "toggleLocationUpdates" and set the event type to "Value Changed." (If you are uncertain of outlets and actions, you can find instructions about how to create them in Chapter 1).

All interaction with the Core Location framework goes through a location manager. With it you can start and stop the location updates. For convenience, set the view controller to be the location manager's delegate; it is the "hub" of action for dealing with all location-based services. Therefore, add CLLocationManagerDelegate as a supported protocol of the view controller's class, as well as the import statement shown in Listing 5-1.

Listing 5-1. Declaring use of the CLLocationManagerDelegate and importing the CoreLocation framework

```
// ...
#import <CoreLocation/CoreLocation.h>

@interface ViewController : UIViewController <CLLocationManagerDelegate>

// ...

@end
```

Now you need an instance variable for your location manager. Add it to the view controller as well, and name it "_locationManager" (See Listing 5-2).

Listing 5-2. Setting an instance variable for the location manager

```
// ...

@interface ViewController : UIViewController<CLLocationManagerDelegate>
{
    CLLocationManager *_locationManager;
}

// ...

@end
```

Your view controller's header file should now look something like Listing 5-3.

Listing 5-3. The ViewController.h file with Listings 5-1 and 5-2 added

```
//
//  ViewController.h
//  Recipe 5-1 Getting Basic Location Info
//

#import <UIKit/UIKit.h>
#import <CoreLocation/CoreLocation.h>

@interface ViewController : UIViewController<CLLocationManagerDelegate>
{
    CLLocationManager *_locationManager;
}

@property (weak, nonatomic) IBOutlet UITextView *locationInformationView;
@property (weak, nonatomic) IBOutlet UISwitch *locationUpdatesSwitch;

- (IBAction)toggleLocationUpdates:(id)sender;

@end
```

Finally, because you are planning to use the location services, you should provide a purpose description. This is done in the application's Info.plist file. Add the key "NSLocationUsageDescription" with the value "We're testing standard location services" (without the quotes), as shown in Figure 5-2. When a user is prompted to allow your application access to his location, that text is displayed, telling the user what you plan to do with his device's location information. Once you type in "NSLocationUsageDescription" the key will change to "Privacy – Location Usage Description" automatically.

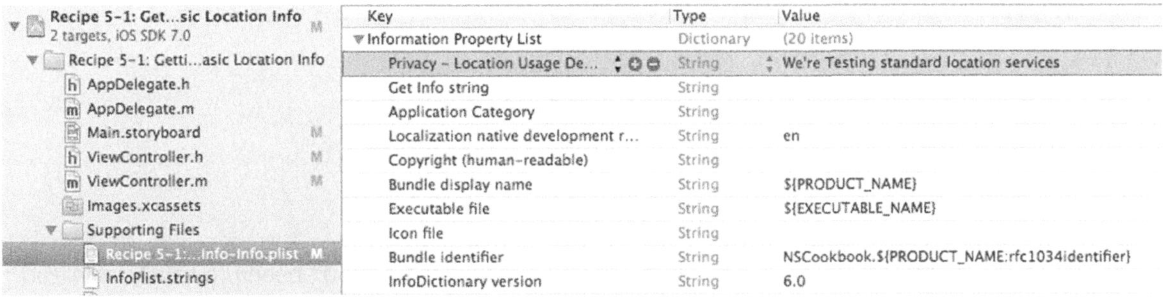

Key	Type	Value
▼ Information Property List	Dictionary	(20 items)
Privacy – Location Usage De... ⬍ ⊕ ⊖	String	⬍ We're Testing standard location services
Get Info string	String	
Application Category	String	
Localization native development r...	String	en
Copyright (human-readable)	String	
Bundle display name	String	${PRODUCT_NAME}
Executable file	String	${EXECUTABLE_NAME}
Icon file	String	
Bundle identifier	String	NSCookbook.${PRODUCT_NAME:rfc1034identifier}
InfoDictionary version	String	6.0

Figure 5-2. Setting the location usage description

Your application skeleton is ready, and now is a good time to build and run it. Nothing interesting will happen, though, when you interact with its user interface; you have yet to implement the code that starts and stops location services, as well as the one that receives the location updates. Let's get started.

Starting and Stopping Location Updates

Now that the interface has been defined, move to the view controller's implementation file (.m) and start implementing these methods and objects. The first thing you will tackle is the toggleLocationUpdates: action, which is invoked when the user touches the switch control.

You need to take a different action depending on whether the user turned the updates on or off, obviously. If the switch was turned on, you should check whether location services are enabled. If they are not, display an alert and turn the switch back to off. Add the code to the toggleLocationUpdates: method, as shown in Listing 5-4.

Listing 5-4. Adding code to toggleLocationUpdates to create a user alert

```
- (IBAction)toggleLocationUpdates:(id)sender
{
    if (self.locationUpdatesSwitch.on == YES)
    {
        if ([CLLocationManager locationServicesEnabled] == NO)
        {
            UIAlertView *locationServicesDisabledAlert =
                [[UIAlertView alloc] initWithTitle:@"Location Services Disabled"
                message:@"This feature requires location services. Enable it in the privacy settings
on your device"
                delegate:nil
                cancelButtonTitle:@"Dismiss"
                otherButtonTitles:nil];
            [locationServicesDisabledAlert show];
            self.locationUpdatesSwitch.on = NO;
            return;
        }
```

```
        // ...

    }
    else
    {
        // Switch was turned off
    }
}
```

Next, if location services *are* enabled, initialize the location manager if it hasn't been previously initialized. For the standard location service, you should always set the desiredAccuracy and distanceFilter properties of the location manager. Also, it's recommended that you set the activityType.

The desiredAccuracy property tells the Core Location framework how accurate (in meters) you want your location information to be. The accuracy, however, is not guaranteed, and the device will try to use the resources available to it to get information as close to your desired accuracy as possible. Apple recommends that you be as conservative as possible with this setting. If you don't need to know the street address of the current device, use a lower accuracy setting. Here are all of the constants available:

- kCLLocationAccuracyBestForNavigation
- kCLLocationAccuracyBest
- kCLLocationAccuracyNearestTenMeters
- kCLLocationAccuracyHundredMeters
- kCLLocationAccuracyKilometer
- kCLLocationAccuracyThreeKilometers

Note   If you are not familiar with the metric system, a meter (m) is slightly longer than a yard (1 yard = 0.9144 m), and a kilometer (km) is just over half a mile (1 mile = 1.609 km).

The distanceFilter property is how far a device has to move (again in meters) before you want to be notified (through your delegate) of its new position. The only constant provided for this property is kCLDistanceFilterNone, which reports all changes in location to your delegate.

The activityType is used by the Core Location framework to better figure out when it should autopause location updates. So if you chose the type CLActivityTypeFitness, Core Location might pause when the runner stops running for a certain amount of time. You have four activity types to choose from:

- *CLActivityTypeAutomotiveNavigation:* This type is best used for navigation in a car. Location updates will pause if no significant change in distance occurs for a while.

- *CLActivityTypeFitness:* This type is best suited for walking or running. The behavior is the same as ClActivityTypeAutomotiveNavigation, except the significant amount of distance is much smaller in the same time period.

- ▦ *CLActivityTypeOtherNavigation:* This works the same as CLActivityTypeAutomotiveNavigation, but is more tailored for train, boat, or plane travel.

- ▦ *CLActivityTypeOther:* Use this type if the other types don't fit your needs.

Once you've set the properties and the delegate in the ViewController.m file, you can start the location services by calling the startUpdatingLocation method on your CLLocationManager, a class for managing the delivery of location and heading updates. Do this by adding the code shown in Listing 5-5.

Listing 5-5. Modify the toggleLocationUpdates method to start updating the location

```
if (self.locationUpdatesSwitch.on == YES)
{
    if ([CLLocationManager locationServicesEnabled] == NO)
    {
        // ...
    }
    if (_locationManager == nil)
    {
        _locationManager = [[CLLocationManager alloc] init];
        _locationManager.desiredAccuracy = kCLLocationAccuracyBest;
        _locationManager.distanceFilter = 1; // meter
        _locationManager.activityType = CLActivityTypeOther;
        _locationManager.delegate = self;
    }

    [_locationManager startUpdatingLocation];

}
else
  // ...
```

That concludes the code used when the user turns updates on. For the "off" part, you simply want to stop the updates if they have been started, as shown in Listing 5-6.

Listing 5-6. Modifying the toggleLocationUpdates method to handle the switch in an "off" position

```
- (IBAction)toggleLocationUpdates:(id)sender
{
    if (self.locationUpdatesSwitch.on == YES)
    {
        // ...
    }
    else
    {
        // Switch was turned off
        // Stop updates if they have been started
```

```
        if (_locationManager != nil)
        {
            [_locationManager stopUpdatingLocation];
        }
    }
}
```

Receiving Location Updates

The delegate methods need to be set up next. These methods are called when a location update is received or when there is an error getting the location. Let's start with the error delegate method (in other words, `locationManager:didFailWithError:`).

The most common source of an error occurs when the user is prompted to allow location services for your app and the user declines. If this happens, you can stop the updates by turning the switch back to off. This triggers a Value Changed event and thus invokes the `toggleLocationUpdates:` method, which turns the updates off.

For any other error, log it to the console. Your code should look something like Listing 5-7.

Listing 5-7. Implementing the locationManager: didFailWithError: delegate method

```
- (void)locationManager:(CLLocationManager *)manager didFailWithError:(NSError *)error
{
    if (error.code == kCLErrorDenied)
    {
        // Turning the switch to off will trigger the
        // toggleLocationServices action,
        // which in turn will stop further updates from coming
        self.locationUpdatesSwitch.on = NO;
    }
    else
    {
        NSLog(@"%@", error);
    }
}
```

The delegate method that handles location updates is a little more involved. The method, `locationM anager:didUpdateLocations:`, delivers an array of locations that have been registered since the last update, the most recent last. For this recipe, you're only interested in the most recent event, so just extract that one, as shown in Listing 5-8.

Listing 5-8. Starting the implementation of the locationManager:didUpdateLocations: delegate method

```
- (void)locationManager:(CLLocationManager *)manager
didUpdateLocations:(NSArray *)locations
{
    CLLocation *lastLocation = [locations lastObject];
    // ...
}
```

The location is represented by a CLLocation object, which contains a lot of valuable information, including the location coordinate, accuracy information, and the timestamp of the location update.

Before your app processes a location object, you should check whether the timestamp of the location object is recent. Core Location often presents the last known location as the first call to the delegate method before it has a lock on the new location. There is often no need to process a location object that represents the device's location at some point in history when you need to know where it is now. Therefore, filter out location events that are more than 30 seconds old, as shown in Listing 5-9.

Listing 5-9. Updating locationManager:didUpdateLocations: to include logic for filtering older locations

```
- (void)locationManager:(CLLocationManager *)manager
didUpdateLocations:(NSArray *)locations
{
    CLLocation *lastLocation = [locations lastObject];
    // Make sure this is a recent location event
    NSTimeInterval eventInterval = [lastLocation.timestamp timeIntervalSinceNow];
    if(abs(eventInterval) < 30.0)
    {
        // This is a recent event
    }
}
```

The other property you need to check before you process an event is its accuracy. Again, there is no need to process an event if it is not within the accuracy bounds that you are expecting. It might be better to wait for the device to obtain a more accurate reading than to present bad information to the user. The location object contains two accuracy properties: horizontalAccuracy and verticalAccuracy.

The horizontalAccuracy property represents the radius of the circle, in meters, within which the location could be located. You can see this circle in the built-in Maps application when you are showing your location. A negative value indicates that the coordinate is invalid.

The verticalAccuracy property is how far, plus or minus in meters, the altitude of the device could be off. Again, a negative value indicates an invalid altitude reading. If the device does not have a GPS, the verticalAccuracy property will always be negative because a GPS is needed to determine the device's altitude.

Listing 5-10 is the code extended with a check that the received location's horizontal accuracy is not invalid and is within 20 meters.

Listing 5-10. Updating locationManager:didUpdateLocations: to check for poor accuracy

```
- (void)locationManager:(CLLocationManager *)manager
didUpdateLocations:(NSArray *)locations
{
    // Make sure this is a recent location event
    CLLocation *lastLocation = [locations lastObject];
    NSTimeInterval eventInterval = [lastLocation.timestamp timeIntervalSinceNow];
```

```
    if(abs(eventInterval) < 30.0)
    {
        // Make sure the event is accurate enough
        if (lastLocation.horizontalAccuracy >= 0 &&
            lastLocation.horizontalAccuracy < 20)
        {
            §self.locationInformationView.text = lastLocation.description;
        }
    }
}
```

The `description` property of a location object returns all the information in one dense string. It is a very easy method for seeing what location information is being returned by the device. We don't recommend showing this string to the end user directly as it contains a great deal of information, but it could be useful for debugging and verifying that location information is being updated and is correct or accurate. For this project, you have set your `locationInfomationView` text to the `lastLocation.description` value, resulting in the preceding completed delegate method.

Your application is now finished and ready for testing.

Testing Location Updates

The iOS simulator contains several convenient ways to test location events. As Figure 5-3 shows, there are functions for setting a custom location or simulating different scenarios, such as a city run or a freeway drive.

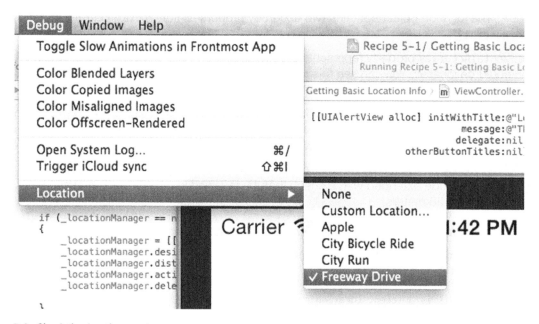

Figure 5-3. Simulating location events

Launch the app on the iOS simulator. When you touch the switch and turn it to "On," you will be prompted to allow this application access to your device's location. Notice in Figure 5-4 that the string you set in the application's property list is displayed.

Figure 5-4. *Your application requesting location permissions*

Click "OK." Notice that the location information label is not updating even though the switch is on. This is because you haven't started any location simulations yet. In the iOS simulator, go to the menu Debug ➤ Location ➤ Freeway Drive, and the label should start to update with information about the prerecorded drive that Apple has provided. Figure 5-5 shows a sample of information delivered by the simulated drive.

Figure 5-5. *Displaying simulated location information*

That concludes Recipe 5-1. The next recipe deals with a way to get location changes that require a lot less battery power.

Recipe 5-2: Significant Location Changes

Being a location-aware app doesn't always mean that it needs the high-accuracy location update that the standard location service provides. Many apps do just fine by knowing which town, city, or even country the device is currently in. For those apps, the significant location change service is the preferred way to retrieve locations; it is faster, requires significantly less battery power, and can run in the background.

This recipe shows you how to set up an application to use the significant location change service to get locations.

Setting Up the Application

Programming the significant location changes services is a lot like programming the standard location services, and the setup is virtually identical. You can either duplicate the project from Recipe 5-1 or create a new single view application and do the following as preparation:

1. Link the application to the Core Location framework.

2. Set a usage description (such as "Testing the significant location change service") for the NSLocationUsageDescription Info.plist key ("Privacy–Location Usage Description" in the property list).

3. Add a label, text view, and a switch control to the main view, which should look something like Figure 5-1 in Recipe 5-1. The text view should contain about five lines and the switch should be initially set to "Off."

4. Create outlets for the text view and the switch and name them "locationInformationView" and "locationUpdatesSwitch," respectively.

5. Create an action for the switch, name it "toggleLocationUpdates," and set the event type to "Value Change."

6. Import the Core Location framework API by adding the following declaration in your view controller's header file: #import <CoreLocation/CoreLocation.h>.

7. Make the view controller a location manager delegate by adding the CLLocationManagerDelegate protocol to the ViewController class.

8. Finally, add a CLLocationManager * instance variable to the view controller and name it "_locationManager."

Refer to Recipe 5-1 for the details regarding the preceding steps. Your view controller's header class should now look like Listing 5-11.

Listing 5-11. The starting setup for the view controller header file

```
//
//  ViewController.h
//  Recipe 5-2: Significant Location Changes
//

#import <UIKit/UIKit.h>
#import <CoreLocation/CoreLocation.h>

@interface ViewController : UIViewController<CLLocationManagerDelegate>
{
    CLLocationManager *_locationManager;
}

@property (strong, nonatomic) IBOutlet UITextView *locationInformationView;
@property (strong, nonatomic) IBOutlet UISwitch *locationUpdatesSwitch;

- (IBAction)toggleLocationUpdates:(id)sender;

@end
```

Build and run the app to make sure everything is ready for the next step.

Enabling Background Updates

For this recipe you will enable location updates to occur even when your app is residing in background mode. To do this you need to add another key to the Info.plist file, so type in the "UIBackgroundModes" key (or "Required background modes," as Xcode translates it to in the user interface). Make sure you set the type to "array" for this item. Next add a sub item with the value "App registers for location updates" with a "string" type, as in Figure 5-6.

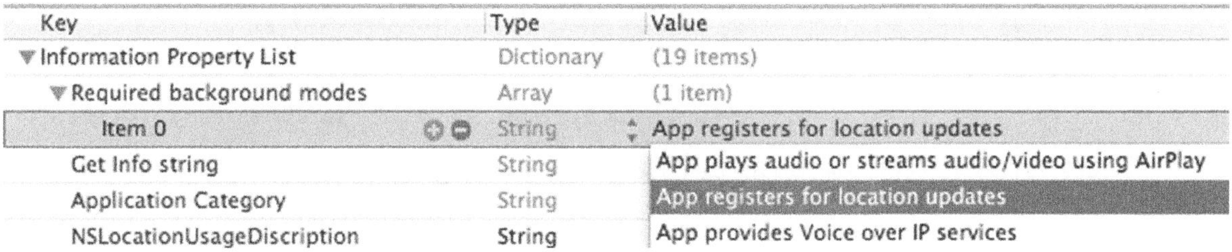

Key	Type	Value
▼ Information Property List	Dictionary	(19 items)
▼ Required background modes	Array	(1 item)
Item 0	String	App registers for location updates
Get Info string	String	App plays audio or streams audio/video using AirPlay
Application Category	String	App registers for location updates
NSLocationUsageDiscription	String	App provides Voice over IP services

Figure 5-6. Specifying location changes as a required background mode

> **Note**   For the most part, Apple does not want you to use background location tracking unless it is absolutely essential for the functionality of the application. They absolutely do not want you to start location services in the background, but they make an exception when it comes to significant location changes.

Now switch focus to the implementation file (.m) of the view controller. Start with the toggleLocationUpdates: method. It gets invoked each time the user changes the value of the switch control.

You'll recognize a lot of the code because it's more or less the same as in Recipe 5-1. The only difference is that you use start and stopMonitoringSignificantLocationChanges instead of start and stopUpdatingLocation. Also, the significant location change service doesn't care about the desiredAccuracy, distanceFilter, and activityType properties, so you can leave them out.

Listing 5-12 shows the new toggleLocationUpdates: method, with differences marked in bold. Go ahead and implement it in your project.

Listing 5-12. Implementing the toggleLocationUpdates method

```
- (IBAction)toggleLocationUpdates:(id)sender
{
    if (self.locationUpdatesSwitch.on == YES)
    {
        if ([CLLocationManager locationServicesEnabled] == NO)
        {
            UIAlertView *locationServicesDisabledAlert = [[UIAlertView alloc]
                initWithTitle:@"Location Services Disabled"
                message:@"This feature requires location services. Enable it in the privacy settings
on your device"
                delegate:nil
                cancelButtonTitle:@"Dismiss"
                otherButtonTitles:nil];
            [locationServicesDisabledAlert show];
            self.locationUpdatesSwitch.on = NO;
            return;
        }
        if (_locationManager == nil)
        {
            _locationManager = [[CLLocationManager alloc] init];
            // Significant location change service does not use desiredAccuracy,
            // distanceFilter or activityType properties so no need to set them
            _locationManager.delegate = self;

        }
        [_locationManager startMonitoringSignificantLocationChanges];
    }
    else
    {
        // Switch was turned off
        // Stop updates if they have been started
        if (_locationManager != nil)
        {
            [_locationManager stopMonitoringSignificantLocationChanges];
        }
    }
}
```

Now you have to set up the delegate methods. They are identical to what you did in the preceding recipe. Listing 5-13 shows the implementation for the `locationManager:didFailWithError` method.

Listing 5-13. Implementing the locationManager:didFailWithError: delegate method

```
- (void)locationManager:(CLLocationManager *)manager didFailWithError:(NSError *)error
{
    if (error.code == kCLErrorDenied)
    {
        // Turning the switch to off will trigger the toggleLocationServices action,
        // which in turn will stop further updates from coming
        self.locationUpdatesSwitch.on = NO;
    }
    else
    {
        NSLog(@"%@", error);
    }
}
```

Listing 5-14 shows the implementation for the `locationManager:didUpdateLocations:` method.

Listing 5-14. Implementing the locationManager:didUpdateLocations: delegate method

```
- (void)locationManager:(CLLocationManager *)manager didUpdateLocations:(NSArray *)locations
{
    // Make sure this is a recent location event
    CLLocation *lastLocation = [locations lastObject];
    NSTimeInterval eventInterval = [lastLocation.timestamp timeIntervalSinceNow];
    if(abs(eventInterval) < 30.0)
    {
        // Make sure the event is accurate enough
        if (lastLocation.horizontalAccuracy >= 0 &&
            lastLocation.horizontalAccuracy < 20)
        {
            self.locationInformationView.text = lastLocation.description;
        }
    }
}
```

The app is nearly finished, so you can build and test it now. Again, you can simulate the location by going to the simulator menu Debug • Location • Freeway Drive. The application text should update when a significant location change has occurred. Next, you'll make the app slightly more interesting by presenting notifications to the user when her location changes significantly.

Adding Local Notifications

Now you are going to make an addition to the `locationManager:didUpdateLocations:` method. If the application is currently in the background state, you'll generate a local notification so the user can see when a location is updated while the app is not running. Listing 5-15 contains these changes.

Listing 5-15. Updating the locationManager:didUpdateLocations: method to include notifications

```
- (void)locationManager:(CLLocationManager *)manager
didUpdateLocations:(NSArray *)locations
{
    // Make sure this is a recent location event
    CLLocation *lastLocation = [locations lastObject];
    NSTimeInterval eventInterval = [lastLocation.timestamp timeIntervalSinceNow];
    if(abs(eventInterval) < 30.0)
    {
        // Make sure the event is accurate enough
        if (lastLocation.horizontalAccuracy >= 0 &&
            lastLocation.horizontalAccuracy < 20)
        {
            self.locationInformationLabel.text = lastLocation.description;

            UILocalNotification *notification = [[UILocalNotification alloc] init];
            notification.alertBody =
              [NSString stringWithFormat:@"New Location: %.3f, %.3f",
                lastLocation.coordinate.latitude, lastLocation.coordinate.longitude];
            notification.alertAction = @"Ok";
            notification.soundName = UILocalNotificationDefaultSoundName;
            //Increment the applicationIconBadgeNumber
            notification.applicationIconBadgeNumber =
              [[UIApplication sharedApplication] applicationIconBadgeNumber] + 1;
            [[UIApplication sharedApplication]
              presentLocalNotificationNow: notification];
        }
    }
}
```

With this new app, you can receive local notifications for each significant location change, even while the application is not in the foreground. These changes are reflected in a notification badge on the app's icon, as well as a normal device notification. Keep in mind that it might take a little while in your simulator for a significant change to happen, as shown in Figure 5-7.

Figure 5-7. A significant change occurrence in the background

Recipe 5-3: Tracking Magnetic Bearing

Modern iPhones and iPads contain magnetometers, hardware that can be used to determine the direction in which the device is being held. The measurement is based on the device's position in relation to the magnetic north pole of the earth.

The magnetic poles are not the same as the geographic poles of the earth. Magnetic north is located in Northern Canada and moves slowly by approximately 55–60 km per year toward the west as the earth's core changes.

Despite being somewhat inaccurate, the magnetic bearing is good enough for most applications, and it's much less expensive in terms of battery power. This recipe shows you how to implement tracking of the magnetic bearing of the device.

About Heading Tracking

Heading tracking gives us the ability to track a user's direction relative to north in real time. Implementing heading tracking is very similar to implementing any of the location tracking services discussed so far: You will include the Core Location framework in your project, create a location manager object, and define its delegate methods.

It is assumed that the device heading is measured while in portrait mode with the top pointing away from the user. You can change this by setting the headingOrientation property on the CLLocationManager object.

The options for this property are as follows:

- CLDeviceOrientationPortrait (default)
- CLDeviceOrientationPortraitUpsideDown
- CLDeviceOrientationLandscapeLeft
- CLDeviceOrientationLandscapeRight

Setting Up the Application

Let's start, as usual, by creating a new single view application project. You will build an application very similar to the preceding two recipes, so either copy one of those projects or create a new one based on the following steps. In case you've decided to make a copy of a previous project, we've marked the differences in bold.

1. Link the application to the Core Location framework.

2. Add a text view and a switch control to the main view, which should look something like Figure 5-2 in Recipe 5-1. The switch should initially be set to "Off."

3. Create outlets for the label and the switch, and name them "**headingInformationView**" and "**headingUpdatesSwitch**," respectively.

4. Create an action for the switch, name it "**toggleHeadingUpdates**," and set the event type to "Value Change."

5. Import the Core Location framework API by adding the following declaration in your view controller's header file: #import <CoreLocation/CoreLocation.h>.

6. Make the view controller a location manager delegate by adding the CLLocationManagerDelegate protocol to the ViewController class.

7. Finally, add a CLLocationManager * instance variable to the view controller and name it "_locationManager."

Refer to Recipe 5-1 for the details regarding the preceding steps. Your view controller's header class should now look something like Listing 5-16.

Listing 5-16. The completed view controller header

```
//
// ViewController.h
// Recipe 5-3 Determining Magnetic Bearing
//

#import <UIKit/UIKit.h>
#import <CoreLocation/CoreLocation.h>
```

```
@interface ViewController : UIViewController<CLLocationManagerDelegate>
{
    CLLocationManager *_locationManager;
}

@property (strong, nonatomic) IBOutlet UITextView *headingInformationView;
@property (strong, nonatomic) IBOutlet UISwitch *headingUpdatesSwitch;

- (IBAction)toggleHeadingUpdates:(id)sender;

@end
```

> **Note**   If you've copied the project, you need to change the names of the outlets and the action. Be sure to use the Rename Refactoring tool in Xcode to do the renaming for you. This way you don't have to reconnect them in Interface Builder.
>
> To bring up the Rename tool, select the outlet (or action) property name that you want to rename. Ctrl-click to bring up the context menu and select Refactor ➤ Rename, as shown in Figure 5-8.

Figure 5-8. Navigation to Refactor ➤ Rename

Starting and Stopping Heading Updates

Switch to the view controller's implementation file (ViewController.m) and scroll to the bottom to start defining the toggleHeadingUpdates method.

Not all iOS devices can deliver heading information. Therefore, when the user has turned the switch to "on," check whether a heading is available. If it's not, turn the switch back to "off" and inform the user by means of the label, as shown in Listing 5-17.

Listing 5-17. Checking for availability of location services

```
- (IBAction)toggleHeadingUpdates:(id)sender
{
    if (self.headingUpdatesSwitch.on == YES)
    {
        // Heading data is not available on all devices
        if ([CLLocationManager headingAvailable] == NO)
        {
            self.headingInformationView.text = @"Heading services unavailable";
            self.headingUpdatesSwitch.on = NO;
            return;
        }

        // ...
```

Now initialize the location manager, as shown in Listing 5-18, if it hasn't already been instantiated. When creating an instance of CLLocationManager that is going to track heading changes, you should specify the headingFilter property. This property specifies how far (in degrees) your heading has to change before your delegate method is called.

Listing 5-18. Initializing the location manager with a tracking filter of 5 degrees

```
if (_locationManager == nil)
{
    _locationManager = [[CLLocationManager alloc] init];
    _locationManager.headingFilter = 5; // degrees
    _locationManager.delegate = self;
}
```

Finally, start and stop heading updates with the startUpdatingHeading and stopUpdatingHeading methods. The complete toggleHeadingUpdates should look like Listing 5-19.

Listing 5-19. The completed toggleheadingUpdates: method

```
- (IBAction)toggleHeadingUpdates:(id)sender
{
    if (self.headingUpdatesSwitch.on == YES)
    {
        // Heading data is not available on all devices
        if ([CLLocationManager headingAvailable] == NO)
        {
            self.headingInformationLabel.text = @"Heading services unavailable";
            self.headingUpdatesSwitch.on = NO;
            return;
        }
        if (_locationManager == nil)
        {
            _locationManager = [[CLLocationManager alloc] init];
            _locationManager.headingFilter = 5; // degrees
            _locationManager.delegate = self;
        }
```

```
    [_locationManager startUpdatingHeading];
    self.headingInformationView.text = @"Starting heading tracking...";
}
else
{
    // Switch was turned off
    self.headingInformationView.text = @"Stopped heading tracking";
    // Stop updates if they have been started
    if (_locationManager != nil)
    {
        [_locationManager stopUpdatingHeading];
    }
}
}
}
```

Implementing Delegate Methods

The delegate methods need to be defined next. With heading tracking services, three delegate methods are required:

- locationManager:didFailWithError:

- locationManager:didUpdateHeading:

- locationManagerShouldDisplayHeadingCalibration:

The first method, didFailWithError, is the same delegate method you have implemented with the location tracking services discussed previously. However, the difference is that the user, unlike location services, cannot deny heading tracking. So if an error occurs, you simply log the error to the console and hope it's temporary. This is adequate for your testing purposes, but in a real-use scenario you probably should find out what kind of errors might occur and take appropriate action. You might also want to read the recipe on default error handling in Chapter 1 for ideas on how you can generally approach errors. This implementation is given in Listing 5-20.

Listing 5-20. Complete implementation of the locationManager:didFailWithError: message

```
-(void)locationManager:(CLLocationManager *)manager didFailWithError:(NSError *)error
{
    NSLog(@"Error while tracking heading: %@", error);
}
```

The next method, didUpdateHeading, gets invoked when the change in the heading of the device exceeds your headingFilter property. As with location updates, first check to see whether the update is a recent reading. Also, make sure that the reading is valid by checking the headingAccuracy property, which will be negative if the heading is invalid. If the reading is both recent and valid, update the label with the value from the magneticHeading property, rounding off to one decimal place. Listing 5-21 shows the complete implementation.

Listing 5-21. Complete implementation of the locationManager:didUpdateHeading: method

```
-(void)locationManager:(CLLocationManager *)manager
didUpdateHeading:(CLHeading *)newHeading
{
    NSTimeInterval headingInterval = [newHeading.timestamp timeIntervalSinceNow];
    // Check if reading is recent
    if(abs(headingInterval) < 30)
    {
        // Check if reading is valid
        if(newHeading.headingAccuracy < 0)
            return;
        self.headingInformationView.text =
          [NSString stringWithFormat:@"%.1f°", newHeading.magneticHeading];
    }
}
```

> **Tip**   You can use Alt+Shift+8 to insert the degree (°) symbol.

The final delegate method you need to implement is locationManagerShouldDisplayHeadingCalibration. This method determines whether the heading calibration screen should be presented. This is the scene that prompts a user to move her device in a figure-eight pattern to calibrate the magnetometer. This is a rather helpful feature, so simply return YES, as shown in Listing 5-22.

Listing 5-22. Implementation for showing the calibration screen

```
-(BOOL)locationManagerShouldDisplayHeadingCalibration:(CLLocationManager *)manager
{
    return YES;
}
```

The application is now finished. Unfortunately, the simulator doesn't support heading simulation, so you'll need to test it on an actual device. When run, it'll look something like Figure 5-9. It displays the heading relative to the magnetic north pole. A value close to 0 or 360 means north, 90 means east, 180 south, and 240 west.

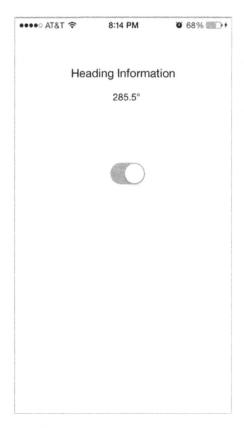

Figure 5-9. *The application displaying magnetic bearing*

That concludes Recipe 5-3. In the next recipe you'll extend this project to include true bearing tracking alongside the magnetic bearing.

> **Note**   Like the other recipes in this chapter that make use of the magnetometer, this functionality works only on a physical device and not in the simulator.

Recipe 5-4: Tracking True Bearing

You have figured out how to get the magnetic north heading, but what about true north? The difference between magnetic north and true north is called *declination*. Declination can vary greatly depending on where you are on the planet, but if you know where you are you can calculate it. The Core Location framework does this for you and provides it in the trueHeading property of a CLHeading object. All you need to do is also call the startUpdatingLocation method on your location manager to get the true north heading.

> **Caution**   In this recipe you extend the project in Recipe 5-3 to include true heading tracking along with the magnetic bearing. Thus, it might be a good idea to make a backup of that project before you start.

Adding True Bearing

Because you are using the location service again, start by adding the `NSLocationUsageDescription` key with a usage description to the info.plist, such as "Testing true bearing." This is similar to what we did in Figure 5-2 except the description should now be "Testing true bearing."

Next, add a second text view and title for displaying the true heading in the main view. Your user interface should now look something like Figure 5-10.

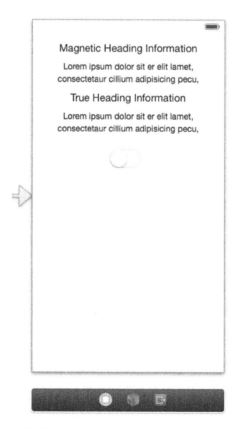

Figure 5-10. New user interface with an added label

Create an outlet named `trueHeadingInformationView` for the new text view. Your view controller's interface file (.h) should now look like Listing 5-23.

Listing 5-23. The complete view controller header file

```
//
// ViewController.h
// Recipe 5-4: Tracking True Bearing
//

#import <UIKit/UIKit.h>
#import <CoreLocation/CoreLocation.h>

@interface ViewController : UIViewController<CLLocationManagerDelegate>
{
    CLLocationManager *_locationManager;
}

@property (strong, nonatomic) IBOutlet UITextView *headingInformationView;
@property (strong, nonatomic) IBOutlet UITextView *trueHeadingInformationView;
@property (strong, nonatomic) IBOutlet UISwitch *headingUpdatesSwitch;

- (IBAction)toggleHeadingUpdates:(id)sender;

@end
```

Only a few changes need to be made to your existing code. Let's start with the toggleHeadingUpdates: method.

Because you will be using location services again, reintroduce the control code from Recipe 5-1 that makes sure location services are enabled. This is shown in Listing 5-24.

Listing 5-24. Adding location services control code from Listing 5-4

```
if (self.headingUpdatesSwitch.on == YES)
{
    // ...

    if ([CLLocationManager locationServicesEnabled] == NO)
    {
        UIAlertView *locationServicesDisabledAlert = [[UIAlertView alloc]
            initWithTitle:@"Location Services Disabled"
            message:@"This feature requires location services. Enable it in the privacy settings on
your device"
            delegate:nil
            cancelButtonTitle:@"Dismiss"
            otherButtonTitles:nil];

        [locationServicesDisabledAlert show];
        self.headingUpdatesSwitch.on = NO;
        return;
    }

    // ...
```

Then, to get true heading readings you need to start the location services in addition to starting heading updates. Listing 5-25 shows the complete toggleHeadingUpdates: method with the changes in bold.

Listing 5-25. The complete toggleHeadingUpdates: method

```
- (IBAction)toggleHeadingUpdates:(id)sender
{
    if (self.headingUpdatesSwitch.on == YES)
    {
        // Heading data is not available on all devices
        if ([CLLocationManager headingAvailable] == NO)
        {
            self.headingInformationView.text = @"Heading services unavailable";
            self.headingUpdatesSwitch.on = NO;
            return;
        }
        if ([CLLocationManager locationServicesEnabled] == NO)
        {
            UIAlertView *locationServicesDisabledAlert =
                [[UIAlertView alloc] initWithTitle:@"Location Services Disabled"
                message:@"This feature requires location services. Enable it in the privacy settings
on your device"
                delegate:nil
                cancelButtonTitle:@"Dismiss"
                otherButtonTitles:nil];

            [locationServicesDisabledAlert show];
            self.headingUpdatesSwitch.on = NO;
            return;
        }

        if (_locationManager == nil)
        {
            _locationManager = [[CLLocationManager alloc] init];
            _locationManager.headingFilter = 5; // degrees
            _locationManager.delegate = self;
}

        [_locationManager startUpdatingHeading];
        // Start location service in order to get true heading
        [_locationManager startUpdatingLocation];
        self.headingInformationView.text = @"Starting heading tracking...";
    }
    else
    {
        // Switch was turned off
        self.headingInformationView.text = @"Stopped heading tracking";
        // Stop updates if they have been started
        if (_locationManager != nil)
        {
            [_locationManager stopUpdatingHeading];
            [_locationManager stopUpdatingLocation];
        }
    }
}
```

Also, insert the error handling code to the locationManager:didFailWithError: delegate method, as shown in Listing 5-26.

Listing 5-26. Implementing the error handling code in the locationManager:didFailWithError: method

```
- (void)locationManager:(CLLocationManager *)manager didFailWithError:(NSError *)error
{
    if (error.code == kCLErrorDenied)
    {
        // Turning the switch to off will indirectly stop
        // further updates from coming
        self.headingUpdatesSwitch.on = NO;
    }
    else
    {
        NSLog(@"%@", error);
    }
}
```

Now, in your locationManager:didUpdateHeading: method, add a new statement to check the trueHeading value, as shown in Listing 5-27. A negative trueHeading value indicates that it's invalid, so you want to use the trueHeading property only if it is greater than or equal to 0.

Listing 5-27. Adding test for invalid reading in locationManager:didUpdateHeading: method

```
-(void)locationManager:(CLLocationManager *)manager
didUpdateHeading:(CLHeading *)newHeading
{
    NSTimeInterval headingInterval = [newHeading.timestamp timeIntervalSinceNow];
    if(abs(headingInterval)<30)
    {
        if (newHeading.headingAccuracy < 0)
            return;
        self.headingInformationView.text =
            [NSString stringWithFormat:@"Magnetic Heading: %.1f°",
                newHeading.magneticHeading];

        if(newHeading.trueHeading >= 0)
            self.trueHeadingInformationView.text =
                [NSString stringWithFormat:@"True Heading: %.1f°",
                    newHeading.trueHeading];
    }
}
```

Upon testing this application, you can get a simple readout of your device's true and magnetic headings. As you can see in Figure 5-11, the two values differ somewhat, more or less depending on your current location.

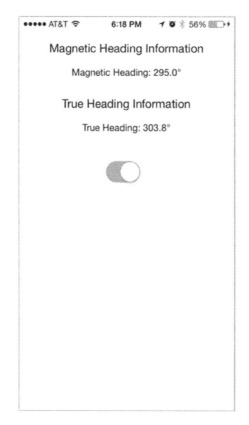

Figure 5-11. *Displaying both magnetic and true heading values*

Recipe 5-5: Region Monitoring

Core Location provides a method for monitoring when a device enters or exits a circular region. This can be a very useful feature for an application; for example, it can trigger an alert when a device enters the vicinity of a certain location, like triggering an alert to pick up milk when you get near the grocery store. You could also use it to send a notification to your family when you leave work to let them know that you are on your way home. Many possibilities are available if you let your imagination do a little wandering.

A Thing or Two About Regions

Regions are defined by a center coordinate and a radius measured in meters. The monitoring method triggers an event only when you cross a region boundary. It will not trigger an event if the device exists in the region when the monitoring starts. Events are triggered only when a device enters or exits a region.

Once you create a CLLocationManager object, you can register multiple regions for monitoring using the startMonitoringForRegion: method. The regions that you register for monitoring are persistent across multiple launches of your application. If your application is not running when a boundary event occurs, your application is automatically relaunched in the background so that it can process the event. All the regions you set up previously are available in the `monitoredRegions` property of the `CLLocationManager` object.

Regions are shared system wide, and only a limited number of regions can be monitored at a given time. You should always limit the number of defined regions that you are currently monitoring so as not to consume the system resources. You should remove regions for monitoring that are not near the device's current location. For instance, there is no need to monitor for regions in Maryland if the device is on the West Coast. The error `kCLErrorRegionMonitoringFailure` will be presented to the `locationManager:monitoringDidFailForRegion:withError:` delegate method if space is unavailable when you try to register a new region for monitoring.

Welcome to Denver!

In this project, you will create a region for the city of Denver, Colorado, and welcome visitors to the city when they enter it. You will start by creating a new single view application.

You will follow the same pattern and build a user interface as in the previous recipes. Follow these steps to set up the application:

1. Link the application to the Core Location framework.

2. Set a usage description (such as "`Testing region monitoring`") for the `NSLocationUsageDescription` key in the application's property list.

3. Add a label, a text view, and a switch control to the main view, which should look something like Figure 5-2 in Recipe 5-1. The switch should be initially set to "Off."

4. Create outlets for the text view and the switch. Name the text view and switch "`regionInformationView`" and "`regionMonitoringSwitch`," respectively.

5. Create an action for the switch; name it "`toggleRegionMonitoring`" and make sure the event type is set to "`Value Change`."

6. Import the core location framework API by adding the following declaration in your view controller's header file: `#import <CoreLocation/CoreLocation.h>`.

7. Make the view controller a location manager delegate by adding the `CLLocationManagerDelegate` protocol to the ViewController class.

8. Finally, add a `CLLocationManager *` instance variable to the view controller and name it "`_locationManager`."

Your view controller's header file should now look like Listing 5-28.

Listing 5-28. The completed view controller header file

```
//
//  ViewController.h
//  Recipe 5-5: Region Monitoring
//

#import <UIKit/UIKit.h>
#import <CoreLocation/CoreLocation.h>

@interface ViewController : UIViewController<CLLocationManagerDelegate>
{
    CLLocationManager *_locationManager;
}

@property (strong, nonatomic) IBOutlet UITextView *regionInformationView;
@property (strong, nonatomic) IBOutlet UISwitch *regionMonitoringSwitch;

- (IBAction)toggleRegionMonitoring:(id)sender;

@end
```

Switching to the implementation file (.m), you can implement your region tracking methods. Let's start with the toggleRegionMonitoring: method, as shown in Listing 5-29. If the switch is turned on, you should check whether region monitoring is available and enabled by the user before you start the monitoring. Note that you check whether monitoring is enabled by using the authorizationStatus class method, which simply returns a Boolean value if the status is authorized or not determined. If the status is kCLAuthorizationStatusNotDetermined, the user will be prompted by the operating system and asked for permission to use the location services.

Listing 5-29. Checking whether or not location monitoring is authorized

```
- (IBAction)toggleRegionMonitoring:(id)sender
{
    if (self.regionMonitoringSwitch.on == YES)
    {
        CLAuthorizationStatus status = [CLLocationManager authorizationStatus];

        if (status == kCLAuthorizationStatusAuthorized ||
            status == kCLAuthorizationStatusNotDetermined)
        {
            // Start monitoring here
        }
        else
        {
            self.regionInformationView.text = @"Region monitoring disabled";
            self.regionMonitoringSwitch.on = NO;
        }
    }
}
```

In the same method, within the "if" statement that checks the authorization status, you will need to instantiate your location manager instance variable if it is not already created. You'll also need to set desiredAccuracy and delegate, as shown in Listing 5-30.

Listing 5-30. Initializing a locationManager instance and setting a delegate and desiredAccuracy

```
if (status == kCLAuthorizationStatusAuthorized ||
    status == kCLAuthorizationStatusNotDetermined)
{
    if(_locationManager == nil)
    {
        _locationManager = [[CLLocationManager alloc] init];
        _locationManager.desiredAccuracy = kCLLocationAccuracyHundredMeters;
        _locationManager.delegate = self;
    }

    // ...
```

You need to define the center coordinate of the region you want to monitor as well as the radius of the region. Be careful when specifying the radius because if it is too large, the monitoring will fail. You can check to make sure your radius is within the radius bounds by comparing it to the maximumRegionMonitoringDistance property of the CLLocationManager object.

Once you have the center coordinate and radius, create the CLCircularRegion object right after the "if" statement, if(_locationManager ==), and provide it with an identifier for future reference, as shown in Listing 5-31.

Listing 5-31. Creating a CLCircularRegion using a coordinate and a region radius

```
if (status == kCLAuthorizationStatusAuthorized ||
    status == kCLAuthorizationStatusNotDetermined)
{
    if(_locationManager == nil)
    {
        _locationManager = [[CLLocationManager alloc] init];
        _locationManager.desiredAccuracy = kCLLocationAccuracyHundredMeters;
        _locationManager.delegate = self;
    }

    CLLocationCoordinate2D denverCoordinate =
    CLLocationCoordinate2DMake(39.7392, -104.9847);
    int regionRadius = 3000; // meters
    if (regionRadius > _locationManager.maximumRegionMonitoringDistance)
    {
        regionRadius = _locationManager.maximumRegionMonitoringDistance;
    }
        CLCircularRegion *denverRegion = [[CLCircularRegion alloc] initWithCenter:denverCoordinate

radius:regionRadius

identifier:@"denverRegion"];
// ...
```

Once the region has been created, you can start monitoring for boundary events of that region by calling the startMonitoringForRegion: method of your location manager immediately after the last code segment, as shown in Listing 5-32.

Listing 5-32. Line of code added to toggleRegionMonitoring to start monitoring

```
[_locationManager startMonitoringForRegion: denverRegion];
```

One last task you should do is turn off region monitoring if the user slides the switch to the "Off" position. To do this, access the monitoredRegions property of your location manager and turn off region monitoring for all the currently monitored regions, as shown in Listing 5-33. You could also choose to selectively turn off specific regions by utilizing the identifier property of the CLCircularRegion.

Listing 5-33. Code added to toggleRegionMonitoring to turn off monitored regions

```
if (self.regionMonitoringSwitch.on == YES)
{
    // ...
}
else
{
    if (_locationManager!=nil)
    {
        for (CLCircularRegion *monitoredRegion in [_locationManager monitoredRegions])
        {
            [_locationManager stopMonitoringForRegion:monitoredRegion];
            self.regionInformationView.Text =
                [NSString stringWithFormat:@"Turned off region monitoring for: %@",
                    monitoredRegion.identifier];
        }
    }
}
```

The delegate methods need to be defined as well. There are two delegate methods for handling boundary events and one for handling errors:

- locationManager:didEnterRegion:
- locationManager:didExitRegion:
- locationManager:monitoringDidFailForRegion:withError:

There are two main error codes that are related to region monitoring. One is kCLErrorRegionMonitoringDenied, which is used when the user of the device has specifically denied access to region monitoring. The other is kCLErrorRegionMonitoringFailure, which is used when monitoring for a specific region has failed, usually because the system has no more region resources available to the application. Add the code in Listing 5-34 to the end of the ViewController.m file.

Listing 5-34. Implementing the locationManager:monitoringDidFailForRegion:withError delegate method

```
-(void)locationManager:(CLLocationManager *)manager
monitoringDidFailForRegion:(CLRegion *)region withError:(NSError *)error
{
    switch (error.code)
    {
        case kCLErrorRegionMonitoringDenied:
        {
            self.regionInformationView.text =
                @"Region monitoring is denied on this device";
            break;
        }
        case kCLErrorRegionMonitoringFailure:
        {
            self.regionInformationView.text =
                [NSString stringWithFormat:@"Region monitoring failed for region: %@",
                    region.identifier];
            break;
        }
        default:
        {
            self.regionInformationView.text =
                [NSString stringWithFormat:@"An unhandled error occured: %@",
                    error.description];
            break;
        }
    }
}
```

locationManager:didEnterRegion: and locationManager:didExitRegion: can perform any function you want. Because the application could be in the background when the boundary event occurs, you will use local notifications in addition to updating the label to let the user know the event occurred, as shown in Listing 5-35.

Listing 5-35. Adding the delegate implementations to detect entering and exiting a region

```
-(void)locationManager:(CLLocationManager *)manager didEnterRegion:(CLRegion *)region
{
    self.regionInformationView.text = @"Welcome to Denver!";

    UILocalNotification *entranceNotification = [[UILocalNotification alloc] init];
    entranceNotification.alertBody = @"Welcome to Denver!";
    entranceNotification.alertAction = @"Ok";
    entranceNotification.soundName = UILocalNotificationDefaultSoundName;
    [[UIApplication sharedApplication]
        presentLocalNotificationNow: entranceNotification];
}
```

```
-(void)locationManager:(CLLocationManager *)manager didExitRegion:(CLRegion *)region
{
    self.regionInformationView.text =
        @"Thanks for visiting Denver! Come back soon!";

    UILocalNotification *exitNotification = [[UILocalNotification alloc] init];
    exitNotification.alertBody=@"Thanks for visiting Denver! Come back soon!";
    exitNotification.alertAction=@"Ok";
    exitNotification.soundName = UILocalNotificationDefaultSoundName;
    [[UIApplication sharedApplication]
        presentLocalNotificationNow:exitNotification];
}
```

To test this functionality using the iOS simulator, you must be able to feed in custom coordinates to be simulated. Like the freeway simulation in previous recipes, you can enter custom coordinates by navigating to Debug ➤ Location ➤ Custom Location, from which you can enter your own coordinates to test with. As an example, you could try latitude 39.7392 and longitude -104.9847, which should bring you inside the Denver region and make your app respond with the welcoming message. Then change the latitude to 39.0 (same longitude as before) and see your app welcome you back. You might also want to try putting the app into the background and switching the locations to verify the notifications pop-up.

Recipe 5-6: Implementing Geocoding

Location coordinates are useful to applications, but they are not very friendly to human beings. When is the last time you wrote your address using latitude and longitude coordinates? It's just not human-friendly. Human locations are expressed in names that reference countries, states, cities, and so on. So when a device's user asks, "Where am I?," the user doesn't want to know the GPS coordinates—the user wants to know what town or city he is in.

Fortunately, Apple has provided a method called *reverse geocoding* that converts location coordinates into a human-readable format. This feature used to be provided by the Map Kit framework, but it has been incorporated into the Core Location framework since iOS 5.

Geocoding, whether forward or reverse, is performed using the CLGeocoder class. You instantiate a CLGeocoder object and then pass it a coordinate and a block of code to perform once it has performed the geocoding. This is a little different than the other location recipes discussed thus far, which used delegate methods.

> **Note**   A device must have network access to perform geocoding requests.

Implementing Reverse Geocoding

Let's create a new single view application. To set up the project, take the following steps:

1. Link the application to the Core Location framework.

2. Set a usage description (such as "Testing geocoding") for the NSLocationUsageDescription key in the application's property list.

3. Add a text view and a button to the main view, which should look something like Figure 5-12. The TextView should contain about five lines (don't forget to set the Lines property in the attributes inspector).

4. Create outlets for the label and the button and name them "geocodingResultsView" and "reverseGeocodingButton," respectively.

5. Create an action for the switch, name it "findCurrentAddress," and make sure the event type is set to "Value Change."

6. Import the Core Location framework API by adding the following declaration in your view controller's header file: #import <CoreLocation/CoreLocation.h>.

7. Make the view controller a location manager delegate by adding the CLLocationManagerDelegate protocol to the ViewController class.

8. Add a CLLocationManager * instance variable to the view controller and name it "_locationManager."

9. Add a second instance variable, this time of the CLGeocoder * type and with the name "_geocoder."

Figure 5-12. Initial user interface for reverse geocoding

Your view controller's header file should now look like Listing 5-36.

Listing 5-36. The completed view controller header file

```
//
//  ViewController.h
//  Recipe 5-6 Implementing Geocoding
//

#import <UIKit/UIKit.h>
#import <CoreLocation/CoreLocation.h>

@interface ViewController : UIViewController<CLLocationManagerDelegate>
{
    CLLocationManager *_locationManager;
    CLGeocoder *_geocoder;
}

@property (strong, nonatomic) IBOutlet UITextView *geocodingResultsView;
@property (strong, nonatomic) IBOutlet UIButton *reverseGeocodingButton;
- (IBAction)findCurrentAddress:(id)sender;

@end
```

Switch to the implementation file (ViewController.m), and scroll to the bottom to implement the method findCurrentAddress. Because this has been covered in preceding recipes in this chapter, we're not going to go into detail about this, but we will cover some highlights.

You should follow the best practices of geocoding and not geocode a location that is too near to one you have already geocoded or that is too recent, so you will set your distanceFilter property on your CLLocationManager object to 500 meters.

In Listing 5-37, you set your desired accuracy to the constant kCLLocationAccuracyHundredMeters so that you get a faster response from the location tracking services and limit the drain on the battery.

Listing 5-37. Implementing the findCurrentAddress action method

```
- (IBAction)findCurrentAddress:(id)sender
{
    if([CLLocationManager locationServicesEnabled])
    {
        if(_locationManager==nil)
        {
            _locationManager=[[CLLocationManager alloc] init];
            _locationManager.distanceFilter = 500;
            _locationManager.desiredAccuracy = kCLLocationAccuracyHundredMeters;
            _locationManager.delegate = self;

        }

        [_locationManager startUpdatingLocation];
        self.geocodingResultsView.text = @"Getting location...";
    }
```

```
    else
    {
        self.geocodingResultsView.text=@"Location services are unavailable";
    }
}
```

Now add your delegate methods for the CLLocationManager object. The first is the locationManager:didFailWithError method, as shown in Listing 5-38.

Listing 5-38. Implementing the locationManager:didFailWithError: method

```
-(void)locationManager:(CLLocationManager *)manager didFailWithError:(NSError *)error
{
    if(error.code == kCLErrorDenied)
    {
        self.geocodingResultsView.text = @"Location information denied";
    }
}
```

Next the locationManager:didUpdateToLocations: delegate method has to be defined. Start with the standard checks to make sure the newLocation timestamp property is recent and that it is valid, as shown in Listing 5-39.

Listing 5-39. The starting implementation of the location: didUpdateLocations: method

```
- (void)locationManager:(CLLocationManager *)manager
didUpdateLocations:(NSArray *)locations
{
    // Make sure this is a recent location event
    CLLocation *newLocation = [locations lastObject];
    NSTimeInterval eventInterval = [newLocation.timestamp timeIntervalSinceNow];
    if(abs(eventInterval) < 30.0)
    {
        // Make sure the event is valid
        if (newLocation.horizontalAccuracy < 0)
            return;

        // ...
    }
}
```

Next check whether the _geocoder instance variable has been instantiated and, if not, create it. Also, make sure that you stop any existing geocoding services before performing a new one, as shown in Listing 5-40.

Listing 5-40. Checking the geocoder instance variable before creation and stopping any existing services

```
- (void)locationManager:(CLLocationManager *)manager
    didUpdateLocations:(NSArray *)locations
{
    // Make sure this is a recent location event
    CLLocation *newLocation = [locations lastObject];
```

```
NSTimeInterval eventInterval = [newLocation.timestamp timeIntervalSinceNow];
if(abs(eventInterval) < 30.0)
{
    // Make sure the event is valid
    if (newLocation.horizontalAccuracy < 0)
        return;

    // Instantiate _geoCoder if it has not been already
    if (_geocoder == nil)
        _geocoder = [[CLGeocoder alloc] init];

    //Only one geocoding instance per action
    //so stop any previous geocoding actions before starting this one
    if([_geocoder isGeocoding])
        [_geocoder cancelGeocode];
}
}
```

Finally, start your reverse geocoding process and define the completion handler. The completion handler receives two objects: an array of placemarks and an error object. The placemarks consist of street, city, and so on. If the array contains one or more objects, then the reverse geocoding was successful. If not, then you can check the error code for details.

The resulting location:didUpdateToLocations: method is shown in Listing 5-41.

Listing 5-41. The completed locationManager:didUpdateLocations: method

```
- (void)locationManager:(CLLocationManager *)manager didUpdateLocations:(NSArray *)locations
{
    // Make sure this is a recent location event
    CLLocation *newLocation = [locations lastObject];
    NSTimeInterval eventInterval = [newLocation.timestamp timeIntervalSinceNow];
    if(abs(eventInterval) < 30.0)
    {
        // Make sure the event is valid
        if (newLocation.horizontalAccuracy < 0)
            return;

        // Instantiate _geoCoder if it has not been already
        if (_geocoder == nil)
            _geocoder = [[CLGeocoder alloc] init];

        //Only one geocoding instance per action
        //so stop any previous geocoding actions before starting this one
        if([_geocoder isGeocoding])
            [_geocoder cancelGeocode];

        [_geocoder reverseGeocodeLocation: newLocation
            completionHandler: ^(NSArray* placemarks, NSError* error)
            {
                if([placemarks count] > 0)
                {
                    CLPlacemark *foundPlacemark = [placemarks objectAtIndex:0];
```

```
            self.geocodingResultsView.text =
                [NSString stringWithFormat:@"You are in: %@",
                    foundPlacemark.description];
        }
        else if (error.code == kCLErrorGeocodeCanceled)
        {
            NSLog(@"Geocoding cancelled");
        }
        else if (error.code == kCLErrorGeocodeFoundNoResult)
        {
            self.geocodingResultsView.text=@"No geocode result found";
        }
        else if (error.code == kCLErrorGeocodeFoundPartialResult)
        {
            self.geocodingResultsView.text=@"Partial geocode result";
        }
        else
        {
            self.geocodingResultsView.text =
                [NSString stringWithFormat:@"Unknown error: %@",
                    error.description];
        }
    }
];

    //Stop updating location until they click the button again
    [manager stopUpdatingLocation];
    }
}
```

You now have an application that can do reverse geocoding and find the address of the current location. Build and run it to verify it works correctly before we move on and extend the functionality of the app with forward geocoding.

Implementing Forward Geocoding

In iOS 5, forward geocoding was introduced. This means that you can pass an address to a geocoder and receive the coordinates for that address. The more information you can provide about an address, the more accurate the resulting forward geocode will be.

Let's extend the application with a feature that translates a given address into coordinates. Start by adding a text field and another button to the user interface. It should resemble Figure 5-13.

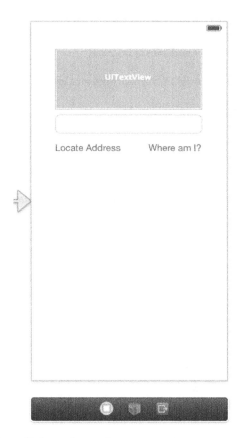

Figure 5-13. *The updated user interface with forward geocoding*

Now, add an outlet called "addressTextField" for the text field. Next, add an action for the button and name it "findCoordinateOfAddress."

In the findCoordinateOfAddress: action, the plan is to take the text the user has entered into the text field and send it to your geocoder object for translation into coordinates. The geocode process may result in multiple matches of possible coordinates, but the best guess is always first. Listing 5-42 shows the implementation of the method.

Listing 5-42. *Implementation of the findCoordinateOfAddress: action method*

```
- (IBAction)findCoordinateOfAddress:(id)sender
{
    // Instantiate _geocoder if it has not been already
    if (_geocoder == nil)
        _geocoder = [[CLGeocoder alloc] init];

    NSString *address = self.addressTextField.text;
    [_geocoder geocodeAddressString:address
```

```
        completionHandler:^(NSArray *placemarks, NSError *error)
        {
            if ([placemarks count] > 0)
            {
                CLPlacemark *placemark = [placemarks objectAtIndex:0];

                self.geocodingResultsView.text = placemark.location.description;
            }
            else
            {
                self.geocodingResultsView.text = error.localizedDescription;
            }
        }
    ];
}
```

In case of an error, the implementation in Listing 5-43 outputs the error message to the label. There are, however, a couple of errors your code should expect and handle. These include network errors, core location denied by user errors, and errors when no geocoding results are found. Listing 5-43 is an updated implementation that extracts these errors and provides (slightly) better error messages in these cases.

Listing 5-43. Adding error handling to the findCoordinateOfAddress: action method

```
- (IBAction)findCoordinateOfAddress:(id)sender
{
    // Instantiate _geocoder if it has not been already
    if (_geocoder == nil)
        _geocoder = [[CLGeocoder alloc] init];

    NSString *address = self.addressTextField.text;
    [_geocoder geocodeAddressString:address
        completionHandler:^(NSArray *placemarks, NSError *error)
        {
            if ([placemarks count] > 0)
            {
                CLPlacemark *placemark = [placemarks objectAtIndex:0];

                self.geocodingResultsView.text = placemark.location.description;
            }
            else if (error.domain == kCLErrorDomain)
            {
                switch (error.code)
                {
                    case kCLErrorDenied:
                        self.geocodingResultsView.text
                            = @"Location Services Denied by User";
                        break;
                    case kCLErrorNetwork:
                        self.geocodingResultsView.text = @"No Network";
                        break;
```

```
                    case kCLErrorGeocodeFoundNoResult:
                        self.geocodingResultsView.text = @"No Result Found";
                        break;
                    default:
                        self.geocodingResultsView.text = error.localizedDescription;
                        break;
                }
            }
            else
            {
                self.geocodingResultsView.text = error.localizedDescription;
            }

        }
    ];
}
```

That concludes Recipe 5-6. Let's end with some best practices advice for geocoding.

Best Practices

Here are some best practices to be aware of when using reverse or forward geocoding:

- You should send only one geocoding request at a time.

- If the user performs an action that will result in the same location being geocoded, the results should be reused rather than requesting the same location multiple times.

- You should not send more than one geocoding request per minute. You should check to see whether the user has moved a significant distance before calling another geocoding request.

- Do not perform a geocoding request if you will not see the results (in other words, if your application is running in the background).

Summary

The Core Location framework is a powerful framework that can be utilized by any number of application features. As demonstrated in this chapter, you can determine where a device is located, which direction a device is facing, and when a device enters or exits a specific region. Beyond those powerful features, you can also perform lookups on geographical coordinates to determine human-readable location information that will be presented to your end user, as well as provide complementary services to perform the reverse.

Apple has walked a fine line of making powerful features available to developers while also respecting a user's privacy and the battery drain on a device. As developers, we should work to deliver exciting features and functionality in our applications while maintaining the same level of respect for our users.

Chapter 6

Motion Recipes

One of the more impressive features of iOS devices is the built-in motion sensor. With motion sensors, iOS developers can create absolutely amazing apps–applications we could only dream about back in early 2000. Nowadays, we can simply point our phones to the night sky and instantly learn the names of stars and constellations. We can play virtual marble labyrinth games that are so close to the real experience that it's almost unbelievable. Motion sensors have truly enriched the field of app development.

Through the Core Motion framework you have easy access to the device's accelerometer, gyroscope, and magnetometer. It is your job to employ these tools to enhance the user's experience and create new, cool features. The recipes in this chapter will help you get started.

All but the first recipe in this chapter require a physical device to test the functionality because there currently is no way to simulate data from the Core Motion framework.

Recipe 6-1: Recognizing Shake Events

Before diving into the Core Motion framework, let's first deal with a related topic: the shaking of a device. A large number of applications utilize this functionality in a variety of ways, with results ranging from the shuffling of songs to the refreshing of information. While this implementation does not necessarily rely on the Core Motion framework, its key action of being able to detect physical changes to your device makes it an important functionality to understand.

Intercepting Shake Events

Although you could use the Core Motion framework to identify shake events, you'll use the more convenient `motionEnded:withEvent:` message created by Apple to handle shake events easily. When a user shakes the device, this message is dispatched to the first responder of your application. The first responder is an object, often a view controller, that receives an event first.

For example, you could set up your application's main view to receive shake events using code, as shown in Listing 6-1.

Listing 6-1. One example of receiving shake events

```objc
@implementation ViewController

// ...

- (BOOL) canBecomeFirstResponder
{
    return YES;
}

- (void) viewWillAppear: (BOOL)animated
{
    [self.view becomeFirstResponder];
    [super viewWillAppear:animated];
}

- (void) viewWillDisappear: (BOOL)animated
{
    [self.view resignFirstResponder];
    [super viewWillDisappear:animated];
}

- (void) motionEnded: (UIEventSubtype)motion withEvent: (UIEvent *)event
{
    if (event.subtype == UIEventSubtypeMotionShake)
    {
        // Device was shaken
    }
}

// ...

@end
```

While the code in Listing 6-1 works for most situations, a slightly more sophisticated solution allows you to recognize shake events from anywhere within your application. The next section shows you how to do it.

Subclassing the Window

If there are no receivers of the motionEnded:withEvent: message within the chain of responders, the message is sent to the application's window object. You should intercept the event, motionEnded:withEvent:, on the window object and implement your own notification scheme. This will let any observing object in your application know when the device has been shaken.

To start, create a new single view application and title it "Recipe 6-1 Recognizing Shake Events." Next, subclass the application's window object. To do that, create a new Objective-C class and name it "MainWindow." Be sure to make it a subclass of UIWindow (see Figure 6-1).

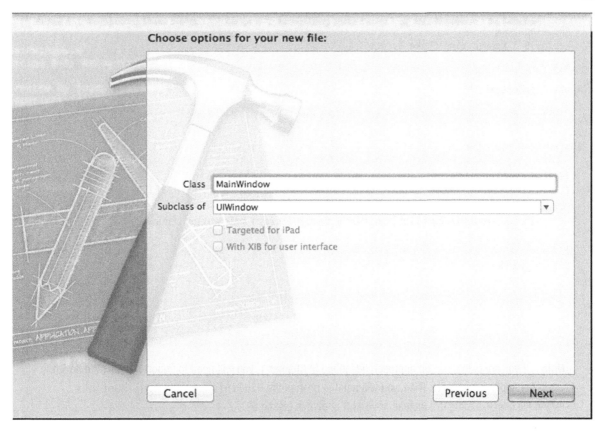

Figure 6-1. *Subclassing UIWindow by creating an Objective-C class*

Next, change the application's setup code to use your custom window class. This is done with a small change in the app delegate. Because we're using the single view application template, which defaults to a storyboard, we'll need to override the getter method for the window to let the system know we're using a custom UIWindow. Listing 6-2 shows you how you should modify your AppDelegate.h and AppDelegate.m files.

Listing 6-2. *Modifying AppDelegate to use a custom UIWindow*

```
//
// AppDelegate.h
// Recipe 6-1 Recognizing Shake Events
//

#import <UIKit/UIKit.h>
#import "MainWindow.h"

@interface AppDelegate : UIResponder <UIApplicationDelegate>

@property (strong, nonatomic) MainWindow *window;

@end
```

```
//
//  AppDelegate.m
//  Recipe 6-1 Recognizing Shake Events
//

#import "AppDelegate.h"

//...

- (MainWindow *)window
{
    if(!_window)
    {

        _window=[[MainWindow alloc] initWithFrame:[UIScreen mainScreen].bounds];

    }
    return _window;
}

//...
```

> **Note**   If you are using the .xib approach described in Chapter 1, you will need to import the MainWindow.h file in the AppDelegate.h file. Then, you will need to change the didFinishLaunchingWithOptions method shown in Listing 6-2 instead of what is shown in Listing 6-1.

Listing 6-3. Setting up the application:didFinishLaunchingWithOptions: method without storyboards

```
- (BOOL)application:(UIApplication *)application didFinishLaunchingWithOptions:(NSDictionary
*)launchOptions
{
    self.window = [[MainWindow alloc] initWithFrame:[[UIScreen mainScreen] bounds]];
    // Override point for customization after application launch.
    self.viewController = [[ViewController alloc] initWithNibName:@"ViewController" bundle:nil];
    self.window.rootViewController = self.viewController;
    [self.window makeKeyAndVisible];
    return YES;
}
```

Now you have an architecture that allows you to intercept events sent to the main window. It's time to implement your application-wide shake notifications.

Implementing Shake Notifications

In `MainWindow.m`, add the code in Listing 6-4.

Listing 6-4. Adding code to mainWindow.m to intercept shake events

```
@implementation MainWindow

// ...

- (void)motionEnded:(UIEventSubtype)motion withEvent:(UIEvent *)event
{
    if (event.type == UIEventTypeMotion && event.subtype == UIEventSubtypeMotionShake)
    {
        [[NSNotificationCenter defaultCenter] postNotificationName:@"NOTIFICATION_SHAKE"
                                        object:self];
    }
}

// ...

@end
```

The code in Listing 6-4 intercepts a shake event and uses the NSNotificationCenter class to post a notification. NSNotificationCenter implements an observer pattern for simple notifications reachable from any part of your application. The type of notification is identified by its name; this recipe uses NOTIFICATION_SHAKE, but you can pick any name you like. An observer pattern is a software design pattern where one object, in this case NSNotificationCenter, notifies its observers when an event occurs, usually by calling one of the observer's methods. As you will shortly see, the observer will be the view controller.

An object interested in your shake notifications can register an action method with the notification center. As an example, let's say you want to be notified about shakes in the application's main view. You could then do something similar to the implementation in Listing 6-5.

Listing 6-5. Implementation of the NSNotification Observer pattern

```
@implementation ViewController

// ...

- (void) viewWillAppear: (BOOL)animated
{
    [[NSNotificationCenter defaultCenter] addObserver:self
                                    selector:@selector(shakeDetected:)
                                    name:@"NOTIFICATION_SHAKE" object:nil];
    [super viewWillAppear:animated];
}
```

```
- (void) viewWillDisappear: (BOOL)animated
{
    [[NSNotificationCenter defaultCenter] removeObserver:self];
    [super viewWillDisappear:animated];
}

-(void)shakeDetected:(NSNotification *)paramNotification
{
    NSLog(@"Shaken not stirred");
}

// ...

@end
```

As you can see in the preceding code, if the view is removed from sight you unregister the observer that listens to the shake notifications in the viewWillDisappear method. This might or might not be what you want. If you want to keep tracking shake events even though the view has disappeared, leave the call to removeObserver: out.

Testing Shake Events

Now you're finished and you can run and test your application. Although Core Motion features require a real device to be tested, shake events can be tested within the simulator. Simply use the Shake Gesture item under the Hardware menu, as shown in Figure 6-2.

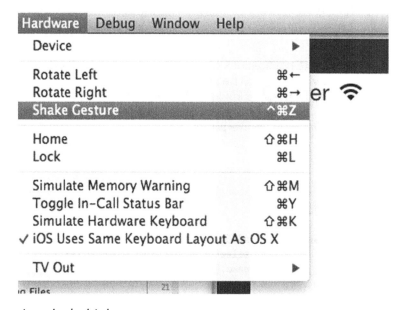

Figure 6-2. Shake events can be simulated

Figure 6-3 shows the test application after it has responded to a shake event.

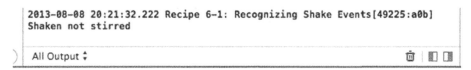

```
2013-08-08 20:21:32.222 Recipe 6-1: Recognizing Shake Events[49225:a0b]
Shaken not stirred
```

| All Output ⬍ | 🗑 ▎ ▊ ▊ |

Figure 6-3. Your test app writes to the output console upon shake events

As you can see from Figure 6-3, the text "Shaken not stirred" is logged to the screen when the notification center calls the shakeDetected method you provided as a selector.

Recipe 6-2: Accessing Raw Core Motion Data

Using this recipe, you'll create a simple application that receives and displays the raw data from the accelerometer, the gyroscope, and the magnetometer sensors. You'll need a real device that has these sensors (such as an iPhone 4 or later) to test the app.

Core Motion Sensors

In Core Motion, you can access three different pieces of hardware on a device, assuming the device is new enough to be equipped with said hardware (see Table 6-1).

- The *accelerometer* measures acceleration, caused by gravity or user acceleration, of the device. The information can provide insight into the current orientation as well as the current general movement of the device.

- The *gyroscope* measures rotation of the device along multiple axes.

- The *magnetometer* provides data regarding the magnetic field passing through the device. This is normally the Earth's magnetic field, but it might also be any other magnetic fields nearby. A magnetic field nearby can interfere with the calibration of the compass. However, this is not permanent; it simply requires a recalibration to fix it.

Table 6-1 shows the availability of the sensors on various iOS devices.

Table 6-1. Sensor Support on Various Devices

Accelerometer	Available on all iPhones, iPads, and iPods
Gyroscope	Available on iPhone 4, iPad2, iPod 4, and later
Magnetometer	Available on iPhone 3GS and later, as well as on all iPads

> **Note** Although Table 6-1 mentions the iPhone 3GS and the first iPad, the oldest devices iOS 7 supports are the iPhone 4 and iPad 2.

For all three sensors, data comes in the form of a three-dimensional vector, with components X, Y, and Z. If you are holding your device facing you with the bottom facing the ground, the x-axis cuts horizontally through your device, the y-axis runs vertically from bottom up, and the z-axis runs through the center of the device toward you.

In the case of the gyroscope, the values are the rotation rate *around* these axes. To find out which direction results in positive rotation rate values, you can use the right-hand rule. Imagine that you hold your open right hand in such a way that your thumb points toward the positive end of the axis. Then a positive rotation around the axis is the direction in which your fingers curve when you close your hand.

Rotation around the X, Y, and Z axes are called pitch, roll, and yaw, respectively. Figure 6-4 shows the axes and the positive directions of these rotations.

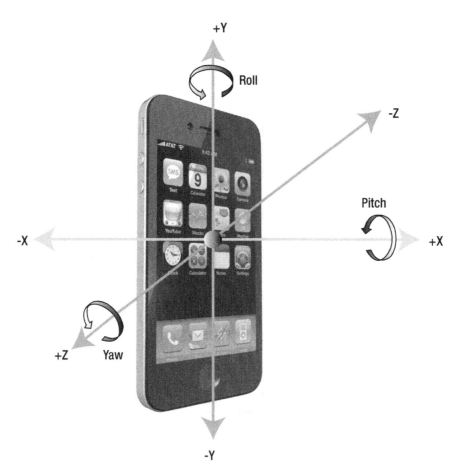

Figure 6-4. *Directions and rotations as defined in iOS*

Setting Up the Project

You will create a simple app that displays the current data from the three sensors. As you move the device around you can see how the movement affects their output.

Begin by creating a new single view application and give it a suitable project name, such as "Raw Motion Data Test." Because you're going to use the Core Motion framework, you need to link the CoreMotion.framework binary to your project.

Next, add labels and a button to the main view and organize them so the view resembles Figure 6-5. You will need 21 labels, 9 of which will be outlets. Make sure you make the label widths large enough so they don't cut off the values too much.

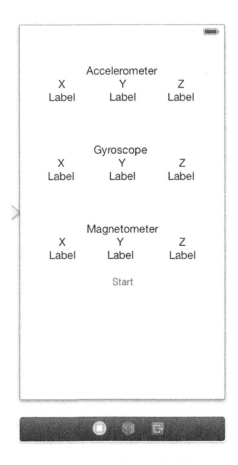

Figure 6-5. Main view interface

Your app will update the labels containing values (in other words, the ones with the text 0.0 in Figure 6-4). Therefore, create outlets for those nine labels so you'll be able to change their text at runtime.

Give the outlets and actions the following names:

- Accelerometer value labels: xAccLabel, yAccLabel, and zAccLabel

- Gyroscope value labels: xGyroLabel, yGyroLabel, and zGyroLabel

- Magnetometer value labels: xMagLabel, yMagLabel, and zMagLabel

- Button outlet: startButton

- Button action: toggleUpdates

For instructions about how to create outlets and actions for view components, see the corresponding recipes in Chapter 1.

When done, your view controller interface declaration should resemble Listing 6-6.

Listing 6-6. The view controller header file with all actions and outlets

```
@interface ViewController : UIViewController

@property (weak, nonatomic) IBOutlet UILabel *xAccLabel;
@property (weak, nonatomic) IBOutlet UILabel *yAccLabel;
@property (weak, nonatomic) IBOutlet UILabel *zAccLabel;
@property (weak, nonatomic) IBOutlet UILabel *xGyroLabel;
@property (weak, nonatomic) IBOutlet UILabel *yGyroLabel;
@property (weak, nonatomic) IBOutlet UILabel *zGyroLabel;
@property (weak, nonatomic) IBOutlet UILabel *xMagLabel;
@property (weak, nonatomic) IBOutlet UILabel *yMagLabel;
@property (weak, nonatomic) IBOutlet UILabel *zMagLabel;

@property (weak, nonatomic) IBOutlet UIButton *startButton;

- (IBAction)toggleUpdates:(id)sender;

@end
```

Now you have the basic structure for the application. It's time to dig out the data from the Core Motion framework.

Accessing Sensor Data

The Core Motion framework relies heavily on a single class called CMMotionManager. This class acts as a hub through which you access the motion sensors. You'll set up a lazy initialization property, a property that initializes when it's needed rather than immediately, to access a single instance of that class.

Make the changes in Listing 6-7 to the view controller's header class. Note that the outlet properties have been removed for the sake of brevity, so don't remove them in your code.

Listing 6-7. Importing the CoreMotion framework and creating a CMMotionManager property

```
#import <UIKit/UIKit.h>
#import <CoreMotion/CoreMotion.h>

@interface ViewController : UIViewController

// ...

@property (strong, nonatomic) CMMotionManager *motionManager;

- (IBAction)toggleUpdates:(id)sender;
;

@end
```

Now switch to ViewController.m and add the code in Listing 6-8 to the view controller's implementation section. Again, code has been removed for brevity.

Listing 6-8. Implementing the lazy initialization property

```
@implementation ViewController

// ...

-(CMMotionManager *)motionManager
{
    // Lazy initialization
    if (_motionManager == nil)
    {
        _motionManager = [[CMMotionManager alloc] init];
    }
    return _motionManager;
}

// ...

@end
```

Because you'll be moving around the device to get different readings, you should stop the autorotation of the user interface. Do that by setting portrait as the only supported interface orientation for this application. You can do that in the Supported Interface Orientations section on the project editor's summary page (see Figure 6-6).

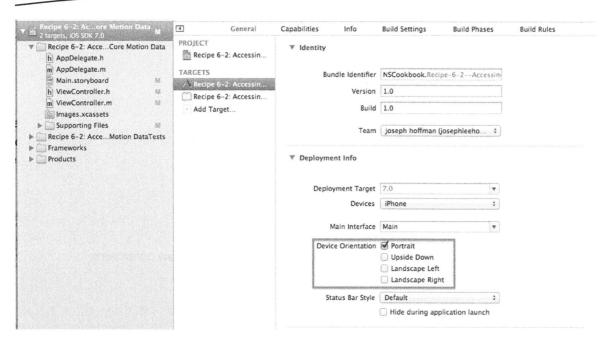

Figure 6-6. Setting supported interface orientations

Next, you need to start receiving data from your sensors and update the respective labels with the information. To do that, perform the following steps:

1. Check whether the sensor in question is available.

2. Set an update interval.

3. Start updating and provide the piece of code that will be invoked on each update.

For example, we can use these steps to set up the accelerometer, as shown in Listing 6-9 (don't start adding code yet).

Listing 6-9. Example code for setting up the accelerometer

```
// Start accelerometer if available
if ([self.motionManager isAccelerometerAvailable])
{
    //Update twice per second
    [self.motionManager setAccelerometerUpdateInterval:1.0/2.0];
    [self.motionManager startAccelerometerUpdatesToQueue:[NSOperationQueue mainQueue]
                    withHandler:
       ^(CMAccelerometerData *data, NSError *error)
        {
            // New data arrived, update accelerometer labels
            self.xAccLabel.text = [NSString stringWithFormat:@"%f",
                                data.acceleration.x];
```

```
                self.yAccLabel.text = [NSString stringWithFormat:@"%f",
                                          data.acceleration.y];
                self.zAccLabel.text = [NSString stringWithFormat:@"%f",
                                          data.acceleration.z];
        }
    ];
}
```

The `startAcceleratorUpdatesToQueue:withHandler:` method retains the code block (the so-called handler) and executes it as a task within the given operation queue repeatedly on the given interval when it updates. In our case, it will result in the accelerator labels being updated with the latest values from the accelerometer.

The other sensors have a similar programming interface. Listing 6-10 shows methods that start and stop all three sensors at once. Add them to your project view controller implementation file.

Listing 6-10. Implementation to start and stop all three sensors

```
- (void)startUpdates
{
    // Start accelerometer if available
    if ([self.motionManager isAccelerometerAvailable])
    {
        [self.motionManager setAccelerometerUpdateInterval:1.0/2.0];
        [self.motionManager startAccelerometerUpdatesToQueue:
                            [NSOperationQueue mainQueue]
                            withHandler:
         ^(CMAccelerometerData *data, NSError *error)
         {
            self.xAccLabel.text = [NSString stringWithFormat:@"%f",
                                      data.acceleration.x];
            self.yAccLabel.text = [NSString stringWithFormat:@"%f",
                                      data.acceleration.y];
            self.zAccLabel.text = [NSString stringWithFormat:@"%f",
                                      data.acceleration.z];
         }];
    }

    // Start gyroscope if available
    if ([self.motionManager isGyroAvailable])
    {
        [self.motionManager setGyroUpdateInterval:1.0/2.0];
        [self.motionManager startGyroUpdatesToQueue:
                            [NSOperationQueue mainQueue]
                            withHandler:
         ^(CMGyroData *data, NSError *error)
         {
            self.xGyroLabel.text = [NSString stringWithFormat:@"%f",
                                       data.rotationRate.x];
            self.yGyroLabel.text = [NSString stringWithFormat:@"%f",
                                       data.rotationRate.y];
```

```
                    self.zGyroLabel.text = [NSString stringWithFormat:@"%f",
                                        data.rotationRate.z];
        }];
    }


    // Start magnetometer if available
    if ([self.motionManager isMagnetometerAvailable])
    {
        [self.motionManager setMagnetometerUpdateInterval:1.0/2.0];
        [self.motionManager startMagnetometerUpdatesToQueue:[NSOperationQueue mainQueue]
                        withHandler:
         ^(CMMagnetometerData *data, NSError *error)
         {
            self.xMagLabel.text = [NSString stringWithFormat:@"%f",
                                    data.magneticField.x];
            self.yMagLabel.text = [NSString stringWithFormat:@"%f",
                                    data.magneticField.y];
            self.zMagLabel.text = [NSString stringWithFormat:@"%f",
                                    data.magneticField.z];
        }];
    }
}


-(void)stopUpdates
{
    if ([self.motionManager isAccelerometerAvailable] &&
        [self.motionManager isAccelerometerActive])
    {
        [self.motionManager stopAccelerometerUpdates];
    }

    if ([self.motionManager isGyroAvailable] &&
        [self.motionManager isGyroActive])
    {
        [self.motionManager stopGyroUpdates];
    }

    if ([self.motionManager isMagnetometerAvailable] &&
        [self.motionManager isMagnetometerActive])
    {
        [self.motionManager stopMagnetometerUpdates];
    }
}
```

Now we will start and stop the motion services from a button with a toggle method tied to our button. To do this, modify the two methods in the ViewController.m, as shown in Listing 6-11.

Listing 6-11. Modifying the viewDidLoad and toggleUpdates: methods to support the start and stop button

```
- (void)viewDidLoad
{
    [super viewDidLoad];
        // Do any additional setup after loading the view, typically from a nib.

    [self.startButton setTitle:@"Stop" forState:UIControlStateSelected];
    [self.startButton setTitle:@"Start" forState:UIControlStateNormal];
}

//...

- (IBAction)toggleUpdates:(id)sender {

    if(![self.startButton isSelected])
    {
        [self startUpdates];
        [self.startButton setSelected:YES];
    }
    else
    {
        [self stopUpdates];
        [self.startButton setSelected:NO];
    }

}
```

Your app is finished and ready to run. Remember, the simulator has no support for any of the three sensors, so nothing interesting will happen during simulation. You need a real device to test this app. Figure 6-7 shows a screen shot of the app in action.

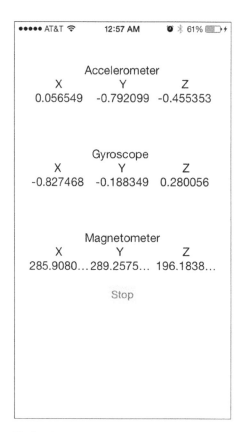

Figure 6-7. *An app displaying raw Core Motion data*

Pushing or Pulling

There are two ways to access updated data from the sensors. In this recipe you used "pushing." What this means is that the motion manager will invoke your code on the given intervals and provide it with the new values. This system is implemented in the `start<Sensor>UpdatesToQueue:withHandler` methods, where you provide the code in the form of a block.

To make the concept of "pushing" clear, think of your email system. With "push" enabled, an email will show up every time one is available. This, of course, can cause battery drain as well as increase data consumption. The other strategy is "pulling," and it's the preferred method if your app has a render loop from which you can query the values yourself on a regular basis. This can be a little more efficient and is generally better suited for game apps. Using the email analogy, this is more of a manual process where the user has to check email first to get the update. Thus, data is provided only when it's needed.

Pulling is implemented in the `start<Sensor>Updates` method. It keeps the properties `accelerometerData`, `gyroData`, and `magnetometerData` on the motion manager updated with the most recent value. Your app can then, at an appropriate time, retrieve the values from those properties, as Listing 6-12 shows.

Listing 6-12. An example of using the pull mode to access accelerometer data

```
// Start updates in pull mode
[self.motionManager startAccelerometerUpdates];

// Pull the values from somewhere within an update loop
self.xMagLabel.text = [NSString stringWithFormat:@"%f",
                        self.motionManager.magnetometerData.magneticField.x];
self.yMagLabel.text = [NSString stringWithFormat:@"%f",
                        self.motionManager.magnetometerData.magneticField.y];
self.zMagLabel.text = [NSString stringWithFormat:@"%f",
                        self.motionManager.magnetometerData.magneticField.z];
```

Selecting an Update Interval

You can set the update interval to as little as one update each ten milliseconds (1/100). However, you should strive to the highest possible value that will work for your application because that will improve battery time. Table 6-2 provides a general guideline for update intervals.

Table 6-2. Guideline Values for Update Intervals

Update Interval	Usage Example
10 ms (1/100)	For detecting high-frequency motion
20 ms (1/50)	Suitable for games that use real-time user input
100 ms (1/10)	Suitable for determining the current orientation of the device

The Nature of Raw Motion Data

When running the app, you might have discovered how incomprehensible the data from the sensors are. This is because the data from the sensors are biased; that is, they are affected by more than one force. The accelerometer, for example, is affected by Earth's gravity as well as the movement from the user's hand. The magnetometer senses not only the magnetic field of the Earth, but also all other magnetic fields in your vicinity.

The biased nature of the raw data makes the data difficult to interpret. You need tricks such as high-pass and low-pass filters to isolate the various components. Fortunately, Core Motion comes with a way to access unbiased data from the sensors, which makes it easy to figure out the device's real orientation and motion. Recipe 6-3 shows you how to use this convenient feature.

Recipe 6-3: Accessing Device Motion Data

The preceding recipe showed you how to access raw motion data from the three sensors. While easy to access, the raw biased data are not easy to use. They require various filtering techniques to isolate the different forces that affect the sensors to make real use of the data. The good news is that Apple has done the difficult work for you, ready to be utilized through the deviceMotion property of the motion manager. This recipe shows you how.

The Device Motion Class

Just like the accelerometer, gyroscope, and magnetometer from the preceding recipe, you can access CMDeviceMotion by starting and stopping updates using very similar methods: startDeviceMotionUpdates and startDeviceMotionUpdatesToQueue:withHandler:. However, you also have two extra methods that allow you to specify a "reference frame": startDeviceMotionUpdatesUsingReferenceFrame: and startDeviceMotionUpdatesUsingReferenceFrame:toQueue:WithHandler:. The reference frame will be discussed shortly.

When retrieving data using an instance of CMDeviceMotion (through the deviceMotion property in your CMMotionManager), you can access six different properties.

- The attitude property is an instance of the CMAttitude class. It gives you detailed insight into the device's orientation at a given time, as compared to a reference frame. Through this class you can access properties such as roll, pitch, and yaw. These values are measured in radians and allow you an accurate measurement of your device's orientation.

- As shown previously in Figure 6-4, roll specifies the device's position of rotation around the *y-axis*, pitch the position of rotation around the *x-axis*, and yaw around the *z-axis*.

- The rotationRate property is just like the one you saw in the preceding recipe, except that it gives a more accurate reading. It does this by reducing device bias that causes a still device to have nonzero rotation values.

- The gravity property represents the acceleration caused solely by gravity on the device.

- The userAcceleration represents the physical acceleration imparted on a device by the user outside gravitational acceleration.

- The magneticField value is similar to the one you saw in Recipe 6-2; however, it removes any device bias, resulting in more accurate readings.

> **Note**   If you are unfamiliar with them, radians are a different way of measuring rotation from the more commonly used degrees. They are based around the value pi (π). A radian value of pi (roughly 3.14) is equivalent to a 180-degree rotation, so any radian value can be converted to degrees by dividing by pi and then multiplying by 180, like so: d = r * 180 / π.

Setting Up the Application

You'll create an application similar to the one you built in Recipe 6-2. So go ahead and create a new single view application project and link the Core Motion framework.

> **Caution**   Failing to link the Core Motion framework results in a linker error, such as the one that follows, when you try to build your application later on.
>
> ```
> Undefined symbols for architecture armv7:
>
>  "_OBJC_CLASS_$_CMMotionManager", referenced from:
>
>    objc-class-ref in ViewController.o
> ```

Now, create a user interface such as the one in Figure 6-8. You'll need 35 label objects, 15 of which are displaying values. You will also need a button. Because you will update those labels at runtime, you'll need to create outlets for them. Use the following names for the outlets and actions:

- Attitude value labels: rollLabel, pitchLabel, and yawLabel
- Rotation rate value labels: xRotLabel, yRotLabel, and zRotLabel
- Gravity value labels: xGravLabel, yGravLabel, and zGravLabel
- User acceleration labels: xAccLabel, yAccLabel, and zAccLabel
- Magnetic field labels: xMagLabel, yMagLabel, and zMagLabel
- Button outlet: startButton
- Button action: toggleUpdates

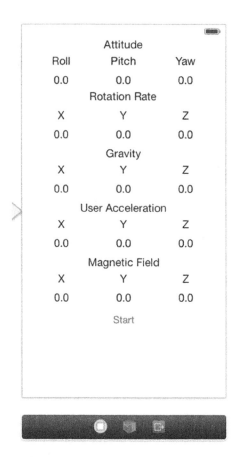

Figure 6-8. *User interface of the device motion app*

As you did in Recipe 6-2, add a motion manager property to the view controller interface file, as shown in Listing 6-13.

Listing 6-13. *Adding the CMMotionManager and CoreMotion import statements to the view controller interface*

```
#import <UIKit/UIKit.h>
#import <CoreMotion/CoreMotion.h>

@interface ViewController : UIViewController

// ...

@property (strong,nonatomic) CMMotionManager *motionManager;

- (IBAction)toggleUpdates:(id)sender;

@end
```

The property should have the same lazy initialization implementation as in the preceding recipe. This is shown again in Listing 6-14.

Listing 6-14. Implementing the lazy initialization property

```
@implementation ViewController

// ...

-(CMMotionManager *)motionManager
{
    // Lazy initialization
    if (_motionManager == nil)
    {
        _motionManager = [[CMMotionManager alloc] init];
    }
    return _motionManager;
}

// ...

@end
```

Also, as in Recipe 6-2, your app should support only portrait orientation (refer to Figure 6-6).

Accessing Device Motion Data

Starting and stopping updates and retrieving data from the device-motion property follow the same pattern that you used for accessing the three sensors' raw data. The difference is that you need only one start statement, which allows you to reach all the data at once.

So, add the methods in Listing 6-15 to your view controller. Be sure to add their declarations to the header file as well because you'll invoke them from the application delegate later.

Listing 6-15. Implementing the startUpdates and stopUpdates methods

```
- (void)startUpdates
{
    // Start device motion updates
    if ([self.motionManager isDeviceMotionAvailable])
    {
        //Update twice per second
        [self.motionManager setDeviceMotionUpdateInterval:1.0/2.0];
        [self.motionManager startDeviceMotionUpdatesToQueue:[NSOperationQueue mainQueue]
                                            withHandler:
         ^(CMDeviceMotion *deviceMotion, NSError *error)
         {
             // Update attitude labels
             self.rollLabel.text =  [NSString stringWithFormat:@"%f",
                                        deviceMotion.attitude.roll];
             self.pitchLabel.text = [NSString stringWithFormat:@"%f",
                                        deviceMotion.attitude.pitch];
             self.yawLabel.text =   [NSString stringWithFormat:@"%f",
                                        deviceMotion.attitude.yaw];
```

```
            // Update rotation rate labels
            self.xRotLabel.text = [NSString stringWithFormat:@"%f",
                                    deviceMotion.rotationRate.x];
            self.yRotLabel.text = [NSString stringWithFormat:@"%f",
                                    deviceMotion.rotationRate.y];
            self.zRotLabel.text = [NSString stringWithFormat:@"%f",
                                    deviceMotion.rotationRate.z];

            // Update user acceleration labels
            self.xGravLabel.text = [NSString stringWithFormat:@"%f",
                                    deviceMotion.gravity.x];
            self.yGravLabel.text = [NSString stringWithFormat:@"%f",
                                    deviceMotion.gravity.y];
            self.zGravLabel.text = [NSString stringWithFormat:@"%f",
                                    deviceMotion.gravity.z];

            // Update user acceleration labels
            self.xAccLabel.text = [NSString stringWithFormat:@"%f",
                                    deviceMotion.userAcceleration.x];
            self.yAccLabel.text = [NSString stringWithFormat:@"%f",
                                    deviceMotion.userAcceleration.y];
            self.zAccLabel.text = [NSString stringWithFormat:@"%f",
                                    deviceMotion.userAcceleration.z];

            // Update magnetic field labels
            self.xMagLabel.text = [NSString stringWithFormat:@"%f",
                                    deviceMotion.magneticField.field.x];
            self.yMagLabel.text = [NSString stringWithFormat:@"%f",
                                    deviceMotion.magneticField.field.y];
            self.zMagLabel.text = [NSString stringWithFormat:@"%f",
                                    deviceMotion.magneticField.field.z];
        }];
    }
}

-(void)stopUpdates
{
    if ([self.motionManager isDeviceMotionAvailable] &&
        [self.motionManager isDeviceMotionActive])
    {
        [self.motionManager stopDeviceMotionUpdates];
    }
}
```

Finally, invoke the start and stop updates methods from the toggleUpdates method as we did in Recipe 6-2 and update the viewDidLoad method, as shown in Listing 6-16.

Listing 6-16. Updating the viewDidLoad and toggleUpdates: methods to add start and stop functionality

```
- (void)viewDidLoad
{
    [super viewDidLoad];
        // Do any additional setup after loading the view, typically from a nib.

    [self.startButton setTitle:@"Stop" forState:UIControlStateSelected];
    [self.startButton setTitle:@"Start" forState:UIControlStateNormal];

}
//...

(IBAction)toggleUpdates:(id)sender
{

    if(![self.startButton isSelected])
    {
        [self startUpdates];
        [self.startButton setSelected:YES];
    }
    else
    {
        [self stopUpdates];
        [self.startButton setSelected:NO];
    }
}

//...
```

If you run this application, you will probably notice that most of your values are more stable than those from the raw sensor data of Recipe 6-2. You might also see all zeros for your magnetometer readings. Move your device in a figure-eight motion to calibrate your magnetometer until these values start updating.

Setting a Reference Frame

Though not required, you can specify a reference frame for your attitude data. This might be handy if you would like to switch the coordinate system or use magnetic north versus true north. Changing the reference frame is done by using the startDeviceMotionUpdatesUsingReferenceFram:toQueue:withHandler: method.

One of the following is a possible value for the reference-frame parameter:

- CMAttitudeReferenceFrameXArbitraryZVertical, which specifies a reference frame with the z-axis along the vertical and the x-axis along any arbitrary direction; simply put, the device is flat and face-up.

- CMAttitudeReferenceFrameXArbitraryCorrectedZVertical, which is the same as the previous value except the magnetometer is used to provide better accuracy. This option increases CPU (central processing unit) usage and requires the magnetometer to be both available and calibrated.

▨ CMAttitudeReferenceFrameXMagneticNorthZVertical, which references a frame that has the z-axis vertical as before, but with the x-axis directed toward "magnetic north." This option requires the magnetometer to be available and calibrated, which means you will probably have to wave your device around a bit before you can get any readings in your application.

▨ CMAttitudeReferenceFrameXTrueNorthZVertical, which is just like the previous, but the x-axis is directed toward "true north" rather than "magnetic north." The location of the device must be available for the device to be able to calculate the difference between the two.

Note   As mentioned earlier in this chapter, there's a difference between "magnetic north" and "true north." Magnetic north is the magnetic north pole of the Earth, which is where any compass will point. This point, however, is not constant due to changes in the Earth's core, and it is moving more than 30 miles per year. True north refers to the direction toward the actual north pole of the Earth, which stays constant.

You will choose the third option, CMAttitudeReferenceFrameXMagneticNorthZVertical, for your application as the direction accuracy doesn't matter that much and using location services is more than is needed. Change your call to the startDeviceMotionUpdatesToQueue:withHandler: method, as shown in Listing 6-17.

Listing 6-17. Adding magnetic north reference to the startDeviceMotionUpdatesToQueue:withHandler method

```
[self.motionManager startDeviceMotionUpdatesUsingReferenceFrame:
                    CMAttitudeReferenceFrameXMagneticNorthZVertical
                    toQueue:[NSOperationQueue mainQueue]
                    withHandler:
 ^(CMDeviceMotion *deviceMotion, NSError *error)
 {
   // ... Update value labels here
 }];
```

When you run your application, you might see "0.0" for all your values. If that's the case, you can move your device around in a figure-eight motion to get your magnetometer calibrated; the values should start updating soon.

You should notice now that if you lay your device on a flat surface and then turn the device around the z-axis, at the moment your x-axis is aligned with the Earth's magnetic field, your yaw value should get close to zero, as in Figure 6-9.

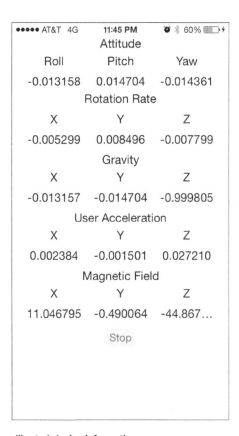

Figure 6-9. Your application receiving calibrated-device information

Recipe 6-4: Moving a Label with Gravity

Recipes 6-2 and 6-3 showed you how to access the various Core Motion data. It's time to put that knowledge to use and make it a little more interesting. Using this recipe, you'll create an application with a single label that you'll be able to move around by tilting your device.

Setting Up the Application

You'll use the same basic architecture that you built in the previous two recipes. So once again start by creating a new single view application and linking it to `CoreMotion.framework`. Then add the following declarations, which should be familiar by now, to your view control's header file, as shown in Listing 6-18.

Listing 6-18. Setting up the ViewController.h file

```
#import <UIKit/UIKit.h>
#import <CoreMotion/CoreMotion.h>

@interface ViewController : UIViewController

@property (strong, nonatomic) CMMotionManager *motionManager;

@end
```

Now switch to ViewController.m and implement the property using lazy initialization; add stubs for the startUpdate and stopUpdate methods. Listing 6-19 shows this code.

Listing 6-19. Creating the custom initializer and adding method stubs

```
@implementation ViewController

- (CMMotionManager *)motionManager
{
    // Lazy initialization
    if (_motionManager == nil)
    {
        _motionManager = [[CMMotionManager alloc] init];
    }
    return _motionManager;
}

- (void)startUpdates
{

}

- (void)stopUpdates
{

}

// ...

@end
```

As in the preceding two recipes, your app should support only the portrait interface orientation, so make sure you make that change in the project settings.

Instead of creating a button in this recipe, we'll start the updates when the view loads. So add the code in Listing 6-20 to the viewDidLoad method in your viewController.m file.

Listing 6-20. Modifying the viewDidLoad method to start updates

```
@implementation ViewController

- (void)viewDidLoad
{
    [super viewDidLoad];

    [self startUpdates];
}
```

Next, you should stop the updates when the view goes away, so add the code in Listing 6-21 right after the viewDidLoad method.

Listing 6-21. Implementing the viewWillDisappear method to stop updates

```
-(void)viewWillDisappear:(BOOL)animated
{

    [self stopUpdates];
}
```

Finally, go to the Main.storyboard and add a label and an outlet for it so you'll be able to change its position at runtime. Name the label's outlet "myLabel." Your user interface should look something like the one in Figure 6-10.

Figure 6-10. The user interface with the label you will move using gravity

Your app is now ready for the next step—implementing gravity-caused movement of the label.

Moving the Label with Gravity

You're going to use a very simple algorithm for the initial version of your label-moving feature. Later you'll spice it up with a little acceleration, but for now you will settle for a linear movement that is proportional to the angle in which you tilt the device.

As you can see, you have increased the update frequency to once per 20 milliseconds (1/50). This enhances the feeling and responsiveness of the app. The next thing to notice is that you use the CMAttitudeReferenceFrameXArbitraryCorrectedZVertical reference frame. This gives you a z-axis that's aligned with Earth's gravity force, which is what you want. Implement the startUpdates and stopUpdates methods, as shown in Listing 6-22.

Listing 6-22. The startUpdates method and stopUpdates method implementation

```
- (void)startUpdates
{
    if ([self.motionManager isDeviceMotionAvailable] &&
        ![self.motionManager isDeviceMotionActive])
    {
        [self.motionManager setDeviceMotionUpdateInterval:1.0/50.0];
        [self.motionManager startDeviceMotionUpdatesUsingReferenceFrame:
                        CMAttitudeReferenceFrameXArbitraryCorrectedZVertical
                        toQueue:[NSOperationQueue mainQueue]
                        withHandler:
         ^(CMDeviceMotion *motion, NSError *error)
         {
             CGRect labelRect = self.myLabel.frame;
             double scale = 5.0;

             // Calculate movement on the x-axis
             double dx = motion.gravity.x * scale;
             labelRect.origin.x += dx;

             // Don't move outside the view's x bounds
             if (labelRect.origin.x < 0)
             {
                 labelRect.origin.x = 0;
             }
             else if (labelRect.origin.x + labelRect.size.width >
                     self.view.bounds.size.width)
             {
                 labelRect.origin.x =
                     self.view.bounds.size.width - labelRect.size.width;
             }

             // Calculate movement on the y-axis
             double dy = motion.gravity.y * scale;
             labelRect.origin.y -= dy;
```

```
            // Don't move outside the view's y bounds
            if (labelRect.origin.y < 0)
            {
                labelRect.origin.y = 0;
            }
            else if (labelRect.origin.y + labelRect.size.height >
                    self.view.bounds.size.height)
            {
                labelRect.origin.y =
                    self.view.bounds.size.height - labelRect.size.height;
            }

            [self.myLabel setFrame:labelRect];
        }];
    }
}

- (void)stopUpdates
{
    if ([self.motionManager isDeviceMotionAvailable] &&
        [self.motionManager isDeviceMotionActive])
    {
        [self.motionManager stopDeviceMotionUpdates];
    }
}
```

The algorithm in the preceding code is the simplest possible. It uses the deviceMotion.gravity property as a velocity value (although it's actually an acceleration) and calculates the delta movement from it. Because each value only reaches between -1.0 and 1.0, use a scaling factor to adjust the general speed of the movement.

If you run the app now, you should see the label moving in the direction you tilt your device; the bigger the tilt, the faster the movement. But the movement feels a bit unnatural. This is because it lacks an important component: acceleration. Acceleration is the topic of the next section.

Adding Acceleration

Adjust the startUpdates method to implement a simple acceleration algorithm. Change your code according to Listing 6-23.

Listing 6-23. Adding an acceleration algorithm to the startUpdates method

```
- (void)startUpdates
{
    if ([self.motionManager isDeviceMotionAvailable] &&
        ![self.motionManager isDeviceMotionActive])
    {
        __block double accumulatedDx = 0;
        __block double accumulatedDy = 0;
```

```objc
    [self.motionManager setDeviceMotionUpdateInterval:1.0/50.0];
    [self.motionManager startDeviceMotionUpdatesUsingReferenceFrame:
                        CMAttitudeReferenceFrameXArbitraryCorrectedZVertical
                        toQueue:[NSOperationQueue mainQueue]
                        withHandler:
     ^(CMDeviceMotion *motion, NSError *error)
     {
         CGRect labelRect = self.myLabel.frame;
         double scale = 1.5;

         double dx = motion.gravity.x * scale;
         accumulatedDx += dx;
         labelRect.origin.x += accumulatedDx;

         if (labelRect.origin.x < 0)
         {
             labelRect.origin.x = 0;
             accumulatedDx = 0;
         }
         else if (labelRect.origin.x + labelRect.size.width >
                 self.view.bounds.size.width)
         {
             labelRect.origin.x =
                 self.view.bounds.size.width - labelRect.size.width;
             accumulatedDx = 0;
         }

         double dy = motion.gravity.y * scale;
         accumulatedDy += dy;
         labelRect.origin.y -= accumulatedDy;

         if (labelRect.origin.y < 0)
         {
             labelRect.origin.y = 0;
             accumulatedDy = 0;
         }
         else if (labelRect.origin.y + labelRect.size.height > self.view.bounds.size.height)
         {
             labelRect.origin.y = self.view.bounds.size.height - labelRect.size.height;
             accumulatedDy = 0;
         }

         [self.myLabel setFrame:labelRect];
     }];
    }
}
```

> **Note**   You might be wondering what the `__block` declarations in front of the `accumulatedDx` and `accumulatedDy` variables are. They are making the variables accessible from within a code block. In addition, they stay accessible even though the surrounding method has gone out of scope. This provides a clean and easy way for blocks to share variables, avoiding the need to create properties or global variables for local needs.

Also notable is that you have decreased the scaling factor. Now it's not a problem if the label moves slowly at first; it'll pick up pace soon enough thanks to the acceleration. You can play around with different values and find the one you like best.

Lastly, but important, if the label reaches a border you reset the speed, as shown in Listing 6-23. Otherwise, it will keep accumulating speed (in the `accumulatedXX` variables) even though the movement has stopped, making it less responsive when you tilt the device in the opposite direction again.

Summary

This chapter discusses specific details about accessing the multiple values and information that the Core Motion framework has to offer. You started with raw data and then used more calibrated, functional values that you could translate into a mildly useful (if not slightly entertaining) application. Core Motion, however, is not a framework that can simply be an entire application in itself. You can use it to acquire values about your device, but you must then have the creativity to put them to use. From a simple application to measure the rotation speed of a person flipping to incorporating the magnetometer into an augmented-reality application, Core Motion provides a basic framework for accessing information, which can then translate into some of the most powerful pieces of software in iOS.

Chapter 7

Map Recipes

The Map Kit framework is an incredibly powerful and useful toolkit that adds immense functionality to the location services that iOS devices offer. The framework's key focus is the ability to place a user-interactive map in an application, with countless other features expanding functionality, allowing for a nearly entirely customizable mapping interface.

With iOS 6, Apple made a fundamental change by replacing the Google Maps backend with a map engine of its own. With the introduction of maps in iOS 6, there were many improvements, including a new cartography that provides great-looking maps at any zoom level, better zooming experience thanks to seamless rendering, and, of course, turn-by-turn navigation.

Apple built upon the maps tools in iOS 7 to give you many more ways in which to create submersive mapping applications. Now you have access to the 3-D APIs used in the Maps application to create your own 3-D mapping applications. Overlays have been improved to allow better readability of content, and a new class has been created for requesting direction-related routes from Apple. In this chapter, we will cover these new features as well as many common, real-world mapping situations.

Recipe 7-1: Showing a Map with the Current Location

The core foundation of any Map Kit application is the actual displaying of the world map. In this section, you will learn how to create an app with a map and how to allow the map to show the user's location.

Setting Up the Application

Create a new single view application and add the Map Kit framework and Core Location framework to the project. You should also provide a location usage description in the application property list. This is done by adding the NSLocationUsageDescription key in the application's Info.plist file (refer to Chapter 5, Figure 5-2). We've set its value to "Testing map views," and that description is used when the user is prompted and asked for permission to use location services. Figure 7-3 provides an example of this system alert box.

Note   Descriptions of how to link frameworks and setting values in the application's property list file can be found in Chapter 1.

When the frameworks have been added, you can start building the user interface. Select the Main. storyboard from the navigation pane and drag a map view from the object library onto the view. Make it fill the entire view.

Next, add a label for displaying the current latitude and longitude of the device. Place it on top of the map, close to the bottom of the screen. Set the label's text alignment to center justified. Also, to make the text easier to read on the map, set a background color (such as white). You will also need to make the width of the label larger. Your user interface should now look something like the one in Figure 7-1.

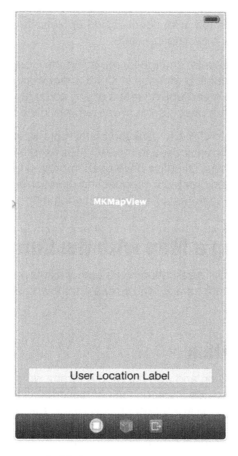

Figure 7-1. *Main view controller with a map and a label*

To make sure the view resizes properly when switching between a 3.5" screen and a 4" screen, select both the MKMapView and the label by command-clicking them and choosing "Add Missing Constraints" from the Resolve Auto Layout Issues menu, which can be found at the bottom of the storyboard (see Chapter 3, Figure 3-7). You should see that the constraint lines are added, as shown in Figure 7-2.

Figure 7-2. *Main view controller with auto layout constraints added*

Create outlets for both the map view and the label. Name the outlets "mapView" and "userLocationLabel," respectively. Because you haven't imported the Map Kit API yet you'll get an error indication next to the mapView property. We'll take care of that next.

> **Note**   Chapter 1 provides detailed instructions about how to create outlets.

Your user interface is fully set up, so you can turn your attention to the view controller's interface file (ViewController.h). You need to make two additions to this class interface before moving to the implementation file. The first is to add the MapKit/MapKit.h and CoreLocation/CoreLocation.h frameworks libraries to the class with import statements, and the second is to make the view controller a map view delegate by adding MKMapViewDelegate as a supported protocol.

Your ViewController.h should now look something like Listing 7-1, with the foregoing changes in bold.

Listing 7-1. Adding import statements and declaring MKMapViewDelegate in ViewController.h

```
//
//  ViewController.h
//  Recipe 7-1 Showing a Map with the Current Location
//

#import <UIKit/UIKit.h>
#import <MapKit/MapKit.h>
#import <CoreLocation/CoreLocation.h>

@interface ViewController : UIViewController <MKMapViewDelegate>

@property (weak, nonatomic) IBOutlet MKMapView *mapView;
@property (weak, nonatomic) IBOutlet UILabel *userLocationLabel;

@end
```

Switch to the implementation file, ViewController.m, and the viewDidLoad method where you'll initialize the map view. We'll begin by explaining the steps and then show you the complete viewDidLoad method.

First, make the view controller be the map view's delegate, as shown in Listing 7-2.

Listing 7-2. Settting the mapView delegate to the viewController

```
self.mapView.delegate = self;
```

Next, set the region of the map view. The region is the portion of the map that is currently being displayed. It consists of a center coordinate and a distance in latitude and longitude surrounding the center coordinate to be shown.

If you are like most people, you don't think of distances in latitudinal and longitudinal degrees, so you can use the method MKCoordinateRegionMakeWithDistance to create a region using a center coordinate and meters surrounding the coordinate, as shown in Listing 7-3. In this recipe, you start with a region of 10 by 10 kilometers over Denver, Colorado, in the United States.

Listing 7-3. Creating the mapView region

```
// Set initial region
CLLocationCoordinate2D denverLocation = CLLocationCoordinate2DMake(39.739, -104.984);
self.mapView.region =
    MKCoordinateRegionMakeWithDistance(denverLocation, 10000, 10000);
```

Two optional properties worth mentioning are zoomEnabled and scrollEnabled. These control whether a user can zoom or pan the map, respectively (shown in Listing 7-4).

Listing 7-4. Optional properties for zoom and scroll

```
// Optional Controls
//   self.mapView.zoomEnabled = NO;
//   self.mapView.scrollEnabled = NO;
```

Finally, define the map as showing the user's location. This is easily done by setting the showUserLocation property to "YES." However, you should set this property only if location services are enabled on the device, as shown in Listing 7-5.

Listing 7-5. Checking for location services and showing the user location

```
//Control User Location on Map
if ([CLLocationManager locationServicesEnabled])
{
    self.mapView.showsUserLocation = YES;
}
```

Keep in mind that the feature to display the user's location in the map requires an authorization from the user, who is asked for permission the first time the app is run.

> **Note**   Just because showUserLocation is set to "YES," the user's location is not automatically visible on the map. To determine whether the location is visible in the current region, use the property userLocationVisible.

When you have specified that you want the map to display the user's location, you can also make it track the user location by setting the userTrackingMode property or by calling the setUserTrackingMode:animated: method.

The tracking mode can be one of three values:

- MKUserTrackingModeNone: Does not track the user's location; the map can be moved to a region that does not contain the user's location.

- MKUserTrackingModeFollow: The map is panned to keep the user's location at the center. The top of the map is north. If the user pans the map manually, tracking stops.

- MKUserTrackingModeFollowWithHeading: The map is panned to keep the user's location at the center, and the map is rotated so that the user's heading is at the top of the map. If the user pans the map manually, tracking stops. This setting won't work in the iOS simulator.

Initially, you are going to set userTrackingMode to MKUserTrackingModeFollow, but later we will show you how to give users the ability to control the tracking mode themselves. Set the user tracking mode, as shown in Listing 7-6.

Listing 7-6. Setting the user tracking mode

```
//Control User Location on Map
if ([CLLocationManager locationServicesEnabled])
{
    self.mapView.showsUserLocation = YES;
    [self.mapView setUserTrackingMode:MKUserTrackingModeFollow animated:YES];
}
```

Your `viewDidLoad` method should now resemble Listing 7-7, which combines Listing 7-2 to 7-6.

Listing 7-7. The completed viewDidLoad method

```
- (void)viewDidLoad
{
    [super viewDidLoad];

    self.mapView.delegate = self;

    // Set initial region
    CLLocationCoordinate2D baltimoreLocation =
        CLLocationCoordinate2DMake(39.303, -76.612);
    self.mapView.region =
        MKCoordinateRegionMakeWithDistance(baltimoreLocation, 10000, 10000);

    // Optional Controls
    //    self.mapView.zoomEnabled = NO;
    //    self.mapView.scrollEnabled = NO;

    // Control User Location on Map
    if ([CLLocationManager locationServicesEnabled])
    {
        self.mapView.showsUserLocation = YES;
        [self.mapView setUserTrackingMode:MKUserTrackingModeFollow animated:YES];
    }
}
```

Finally, respond to location updates and update the label with the new location data. This is done in the `mapView:didUpdateUserLocation:` delegate method that you add to your view controller. Your implementation of the method should look like Listing 7-8.

Listing 7-8. Implementing the mapView:didUpdateUserLocation: method

```
-(void)mapView:(MKMapView *)mapView didUpdateUserLocation:(MKUserLocation *)userLocation
{
    self.userLocationLabel.text =
        [NSString stringWithFormat:@" Location: %.5f°, %.5f°",
         userLocation.coordinate.latitude, userLocation.coordinate.longitude];
}
```

You have enough of a start that you can now run your app on the simulator. When the app launches on the simulator, the user is prompted to allow the app access to his location. Figure 7-3 shows your application displaying this prompt. Note that the message includes the location usage description if you provided it in the `.plist` file.

Figure 7-3. *The app's prompt to access location*

If you tap "OK" and there is no sign of your location on the map, start one of the location debug services from the simulator by choosing option Debug ➤ Location ➤ Freeway Drive. This starts the location simulation services on the simulator, showing a map that should pan to the new location. Because you chose freeway drive, you will see the location move as if you were driving in California near Apple. You can, of course, choose one of the other location simulations if you want. See "Testing Location Updates" in Chapter 4 for more information.

User-Controlled Tracking

If users try to pan the map manually, one of the problems they will encounter is that the user location tracking stops. Apple provided a `UIBarButtonItem` class named `MKUserTrackingBarButtonItem`. This button can be added to any `UIToolBar` or `UINavigationbar` and toggles the user tracking modes on the specified map view.

To set this up, add a toolbar to your user interface. Select both the map view and the location label and clear auto layout constraints by selecting "Clear Constraints" in the Resolve Auto Layout Issues menu. From the same menu, choose "add missing constraints" with the toolbar, label, and map view selected. Then create an outlet named "`mapToolbar`" to reference the toolbar.

Delete the button that is added to the toolbar by default, as you will not need it. You will add a button programmatically in just a moment, but for now your user interface should resemble Figure 7-4.

Figure 7-4. Adding a toolbar to the bottom of the view

Now you will add the `MKUserTrackingBarButtonItem` in code. Switch to the view controller's implementation file and scroll to the `viewDidLoad` method. Add the code in Listing 7-9 to the bottom of the method.

Listing 7-9. Adding MKUserTrackingBarButtonItem to viewDidLoad method

```
// Add button for controlling user location tracking
MKUserTrackingBarButtonItem *trackingButton =
    [[MKUserTrackingBarButtonItem alloc] initWithMapView:self.mapView];
[self.mapToolbar setItems: [NSArray arrayWithObject: trackingButton] animated:YES];
```

With this new addition, users can manually pan the map and get back to tracking their location with a tap of the new bar button. Figure 7-5 demonstrates the user-tracking functionality you have implemented.

Figure 7-5. Simulated application with panning and user tracking

Recipe 7-2: Marking Locations with Pins

A common usage of maps is to mark not only your current location and destination, but also various points of interest along the route. In iOS, these highlighted points within the map are called *annotations*. By default, annotations look like pins. This recipe shows you how to add them to your map.

In this recipe, you will build an application similar to the one in Recipe 7-1. Follow these steps to set up the application:

1. Create a new single view application project.

2. Add the Map Kit framework to the project.

3. Add the Core Location framework to the project. In this recipe, you won't use the location services so there's no need to provide a location usage description. You still need to link in the framework, though, or you'll get linker errors when building later.

4. Add a map view to the application's main view from the object library.

5. Create an outlet for referencing the map view in the viewController.h file. Name the outlet "`mapView`."

6. Import the MapKit framework and make your view controller class conform to the `MKMapViewDelegate` protocol. The view controller's header file should now resemble Listing 7-10, with changes from this step in bold.

Listing 7-10. The completed ViewController.h file

```
//
//  ViewController.h
//  Recipe 7-2 Marking Locations wiht Pins
//

#import <UIKit/UIKit.h>
#import <MapKit/MapKit.h>
#import <CoreLocation/CoreLocation.h>

@interface ViewController : UIViewController<MKMapViewDelegate>

@property (weak, nonatomic) IBOutlet MKMapView *mapView;

@end
```

7. Finally, initialize the map view delegate property in the `viewDidLoad` method of the view controller, as shown in Listing 7-11.

Listing 7-11. Initializing the mapView delegate property

```
- (void)viewDidLoad
{
    [super viewDidLoad];
        // Do any additional setup after loading the view, typically from a nib.
    self.mapView.delegate = self;
}
```

Your application is now set up, and you should build and run it to make sure everything is working properly before moving on.

Adding Annotation Objects

Two objects are involved when you display an annotation on the map: the annotation object and the annotation view. The job of the annotation view is to draw an annotation. The annotation view is provided with a drawing context and an annotation object, which holds the data associated with the annotation. In its simplest form, an annotation object contains a title and a coordinate.

To create an annotation object, you can use the built-in `MKPointAnnotation` class that holds properties for title, subtitle, and location. Then all you need to do is to add the annotations to the map view with its `addAnnotation:` or `addAnnotations:` method.

Let's add a few annotations to the map view. Add the code in Listing 7-12 to the `viewDidLoad` method.

Listing 7-12. Creating annotations in the viewDidLoad method

```
- (void)viewDidLoad
{
    [super viewDidLoad];
        // Do any additional setup after loading the view, typically from a nib.
    self.mapView.delegate = self;

    MKPointAnnotation *annotation1 = [[MKPointAnnotation alloc] init];
    annotation1.title = @"Miami";
    annotation1.subtitle = @"Annotation 1";
    annotation1.coordinate = CLLocationCoordinate2DMake(25.802, -80.132);

    MKPointAnnotation *annotation2 = [[MKPointAnnotation alloc] init];
    annotation2.title = @"Denver";
    annotation2.subtitle = @"Annotation 2";
    annotation2.coordinate = CLLocationCoordinate2DMake(39.733, -105.018);

    [self.mapView addAnnotation:annotation1];
    [self.mapView addAnnotation:annotation2];
}
```

We chose to make the pins drop in Miami and Denver, but any coordinates work just as well. If you run this app now, you should see your map with two pins stuck in, as in Figure 7-6. You might need to zoom out to see them; this can be done in the simulator by holding Alt (⌥) to simulate a pinch and dragging outward from the middle of the screen.

Figure 7-6. Application with map and pins

In the beginning of this section, we spoke of two objects being necessary to display an annotation. You might be wondering what happened to the second object, the annotation view. We didn't create one yet, but the annotation objects still show up on the map. The reason is that if you don't provide it, the framework will create instances of the `MKPinAnnotationView` class and use them as annotation views. In the next section, we will create an annotation view.

Changing the Pin Color

The default annotation view displays your annotation as a red pin on the map. Usually, the red color indicates a destination location. The other two possible pin colors of an `MKPinAnnotationView` are green (for starting points) and purple (for user-defined points). If you want a color other than red for your pin, you'll need to create the views yourself, which can be done in the `mapView:viewForAnnotation:` delegate method.

Let's change the pin color to purple for the annotations. Start by adding the `mapView:viewForAnnotation:` method to your view controller, as shown in Listing 7-13.

Listing 7-13. Implementing the mapView:viewForAnnotation: method

```
- (MKAnnotationView *)mapView:(MKMapView *)mapView
viewForAnnotation:(id<MKAnnotation>)annotation
{
    // Returning nil will result in a default annotation view being used
    return nil;
}
```

The map view sends all annotations that are within its current range to the `mapView:viewForAnnotation:` method to retrieve the annotation view it uses to do the drawing. The user location, which is a special kind of annotation, is also sent to this method, so you need to make sure the provided annotation is of the type you expect. Add the bold code in Listing 7-14 to the mapView:viewForAnnotation: method to check for this.

Listing 7-14. Checking for the correct annotation type

```
- (MKAnnotationView *)mapView:(MKMapView *)mapView
viewForAnnotation:(id<MKAnnotation>)annotation
{
    // Don't create annotation views for the user location annotation
    if ([annotation isKindOfClass:[MKPointAnnotation class]])
    {
        // Create and return our own annotation view here
    }

    // Returning nil will result in a default annotation view being used
    return nil;
}
```

To minimize the number of annotation views needed, map views provide a way to reuse annotation views by caching them. The code shown in Listing 7-15 to cache the views looks a lot like the code used to create cells for table views (see Chapter 4).

Listing 7-15. Adding code for caching annotation views in the mapView:viewForAnnotation: method

```
- (MKAnnotationView *)mapView:(MKMapView *)mapView
viewForAnnotation:(id<MKAnnotation>)annotation
{
    // Don't create annotation views for the user location annotation
    if ([annotation isKindOfClass:[MKPointAnnotation class]])
    {
        static NSString *userPinAnnotationId = @"userPinAnnotation";

        // Create an annotation view, but reuse a cached one if available
        MKPinAnnotationView *annotationView =
            (MKPinAnnotationView *)[self.mapView
            dequeueReusableAnnotationViewWithIdentifier:userPinAnnotationId];
        if(annotationView)
        {
            // Cached view found. It'll have the pin color set but not annotation.
            annotationView.annotation = annotation;
        }
        else
        {
            // No cached view were available, create a new one
            annotationView = [[MKPinAnnotationView alloc] initWithAnnotation:annotation
                            reuseIdentifier:userPinAnnotationId];

            // Purple indicates user defined pin
            annotationView.pinColor = MKPinAnnotationColorPurple;
        }

        return annotationView;
    }
    return nil;
}
```

> **Note** The identifier string should be different for every type of annotation view you create. For example, an annotation view that draws red pins should have a different ID than one that draws purple pins. Otherwise, you might get unexpected behavior when you retrieve views from the cache.

If you build and run now you should see the same pins as those in Figure 7-5, but they'll be purple instead of red. Besides changing pin color, a lot more can be done to customize annotations. This is the topic of Recipe 7-3.

Recipe 7-3: Creating Custom Annotations

Most of the time the default `MKPinAnnotationView` objects are incredibly useful, but you might at some point decide you want a different image instead of a pin to represent an annotation on your map. Likewise, you might want to display more usable and attractive callouts when the user taps your annotations. To create a custom annotation view, you will be subclassing the `MKAnnotationView` class. Using Recipe 7-3, you also will create a custom annotation object to hold additional data as well as a detailed view, which is displayed when the user taps your callouts.

Setting Up the Application

To set up the application, you first must create your project the same way you did in the preceding recipes. Follow these steps to set up your app skeleton:

1. Create a new single view application project.

2. Add the Map Kit framework to the project.

3. Add the Core Location framework to the project. In this recipe, you will not use the location services, so there's no need to provide a location usage description. You still need to link in the framework, though, or you'll get linker errors when building later.

4. Add a map view to the application's main view from the object library.

5. Create an outlet for referencing the map view from the object library. Name the outlet "mapView."

6. Import the Map Kit API in `ViewController.h`.

7. Import the MapKit framework and make your view controller class conform to the `MKMapViewDelegate` protocol. The view controller's header file should now look like Listing 7-16, with changes from this step in bold.

Listing 7-16. The finished ViewController.h file

```
//
//  ViewController.h
//  Recipe 7-3 Creating Custom Annotations
//

#import <UIKit/UIKit.h>
#import <MapKit/MapKit.h>

@interface ViewController : UIViewController<MKMapViewDelegate>

@property (weak, nonatomic) IBOutlet MKMapView *mapView;

@end
```

8. Finally, initialize the map view delegate property in the `viewDidLoad` method of the view controller.

```
- (void)viewDidLoad
{
    [super viewDidLoad];
        // Do any additional setup after loading the view, typically from a nib.
    self.mapView.delegate = self;
}
```

Before going any further, you must add an image to be used instead of a pin. For Recipe 7-3 we have chosen a small image, `overlay.png`, shown here in Figure 7-7. You can get this image from the source code download available on the Apress website page for this book. You can, of course, pick any image you like.

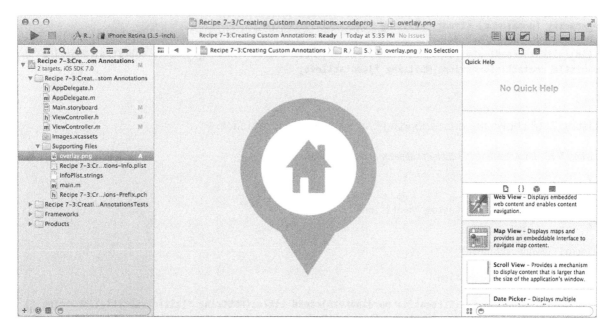

Figure 7-7. *The custom annotation image added to the project*

The image is a bit large to use on a map, so you will be scaling it down later. However, in a real scenario you would scale down the image to the size of your annotation before adding it to the project. This way you save some space and clock cycles because the application won't have to do the scaling at runtime.

Creating a Custom Annotation Class

The next step is to create your custom annotation class. Use the built-in `Objective-C` class template to create a new subclass of `MKPointAnnotation`. Name the new class "MyAnnotation."

MKPointAnnotation already contains properties for the title and the subtitle, so you don't have to declare them in your class. However, to show you how to attach custom data to your annotation objects, you'll extend the class with an additional property to keep contact information. You'll also add a designated initialization method to contain all the annotation setup code. Now make changes to MyAnnotation.h, as shown in Listing 7-17.

Listing 7-17. Adding a custom initializer and contact info property to the MyAnnotation.h file

```
//
//  MyAnnotation.h
//  Recipe 7-3 Customizing Annotations
//

#import <MapKit/MapKit.h>

@interface MyAnnotation : MKPointAnnotation

@property (nonatomic, strong) NSString *contactInformation;

-(id)initWithCoordinate:(CLLocationCoordinate2D)coord title:(NSString *)title subtitle:(NSString *)
subtitle contactInformation:(NSString *)contactInfo;

@end
```

Listing 7-18 shows the corresponding changes to MyAnnotation.m.

Listing 7-18. Implementing the custom initializer and setting properties

```
//
//  MyAnnotation.m
//  Recipe 7-3 Creating Custom Annotations
//

#import "MyAnnotation.h"

@implementation MyAnnotation

-(id)initWithCoordinate:(CLLocationCoordinate2D)coord title:(NSString *)title subtitle:(NSString *)
subtitle contactInformation:(NSString *)contactInfo
{
    self = [super init];
    if (self)
    {
        self.coordinate = coord;
        self.title = title;
        self.subtitle = subtitle;
        self.contactInformation = contactInfo;
    }

    return self;
}

@end
```

Creating a Custom Annotation View

Now you can proceed to create your custom annotation view. As before, create a new Objective-C class, this time with the name "MyAnnotationView" and with "MKAnnotationView" as the parent class.

The only thing you do in the custom annotation view class is to override the initWithAnnotation:r esuseIdentifier: method. That's where all the customization takes place. But before we go ahead and do that, let's take a quick look at the code that's been generated for you in MyAnnotationView.m, as shown in Listing 7-19.

Listing 7-19. Automatically generated code in MyAnnotationView.m

```
// ...

@implementation MyAnnotationView

- (id)initWithFrame:(CGRect)frame
{
    // ...
}

/*
// Only override drawRect: if you perform custom drawing.
// An empty implementation adversely affects performance during animation.
- (void)drawRect:(CGRect)rect
{
    // Drawing code
}
*/

@end
```

Xcode has added an initWithFrame: method to your class. You will not need it so feel free to remove it. For your convenience, Xcode has also added the drawRect: method but commented it out. The drawRect: method is interesting because it provides a way to completely control the drawing of your annotation. We will not use it in this recipe so you can remove it as well.

Add the code in Listing 7-20 to replace the code that was provided for you. This code creates the custom annotation image to be used instead of the pin. Also, the frame of the annotation view is adjusted to the 40 by 40 points that the image is scaled down to.

Listing 7-20. MyAnnotationView with the added custom initializer

```
//
//  MyAnnotationView.m
//  Recipe 7-3 Creating Custom Annotations
//

#import "MyAnnotationView.h"

@implementation MyAnnotationView
```

```
- (id)initWithAnnotation:(id <MKAnnotation>)annotation
reuseIdentifier:(NSString *)reuseIdentifier
{
    self = [super initWithAnnotation:annotation reuseIdentifier:reuseIdentifier];
    if (self)
    {
        UIImage *myImage = [UIImage imageNamed:@"overlay.png"];
        self.image = myImage;
        self.frame = CGRectMake(0, 0, 40, 40);
        // Use contentMode to ensure best scaling of image
        self.contentMode = UIViewContentModeScaleAspectFill;
        // Use centerOffset to adjust the position of the image
        self.centerOffset = CGPointMake(0, -20);
    }
    return self;
}

@end
```

If necessary, you can also adjust the position of the image relative to the coordinates by using the centerOffset property. This is especially useful if the image you are using has a particular point, such as a pin or arrow, that you would like to have at the exact coordinates. As you can see in Listing 7-20, an offset was created for this example using CGMake(0,-20), which moved the relative position of the image up by 20 points. This was necessary to align the point of the image to the coordinate.

Now that your custom classes are all set up, you can return to your view controller to implement your map's delegate method (Listing 7-21). You'll probably recognize a lot of it from the preceding recipes. The main difference is that you don't create instances from MKPinAnnotationView, but rather from the custom MyAnnotationView class.

Listing 7-21. Implementing the map delegate method

```
//
//  ViewController.m
//  Recipe 7-3 Creating Custom Annotations
//

#import "ViewController.h"
#import "MyAnnotation.h"
#import "MyAnnotationView.h"

// ...

@implementation ViewController

// ...

- (MKAnnotationView *)mapView:(MKMapView *)mapView
viewForAnnotation:(id<MKAnnotation>)annotation
```

```
{
    // Don't create annotation views for the user location annotation
    if ([annotation isKindOfClass:[MyAnnotation class]])
    {
        static NSString *myAnnotationId = @"myAnnotation";

        // Create an annotation view, but reuse a cached one if available
        MyAnnotationView *annotationView =
        (MyAnnotationView *)[self.mapView
                            dequeueReusableAnnotationViewWithIdentifier:myAnnotationId];
        if(annotationView)
        {
            // Cached view found, associate it with the annotation
            annotationView.annotation = annotation;
        }
        else
        {
            // No cached view were available, create a new one
            annotationView = [[MyAnnotationView alloc] initWithAnnotation:annotation
                                                        reuseIdentifier:myAnnotationId];
        }

        return annotationView;
    }

    // Use a default annotation view for the user location annotation
    return nil;
}
@end
```

Finally, all you need to run this is some test data. In the viewDidLoad method, add the bold lines in Listing 7-22 to create a couple of annotations and add them to your map.

Listing 7-22. Creating some test data

```
@implementation ViewController

// ...

- (void)viewDidLoad
{
    [super viewDidLoad];
        // Do any additional setup after loading the view, typically from a nib.
    self.mapView.delegate = self;

    MyAnnotation *ann1 = [[MyAnnotation alloc]
        initWithCoordinate: CLLocationCoordinate2DMake(37.68, -97.33)
        title: @"Company 1"
        subtitle: @"Something Catchy"
        contactInformation: @"Call 555-123456"];
```

```
MyAnnotation *ann2 = [[MyAnnotation alloc]
    initWithCoordinate:CLLocationCoordinate2DMake(41.500, -81.695)
    title:@"Company 2"
    subtitle:@"Even More Catchy"
    contactInformation:@"Call 555-654321"];

NSArray *annotations = [NSArray arrayWithObjects: ann1, ann2, nil];
[self.mapView addAnnotations:annotations];
}

// ...

@end
```

At this point, when you run the app you should see your two annotations appear on the map with your image (shrunk down to a reasonable size) over Wichita, Kansas and Cleveland, Ohio. Figure 7-8 provides a simulation of this app.

Figure 7-8. *Application with map and custom annotations*

Customizing the Callouts

Now you will add a few extra lines of code to customize your callouts. First, you will place an image to the left of the annotation's title and subtitle. This is done through the use of the annotationView's property "leftCalloutAccessoryView." You will also add an accessory button to the right side of the callout. You'll use it later to display a detailed view of the annotation.

Return to MyAnnotationView.m and extend the initWithAnnotation:reuseidentifier: method with the code shown in Listing 7-23.

Listing 7-23. Modifying the annotation view in the custom initializer

```
- (id)initWithAnnotation:(id <MKAnnotation>)annotation
reuseIdentifier:(NSString *)reuseIdentifier
{
    self = [super initWithAnnotation:annotation reuseIdentifier:reuseIdentifier];
    if (self)
    {
        UIImage *myImage = [UIImage imageNamed:@"overlay.png"];
        self.image = myImage;
        self.frame = CGRectMake(0, 0, 40, 40);
        //Use contentMode to ensure best scaling of image
        self.contentMode = UIViewContentModeScaleAspectFill;
        //Use centerOffset to adjust the position of the image
        self.centerOffset = CGPointMake(1, 1);

        self.canShowCallout = YES;

        // Left callout accessory view
        UIImageView *leftAccessoryView = [[UIImageView alloc] initWithImage:myImage];
        leftAccessoryView.frame = CGRectMake(0, 0, 20, 20);
        leftAccessoryView.contentMode = UIViewContentModeScaleAspectFill;
        self.leftCalloutAccessoryView = leftAccessoryView;

        // Right callout accessory view
        self.rightCalloutAccessoryView =
            [UIButton buttonWithType:UIButtonTypeDetailDisclosure];
    }
    return self;
}
```

As you can see, we're reusing the annotation image but wrapping it into an image view to scale it down, this time to 20 by 20 points.

If you build and run your application now, your annotations will present callouts such as the one in Figure 7-9.

Figure 7-9. Map with custom annotations, one of which is showing a callout

Adding a Detailed View

At this point, your callouts are set up visually, but there's a massive amount of potential in having those buttons inside the callouts that you haven't tapped into yet. Most map-based apps that use buttons on their callouts usually use the button to push another view controller onto the screen. An application focused on displaying the locations of a specific business on the map might allow the user to view all the details or pictures from a specific location. In the Apple Maps application you can see a similar behavior when you select a business that has been provided by a map search. Selecting the info button gives you details about the business, such as the address and rating.

To increase your functionality, you will implement another one of your map's delegate methods, -mapView:annotationView:calloutAccessoryControlTapped:, and have it present a modal view controller. For the purpose of this recipe, you will have it display only your particular annotation's title, subtitle, and contact information texts.

For this example, we're going to use a mix of storyboards and .xib view files. Start by creating the new class. Name the new class DetailedViewController and make sure it's a subclass of UIViewController. On the file options screen, select the "With XIB for user interface" option. This will create a new class, and a .xib file will now appear with the same class name.

Select the .xib file of DetailedViewController from the project navigator and add three labels to the provided view. Place them near the bottom of the view, as shown in Figure 7-10.

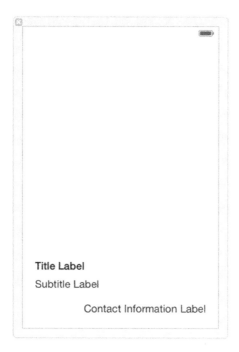

Figure 7-10. DetailedViewController.xib view

Now, create outlets for the three labels. Name them `titleLabel`, `subtitleLabel`, and `contactInformationLabel`, respectively. Also, make additions to the header file, as shown in Listing 7-24.

Listing 7-24. The DetailedViewController.h implementation

```
//
//  DetailedViewController.h
//  Recipe 7-3 Creating Custom Annotations
//

#import <UIKit/UIKit.h>
#import "MyAnnotation.h"

@interface DetailedViewController : UIViewController

@property (weak, nonatomic) IBOutlet UILabel *titleLabel;
@property (weak, nonatomic) IBOutlet UILabel *subtitleLabel;
@property (weak, nonatomic) IBOutlet UILabel *contactInformationLabel;

@property (strong, nonatomic) MyAnnotation *annotation;

-(id)initWithAnnotation:(MyAnnotation *)annotation;

@end
```

In DetailedViewController.m, start by removing the initWithNibName:bundle: method that Xcode added to your class. In its place, implement the initWithAnnotation: method you declared earlier, as shown in Listing 7-25.

Listing 7-25. Implementing the custom initializer in the DetailViewController.m file

```
//
//  DetailedViewController.m
//  Recipe 7-3 Creating Custom Annotations
//

// ...

@implementation DetailedViewController

// ...

-(id)initWithAnnotation:(MyAnnotation *)annotation
{
    self = [super init];
    if (self)
    {
        self.annotation = annotation;
    }

    return self;
}

// ...

@end
```

In the viewDidLoad method of the detailed view controller, add code to initialize the labels with texts from the stored annotation object, as shown in Listing 7-26.

Listing 7-26. The viewDidLoad implementation

```
- (void)viewDidLoad
{
    [super viewDidLoad];
    // Do any additional setup after loading the view from its nib.
    self.titleLabel.text = self.annotation.title;
    self.subtitleLabel.text = self.annotation.subtitle;
    self.contactInformationLabel.text = self.annotation.contactInformation;
}
```

Finally, you are ready to implement your map's delegate method back in your main view controller. In this method, you create and present your DetailedViewController. For this recipe we chose the partial curl transition, which is a pretty cool effect. Listing 7-27 shows how you set it up. Don't forget to import the DetailedViewController into the ViewController.m class.

Listing 7-27. Implementing the mapView:annotationView:calloutAccessoryControlTapped: method

```
#import "ViewController.h"
#import "MyAnnotation.h"
#import "MyAnnotationView.h"
#import "DetailedViewController.h"

@interface ViewController ()
//...

-(void)mapView:(MKMapView *)mapView annotationView:(MKAnnotationView *)view
calloutAccessoryControlTapped:(UIControl *)control
{
    DetailedViewController *dvc = [[DetailedViewController alloc]
        initWithAnnotation:view.annotation];
    dvc.modalTransitionStyle = UIModalTransitionStylePartialCurl;
    [self presentViewController:dvc animated:YES completion:^{}];
}

@end
```

Now you're done with Recipe 7-3. Your application should resemble Figure 7-11 when you tap a detail disclosure button in one of your customized callouts.

Figure 7-11. Application responding to the tapping of callouts

Recipe 7-4: Dragging a Pin

Using this recipe, you'll make a little tool that allows you to drag a pin on a map and read its location from the console.

Start by creating a new map-based application, just as you did in the preceding recipes. Here are the steps again:

1. Create a new single view application project.

2. Add the Map Kit framework to the project.

3. Add the Core Location framework to the project.

4. Add a map view to the application's main view.

5. Create an outlet for referencing the map view. Name the outlet "mapView."

6. Import the MapKit framework and make your view controller class conform to the MKMapViewDelegate protocol. The view controller's header file should now look like Listing 7-28.

Listing 7-28. The finished ViewController.h file

```
//
// ViewController.h
// Recipe 7-4 Dragging a Pin
//

#import <UIKit/UIKit.h>
#import <MapKit/MapKit.h>

@interface ViewController : UIViewController<MKMapViewDelegate>

@property (weak, nonatomic) IBOutlet MKMapView *mapView;

@end
```

7. Finally, initialize the map view delegate property in the viewDidLoad method of the view controller, as shown in Listing 7-29.

Listing 7-29. Initializing the delegate property in the viewDidLoad method

```
- (void)viewDidLoad
{
    [super viewDidLoad];
        // Do any additional setup after loading the view, typically from a nib.
    self.mapView.delegate = self;
}
```

Adding a Draggable Pin

You're going to make a really simple tool with a single pin on the map that the user can drag around. Let's start by placing the pin in the map when the application has loaded the main view by modifying the viewDIdLoad method, as shown in Listing 7-30.

Listing 7-30. Placing a pin on the map when the application loads

```
- (void)viewDidLoad
{
    [super viewDidLoad];
        // Do any additional setup after loading the view, typically from a nib.
    self.mapView.delegate = self;

    MKPointAnnotation *annotation = [[MKPointAnnotation alloc] init];
    annotation.coordinate = CLLocationCoordinate2DMake(39.303, -76.612);
    [self.mapView addAnnotation:annotation];
}
```

We've put the pin in Denver, but soon you'll be able to replace it with coordinates of your own using this tool. But first you need to make the pin draggable. To do that you need to customize the annotation view that displays your pin, as shown in Listing 7-31. The code is nearly identical to the one used in Recipes 7-2 and 7-3, except that you now set the draggable property.

Listing 7-31. The mapView:viewForAnnotation: method implementation

```
- (MKAnnotationView *)mapView:(MKMapView *)mapView
viewForAnnotation:(id<MKAnnotation>)annotation
{
    // Don't create annotation views for the user location annotation
    if ([annotation isKindOfClass:[MKPointAnnotation class]])
    {
        static NSString *draggableAnnotationId = @"draggableAnnotation";

        // Create an annotation view, but reuse a cached one if available
        MKPinAnnotationView *annotationView =
        (MKPinAnnotationView *)[self.mapView
            dequeueReusableAnnotationViewWithIdentifier:draggableAnnotationId];
        if(annotationView)
        {
            // Cached view found, associate it with the annotation
            annotationView.annotation = annotation;
        }
        else
        {
            // No cached view was available; create a new one
            annotationView = [[MKPinAnnotationView alloc] initWithAnnotation:annotation
                reuseIdentifier:draggableAnnotationId];
            annotationView.pinColor = MKPinAnnotationColorPurple;
            annotationView.draggable = YES;
        }
```

```
        return annotationView;
    }

    // Use a default annotation view for the user location annotation
    return nil;
}
```

If you run the application now, you can drag the pin from Denver to any other place of your choice. However, let's turn this cool but somewhat useless app into a tool. You will intercept when the user drops the pin and output the new location to the console. To do this you will make use of the `mapVie w:annotationView:didChangeDragState:fromOldState:` delegate method. The method name is long but self-explanatory. Add Listing 7-32 to your view controller.

Listing 7-32. Implementing the delegate for detecting the changed state of a pin

```
-(void)mapView:(MKMapView *)mapView annotationView:(MKAnnotationView *)view
didChangeDragState:(MKAnnotationViewDragState)newState
fromOldState:(MKAnnotationViewDragState)oldState
{
    if (newState == MKAnnotationViewDragStateEnding)
    {
        MKPointAnnotation *annotation = view.annotation;
        NSLog(@"\nPin Location: %f, %f (Lat, Long)",
            annotation.coordinate.latitude, view.annotation.coordinate.longitude);
    }

}
```

Run the application in the simulator and drag the pin to a new location. The console now shows the world coordinates of the pin, as in Figure 7-12. The tool can be quite useful if you want to create some location test data of your own.

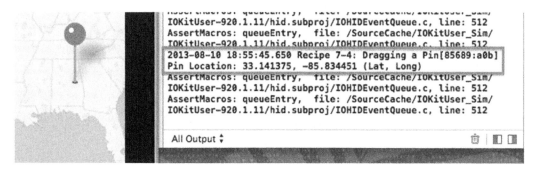

Figure 7-12. The tool prints new pin locations to the console

Not bad for a few lines of code. Now let's move on to adding overlays in a map.

Recipe 7-5: Adding Overlays to a Map

An annotation, as you've seen in the preceding recipes, is a marking on a map. Because annotations are associated with a single coordinate, they stay the same size at all times, even when the user zooms in or out in the map.

This recipe looks at another type of map marking called *overlays*. These are shapes such as circles or polygons and, unlike annotations, they scale when the map zoom changes.

You will be adding three kinds of overlays to your MapView: circle, polygon, and line overlays. The process to add these is very similar to that of adding annotations, but this time you will not create a custom class for the overlays as you did with annotations in Recipe 7-3.

Again, start by setting up a new map-based application. We trust you know the steps by now, but you could always refer to the preceding recipes for guidance.

Creating the Overlays

Again, you will create your test data in the viewDidLoad method of your view controller. First is a circle overlay over large parts of Mexico. Add Listing 7-33 to the viewDidLoad method.

Listing 7-33. Creating a circle overlay

```
CLLocationCoordinate2D mexicoCityLocation = CLLocationCoordinate2DMake(19.808, -98.965);
MKCircle *circleOverlay = [MKCircle circleWithCenterCoordinate:mexicoCityLocation
                           radius:500000];
```

Next, create a polygon overlay. Note that a polygon must always start and end in the same location. Add Listing 7-34 to the viewDidLoad method.

Listing 7-34. Creating a polygon overlay

```
CLLocationCoordinate2D polyCoords[5] =
{
    CLLocationCoordinate2DMake(39.9, -76.6),
    CLLocationCoordinate2DMake(36.7, -84.0),
    CLLocationCoordinate2DMake(33.1, -89.4),
    CLLocationCoordinate2DMake(27.3, -80.8),
    CLLocationCoordinate2DMake(39.9, -76.6)
};
MKPolygon *polygonOverlay = [MKPolygon polygonWithCoordinates:polyCoords count:5];
```

Add a line overlay to the viewDidLoad method. Listing 7-35 shows this code.

Listing 7-35. Creating a line overlay

```
CLLocationCoordinate2D pathCoords[2] =
{
    CLLocationCoordinate2DMake(46.8, -100.8),
    CLLocationCoordinate2DMake(43.7, -70.4)
};
MKPolyline *pathOverlay = [MKPolyline polylineWithCoordinates:pathCoords count:2];
```

Finally, add the three overlays to the map. In iOS 7, Apple provides a new feature with overlays. Now you can specify a level. You have two options for the overlays: they are drawn either above the roads or above the roads and labels. You can use the properties MKOverlayLevelAboveRoads or MKOverlayLevelAboveLabels, respectively. In our example, we'll put the label above the roads so the text is easier to read; in other words, the labels will be above the overlay. Add the code in Listing 7-36 to the viewDidLoad method to do this.

Listing 7-36. Adding the overlays to the map above the roads but below the labels

```
[self.mapView addOverlays:[NSArray arrayWithObjects: circleOverlay, polygonOverlay, pathOverlay, nil]
                level:MKOverlayLevelAboveRoads];
```

If you build and run your application at this point you'll see a map, but none of the overlays you've created have been added. This is because you haven't provided the overlay view objects. This is done in the mapView:rendererForOverlay: delegate method, which you'll add to your view controller. Add the implementation in Listing 7-37 to the view controller.

Listing 7-37. Implementing the mapView:rendererForOverlay: delegate method

```
-(MKOverlayRenderer *)mapView:(MKMapView *)mapView rendererForOverlay:(id )overlay
{
    if([overlay isKindOfClass:[MKCircle class]])
    {
        MKCircleRenderer *renderer = [[MKCircleRenderer alloc] initWithOverlay:overlay];

        //Display settings
        renderer.lineWidth = 1;
        renderer.strokeColor = [UIColor blueColor];
        renderer.fillColor = [[UIColor blueColor] colorWithAlphaComponent:0.5];
        return renderer;
    }
    if([overlay isKindOfClass:[MKPolygon class]])
    {
        MKPolygonRenderer *renderer= [[MKPolygonRenderer alloc] initWithOverlay:overlay];

        //Display settings
        renderer.lineWidth=1;
        renderer.strokeColor=[UIColor blueColor];
        renderer.fillColor=[[UIColor blueColor] colorWithAlphaComponent:0.5];
        return renderer;
    }
    else if ([overlay isKindOfClass:[MKPolyline class]])
    {
        MKPolylineRenderer *renderer = [[MKPolylineRenderer alloc] initWithOverlay:overlay];

        //Display settings
        renderer.lineWidth = 3;
        renderer.strokeColor = [UIColor blueColor];
        return renderer;
    }

    return nil;
}
```

As you can see from the preceding code, each overlay shape type has a corresponding overlay view type that you use to instantiate the view objects. Each view class has similar properties for customizing the appearance of the overlay, such as colors and a transparency (alpha) component.

You're finished with this recipe. When you build and run the application, you should see a screen resembling the one in Figure 7-13.

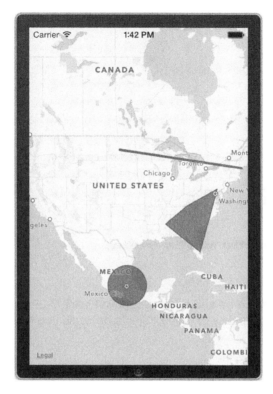

Figure 7-13. *An app with a circle, a polygon, and a line overlay*

Recipe 7-6: Grouping Annotations Dynamically

When it comes to using annotations on a map view, a common problem is the possibility of having many annotations appear very close to each other, cluttering up the screen and making the application difficult to use. One solution is to group annotations based on the location and the size of the visible map. Recipe 7-6 employs a simple algorithm that, when the visible region changes, compares the location of the annotations and temporarily removes those that are too close to others.

First, you need to create a new map-based application project. Refer to Recipe 7-1 for details on how to do this.

A Forest of Pins

Let's start by creating the test data, 1,000 pins randomly distributed within a relatively small area on the map. First, you need a couple of instance variables, one to keep track of your current zoom level and a mutable array to hold your annotations. Make the changes shown in bold in Listing 7-38 to your ViewController.h file.

Listing 7-38. The ViewController.h file with added property and instance variables

```
//
//  ViewController.h
//  Recipe 7-6 Grouping Annotations Dynamically
//

#import <UIKit/UIKit.h>
#import <MapKit/MapKit.h>

@interface ViewController : UIViewController<MKMapViewDelegate>
{
    CLLocationDegrees _zoomLevel;
    NSMutableArray *_annotations;
}

@property (weak, nonatomic) IBOutlet MKMapView *mapView;

@end
```

Now switch to the implementation file and add the code in Listing 7-39 to instantiate the _annotations array. Give the array an initial capacity of 1,000 objects because you'll be making that many annotations soon.

Listing 7-39. Adding code to instantiate the _annotations array

```
- (void)viewDidLoad
{
    [super viewDidLoad];
    // Do any additional setup after loading the view, typically from a nib.
    self.mapView.delegate = self;

    _annotations = [[NSMutableArray alloc] initWithCapacity:1000];
}
```

Next, create a custom annotation class. As usual, use the Objective-C class template to add the files to your project. Make sure to use NSObject as the parent class and name the new class "Hotspot."

To make the new class an annotation class, make it conform to the MKAnnotation protocol. Also, to make it easy to instantiate annotations with your new class, add an initializing method that takes a coordinate, a title, and a subtitle. The header file should now look like Listing 7-40.

Listing 7-40. The completed Hotspot.h file

```
//
//  Hotspot.h
//  Recipe 7-6 Grouping Annotations Dynamically
//
#import <Foundation/Foundation.h>
#import <MapKit/MapKit.h>

@interface Hotspot : NSObject<MKAnnotation>
{
    CLLocationCoordinate2D _coordinate;
    NSString *_title;
    NSString *_subtitle;
}

@property (nonatomic) CLLocationCoordinate2D coordinate;
@property (nonatomic, readonly, copy) NSString *title;
@property (nonatomic, readonly, copy) NSString *subtitle;

-(id)initWithCoordinate:(CLLocationCoordinate2D)coordinate title:(NSString *)title
subtitle:(NSString *)subtitle;

@end
```

And the corresponding implementation, as shown in Listing 7-41.

Listing 7-41. Starting implementation of the Hotspot.m file

```
//
//  Hotspot.m
//  Recipe 7-6 Grouping Annotations Dynamically
//

#import "Hotspot.h"

@implementation Hotspot

-(id)initWithCoordinate:(CLLocationCoordinate2D)coordinate
title:(NSString *)title subtitle:(NSString *)subtitle
{
    self = [super init];
    if (self) {
        self.coordinate = coordinate;
        self.title = title;
        self.subtitle = subtitle;
    }
    return self;
}
```

```objc
-(CLLocationCoordinate2D)coordinate
{
    return _coordinate;
}

-(void)setCoordinate:(CLLocationCoordinate2D)coordinate
{
    _coordinate = coordinate;
}

-(NSString *)title
{
    return _title;
}

-(void)setTitle:(NSString *)title
{
    _title = title;
}

-(NSString *)subtitle
{
    return _subtitle;
}

-(void)setSubtitle:(NSString *)subtitle
{
    _subtitle = subtitle;
}
```

@end

You'll also define a few constants that set up your starting coordinates and grouping parameters. These are also used to help generate some random locations for demonstration purposes. Place the statements in Listing 7-42 before your import statements in the ViewController.m file.

Listing 7-42. Constant definitions

```objc
#define centerLat 39.7392
#define centerLong -104.9842
#define spanDeltaLat 4.9
#define spanDeltaLong 5.8
#define scaleLat 9.0
#define scaleLong 11.0
```

Next, you need some testing data. Begin by importing Hotspot.h in at the top of your ViewController.m file (Listing 7-43).

Listing 7-43. Hotspot.h import statement

```objc
#import "Hotspot.h"
```

Listing 7-44 shows two methods that generate some 1,000 hotspots for you to use, all within fairly close proximity to each other, so that you can see what kind of issue you are working with. Add these to the view controller.

Listing 7-44. Methods to generate 1,000 hotspots

```
-(float)randomFloatFrom:(float)a to:(float)b
{
    float random = ((float) rand()) / (float) RAND_MAX;
    float diff = b - a;
    float r = random * diff;
    return a + r;
}

-(void)generateAnnotations
{
    srand((unsigned)time(0));

    for (int i=0; i<1000; i++)
    {
        CLLocationCoordinate2D randomLocation =
            CLLocationCoordinate2DMake(
                                [self randomFloatFrom:37.0 to:42.0],
                                [self randomFloatFrom:-103.0 to:-107.0]         );

        Hotspot *place = [
            [Hotspot alloc]
            initWithCoordinate:randomLocation
            title: [NSString stringWithFormat:@"Place %d title", i]
            subtitle: [NSString stringWithFormat:@"Place %d subtitle", i]
        ];
        [_annotations addObject:place];
    }
}
```

Now that you have your method for generating testing data, you'll make sure to invoke it in your viewDidLoad method, then add the annotations to the map and adjust its region to display them all. Listing 7-45 shows the code necessary to do that.

Listing 7-45. Updating the viewDidLoad method to invoke new methods and add annotations

```
- (void)viewDidLoad
{
    [super viewDidLoad];
        // Do any additional setup after loading the view, typically from a nib.
    self.mapView.delegate = self;

    _annotations = [[NSMutableArray alloc] initWithCapacity:1000];

    [self generateAnnotations];
    // The line below is for setup purposes only. It will be unnecessary
    // when grouping is implemented.
    [self.mapView addAnnotations:_annotations];
```

```
    CLLocationCoordinate2D centerPoint = {centerLat, centerLong};
    MKCoordinateSpan coordinateSpan = MKCoordinateSpanMake(spanDeltaLat, spanDeltaLong);
    MKCoordinateRegion coordinateRegion =
        MKCoordinateRegionMake(centerPoint, coordinateSpan);

    [self.mapView setRegion:coordinateRegion];
    [self.mapView regionThatFits:coordinateRegion];
}
```

Finally, you need to implement your map's viewForAnnotation method so you can correctly display your pins. Listing 7-46 is similar to the one used in the preceding recipes.

Listing 7-46. Implementing the mapView:viewForAnnotation: method

```
- (MKAnnotationView *)mapView:(MKMapView *)mapView viewForAnnotation:(id <MKAnnotation>)annotation
{
    // if it's the user location, just return nil.
    if ([annotation isKindOfClass:[MKUserLocation class]])
        return nil;
        else
    {
        static NSString *startPinId = @"StartPinIdentifier";
        MKPinAnnotationView *startPin =
            (id)[mapView dequeueReusableAnnotationViewWithIdentifier:startPinId];
                if (startPin == nil)
        {
            startPin = [[MKPinAnnotationView alloc]
                        initWithAnnotation:annotation
                        reuseIdentifier:startPinId];
            startPin.canShowCallout = YES;
            startPin.animatesDrop = YES;
        }
        return startPin;
    }
}
```

At this point, if you run the application you should see a view resembling Figure 7-14, which a nice illustration of the problem you are trying to solve.

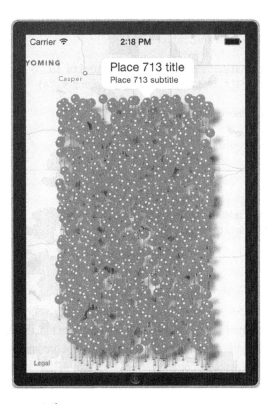

Figure 7-14. A map with far too many annotations

Implementing a Solution

To properly iterate through your annotations and group them, you will be going through each pin and determining how it should be placed. If it is close to another pin that has already been dropped, it will be considered "found," and it will be removed from the map. If not, you will add it to the list of those already in the map, and add it to the map itself as an annotation. The method in Listing 7-47 provides an efficient implementation and should be placed in your view controller's .m file.

Listing 7-47. Method for iterating through annotations and grouping them

```
-(void)group:(NSArray *)annotations
{
    float latDelta = self.mapView.region.span.latitudeDelta / scaleLat;
    float longDelta = self.mapView.region.span.longitudeDelta / scaleLong;
    NSMutableArray *visibleAnnotations = [[NSMutableArray alloc] initWithCapacity:0];

    for (Hotspot *current in annotations)
    {
        CLLocationDegrees lat = current.coordinate.latitude;
        CLLocationDegrees longi = current.coordinate.longitude;
```

```
        bool found = FALSE;
        for (Hotspot *temp in visibleAnnotations)
        {
            if(fabs(temp.coordinate.latitude - lat) < latDelta &&
               fabs(temp.coordinate.longitude - longi) < longDelta)
            {
                [self.mapView removeAnnotation:current];
                found = TRUE;
                break;
            }
        }
        if (!found)
        {
            [visibleAnnotations addObject:current];
            [self.mapView addAnnotation:current];
        }
    }
}
```

> **Note**   In this method, you use the fabs function. This is different from the abs function in that it is
> specifically used for floats. Using the abs function here would result in grouping only at the integer level of
> coordinates, and your app would not work correctly.

Next, you need to deal with your application's regrouping the points every time the visible section
of the map is changed. This is fairly easy to do by implementing the delegate method shown in
Listing 7-48.

Listing 7-48. Implementation of the mapView:regionDidChangeAnimated: delegate method

```
-(void)mapView:(MKMapView *)mapView regionDidChangeAnimated:(BOOL)animated
{
    if (_zoomLevel != mapView.region.span.longitudeDelta)
    {
        [self group:_annotations];
        _zoomLevel = mapView.region.span.longitudeDelta;
    }
}
```

> **Note**   When implementing these methods, make sure that any methods that use the -group: method are
> implemented after it, otherwise the compiler will complain. Another way to solve this problem is to simply
> declare the (void)group(NSArray *)annotations method in your header file or in a private
> @interface section.

Now you can remove the following line from the `viewDidLoad method`, as its function will be performed by your group: method.

```
[self.mapView addAnnotations:_annotations];
```

You don't need to call the group: method at the end of your `viewDidLoad` method because when the map is first displayed, your delegate method -`mapView: regionDidChangeAnimated:` is called and does the initial grouping automatically.

Upon running the app now, you should see your map populated with significantly fewer annotations, somewhat regularly distributed, as in Figure 7-15. When zooming in or out, you can see annotations appear or disappear, respectively, as the map changes.

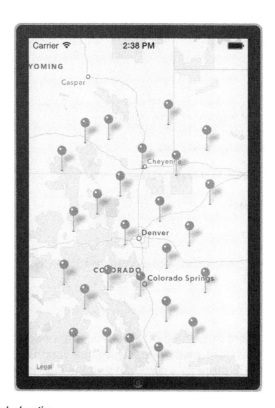

Figure 7-15. Grouped annotations by location

Adding Color Coding

Your annotations are correctly grouping at this point, but you have a new issue. You cannot easily tell whether a single annotation is standing on its own or whether it is encapsulating multiple hotspots. To correct this problem, you can add functionality to allow hotspots to keep track of the number of other hotspots they represent.

First, you need to go to your `Hotspot` class and add a mutable array property—`places`. You also need to add a few method definitions that you can use shortly to help manage this array. Listing 7-49 shows lines in bold that need to be added to `Hotspot.h`.

Listing 7-49. Modification of the Hotspot.h to add method definitions and a mutable array

```
//
//  Hotspot.h
//  Recipe 7-6 Grouping Annotations Dynamically
//

#import <MapKit/MapKit.h>

@interface Hotspot : NSObject<MKAnnotation>
{
    CLLocationCoordinate2D _coordinate;
    NSString *_title;
    NSString *_subtitle;
}

@property (nonatomic) CLLocationCoordinate2D coordinate;
@property (nonatomic, copy) NSString *title;
@property (nonatomic, copy) NSString *subtitle;

@property (nonatomic, strong) NSMutableArray *places;

-(void)addPlace:(Hotspot *)hotspot;
-(int)placesCount;
-(void)cleanPlaces;

-(id)initWithCoordinate:(CLLocationCoordinate2D)coordinate title:(NSString *)title
subtitle:(NSString *)subtitle;

@end
```

Not only do you need to implement these methods, but you also need to change your `-initWithCoordinate:title:subtitle:` method to ensure that your `places` array is correctly created. You also have to change the `title` property's getter so that the callout title shows the number of hotspots represented. Your implementation file should now look like Listing 7-50 (some unchanged getters and setters have been removed for brevity).

Listing 7-50. The refactored Hotspot.m file

```
//
//  Hotspot.m
//  Recipe 7-6 Grouping Annotations Dynamically
//

#import "Hotspot.h"

@implementation Hotspot
```

```
-(id)initWithCoordinate:(CLLocationCoordinate2D)coordinate title:(NSString *)title
subtitle:(NSString *)subtitle
{
    self = [super init];
    if (self) {
        self.coordinate = coordinate;
        self.title = title;
        self.subtitle = subtitle;
        self.places = [[NSMutableArray alloc] initWithCapacity:0];
    }
    return self;
}

// ...

-(NSString *)title
{
    if ([self placesCount] == 1)
    {
        return _title;
    }
    else
        return [NSString stringWithFormat:@"%i Places", [self.places count]];
}

-(void)addPlace:(Hotspot *)hotspot
{
    [self.places addObject:hotspot];
}

-(int)placesCount
{
    return [self.places count];
}

-(void)cleanPlaces
{
    [self.places removeAllObjects];
    [self.places addObject:self];
}

@end
```

The foregoing placesCount method is not necessary; it just makes accessing the number of places represented by a single hotspot slightly easier. Your cleanPlaces method is used simply to reset the places array whenever you regroup your annotations. All you have to do now is add the two lines to the group: method:, as shown in Listing 7-51.

Listing 7-51. Modifying the group: method to includes methods for counting and clearing places

```
-(void)group:(NSArray *)annotations
{
    float latDelta = self.mapView.region.span.latitudeDelta / scaleLat;
    float longDelta = self.mapView.region.span.longitudeDelta / scaleLong;
    [_annotations makeObjectsPerformSelector:@selector(cleanPlaces)];
    NSMutableArray *visibleAnnotations = [[NSMutableArray alloc] initWithCapacity:0];

    for (Hotspot *current in annotations)
    {
        CLLocationDegrees lat = current.coordinate.latitude;
        CLLocationDegrees longi = current.coordinate.longitude;

        bool found = FALSE;
        for (Hotspot *temp in visibleAnnotations)
        {
            if(fabs(temp.coordinate.latitude - lat) < latDelta &&
                fabs(temp.coordinate.longitude - longi) < longDelta)
            {
                [self.mapView removeAnnotation:current];
                found = TRUE;
                [temp addPlace:current];
                break;
            }
        }
        if (!found)
        {
            [visibleAnnotations addObject:current];
            [self.mapView addAnnotation:current];
        }
    }
}
```

Now you have a fairly easy way to determine whether any given hotspot is representing any other hotspot, but only by selecting that specific hotspot. It would be much better if you could easily see which hotspots are groups and which are individuals. To do this, give each hotspot a pointer to its own MKPinAnnotationView. This allows you to control how an annotation is presented based on the number of places it represents. In this case, you use this reference to display a red pin for an individual and a green pin for a grouped hotspot.

First, you will add the following property to your Hotspot.h file:

```
@property (nonatomic, strong) MKPinAnnotationView *annotationView;
```

Next, you need to tell your map's delegate how to display the pins correctly, as shown in the new version of your viewForAnnotation: method, located in the ViewController.m file. Listing 7-52 shows the delegate method implementation.

Listing 7-52. New implementation of the mapView: viewForAnnotation: method

```
- (MKAnnotationView *)mapView:(MKMapView *)mapView viewForAnnotation:(id <MKAnnotation>)annotation
{
    // if it's the user location, just return nil.
    if ([annotation isKindOfClass:[MKUserLocation class]])
        return nil;
        else
    {
        static NSString *startPinId = @"StartPinIdentifier";
        MKPinAnnotationView *startPin =
            (id)[mapView dequeueReusableAnnotationViewWithIdentifier:startPinId];
                if (startPin == nil)
        {
            startPin = [[MKPinAnnotationView alloc]
                        initWithAnnotation:annotation reuseIdentifier:startPinId];
            startPin.canShowCallout = YES;
            startPin.animatesDrop = YES;

            Hotspot *place = annotation;
            place.annotationView = startPin;
            if ([place placesCount] > 1)
            {
                startPin.pinColor = MKPinAnnotationColorGreen;
            }
            else if ([place placesCount] == 1)
            {
                startPin.pinColor = MKPinAnnotationColorRed;
            }
        }

        return startPin;
    }
}
```

This makes all your annotations correctly appear as either green or red, depending on whether they are groups or individual hotspots. However, if you zoom in on a specific green annotation, it will not correctly change color as it goes from a group to an individual. As your final step to correct this problem, add code to the mapView:regionDidChangeAnimated: method to change the pin color based on the number of places represented, as shown in Listing 7-53.

Listing 7-53. The updated mapView:regionDidChangeAnimated: method

```
-(void)mapView:(MKMapView *)mapView regionDidChangeAnimated:(BOOL)animated
{
    if (_zoomLevel != mapView.region.span.longitudeDelta)
    {
        [self group:_annotations];
        _zoomLevel = mapView.region.span.longitudeDelta;

        NSSet *visibleAnnotations =
            [mapView annotationsInMapRect:mapView.visibleMapRect];
        for (Hotspot *place in visibleAnnotations)
```

```
    {
        if ([place placesCount] > 1)
            place.annotationView.pinColor = MKPinAnnotationColorGreen;
        else
            place.annotationView.pinColor = MKPinAnnotationColorRed;
    }

  }
}
```

Now any pins that represent groups of hotspots are green, while individual ones are red, as demonstrated in Figure 7-16.

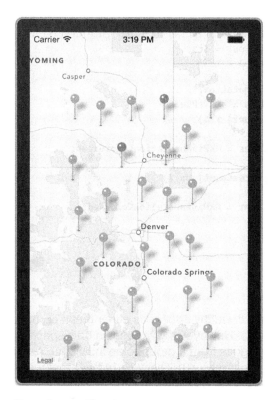

Figure 7-16. *Grouped annotations with number-specific colors*

Recipe 7-7: Starting Maps from Your App

In iO7, an API called MKMapItem is available that makes it easy to interact with the built-in Maps app. Instead of building your own half-baked map features you can now, with only a couple of lines of code, turn your users over to the one app that specializes in providing maps and directions. For many apps, this makes perfect sense. After all, map support is a nice feature but not the main focus for most apps.

Let's build a really simple application with three buttons that start Maps in different ways. Use the following steps to get started:

1. Start by creating a new single view application and link the Map Kit and the Core Location frameworks to it.

2. Import the Mapkit framework in the header file.

3. Add three buttons and configure them to look like Figure 7-17.

Figure 7-17. User interface for starting Maps in three ways

4. Create actions for the buttons with the following respective names:

    ▫ Button Action: `startWithOnePlacemark`

    ▫ Button Action: `startWithMultiplePlacemarks`

    ▫ Button Action: `startInDirectionsMode`

Adding Map Items

We'll start with the simplest case, launching Maps with a single map item. We'll show you the steps first and then the complete implementation of the `startWithOnePlacemark:` action method.

First, create a new map item for the location of the famous Big Ben in London, as shown in Listing 7-54. A map item encapsulates a placemark that in turn represents a location coordinate, so start by defining the coordinate.

Listing 7-54. Creating a map item for the Big Ben location

```
CLLocationCoordinate2D bigBenLocation =
    CLLocationCoordinate2DMake(51.50065200, -0.12483300);
```

Listing 7-55 shows how to create a placemark. The address dictionary can be used to provide address information for the placemark to the Maps app. Keep it simple, though, and send in `nil`.

Listing 7-55. Creating a placemark

```
MKPlacemark *bigBenPlacemark =
    [[MKPlacemark alloc] initWithCoordinate:bigBenLocation addressDictionary:nil];
```

With the placemark you are ready to create the map item that you will send to the Maps app later. Listing 7-56 shows how to create this. Besides the address dictionary of the placemark object, `MKMapItem` has properties for providing three additional pieces of information associated with the map item: name, phone, and URL. For this recipe, the name property is sufficient.

Listing 7-56. Creating a map item

```
MKMapItem *bigBenItem = [[MKMapItem alloc] initWithPlacemark:bigBenPlacemark];
bigBenItem.name = @"Big Ben";
```

> **Note**   Often, you'll need to deal with placemarks you receive from the Core Location framework. These placemarks have a different class (`CLPlacemark`) from the one in the Map Kit framework (`MKPlacemark`). However, you can use the `initWithPlacemark:` method to initialize a Map Kit placemark with one from Core Location.

Listing 7-57 shows how to ask Maps to launch with your map item using the `openInMapsWithLaunchOptions:` method.

Listing 7-57. Asking Maps to launch with a map item

```
[bigBenItem openInMapsWithLaunchOptions:nil];
```

Combining Listing 7-54 to 7-57, the complete action method looks like Listing 7-58.

Listing 7-58. The complete startWithOnePlacemark: method

```
- (IBAction)startWithOnePlacemark:(id)sender
{
    CLLocationCoordinate2D bigBenLocation = CLLocationCoordinate2DMake(51.50065200, -0.12483300);
    MKPlacemark *bigBenPlacemark = [[MKPlacemark alloc] initWithCoordinate:bigBenLocation
addressDictionary:nil];
    MKMapItem *bigBenItem = [[MKMapItem alloc] initWithPlacemark:bigBenPlacemark];
    bigBenItem.name = @"Big Ben";

    [bigBenItem openInMapsWithLaunchOptions:nil];
}
```

If you build and run now, you can press the first button and launch Maps with a pin showing the location of the famous clock tower of London, as in Figure 7-18.

Figure 7-18. Maps launched showing Big Ben

When launching Maps with multiple map items, you'll need to use the openMapsWithItems:launchOpt ions: class method of MKMapItem. It takes an array with map items, but the rest is the same.

Go to the next action method, startWithMultiplePlacemarks, and implement it as shown in Listing 7-59.

Listing 7-59. The startWithMultiplePlacemarks: method implementation

```
- (IBAction)startWithMultiplePlacemarks:(id)sender
{
    CLLocationCoordinate2D bigBenLocation = CLLocationCoordinate2DMake(51.50065200, -0.12483300);
    MKPlacemark *bigBenPlacemark = [[MKPlacemark alloc] initWithCoordinate:bigBenLocation
addressDictionary:nil];
    MKMapItem *bigBenItem = [[MKMapItem alloc] initWithPlacemark:bigBenPlacemark];
    bigBenItem.name = @"Big Ben";

    CLLocationCoordinate2D westminsterLocation = CLLocationCoordinate2DMake(51.50054300,
-0.13570200);
    MKPlacemark *westminsterPlacemark = [[MKPlacemark alloc] initWithCoordinate:westminsterLocation
addressDictionary:nil];
    MKMapItem *westminsterItem = [[MKMapItem alloc] initWithPlacemark:westminsterPlacemark];
    westminsterItem.name = @"Westminster Abbey";

    NSArray *items = [[NSArray alloc] initWithObjects:bigBenItem, westminsterItem, nil];
    [MKMapItem openMapsWithItems:items launchOptions:nil];
}
```

If you build and run now you can see two pins, one for Big Ben and one for Westminster Abbey, as in Figure 7-19.

Figure 7-19. Maps launched with two map items

Launching in Directions Mode

Another cool feature is providing the user with turn-by-turn directions in the Maps app. From there, the user can select any placemark and ask Maps how to get there by car or by foot. It is possible for your app to employ this great feature to provide value to your users in a more direct way by launching Maps in directions mode. Let's go ahead and do that in the last action.

To start Maps in directions mode, all you need to do is to provide an options dictionary with the MKLaunchOptionsDirectionsModeKey set to either MKLaunchOptionsDirectionsModeWalking or MKLaunchOptionsDirectionsModeDriving. The code in Listing 7-60 launches Maps in directions mode, showing the walking path between Westminster Abbey and Big Ben, as in Figure 7-20. Add it to the startInDirectionsMode action method so that it gets triggered when the user hits the third button in your app, as seen in Listing 7-60.

Figure 7-20. Maps launched in directions mode

Listing 7-60. Implementation of the startInDirectionsMode: method

```
- (IBAction)startInDirectionsMode:(id)sender
{
    CLLocationCoordinate2D bigBenLocation =
        CLLocationCoordinate2DMake(51.50065200, -0.12483300);
    MKPlacemark *bigBenPlacemark = [[MKPlacemark alloc]
        initWithCoordinate:bigBenLocation addressDictionary:nil];
```

```
    MKMapItem *bigBenItem = [[MKMapItem alloc] initWithPlacemark:bigBenPlacemark];
    bigBenItem.name = @"Big Ben";

    CLLocationCoordinate2D westminsterLocation =
        CLLocationCoordinate2DMake(51.50054300, -0.13570200);
    MKPlacemark *westminsterPlacemark = [[MKPlacemark alloc]
        initWithCoordinate:westminsterLocation addressDictionary:nil];
    MKMapItem *westminsterItem = [[MKMapItem alloc]
        initWithPlacemark:westminsterPlacemark];
    westminsterItem.name = @"Westminster Abbey";

    NSArray *items = [[NSArray alloc] initWithObjects:bigBenItem, westminsterItem, nil];
    NSDictionary *options =
        @{MKLaunchOptionsDirectionsModeKey: MKLaunchOptionsDirectionsModeWalking};
    [MKMapItem openMapsWithItems:items launchOptions:options];
}
```

When launching in directions mode, Maps takes the first item in the array as the starting point and the last as the destination. However, if the array contains only one placemark, Maps will consider that to be the destination and the device's current location to be the starting point.

But what if you want to find the route *from* a point *to* your current location? That's possible too. MKMapItem provides a way to create a symbolic map item that points out the current location. All you have to do is to add that map to the end of the array of map items. Here's an example that asks Maps for directions from Big Ben to the current location:

```
NSArray *items = [[NSArray alloc]
    initWithObjects:bigBenItem, [MKMapItem mapItemForCurrentLocation], nil];
[MKMapItem openMapsWithItems:items launchOptions:nil];
```

Before finishing this recipe, we want to point out that there are more options that can control how Maps will launch—for example, in satellite map mode or with a specific region. Refer to Apple's documentation for details about these and other Maps launch options.

Recipe 7-8: Registering a Routing App

The preceding recipe used an API to launch Maps directly from your app. Another feature of iOS 7 is that it's possible to go the other way around; if your app is a registered routing app, it might be launched from within Maps.

As an example of how this might work, consider users who have localized Big Ben as a point of interest in Maps. They now want to know how to get there by bus, so they press the directions button, select the routing mode, and then browse through available routing apps and discover one that seems to fit their needs. They select it, and the routing app is launched by Maps.

Recipe 7-8 shows you how you can register your app as a routing app.

Declaring a Routing App

For Recipe 7-8 we'll just create a simple dummy app that does nothing more than display the starting point and destination point provided by Maps upon launch. So start by creating a new single view application and link the Map Kit and Core Location frameworks to it. Make sure you import the Map Kit framework in the header file.

Next, add a label to the user interface. Make it big enough to contain at least five rows of text. Your main view should look something like the one in Figure 7-21. Also, create an outlet named "routingLabel" that's connected to the label.

Figure 7-21. *A dummy routing app with a single label*

To allow your app to be launchable from Maps, you need to declare it as a routing app. This is done in the application's property list file, but there's a convenient user interface for it in Xcode.

Select the root node in the project navigator, select the Capabilities tab, and scroll down to the Maps section. Make sure the switch is set to "ON" and, because this app doesn't support any of the available transportation types, select Other. (See Figure 7-22.)

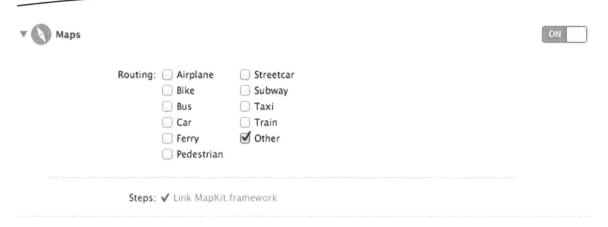

Figure 7-22. Declaring a routing app

Handling Launches

Now that your app is registered as a routing app, Maps can integrate with it through URL requests. To respond to such a request, add the application:openURL:sourceApplication:annotation: delegate method to your app delegate. Make sure the request is a directions request by using the isDirectionsRequestURL: convenience method of the MKDirectionsRequest class, as shown in Listing 7-61.

Listing 7-61. Implementation of the application:openURL:sourceApplication:annotation: delegate

```
- (BOOL)application:(UIApplication *)application openURL:(NSURL *)url
sourceApplication:(NSString *)sourceApplication annotation:(id)annotation
{
    if ([MKDirectionsRequest isDirectionsRequestURL:url])
    {
        // Code to handle request goes here

        return YES;
    }

    return NO;
}
```

The request contains a starting point and an end point that your app can use to adjust to the user's needs. You extract the request from the URL using the initWithContentsOfURL: method. Modify the code in Listing 7-61, as shown in Listing 7-62.

Listing 7-62. Extracting the request

```
- (BOOL)application:(UIApplication *)application openURL:(NSURL *)url
sourceApplication:(NSString *)sourceApplication annotation:(id)annotation
{
    if ([MKDirectionsRequest isDirectionsRequestURL:url])
```

```
{
    MKDirectionsRequest *request = [[MKDirectionsRequest alloc]
        initWithContentsOfURL:url];

    MKMapItem *source = [request source];
    MKMapItem *destination = [request destination];

return YES;
}
return NO;
}
```

For the purpose of this recipe we'll simply display these points in the routing label of our application. One important aspect is that any of the provided map items might be the symbolic Current Location item, which won't have an actual placemark attached. You can use the isCurrentLocation property to detect whether that is the case and take appropriate action. In this case you'll just display the text "Current Location." Listing 7-63 shows the final launch response.

Listing 7-63. Adding to launch response to code in Listing 7-62

```
- (BOOL)application:(UIApplication *)application openURL:(NSURL *)url
sourceApplication:(NSString *)sourceApplication annotation:(id)annotation
{
    if ([MKDirectionsRequest isDirectionsRequestURL:url])
    {
        MKDirectionsRequest *request = [[MKDirectionsRequest alloc]
            initWithContentsOfURL:url];

        MKMapItem *source = [request source];
        MKMapItem *destination = [request destination];

        NSString *sourceString;
        NSString *destinationString;

        if (source.isCurrentLocation)
            sourceString = @"Current Location";
        else
            sourceString = [NSString stringWithFormat:@"%f, %f",
                            source.placemark.location.coordinate.latitude,
                            source.placemark.location.coordinate.longitude];

        if (destination.isCurrentLocation)
            sourceString = @"Current Location";
        else
            destinationString = [NSString stringWithFormat:@"%f, %f",
                                 destination.placemark.location.coordinate.latitude,
                                 destination.placemark.location.coordinate.longitude];

                self.viewController= (ViewController*)self.window.rootViewController;
        self.viewController.routingLabel.text =
            [NSString stringWithFormat:@"Start at: %@\nStop at: %@",
             sourceString, destinationString];
```

```
        return YES;
    }
    return NO;
}
```

Let's not forget to update the AppDelegate.h file to include our imports and a property for the view controller class, as shown in Listing 7-64.

Listing 7-64. Adding an import statement and a property for the view controller class in the AppDelegate.h file

```
//
//  AppDelegate.h
//  Recipe 7-8 Registering a Routing App
//
#import <UIKit/UIKit.h>
#import <MapKit/MapKit.h>
#import "ViewController.h"

@interface AppDelegate : UIResponder <UIApplicationDelegate>

@property (strong, nonatomic) UIWindow *window;
@property (strong,nonatomic) ViewController *viewController;

@end
```

Testing the Routing App

It's time to take your app on a test run. Build and run it in the simulator. When your app launches, click the "home" button to close the app. You will test a routing between Westminster Abbey and Big Ben in London, so start by setting the current location of the simulator to the coordinates of Westminster Abbey. This can be done in the main menu of the simulator, under Debug ➤ Location ➤ Custom Location. Enter 51.500543 for latitude and -0.135702 for longitude in the dialog box (see Figure 7-23).

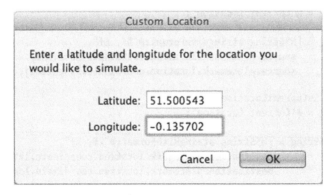

Figure 7-23. Setting a custom location for the simulator

When the custom location has been set, locate and launch the Maps app on the simulator. Enter "Big Ben, London" in the search field and let the Maps app find it. You should eventually see a screen like the one in Figure 7-24 (you'll need to pan a little to the left to get Westminster Abbey within the visible region).

Figure 7-24. *The simulator with the Big Ben point of interest selected and the current-location dot at Westminster Abbey*

With the Big Ben placemark selected, click the "Directions" button located to the left of the search field at the top of the Maps app screen, as shown in Figure 7-25.

Figure 7-25. *The "Directions" button in Maps app*

In the Directions screen, select the "routing apps mode" button. This is the button that looks like a bus, next to the "walking mode" button (see Figure 7-26). With the routing apps mode selected, click the routing button on the upper-right side of the screen. You can also press the list item if it has a bus icon next to it.

Figure 7-26. Maps' Directions screen with the routing app mode selected

You're now presented with a screen of available routing apps. If everything is set up correctly, your app should be in the list with a "Route" button next to it, as in Figure 7-27.

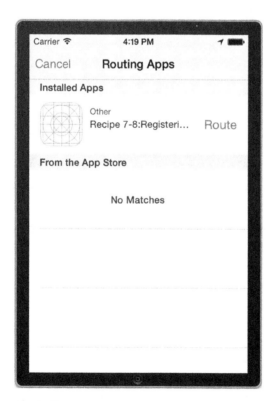

Figure 7-27. Your app as a routing option in Maps

Now if you tap the "Route" button, your app will be launched and, if you've implemented the `appl ication:openURL:sourceApplication:annotation:` method correctly, your app should look like the one in Figure 7-28.

Figure 7-28. Your routing app launched from within Maps

Specifying a Coverage Area

Even though your routing app successfully integrates with the Maps app, there's actually one essential piece missing: You need to tell Maps in which region your app provides the routing service. This is done using a special file, a GeoJSON file, to declare the geographic coverage area. Maps uses the information to filter among the available routing apps so that the user won't be flooded with irrelevant choices.

The reason it worked for you without the GeoJSON file is that for testing purposes, all routing apps installed on the simulator are available and considered valid. However, an app cannot be approved for the app store without submitting a valid GeoJSON file.

Now create a GeoJSON file for your app. Add a file to the Supporting Files folder in the project navigator. Pick the GeoJSON template under the Resource section (see Figure 7-29). Name the file "London.geojson." You don't need to add it to the target because it should be submitted with your app and not as part of its bundle.

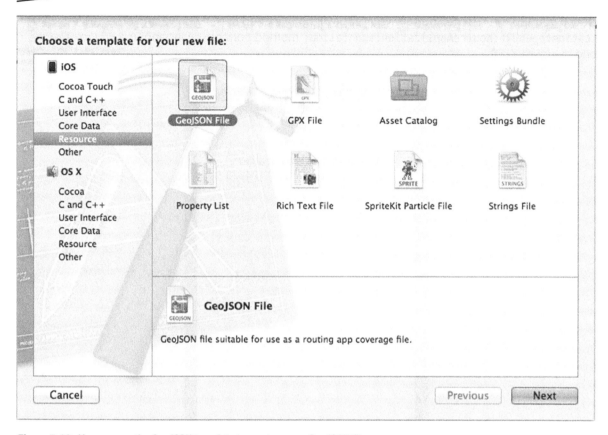

Figure 7-29. *You can use the GeoJSON template to create a new GeoJSON file*

Make the content of the new file as follows:

```
{
    "type": "MultiPolygon",
    "coordinates": [
                    [[[52.257770, -0.989542],
                      [51.001232, -0.943830],
                      [51.050521, 0.303471],
                      [51.848169, 0.362244],
                      [52.257770, -0.989542]]]
                    ]
}
```

The numbers in the file represent world coordinates, and together they make a closed polygon. Because the polygon must be closed, the first and the last coordinate must also be the same.

You can test your GeoJSON file by pointing it out in your Xcode Scheme for the project. Go to Product ➤ scheme ➤ Edit Scheme in the menu. In the Options page, there's a setting for Routing App Coverage file. Click it and select your GeoJSON file. (See Figure 7-30.)

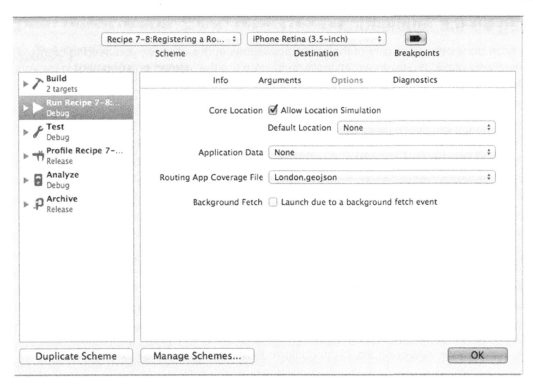

Figure 7-30. Setting the Routing App Coverage file for testing purposes

You now can test whether your file works by selecting points of interests in or out of the coverage area. Be sure to have both the starting and the ending points within the coverage area if you want to test whether your app shows up in the list of available routing apps.

> **Note**   If your app doesn't show up as a choice for routing as you expect it to, there might be an error in your GeoJSON file. Check the console, because Maps reports any errors with the GeoJSON file there.

A final note before closing this recipe. When you design your own GeoJSON file, we recommend that you keep it simple. Apple suggests no more than 20 polygons containing at most 20 points each. There is no need to be exact, so a simple bounding rectangle will do in most cases.

Recipe 7-9: Getting Directions

A new API added in iOS 7 lets you get driving or walking directions from within your app. These directions come with everything you would expect from a maps application, including alternate routes and route finding. As an added bonus, you also have time estimates that are based on current traffic and even historical data.

Setting Up the Application

As you have done before in many of the map applications in this chapter, you need to create a new single view application with a map view on it. Here are the instructions once again for your convenience:

1. Create a new single view application project.

2. Add the Map Kit framework to the project.

3. Add the Core Location framework to the project. In this recipe, you will not use the location services so there's no need to provide a location usage description. You still need to link in the framework, though, or you'll get linker errors when building later.

4. Add a map view to the application's main view.

5. Create an outlet for referencing the map view. Name the outlet "`mapView`."

6. Import the Map Kit API into `ViewController.h`.

7. Add the `NSLocationUsageDescription` key to the application.info plist file and give it a suitable identifier, such as "Testing Getting Directions."

8. Make your view controller class conform to the `MKMapViewDelegate` protocol.

Drawing Directions on the Map

To start, we will create a new method for finding our directions. In this method, we need to make a request using both our source and destination coordinates. For our example, we have chosen Red Rocks Amphitheatre and the Sports Authority Field in Denver as the source and destination for the directions, respectively. Add the code shown in Listing 7-65 to the ViewController.h and ViewController.m files.

Listing 7-65. Setting up the viewController.h and .m files

```
//
//  ViewController.h
//  Recipe 7-9 Getting Directions
//
#import <UIKit/UIKit.h>
#import <MapKit/MapKit.h>
#import <CoreLocation/CoreLocation.h>

@interface ViewController : UIViewController <MKMapViewDelegate>

@property (weak, nonatomic) IBOutlet MKMapView *mapView;
@property (strong, nonatomic) MKDirectionsResponse *response;

@end
```

```
//
// ViewController.m
// Recipe 7-9 Getting Directions
//
//...

-(void)findDirectionsFrom: (MKMapItem *)source to:(MKMapItem *)destination
{
    //Make request and provide it with source and destination MKMapItems
    MKDirectionsRequest *request = [[MKDirectionsRequest alloc] init];
    request.source = source;
    request.destination = destination;
    request.requestsAlternateRoutes = NO;

    MKDirections *directions = [[MKDirections alloc] initWithRequest:request];

    //Find directions and call a method to show directions
    [directions calculateDirectionsWithCompletionHandler:^(MKDirectionsResponse *response,
NSError *error) {
        if(error)
        {
            NSLog(@"Bummer, we got an error: %@",error);
        }
        else
        {
            [self showDirectionsOnMap:response];

        }
    }];

}

-(void)showDirectionsOnMap:(MKDirectionsResponse *)response
{
    self.response = response;

    for (MKRoute *route in self.response.routes)
    {
        [self.mapView addOverlay:route.polyline level:MKOverlayLevelAboveRoads];
    }

    [self.mapView addAnnotation:self.response.source.placemark];
    [self.mapView addAnnotation:self.response.destination.placemark];

}
```

The two methods here receive a request for directions and then create a route on the map in the form of a polyline, with both the source and destination points marked with a pin. We'll need to add one more delegate method to the view controller to actually draw the route on the map. You'll do that by adding the the code shown in Listing 7-66.

Listing 7-66. Adding the mapView:rendererForOverlay: delegate method

```
//
//  ViewController.m
//  Recipe 7-9 Getting Directions
//

//...

-(MKOverlayRenderer *)mapView:(MKMapView *)mapView rendererForOverlay:(id )overlay
{

    if([overlay isKindOfClass:[MKPolyline class]])
    {
        MKPolylineRenderer *renderer = [[MKPolylineRenderer alloc] initWithOverlay:overlay];
        renderer.lineWidth = 3;
        renderer.strokeColor = [UIColor blueColor];
        return renderer;

    }
    else
    {
        return nil;
    }
}
```

Lastly, we need to set some coordinates in the viewDidLoad method and call the newly created methods for finding directions and putting them on the map. First, add some constants to the ViewController.m file above the "import," as shown in Listing 7-67.

Listing 7-67. Defining constants

```
#define centerLat 39.6653
#define centerLong -105.2058
#define spanDeltaLat .5
#define spanDeltaLong .5

#import "ViewController.h"

//...
```

Then create some MKMapItems using the coordinates for both Red Rocks and Sports Authority and use them to call the findDirectionsFrom: to: method we just created in the viewDidLoad method, as shown in Listing 7-68. As mentioned before, an MKMapItem holds information about a place such as the placemark and the name.

Listing 7-68. Updating the viewDidLoad method to call the findDirectionsFrom: to: method

```
- (void)viewDidLoad
{
    [super viewDidLoad];
        // Do any additional setup after loading the view, typically from a nib.
    self.mapView.delegate = self;
```

```
    CLLocationCoordinate2D centerPoint = {centerLat, centerLong};
    MKCoordinateSpan coordinateSpan = MKCoordinateSpanMake(spanDeltaLat, spanDeltaLong);
    MKCoordinateRegion coordinateRegion =
    MKCoordinateRegionMake(centerPoint, coordinateSpan);

    [self.mapView setRegion:coordinateRegion];
    [self.mapView regionThatFits:coordinateRegion];

    CLLocationCoordinate2D redRocksAmphitheatre= CLLocationCoordinate2DMake(39.6653, -105.2058);
    MKPlacemark *redRocksPlacemark = [[MKPlacemark alloc] initWithCoordinate:
redRocksAmphitheatre addressDictionary:nil];
    MKMapItem *redRocksItem = [[MKMapItem alloc] initWithPlacemark:redRocksPlacemark];
    redRocksItem.name = @"Red Rocks Amphitheatre";

    CLLocationCoordinate2D sportsAuthorityField = CLLocationCoordinate2DMake(39.7439, -105.0200);
    MKPlacemark *sportsAuthorityPlacemark = [[MKPlacemark alloc]
initWithCoordinate:sportsAuthorityField addressDictionary:nil];
    MKMapItem *sportsAuthorityItem = [[MKMapItem alloc] initWithPlacemark:sportsAuthorityPlacemark];
    sportsAuthorityItem.name = @"Sports Authority Field";

    [self findDirectionsFrom:redRocksItem to: sportsAuthorityItem];
}
```

If you build and run your app, you will see a polyline route is drawn from the Red Rocks Amphitheatre to the Sports Authority Field, as shown in Figure 7-31. We didn't do it in this example, but you can also draw multiple routes by changing `request.requestsAlternateRoutes` from NO to YES in the `findDirectionsFrom: to:` method.

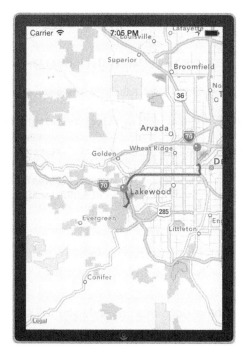

Figure 7-31. Drawing directions on a map

Adding ETA

Before concluding this recipe, we will explore one more handy feature included in the MKDirections class that allows you to get the estimated time of arrival (ETA). The ETA is based on current traffic conditions and can be a nice feature to add to your mapping applications.

Listing 7-69 shows how to modify the findDirectionsFrom: to: method to add an ETA alert. Basically, all you are doing is calling a class method, calculateETAWithCompletionHandler, inside the calculateDirectionsWIthCompletionHandler: method's completion handler. You need to do this because the calculateDirectionsWithCompletionHandler: method is carried out asynchronously, and you will get an error if you try to carry out two MKDirections method calls at the same time. By adding the second method to the first method's completion block, you ensure that the first method has completed first.

Listing 7-69. Creating an alert view to display ETA

```
 -(void)findDirectionsFrom: (MKMapItem *)source to:(MKMapItem *)destination
{
//...

    [directions calculateDirectionsWithCompletionHandler:^(MKDirectionsResponse *response,
NSError *error) {
        if(error)
        {
            NSLog(@"Bummer, we got an error: %@",error);

        }
        else
        {
            [self showDirectionsOnMap:response];

            [directions calculateETAWithCompletionHandler:^(MKETAResponse *response, NSError *error)
                {
                NSLog(@"You will arive in: %.1f Mins%@", response.expectedTravelTime/60.0,error);

                UIAlertView *alert = [[UIAlertView alloc] initWithTitle:@"ETA!"
                                                        message:[NSString
stringWithFormat:@"Estimated Time of Arrival in: %.1f Mins.",response.expectedTravelTime/60.0]
                                                        delegate:nil
                                                        cancelButtonTitle:@"Dismiss"
                                                        otherButtonTitles: nil];
                [alert show];
            }];

        }
    }];
}
```

That concludes this recipe. If you have done this correctly you will see an alert with the ETA, as shown in Figure 7-32.

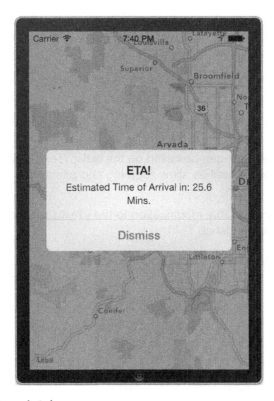

Figure 7-32. Displaying the ETA in an alert view

Recipe 7-10: Using 3-D Mapping

Before iOS 7, 3-D features were limited solely to the Maps app. Now Apple has given us some new APIs that let us take advantage of 3-D mapping features such as choosing camera position and even animating 3-D views. In this recipe, we will explore two methods of displaying a 3-D map view as well as creating a fly-over.

Using the Properties Approach

As you did in many of the recipes in this chapter, you need to set up a new map-view single view application to get started. The new MKMapCamera API lets you choose a camera location when viewing a map. You can set a camera using either a convenience method or by setting some properties. We'll start with setting properties, and then we'll show you how to get the same effect using the convenience method.

The MKMapCamera API actually makes it pretty easy to put your map in a 3-D view. All that is needed is setting four properties and setting the mapView camera to the MKMapCamera object we create. The four properties are as follows:

- Pitch: This is the angle of the camera lens in degrees. A zero value will look straight at the ground and a nonzero value will be toward the horizon.

- ▨ Altitude: This is the distance in meters above the ground. Generally, if you want to see buildings this should be in the ball park of 600 or less. This value changes depending on the height of the buildings.

- ▨ Heading: This is the degree heading where north is 0 degrees and south is 180 degrees.

- ▨ centerCoordinate: This is a CLLocationCoordinate type input that specifies where the camera is located.

There are also a few properties that can be called on the MKMapView object to show items such as buildings and points of interest as well as allow zooming and pitch. We'll be using a few of these in our code example.

All that is needed in the recipe is a little modification to the viewDidLoad method. Modify the viewDidLoad method as shown in Listing 7-70.

Listing 7-70. Modifying the viewDidLoad method to create a 3-D map view

```
- (void)viewDidLoad
{
    [super viewDidLoad];

    self.mapView.delegate = self;

    //Create a new MKMapCamera object
    MKMapCamera *mapCamera = [[MKMapCamera alloc] init];

    //set MKMapCamera properties
    mapCamera.centerCoordinate = CLLocationCoordinate2DMake(40.7130,-74.0085);
    mapCamera.pitch = 57;
    mapCamera.altitude = 650;
    mapCamera.heading = 90;

    //Set MKmapView camera property
    self.mapView.camera = mapCamera;

    //Set a few MKMapView Properties to allow pitch, building view, points of interest, and zooming.
    self.mapView.pitchEnabled = YES;
    self.mapView.showsBuildings = YES;
    self.mapView.showsPointsOfInterest = YES;
    self.mapView.zoomEnabled = YES;

}
```

The code in Listing 7-70 simply initializes the map-view delegate and then creates an MKMapCamera instance with the needed coordinate, pitch, altitude, and heading. Next, add that camera to the map view and set properties on the map view to make it look and behave better.

Now if you build and run the application, you'll find a nice building view of the One World Trade Center Building in New York City, as shown in Figure 7-33.

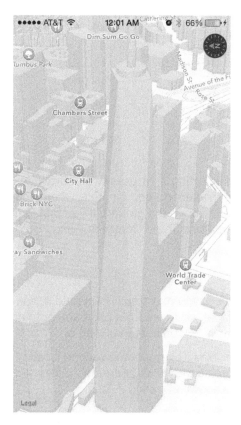

Figure 7-33. *Using MKMapCamera to view a 3-D map*

Using the Convenience Method Approach

The property approach is concise and easy to understand, but there is a faster and easier method for showing a 3-D view. Apple has provided a convenience method that can do all of this when you initialize your MKMapCamera object. The ViewDidLoad method would look like Listing 7-71 instead of Listing 7-70.

Listing 7-71. *Modifying the viewDidLoad method to create a 3-D map view using the convenience method*

```
- (void)viewDidLoad
{
    [super viewDidLoad];

    self.mapView.delegate = self;

    //Using the Convenience Method
    CLLocationCoordinate2D ground = CLLocationCoordinate2DMake(40.7128,-74.0117);
    CLLocationCoordinate2D eye = CLLocationCoordinate2DMake(40.7132,-74.0150);
    MKMapCamera *mapCamera = [MKMapCamera cameraLookingAtCenterCoordinate:ground
fromEyeCoordinate:eye eyeAltitude:740];
```

```
//Set MKmapView camera property
self.mapView.camera = mapCamera;

//Set a few MKMapView Properties to allow pitch, building view, points of interest, and zooming.
self.mapView.pitchEnabled = YES;
self.mapView.showsBuildings = YES;
self.mapView.showsPointsOfInterest = YES;
self.mapView.zoomEnabled = YES;

}
```

The convenience method shown in Listing 7-71 uses two coordinates. The first coordinate is where you want the camera to look and the second coordinate is where you want the camera to be. The last parameter is simply the altitude above the ground. If you build and run this app, you should see a slightly different view of the One World Trade Center Building.

Creating a Fly-Over

Because MKMapView is a type of view, you can actually animate it. You will take advantage of this fact by creating a nice fly-over effect that will move from one camera to another. This is actually very simple to do using the UIView animateWithDuration: method.

To start, you need to create a new MKMapCamera for the second location. For this demonstration, we will use the convenience method to create the MKMapCamera instances. Modify the code from Listing 7-71 to add a new camera instance, as shown in Listing 7-72.

Listing 7-72. Adding a new MKMapCamera instance to the viewDidLoad method

```
- (void)viewDidLoad
{
    [super viewDidLoad];

    self.mapView.delegate = self;

    //Using the Convenience Method
    CLLocationCoordinate2D ground = CLLocationCoordinate2DMake(40.7128,-74.0117);
    CLLocationCoordinate2D eye = CLLocationCoordinate2DMake(40.7132,-74.0150);
    MKMapCamera *mapCamera = [MKMapCamera cameraLookingAtCenterCoordinate:ground
fromEyeCoordinate:eye eyeAltitude:740];

    CLLocationCoordinate2D ground2 = CLLocationCoordinate2DMake(40.7,-73.99);
    CLLocationCoordinate2D eye2 = CLLocationCoordinate2DMake(40.7,-73.98);
    MKMapCamera *mapCamera2 = [MKMapCamera cameraLookingAtCenterCoordinate:ground2
fromEyeCoordinate:eye2 eyeAltitude:700];

//...
}
```

In Listing 7-72, you can see that the code added is identical to the implementation of the first camera, except the coordinates are now slightly different. The last step is to create the animation. To make a nice, smooth animation, we'll cover a short distance over a fair amount of time (25 seconds). Add the code in Listing 7-73 to the `viewDidLoad` method.

Listing 7-73. Creating a 25-second animation to the second camera view

```
[UIView animateWithDuration:25.0 animations:^{

    self.mapView.camera = mapCamera2;

}];
```

If you build and run the application now, you should see a very nice fly-over from the One World Trade Center Building across the Brooklyn Bridge. We encourage you to play with the coordinates and altitudes to see how it affects the appearance of the animation.

It's worth pointing out that if you try to move over a distance too fast or if you add too many annotations and details to the map, the animation will be choppy or the items will not load at all. Debugging these issues are beyond the scope of this book, but you can view the "Putting Map Kit in Perspective" video found at `https://developer.apple.com/wwdc/videos/` for more details.

Summary

The Map Kit framework is one of the most popular frameworks because of its powerful yet incredibly flexible ability to provide a fully customizable yet simplistic map interface. In this chapter, you have seen the major capabilities of Map Kit, from locating the user to adding annotations and overlays to the new 3-D capabilities with Maps. However, you have only scratched the surface of the capabilities of Map Kit, especially in the areas of map-based problem solving. A quick look at the Map Kit documentation[1] reveals various other commands, methods, and properties we did not cover, which range from isolating particular sections of a map to entirely customizing how touch events are handled by the map. The effectiveness of these countless capabilities is limited only by the developer's imagination.

---

[1]`http://developer.apple.com/library/ios/#documentation/MapKit/Reference/MapKit_Framework_Reference.`

Chapter **8**

Social Network Recipes

Social networking is perhaps the strongest trend on the Internet right now. People with an online presence are sharing and consuming content on one or more of the many sites that offer such services. Because forming communities is part of our nature, and the Internet platform makes it so easy, we can be sure the trend will last and get stronger as more and more services join in.

In iOS 6, Apple introduced the Social framework, making it easy to integrate your apps with social networks. In iOS 7, the framework has been expanded to support Vimeo and Flicker as well as Facebook, Twitter, and the China-based Weibo networks.

> **Note** The Twitter framework that was introduced in iOS 5 is now deprecated and has been superseded by the Social framework.

In this chapter, we will show you how you can share the content in your app with social networking applications using the convenient UIActivityViewController. We'll also show you how you can implement more advanced integration with Twitter and Facebook using the new Social framework.

Recipe 8-1: Sharing Content with the Activity View

Most apps are not in the social networking business. However, many that are not do have content their users would benefit from sharing. Fortunately, Apple has an API that makes this easy. The UIActivityViewController takes the content you provide and presents the user with relevant "activities," such as posting to Facebook or Twitter. UIActivityViewController is a convenient view class that provides a configurable interface. The interface allows you to share content on social networks or take advantage of standard services such as sending emails or even sharing files with nearby iOS 7 devices using Airdrop. The UIActivityViewController interface is the same one that appears when you click the "share" button in Safari. The only difference is the configuration. In this recipe, we'll show you how to set up UIActivityViewController to share a snippet of text and a URL.

Start by creating a new single view application. Select the Main.storyboard and add a text view, a text field, and a navigation bar to the main view and arrange them so that the main view resembles Figure 8-1. To create the button with the activity icon you see in the upper-right corner of Figure 8-1, drag a bar button to the navigation bar. In the attribute inspector, set the button's Identifier attribute to "Action."

Figure 8-1. *A simple user interface for sharing some text and a URL*

The text field is used to input URL links, so set its Placeholder attribute to read "URL to share" in the attributes inspector. You might also want to change its Keyboard attribute to "URL" to better match the data that will be entered there.

As usual, you need to reference the edit controls from your code, so create the following respective outlets and actions:

- Outlet: messageTextView

- Outlet: urlTextField

- Navigation button action: shareContent

Setting Up an Activity View Controller

Now that you have the user interface set up, you can go to ViewController.m to implement the shareContent action method. Add the code to the shareContent: method to initialize and present a UIActivityViewController to share the text and the URL, as shown in Listing 8-1.

Listing 8-1. Implementation of the shareContent: method

```
- (IBAction)shareContent:(id)sender
{
    NSString *text = self.messageTextView.text;
    NSURL *url = [NSURL URLWithString:self.urlTextField.text];
    NSArray *items = @[text, url];

    UIActivityViewController *vc = [[UIActivityViewController alloc]
        initWithActivityItems:items applicationActivities:nil];
    [self presentViewController:vc animated:YES completion:nil];
}
```

Note   In this bit of code we are using literals for creating arrays. As of Xcode 4.5, you can write arrays as @[object1, object2] instead of [NSArray arrayWithObjects:object1, object2, nil].

That's it! That's all the code you need for sharing the content on Facebook, Twitter, or any of the other ways Apple provides. You can now build and run the application, enter some text and a URL, and then tap the activity button to bring up the activity view, as shown in Figure 8-2.

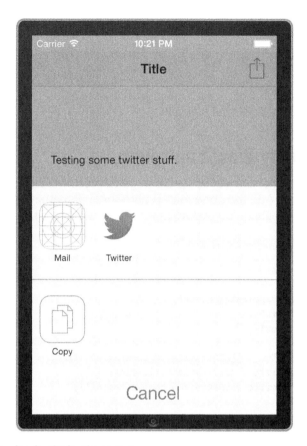

Figure 8-2. The built-in activity view for sharing the content

Once the activity view is presented, you have turned the control of the sharing over to iOS. It uses the accounts that have been set up on the device or asks the user for login details if the accounts haven't been configured. Users new to Facebook, Twitter, Vimeo, Flickr, and other social media networks can create new accounts and get a seamless experience, depending on location. You get all of this with only about five lines of code.

Figure 8-3 shows an example of when a user of this app has selected to share the content to Twitter. The user is allowed to change the text before sending it to the service. The user can also change the account (if more than one is available) from which the tweet will be sent. The Facebook integration has a similar sheet in which the user can lay the final touch. However, due to the nature of Facebook, only one account is allowed on any single device.

Figure 8-3. The tweet sheet in which the user can lay the last touch to the content before it's shared

Excluding Activity View Items

When the activity view is shown, iOS looks at the content and tries to parse the content to show only relevant options. For example, the Weibo service shows only if you have a Chinese keyboard installed.

> **Note**   The number of options also depends on the availability of the services. For example, sending text messages isn't available if you run your app in the iOS simulator, so it won't appear as an option.

In addition to the system limiting options, there might be situations where you want to reduce the number of options even more yourself. For example, if you know that your users will never email the content, it makes no sense to have that option.

Fortunately, you can exclude items from the activity view by using the excludeActivityTypes property of the UIActivityViewController. For instance, if you want to exclude the "Mail" and the "Copy to Pasteboard" services, add the code to the shareContent: method, as shown in Listing 8-2.

Listing 8-2. Updating the shareContent: method to exclude copy and mail options

```
- (IBAction)shareContent:(id)sender
{
    NSString *text = self.messageTextView.text;
    NSURL *url = [NSURL URLWithString:self.urlTextField.text];
    NSArray *items = @[text, url];

    UIActivityViewController *vc = [[UIActivityViewController alloc]
        initWithActivityItems:items applicationActivities:nil];
    vc.excludedActivityTypes = @[UIActivityTypeMail, UIActivityTypeCopyToPasteboard];
    [self presentViewController:vc animated:YES completion:nil];
}
```

If you make the change shown in Listing 8-2 and build and run the app again, you'll see (as shown in Figure 8-4) that both "Mail" and "Copy" are no longer visible in the activity view.

Figure 8-4. *The activity view without "Mail" and "Copy" options*

Table 3-1 shows a complete set of valid activity types and the type of objects you can send to them as data.

Table 3-1. Activity Types

Constant	Valid Data Items	Usage
UIActivityTypePostToFacebook	NSString, NSAttributedString, UIImage, AVAsset, NSURL	For posting mostly text and images to Facebook
UIActivityTypePostToTwitter	NSString, NSAttributedString, UIImage, AVAsset, NSURL	For posting mostly text and images to Twitter
UIActivityTypePostToWeibo	NSString, NSAttributedString, UIImage, AVAsset, NSURL	For posting mostly text and images to China-based Weibo
UIActivityTypeMessage	NSString, NSAttributedString, NSURL (with the sms: scheme)	For sending an SMS message
UIActivityTypeMail	NSString, UIImage, NSURL (local files, or using the mailto: scheme)	For adding strings, images, and URLs to email messages
UIActivityTypePrint	UIImage, NSData, NSURL (local files only), UIPrintPageRenderer, UIPrintFormatter, UIPrintInfo	For sending a multitude of data objects to an air printer
UIActivityTypeCopyToPasteboard	NSString, UIImage, NSURL, UIColor, NSDictionary	For copying content to the Clipboard
UIActivityTypeAssignToContact	UIImage	For assigning an image to a contact
UIActivityTypeSaveToCameraRoll	UIImage, NSURL (for video)	For adding images or video URLs to a camera roll
UIActivityTypeAddToReadingList	NSURL	For adding a URL to a reading list
UIActivityTypePostToFlickr	UIImage, ALAsset, NSURL (With Image and file scheme), NSData (Image Data)	For posting images or URLs of images to Flickr
UIActivityTypePostToVimeo	ALAsset, NSURL (File scheme and point to video), NSData (Video data)	For mostly posting videos or URLs to Vimeo
UIActivityTypePostToTencentWeibo	NSString, NSAttributedString, UIImage, AVAsset, NSURL (data for activity items)	For posting strings, URLs, and images to Tencent Weibo
UIActivityTypeAirDrop	NSString, NSAttributedString, UIImage, AVAsset, NSURL (data for activity items), NSArray (provided contents are first five items), NSDictionary (provided contents are first five items)	For sharing a multitude of files with users in close proximity

Including Activity View Items

Excluding items from the activity view is easy. In contrast, including activities not currently supported in iOS requires a little more work on your behalf. You will need to create a subclass of UIActivity, an abstract class used in conjunction with UIActivityViewController, to present the user with a custom service.

To show you how that is done, we will implement a simple logging service that accepts text and URL objects and sends them to stdout (the Standard Output Stream). Start by creating a new subclass of UIActivity with the name "MyLogActivity" (by going to File ➤ New ➤ File... and selecting Objective-C class).

In the MyLogActivity.h, add the property shown in Listing 8-3 to hold the text message that should be sent to stdout.

Listing 8-3. MyLogActivity.h with the logMessage property

```
//
//  MyLogActivity.h
//  Recipe 8-1 Sharing content with the Activity View
//

#import <UIKit/UIKit.h>

@interface MyLogActivity : UIActivity

@property (strong, nonatomic)NSString *logMessage;

@end
```

Add an image to your project to use as the icon for your activity. For best results, use a 72 × 72 dpi PNG image with only white color in combination with the alpha channel to produce a white icon. (Apple doesn't allow multi-color icons for custom activities yet.) You *can* provide an image with no transparency, which is what we did in this example; however, you will get a plain, all-white icon (this is shown later in Figure 8-5). Create an image asset for this icon and title it "nscup" or whatever you choose to call your image. To do this, select the image.xcassets file from the project navigator and click the "+" button in the lower-left corner of the editor window. This will add a new asset to the .xcassets file. Click the asset to rename it and drag your image to one of the image placeholders. You can find more details on this procedure in Recipe 1-8 in Chapter 1.

With an icon asset created in your project, you can turn your attention to the implementation of the MyLogActivity class. A UIActivity subclass must provide the following pieces of information:

- *Activity Type:* A unique identifier for the activity, which is not shown to the user. Table 3-1 contains constants for the identifiers of the built-in services.

- *Activity Title:* The title displayed to the user in the activity view.

- *Activity Image:* The icon displayed along with the title in the activity view.

- *Can Perform on Activity Items:* Whether the activity can handle the provided data objects.

To provide the preceding information, modify the `MyLogActivity.m` file, as shown in Listing 8-4.

Listing 8-4. Modifying the MyLogActivity implementation to include necessary components

```objc
//
//  MyLogActivity.m
//  Recipe 8-1 Sharing content with the Activity View
//

#import "MyLogActivity.h"

@implementation MyLogActivity

-(NSString *)activityType
{
    return @"MyLogActivity";
}

-(NSString *)activityTitle
{
    return @"Log";
}

-(UIImage *)activityImage
{
    // Replace the file name with the one of the file you imported into your project
    return [UIImage imageNamed:@"nscup.png"];
}

-(BOOL)canPerformWithActivityItems:(NSArray *)activityItems
{
    for (NSObject *item in activityItems)
    {
        if (![item isKindOfClass:[NSString class]] && ![item isKindOfClass:[NSURL class]])
        {
            return NO;
        }
    }
    return YES;
}

@end
```

If your activity has been displayed and the user taps its button, the custom activity class will be sent a `prepareWithActivityItems:` message. In this case, we simply append the content for each item and store the result in the `logMessage` property. Add the method with the implementation shown in Listing 8-5 to the `MyLogActivity.m` file.

Listing 8-5. Implementation of the prepareWithActivityitems: method

```
-(void)prepareWithActivityItems:(NSArray *)activityItems
{
    self.logMessage = @"";
    for (NSObject *item in activityItems)
    {
        self.logMessage = [NSString stringWithFormat:@"%@\n%@",
                        self.logMessage, item];
    }
}
```

Finally, the activity is asked to perform whatever it's supposed to do. If your custom activity wants to display an additional user interface, like the Twitter activity does with its tweet sheet, the custom activity should override the `activityViewController` method of `UIActivity`.

However, because we're not interested in displaying a user interface for our logging service, we instead override the `performActivity` method, as shown in Listing 8-6.

Listing 8-6. Implementation of the performActivity override method

```
-(void)performActivity
{
    NSLog(@"%@", self.logMessage);
    [self activityDidFinish:YES];
}
```

Your custom log service is finished and you can now return to the `shareContent:` action method in `ViewController.m` to set up the view controller to include the new activity. The new changes are shown in Listing 8-7.

Listing 8-7. Adding support for the new activity in the viewController.m file

```
//
//  ViewController.m
//  Recipe 8-1 Sharing content with the Activity View
//

#import "ViewController.h"
#import "MyLogActivity.h"

@implementation ViewController

// ...
```

```
- (IBAction)shareContent:(id)sender
{
    NSString *text = self.messageTextView.text;
    NSURL *url = [NSURL URLWithString:self.urlTextField.text];
    NSArray *items = @[text, url];
    MyLogActivity *myLogService = [[MyLogActivity alloc] init];
    NSArray *customServices = @[myLogService];

    UIActivityViewController *vc = [[UIActivityViewController alloc]
        initWithActivityItems:items applicationActivities:customServices];
    vc.excludedActivityTypes = @[UIActivityTypeMail, UIActivityTypeCopyToPasteboard];
    [self presentViewController:vc animated:YES completion:nil];
}

@end
```

If you run the code now and tap the activity button, you'll see that your log activity is among the valid options, as shown in Figure 8-5.

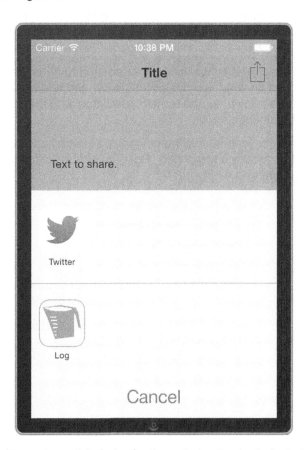

Figure 8-5. The activity view with a custom activity for logging the content on the standard output

If you tap the "Log" icon, your content is sent to the standard output stream, as Figure 8-6 shows.

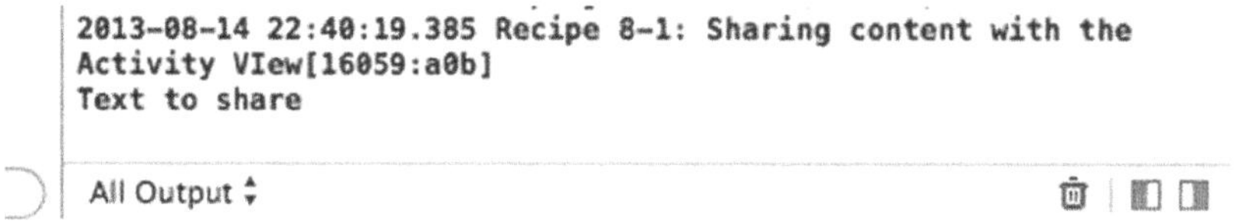

```
2013-08-14 22:40:19.385 Recipe 8-1: Sharing content with the
Activity VIew[16059:a0b]
Text to share
```

All Output ⬍   🗑 | 🔳 🔲

Figure 8-6. *The sharing test app after it sends its content to the custom log activity item*

Recipe 8-2: Sharing Content Using a Compose View

The activity view, as you saw in the previous recipe, provides a standardized way to share content through several different channels. In most cases, this is what you want; the user recognizes the user interface from other apps and can choose to share the content in all the ways that make sense to them. However, what if you want to skip that step and take the user straight to the place where they compose the tweet? For these situations, you can use SLComposeViewController, a class that presents a standard view to the user where they can compose a post in one of the supported social networks. This is the same compose view you would see if you tap the "Twitter" button in the activity view.

The SLComposeViewController currently has support for posting to Facebook, Twitter, and Weibo. In this recipe, you build on what you did in Recipe 8-1 and add a button that uses SLComposeViewController to display a compose view populated with the content, and from which the user can post directly to Facebook.

SLComposeViewController resides in the Social framework, so start by adding it to your project (refer to Recipe 1-2 in Chapter 1). Then add a button titled "Post to Facebook" to the main view. Make the new user interface look something like Figure 8-7.

Figure 8-7. *A user interface with a button for direct targeting of Facebook sharing*

For the new button, create an action named "shareOnFacebook." Also, import the Social framework API into your view controller's header file. The ViewController.h file should look like Listing 8-8.

Listing 8-8. The complete ViewController.h file

```
//
//  ViewController.h
//  Recipe 8-1 Sharing content with the Activity View
//

#import <UIKit/UIKit.h>
#import <Social/Social.h>

@interface ViewController : UIViewController

@property (weak, nonatomic) IBOutlet UITextView *messageTextView;
@property (weak, nonatomic) IBOutlet UITextField *urlTextField;
```

```
- (IBAction)shareContent:(id)sender;
- (IBAction)shareOnFacebook:(id)sender;

@end
```

Finally, implement the shareOnFacebook: action method. Listing 8-9 shows the implementation file.

Listing 8-9. Modification of the shareOnFacebook: method in the ViewController.m file

```
//
//  ViewController.m
//  Recipe 8-1 Sharing content with the Activity View
//

#import "ViewController.h"
#import "MyLogActivity.h"

@implementation ViewController

// ...

- (IBAction)shareOnFacebook:(id)sender
{
    NSString *text = self.messageTextView.text;
    NSURL *url = [NSURL URLWithString:self.urlTextField.text];

    SLComposeViewController *cv =
        [SLComposeViewController composeViewControllerForServiceType:SLServiceTypeFacebook];
    [cv setInitialText:text];
    [cv addURL:url];

    [self presentViewController:cv animated:YES completion:nil];
}

@end
```

> **Note**   Besides URL objects, the compose view also supports the adding of image objects by means of the addImage: method.

As you can see, you initialize the compose view with the text from the text view and the URL from the text field. If you build and run the project now and tap the "Post to Facebook" button, you'll be presented with a Facebook compose sheet from which you can post the content to your Facebook account. As with the activity view, you get all the built-in integration for free, so if a user doesn't have an account installed she will be asked whether she wants to set one up. Figure 8-8 shows an example of this.

Figure 8-8. If the user has no account for the selected service, iOS asks whether one should be set up

In this example, you initialized the compose view to target Facebook. The code for setting up Twitter or Weibo is nearly identical. The only action you need to take is to replace the SLServiceTypeFacebook constant with SLServiceTypeTwitter or SLServiceTypeWeibo, respectively, as shown in the following example:

```
SLComposeViewController *cv =
    [SLComposeViewController composeViewControllerForServiceType:SLServiceTypeTwitter];
```

Recipe 8-3: Sharing Content Using SLRequest

In Recipes 8-1 and 8-2 you learned how to use the built-in user interfaces for sharing content. For some apps, however, it makes sense to build a completely customized user interface. For example, if you are planning to build the best Twitter or Facebook app ever, or if your users aren't interested in the last-touch editing possibility that the built-in compose views are offering, perhaps they would benefit from a more automatic posting experience.

These apps want to use the native API of the respective social network service. Fortunately, iOS 7 offers great help in the SLRequest class. It takes care of the complicated authentication handling for you, making your job a lot easier.

In this recipe, we'll show you how to send a tweet using SLRequest. You'll need a new single view application project. You also will use two external frameworks, the Social framework and the Accounts framework, which is used by the Social framework to handle authorizations. Make sure you add these frameworks to your project before you continue.

Setting Up the Main View

Start by setting up the user interface so that it resembles Figure 8-9. You'll need a text view, a button, and a label. Make the label centered, with two lines, and word wrapped.

Figure 8-9. A simple user interface for posting to Twitter

Create the following outlets and actions:

- Outlet: textView
- Outlet: statusLabel
- Button action: shareOnTwitter

Finally, import the Social and the Accounts framework APIs. Your ViewController.h should now look like Listing 8-10.

Listing 8-10. The modified ViewController.h file

```
//
//  ViewController.h
//  Recipe 8-3 Sharing Content Using SLRequest
//

#import <UIKit/UIKit.h>
#import <Social/Social.h>
#import <Accounts/Accounts.h>

@interface ViewController : UIViewController

@property (weak, nonatomic) IBOutlet UITextView *textView;
@property (weak, nonatomic) IBOutlet UILabel *statusLabel;

- (IBAction)shareOnTwitter:(id)sender;

@end
```

Requesting Access to Twitter Accounts

The first action you need to take when preparing an SLRequest object is to request access to the account type in question. For this, you need an ACAccountStore instance. What's important with this instance is that it needs to stay alive through the entire process of sending requests. The easiest way to do that is to assign it to a property where it'll be retained.

Add the following property declaration, as shown in bold in Listing 8-11, to the ViewController.h file.

Listing 8-11. Adding an ACAccountStore property to the ViewController.h file

```
//
//  ViewController.h
//  Recipe 8-3 Sharing Content Using SLRequest
//

#import <UIKit/UIKit.h>
#import <Social/Social.h>
#import <Accounts/Accounts.h>

@interface ViewController : UIViewController

@property (weak, nonatomic) IBOutlet UITextView *textView;
@property (weak, nonatomic) IBOutlet UILabel *statusLabel;
@property (strong, nonatomic) ACAccountStore *accountStore;

- (IBAction)shareOnTwitter:(id)sender;

@end
```

Now you can start implementing the shareOnTwitter: action method in ViewController.m. Begin by adding the code in bold in Listing 8-12 to request access to the Twitter accounts registered on the device.

Listing 8-12. Completing the implementation of the shareOnTwitter: method

```
- (IBAction)shareOnTwitter:(id)sender
{
    self.accountStore = [[ACAccountStore alloc] init];

    ACAccountType *accountType =
        [self.accountStore accountTypeWithAccountTypeIdentifier:ACAccountTypeIdentifierTwitter];

    [self.accountStore requestAccessToAccountsWithType:accountType options:nil
        completion:^(BOOL granted, NSError *error)
        {

            if (granted)
            {
                //TODO: Get Twitter account and send tweet to it
            }
            else
            {
                //TODO: Handle not granted
            }
        }
    ];
}
```

What's interesting in Listing 8-12 is the requestAccessToAccountsWithType:options:completion: method. It's asynchronous, so you should provide a block, which will be invoked when the method is finished. You then know whether the request was granted by checking the argument with the same name.

If access to the Twitter account was denied, simply update the status label. However, the fact that you are in a code block complicates things a bit. The problem is that the completion block might be invoked on any arbitrary thread, but you shouldn't update the user interface from anything but the main thread. To handle that, use the dispatch_async function, which also takes a code block argument, to perform the updating of the status label from the main thread, as shown in Listing 8-13.

Listing 8-13. Adding code to the requestAccessToAccountsWithType:options:completion: method to update the label

```
[self.accountStore requestAccessToAccountsWithType:accountType options:nil
completion:^(BOOL granted, NSError *error)
{
    __block NSString *statusText = @"";

    if (granted)
    {
        //TODO: Get Twitter account and send tweet to it
    }
```

```
    else
    {
        statusText = @"Access to Twitter accounts was not granted";
    }

    dispatch_async(dispatch_get_main_queue(), ^(void)
    {
        self.statusLabel.text = statusText;
    });
}
```

Now we're going to switch gears and implement the sendText:toTwitterAccount: helper method. This method is what actually posts to Twitter. It's the main lesson of this recipe, so we'll explain its parts.

First, it builds an SLRequest object for the operation. In this case, you will ask Twitter to update the status text, as shown in Listing 8-14.

Listing 8-14. Adding a Twitter request to the sendText:toTwitterAccount: method

```
- (void)sendText:(NSString *)text toTwitterAccount:(ACAccount *)twitterAccount
{
    NSURL *requestURL = [NSURL URLWithString:@"http://api.twitter.com/1/statuses/update.json"];
    SLRequest *tweetRequest = [SLRequest requestForServiceType:SLServiceTypeTwitter
        requestMethod:SLRequestMethodPOST URL:requestURL
        parameters:[NSDictionary dictionaryWithObject:text forKey:@"status"]];

    // ...
}
```

Next, it assigns the account to the request. This step is really important because it's what allows the Service framework to handle all the authentication communication with Twitter. Listing 8-15 shows the addition of the new code in bold.

Listing 8-15. Adding code to Listing 8-14 to set the Twitter account

```
- (void)sendText:(NSString *)text toTwitterAccount:(ACAccount *)twitterAccount
{
    NSURL *requestURL = [NSURL URLWithString:@"http://api.twitter.com/1/statuses/update.json"];
    SLRequest *tweetRequest = [SLRequest requestForServiceType:SLServiceTypeTwitter
        requestMethod:SLRequestMethodPOST URL:requestURL
        parameters:[NSDictionary dictionaryWithObject:text forKey:@"status"]];

    [tweetRequest setAccount:twitterAccount];

    // ...
}
```

Finally, the method sends the request asynchronously and provides a code block that will be invoked on completion. This addition is shown in Listing 8-16.

Listing 8-16. Adding code to Listing 8-15 for sending an asynchronous request

```
- (void)sendText:(NSString *)text toTwitterAccount:(ACAccount *)twitterAccount
{
    NSURL *requestURL = [NSURL URLWithString:@"http://api.twitter.com/1/statuses/update.json"];
    SLRequest *tweetRequest = [SLRequest requestForServiceType:SLServiceTypeTwitter
        requestMethod:SLRequestMethodPOST URL:requestURL
        parameters:[NSDictionary dictionaryWithObject:text forKey:@"status"]];

    [tweetRequest setAccount:twitterAccount];

    [tweetRequest performRequestWithHandler:
     ^(NSData *responseData, NSHTTPURLResponse *urlResponse, NSError *error)
     {
         __block NSString *status;

         if ([urlResponse statusCode] == 200)
         {
             status = [NSString stringWithFormat:@"Tweeted successfully to %@",
                 twitterAccount.accountDescription];
         }
         else
         {
             status = @"Error occurred!";
             NSLog(@"%@", error);
         }

         dispatch_async(dispatch_get_main_queue(), ^(void)
         {
             self.statusLabel.text = status;
         });

     }];
}
```

> **Note** As shown in the preceding method, you can evaluate the results of an SLRequest by checking the
> statusCode of the urlResponse. If this value is 200, the request was successfully completed. Otherwise,
> there was some sort of error. Refer to the Twitter API at https://dev.twitter.com/docs/error-
> codes-responses for specific details about all the various error codes.

Now that the sendText:toTwitterAccount is finished, you'll complete the "TODO" case from Listing 8-12. Here you will take advantage of the new method, although you can use the accountsWithAccountType method of the account store to get an array of available accounts. A user might have several Twitter accounts installed on the device. For now, you will make it simple and grab the first in the list, as shown in Listing 8-17. Later, you will add code that allows a user to choose which Twitter account to use.

Listing 8-17. Completing the "granted if" statement in the requestToAccountsWithType: method completion block

```
- (IBAction)shareOnTwitter:(id)sender
{
    self.accountStore = [[ACAccountStore alloc] init];

    ACAccountType *accountType =
        [self.accountStore accountTypeWithAccountTypeIdentifier:ACAccountTypeIdentifierTwitter];

    [self.accountStore requestAccessToAccountsWithType:accountType options:nil
     completion:^(BOOL granted, NSError *error)
     {
         __block NSString *statusText = @"";

         if (granted)
         {
             NSArray *availableTwitterAccounts =
                 [self.accountStore accountsWithAccountType:accountType];

             if (availableTwitterAccounts.count == 0)
             {
                 statusText = @"No Twitter accounts available";
             }
             else
             {
                 ACAccount *account = [availableTwitterAccounts objectAtIndex:0];
                 [self sendText:self.textView.text toTwitterAccount:account];
             }
         }
         else
         {
             statusText = @"Access to Twitter accounts was not granted";
         }

         dispatch_async(dispatch_get_main_queue(), ^(void)
         {
             self.statusLabel.text = statusText;
         });
    }];
}
```

If you build and run now (and have at least one Twitter account set up on the device) you should, as Figure 8-10 shows, be able to tweet from your app.

Figure 8-10. A tweet successfully sent from the app

Handling Multiple Accounts

What if the user has more than one Twitter account set up on the device? Currently, our app uses the first in the list, but you will add a feature to it that allows the user to actually choose which to use.

You will use an alert view to present the available accounts from which the user will pick. This will require the following steps:

1. Promote the availableTwitterAccounts array, which is currently a local variable in the shareOnTwitter: method, into an instance variable.

2. Reference that array from the delegate method of the alert view.

3. Make the view controller an alert view delegate by adding the UIAlertViewDelegate protocol to your view controller class.

To perform these steps in code, add the bold items in Listing 8-18 to your ViewController.h file.

Listing 8-18. Setting up the view controller header to allow for account selection alert view

```
//
//  ViewController.h
//  Recipe 8-3 Sharing Content Using SLRequest
//

#import <UIKit/UIKit.h>
#import <Social/Social.h>
#import <Accounts/Accounts.h>

@interface ViewController : UIViewController <UIAlertViewDelegate>
{
    @private
    NSArray *availableTwitterAccounts;
}
```

```
@property (weak, nonatomic) IBOutlet UITextView *textView;
@property (weak, nonatomic) IBOutlet UILabel *statusLabel;
@property (strong, nonatomic) ACAccountStore *accountStore;

- (IBAction)shareOnTwitter:(id)sender;

@end
```

And in the shareOnTwitter: method in ViewController.m, make the changes shown in Listing 8-19.

Listing 8-19. Updating the shareOnTwitter method to handle multiple accounts

```
- (IBAction)shareOnTwitter:(id)sender
{
    self.accountStore = [[ACAccountStore alloc] init];

    ACAccountType *accountType =
        [self.accountStore accountTypeWithAccountTypeIdentifier:ACAccountTypeIdentifierTwitter];

    [self.accountStore requestAccessToAccountsWithType:accountType options:nil
     completion:^(BOOL granted, NSError *error)
     {
         __block NSString *statusText = @"";

         if (granted)
         {
             availableTwitterAccounts = [self.accountStore accountsWithAccountType:accountType];

             if (availableTwitterAccounts.count == 0)
             {
                 statusText = @"No Twitter accounts available";
             }
             if (availableTwitterAccounts.count == 1)
             {
                 ACAccount *account = [availableTwitterAccounts objectAtIndex:0];
                 [self sendText:self.textView.text toTwitterAccount:account];
             }
             else if (availableTwitterAccounts.count > 1)
             {
                 dispatch_async(dispatch_get_main_queue(), ^(void)
                 {
                     UIAlertView *alert =
                         [[UIAlertView alloc] initWithTitle:@"Select Twitter Account"
                             message:@"Select the Twitter account you want to use."
                             delegate:self
                             cancelButtonTitle:@"Cancel"
                             otherButtonTitles:nil];
```

```
                    for (ACAccount *twitterAccount in availableTwitterAccounts)
                    {
                        [alert addButtonWithTitle:twitterAccount.accountDescription];
                    }

                    [alert show];
                });
            }
        }
        else
        {
            statusText = @"Access to Twitter accounts was not granted";
        }

        dispatch_async(dispatch_get_main_queue(), ^(void)
        {
            self.statusLabel.text = statusText;
        });
    }];
}
```

Note that you are wrapping the alert view in the same `dispatch_async()` call as you did with the updating of the status label. The reason is the same: alert views must run on the main thread or you might experience problems.

The only task left is to respond when the user selects one of the accounts in the alert view. Do that by adding the delegate method shown in Listing 8-20.

Listing 8-20. Implementation of the alertView:clickedButtonAtIndex: method

```
-(void)alertView:(UIAlertView *)alertView clickedButtonAtIndex:(NSInteger)buttonIndex
{
    if (buttonIndex == 0)
    {
        // User Canceled
        return;
    }

    NSInteger indexInAvailableTwitterAccountsArray = buttonIndex - 1;
    ACAccount *selectedAccount = [availableTwitterAccounts
                            objectAtIndex:indexInAvailableTwitterAccountsArray];
    [self sendText:self.textView.text toTwitterAccount:selectedAccount];
}
```

Before you build and run your app again, make sure you have more than one Twitter account set up on the device (or the iOS simulator). The next time you tap the "Tweet" button, you'll get to choose which of your accounts to send the tweet to. Figure 8-11 shows an example of the alert view.

Figure 8-11. An alert view that allows the user to pick which Twitter account to post to

Recipe 8-4: Retrieving Tweets

Now that you have covered several different methods by which you can post updates to Twitter, you can apply the concepts from the preceding recipe that revolve around the SLRequest class to build an application that can acquire and display tweets.

In this recipe, you will build a simple Twitter reader app that allows the user to view the recent tweets from a Twitter timeline. This timeline will display based on available accounts the user has installed on the device. This will be done using a new application consisting of a navigation controller in combination with table view controllers for the basic tweet navigation.

Setting Up a Navigation-Based Application

Start by setting up the new project from scratch. This time use the Empty Application template. You can name the project "Recipe 8-4 Retrieving Tweets". For this recipe, we'll create the interface programmatically. As in the preceding recipe, you use both the Social and the Accounts frameworks, so go ahead and link those to your project. We'll need to import those frameworks into the view controller we will create shortly.

Next, create the main view controller. It displays a list of Twitter feeds, so create a new class titled MainTableViewController and give it a subclass of UITableViewController. You do not need a .xib file to design any user interface, so be sure the option "With XIB for user interface" is unchecked.

Before you implement the new view controller, go to the app delegate to put in code necessary to implement a navigation controller. Open the AppDelegate.h file and add a property for the navigation controller, as shown in Listing 8-21.

Listing 8-21. Modifying the AppDelegate.h file to include the UINavigationController property

```
//
//  AppDelegate.h
//  Recipe 8-4 Retrieving Tweets
//

#import <UIKit/UIKit.h>

@interface AppDelegate : UIResponder <UIApplicationDelegate>

@property (strong, nonatomic) UIWindow *window;
@property (strong, nonatomic) UINavigationController *navigationController;

@end
```

The corresponding implementation for the AppDelegate.m file is shown in bold in Listing 8-22. Here we are simply creating an instance of the MainTableViewController class we created. We are also setting it to the root view controller, as well as setting up a navigation controller.

Listing 8-22. Modifying the appDelegate.m file to create a MainTableViewController instance

```
//
//  AppDelegate.m
//  Recipe 8-4 Retrieving Tweets
//

#import "AppDelegate.h"
#import "MainTableViewController.h"

@implementation AppDelegate

- (BOOL)application:(UIApplication *)application didFinishLaunchingWithOptions:(NSDictionary *)launchOptions
{
    self.window = [[UIWindow alloc] initWithFrame:[[UIScreen mainScreen] bounds]];
    // Override point for customization after application launch.
    UITableViewController *mainViewController =
        [[MainTableViewController alloc] initWithStyle:UITableViewStyleGrouped];
    self.navigationController =
        [[UINavigationController alloc] initWithRootViewController:mainViewController];
    self.window.rootViewController = self.navigationController;
```

```
    self.window.backgroundColor = [UIColor whiteColor];
    [self.window makeKeyAndVisible];
    return YES;
}

// ...

@end
```

Displaying Available Feeds

Now that you have hooked up the navigation controller and the main table view controller, you can start implementing the table view. The table view displays a number of Twitter feeds that the user can choose to view. In this recipe, you add the feeds of the currently installed Twitter accounts.

To retrieve the installed accounts, you need an account store and an array to store the available accounts. Go to MainTableViewController.h and add the declarations, as shown in bold in Listing 8-23.

Listing 8-23. Modifying the MainTableViewController.h file to include properties for managing accounts

```
//
//  MainTableViewController.h
//  Recipe 8-4 Retrieving Tweets
//

#import <UIKit/UIKit.h>
#import <Accounts/Accounts.h>

@interface MainTableViewController : UITableViewController

@property (strong, nonatomic) ACAccountStore *accountStore;
@property (strong, nonatomic) NSArray *twitterAccounts;

@end
```

Next, go to MainTableViewController.m and add code to the viewDidLoad method to set the navigation title as well as initialize and call the retrieveAccounts method, which we'll create next. Modify the viewDidLoad method, as shown in Listing 8-24.

Listing 8-24. Modifying the viewDidLoad method to set the navigation title and initialize and retrieve accounts

```
- (void)viewDidLoad
{
    [super viewDidLoad];

    self.navigationItem.title = @"My Twitter Reader";
    self.accountStore = [[ACAccountStore alloc] init];
    [self retrieveAccounts];
}
```

In the retrieveAccounts helper method, we're going to ask for permission to access the Twitter accounts. You might recognize the implementation, shown in Listing 8-25, from the preceding recipe.

Listing 8-25. Implementing the retrieveAccounts method

```
- (void)retrieveAccounts
{
    ACAccountType *accountType =
        [self.accountStore accountTypeWithAccountTypeIdentifier:ACAccountTypeIdentifierTwitter];

    [self.accountStore requestAccessToAccountsWithType:accountType options:nil
                                        completion:^(BOOL granted, NSError *error)
    {
        if (granted)
        {
            self.twitterAccounts = [self.accountStore accountsWithAccountType:accountType];
            dispatch_async(dispatch_get_main_queue(), ^(void)
                    {
                        [self.tableView reloadData];
                    });
        }
    }];
}
```

Next, implement the table view data source delegate methods that let the table view know how many rows and sections it should display. You are using only one section, in which you display the public feed plus the available Twitter accounts. Listing 8-26 shows the two methods.

Listing 8-26. Implementation of delegate methods needed to display the correct amount of rows and sections

```
- (NSInteger)numberOfSectionsInTableView:(UITableView *)tableView
{
    // Return the number of sections.
    return 1;
}

- (NSInteger)tableView:(UITableView *)tableView numberOfRowsInSection:(NSInteger)section
{
    // Return the number of rows in the section.
    return self.twitterAccounts.count;
}
```

Next, create a table view cell class that displays the items in the table view. To do this, create a new UITableViewCell class and name it "TwitterFeedCell." Open the header file of the new class and add the code shown in bold in Listing 8-27.

Listing 8-27. Modifying the AppDelegate.h file to include the UINavigationController property

```
//
//  TwitterFeedCell.h
//  Recipe 8-4 Retrieving Tweets
//

#import <UIKit/UIKit.h>
#import <Accounts/Accounts.h>

extern NSString * const TwitterFeedCellId;

@interface TwitterFeedCell : UITableViewCell

@property (strong, nonatomic) ACAccount *twitterAccount;

@end
```

> **Note**   In Listing 8-27, you'll see a new way of creating a variable using *extern*. This creates a variable that can be accessed anywhere in the application. Other programming languages might call this a *global variable*. You'll see later in this recipe that we use this variable from a different class.

Now you will set up a very simple cell with the default look. However, you need to add a disclosure indicator that signals the user that there's a detailed view waiting if the user taps the cell. Open the TwitterFeedCell.m file and change the initWithStyle:reuseIdentifier: method that Xcode generated for you, as shown in Listing 8-28.

Listing 8-28. Creating a cell disclosure indicator in the initializer

```
- (id)initWithStyle:(UITableViewCellStyle)style reuseIdentifier:(NSString *)reuseIdentifier
{
    self = [super initWithStyle:style reuseIdentifier:reuseIdentifier];
    if (self) {
        // Initialization code
        self.accessoryType = UITableViewCellAccessoryDisclosureIndicator;
    }
    return self;
}
```

You'll also set up the reuse constant that you'll use later to "dequeue" cells from the cell cache of the table view. Listing 8-29 shows the line of code you need to add.

Listing 8-29. Setting the cell reuse constant

```
//
//  TwitterFeedCell.m
//  Recipe 8-4 Retrieving Tweets
//
```

```
#import "TwitterFeedCell.h"

NSString * const TwitterFeedCellId = @"TwitterFeedCell";

@implementation TwitterFeedCell

// ...

@end
```

Finally, you'll add a custom setter method for the `twitterAccount` property in the twitterFeedCell.m file. The setter sets the property and also updates the label text of the cell. If the account property is nil, you can assume the cell is representing the public Twitter feed. Listing 8-30 shows the implementation of the setter.

Listing 8-30. Implementing the custom setter method, setTwitterAccount:

```
- (void)setTwitterAccount:(ACAccount *)account
{
    _twitterAccount = account;
    if (_twitterAccount)
    {
        self.textLabel.text = _twitterAccount.accountDescription;
    }
    else
    {
        NSLog(@"No Twitter Account Given!");
    }
}
```

With the cell class finished, you can return to the main table view controller to finish the implementation. First, you'll need to register the `TwitterFeedCell` class with the table view. You can do that in the `viewDidLoad` method, as shown in Listing 8-31.

Listing 8-31. Registering the TwitterFeedCell class in the MainTableViewController class

```
//
//  MainTableViewController.m
//  Recipe 8-4 Retrieving Tweets
//

#import "MainTableViewController.h"
#import "TwitterFeedCell.h"

@implementation MainTableViewController

// ...
```

```objc
- (void)viewDidLoad
{
    [super viewDidLoad];

    //Note the use of the extern variable here
    [self.tableView registerClass:TwitterFeedCell.class
        forCellReuseIdentifier:TwitterFeedCellId];

    self.navigationItem.title = @"Twitter Feeds";
    self.accountStore = [[ACAccountStore alloc] init];
    [self retrieveAccounts];
}

// ...

@end
```

Now you can implement the creation of the cells in the tableView:cellForRowAtIndexPath: delegate method, as shown in Listing 8-32. This code is relatively simple. First, create an instance of the cell for each account; because these are registered cells, they will use the custom class we created. For each cell, set the twitterAccount property, which in turn calls the custom setter that sets the cell label text.

Listing 8-32. Implementation of the tableView:cellForRowAtIndexPath: delegate method

```objc
- (UITableViewCell *)tableView:(UITableView *)tableView cellForRowAtIndexPath:(NSIndexPath
*)indexPath
{

    TwitterFeedCell *cell = [tableView dequeueReusableCellWithIdentifier:TwitterFeedCellId
forIndexPath:indexPath];
    // Configure the cell...

    cell.twitterAccount = [self.twitterAccounts objectAtIndex:indexPath.row];

    return cell;
}
```

If you build and run your app now, you should see a screen similar to the one in Figure 8-12.

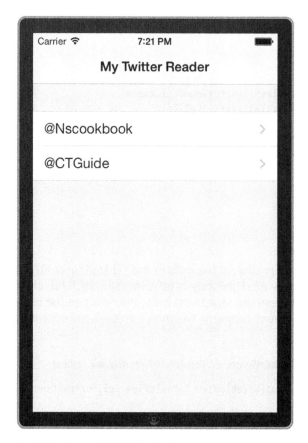

Figure 8-12. A simple Twitter reader displaying available Twitter feeds

Displaying Tweets

With the main view in place and working, you can move on to add another view to display the selected timeline. You will also implement this view with a table view, so begin by creating a new UITableViewController class, this time with the name "TweetTableViewController". Again, you do not need a .xib file for the user interface, so leave that option unselected.

The new view takes a Twitter account and displays its timeline in the table view. You'll start by setting up the header file. Add the code shown in bold in Listing 8-33 to the TweetTableViewController.h file.

Listing 8-33. Setting up the TweetTableViewController.h header file

```
//
//  TweetTableViewController.h
//  Recipe 8-4 Retrieving Tweets
//

#import <UIKit/UIKit.h>
#import <Accounts/Accounts.h>
#import <Social/Social.h>
```

```
@interface TweetTableViewController : UITableViewController
```

@property (strong, nonatomic) ACAccount *twitterAccount;
@property (strong, nonatomic) NSMutableArray *tweets;

-id)initWithStyle:(UITableViewStyle)style;
-(id)initWithTwitterAccount:(ACAccount *)account;

```
@end
```

In the implementation file, start by implementing the initialization methods. Add the code shown in bold in Listing 8-34.

Listing 8-34. Implementing the initialization methods

```
- (id)initWithStyle:(UITableViewStyle)style
{
    self = [super initWithStyle:style];
    if (self) {
        // Custom initialization
        self.tweets = [[NSMutableArray alloc] initWithCapacity:50];
    }
    return self;
}

-(id)initWithTwitterAccount:(ACAccount *)account
{
    self = [self initWithStyle:UITableViewStylePlain];
    if (self) {
        self.twitterAccount = account;
    }
    return self;
}
```

As you'll see later, you use the initWithTwitterAccount: method to set up the view controller. However, by separating the initialization into two methods, you make sure the view controller works in a default setup scenario as well. This might be useful if you decide to reuse this class and try to initialize it without specifying the account, such as [[TweetTableViewController alloc] init].

In the viewDidLoad method, update the title of the navigation bar and call the method to retrieve the timeline, which we will implement next. Modify the viewDidLoad method, as shown in Listing 8-35.

Listing 8-35. Modifying the viewDidLoad method to set the navigation title and call the retrieveTweets method

```
    - (void)viewDidLoad
{
    [super viewDidLoad];

        self.navigationItem.title = self.twitterAccount.accountDescription;

    [self retrieveTweets];
}
```

The `retrieveTweets` method is the essence of this recipe. It's the one that retrieves the tweets from the given Twitter feed. The Twitter feed will be the home timeline of the user. Listing 8-36 shows the method implementation.

Listing 8-36. Implementing the retrieveTweets method

```
-(void)retrieveTweets
{
    [self.tweets removeAllObjects];

    SLRequest *request;

    if (self.twitterAccount)
    {
        // Get home timeline of the Twitter account
        NSURL *requestURL =
            [NSURL URLWithString:@"http://api.twitter.com/1.1/statuses/home_timeline.json"];
        request = [SLRequest requestForServiceType:SLServiceTypeTwitter
            requestMethod:SLRequestMethodGET URL:requestURL parameters:nil];
        [request setAccount:self.twitterAccount];
    }
    else
    {

        NSLog(@"Uh oh, there's no Twitter account!");

    }


    [request performRequestWithHandler:
    ^(NSData *responseData, NSHTTPURLResponse *urlResponse, NSError *error)
    {
        if ([urlResponse statusCode] == 200)
        {
            NSError *jsonParsingError;
            self.tweets = [NSJSONSerialization JSONObjectWithData:responseData
                options:0 error:&jsonParsingError];
        }
        else
        {
            NSLog(@"HTTP response status: %i\n", [urlResponse statusCode]);
        }
        dispatch_async(dispatch_get_main_queue(), ^(void)
                    {
                        [self.tableView reloadData];
                    });
    }];
}
```

There's a lot going on in Listing 8-36, so we'll take a moment to break it down. The first thing we're doing is removing any tweets from the tweets array. If there are available accounts, then we create a request using the Twitter API URL to get statuses: "`http://api.twitter.com/1.1/statuses/home_timeline.json`." Then we perform the request and populate the tweets array once it is finished.

Note that the response from Twitter comes in a JSON format, which you decode using the NSJSONSerialization class. The result is an array of dictionaries, one for each tweet.

With the data in place, you can start implementing the table view to display it. As in the main table view, you will have only one section that contains the recent tweets. Make the changes to the numberOfSectionsInTableView: and the tableView:numberOfRowsInSection: methods, as shown in Listing 8-37.

Listing 8-37. Implementing the delegate methods for displaying the correct number of rows and sections

```
- (NSInteger)numberOfSectionsInTableView:(UITableView *)tableView
{
    // Return the number of sections.
    return 1;
}

- (NSInteger)tableView:(UITableView *)tableView numberOfRowsInSection:(NSInteger)section
{
    // Return the number of rows in the section.
    return self.tweets.count;
}
```

Because the cells in this table view have a slightly different look and content than the ones in the main table view, you need to create a new UITableViewCell subclass. This time, name the class "TweetCell."

Open TweetCell.h and make the changes shown in Listing 8-38.

Listing 8-38. Setting up the TweetCell.h file

```
//
//  TweetCell.h
//  Recipe 8-4 Retrieving Tweets
//

#import <UIKit/UIKit.h>

extern NSString * const TweetCellId = @"TweetCell";

@interface TweetCell : UITableViewCell

@property (strong, nonatomic)NSDictionary *tweetData;

@end
```

This cell type uses the standard look with a subtitle and a disclosure indicator. Make these changes to the initWithStyle:reuseIdentifier: method (in the TweetCell.m file), as shown in Listing 8-39.

Listing 8-39. Implementing the custom TweetCell initializer

```
- (id)initWithStyle:(UITableViewCellStyle)style reuseIdentifier:(NSString *)reuseIdentifier
{
    self = [super initWithStyle:UITableViewCellStyleSubtitle reuseIdentifier:reuseIdentifier];
    if (self)
    {
        // Initialization code
        self.accessoryType = UITableViewCellAccessoryDisclosureIndicator;
    }
    return self;
}
```

The cell updates its labels when it receives new tweet data. To accomplish that, you'll add a custom setter method for the tweetData property, as shown in Listing 8-40.

Listing 8-40. Implementing the setTweetData: method

```
-(void)setTweetData:(NSDictionary *)tweetData
{
    _tweetData = tweetData;
    // Update cell
    NSDictionary *userData = [_tweetData objectForKey:@"user"];
    self.textLabel.text = [userData objectForKey:@"name"];
    self.detailTextLabel.text = [_tweetData objectForKey:@"text"];
}
```

Let's complete the implementation of the table view. Go back to TweetTableViewController.m and make changes, as shown in Listing 8-41.

Listing 8-41. Registering the TweetCell class and adding the cells to the table

```
//
//  TweetTableViewController.m
//  Recipe 8-4 Retrieving Tweets
//

#import "TweetTableViewController.h"
#import "TweetCell.h"

@implementation TweetTableViewController

- (void)viewDidLoad
{
    [super viewDidLoad];

    [self.tableView registerClass:TweetCell.class forCellReuseIdentifier:TweetCellId];

        self.navigationItem.title = self.twitterAccount.accountDescription;

    [self retrieveTweets];
}
// ...
```

```
- (UITableViewCell *)tableView:(UITableView *)tableView cellForRowAtIndexPath:(NSIndexPath *)indexPath
{
    TweetCell *cell = [tableView dequeueReusableCellWithIdentifier:TweetCellId
forIndexPath:indexPath];
    // Configure the cell...
    cell.tweetData = [self.tweets objectAtIndex:indexPath.row];

    return cell;
}

// ...

@end
```

You're done for now with the tweet table view, so let's return to the main table view and implement the code that displays the new view controller. Open MainTableViewController.m and add the table View:didSelectRowAtIndexPath: delegate method, as shown in Listing 8-42.

Listing 8-42. Adding code to the tableView:didSelectRowAtIndexPath: method to display the tweet table view

```
#import "TweetTableViewController.h"
#import "MainTableViewController.h"
#import "TwitterFeedCell.h"
#import "TweetTableViewController.h"

@interface MainTableViewController ()
//...

- (void)tableView:(UITableView *)tableView didSelectRowAtIndexPath:(NSIndexPath *)indexPath
{
    // Navigation logic may go here. Create and push another view controller.
    ACAccount *account = nil;

        account = [self.twitterAccounts objectAtIndex:indexPath.row];

    TweetTableViewController *detailViewController = [[TweetTableViewController alloc]
initWithTwitterAccount:account];
    // ...
    // Pass the selected object to the new view controller.
    [self.navigationController pushViewController:detailViewController animated:YES];
}
//...
```

It's again time to build and run your app. This time you should be able to select one of the timelines and get a list of the most recent tweets. Figure 8-13 shows an example of this new table view.

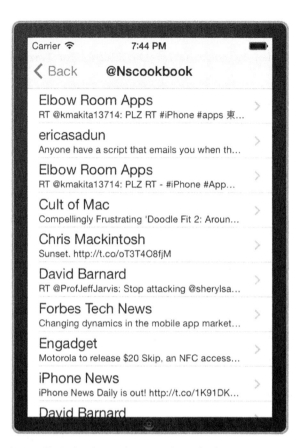

Figure 8-13. A simple tweet reader app displaying the public tweets feed of Twitter

Showing Individual Tweets

When the user taps a tweet cell, we should display a detailed view of that tweet. This will be a simple view controller, so you will create a new UIViewController subclass with the name "TweetViewController." This time, however, you will build its user interface in Interface Builder, so make sure to select the "With XIB for user interface" option.

Open the new TweetViewController.xib file to bring up Interface Builder. The first thing you're going to do is to make sure you design the user interface with the navigation bar in mind. Select the view and go to the attribute inspector. In the Simulated Metrics section, change the value of the Top Bar attribute from "None" to "Translucent Navigation Bar" (see Figure 8-14). This displays a navigation bar in the view, which is helpful when you're creating your layout.

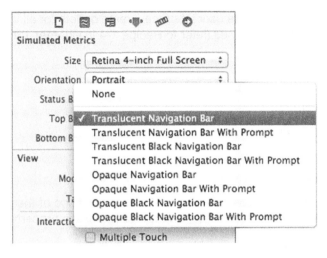

Figure 8-14. Simulating a navigation bar to help in user interface design

You're going to create a user interface for displaying the tweet details. You'll need an image view, four labels, and a text view to display the actual tweet. Drag those items onto the view from the object library and arrange them as shown in Figure 8-15. Make sure you change your "Description" label to two lines and make the size of the label a little bigger so it has room to grow. The image view shown in Figure 8-15 has a size of 64 points x 64 points.

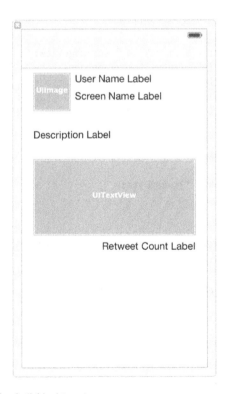

Figure 8-15. A user interface for showing individual tweets

When you're done with the layout of the user interface, create outlets for all the components. Give the outlets the following respective names (refer to Recipe 1-4 in Chapter 1 for creating outlets):

- userImageView
- userNameLabel
- userScreenNameLabel
- userDescriptionLabel
- tweetTextView
- retweetCountLabel

With the outlets created, you should see property outlets for each one of them in the TweetViewController.h file. In addition to those, add an NSDictionary property and declare a custom initializer method, as shown in Listing 8-43.

Listing 8-43. Adding an NSDictionary property and custom initializer to TweetViewController.h

```
//
//  TweetViewController.h
//  Recipe 8-4 Retrieving Tweets
//

#import <UIKit/UIKit.h>

@interface TweetViewController : UIViewController

@property (weak, nonatomic) IBOutlet UIImageView *userImageView;
@property (weak, nonatomic) IBOutlet UILabel *userNameLabel;
@property (weak, nonatomic) IBOutlet UILabel *userScreenNameLabel;
@property (weak, nonatomic) IBOutlet UILabel *userDescriptionLabel;
@property (weak, nonatomic) IBOutlet UITextView *tweetTextView;
@property (weak, nonatomic) IBOutlet UILabel *retweetCountLabel;

@property (strong, nonatomic) NSDictionary *tweetData;

-(id)initWithTweetData:(NSDictionary *)tweetData;

@end
```

The implementation of the initializer is pretty straightforward. Add the initializer to the TweetViewController.m file, as shown in Listing 8-44.

Listing 8-44. Adding the custom initializer method to the TweetViewController.m file

```
//
//  TweetViewController.m
//  Recipe 8-4 Retrieving Tweets
//
```

```
#import "TweetViewController.h"

@implementation TweetViewController

-(id)initWithTweetData:(NSDictionary *)tweetData
{
    self = [super initWithNibName:nil bundle:nil];
    if (self) {
        _tweetData = tweetData;
    }
    return self;
}

// ...

@end
```

If someone changes the tweetData property, you need to update the view with the new data. Therefore, add a custom setter with the implementation shown in Listing 8-45.

Listing 8-45. Implementing the setTweetData method

```
-(void)setTweetData:(NSDictionary *)tweetData
{
    _tweetData = tweetData;
    [self updateView];
}
```

The updateView helper method takes the tweet data and updates the controls in the view, including the image view. Implement this method, as shown in Listing 8-46.

Listing 8-46. Implementation of the updateView method

```
-(void)updateView
{
    NSDictionary *userData = [self.tweetData objectForKey:@"user"];

    NSString *imageURLString = [userData objectForKey:@"profile_image_url"];
    NSURL *imageURL = [NSURL URLWithString:imageURLString];
    NSData *imageData = [NSData dataWithContentsOfURL:imageURL];
    self.userImageView.image = [UIImage imageWithData:imageData];

    self.userNameLabel.text = [userData objectForKey:@"name"];
    self.userScreenNameLabel.text = [userData objectForKey:@"screen_name"];
    self.userDescriptionLabel.text = [userData objectForKey:@"description"];

    self.tweetTextView.text = [self.tweetData objectForKey:@"text"];
    self.retweetCountLabel.text = [NSString stringWithFormat:@"Retweet Count: %@",
        [self.tweetData objectForKey:@"retweet_count"]];
}
```

Finally, in the `viewDidLoad` method set the title of the navigation bar and call the method from Listing 8-46. The `viewDidLoad` method should now look like Listing 8-47.

Listing 8-47. The modified viewDidLoad method

```
- (void)viewDidLoad
{
    [super viewDidLoad];
    // Do any additional setup after loading the view from its nib.
    self.navigationItem.title = @"Tweet";
    [self updateView];
}
```

Your tweet view controller is now ready to use. Let's implement the code that will display it. Return to TweetTableViewController.m and modify the implementation of the `tableView:didSelectRowAtIndexPath:` method, as shown in Listing 8-48. This step should look very familiar, as it is nearly the same as adding the TweetTableViewController to the MainTableViewController's table view cells.

Listing 8-48. Adding code to display the tweetViewController

```
#import "TweetTableViewController.h"
#import "TweetCell.h"
#import "TweetViewController.h"

@interface TweetTableViewController ()
//...

- (void)tableView:(UITableView *)tableView didSelectRowAtIndexPath:(NSIndexPath *)indexPath
{
    // Navigation logic may go here. Create and push another view controller.
    NSDictionary *tweetData = [self.tweets objectAtIndex:indexPath.row];
    TweetViewController *detailViewController =
        [[TweetViewController alloc] initWithTweetData:tweetData];
    // ...
    // Pass the selected object to the new view controller.
    [self.navigationController pushViewController:detailViewController animated:YES];
}
//...
```

With the individual tweet view, your app is finished. You can now select a feed, then a tweet, and see its detail, as shown in Figure 8-16.

Figure 8-16. A view displaying a tweet

Summary

In this chapter, you learned the three major ways in which you can implement social networking features in iOS 7. You've seen UIActivityViewController, which is the easiest way to share your app's content; you've looked at a more direct way to target Twitter, Facebook, and other social media using SLComposeViewController; and, finally, you've seen how you can use SLRequest to use every aspect of the native APIs of these social networks. Social networking is a thing of the past, the present, as well as the future, and iOS 7 has the tools you need to help your users share and connect through your apps.

Chapter 9

Camera Recipes

A great number of mobile applications can interact with your device's camera, including apps that take pictures, record videos, and provide overlays (for example, augmented-reality applications such as a constellation app). iOS developers have a great deal of control in how they can interact with any given device's hardware. With iOS 7, a number of features have been added to improve capture quality and give developers more to work with, such as increased frame rate and smoother auto focus. One exciting new feature is the ability to use real-time discovery of machine-readable metadata (barcodes). In this chapter, you will learn multiple ways to access and use these functionalities, from simple, predefined interfaces to incredibly flexible, custom implementations, as well as capturing machine-readable metadata.

> **Note** The iOS simulator does not support camera hardware. To test most recipes in this chapter, you must run them on a physical device.

Recipe 9-1: Taking Pictures

iOS has an incredibly handy and simple interface to your device's camera. With this interface you can allow users to take pictures and record video from inside an app. Here, you learn the basics of starting the camera interface to capture a still image.

To begin, you will create a simple project that allows you to pull up your camera, take a picture, and then display the most recently taken image on your screen. First, create a new single view application project. For this recipe, you don't need to import any extra frameworks into your project.

Setting Up the User Interface

Set up a simple user interface containing an image view and a button. Switch over to the view in your Main.storyboard file. Then drag an image view from the object library and make it fill the entire view. Next, drag out a UIButton into your view. The button accesses the camera, so set its text to "Take Picture." Your view should now resemble the view in Figure 9-1. You may want to position the button high enough or add a constraint so it won't be cut off on a 3.5" screen (see Chapter 3 for adding Auto Layout constraints).

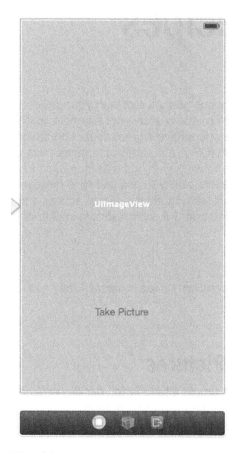

Figure 9-1. A simple user interface for taking pictures

Create outlets for your image view and your button and name them "imageView" and "cameraButton," respectively. Also, create an action with the name "takePicture" for your button.

Your ViewController.h file should now resemble the code in Listing 9-1.

Listing 9-1. The ViewController.h file with added outlets and the takePicture: method

```
//
//   ViewController.h
//   Recipe 9-1 Taking Pictures
//

#import <UIKit/UIKit.h>

@interface ViewController : UIViewController

@property (weak, nonatomic) IBOutlet UIImageView *imageView;
@property (weak, nonatomic) IBOutlet UIButton *cameraButton;

- (IBAction)takePicture:(id)sender;

@end
```

Accessing the Camera

To access the camera you will use the UIImagePickerController class, which presents an interface for choosing photos or taking them. Whenever dealing with the camera hardware on iOS, it is essential that, as a developer, you include a function to have your app check for hardware availability. This is done through the isSourceTypeAvailable: class method of UIImagePickerController. The method takes one of the following predefined constants as an argument:

- UIImagePickerControllerSourceTypeCamera

- UIImagePickerControllerSourceTypePhotoLibrary

- UIImagePickerControllerSourceTypeSavedPhotosAlbum

For this recipe you'll use the first choice, UIImagePickerControllerSourceTypeCamera. UIImagePickerControllerPhotoLibrary is used to access all the stored photos on the device, while UIImagePickerControllerSavedPhotosAlbum is used to access only the Camera Roll album.

Now, switch to the ViewController.m file and locate the stubbed out takePicture: action method. There, you'll begin by checking whether the camera source type is available and, if not, display a UIAlertView saying so. Fill out the takePicture method, as shown in Listing 9-2.

Listing 9-2. The takePicture: method implementation

```
- (IBAction)takePicture:(id)sender
{
    // Make sure camera is available
    if ([UIImagePickerController
        isSourceTypeAvailable:UIImagePickerControllerSourceTypeCamera] == NO)
    {
        UIAlertView *alert = [[UIAlertView alloc] initWithTitle:@"Error"
                                                        message:@"Camera Unavailable"
                                                       delegate:self
```

```
                                    cancelButtonTitle:@"Cancel"
                                    otherButtonTitles:nil, nil];
        [alert show];
        return;
    }
}
```

The iOS simulator does not have camera functionality. Therefore, you'll see only the error message, demonstrated in Figure 9-2, when you run your app there. To fully test this application, you will need to run it on a physical device.

Figure 9-2. The simulator does not have camera support, so you need to test your app on a real device

Before you expand the takePicture: method in the case in which the camera is in fact available, you need to make a couple of changes in ViewController.h. The first is to add a property to hold the image-picker instance through which interface you'll access the camera. The second change is to prepare the view controller for receiving events from the image picker. Such a delegate needs to conform to both UIImagePickerControllerDelegate and UINavigationControllerDelegate protocols. Update the header file with the changes in bold shown in Listing 9-3.

Listing 9-3. The updated ViewController.h file with delegates and the UIImagePickerController property

```
//
//  ViewController.h
//  Recipe 9-1 Taking Pictures
//

#import <UIKit/UIKit.h>

@interface ViewController : UIViewController<UIImagePickerControllerDelegate,
                                             UINavigationControllerDelegate>

@property (weak, nonatomic) IBOutlet UIImageView *imageView;
@property (weak, nonatomic) IBOutlet UIButton *cameraButton;
@property (strong, nonatomic) UIImagePickerController *imagePicker;


- (IBAction)takePicture:(id)sender;

@end
```

Now you can fill out the code in your takePicture: action method in ViewController.m. It creates and initializes the image-picker instance—if it hasn't already done so—and presents it to handle the camera device (Listing 9-4).

Listing 9-4. Adding code to the takePicture: method to initialize and present the camera

```
- (IBAction)takePicture:(id)sender
{
        // Make sure camera is available
    if ([UIImagePickerController
          isSourceTypeAvailable:UIImagePickerControllerSourceTypeCamera] == NO)
    {
        UIAlertView *alert = [[UIAlertView alloc] initWithTitle:@"Error"
                                                        message:@"Camera Unavailable"
                                                       delegate:self
                                              cancelButtonTitle:@"Cancel"
                                              otherButtonTitles:nil, nil];
        [alert show];
        return;
    }
    if (self.imagePicker == nil)
    {
        self.imagePicker = [[UIImagePickerController alloc] init];
        self.imagePicker.delegate = self;
        self.imagePicker.sourceType = UIImagePickerControllerSourceTypeCamera;

    }
    [self presentViewController:self.imagePicker animated:YES completion:NULL];
}
```

If you run your app now (on a real device) and tap the button, you should be presented with a simple camera interface that allows you to take a picture and select it for the purpose of your app (or retake it if you're not satisfied). Figure 9-3 shows the user interface of UIImagePickerController.

Figure 9-3. The user interface of a UIImagePickerViewController

Retrieving a Picture

Now that you have set up your view controller to successfully present your UIImagePickerController, you need to handle how your view controller reacts to the completion of the UIImagePickerController's selection, when a picture has been taken and selected for use. Do this by using the delegate method i magePickerController:didFinishPickingMediaWithInfo:. Retrieve the picture, update the image view, and finally dismiss the image picker, as shown in Listing 9-5.

Listing 9-5. Implementing the imagePickerController:didFinishPickingMediaWithInfo: delegate method

```
-(void)imagePickerController:(UIImagePickerController *)picker
didFinishPickingMediaWithInfo:(NSDictionary *)info
{
    UIImage *image = [info objectForKey:UIImagePickerControllerOriginalImage];
    self.imageView.image = image;
    self.imageView.contentMode = UIViewContentModeScaleAspectFill;
    [self dismissViewControllerAnimated:YES completion:NULL];
}
```

> **Note** By setting the content-mode property of the image view to `UIViewContentModeScaleAspectFill`,
> we ensure that the picture will fill the entire view while still maintaining its aspect ratio. This usually
> results in the picture's being cropped instead of looking stretched. Alternatively, you could use
> `UIViewContentModeScaleAspectFit`, which displays the entire picture with a retained aspect ratio but
> does not necessarily fill the entire view.

Another delegate method needs to be implemented to handle the cancellation of an image selection.
The only action you need to take is to dismiss the image-picker view. Add the code in Listing 9-6 to
the implementation file.

Listing 9-6. Implementing the imagePickerControllerDidCancel: delegate method

```
- (void) imagePickerControllerDidCancel: (UIImagePickerController *) picker
{
    [self dismissViewControllerAnimated:YES completion:NULL];
}
```

Your app can now access the camera, take a picture, and set it as the background of the app, as
Figure 9-4 shows.

Figure 9-4. Your app with a photo set as the background

> **Note**   The `UIImagePickerController` class does not support landscape orientation for taking pictures. Although you *can* take pictures that way, the view does not adjust according to the landscape orientation, which results in a rather weird user experience.

Implementing Basic Editing

As an optional setting, you could allow your camera interface to be editable, enabling the user to crop and frame the picture he has taken. To do this, you simply have to set the `UIImagePickerController`'s `allowsEditing` property to `YES`, as shown in Listing 9-7.

Listing 9-7. Modifying the takePicture: action method to allow editing

```
- (IBAction)takePicture:(id)sender
{
    // ...

    if (self.imagePicker == nil)
    {
```

```
        self.imagePicker = [[UIImagePickerController alloc] init];
        self.imagePicker.delegate = self;
        self.imagePicker.sourceType = UIImagePickerControllerSourceTypeCamera;
        self.imagePicker.allowsEditing = YES;


    }
    [self presentViewController:self.imagePicker animated:YES completion:NULL];
}
```

Then, to acquire the edited image, you also need to make a change in the imagePickerController:didFinishPickingMediaWithInfo: method, as shown in Listing 9-8.

Listing 9-8. Modifying imagePickerController:didFinishPickingMediaWithInfo: to receive edited image

```
-(void)imagePickerController:(UIImagePickerController *)picker
didFinishPickingMediaWithInfo:(NSDictionary *)info
{
    UIImage *image = [info objectForKey:UIImagePickerControllerEditedImage];
    self.imageView.image = image;
    self.imageView.contentMode = UIViewContentModeScaleAspectFill;
    [self dismissViewControllerAnimated:YES completion:NULL];
}
```

Saving Pictures to a Photos Album

You might want to save the pictures you take to the device's saved-photos album. This is easily done with the UIImageWriteToSavedPhotosAlbum() function. Add a line to your imagePickerViewController:didFinishPickingMediaWithInfo: method, as shown in Listing 9-9.

Listing 9-9. Modifying the imagePickerController:didFinishPickingMediaWithInfo: method to add a save option

```
-(void)imagePickerController:(UIImagePickerController *)picker
didFinishPickingMediaWithInfo:(NSDictionary *)info
{
    UIImage *image = (UIImage *)[info objectForKey:UIImagePickerControllerEditedImage];
    UIImageWriteToSavedPhotosAlbum (image, nil, nil , nil);
    self.imageView.image = image;
    self.imageView.contentMode = UIViewContentModeScaleAspectFill;
    [self dismissViewControllerAnimated:YES completion:NULL];
}
```

However, as of iOS 6 privacy restrictions have been applied to the saved-photos album; an app that wants to access it now needs an explicit authorization from the user. Therefore, you should also provide an explanation as to why your app requests access to the saved-photos library. This is done in the application's Info.plist file (found in the Supporting Files folder in the project navigator) and the key NSPhotoLibraryUsageDescription (or "Privacy—Photo Library Usage Description," as it's displayed in the property list).

You can enter any text you want for the usage description; we chose "Testing the camera." The important thing to know is that the text will be displayed to the user when he is prompted for authorizing the app access to the photo album, as in Figure 9-5.

Figure 9-5. Saving the picture to the photos library will need an authorization from the user

Recipe 9-2: Recording Video

Your UIImagePickerController is actually a lot more flexible than you've seen so far, especially because you've been using it exclusively for still images. Here, you'll learn how to set up your UIImagePickerController to handle both still images and video.

For this recipe, you build off the code from Recipe 9-1 because it already includes the setup you need. You add to its functionality by implementing the option to record and save videos.

Start by setting the image picker's allowed media types to all available types for the camera. This can be done using the availableMediaTypesForSourceType: class method of the UIImagePickerController, as shown in Listing 9-10.

Listing 9-10. Updating the takePicture: method to allow video recording

```
- (IBAction)takePicture:(id)sender
{
    // Make sure camera is available
    if ([UIImagePickerController
        isSourceTypeAvailable:UIImagePickerControllerSourceTypeCamera] == NO)
    {
        UIAlertView *alert = [[UIAlertView alloc] initWithTitle:@"Error"
                                                    message:@"Camera Unavailable"
                                                    delegate:self
                                            cancelButtonTitle:@"Cancel"
                                            otherButtonTitles:nil, nil];
        [alert show];
        return;
    }
    if (self.imagePicker == nil)
    {
        self.imagePicker = [[UIImagePickerController alloc] init];
        self.imagePicker.delegate = self;
        self.imagePicker.sourceType = UIImagePickerControllerSourceTypeCamera;
        self.imagePicker.mediaTypes = [UIImagePickerController
            availableMediaTypesForSourceType:UIImagePickerControllerSourceTypeCamera];
        self.imagePicker.allowsEditing = YES;

    }
    [self presentViewController:self.imagePicker animated:YES completion:NULL];
}
```

Next, you need to instruct your application on how to handle when the user records and uses a video. To do this, link the Mobile Core Services framework to your project and import its API in your view controller's header file, as shown in Listing 9-11.

Listing 9-11. Importing the framework to the ViewController.h file

```
//
//  ViewController.h
//  Recipe 9-2 Recording Videos
//

#import <UIKit/UIKit.h>
#import <MobileCoreServices/MobileCoreServices.h>

@interface ViewController : UIViewController<UIImagePickerControllerDelegate,
UINavigationControllerDelegate>

@property (weak, nonatomic) IBOutlet UIImageView *imageView;
@property (weak, nonatomic) IBOutlet UIButton *cameraButton;
@property (strong, nonatomic) UIImagePickerController *imagePicker;

- (IBAction)takePicture:(id)sender;

@end
```

Now add the bold code in Listing 9-12 to your UIImagePickerController's delegate method.

Listing 9-12. Adding video comparison to the imagePickerController:didFinishPickingMediaWithInfo: method

```
-(void)imagePickerController:(UIImagePickerController *)picker
didFinishPickingMediaWithInfo:(NSDictionary *)info
{
    NSString *mediaType = [info objectForKey: UIImagePickerControllerMediaType];

    if (CFStringCompare((__bridge CFStringRef) mediaType, kUTTypeMovie, 0) ==
        kCFCompareEqualTo)
    {
        // Movie Captured
        NSString *moviePath =
            (NSString *) [[info objectForKey: UIImagePickerControllerMediaURL] path];

        if (UIVideoAtPathIsCompatibleWithSavedPhotosAlbum (moviePath))
        {
            UISaveVideoAtPathToSavedPhotosAlbum (moviePath, nil, nil, nil);
        }
    }
    else
    {
        // Picture Taken
        UIImage *image =
            (UIImage *)[info objectForKey:UIImagePickerControllerEditedImage];
```

```
        UIImageWriteToSavedPhotosAlbum (image, nil, nil , nil);
        self.imageView.image = image;
        self.imageView.contentMode = UIViewContentModeScaleAspectFill;
    }
    [self dismissViewControllerAnimated:YES completion:NULL];
}
```

Essentially, what you are doing in Listing 9-12 is comparing the media type of the saved file. The main issue comes into play when you attempt to compare mediaType, which is an NSString, with kUTTypeMovie, which is of the type CFStringRef. You accomplish this by casting your NSString down to a CFStringRef. In iOS 5+ this process became slightly more complicated with the introduction of Automatic Reference Counting (ARC) because ARC deals with Objective-C object types such as NSString, but not with C types like CFStringRef. You create a bridged casting by placing __bridge before your CFStringRef, as shown earlier, to instruct ARC not to deal with this object.

If all has gone well, your app should now be able to record video by selecting the video mode in the image-picker view, as shown in Figure 9-6. The video is then saved (if allowed by the user) to the private photos library.

Figure 9-6. The image-picker view with a switch control between photo and video modes

Recipe 9-3: Editing Videos

Although your UIImagePickerController offers a convenient way to record and save video files, it does nothing to allow you to edit them. Fortunately, iOS has another built-in controller called UIVideoEditorController, which you can use to edit your recorded videos.

You can build this fairly simple recipe off your second project from Recipe 9-2, in which you added video functionality to your UIImagePickerController.

Start by adding a second button with the title "Edit Video" to your view controller's interface file. Arrange the two buttons, as shown in Figure 9-7.

Figure 9-7. New user interface with a button for editing the video

Next, create an action named editVideo for when the user taps the "Edit Video" button.

You'll also need a property to store the path to the video that the user records. Define it in the view controller's header file, as shown in Listing 9-13.

Listing 9-13. The ViewController.h file with the new additions

```
//
//  ViewController.h
//  Recipe 9-3 Editing Videos
//

#import <UIKit/UIKit.h>
#import <MobileCoreServices/MobileCoreServices.h>

@interface ViewController : UIViewController<UIImagePickerControllerDelegate,
UINavigationControllerDelegate>

@property (weak, nonatomic) IBOutlet UIImageView *imageView;
@property (weak, nonatomic) IBOutlet UIButton *cameraButton;
@property (strong, nonatomic) UIImagePickerController *imagePicker;
@property (strong, nonatomic) NSString *pathToRecordedVideo;

- (IBAction)takePicture:(id)sender;
- (IBAction)editVideo:(id)sender;

@end
```

Now, in the imagePickerController:didFinishPickingMediaWithInfo: method, make sure the pathToRecordedVideo property gets updated with the path to the newly recorded video, as shown in Listing 9-14.

Listing 9-14. Adding the video path for the newly recorded video

```
-(void)imagePickerController:(UIImagePickerController *)picker
didFinishPickingMediaWithInfo:(NSDictionary *)info
{
    NSString *mediaType = [info objectForKey: UIImagePickerControllerMediaType];

    if (CFStringCompare((__bridge CFStringRef) mediaType, kUTTypeMovie, 0) ==
        kCFCompareEqualTo)
    {
        NSString *moviePath = (NSString *)[[info objectForKey: UIImagePickerControllerMediaURL] path];
        self.pathToRecordedVideo = moviePath;

        if (UIVideoAtPathIsCompatibleWithSavedPhotosAlbum (moviePath))
        {
            UISaveVideoAtPathToSavedPhotosAlbum (moviePath, nil, nil, nil);
        }
    }
    else
    {
        //...
    }
}
```

With the `pathToRecordedVideo` property in place, you can turn your focus to your `editVideo` action. This action opens the last recorded video for editing in a video editor controller, or displays an error if no video was recorded. Listing 9-15 shows this method implementation.

Listing 9-15. The editVideo method implementation

```
- (IBAction)editVideo:(id)sender
{
    if (self.pathToRecordedVideo)
    {
        UIVideoEditorController *editor = [[UIVideoEditorController alloc] init];
        editor.videoPath = self.pathToRecordedVideo;
        editor.delegate = self;
        [self presentViewController:editor animated:YES completion:NULL];
    }
    else
    {
        UIAlertView *alert = [[UIAlertView alloc] initWithTitle:@"Error"
            message:@"No Video Recorded Yet"
            delegate:self
            cancelButtonTitle:@"Cancel"
            otherButtonTitles:nil, nil];
        [alert show];
    }
}
```

Because the video editor's receiving delegate is your view controller, you need to make sure it conforms to the `UIVideoEditorControllerDelegate` protocol. Add the protocol to the header file, as shown in Listing 9-16.

Listing 9-16. Declaring the UIVideoEditorControllerDelegate protocol

```
// ...

@interface ViewController : UIViewController<UIImagePickerControllerDelegate,
                                             UINavigationControllerDelegate,
                                             UIVideoEditorControllerDelegate>

// ...

@end
```

Finally, you need to implement a few delegate methods for your `UIVideoEditorController`. First, you need a delegate method to handle a successful editing/trimming. Listing 9-17 shows this method.

Listing 9-17. The VideoEditorController:didSaveEditedVideoToPath: delegate method implementation

```
-(void)videoEditorController:(UIVideoEditorController *)editor
didSaveEditedVideoToPath:(NSString *)editedVideoPath
{
    self.pathToRecordedVideo = editedVideoPath;
    if (UIVideoAtPathIsCompatibleWithSavedPhotosAlbum (editedVideoPath))
```

```
    {
        UISaveVideoAtPathToSavedPhotosAlbum (editedVideoPath, nil, nil, nil);
    }
    [self dismissViewControllerAnimated:YES completion:NULL];
}
```

As you can see, your application sets the newly edited video as your next video to be edited so that you can create increasingly trimmed clips. It also saves each edited version to your photo album, if possible.

You need one more delegate method to handle the cancellation of your UIVideoEditorController. Add the implementation of the method shown in Listing 9-18.

Listing 9-18. Implementation of the videoEditorControllerDidCancel: delegate method

```
-(void)videoEditorControllerDidCancel:(UIVideoEditorController *)editor
{
    [self dismissViewControllerAnimated:YES completion:NULL];
}
```

Upon testing on a physical device, your application should now successfully allow you to edit your videos. Figure 9-8 shows a view of your application giving you the option to edit a recorded video.

Figure 9-8. Editing (trimming) a video using UIVideoEditorController

> **Note** You might have noticed that the recording quality is a little lower when you are in the editor. The default video quality is set to medium. If you would like high quality, simply set the video quality property in the `takePicture:` method; for example, `Self.imagePicker.videoQuality = UIImagePickerControllerQualityTypeHigh`.

Recipe 9-4: Using Custom Camera Overlays

There are a variety of applications that implement the camera interface but also implement a custom overlay—for example, to display constellations on the sky or simply to implement their own custom camera controls. In this recipe, you'll continue building on the project from the preceding recipes and implement a very basic custom camera screen overlay. Specifically, you replace the default button controls with your own versions of them. Although simple, the example should give you an idea of how to create your own, more useful overlay functionalities.

You build your custom overlay view directly in code in a method you'll name "`customViewForImagePicker:`." This method creates an overlay view and populates it with three buttons: one for taking the picture, one for turning the flash on and off, and one to toggle between the front and rear cameras. Listing 9-19 shows this code, which you add to the `ViewController.m` from Recipe 9-3.

Listing 9-19. Implementation of the customViewForImagePicker: method

```objc
-(UIView *)customViewForImagePicker:(UIImagePickerController *)imagePicker;
{
    UIView *view = [[UIView alloc] initWithFrame:CGRectMake(0, 20, 280, 480)];
    view.backgroundColor = [UIColor clearColor];

    UIButton *flashButton =
        [[UIButton alloc] initWithFrame:CGRectMake(10, 10, 120, 44)];
    flashButton.backgroundColor = [UIColor colorWithRed:.5 green:.5 blue:.5 alpha:.5];
    [flashButton setTitle:@"Flash Auto" forState:UIControlStateNormal];
    [flashButton setTitleColor:[UIColor whiteColor] forState:UIControlStateNormal];
    flashButton.layer.cornerRadius = 10.0;

    UIButton *changeCameraButton =
        [[UIButton alloc] initWithFrame:CGRectMake(190, 10, 120, 44)];
    changeCameraButton.backgroundColor =
        [UIColor colorWithRed:.5 green:.5 blue:.5 alpha:.5];
    [changeCameraButton setTitle:@"Rear Camera" forState:UIControlStateNormal];
    [changeCameraButton setTitleColor:[UIColor whiteColor]
        forState:UIControlStateNormal];
    changeCameraButton.layer.cornerRadius = 10.0;

    UIButton *takePictureButton =
        [[UIButton alloc] initWithFrame:CGRectMake(100, 432, 120, 44)];
    takePictureButton.backgroundColor =
        [UIColor colorWithRed:.5 green:.5 blue:.5 alpha:.5];
```

```
    [takePictureButton setTitle:@"Click!" forState:UIControlStateNormal];
    [takePictureButton setTitleColor:[UIColor whiteColor]
        forState:UIControlStateNormal];
    takePictureButton.layer.cornerRadius = 10.0;

    [flashButton addTarget:self action:@selector(toggleFlash:)
        forControlEvents:UIControlEventTouchUpInside];
    [changeCameraButton addTarget:self action:@selector(toggleCamera:)
        forControlEvents:UIControlEventTouchUpInside];
    [takePictureButton addTarget:imagePicker action:@selector(takePicture)
        forControlEvents:UIControlEventTouchUpInside];

    [view addSubview:flashButton];
    [view addSubview:changeCameraButton];
    [view addSubview:takePictureButton];

    return view;
}
```

In Listing 9-19, you have defined your UIView as well as the buttons to be put in it, given them their actions to perform and added them into the view, set the title of each button to be either its starting value or its purpose, and also set their cornerRadius so that the buttons will have rounded corners. One of the most important details here is that you set your buttons to be semitransparent, as they are placed over your camera's display. You do not want to cover up any of your picture, so the buttons have to be at least partially see-through.

As you may have noticed, the action for the takePictureButton is directly connected to the takePicture method on the image picker. The other two buttons, on the other hand, are connected to methods (toggleFlash and toggleCamera, respectively) on your view controller. At this point, those two methods don't exist, so you need to implement them. Listing 9-20 shows their implementation.

Listing 9-20. Implementation for the toggleFlash: and toggleCamera: methods

```
-(void)toggleFlash:(UIButton *)sender
{
    if (self.imagePicker.cameraFlashMode == UIImagePickerControllerCameraFlashModeOff)
    {
        self.imagePicker.cameraFlashMode = UIImagePickerControllerCameraFlashModeOn;
        [sender setTitle:@"Flash On" forState:UIControlStateNormal];
    }
    else
    {
        self.imagePicker.cameraFlashMode = UIImagePickerControllerCameraFlashModeOff;
        [sender setTitle:@"Flash Off" forState:UIControlStateNormal];
    }
}
```

```
-(void)toggleCamera:(UIButton *)sender
{
    if (self.imagePicker.cameraDevice == UIImagePickerControllerCameraDeviceRear)
    {
        self.imagePicker.cameraDevice = UIImagePickerControllerCameraDeviceFront;
        [sender setTitle:@"Front Camera" forState:UIControlStateNormal];
    }
    else
    {
        self.imagePicker.cameraDevice = UIImagePickerControllerCameraDeviceRear;
        [sender setTitle:@"Rear Camera" forState:UIControlStateNormal];
    }
}
```

Next, hide the default camera buttons and provide the image picker with your custom overlay view. Add the two lines of code shown in Listing 9-21 to your takePicture: method. You can also comment out the setting of the allowsEditing property because the new way of taking pictures doesn't support that.

Listing 9-21. Modifying the takePicture method to hide the default camera buttons and to set the custom overlay

```
- (IBAction)takePicture:(id)sender
{
        // Make sure camera is available
    if ([UIImagePickerController
        isSourceTypeAvailable:UIImagePickerControllerSourceTypeCamera] == NO)
    {
        UIAlertView *alert = [[UIAlertView alloc] initWithTitle:@"Error"
                                                    message:@"Camera Unavailable"
                                                    delegate:self
                                            cancelButtonTitle:@"Cancel"
                                            otherButtonTitles:nil, nil];
        [alert show];
        return;
    }
    if (self.imagePicker == nil)
    {
        self.imagePicker = [[UIImagePickerController alloc] init];
        self.imagePicker.delegate = self;
        self.imagePicker.sourceType = UIImagePickerControllerSourceTypeCamera;
        self.imagePicker.mediaTypes = [UIImagePickerController
            availableMediaTypesForSourceType:UIImagePickerControllerSourceTypeCamera];
        // self.imagePicker.allowsEditing = YES;
        self.imagePicker.showsCameraControls = NO;
        self.imagePicker.cameraOverlayView =
            [self customViewForImagePicker:self.imagePicker];
    }
    [self presentViewController:self.imagePicker animated:YES completion:NULL];
}
```

Finally, you need to make a small change to the imagePickerController:didFinishPickingMedia WithInfo: method. As mentioned earlier, the takePicture method of the image picker doesn't support editing. This means that you have to retrieve your picture from the info dictionary using the UIImagePickerControllerOriginalImage key instead of UIImagePickerControllerEditedImage, as shown in Listing 9-22.

Listing 9-22. Modifying the imagePickerController: didFinishPickingMediaWithInfo: to use the original image

```
-(void)imagePickerController:(UIImagePickerController *)picker
didFinishPickingMediaWithInfo:(NSDictionary *)info
{
    NSString *mediaType = [info objectForKey: UIImagePickerControllerMediaType];

    if (CFStringCompare((__bridge CFStringRef) mediaType, kUTTypeMovie, 0) ==
        kCFCompareEqualTo)
    {
        NSString *moviePath =
            (NSString *) [[info objectForKey: UIImagePickerControllerMediaURL] path];
        self.pathToRecordedVideo = moviePath;

        if (UIVideoAtPathIsCompatibleWithSavedPhotosAlbum (moviePath))
        {
            UISaveVideoAtPathToSavedPhotosAlbum (moviePath, nil, nil, nil);
        }
    }
    else
    {
        UIImage *image =
            (UIImage *)[info objectForKey:UIImagePickerControllerOriginalImage];
        UIImageWriteToSavedPhotosAlbum(image, nil, nil , nil);
        self.imageView.image = image;
        self.imageView.contentMode = UIViewContentModeScaleAspectFill;
    }
    [self dismissViewControllerAnimated:YES completion:NULL];
}
```

If you run your app now, your camera should, as shown in Figure 9-9, display your three buttons in an overlay.

Figure 9-9. *An image-picker controller with a custom overlay view replacing the standard buttons*

From here you can create your own custom overlays and easily change their functions to fit nearly any situation. The following recipes leave the image-picker controller and instead look into the Audiovisual (AV) Foundation framework for capturing your pictures and videos.

Recipe 9-5: Displaying Camera Preview with AVCaptureSession

While the UIImagePickerController and UIVideoEditorController interfaces are incredibly useful, they certainly aren't as customizable as they could be. With the AV Foundation framework, however, you can create your camera interfaces from scratch, making them just the way you want. The AV Foundation framework gives you access to more audio and video tools so you can fully customize the user experience.

In this recipe and the ones that follow, you will use the AVCaptureSession API to essentially create your own version of the camera. You'll do this in steps, starting with the displaying of a camera preview.

Begin by creating a new single-view project. You'll use the same project for the rest of this chapter, so name it accordingly (such as "MyCamera"). Also, make sure to add the AVFoundation framework to your project or you'll run into linker errors later.

Now, add a property to your view controller to hold your AVCaptureSession instance and one to hold the video input instance by making the changes in Listing 9-23 to your ViewController.h file.

Listing 9-23. The ViewController.h file with added AVCaptureSession and AVCaptureDeviceInput properties

```
//
//  ViewController.h
//  Recipe 9-5 Displaying Camera Preview With AVCaptureSession
//

#import <UIKit/UIKit.h>
#import <AVFoundation/AVFoundation.h>

@interface ViewController : UIViewController

@property (strong, nonatomic) AVCaptureSession *captureSession;
@property (strong, nonatomic) AVCaptureDeviceInput *videoInput;

@end
```

Next, switch to the ViewController.m file and locate the viewDidLoad method. There you set up the capture session to receive input from the camera. We'll show you step-by-step now and later will present you with the complete viewDidLoad implementation.

First, create your AVCaptureSession. Optionally, you might also want to change the resolution preset, which is set to AVCaptureSessionPresetHigh by default. Add the code in Listing 9-24 to the viewDidLoad method.

Listing 9-24. Creating and initializing an AVCaptureSession instance

```
self.captureSession = [[AVCaptureSession alloc] init];
//Optional: self.captureSession.sessionPreset = AVCaptureSessionPresetMedium;
```

Next, specify your input device, which is your rear camera (assuming one is accessible), as shown in Listing 9-25. You specify this through the use of the AVCaptureDevice class method +defaultDeviceWithMediaType:, which can take a variety of different arguments depending on the type of media desired, the most prominent of which are AVMediaTypeVideo and AVMediaTypeAudio.

Listing 9-25. Specifying the capture device

```
AVCaptureDevice *device = [AVCaptureDevice defaultDeviceWithMediaType:AVMediaTypeVideo];
```

Next, you need to set up the instance of AVCaptureDeviceInput to specify your chosen device as an input for your capture session. Also, include a check to make sure the input has been correctly created before adding it to your session. Listing 9-26 shows this instance and check statement.

Listing 9-26. Setting the input instance and checking its existence before assigning the video input

```
NSError *error = nil;
self.videoInput = [AVCaptureDeviceInput deviceInputWithDevice:device error:&error];
if (self.videoInput)
{
    [self.captureSession addInput:self.videoInput];
}
else
{
    NSLog(@"Input Error: %@", error);
}
```

The last part of your videoDidLoad, as shown in Listing 9-27, is the creation of a preview layer, with which you can see what your camera is viewing. Set your preview layer to be the layer of your main view, but with a slightly altered height so as not to block a button that you'll set up in the next recipe.

Listing 9-27. Creating the preview layer

```
AVCaptureVideoPreviewLayer *previewLayer =
    [AVCaptureVideoPreviewLayer layerWithSession:self.captureSession];
UIView *aView = self.view;
previewLayer.frame =
    CGRectMake(0, 20, self.view.frame.size.width, self.view.frame.size.height-70);
[aView.layer addSublayer:previewLayer];
```

Once all these steps are complete, the viewDidLoad method should look like Listing 9-28.

Listing 9-28. The complete viewDidLoad method

```
- (void)viewDidLoad
{
    [super viewDidLoad];
    // Do any additional setup after loading the view, typically from a nib.

    self.captureSession = [[AVCaptureSession alloc] init];
    //Optional: self.captureSession.sessionPreset = AVCaptureSessionPresetMedium;

    AVCaptureDevice *device =
        [AVCaptureDevice defaultDeviceWithMediaType:AVMediaTypeVideo];

    NSError *error = nil;
    self.videoInput = [AVCaptureDeviceInput deviceInputWithDevice:device error:&error];
    if (self.videoInput)
    {
        [self.captureSession addInput:self.videoInput];
    }
    else
    {
        NSLog(@"Input Error: %@", error);
    }
```

```
AVCaptureVideoPreviewLayer *previewLayer =
    [AVCaptureVideoPreviewLayer layerWithSession:self.captureSession];
UIView *aView = self.view;
previewLayer.frame =
    CGRectMake(0, 0, self.view.frame.size.width,
        self.view.frame.size.height-70);
[aView.layer addSublayer:previewLayer];
}
```

> **Note**   Just like any other CALayer, an AVCaptureVideoPreviewLayer can be repositioned, rotated, resized, and even animated. With it, you are no longer bound to using the entire screen to record video as you are with the UIImagePicker, meaning you could have your preview layer in one part of the screen and other information for the user in another. As with almost every part of iOS development, the possibilities of use are limited only by the developer's imagination.

Now the only thing that needs to be added is code to start and stop your capture session. In this app, you'll display the camera preview upon application launch, so a good place to put the start code is in the viewWillAppear: method, as shown in Listing 9-29.

Listing 9-29. Implementation of the viewWillAppear method

```
- (void)viewWillAppear:(BOOL)animated
{
    [super viewWillAppear:animated];
    [self.captureSession startRunning];
}
```

You will also add the corresponding stopping code for the capture session, as shown in Listing 9-30.

Listing 9-30. Implementation of the viewWillDisappear method

```
- (void)viewWillDisappear:(BOOL)animated
{
    [super viewWillDisappear:animated];
    [self.captureSession stopRunning];
}
```

If you build and run your application now, it should display a live camera preview, as shown in Figure 9-10.

Figure 9-10. *Displaying a camera preview with AVCaptureSession*

Recipe 9-6: Capturing Still Images with AVCaptureSession

In the preceding recipe, you learned how to set up an AVCaptureSession with input from the camera. You also saw how you can connect an AVCaptureVideoPreviewLayer to display a live camera preview in your app. Now you will expand the project by connecting an AVCaptureStillImageOutput object to take still images and save them to the saved photos library on the device.

Before digging into the coding, you need to make a couple of changes to the project. The first is to add the AssetsLibrary.framework to your project. You use functionality from that framework to write the photos to the photos library.

Because you access the shared photos library of the device, you need to provide a usage description in the application's Info.plist file. Go ahead and add the NSPhotoLibraryUsageDescription key (displayed as "Privacy—Photo Library Usage Description" in the property editor) with a brief text containing the reason why your app seeks the access (such as "Testing AVCaptureSession"). Refer to Recipe 1-7 in Chapter 1 for a refresher on this procedure.

Adding a Capture Button

You need a way to trigger a still image capture. Start by adding a button with the title "Capture" to your view controller's storyboard view. Also make sure to create an action named "capture" for the button. To ensure the button moves with the size of the screen, select the button and choose

"Add Missing Constraints" from the Resolve Auto Layout Issues menu in the lower-right corner of the storyboard editor screen. When you're done, the view should resemble Figure 9-11 with the button selected.

Figure 9-11. A user interface with a button to capture a video frame

Switch to your ViewController.h file and import the AssetsLibrary framework. Also, add a property to hold your still image output instance, as shown in bold in Listing 9-31.

Listing 9-31. The finished ViewController.h file

```
//
// ViewController.h
// Recipe 9-6: Taking Still Images With AVCaptureSession
//

#import <UIKit/UIKit.h>
#import <AVFoundation/AVFoundation.h>
#import <AssetsLibrary/AssetsLibrary.h>

@interface ViewController : UIViewController
```

```
@property (strong, nonatomic) AVCaptureSession *captureSession;
@property (strong, nonatomic) AVCaptureDeviceInput *videoInput;
@property (strong, nonatomic) AVCaptureStillImageOutput *stillImageOutput;

- (IBAction)capture:(id)sender;

@end
```

In ViewController.m, add the code in Listing 9-32 to the viewDidLoad method. The new code (marked in bold) allocates and initializes your still image output object and connects it to the capture session.

Listing 9-32. Adding the still image output object and connecting it to the capture session

```
- (void)viewDidLoad
{
    [super viewDidLoad];
        // Do any additional setup after loading the view, typically from a nib.
    self.captureSession = [[AVCaptureSession alloc] init];
    //Optional: self.captureSession.sessionPreset = AVCaptureSessionPresetMedium;

    AVCaptureDevice *device =
        [AVCaptureDevice defaultDeviceWithMediaType:AVMediaTypeVideo];

    NSError *error = nil;
    self.videoInput = [AVCaptureDeviceInput deviceInputWithDevice:device error:&error];
    if (self.videoInput)
    {
        [self.captureSession addInput:self.videoInput];
    }
    else
    {
        NSLog(@"Input Error: %@", error);
    }

    self.stillImageOutput = [[AVCaptureStillImageOutput alloc] init];
    NSDictionary *stillImageOutputSettings =
        [[NSDictionary alloc] initWithObjectsAndKeys:
            AVVideoCodecJPEG, AVVideoCodecKey, nil];
    [self.stillImageOutput setOutputSettings:stillImageOutputSettings];
    [self.captureSession addOutput:self.stillImageOutput];

    AVCaptureVideoPreviewLayer *previewLayer =
        [AVCaptureVideoPreviewLayer layerWithSession:self.captureSession];
    UIView *aView = self.view;
    previewLayer.frame =
        CGRectMake(0, 0, self.view.frame.size.width, self.view.frame.size.height-70);
    [aView.layer addSublayer:previewLayer];
}
```

> **Note** Besides AVCaptureStillImageOutput, you can use a number of other output formats—for example,
> the AVCaptureMovieFileOutput, which you use in the next recipe, the AVCaptureVideoDataOutput,
> with which you can access the raw video output frame by frame, AVCaptureAudioFileOutput for saving
> audio files, and AVCaptureAudioDataOutput for processing audio data.

Now it's time to implement the action method. All it should do is trigger the capturing of a still image.
We chose to extract the capturing code into a helper method for the sake of making changes that
will come in the next recipe easier. Add the method call to the capture action method, as shown in
Listing 9-33.

Listing 9-33. Implementing the capture: action method

```
- (IBAction)capture:(id)sender
{
    [self captureStillImage];
}
```

The implementation of captureStillImage method can seem daunting at first, so we'll take it in steps
and then show you the complete method.

First, acquire the capture connection and make sure it uses the portrait orientation to capture the
image. Listing 9-34 shows this step.

Listing 9-34. Starting the captureStillImage method and adding the capture connection with portrait orientation

```
- (void) captureStillImage
{
    AVCaptureConnection *stillImageConnection =
        [self.stillImageOutput.connections objectAtIndex:0];
    if ([stillImageConnection isVideoOrientationSupported])
        [stillImageConnection setVideoOrientation:AVCaptureVideoOrientationPortrait];

    // ...
}
```

Then, as Listing 9-35 shows you run the captureStillImageAsynchronouslyFromConnection method
and provide a code block that is invoked when the still image capture has been completed.

Listing 9-35. Adding code to capture the still image

```
[self.stillImageOutput
    captureStillImageAsynchronouslyFromConnection:stillImageConnection
    completionHandler:^(CMSampleBufferRef imageDataSampleBuffer, NSError *error)
    {
        // ...
    }
];
```

When the capture has completed, check to see whether it was successful; otherwise, log the error as shown in Listing 9-36.

Listing 9-36. Checking for captured image success or failure

```
[self.stillImageOutput
    captureStillImageAsynchronouslyFromConnection:stillImageConnection
    completionHandler:^(CMSampleBufferRef imageDataSampleBuffer, NSError *error)
    {
        if (imageDataSampleBuffer != NULL)
        {
            // ...
        }
        else
        {
            NSLog(@"Error capturing still image: %@", error);
        }
    }
];
```

If the capture was successful, extract the image from the buffer, as shown in Listing 9-37.

Listing 9-37. Completing code for image-capture success

```
if (imageDataSampleBuffer != NULL)
{
    NSData *imageData = [AVCaptureStillImageOutput
        jpegStillImageNSDataRepresentation:imageDataSampleBuffer];
    UIImage *image = [[UIImage alloc] initWithData:imageData];

    // ...
}
```

Next, save the image to the photo library. This is also an asynchronous task, so provide a block for when it completes. Whether the task completed successfully or with an error (in other words, if the user didn't allow access to the photo library), display an alert to notify the user, as shown in Listing 9-38.

Listing 9-38. Adding code to save asynchronously and alert the user of success or error

```
ALAssetsLibrary *library = [[ALAssetsLibrary alloc] init];
[library writeImageToSavedPhotosAlbum:[image CGImage]
    orientation:(ALAssetOrientation)[image imageOrientation]
    completionBlock:^(NSURL *assetURL, NSError *error)
    {
        UIAlertView *alert;
        if (!error)
        {
            alert = [[UIAlertView alloc] initWithTitle:@"Photo Saved"
                message:@"The photo was successfully saved to your photos library"
                delegate:nil
                cancelButtonTitle:@"OK"
                otherButtonTitles:nil, nil];
        }
```

```
            else
            {
                alert = [[UIAlertView alloc] initWithTitle:@"Error Saving Photo"
                    message:@"The photo was not saved to your photos library"
                    delegate:nil
                    cancelButtonTitle:@"OK"
                    otherButtonTitles:nil, nil];
            }

            [alert show];
        }
];
```

Listing 9-39 shows the captureStillImage method in its entirety.

Listing 9-39. The full captureStillImage implementation

```
- (void) captureStillImage
{
    AVCaptureConnection *stillImageConnection =
        [self.stillImageOutput.connections objectAtIndex:0];
    if ([stillImageConnection isVideoOrientationSupported])
        [stillImageConnection setVideoOrientation:AVCaptureVideoOrientationPortrait];

    [self.stillImageOutput
        captureStillImageAsynchronouslyFromConnection:stillImageConnection
        completionHandler:^(CMSampleBufferRef imageDataSampleBuffer, NSError *error)
        {
            if (imageDataSampleBuffer != NULL)
            {
                NSData *imageData = [AVCaptureStillImageOutput
                    jpegStillImageNSDataRepresentation:imageDataSampleBuffer];
                ALAssetsLibrary *library = [[ALAssetsLibrary alloc] init];
                UIImage *image = [[UIImage alloc] initWithData:imageData];
                [library writeImageToSavedPhotosAlbum:[image CGImage]
                    orientation:(ALAssetOrientation)[image imageOrientation]
                    completionBlock:^(NSURL *assetURL, NSError *error)
                    {
                        UIAlertView *alert;
                        if (!error)
                        {
                            alert = [[UIAlertView alloc] initWithTitle:@"Photo Saved"
                                message:@"The photo was successfully saved to your photos library"
                                delegate:nil
                                cancelButtonTitle:@"OK"
                                otherButtonTitles:nil, nil];
                        }
                        else
                        {
                            alert = [[UIAlertView alloc] initWithTitle:@"Error Saving Photo"
                                message:@"The photo was not saved to your photos library"
                                delegate:nil
```

```
                                cancelButtonTitle:@"OK"
                                otherButtonTitles:nil, nil];
                    }

                    [alert show];
                }
            ];
        }
        else
        {
            NSLog(@"Error capturing still image: %@", error);
        }
    }
];
}
```

That completes Recipe 9-6. You now can run your app and tap the "Capture" button to take a picture that is saved in your photo library, as in Figure 9-12.

Figure 9-12. *A still image captured and saved to the photo library*

While you haven't included any fancy animations to make it look like a camera, this is quite useful as far as a basic camera goes. Recipe 9-7 takes it to the next level and shows you how to record a video using `AVCaptureSession`.

Recipe 9-7: Capturing Video with AVCaptureSession

Now that you have covered some of the basics of using AVFoundation, you will use it to implement a slightly more complicated project. This time, you'll extend your app to include a capturing video mode. To do this, you'll need to allow the user to switch between taking pictures and recording videos. First you will build the functionality to switch modes, then you will implement the video capture using AVCaptureSession. You'll build on the same project that you have been working on since Recipe 9-5.

Adding a Video Recording Mode

Add a new component to your user interface that lets the user switch between still image and video recording modes. A simple segmented control works for the purpose of this recipe, so go ahead and add one from the object library. Change the default text on the two segments to "Take Photo" and "Record Video" and place them so that your view resembles Figure 9-13.

Figure 9-13. A simple user interface that allows the user to switch modes between photo and video capturing

To access both the segmented control and the button from your code, you will need to add outlets for them. Use the names "modeControl" and "captureButton," respectively. You also need to respond when the segment control's value changes, so create an action for that event. Name the action "updateMode."

Now switch over to your ViewController.h file. Add a couple of properties that are for the video recording setup of your capture session—one for audio input and one for movie file output. Also, to prepare the view controller for being an output delegate for the movie file recording, you will add an AVCaptureFileOutputRecordingDelegate protocol to the header. Listing 9-40 shows the code with all these changes, which are marked in bold.

Listing 9-40. Setting up the ViewController.h file

```
//
//  ViewController.h
//  Recipe 9-7 Recording Video With AVCaptureSession
//

#import <UIKit/UIKit.h>
#import <AVFoundation/AVFoundation.h>
#import <AssetsLibrary/AssetsLibrary.h>

@interface ViewController : UIViewController <AVCaptureFileOutputRecordingDelegate>

@property (strong, nonatomic) AVCaptureSession *captureSession;
@property (strong, nonatomic) AVCaptureDeviceInput *videoInput;
@property (strong, nonatomic) AVCaptureDeviceInput *audioInput;
@property (strong, nonatomic) AVCaptureStillImageOutput *stillImageOutput;
@property (strong, nonatomic) AVCaptureMovieFileOutput *movieOutput;

@property (weak, nonatomic) IBOutlet UIButton *captureButton;
@property (weak, nonatomic) IBOutlet UISegmentedControl *modeControl;

- (IBAction)capture:(id)sender;
- (IBAction)updateMode:(id)sender;

@end
```

Now that your header file is set up, switch to your implementation file. To start, you will make several changes to the viewDidLoad method. The first is to set up an audio input object to capture sound from the device's microphone while recording video. These changes are shown in bold in Listing 9-41.

Listing 9-41. Setting up the audio input object

```
- (void)viewDidLoad
{
    [super viewDidLoad];
    self.captureSession = [[AVCaptureSession alloc] init];
    //Optional: self.captureSession.sessionPreset = AVCaptureSessionPresetMedium;

    AVCaptureDevice *videoDevice =
        [AVCaptureDevice defaultDeviceWithMediaType:AVMediaTypeVideo];
```

```
AVCaptureDevice *audioDevice =
    [AVCaptureDevice defaultDeviceWithMediaType:AVMediaTypeAudio];

NSError *error = nil;

self.videoInput =
    [AVCaptureDeviceInput deviceInputWithDevice:videoDevice error:nil];
self.audioInput =
    [[AVCaptureDeviceInput alloc] initWithDevice:audioDevice error:nil];


// ...
}
```

Now we'll replace the existing if-else statement you added in Listing 9-26 from the preceding recipe. The replacement consists of an if-else statement that encompasses some of the image output initialization code already written and a new if statement to check for errors on the audio input. Listing 9-42 shows these changes.

Listing 9-42. Adding error checks to the audio and video inputs

```
- (void)viewDidLoad
{

    [super viewDidLoad];
    self.captureSession = [[AVCaptureSession alloc] init];
    //Optional: self.captureSession.sessionPreset = AVCaptureSessionPresetMedium;

    AVCaptureDevice *videoDevice =
    [AVCaptureDevice defaultDeviceWithMediaType:AVMediaTypeVideo];
    AVCaptureDevice *audioDevice =
    [AVCaptureDevice defaultDeviceWithMediaType:AVMediaTypeAudio];

    NSError *error = nil;

    self.videoInput =
    [AVCaptureDeviceInput deviceInputWithDevice:videoDevice error:&error];
    self.audioInput =
    [[AVCaptureDeviceInput alloc] initWithDevice:audioDevice error:&error];


    if (self.videoInput)
    {

        self.stillImageOutput = [[AVCaptureStillImageOutput alloc] init];
        NSDictionary *stillImageOutputSettings = [[NSDictionary alloc]
                                            initWithObjectsAndKeys:AVVideoCodecJPEG,
AVVideoCodecKey, nil];
        [self.stillImageOutput setOutputSettings:stillImageOutputSettings];
        [self.captureSession addOutput:self.stillImageOutput];
    }
```

```
      else
      {
          NSLog(@"Video Input Error: %@", error);
      }
      if (!self.videoInput)
      {
          NSLog(@"Audio Input Error: %@", error);
      }
//...
}
```

Next, set up an output object that records the data from the input objects and produces a movie file, as shown in Listing 9-43.

Listing 9-43. Setting up the movie output object

```
- (void)viewDidLoad
{
    // ...

    self.stillImageOutput = [[AVCaptureStillImageOutput alloc] init];
    NSDictionary *stillImageOutputSettings = [[NSDictionary alloc]
        initWithObjectsAndKeys:AVVideoCodecJPEG, AVVideoCodecKey, nil];
    [self.stillImageOutput setOutputSettings:stillImageOutputSettings];

    self.movieOutput = [[AVCaptureMovieFileOutput alloc] init];

    [self.captureSession addOutput:self.stillImageOutput];

    // ...
}
```

Finally, set up the capture session in the picture-taking mode and adjust the size of the preview layer so it won't cover the new segment control. Listing 9-44 shows this change.

Listing 9-44. Adding the video input to the capture session and changing the frame size

```
if (self.videoInput)
{

    self.stillImageOutput = [[AVCaptureStillImageOutput alloc] init];
    NSDictionary *stillImageOutputSettings = [[NSDictionary alloc]
                                      initWithObjectsAndKeys:AVVideoCodecJPEG,
AVVideoCodecKey, nil];
    [self.stillImageOutput setOutputSettings:stillImageOutputSettings];

    self.movieOutput = [[AVCaptureMovieFileOutput alloc] init];

    // Setup capture session for taking pictures
    [self.captureSession addInput:self.videoInput];
    [self.captureSession addOutput:self.stillImageOutput];
}
```

With all these changes, your `viewDidLoad` method should resemble Listing 9-45.

Listing 9-45. The complete viewDidLoad method

```
- (void)viewDidLoad
{

        [super viewDidLoad];
        self.captureSession = [[AVCaptureSession alloc] init];
        //Optional: self.captureSession.sessionPreset = AVCaptureSessionPresetMedium;

        AVCaptureDevice *videoDevice =
        [AVCaptureDevice defaultDeviceWithMediaType:AVMediaTypeVideo];
        AVCaptureDevice *audioDevice =
        [AVCaptureDevice defaultDeviceWithMediaType:AVMediaTypeAudio];

        NSError *error = nil;

        self.videoInput =
        [AVCaptureDeviceInput deviceInputWithDevice:videoDevice error:&error];
        self.audioInput =
        [[AVCaptureDeviceInput alloc] initWithDevice:audioDevice error:&error];

        if (self.videoInput)
        {

            self.stillImageOutput = [[AVCaptureStillImageOutput alloc] init];
            NSDictionary *stillImageOutputSettings = [[NSDictionary alloc]
                                                    initWithObjectsAndKeys:AVVideoCodecJPEG,
AVVideoCodecKey, nil];
            [self.stillImageOutput setOutputSettings:stillImageOutputSettings];

            self.movieOutput = [[AVCaptureMovieFileOutput alloc] init];

            // Setup capture session for taking pictures
            [self.captureSession addInput:self.videoInput];
            [self.captureSession addOutput:self.stillImageOutput];
        }
        else
        {
            NSLog(@"Video Input Error: %@", error);
        }
        if (!self.videoInput)
        {
            NSLog(@"Audio Input Error: %@", error);
        }

        AVCaptureVideoPreviewLayer *previewLayer =
        [AVCaptureVideoPreviewLayer layerWithSession:self.captureSession];
        UIView *aView = self.view;
```

```
previewLayer.frame =
CGRectMake(0, 70, self.view.frame.size.width, self.view.frame.size.height-140);
[aView.layer addSublayer:previewLayer];
```

}

Note that you're not adding `audioInput` and `movieOutput` objects to the capture session. Later, you'll add and remove input objects, depending on which mode the user selects, but for now it's assumed to be the "Take Photo" mode. Therefore, only input and output objects associated with that particular mode are added in the `viewDidLoad` method. (For the same reason, it's also important that the segment control has the correct selected index value set.)

Now, update the `capture` action method, as shown in Listing 9-46. It now should check what mode the application is in; if it is in the "Take Photo" mode, it should do what it used to do, which is to capture a still image.

Listing 9-46. Adding a condition statement to the capture: method

```
- (IBAction)capture:(id)sender
{
    if (self.modeControl.selectedSegmentIndex == 0)
    {
        // Picture Mode
        [self captureStillImage];
    }
    else
    {
        // Video Mode
    }
}
```

If in video recording mode, however, it should toggle between a start and stop recording mode, depending on whether or not a movie is currently being recorded, as shown in Listing 9-47.

Listing 9-47. Adding code to the capture: method to handle video operation

```
- (IBAction)capture:(id)sender
{
    if (self.modeControl.selectedSegmentIndex == 0)
    {
        // Picture Mode
        [self captureStillImage];
    }
    else
    {
        // Video Mode
        if (self.movieOutput.isRecording == YES)
        {
            [self.captureButton setTitle:@"Capture" forState:UIControlStateNormal];
            [self.movieOutput stopRecording];
        }
```

```
        else
        {
            [self.captureButton setTitle:@"Stop" forState:UIControlStateNormal];
            [self.movieOutput startRecordingToOutputFileURL:[self tempFileURL]
                recordingDelegate:self];
        }
    }
}
```

You have probably noticed that you called the method `tempFileURL` to set up your `AVCaptureOutput` earlier. This method, in short, returns a path for your recorded video to be temporarily saved on your device. If there is already a file saved at the location, it will delete that file. (This way, you never use more than one video's worth of disk space.) In a real application, you might want to prompt the user and inform the user of an overwrite, but for simplicity we'll skip the prompt code. Listing 9-48 shows the `tempFileURL` implementation.

Listing 9-48. Implementing the tempFileURL method

```
- (NSURL *) tempFileURL
{
    NSString *outputPath = [[NSString alloc] initWithFormat:@"%@%@",
        NSTemporaryDirectory(), @"output.mov"];
    NSURL *outputURL = [[NSURL alloc] initFileURLWithPath:outputPath];
    NSFileManager *manager = [[NSFileManager alloc] init];
    if ([manager fileExistsAtPath:outputPath])
    {
        [manager removeItemAtPath:outputPath error:nil];
    }
    return outputURL;
}
```

The next step is to set up your `AVCaptureMovieFileOutput`'s delegate method to be invoked when an `AVCaptureSession` has finished recording a movie. The method starts by checking whether there were any errors in recording the video to a file and then saves your video file into your asset library. The process of writing a video to the photo album is nearly the same as with photos, so you'll probably recognize a lot of that code from the preceding recipe. Listing 9-49 shows the implementation.

Listing 9-49. Implementation of the captureOutputdidFinishRecordingToOutputFileAtUrl:fromConnections:error method

```
- (void)captureOutput:(AVCaptureFileOutput *)captureOutput
didFinishRecordingToOutputFileAtURL:(NSURL *)outputFileURL
    fromConnections:(NSArray *)connections
              error:(NSError *)error
{
    BOOL recordedSuccessfully = YES;
    if ([error code] != noErr)
    {
        // A problem occurred: Find out if the recording was successful.
        id value = [[error userInfo]
            objectForKey:AVErrorRecordingSuccessfullyFinishedKey];
```

```
        if (value)
            recordedSuccessfully = [value boolValue];
        // Logging the problem anyway:
        NSLog(@"A problem occurred while recording: %@", error);
    }
    if (recordedSuccessfully)
    {
        ALAssetsLibrary *library = [[ALAssetsLibrary alloc] init];

        [library writeVideoAtPathToSavedPhotosAlbum:outputFileURL
            completionBlock:^(NSURL *assetURL, NSError *error)
            {
                UIAlertView *alert;
                if (!error)
                {
                    alert = [[UIAlertView alloc] initWithTitle:@"Video Saved"
                        message:@"The movie was successfully saved to your photos library"
                        delegate:nil
                        cancelButtonTitle:@"OK"
                        otherButtonTitles:nil, nil];
                }
                else
                {
                    alert = [[UIAlertView alloc] initWithTitle:@"Error Saving Video"
                        message:@"The movie was not saved to your photos library"
                        delegate:nil
                        cancelButtonTitle:@"OK"
                        otherButtonTitles:nil, nil];
                }

                [alert show];
            }
        ];
    }
}
```

Finally, as shown in Listing 9-50, you implement the action method that's invoked when the user switches between the two modes. This method updates the capture session with the correct input and output objects that are associated with the corresponding mode. It also sets the orientation mode for the video mode output objects. (This is already taken care of for the still image mode; see Recipe 9-6 for details.) Finally, it resets the title of the capture button. In iOS 7, the user has the option of denying access to the microphone; there is also an if statement to check that you can add the audio input to the session. If not, it prompts the user with directions about how to fix the problem and switches the user back to the camera.

Listing 9-50. Implementation of the updateMode: action

```
- (IBAction)updateMode:(id)sender
{
    [self.captureSession stopRunning];
    if (self.modeControl.selectedSegmentIndex == 0)
```

```
    {
        // Still Image Mode
        if (self.movieOutput.isRecording == YES)
        {
            [self.movieOutput stopRecording];
        }
        [self.captureSession removeInput:self.audioInput];
        [self.captureSession removeOutput:self.movieOutput];
        [self.captureSession addOutput:self.stillImageOutput];
    }
    else
    {
        if([self.captureSession canAddInput:self.audioInput])
        {
            // Video Mode
            [self.captureSession removeOutput:self.stillImageOutput];
            [self.captureSession addInput:self.audioInput];
            [self.captureSession addOutput:self.movieOutput];

            // Set orientation of capture connections to portrait
            NSArray *array = [[self.captureSession.outputs objectAtIndex:0] connections];
            for (AVCaptureConnection *connection in array)
            {
                connection.videoOrientation = AVCaptureVideoOrientationPortrait;
            }
        }
        else
        {
            self.modeControl.selectedSegmentIndex = 0;
            NSLog(@"User turned off access to microphone");
            UIAlertView *alert = [[UIAlertView alloc] initWithTitle:@"Can't Access Audio"
message:@"Verify microphone access is turned on in Settings->Privacy->Microphone" delegate:nil
cancelButtonTitle:@"OK" otherButtonTitles:nil];
            [alert show];

        }
    }
    [self.captureButton setTitle:@"Capture" forState:UIControlStateNormal];

    [self.captureSession startRunning];
}
```

Now you are ready to build and run your app. You should be able to switch between taking photos and recording videos, and the results should be stored in the photos library of your device. Figure 9-14 shows the app in action. If you turn off the access to the microphone by going to Settings ➤ Privacy ➤ Microphone, the app will prompt you and let you know that it failed to add an audio input and how to fix it.

Figure 9-14. *An app that can take photos and record videos*

Recipe 9-8: Capturing Video Frames

For many applications that utilize videos, a thumbnail image is a useful way to "represent" a given video. In this recipe, you expand the preceding recipe and generate and display a thumbnail image when a video has been recorded.

Start by adding the CoreMedia framework to your project. You use it to generate the thumbnail.

Next, add an image view to the lower-left corner of your main view's user interface so that it resembles Figure 9-15. Once again, you will want to add some constraints to the image view by selecting "Add Missing Constraints" from the Resolve Auto Layout Issues menu in the lower-right corner of the storyboard window. This will ensure it looks fine on a 3.5" device. With UIImage selected, add a width and height constraint from the pin menu, as shown in Figure 9-16.

Figure 9-15. *The user interface with a thumbnail image view in the lower-left corner*

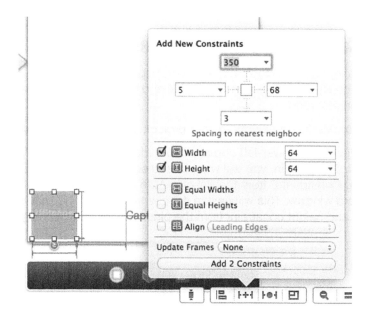

Figure 9-16. *Adding width and height constraints*

Add an outlet with the name "thumbnailImageView" for the image view so you can reference it later from your code.

Now, let's get to the core of this recipe. The method in Listing 9-51 extracts an image from the halfway point of the movie and updates the thumbnail image view. This method basically creates an asset using a URL and creates an image generator from it. Then we check for proper rotation and set the time of the clip we want to take the image from. Then we generate the image asynchronously.

Listing 9-51. Implementation of createThumbnailForVideoURL

```
-(void)createThumbnailForVideoURL:(NSURL *)videoURL
{
    AVURLAsset *myAsset = [[AVURLAsset alloc] initWithURL:videoURL options:[NSDictionary
dictionaryWithObject:@"YES" forKey:AVURLAssetPreferPreciseDurationAndTimingKey]];

    AVAssetImageGenerator *imageGenerator =
        [AVAssetImageGenerator assetImageGeneratorWithAsset:myAsset];
    //Make sure images are correctly rotated.
    imageGenerator.appliesPreferredTrackTransform = YES;
    Float64 durationSeconds = CMTimeGetSeconds([myAsset duration]);
    CMTime half = CMTimeMakeWithSeconds(durationSeconds/2.0, 600);
    NSArray *times = [NSArray arrayWithObjects: [NSValue valueWithCMTime:half], nil];

    [imageGenerator generateCGImagesAsynchronouslyForTimes:times
        completionHandler:^(CMTime requestedTime, CGImageRef image, CMTime actualTime,
                            AVAssetImageGeneratorResult result, NSError *error)
        {
            if (result == AVAssetImageGeneratorSucceeded)
            {
                self.thumbnailImageView.image = [UIImage imageWithCGImage:image];
            }
            else if (result == AVAssetImageGeneratorFailed)
            {
                NSLog(@"Failed with error: %@", [error localizedDescription]);
            }
        }
    ];
}
```

Now all that's left is to call the method when a video has been recorded, as shown in Listing 9-52. All that we're doing here is adding one line of code that calls the method in Listing 9-51 when a video is successfully captured.

Listing 9-52. Modifying the captureOutput:didFinishRecordingToOutputFuleAtURL:fromConnections: method

```
- (void)captureOutput:(AVCaptureFileOutput *)captureOutput
didFinishRecordingToOutputFileAtURL:(NSURL *)outputFileURL
        fromConnections:(NSArray *)connections
                  error:(NSError *)error
{
    BOOL recordedSuccessfully = YES;
    if ([error code] != noErr)
```

```
    {
        // A problem occurred: Find out if the recording was successful.
        id value =
            [[error userInfo] objectForKey:AVErrorRecordingSuccessfullyFinishedKey];
        if (value)
            recordedSuccessfully = [value boolValue];
        // Logging the problem anyway:
        NSLog(@"A problem occurred while recording: %@", error);
    }
    if (recordedSuccessfully)
    {
        [self createThumbnailForVideoURL:outputFileURL];
        ALAssetsLibrary *library = [[ALAssetsLibrary alloc] init];

        [library writeVideoAtPathToSavedPhotosAlbum:outputFileURL
            completionBlock:^(NSURL *assetURL, NSError *error)
            {
                UIAlertView *alert;
                if (!error)
                {
                    alert = [[UIAlertView alloc] initWithTitle:@"Video Saved"
                        message:@"The movie was successfully saved to your photos library"
                        delegate:nil
                        cancelButtonTitle:@"OK"
                        otherButtonTitles:nil, nil];
                }
                else
                {
                    alert = [[UIAlertView alloc] initWithTitle:@"Error Saving Video"
                        message:@"The movie was not saved to your photos library"
                        delegate:nil
                        cancelButtonTitle:@"OK"
                        otherButtonTitles:nil, nil];
                }

                [alert show];
            }
        ];
    }
}
```

Now build and run your application and switch to the "Record Video" mode when it has launched. Record a video by clicking the "Capture" button twice (once for start and again for stop). A few seconds later a thumbnail from halfway into your movie will be displayed in the lower-left corner, as Figure 9-17 shows.

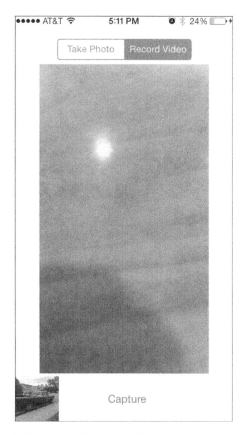

Figure 9-17. Your app displaying a movie thumbnail in the lower-left corner

Note   As you might have noticed, the method used in Recipe 9-8 is rather slow, and it usually takes a couple of seconds to extract the image. There are other ways you might want to try—for example, adding an AVCaptureStillImageOutput to your capture session (it's possible to have several output objects connected) and taking a snapshot when the recording starts. You can use what you learned in Recipe 9-6. Another way is to use the AVCaptureVideoDataOutput mentioned earlier. With that method you can grab any frame you like during recording and extract an image.

Recipe 9-9: Capturing Machine-Readable Codes

With iOS 7 we now have a new functionality in the AVCaptureMetadataOutput class that makes reading machine-readable codes very easy to implement. Machine-readable codes are basically just one-dimensional or two-dimensional barcodes such as UPC-E or QR codes. As an example, Apple's passbook app uses this functionality to read various types of codes. Now you, too, can add this functionality to your app with very little code. This class now gives us the ability to read any of the following types of machine-readable codes:

One–Dimensional

- UPC-E
- EAN-8, EAN-13
- Code 39 (with and without checksum)
- Code 93
- Code 128

Two–Dimensional

- PDF417
- QR
- Aztec

To start, you will be creating a new single view application that is similar to Recipe 9-5. As you did before, you need to add the AssetsLibrary, AVFoundation, and CoreGraphics frameworks. Drag a label to the screen and arrange it as shown in Figure 9-18. Make the label three lines high and resize it to be the width of the screen. Select the label and add some constraints by choosing "Add Missing Constraints" from the Resolve Auto Layout Issues menu in the lower-right side of the storyboard editor.

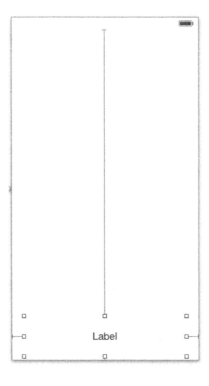

Figure 9-18. The finished interface

Next, create an outlet for the text label with the name "codeLabel."

Now that you have a starting place set up, add a few properties as well as a delegate declaration to the view controller header file. The properties will be used to handle a capture session, the input device, and the metadata output. We'll need to add a delegate to our view controller to retrieve information when a bar code or QR code is scanned. Listing 9-53 shows the completed ViewController.h file.

Listing 9-53. The completed ViewController.h file with required properties and delegate declaration

```
//
//  ViewController.h
//  Recipe 9-9 Capturing Machine-Readable Codes
//

#import <UIKit/UIKit.h>
#import <AVFoundation/AVFoundation.h>

@interface ViewController : UIViewController <AVCaptureMetadataOutputObjectsDelegate>

@property (weak, nonatomic) IBOutlet UILabel *codeLabel;
@property (strong, nonatomic) AVCaptureSession *captureSession;
@property (strong, nonatomic) AVCaptureDeviceInput *videoInput;
@property (strong, nonatomic) AVCaptureMetadataOutput *metadataOutput;

@end
```

Next, we need to add a little bit of code to the viewDidLoad: method and add the delegates. Because there are a few different things we'll be adding to the viewDidLoad method, we'll first explain each piece and reveal the complete viewDidLoad method when we're done.

To begin, we'll create an AVCaptureSession and provide the input type and the input device, as shown in Listing 9-54. As we did in the preceding two recipes, we are checking for errors and the existence of the video input before assigning the input.

Listing 9-54. Adding an AVCaptureSession and video input

```
//
//  ViewController.m
//  Recipe 9-9 Capturing Machine-Readable Codes
//

//...
- (void)viewDidLoad
{

    [super viewDidLoad];

    self.captureSession = [[AVCaptureSession alloc] init];

    AVCaptureDevice *device =
    [AVCaptureDevice defaultDeviceWithMediaType:AVMediaTypeVideo];
```

```
    NSError *error = nil;
    self.videoInput = [AVCaptureDeviceInput deviceInputWithDevice:device error:&error];
    if (self.videoInput)
    {
        [self.captureSession addInput:self.videoInput];
    }
    else
    {
        NSLog(@"Input Error: %@", error);
    }

//...
}
```

Next, you should allocate and initialize your metadataOutput property and then set the delegate and the dispatch queue to the main thread. Because QR codes aren't really that intensive, the main thread should be fine for handling these operations. You also need to set a couple of metadata types. For this example, we will use UPC-E code and QR code types. You can expand these as much as you please using any of the types listed earlier. Add the code in Listing 9-55 to the viewDidLoad method.

Listing 9-55. Creating an AVCaptureMetadagaOutput instance and setting the object types

```
self.metadataOutput = [[AVCaptureMetadataOutput alloc] init];
[self.captureSession addOutput:self.metadataOutput];

[self.metadataOutput setMetadataObjectsDelegate:self queue:dispatch_get_main_queue()];

self.metadataOutput.metadataObjectTypes = @[AVMetadataObjectTypeUPCECode, AVMetadataObjectTypeQRCode];
```

As we did in Recipe 9-5, we'll create a new preview layer and set it to a view that will allow us to view what the camera is seeing. Add the code in Listing 9-56 to the viewDidLoad method as well.

Listing 9-56. Creating a preview layer to view the current camera view

```
AVCaptureVideoPreviewLayer *previewLayer =
[AVCaptureVideoPreviewLayer layerWithSession:self.captureSession];
UIView *aView = self.view;
previewLayer.frame =
CGRectMake(0, 20, self.view.frame.size.width,
            self.view.frame.size.height-100);
[aView.layer addSublayer:previewLayer];
```

When you are done, your viewDidLoad method should look like Listing 9-57.

Listing 9-57. The completed viewDidLoad method

```
- (void)viewDidLoad
{
    [super viewDidLoad];
    // Do any additional setup after loading the view, typically from a nib.

    self.captureSession = [[AVCaptureSession alloc] init];

    AVCaptureDevice *device =
    [AVCaptureDevice defaultDeviceWithMediaType:AVMediaTypeVideo];

    NSError *error = nil;
    self.videoInput = [AVCaptureDeviceInput deviceInputWithDevice:device error:&error];
    if (self.videoInput)
    {
        [self.captureSession addInput:self.videoInput];
    }
    else
    {
        NSLog(@"Input Error: %@", error);
    }

    self.metadataOutput = [[AVCaptureMetadataOutput alloc] init];
    [self.captureSession addOutput:self.metadataOutput];

    [self.metadataOutput setMetadataObjectsDelegate:self queue:dispatch_get_main_queue()];

    self.metadataOutput.metadataObjectTypes = @[AVMetadataObjectTypeUPCECode, AVMetadataObjectTypeQRCode];

    AVCaptureVideoPreviewLayer *previewLayer =
    [AVCaptureVideoPreviewLayer layerWithSession:self.captureSession];
    UIView *aView = self.view;
    previewLayer.frame =
    CGRectMake(0, 20, self.view.frame.size.width,
                self.view.frame.size.height-70);
    [aView.layer addSublayer:previewLayer];

}
```

Now the only action left is to create the delegate method. All we'll do here is simply set the text label to the value received. Add the code in Listing 9-58 to the implementation file.

Listing 9-58. The captureOutput:didOutputMetadataObjects:fromConnection: method implementation

```
- (void)captureOutput:(AVCaptureOutput *)captureOutput didOutputMetadataObjects:(NSArray *)
metadataObjects fromConnection:(AVCaptureConnection *)connection
{

    self.codeLabel.text = [NSString stringWithFormat:@" Type - %@: Value - %@",object.
type,object.stringValue];

}
```

The last step is to start and stop the capture session using the `viewWillAppear` and `viewWillDisappear` methods, as we did in Recipe 9-5. Add the two methods and their code shown in Listing 9-59 to the view controller as well.

Listing 9-59. Adding the viewWillAppear and viewWillDisappear method implementations

```
- (void)viewWillAppear:(BOOL)animated
{
    [super viewWillAppear:animated];
    [self.captureSession startRunning];
}
- (void)viewWillDisappear:(BOOL)animated
{
    [super viewWillDisappear:animated];
    [self.captureSession stopRunning];
}
```

That's it! If you run it and find either a UPC-E or QR code, your app should look similar to Figure 9-19.

Figure 9-19. The finished app with the text of the code type and value

Summary

As a developer, you have a great deal of choice when it comes to dealing with your device's camera. The predefined interfaces, such as `UIImagePickerController` and `UIVideoEditorController`, are incredibly useful and well designed, but Apple's implementation of the AV Foundation framework allows for more possibilities. Everything from dealing with video and audio to handling barcodes and still images is possible. Even a quick glance at the full documentation reveals countless other functionalities not discussed here, including everything from device capabilities (such as the video camera's LED "torch") to the implementation of your own "Touch-To-Focus" functionality. We live in a world where images, audio, and video fly around the world in a matter of seconds, and as developers we must be able to design and create innovative solutions that fit in with our media-based community.

Chapter 10

Multimedia Recipes

In the words of Aldous Huxley, "After silence, that which comes nearest to expressing the inexpressible is music." We live in a world where we are surrounded by sound and music. From the most subtle background tune in an advertisement to the immense blast of an electric guitar at a rock concert, sound has a tremendous impact on and plays an integral part in our lives. It is our responsibility as developers to translate this force into our applications and bring the most complete and ideal experience to users.

Throughout this chapter, a variety of recipes make use of accessing the music library. Therefore, to fully test these recipes you should ensure there are at least a few songs in your device's music library.

Recipe 10-1: Playing Audio

If you ask most people what they think of when they hear the words "iPhone" and "audio," they will probably think along the lines of their iPod and the thousands of songs they have downloaded. What most users tend to overlook, despite its immense importance, is the concept of background audio and sound effects. These sound clips and tunes might go completely unnoticed by the user in normal use, but in terms of app functionality and design they can tremendously improve the quality of an app. It might be the little "shutter click" when you take a picture or some background music that gets stuck in your head after you play a game for too long; regardless of whether the user notices it, sound can make a world of difference. The iOS AV Foundation framework provides a simple way to access, play, and manipulate sound files using AVAudioPlayer. In this recipe, you will create a sample project that allows you to play an audio file and, in addition, allows the user to manipulate the clip's playback.

Setting Up the Application

Start by creating a new single view application project. In this recipe, you will utilize two frameworks that aren't linked by default, so you need to add them to your project. These are AVFoundation.framework, which includes the AVAudioPlayer class, and AudioToolbox.framework, which you'll use to vibrate the device.

Next, to import the APIs for these frameworks, switch to your view controller's header file and add the following statements:

```
//
//  ViewController.h
//  Recipe 10-1 Playing Audio
//

#import <UIKit/UIKit.h>
#import <AVFoundation/AVFoundation.h>
#import <AudioToolbox/AudioToolbox.h>

@interface ViewController : UIViewController

@end
```

Now build your view in the Main.storyboard file using the following components to resemble Figure 10-1:

- 3 sliders: Rate, Pan, and Volume

- 5 title labels: Average, Peak, Rate, Pan, and Volume

- 2 value labels: Both with default value "0.0"

- 3 buttons: Vibrate, Play, and Pause

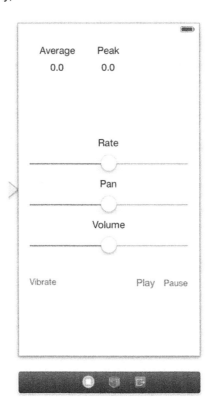

Figure 10-1. A user interface to control an AVAudioPlayer

You need your slider's values to match the possible values of the properties they control. Using the attribute inspector, adjust the minimum and maximum values of your Rate slider to **0.5** and **2.0** (corresponding to half speed and 2x speed). Also, set its current value to **1**. The values for the Pan slider should be **-1** and **1** (corresponding to left pan and right pan) with **0** as the current value. The Volume slider's default values should already be fine, as the volume property goes from 0 to 1. Just set its current value to **1** (maximum volume).

As you have done in preceding recipes, create outlets for the controls that are referenced from your code and actions for the events you need to respond to. Create the following outlets:

- `rateSlider`, `panSlider`, and `volumeSlider` for the sliders
- `averageLabel` and `peakLabel` for your two level-monitoring labels (the ones with the texts "0.0" in Figure 10-1)

Create the following actions:

- `updateRate`, `updatePan`, and `updateVolume` for the Value Changed events of the respective sliders
- `playVibrateSound`, `startPlayer`, and `pausePlayer` for the Touch Up Inside events of the buttons

Add two properties to your header file to keep track of your AVAudioPlayer and your AVAudioSession:

```
@property (strong, nonatomic) AVAudioPlayer *player;
```

The last step in your header file is to make your view controller conform to the AVAudioPlayerDelegate protocol. Your ViewController.h file should now resemble Listing 10-1.

Listing 10-1. The initial ViewController.h setup

```
//
//  ViewController.h
//  Recipe 9.1 Playing Audio
//

#import <UIKit/UIKit.h>
#import <AVFoundation/AVFoundation.h>
#import <AudioToolbox/AudioToolbox.h>

@interface ViewController : UIViewController<AVAudioPlayerDelegate>

@property (weak, nonatomic) IBOutlet UISlider *rateSlider;
@property (weak, nonatomic) IBOutlet UISlider *panSlider;
@property (weak, nonatomic) IBOutlet UISlider *volumeSlider;

@property (weak, nonatomic) IBOutlet UILabel *averageLabel;
@property (weak, nonatomic) IBOutlet UILabel *peakLabel;

@property (strong, nonatomic) AVAudioPlayer *player;
```

```
- (IBAction)updateRate:(id)sender;
- (IBAction)updatePan:(id)sender;
- (IBAction)updateVolume:(id)sender;

- (IBAction)playVibrateSound:(id)sender;
- (IBAction)startPlayer:(id)sender;
- (IBAction)pausePlayer:(id)sender;

@end
```

Before you proceed, you need to select and import the sound file that your application will be playing. The file we use is called `midnight-ride.mp3`, and the code reflects this file name. You need to change any filename or file type according to the file you choose. You should consult Apple's documentation on which file types are appropriate at `https://developer.apple.com/library/ios/ DOCUMENTATION/AudioVideo/Conceptual/MultimediaPG/UsingAudio/UsingAudio.html#//apple_ref/ doc/uid/TP40009767-CH2`. However, it is fairly safe to assume that most commonly used file types, such as .wav or .mp3, will work.

Tip   We downloaded our sound file from Sound Jay, which offers sound and music files free of charge. Be sure to read the terms of use (`http://www.soundjay.com/tos.html`) for how you may use Sound Jay's files in your projects.

Add the sound file to your project by dragging and dropping it into the Supported Files folder. For more information about adding resource files, see Chapter 1, Recipe 1-8.

Setting Up the Audio Player

Switch to `ViewController.m` and locate the `viewDidLoad` method. Add the code in Listing 10-2 to set up `AVAudioPlayer`.

Listing 10-2. Updating the viewDidLoad method to set up AVAudioPlayer

```
- (void)viewDidLoad
{
    [super viewDidLoad];
    // Do any additional setup after loading the view, typically from a nib.
    NSString *fileName = @"midnight-ride"; // Change this to your own file
    NSString *fileType = @"mp3";
    NSString *soundFilePath =
        [[NSBundle mainBundle] pathForResource:fileName ofType:fileType];
    NSURL *soundFileURL = [NSURL fileURLWithPath:soundFilePath];

    NSError *error;
    self.player =
        [[AVAudioPlayer alloc] initWithContentsOfURL:soundFileURL error:&error];
```

```
    if (error)
    {
        NSLog(@"Error creating the audio player: %@", error);
    }
    self.player.enableRate = YES; //Allows us to change the playback rate.
    self.player.meteringEnabled = YES; //Allows us to monitor levels
    self.player.delegate = self;
    self.volumeSlider.value = self.player.volume;
    self.rateSlider.value = self.player.rate;
    self.panSlider.value = self.player.pan;

    [self.player prepareToPlay]; //Preload audio to decrease lag

    [NSTimer scheduledTimerWithTimeInterval:0.1
        target:self selector:@selector(updateLabels) userInfo:nil repeats:YES];
}
```

From Listing 10-2, you can see that you set the URL for your sound file and initialized your AVAudioPlayer with it, set the enableRate property to allow you to change the playback rate, and set the meteringEnabled property to allow you to monitor the player's levels. The optional prepareToPlay on your player gets called to pre-load the sound file, which hopefully makes your application slightly faster. At the end you created a timer, which performs your updateLabels method at a rate of ten times per second. This way your labels will update at a nearly constant rate.

Now add a simple implementation of the updateLabels method, as shown in Listing 10-3.

Listing 10-3. Implementing the updateLabels method

```
-(void)updateLabels
{
    [self.player updateMeters];
    self.averageLabel.text =
        [NSString stringWithFormat:@"%f", [self.player averagePowerForChannel:0]];
    self.peakLabel.text =
        [NSString stringWithFormat:@"%f", [self.player peakPowerForChannel:0]];
}
```

The updateMeters method needs to be called any time you use the averagePowerForChannel or peakPowerForChannel methods to get up-to-date values. Both methods take an NSUInteger, which is an unsigned integer argument that specifies the channel for which to retrieve information. By giving it the value of 0, you specify the left channel for a stereo track or the single channel for a mono track. Given that you are dealing with only a basic use of the functionality, channel 0 is a good default.

Next, implement your action methods for your sliders, as shown in Listing 10-4. These actions are called every time the respective slider's value is changed.

Listing 10-4. Implementation of the updateRate, updatePan, and updateVolume methods

```
- (IBAction)updateRate:(id)sender
{
    self.player.rate = self.rateSlider.value;
}
```

```
- (IBAction)updatePan:(id)sender
{
    self.player.pan = self.panSlider.value;
}

- (IBAction)updateVolume:(id)sender
{
    self.player.volume = self.volumeSlider.value;
}
```

Next, implement your button action methods, which are also quite simple. This implementation is shown in Listing 10-5.

Listing 10-5. Implementation of the playVibrateSound, startPlayer, and pausePlayer action methods

```
- (IBAction)playVibrateSound:(id)sender
{
    AudioServicesPlaySystemSound(kSystemSoundID_Vibrate);
}

- (IBAction)startPlayer:(id)sender
{
    [self.player play];
}

- (IBAction)pausePlayer:(id)sender
{
    [self.player pause];
}
```

> **Note**   Although most of the AV Foundation functionalities you are currently working with will work on the simulator (using your computer's microphone and speakers), the vibrate sound will not. You need a physical device to test this functionality.

Handling Errors and Interruptions

At this point, your app can successfully play and pause your music, and you can adjust your playback rate, pan, and volume as well as monitor your output levels. However, it lacks some basic error handling and interruption handling.

To catch any errors in playing files, you can implement the method in Listing 10-6 from the AVAudioPlayerDelegate protocol.

Listing 10-6. Implementation of the audioPlayerDecodeErrorDidOccur:error: delegate method

```
-(void)audioPlayerDecodeErrorDidOccur:(AVAudioPlayer *)player error:(NSError *)error
{
    NSLog(@"Error playing file: %@", [error localizedDescription]);
}
```

Whenever you are dealing with an app that has sound or music involved, there is always a concern that your app might be interrupted by a phone call or text message, so you should always include functionality to deal with these concerns. This can be done through a couple of AVAudioPlayer delegate methods. The audioPlayerBeginInterruption: method is called when an audio player has been interrupted while playing. For most cases, you don't have to provide an implementation for that method because your player is automatically paused by the system. However, if you want your player to resume playing after such an interruption, you need to implement the audioPlayerEndInterruption: method. In this recipe you want the audio player to resume, so add the code in Listing 10-7 to your view controller.

Listing 10-7. Implementing the audioPlayerEndInterruption:withOptions: method

```
- (void)audioPlayerEndInterruption:(AVAudioPlayer *)player withOptions:(NSUInteger)flags
{
    if (flags == AVAudioSessionInterruptionOptionShouldResume)
    {
        [player play];
    }
}
```

You can now see the flexibility with which you can use the AVAudioPlayer, despite its simplistic use. By using multiple instances of AVAudioPlayer, you can implement complex audio designs using multiple sounds at the same time. One could possibly have a background music track running in one AVAudioPlayer and have one or two others handling event-based sound effects. The power, simplicity, and flexibility of the AVAudioPlayer class are what make it so popular among iOS developers.

Recipe 10-2: Recording Audio

Now that you have dealt with the key concept of playing audio, you can familiarize yourself with the reverse: recording audio. This process is very similar in both structure and implementation to playing audio. You use the AVAudioRecorder class to do your recording in conjunction with an AVAudioPlayer to handle the playback of your recording. We also make this project slightly more complicated by setting up two multifunctional buttons; one for starting and stopping a recording, and one for playing and pausing a recording.

Start by creating a new single view application project. You need to link and import the AVFoundation framework into your project again, as you did in the preceding recipe. Unlike the preceding recipe, however, you do not need the Audio Toolbox framework.

Now set up the user interface so that it looks like Figure 10-2 with the following items:

- 2 title labels: Average and Peak
- 2 value labels: Both with a "0.0" value
- 2 buttons: Record and Play

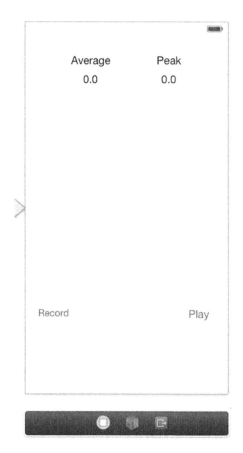

Figure 10-2. *User interface for recording and playing audio*

Create the following outlets:

- averageLabel and peakLabel for the level-monitoring labels
- recordButton and playButton for the buttons

Create the following actions:

- toggleRecording for the Change Value event of the "Record" button
- togglePlaying for the Change Value event of the "Play" button

Before you proceed to your implementation file, you'll make some additional changes to the ViewController.h file, as shown in Listing 10-8. The first is to prepare the view controller for being a delegate for both the audio player and audio recorder by conforming to the AVAudioPlayerDelegate and the AVAudioRecorderDelegate protocols.

Listing 10-8. *Declaring delegates in the ViewController.h file*

```
@interface ViewController : UIViewController<AVAudioPlayerDelegate,
                                              AVAudioRecorderDelegate>
```

Next, add an instance variable to flag when a new recording is available, as shown in Listing 10-9.

Listing 10-9. Adding an instance variable to the ViewController.h file

```
@interface ViewController : UIViewController<AVAudioPlayerDelegate,
                                             AVAudioRecorderDelegate>
{
    @private
    BOOL _newRecordingAvailable;
}

// ...

@end
```

Finally, add four properties for holding the instance of the audio player, the audio recorder, the audio session, and the file path to the recorded file. With these and the preceding changes, your ViewController.h file should resemble Listing 10-10, with changes in bold.

Listing 10-10. The complete ViewController.h file

```
//
//  ViewController.h
//  Recipe 9.2 Recording Audio
//

#import <UIKit/UIKit.h>
#import <AVFoundation/AVFoundation.h>

@interface ViewController : UIViewController<AVAudioPlayerDelegate, AVAudioRecorderDelegate>
{
    BOOL _newRecordingAvailable;
}

@property (weak, nonatomic) IBOutlet UILabel *averageLabel;
@property (weak, nonatomic) IBOutlet UILabel *peakLabel;
@property (weak, nonatomic) IBOutlet UIButton *recordButton;
@property (weak, nonatomic) IBOutlet UIButton *playButton;
@property (strong, nonatomic) AVAudioPlayer *player;
@property (strong, nonatomic) AVAudioRecorder *recorder;
@property (strong, nonatomic) AVAudioSession *session;
@property (strong, nonatomic) NSString *recordedFilePath;

- (IBAction)toggleRecording:(id)sender;
- (IBAction)togglePlaying:(id)sender;

@end
```

Setting Up an Audio Recorder

Now it's time to implement the viewDidLoad method in the ViewController.m file. First, you will set up the audio session and an error variable. The initialization of the AVAudioSession is different because we are initializing it with SharedInstance. The system creates a singleton, a single instance for the audio session that is shared between all apps that use audio. By initializing it, you have access to audio, but because it's shared you might have interruptions from the music app or the phone. Add the code shown in Listing 10-11 to your viewDidLoad method.

Listing 10-11. Setting an AVAudioSession and an error variable

```
self.session = [AVAudioSession sharedInstance];
[self.session setActive:YES error:nil];

NSError *error;

[[AVAudioSession sharedInstance] setCategory:AVAudioSessionCategoryRecord error:&error];
```

Next, you'll define a file path for the recording, as shown in Listing 10-12.

Listing 10-12. Defining a recording file path

```
self.recordedFilePath = [[NSString alloc] initWithFormat:@"%@%@",
    NSTemporaryDirectory(), @"recording.wav"];
```

Next, you'll initialize the audio recorder with the file path converted to a URL. Listing 10-13 shows this initialization.

Listing 10-13. Initializing the audio recorder

```
NSURL *url = [[NSURL alloc] initFileURLWithPath:self.recordedFilePath];
NSError *error;
self.recorder = [[AVAudioRecorder alloc] initWithURL:url settings:nil error:&error];
if (error)
{
    NSLog(@"Error initializing recorder: %@", error);
}
self.recorder.meteringEnabled = YES;
self.recorder.delegate = self;
[self.recorder prepareToRecord];
```

The call to prepareToRecord in Listing 10-13 assures that when the user taps the "Record" button later, the recording will start immediately (assuming the user granted permission to the microphone).

Finally, as in Recipe 10-1, start a timer that triggers updating of the level-monitoring labels. The viewDidLoad method should now look like Listing 10-14.

Listing 10-14. The complete viewDidLoad method

```
- (void)viewDidLoad
{
    [super viewDidLoad];

    self.session = [AVAudioSession sharedInstance];
    [self.session setActive:YES error:nil];

    NSError *error;

    [[AVAudioSession sharedInstance] setCategory:AVAudioSessionCategoryPlayAndRecord error:&error];


    self.recordedFilePath = [[NSString alloc] initWithFormat:@"%@%@",
                                NSTemporaryDirectory(), @"recording.wav"];
    NSURL *url = [[NSURL alloc] initFileURLWithPath:self.recordedFilePath];

    self.recorder = [[AVAudioRecorder alloc] initWithURL:url settings:nil error:&error];
    if (error)
    {
        NSLog(@"Error initializing recorder: %@", error);
    }
    self.recorder.meteringEnabled = YES;
    self.recorder.delegate = self;
    [self.recorder prepareToRecord];

    [NSTimer scheduledTimerWithTimeInterval:0.01 target:self
}
```

You might be wondering why you aren't also initializing the audio player in the viewDidLoad method. The reason is that the player's initializer requires a URL that points to an audio file, but at the time of the view loading there are no audio files recorded. Therefore, as you'll see later, you create the player when the user taps the "Play" button.

Add the updateLabels method as shown in Listing 10-15, which resembles the one in Recipe 10-1 with the exception that now it's the audio recorder that's being monitored and not the audio player.

Listing 10-15. Implementation of the updateLabels method

```
-(void)updateLabels
{
    [self.recorder updateMeters];
    self.averageLabel.text =
        [NSString stringWithFormat:@"%f", [self.recorder averagePowerForChannel:0]];
    self.peakLabel.text =
        [NSString stringWithFormat:@"%f", [self.recorder peakPowerForChannel:0]];
}
```

Now let's turn to the action methods. Start with toggleRecordinxg:. It has only two cases. If the recorder is currently active, it should stop the recording and reset the title of the "Record" button; if not, it should start recording and change the title of the "Record" button to "Stop." Because the user now can potentially deny access to the microphone, we also added the completion block that tests this case. If permission to record is granted, then recording starts. Otherwise, an alert pops up to notify the user that she needs to enable the microphone in the privacy settings. Listing 10-16 shows the completed method.

Listing 10-16. Implementation of the toggleRecording: method

```
- (IBAction)toggleRecording:(id)sender
{

    if ([self.recorder isRecording])
    {
        [self.recorder stop];
        [self.recordButton setTitle:@"Record" forState:UIControlStateNormal];
    }
    else
    {
        [self.session requestRecordPermission:^(BOOL granted) {

            if(granted)
            {
            [self.recorder record];
            [self.recordButton setTitle:@"Stop" forState:UIControlStateNormal];
            }
            else
            {

                UIAlertView *alert = [[UIAlertView alloc] initWithTitle:@"Recording Permission
Denied" message:@"Verify microphone access is turned on in Settings->Privacy->Microphone"
delegate:nil cancelButtonTitle:@"OK" otherButtonTitles:nil];
                [alert show];
            }
        }];

    }
}
```

Next, implement the AVAudioRecorderDelegate method protocol, as shown in Listing 10-17. It will be called when a recording has finished, with a flag that indicates whether the recording was completed successfully.

Listing 10-17. Implementing the audioRecorderDidFinishRecording:successfully: delegate method

```
- (void)audioRecorderDidFinishRecording:(AVAudioRecorder *)recorder successfully:(BOOL)flag
{
    _newRecordingAvailable = flag;
    [self.recordButton setTitle:@"Record" forState:UIControlStateNormal];
}
```

As you can see, if the recording is successful you indicate that a new recording is available by setting an instance variable flag. You also reset the title of the button to read "Record" again.

Now to the slightly more complicated "Play" button. When the user taps it, there are four possible states (we'll need to consider only three):

1. The audio player is active, in which case you pause it and reset the button's title to "Play."

2. A new recording is available, which forces you to recreate the audio player with the new file. Then start the player and set the button's title to "Pause."

3. A player has been created but is currently not active, which means it has been paused and should be restarted. Start the player and set the button title to "Pause."

4. No player has been created yet. This means that there is no valid recording available. Simply ignore this case.

Listing 10-18 shows the preceding points translated into code.

Listing 10-18. Implementation of the togglePlaying: method

```objc
- (IBAction)togglePlaying:(id)sender
{
    if (self.player.playing)
    {
        [self.player pause];
        [self.playButton setTitle:@"Play" forState:UIControlStateNormal];
    }
    else if (_newRecordingAvailable)
    {
        NSURL *url = [[NSURL alloc] initFileURLWithPath:self.recordedFilePath];
        NSError *error;
        self.player = [[AVAudioPlayer alloc] initWithContentsOfURL:url error:&error];
        if (!error)
        {
            self.player.delegate = self;
            [self.player play];
        }
        else
        {
            NSLog(@"Error initializing player: %@", error);
        }
        [self.playButton setTitle:@"Pause" forState:UIControlStateNormal];
        _newRecordingAvailable = NO;
    }
    else if (self.player)
    {
        [self.player play];
        [self.playButton setTitle:@"Pause" forState:UIControlStateNormal];
    }
}
```

When the player has finished playing, the button's title should be reset. The delegate method in Listing 10-19 takes care of that.

Listing 10-19. Implementation of the audioPlayerDidFinishPlaying:successfully: delegate method

```
-(void)audioPlayerDidFinishPlaying:(AVAudioPlayer *)player successfully:(BOOL)flag
{
    [self.playButton setTitle:@"Play" forState:UIControlStateNormal];
}
```

Handling Interruptions

At this point, your application successfully records and plays a sound. As with the previous recipe, you should implement the delegate methods to handle interruptions such as phone calls or text messages. Listing 10-20 shows the methods for handling interruptions for both the audio player and the recorder.

Listing 10-20. Implementation of the two delegate methods to handle interruptions

```
- (void)audioPlayerEndInterruption:(AVAudioPlayer *)player withOptions:(NSUInteger)flags
{
    if (flags == AVAudioSessionInterruptionOptionShouldResume)
    {
        [player play];
    }
}

- (void)audioRecorderEndInterruption:(AVAudioRecorder *)recorder withOptions:(NSUInteger)flags
{
    if (flags == AVAudioSessionInterruptionOptionShouldResume)
    {
        [recorder record];
    }
}
```

Now you have a fully functional app to record and play sounds from your device. As you can see, the AVAudioRecorder and AVAudioPlayer work well together to provide a complete yet simple audio interface for the user.

Recipe 10-3: Accessing the Music Library

So far you have been able to deal with playing and manipulating sound files that you have included in your project. However, an easy way to access a significantly larger supply of sound files is by accessing the user's music library.

In this recipe, you will make another new single view application. This time you need to link it with the Media Player framework, which allows you to play music, movies, podcasts, and audio books. The other benefit is that it gives you access to the iPod library. As usual, add an import statement for the framework to your view controller.

Setting Up a Basic Music Player

Set up your view to work as a basic music player. Add the following components so it looks like Figure 10-3:

- 4 buttons: Add Music to Queue, Prev, Play, Next
- 3 labels: Now Playing:, Info, Volume
- 1 view: Make it 20 points x 276 points

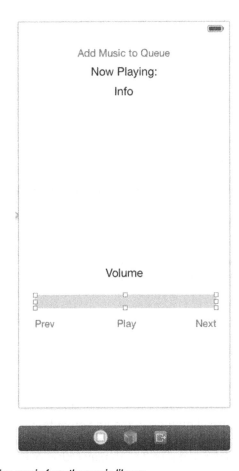

Figure 10-3. User interface for queuing music from the music library

Create the following outlets for the controls that are referenced from your code:

- `infoLabel`
- `volumeView`; change the property type to `MPVolumeView` instead of `UIView`
- `playButton`

Create the following actions:

- addItems, for the Touch Up Inside event of the "Add Music to Queue" button

- prevTapped, playTapped, and nextTapped, respectively, for the three buttons at the bottom

Define two properties in your header file—one of type MPMusicPlayerController called "player," which you use to play music, and one of type MPMediaItemCollection called "myCollection," which helps you keep track of your chosen tracks to play. Finally, make your view controller the delegate for a class called "MPMediaPickerController," which allows your user to select music to play. Overall, your header file should now look like Listing 10-21.

Listing 10-21. The finished ViewController.h file

```
//
//  ViewController.h
//  Recipe 10-3 Accessing Music Library
//

#import <UIKit/UIKit.h>
#import <MediaPlayer/MediaPlayer.h>

@interface ViewController : UIViewController<MPMediaPickerControllerDelegate>

@property (weak, nonatomic) IBOutlet UILabel *infoLabel;
@property (weak, nonatomic) IBOutlet MPVolumeView *volumeView;
@property (weak, nonatomic) IBOutlet UIButton *playButton;
@property (strong, nonatomic) MPMediaItemCollection *myCollection;
@property (strong, nonatomic) MPMusicPlayerController *player;

- (IBAction)addItems:(id)sender;
- (IBAction)prevTapped:(id)sender;
- (IBAction)playTapped:(id)sender;
- (IBAction)nextTapped:(id)sender;
- (IBAction)updateVolume:(id)sender;

@end
```

Now you can set up your viewDidLoad method in the implementation file. Listing 10-22 shows that you set the player, call the setNotifications method, and setup the volumeView. The MPVolumeView is a class that inserts a volume slider and a button to play music over Apple TV or a wireless streaming airplay standard device. The nice thing about this view is that it handles volume and airplay logic without any further configuration.

Listing 10-22. The viewDidLoad implementation

```
- (void)viewDidLoad
{
    [super viewDidLoad];
        // Do any additional setup after loading the view, typically from a nib.
    self.infoLabel.text = @"...";
```

```
self.player = [MPMusicPlayerController applicationMusicPlayer];

[self setNotifications];

[self.player beginGeneratingPlaybackNotifications];

[self.player setShuffleMode:MPMusicShuffleModeOff];
self.player.repeatMode = MPMusicRepeatModeNone;

self.volumeView.backgroundColor = [UIColor clearColor];
MPVolumeView *myVolumeView =
[[MPVolumeView alloc] initWithFrame: self.volumeView.bounds];
[self.volumeView addSubview: myVolumeView];

}
```

> **Note**   The MPMusicPlayerController class has two important class methods that allow you to access an instance of the class. The one you used previously, applicationMusicPlayer, returns an application-specific music player. This option can be useful for keeping your music separate from the device's music player, but it has the downside of being unable to play once the app enters the background. Alternatively, you can use the iPodMusicPlayer, which allows for continuous play despite being in the background. The main thing to keep in mind in this case, however, is that your player might already have a nowPlayingItem from the actual iPod that you should be able to handle.

Handling Notifications

Whenever you use an instance of MPMusicPlayerController, it is recommended you register for notifications for whenever the playback state changes or whenever the currently playing song changes. We have extracted this code into a helper method named "setNotifications." Listing 10-23 shows the implementation for the setNotifications method.

Listing 10-23. Implementation of the setNotifications method

```
-(void)setNotifications
{
    NSNotificationCenter *notificationCenter = [NSNotificationCenter defaultCenter];

    [notificationCenter
     addObserver: self
     selector:    @selector(handleNowPlayingItemChanged:)
     name:        MPMusicPlayerControllerNowPlayingItemDidChangeNotification
     object:      self.player];
```

```
[notificationCenter
 addObserver: self
 selector:    @selector(handlePlaybackStateChanged:)
 name:        MPMusicPlayerControllerPlaybackStateDidChangeNotification
 object:      self.player];

}
```

Next, the method to handle the playback state-change notification simply updates the title of the "Play" button to reflect the new state, as shown in Listing 10-24.

Listing 10-24. Implementation of the handlePlaybackStateChange: method

```
- (void) handlePlaybackStateChanged: (id) notification
{
    MPMusicPlaybackState playbackState = [self.player playbackState];

    if (playbackState == MPMusicPlaybackStateStopped)
    {
        [self.playButton setTitle:@"Play" forState:UIControlStateNormal];
    }
    else if (playbackState == MPMusicPlaybackStatePaused)
    {
        [self.playButton setTitle:@"Play" forState:UIControlStateNormal];
    }
    else if (playbackState == MPMusicPlaybackStatePlaying)
    {
        [self.playButton setTitle:@"Pause" forState:UIControlStateNormal];
    }
}
```

Finally, whenever the currently playing song is changed, the info label should be updated. The code in Listing 10-25 handles this case.

Listing 10-25. Implementation of the handleNowPlayingItemChanged: method

```
- (void) handleNowPlayingItemChanged: (id) notification
{
    MPMediaItem *currentItemPlaying = [self.player nowPlayingItem];
    if (currentItemPlaying)
    {
        NSString *info = [NSString stringWithFormat:@"%@ - %@",
            [currentItemPlaying valueForProperty:MPMediaItemPropertyTitle],
            [currentItemPlaying valueForProperty:MPMediaItemPropertyArtist]];
        self.infoLabel.text = info;
    }
    else
    {
        self.infoLabel.text = @"...";
    }
}
```

Picking Media to Play

To add music to your list of tunes, use the MPMediaPickerController class. This class provides, as shown in Figure 10-4, a standardized way to make a music selection. Add the code in Listing 10-26 to the addItems action method to set up and display a media picker.

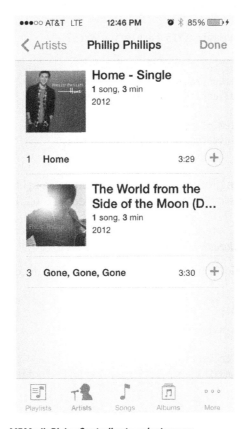

Figure 10-4. *The user interface of the MPMediaPickerController to select songs*

Listing 10-26. *Completing the implementation for the additems: action method*

```
- (IBAction)addItems:(id)sender
{
    MPMediaPickerController *picker =
        [[MPMediaPickerController alloc] initWithMediaTypes:MPMediaTypeMusic];
    picker.delegate = self;
    picker.allowsPickingMultipleItems = YES;
    picker.prompt = NSLocalizedString (@"Add songs to play",
        "Prompt in media item picker");
    [self presentViewController:picker animated:YES completion:NULL];
}
```

The media picker communicates with your view controller through the MPMediaPickerControllerDelegate protocol you added to the header earlier. Implement the following two delegate methods to handle both cancellation and successful selection of media, as shown in Listing 10-27.

Listing 10-27. Implementing methods to handle cancellation and successful selection of media

```
-(void)mediaPickerDidCancel:(MPMediaPickerController *)mediaPicker
{
    [self dismissViewControllerAnimated:YES completion:NULL];
}

-(void)mediaPicker:(MPMediaPickerController *)mediaPicker
didPickMediaItems:(MPMediaItemCollection *)mediaItemCollection
{
    [self updateQueueWithMediaItemCollection:mediaItemCollection];
    [self dismissViewControllerAnimated:YES completion:NULL];
}
```

An MPMediaItemCollection is the group of media items that were selected by the user. Use it to update the media player's queue in the updateQueueWithMediaItemCollection: method, as shown in Listing 10-28.

Listing 10-28. Implementing the updateQueueWithMediaItemCollection: method

```
-(void)updateQueueWithMediaItemCollection:(MPMediaItemCollection *)collection
{
    if (collection)
    {
        if (self.myCollection == nil)
        {
            self.myCollection = collection;
            [self.player setQueueWithItemCollection: self.myCollection];
            [self.player play];
        }
        else
        {
            BOOL wasPlaying = NO;
            if (self.player.playbackState == MPMusicPlaybackStatePlaying)
            {
                wasPlaying = YES;
            }

            MPMediaItem *nowPlayingItem       = self.player.nowPlayingItem;
            NSTimeInterval currentPlaybackTime = self.player.currentPlaybackTime;

            NSMutableArray *combinedMediaItems =
                [[self.myCollection items] mutableCopy];
            NSArray *newMediaItems = [collection items];
            [combinedMediaItems addObjectsFromArray: newMediaItems];
```

```
            self.myCollection =
                [MPMediaItemCollection collectionWithItems:combinedMediaItems];

            [self.player setQueueWithItemCollection:self.myCollection];

            self.player.nowPlayingItem      = nowPlayingItem;
            self.player.currentPlaybackTime = currentPlaybackTime;

            if (wasPlaying)
            {
                [self.player play];
            }
        }
    }
}
```

Listing 10-28 might seem complex, but it is actually a fairly linear progression. First, after checking to make sure the collection of newly selected items is not nil, check to see whether there is a previous queue set up. If not, simply set your player's queue to this collection. On the other hand, if a collection does exist, then combine the two, set your player's queue as the result, and restore your playback to where it previously was.

The remaining action methods' implementations are pretty straightforward. Listing 10-29 shows the one that responds to a user tapping the "Prev" button.

Listing 10-29. Implementing the prevTapped: action method

```
- (IBAction)prevTapped:(id)sender
{
    if ([self.player currentPlaybackTime] > 5.0)
    {
        [self.player skipToBeginning];
    }
    else
    {
        [self.player skipToPreviousItem];
    }
}
```

As you can see, in Listing 10-29 we've given the "Prev" button two functionalities: If the media player is at the beginning of the current song, tapping the button will skip to the previous song; however, if the playback is more than five seconds into the current song, tapping the button will skip to the beginning of the current song.

The next button is even simpler. It simply skips to the next song, as shown in Listing 10-30.

Listing 10-30. Implementation of the nextTapped: action method

```
- (IBAction)nextTapped:(id)sender
{
    [self.player skipToNextItem];
}
```

The "Play" button toggles between "Play" and "Pause" and updates the button title accordingly, as shown in Listing 10-31.

Listing 10-31. Implementation of the playTapped: action method

```
- (IBAction)playTapped:(id)sender
{
    if ((self.myCollection != nil) &&
        (self.player.playbackState != MPMusicPlaybackStatePlaying))
    {
        [self.player play];
        [self.playButton setTitle:@"Pause" forState:UIControlStateNormal];
    }
    else if (self.player.playbackState == MPMusicPlaybackStatePlaying)
    {
        [self.player pause];
        [self.playButton setTitle:@"Play" forState:UIControlStateNormal];
    }
}
```

Your application is now ready to build and run. One thing to note when you run this application is that until the music is playing, whether that be from the app or the music player, you cannot adjust your AVAudioPlayer's volume by using the external volume buttons. These buttons still control the ringer volume, as opposed to the playback volume. After a song is playing, you receive full control over the playback volume through these buttons.

You'll now go on by adding the possibility to search the music library for media to add to the playback queue.

Querying Media

The media player comes with a powerful querying capability with which you can search the music library. To give you an idea of its possibilities, we're going to add an MPMediaQuery feature to the application. This feature allows the user to query the music library for items containing a certain text and have them added to the media player's queue.

First, add a UIButton as well as a UITextField to your view so that your view now looks like Figure 10-5.

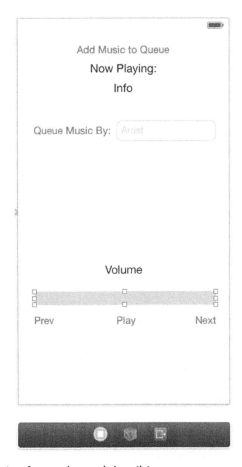

Figure 10-5. User interface with a feature for querying music by artist

Create an outlet with the name "artistTextField" for referencing the text field and an action named "queueMusicByArtist" for the button.

The first thing you do with your new UITextField is to set its delegate to your view controller by adding the lines in Listing 10-32 to the viewDidLoad method.

Listing 10-32. Adding the artistTextField delegate to the viewDidLoad method

```
- (void)viewDidLoad
{
    // ...

    self.artistTextField.delegate = self;
    self.artistTextField.enablesReturnKeyAutomatically = YES;
}
```

Make sure to adjust your header file to declare that your view controller conforms to the UITextFieldDelegate protocol, as shown in Listing 10-33.

Listing 10-33. Declaring the UITextFieldDelegate protocol

```
@interface ViewController : UIViewController<MPMediaPickerControllerDelegate,
                                        UITextFieldDelegate>

// ...

@end
```

Next, implement the delegate method to have your text field dismiss the keyboard and automatically perform the query when the user taps the return key, as shown in Listing 10-34.

Listing 10-34. Implementation of the textFieldShouldReturn: delegate method

```
-(BOOL)textFieldShouldReturn:(UITextField *)textField
{
    [textField resignFirstResponder];
    [self queueMusicByArtist:self];
    return NO;
}
```

Finally, the queueMusicByArtist: method is implemented, as shown in Listing 10-35. This method basically takes the value in the text field and checks to make sure it's not blank. If it's not blank, create a predicate, a logical condition in which to test media items against and return the correct list of items. Then populate the queue with the results.

Listing 10-35. Implementation of the queueMusicByArtist: method

```
- (IBAction)queueMusicByArtist:(id)sender
{
    NSString *artist = self.artistTextField.text;
    if (artist != nil && ![artist isEqual: @""])
    {
        MPMediaPropertyPredicate *artistPredicate =
            [MPMediaPropertyPredicate
                predicateWithValue:artist
                forProperty:MPMediaItemPropertyArtist
                comparisonType:MPMediaPredicateComparisonContains];
        MPMediaQuery *query = [[MPMediaQuery alloc] init];
        [query addFilterPredicate:artistPredicate];

        NSArray *result = [query items];
        if ([result count] > 0)
        {
            [self updateQueueWithMediaItemCollection:
                [MPMediaItemCollection collectionWithItems:result]];
        }
        else
            self.infoLabel.text = @"Artist Not Found.";
    }
}
```

You can now run and test the new feature. Enter a search string in the artist text field and press "Return" (or tap the "Queue Music By" button); the media player should start playing all songs from artists whose names contain the provided text.

As you can see, querying the media library is a fairly simple process, which at its bare minimum requires only an instance of the MPMediaQuery class. You can then add MPMediaPropertyPredicates to a query to make it more specific. The MPMediaPropertyPredicates is basically a configurable operation that can be used to query media and return a list of media items based on the conditions of the operation.

Using MPMediaPropertyPredicates requires a decent knowledge of the different MPMediaItemProperties so you can know exactly what kind of information you can acquire. Not all MPMediaItemProperties are filterable, and the filterable properties are also different if you are dealing specifically with a podcast. You should refer to the Apple documentation about MPMediaItem for a full list of properties, but the following is a list of the most commonly used ones:

- MPMediaItemPropertyMediaType: The media type, such as MP3, M4V, and so on

- MPMediaItemPropertyTitle: The media item title, such as a song title

- MPMediaItemPropertyAlbumTitle: The album title

- MPMediaItemPropertyArtist: The artist

- MPMediaItemPropertyArtwork: The album artwork image

> **Tip** Whenever you use MPMediaItemPropertyArtwork, you can use the imageWithSize: method defined in MPMediaItemPropertyArtwork to create a UIImage from the artwork.

We have barely scratched the surface of media-item queries, but here are a few points to keep in mind when dealing with them:

- Whenever multiple filter predicates specifying different properties are added to a query, the predicates are evaluated using the AND operator, meaning that if you specify an artist name and an album name, you will receive only songs by that artist AND from that specific album.

- Do not add two filter predicates of the same property to a query because the resulting behavior is not defined. If you wish to query a database for multiple specific values of the same property, such as filtering for all songs by two different artists, a better method is simply to create two queries and then combine their results afterward.

- The comparisonType property of an MPMediaPropertyPredicate helps specify how exact you want your predicate to be. A value of MPMediaPredicateComparisonEqualTo returns only items with the string exactly equal to the given one, while a value of MPMediaPredicateComparisonContains, as shown earlier, returns items that contain the given string, which is a less specific search.

MPMediaQuery instances can also be given a "grouping property" so they automatically group their results. You could, for example, filter a query by a specific artist but group according to the album name:

```
[query setGroupingType: MPMediaGroupingAlbum];
```

In this way, you can retrieve all the songs by a specific artist but iterate through them as if they were in albums, as demonstrated by Listing 10-36.

Listing 10-36. An example of querying all artists and iterating through them as if they were albums

```
NSArray *albums = [query collections];
for (MPMediaItemCollection *album in albums)
{
    MPMediaItem *representativeItem = [album representativeItem];
    NSString *albumName =
        [representativeItem valueForProperty: MPMediaItemPropertyAlbumTitle];
    NSLog (@"%@", albumName);
}
```

You can also set a grouping type by using MPMediaQuery class methods, such as albumsQuery, which creates your query instance with a pre-set grouping property.

Even though we haven't dug deep into the Media Player framework, you can probably see the power of it. Accessing the user's own library opens up an entirely new level of audio customization for your applications, possibilities such as selecting music to wake up to or allowing the user to specify her own background music for your game. You're probably coming up with several other uses yourself right now. Why not go ahead and implement them?

Recipe 10-4: Playing Background Audio

In this recipe, you'll build a basic music player app that can keep playing even in background mode. Additionally, you'll use MPNowPlayingInfoCenter to allow your app to be controlled from the multitasking bar and to display information about the current tune on the lock screen.

Start by creating a new single view application project. You'll need the following frameworks, so make sure you link their binaries to your project:

- AVFoundation.framework: To play your audio files.
- MediaPlayer.framework: To access your library of media files.
- CoreMedia.framework: You won't use any classes from this framework, but you will need some of the CMTime functions to help deal with your audio player.

Also, add the following import statements to your view controller's header file. You do not need one for the Core Media framework in this project:

```
#import <MediaPlayer/MediaPlayer.h>
#import <AVFoundation/AVFoundation.h>
```

Setting Up the User Interface

It's usually a good idea to start with the design of the user interface. You'll build a simple media player with the following features:

- Add items from the music library to the playlist

- Start and pause playback

- Navigate backward and forward in the playlist

- Clear the playlist

- Provide information about the current song and album

Create the user interface, as shown in Figure 10-6, with an info label, an image view, and five buttons: Library, <<, Play, >>, and Clear.

Figure 10-6. A user interface for a simple media player with background playback

Create the following outlets:

- ▦ playButton
- ▦ infoLabel
- ▦ artworkImageView

Create the following actions:

- ▦ queueFromLibrary
- ▦ goToPrevTrack
- ▦ togglePlay
- ▦ goToNextTrack
- ▦ clearPlaylist

Declaring Background Mode Playback

Now set up your app to continue playing music after the app has entered a background state of operation. The first thing you need to do is declare a property of type AVAudioSession, called session.

```
@property (nonatomic, strong) AVAudioSession *session;
```

Next, add the code in Listing 10-37 to your viewDidLoad method.

Listing 10-37. Filling out the ViewDidLoad method

```
- (void)viewDidLoad
{
    [super viewDidLoad];
    self.session = [AVAudioSession sharedInstance];
    NSError *error;
    [self.session setCategory:AVAudioSessionCategoryPlayback error:&error];
    if (error)
    {
        NSLog(@"Error setting audio session category: %@", error);
    }
    [self.session setActive:YES error:&error];
    if (error)
    {
        NSLog(@"Error activating audio session: %@", error);
    }
}
```

By specifying that your session category is of type AVAudioSessionCategoryPlayback, you are telling your device that your application's main focus is playing music and should therefore be allowed to continue playing audio while the application is in the background.

Now that you have configured your AVAudioSession, you need to edit your application's .plist file to specify that your application, when in the background mode, must be allowed to run audio. You do that by adding audio as a required background mode in the properties list (.plist file), as shown in Figure 10-7. For more information on this procedure, refer to Chapter 1, Recipe 1-7.

Key	Type	Value
▼ Information Property List	Dictionary	(15 items)
▼ Required background modes	Array	(1 item)
Item 0	String	App plays audio or streams audio/video using AirPlay
Localization native develop... ○ ○	String	en
Bundle display name	String	${PRODUCT_NAME}
Executable file	String	${EXECUTABLE_NAME}
Bundle identifier	String	NSCookbook.${PRODUCT_NAME:rfc1034identifier}
InfoDictionary version	String	6.0

Figure 10-7. Setting audio as a required background mode

To allow the user to control your media player remotely, either from the buttons of her earphones or from the activity bar, you need to respond to remote control events. For these events to work, your view controller needs to be the first responder, so enable this by overriding the canBecomeFirstResponder method, as shown in Listing 10-38.

Listing 10-38. Implementation of the canBecomeFirstResponder: override method

```
-(BOOL)canBecomeFirstResponder
{
    return YES;
}
```

Now, implement the viewDidAppear: and viewWillDisappear: methods to set the first responder status and register for the remote control events, as shown in Listing 10-39.

Listing 10-39. Implementation of the viewDidAppear: and viewWillDisappear: methods

```
- (void)viewDidAppear:(BOOL)animated
{
    [super viewDidAppear:animated];
    [[UIApplication sharedApplication] beginReceivingRemoteControlEvents];
    [self becomeFirstResponder];
}

- (void)viewWillDisappear:(BOOL)animated
{
    [[UIApplication sharedApplication] endReceivingRemoteControlEvents];
    [self resignFirstResponder];
    [super viewWillDisappear:animated];
}
```

To receive and respond to remote control events, implement the method shown in Listing 10-40.

Listing 10-40. Implementation of the remoteControlRecievedWithEvent: method

```
- (void)remoteControlReceivedWithEvent: (UIEvent *) receivedEvent
{
    if (receivedEvent.type == UIEventTypeRemoteControl)
    {
```

```
        switch (receivedEvent.subtype)
        {
            case UIEventSubtypeRemoteControlTogglePlayPause:
                [self togglePlay:self];
                break;

            case UIEventSubtypeRemoteControlPreviousTrack:
                [self goToPrevTrack:self];
                break;

            case UIEventSubtypeRemoteControlNextTrack:
                [self goToNextTrack:self];
                break;

            default:
                break;
        }
    }
}
```

As you can see, you only redirect the events by invoking the respective action method, which you'll implement shortly.

Implementing the Player

You use an AVPlayer to do the playback. It differs from the MPMusicPlayerController you saw in the preceding recipe in that it can continue playing in background mode. However, it doesn't work directly with items from your music library, which requires a little more coding than with MPMusicPlayerController.

Add the following properties to your view controller:

```
@property (nonatomic, strong) AVPlayer *player;
@property (nonatomic, strong) NSMutableArray *playlist;
@property (nonatomic)NSInteger currentIndex;
```

The playlist property holds an array of items from the music library, and the currentIndex holds the index of the current track within the playlist. Return to the viewDidLoad method and add the code in Listing 10-41 to initialize the player and the playlist.

Listing 10-41. Updating the viewDidLoad method to initialize the playlist and player

```
- (void)viewDidLoad
{
    [super viewDidLoad];

    // ...

    self.playlist = [[NSMutableArray alloc] init];
    self.player = [[AVPlayer alloc] init];
}
```

Now let's start by implementing the "Library" button. It should present a media picker controller, as shown previously in Figure 10-4, and append the selected items to the playlist. Listing 10-42 shows this implementation.

Listing 10-42. Implementation of the queueFromLibrary: method

```
- (IBAction)queueFromLibrary:(id)sender
{
    MPMediaPickerController *picker =
        [[MPMediaPickerController alloc] initWithMediaTypes:MPMediaTypeMusic];
    picker.delegate = self;
    picker.allowsPickingMultipleItems = YES;
    picker.prompt = @"Choose Some Music!";
    [self presentViewController:picker animated:YES completion:NULL];
}
```

You also need to add the MPMediaPickerControllerDelegate protocol to your view controller. Modify the line in Listing 10-5, as shown in Listing 10-43.

Listing 10-43. Adding the MPMediaPickerControllerDelegate protocol

```
@interface ViewController : UIViewController<MPMediaPickerControllerDelegate>
```

Now implement the delegate methods that receive the selected items. It should append them to the list and dismiss the media picker. Also, if these are the first items added, playback should be started (Listing 10-44).

Listing 10-44. Implementation of the mediaPicker:didPickMediaItems: delegate method

```
-(void)mediaPicker:(MPMediaPickerController *)mediaPicker
didPickMediaItems:(MPMediaItemCollection *)mediaItemCollection
{
    BOOL shallStartPlayer = self.playlist.count == 0;

    [self.playlist addObjectsFromArray:mediaItemCollection.items];

    if (shallStartPlayer)
        [self startPlaybackWithItem:[self.playlist objectAtIndex:0]];

    [self dismissViewControllerAnimated:YES completion:NULL];
}
```

This leads us to the startPlaybackWithItem: method. This method replaces the currently played item (if any), resets the current playback position (in case the item has been played before), and starts the playback, as shown in Listing 10-45.

Listing 10-45. Implementation of the startPlaybackWithItem: method

```
-(void)startPlaybackWithItem:(MPMediaItem *)mpItem
{
    [self.player replaceCurrentItemWithPlayerItem:[self avItemFromMPItem:mpItem]];
    [self.player seekToTime:kCMTimeZero];
    [self startPlayback];
}
```

Because the AVPlayer is working with AVPlayerItems and not MPMediaItems, you need to create one. This is the job of the avItemFromMPItem: method shown in Listing 10-46.

Listing 10-46. Implementation of the avItemFromMPItem: method

```
-(AVPlayerItem *)avItemFromMPItem:(MPMediaItem *)mpItem
{
    NSURL *url = [mpItem valueForProperty:MPMediaItemPropertyAssetURL];

    AVPlayerItem *item = [AVPlayerItem playerItemWithURL:url];

    [[NSNotificationCenter defaultCenter]
     addObserver:self
     selector:@selector(playerItemDidReachEnd:)
     name:AVPlayerItemDidPlayToEndTimeNotification
     object:item];

    return item;
}
```

What's interesting in Listing 10-46 is that you not only create the AVPlayerItem, but you also register a method to receive a notification when the song has reached its end. This is so you can continue to the next tune in the playlist using the playerItemDidReachEnd: method shown in Listing 10-47.

Listing 10-47. Implementation of the playerItemDidReachEnd: method

```
- (void)playerItemDidReachEnd:(NSNotification *)notification
{
    [self goToNextTrack:self];
}
```

The next stop is the startPlayback method. It starts the player, changes the title of the "Play" button to "Pause," and calls updateNowPlaying. This implementation is shown in Listing 10-48.

Listing 10-48. Implementation of the startPlayback method

```
-(void)startPlayback
{
    [self.player play];
    [self.playButton setTitle:@"Pause" forState:UIControlStateNormal];
    [self updateNowPlaying];
}
```

Finally, the last method to implement in this chain of calls is updateNowPlaying, as shown in Listing 10-49. The method, aside from updating your user interface to display the current song information, also uses the MPNowPlayingInfoCenter. This class allows the developer to place information on the device's lock screen (see Figure 10-8 for an example) or on other devices when the application is displaying info through AirPlay. You can pass information to it by setting the nowPlayingInfo property of the defaultCenter to a dictionary of values and properties that you created.

Listing 10-49. Implementation of the updateNowPlaying method

```
-(void)updateNowPlaying
{
    if (self.player.currentItem != nil)
    {
        MPMediaItem *currentMPItem = [self.playlist objectAtIndex:self.currentIndex];

        self.infoLabel.text =
            [NSString stringWithFormat:@"%@ - %@",
                [currentMPItem valueForProperty:MPMediaItemPropertyTitle],
                [currentMPItem valueForProperty:MPMediaItemPropertyArtist]];

        UIImage *artwork =
            [[[currentMPItem valueForProperty:MPMediaItemPropertyArtwork]
                imageWithSize:self.artworkImageView.frame.size];
        self.artworkImageView.image = artwork;

        NSString *title = [currentMPItem valueForProperty:MPMediaItemPropertyTitle];
        NSString *artist =
            [currentMPItem valueForProperty:MPMediaItemPropertyArtist];
        NSString *album =
            [currentMPItem valueForProperty:MPMediaItemPropertyAlbumTitle];

        NSDictionary *mediaInfo =
            [NSDictionary dictionaryWithObjectsAndKeys:
                artist, MPMediaItemPropertyArtist,
                title, MPMediaItemPropertyTitle,
                album, MPMediaItemPropertyAlbumTitle,
                [currentMPItem valueForProperty:MPMediaItemPropertyArtwork],
                    MPMediaItemPropertyArtwork,
                nil];
        [MPNowPlayingInfoCenter defaultCenter].nowPlayingInfo = mediaInfo;
    }
    else
    {
        self.infoLabel.text = @"...";
        [self.playButton setTitle:@"Play" forState:UIControlStateNormal];
        self.artworkImageView.image = nil;
    }
}
```

Figure 10-8. Information on the lock screen about the current track

The next action method is `togglePlay`, which should toggle between play and pause modes. An edge case here is that if the player has not yet been initialized, you need to initialize it with the first item in your playlist. Listing 10-50 shows this implementation.

Listing 10-50. Implementation of the togglePlay: method

```
- (IBAction)togglePlay:(id)sender
{
    if (self.playlist.count > 0)
    {
        if (self.player.currentItem == nil)
        {
            [self startPlaybackWithItem:[self.playlist objectAtIndex:0]];
        }
        else
        {
            // Player has an item, pause or resume playing it
            BOOL isPlaying = self.player.currentItem && self.player.rate != 0;
            if (isPlaying)
            {
                [self pausePlayback];
            }
```

```
        else
        {
            [self startPlayback];
        }
      }
    }
}
```

From the code in Listing 10-50, you can see a call to the `pausePlayback` method that you haven't yet implemented. That's easily fixed. All it needs to do is pause the player and update the "Play" button title, as shown in Listing 10-51.

Listing 10-51. Implementation of the pausePlayback method

```
-(void)pausePlayback
{
    [self.player pause];
    [self.playButton setTitle:@"Play" forState:UIControlStateNormal];
}
```

Next, add the `goToPrevTrack:` and `goToNextTrack:` action methods shown in Listing 10-52. They are pretty straightforward. In this method, we created the functionality that checks if playback is more than five seconds into the song. If it is past five seconds, the "Back" button will rewind the current song and will not skip to the previous item in the playlist. This is expected behavior for most media players.

Listing 10-52. Implementation of the goToPrevTrack: and goToNextTrack: methods

```
- (IBAction)goToPrevTrack:(id)sender
{
    if (self.playlist.count == 0)
        return;

    if (CMTimeCompare(self.player.currentTime, CMTimeMake(5.0, 1)) > 0)
    {
        [self.player seekToTime:kCMTimeZero];
    }
    else
    {
        if (self.currentIndex == 0)
        {
            self.currentIndex = self.playlist.count - 1;
        }
        else
        {
            self.currentIndex -= 1;
        }
        MPMediaItem *previousItem = [self.playlist objectAtIndex:self.currentIndex];
        [self startPlaybackWithItem:previousItem];
    }
}
```

```
- (IBAction)goToNextTrack:(id)sender
{
    if (self.playlist.count == 0)
        return;

    if (self.currentIndex == self.playlist.count - 1)
    {
        self.currentIndex = 0;
    }
    else
    {
        self.currentIndex += 1;
    }
    MPMediaItem *nextItem = [self.playlist objectAtIndex:self.currentIndex];
    [self startPlaybackWithItem: nextItem];
}
```

The CMTimeMake() function you used in Listing 10-52 is a very flexible function that takes two inputs. The first represents the number of time units you want, and the second represents the timescale, where 1 represents a second, 2 represents half a second, and so on. A call of CMTimeMake(100, 10) would make 100 units of (1/10) seconds each, resulting in 10 seconds.

There's only one feature remaining unimplemented: clearing the playlist. Listing 10-53 shows this implementation.

Listing 10-53. Implementation of the clearPlaylist: method

```
- (IBAction)clearPlaylist:(id)sender
{
    [self.player replaceCurrentItemWithPlayerItem:nil];
    [self.playlist removeAllObjects];
    [self updateNowPlaying];
    [self.playButton setTitle:@"Play" forState:UIControlStateNormal];
}
```

Finally, your app is now ready to build and run. When you test the app, it should continue to play music even after the application has entered the background. Figure 10-9 shows the multitasking bar with which you can control your media player even when another app is active.

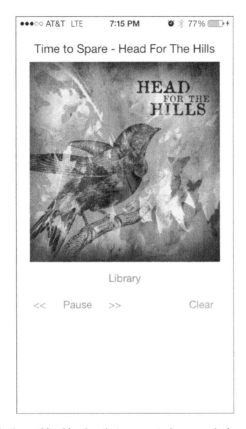

Figure 10-9. The "remote" controls in the multitasking bar that can control an app playing audio in the background

Tip   This recipe used AVPlayer to do the playback. It can handle only one item at a time, which is why we had to implement an external playlist. However, there is an alternative player that you can use to play queued items. The AVQueuePlayer is suitable for applications that need to play a sequence of items, but don't need complex navigation within the playlist.

Summary

The complete multimedia experience is one that goes beyond a simple matter of listening to music. Sound, as a product, is about the tiny details that make things just a little bit better. From recording music to filtering media items to creating volume ramps, every little detail that you, as a developer, take care to include will eventually result in more powerful and enjoyable tools. In iOS development, Apple has provided us with an incredibly powerful set of multimedia-based functionalities. We should not let it go to waste.

Chapter 11

Image Recipes

Now that the majority of the global population uses smartphones with cameras, most photos are taken with smartphones instead of point–and-shoot cameras. For this reason, images are always available and play a central role in how users utilize their smartphones. Fortunately, you have several different methods by which to create, utilize, manipulate, and display images. In addition, you can add filters to images, allowing for drastic alteration of the display with very little code. By understanding these inherent functionalities and techniques in iOS, you can more easily implement stronger, more powerful, and more informative applications.

Recipe 11-1: Using Image Views

The easiest way to display an image in your application is to use the UIImageView class, which is a view-based container for displaying images and image animations. In this recipe, you create a simple app that displays an image chosen by the user. Later, you'll build on top of it to take full advantage of the image-processing power of iOS.

To enhance the functionality of your application, you will specifically design it for the iPad and then make use of the UISplitViewController. Create a new project and select the Master-Detail Application template. On the next screen, after entering the project name as "Image Recipes," ensure the application's device-family is set to "iPad," as shown in Figure 11-1.

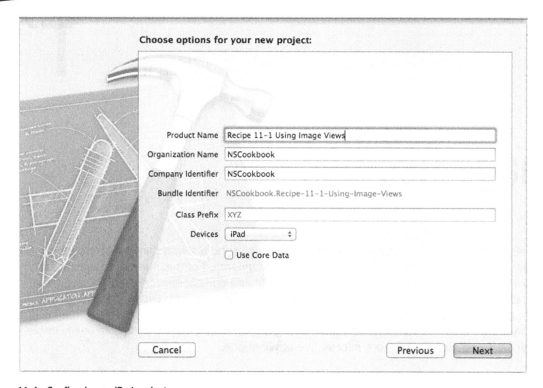

Figure 11-1. *Configuring an iPad project*

After you create your application, Xcode generates a project with a `UISplitViewController` set up with master and detail view controllers. If your simulator or device is in portrait mode, you will see only the view of the detail view controller; however, if you rotate to landscape mode you will get a nice mix of both views. You will see a storyboard scene in your main.storyboard file. If you simulate the app, the generic view will resemble Figure 11-2.

Figure 11-2. An empty UISplitViewController

If you have looked at the MasterViewController files, you might have noticed there is a lot of added boilerplate functionality for adding and removing rows. For now you can just ignore this boilerplate. We won't be touching the MasterViewController for this recipe.

Now you can configure the detail view controller to include some content. Select the detail view controller from the main.storyboard file and use Interface Builder to create the user interface. Add a label (or reuse the one created by default by the template), an image view, and two buttons. The label text should be "Select an image to be displayed," and the text for the buttons should be "Select Image" and "Clear Image." Arrange these objects as shown in Figure 11-3. Also, change the background color of the image view to black by selecting the image view and changing the background value from the attributes inspector.

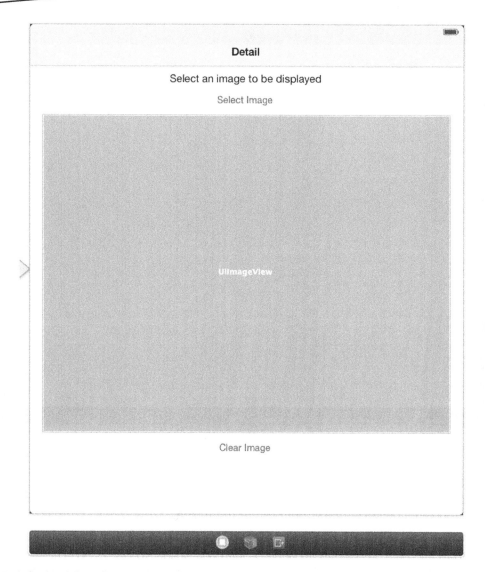

Figure 11-3. A simulated view of your configured user interface

Select the image view and open the attributes inspector. In the view section, change the Mode attribute from "Scale to Fill" to "Aspect Fill." This makes the image view scale its content so that it fills the image view's bounds while preserving the proportions of the image. This usually means that a part of the image is drawn outside the frame of the image view. To prevent this, you should also select the Drawing option "Clip Subviews." Figure 11-4 shows these settings.

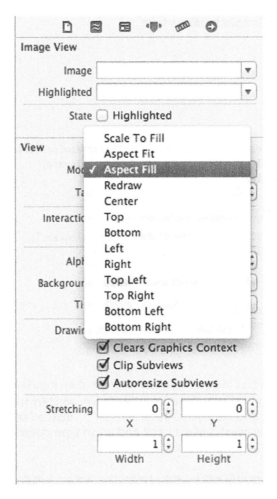

Figure 11-4. Configuring an image view to fill with maintained proportions and clip to its bounds

Create the following outlets:

- detailDescriptionLabel
- imageView

Create the following actions:

- selectImage
- clearImage

Configure your application to display a UIPopoverController containing a UIImagePickerController to allow users to select an image from their iPads. To do this, you need your detail view controller to conform to several extra protocols: UIImagePickerControllerDelegate, UINavigationControllerDelegate, and UIPopoverControllerDelegate. You also need to add a property to reference the UIPopoverController. To incorporate these changes, add the code in bold shown in Listing 11-1 to the DetailViewController.h file.

Listing 11-1. The starting DetailViewController.h implementation

```
//
//  DetailViewController.h
//  Recipe 11-1 Using Image Views
//

#import <UIKit/UIKit.h>

@interface DetailViewController : UIViewController <UISplitViewControllerDelegate,
    UIImagePickerControllerDelegate,UINavigationControllerDelegate,
    UIPopoverControllerDelegate>

@property (strong, nonatomic) id detailItem;

@property (weak, nonatomic) IBOutlet UILabel *detailDescriptionLabel;
@property (weak, nonatomic) IBOutlet UIImageView *imageView;

@property (strong, nonatomic) UIPopoverController *pop;

- (IBAction)selectImage:(id)sender;
- (IBAction)clearImage:(id)sender;

@end
```

Now you can implement the selectImage: method to present an interface to select an image to display. Modify this method in the DetailViewController.m file, as shown in Listing 11-2. Take note that we changed the input type to the sender to "UIButton *" instead of "id." This is because we use this input in the presentPopoverFromRect: call and an id type doesn't have a "frame" property, which would throw an error.

Listing 11-2. Configuring an image view to fill with maintained proportions and clip to its bounds

```
-(void)selectImage:(UIButton *)sender
{
    UIImagePickerController *picker = [[UIImagePickerController alloc] init];
    if ([UIImagePickerController
            isSourceTypeAvailable:UIImagePickerControllerSourceTypePhotoLibrary])
    {
        picker.sourceType = UIImagePickerControllerSourceTypePhotoLibrary;
        picker.delegate = self;

        self.pop = [[UIPopoverController alloc] initWithContentViewController:picker];
        self.pop.delegate = self;
        [self.pop presentPopoverFromRect:sender.frame inView:self.view
            permittedArrowDirections:UIPopoverArrowDirectionAny animated:YES];
    }
}
```

You can then implement your UIImagePickerController delegate methods to properly handle the selection of an image or cancellation. Listing 11-3 shows the first one, which handles the cancellation.

Listing 11-3. Implementing the imagePickerControllerDidCancel: delegate method

```
-(void)imagePickerControllerDidCancel:(UIImagePickerController *)picker
{
    [self.pop dismissPopoverAnimated:YES];
}
```

Listing 11-4 shows the second `UIImagePickerController` delegate method for handling image selection.

Listing 11-4. Implementing the imagePickerController:didFinishPickingMediaWithInfo:

```
-(void)imagePickerController:(UIImagePickerController *)picker
didFinishPickingMediaWithInfo:(NSDictionary *)info
{
    UIImage *image = [info valueForKey:@"UIImagePickerControllerOriginalImage"];
    self.imageView.image = image;


    [self.pop dismissPopoverAnimated:YES];
}
```

As you can see from Listing 11-4, you configure the image view to display the selected image by using the `image` property.

Finally, you can implement the `clearImage: action` method shown in Listing 11-5 to allow your view to be reset.

Listing 11-5. Implementing the clearImage: method

```
- (IBAction)clearImage:(id)sender
{
    self.imageView.image = nil;
}
```

At this point, you can run your application, select an image, and display it in a `UIImageView`, as shown in Figure 11-5. Because you set the view mode to aspect fill and chose the "Clip Subviews" option, the image will size to the smaller dimension and clip the rest.

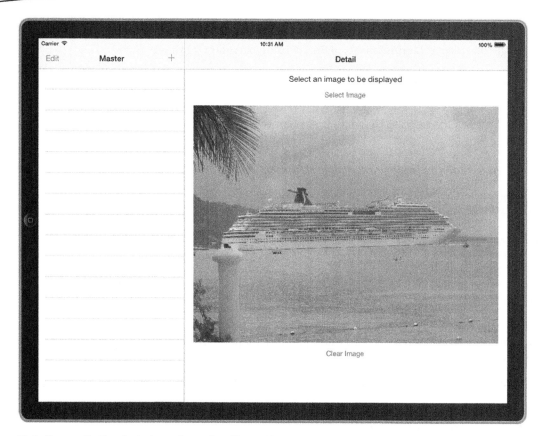

Figure 11-5. Your application displaying an image in a UIImageView

> **Tip**   If you are testing the application on the iOS simulator, you will need to have some images to display. The easiest way to save images to the simulator's photos library is to drag and drop them onto the simulator window. This brings up Safari, where you can click and hold the mouse on the image. You then are given an option to save the image, and after this you can use it in your application.

Recipe 11-2: Scaling Images

Often the images that your applications deal with come from a variety of sources and usually do not fit your specific view's display perfectly. To adjust for this, you can implement methods to scale and resize your images.

With an image view, scaling and resizing are easy. For example, in the preceding recipe you used Aspect Fill in combination with Clip Subviews to scale proportionally and still fill the entire image view. This results in a clipped but nice-looking image. Another option is to use the Aspect Fit mode, which also scales the image with retained aspect ratio but displays the entire image. This, of course, might cause unused space in your image view, which might resemble a widescreen movie on a non-widescreen television. If you don't care about image aspect, you can use the default mode "Scale to Fill." Use these and other options by simply changing the Mode attribute of the image view from the attributes inspector.

However, sometimes you might like to scale the actual image programmatically, such as if you want to save the resulting image or just optimize the display by providing an already scaled image. In this recipe, we'll show you how to scale an image using code. You will implement two different methods corresponding to the Scale to Fill and the Aspect Fit modes of an image view.

You will build on the previous recipe, but for now use the master view's table view, which contains three functions: Select Image, Resize Image, and Scale Image. Because these functions operate directly on a UIImage, you need to turn off the inherent scaling function of the image view. Do this by changing its Mode attribute to "Center" instead of Aspect Fill from the attributes inspector.

Before moving on, remove some of the boilerplate code that was provided with the Master-Detail Application template mentioned in the last recipe. This boilerplate code allows for creation and deletion of rows, which is functionality we won't be using. In the MasterViewController.m file you can remove the following items from the viewDidLoad method.

```
self.navigationItem.leftBarButtonItem = self.editButtonItem;

    UIBarButtonItem *addButton = [[UIBarButtonItem alloc]
initWithBarButtonSystemItem:UIBarButtonSystemItemAdd target:self action:@selector(insertNewObject:)];
    self.navigationItem.rightBarButtonItem = addButton;
```

You also can remove the following methods from the MasterViewController:

```
insertNewObject:
tableView: canEditRowAtIndexPath:
tableView: commitEditingStyle:forRowAtIndexPath:
tableView: canMoveRowAtIndexPath:
```

Now that you've cleaned up your code, add a couple of outlets to the two buttons in the DetailViewController class. The outlets should be named "selectImageButton" and "clearImageButton," respectively.

Next, create a method to configure the user interface of your detail view controller. Listing 11-6 shows the method declaration in the DetailViewController.h file.

Listing 11-6. Adding the method declaration for handling user interface configuration

```
//
//  DetailViewController.h
//  Recipe 11-2 Scaling Images
//

#import <UIKit/UIKit.h>
```

```
@interface DetailViewController : UIViewController <UISplitViewControllerDelegate,
                                                    UIImagePickerControllerDelegate,
                                                    UINavigationControllerDelegate,
                                                    UIPopoverControllerDelegate>

@property (strong, nonatomic) id detailItem;

@property (weak, nonatomic) IBOutlet UILabel *detailDescriptionLabel;
@property (weak, nonatomic) IBOutlet UIImageView *imageView;
@property (weak, nonatomic) IBOutlet UIButton *selectImageButton;
@property (weak, nonatomic) IBOutlet UIButton *clearImageButton;

@property (strong, nonatomic) UIPopoverController *pop;

- (IBAction)selectImage:(id)sender;
- (IBAction)clearImage:(id)sender;

- (void)configureDetailsWithImage:(UIImage *)image label:(NSString *)label showsButtons:(BOOL)
showButton;

@end
```

The method declared in Listing 11-6 should be added to the DetailViewController.h file. The implementation is shown in Listing 11-7.

Listing 11-7. Implementing the configureDetailsWithImage:label:showbuttons: method

```
-(void)configureDetailsWithImage:(UIImage *)image label:(NSString *)label
showsButtons:(BOOL)showsButton
{
    self.imageView.image = image;
    self.detailDescriptionLabel.text = label;
    if (showsButton == NO)
    {
        self.selectImageButton.hidden = YES;
        self.clearImageButton.hidden = YES;
    }
    else if (showsButton == YES)
    {
        self.selectImageButton.hidden = NO;
        self.clearImageButton.hidden = NO;
    }
}
```

Because we will be communicating between the master view controller and the detail view controller, it's best to set up a delegate so the detail view controller can notify the master view controller when an image change has occurred. Then the master view controller can set that image directly. To start with, implement the protocol in the DetailViewController.h file, as shown in Listing 11-8. In this modification, you first declare that you're going to use a protocol. Next, you create a property for the delegate. Then you declare the protocol methods.

Listing 11-8. Setting up a protocol for communication between the master and detail view controllers

```
//
//  DetailViewController.h
//  Recipe 11-2 Scaling Images
//

#import <UIKit/UIKit.h>

@protocol DetailViewControllerDelegateProtocol;

@interface DetailViewController : UIViewController <UISplitViewControllerDelegate,
                                                    UIImagePickerControllerDelegate,
                                                    UINavigationControllerDelegate,
                                                    UIPopoverControllerDelegate>
@property (strong, nonatomic) id detailItem;

@property (nonatomic, weak) id <DetailViewControllerDelegateProtocol> delegate;

@property (weak, nonatomic) IBOutlet UILabel *detailDescriptionLabel;
@property (weak, nonatomic) IBOutlet UIImageView *imageView;

@property (nonatomic, strong) IBOutlet UIButton *selectImageButton;
@property (nonatomic, strong) IBOutlet UIButton *clearImageButton;

@property (strong, nonatomic) UIPopoverController *pop;

- (IBAction)selectImage:(id)sender;
- (IBAction)clearImage:(id)sender;

- (void)configureDetailsWithImage:(UIImage *)image label:(NSString *)label showsButtons:(BOOL)
showsButton;

@end

@protocol DetailViewControllerDelegateProtocol <NSObject>

- (void)detailViewController:(DetailViewController *)controller didSelectImage:(UIImage *)image;
- (void)detailViewControllerDidClearImage:(DetailViewController *)controller;

@end
```

Now, add a property to your master view controller class to store the chosen image, as shown in Listing 11-9.

Listing 11-9. Adding a UIImage property to the MasterViewController.h file

```
//
//  MasterViewController.h
//  Recipe 11-2 Scaling Images
//
```

```
#import <UIKit/UIKit.h>

@interface MasterViewController : UITableViewController

@property (strong, nonatomic) DetailViewController *detailViewController;
@property (strong, nonatomic) UIImage *mainImage;

@end
```

Back in your detail view controller, you will need to update the imagePickerController:
didFinishPickingMediaWithInfo: delegate method to update the image of the master view
controller. Do this by calling the protocol method, as shown in Listing 11-10.

Listing 11-10. Modifying the imagePickerController: to call the new protocol

```
-(void)imagePickerController:(UIImagePickerController *)picker didFinishPickingMediaWithInfo:(NSDic
tionary *)info
{
    UIImage *image = [info valueForKey:@"UIImagePickerControllerOriginalImage"];
        self.imageView.image = image;
    [self.pop dismissPopoverAnimated:YES];

    [self.delegate detailViewController:self didSelectImage:image];
}
```

You also need to adjust the implementation of the clearImage: action method. Again, we are calling
a protocol method, as you can see from Listing 11-11.

Listing 11-11. Modifying the clearImage: method to take advantage of the detailViewControllerDidClearImage: protocol method

```
- (IBAction)clearImage:(id)sender
{
    self.imageView.image = nil;
    [self.delegate detailViewControllerDidClearImage:self];
}
```

In your master view controller, you should declare that you are conforming to
DetailViewControllerDelegateProtocol. So modify the MasterViewController.h file to accommodate
this change, as shown in Listing 11-12.

Listing 11-12. Declaring the DetailViewControllerDelegateProtocol

```
//
//  MasterViewController.h
//  Recipe 11-2 Scaling Images
//

#import <UIKit/UIKit.h>
#import "DetailViewController.h"

@interface MasterViewController : UITableViewController <DetailViewControllerDelegateProtocol>
```

```
@property (strong, nonatomic) DetailViewController *detailViewController;
@property (strong, nonatomic) UIImage *mainImage;

@end
```

You also should set the delegate for the master view controller in the ViewDidLoad method, as shown in Listing 11-13.

Listing 11-13. Setting the delegate in the viewDidLoad method of the MasterViewController.m file

```
//
//  MasterViewController.m
//  Recipe 11-2 Scaling Images
//
//...
- (void)viewDidLoad
{
    [super viewDidLoad];
    self.detailViewController = (DetailViewController *)[[self.splitViewController.viewControllers
lastObject] topViewController];
    self.detailViewController.delegate = self;
}
```

Next, create two different methods to resize an image. Add the two class methods shown in Listing 11-14 to your MasterViewController.m file. You do not need to declare these in the MasterViewController.h file because the only class that needs to use them is the MasterViewController class.

Listing 11-14. Implementing the scaleImage and aspectScaleImage: toSize methods

```
//
//  MasterViewController.m
//  Recipe 11-2 Scaling Images
//

#import "MasterViewController.h"

@interface MasterViewController ()
//...
-(UIImage *)scaleImage:(UIImage *)image toSize:(CGSize)size
{
    UIGraphicsBeginImageContext(size);
    [image drawInRect:CGRectMake(0, 0, size.width, size.height)];
    UIImage *scaledImage = UIGraphicsGetImageFromCurrentImageContext();
    UIGraphicsEndImageContext();
    return scaledImage;
}
```

```
-(UIImage *)aspectScaleImage:(UIImage *)image toSize:(CGSize)size
{
    if (image.size.height < image.size.width)
    {
        float ratio = size.height / image.size.height;
        CGSize newSize = CGSizeMake(image.size.width * ratio, size.height);
        UIGraphicsBeginImageContext(newSize);
        [image drawInRect:CGRectMake(0, 0, newSize.width, newSize.height)];
    }
    else {
        float ratio = size.width / image.size.width;
        CGSize newSize = CGSizeMake(size.width, image.size.height * ratio);
        UIGraphicsBeginImageContext(newSize);
        [image drawInRect:CGRectMake(0, 0, newSize.width, newSize.height)];
    }
    UIImage *aspectScaledImage = UIGraphicsGetImageFromCurrentImageContext();
    UIGraphicsEndImageContext();
    return aspectScaledImage;
}

//...
```

In Listing 11-14 the first method simply recreates the image within a specified size, ignoring the aspect ratio of the image. The second method, with a little calculation, determines the best way to resize the image to both preserve the aspect ratio and fit inside the given size.

To make sure your view controllers are properly interacting, add the DetailViewControllerDelegateProtocol methods shown in Listing 11-15, which set the image or clear the image and reload the table.

Listing 11-15. Implementing the DetailViewControllerDelegateProtocol methods

```
- (void)detailViewController:(DetailViewController *)controller didSelectImage:(UIImage *)image
{
    self.mainImage = image;
    [self.tableView reloadData];
}

- (void)detailViewControllerDidClearImage:(DetailViewController *)controller
{
    self.mainImage = nil;
    [self.tableView reloadData];
}
```

To finish configuring the behavior of the master view controller, you'll need to fill in the data source data for the table view.

First, set the number of sections to one. You will need to replace the boilerplate code that was provided in this method as part of the Master-Detail View Controller template. The new implementation is shown in Listing 11-16.

Listing 11-16. Modifying the numberOfSectionsInTableView: delegate method

```
- (NSInteger)numberOfSectionsInTableView:(UITableView *)tableView
{
    return 1;
}
```

Next, update the number of rows depending on whether or not you have an image to work with. If there is no image, then you should display only the text "Selected Image," which will require only one row. Again, you will replace the boilerplate code with the new code shown in Listing 11-17.

Listing 11-17. Implementing the tableView:numberOfRowsInSection: delegate method

```
- (NSInteger)tableView:(UITableView *)tableView numberOfRowsInSection:(NSInteger)section
{
    if (self.mainImage == nil)
        return 1;
    else
        return 3;
}
```

Next, set the cell labels depending on whether the current cell is 0, 1, or 2. This implementation is shown in Listing 11-18.

Listing 11-18. Implementing the tableView: cellForRowAtIndexPath: method

```
- (UITableViewCell *)tableView:(UITableView *)tableView cellForRowAtIndexPath:(NSIndexPath *)
indexPath
{
    UITableViewCell *cell = [tableView dequeueReusableCellWithIdentifier:@"Cell"
forIndexPath:indexPath];

    if (indexPath.row == 0)
        cell.textLabel.text = NSLocalizedString(@"Selected Image", @"Detail");
    else if (indexPath.row == 1)
        cell.textLabel.text = NSLocalizedString(@"Resized Image", @"Detail");
    else if (indexPath.row == 2)
        cell.textLabel.text = NSLocalizedString(@"Scaled Image", @"Detail");
    return cell;
}
```

Lastly, if a cell is selected, you should determine which cell it was and then set the image and title for the `DetailViewController` using the `configureDetailsWithImage:showsButtons:` protocol method. Listing 11-19 shows the new method with the boilerplate code replaced.

Listing 11-19. The new implementation of the tableView:didSelectRowAtIndexPath: delegate method

```
- (void)tableView:(UITableView *)tableView didSelectRowAtIndexPath:(NSIndexPath *)indexPath
{
    if (self.mainImage != nil)
    {
        UIImage *image;
        NSString *label;
        BOOL showsButtons = NO;
        if (indexPath.row == 0)
        {
            image = self.mainImage;
            label = @"Select an Image to Display";
            showsButtons = YES;
        }
        else if (indexPath.row == 1)
        {
            image = [self scaleImage:self.mainImage
                                        toSize:self.detailViewController.imageView.frame.size];
            label = @"Chosen Image Resized";
        }
        else if (indexPath.row == 2)
        {
            image = [self aspectScaleImage:self.mainImage
                                        toSize:self.detailViewController.imageView.frame.size];
            label = @"Chosen Image Scaled";
        }
        [self.detailViewController configureDetailsWithImage:image label:label
                                        showsButtons:showsButtons];
    }
}
```

You are done and can now build and run the application. This time, when you select an image you'll see that it doesn't scale and (assuming the image is larger than the image view) will be clipped, such as the one in Figure 11-6.

Figure 11-6. An image of a geyser in Yellowstone National Park

Now if you select the Resized Image cell in the master view you will see the same picture, this time run through the `scaleImage:toSize:` method you created. The image has been scaled, without considering its original proportions, to the same size as the image view. Figure 11-7 shows an example of this.

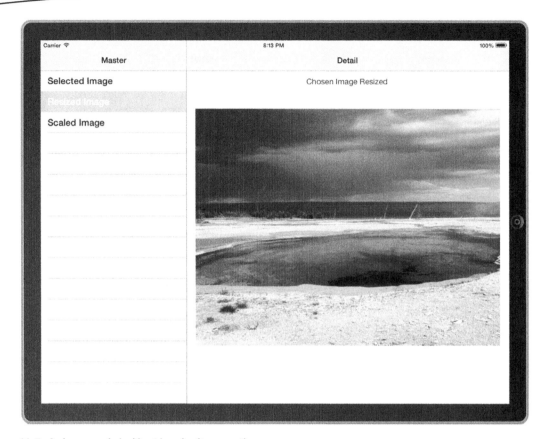

Figure 11-7. An image scaled without keeping its proportions

The issue with this option, however, is that the picture has become slightly deformed. This might not be quite obvious with this particular image, but when dealing with images of people the distortion of physical features is quite obvious and unsightly. To solve this, use the Aspect-Scaled image option.

When you select the Scaled Image cell you'll see the effect of your `aspectScaleImage:toSize:` method. This method has created a `UIImage` of a size that fits within the image view but with maintained original proportions. This results in an image without any size distortions, but will scale the image to either the width or height. Depending on the image, the background of the image view might be showing. The image we chose scaled to the width and cut off the top and bottom, as shown in Figure 11-8.

Figure 11-8. *An alternative method of scaling to remove distortion*

That's it for this recipe! To review, you have covered two simple methods for resizing a UIImage, each with their own advantages and issues.

1. Your first method simply resized the image to a given size, regardless of aspect ratio. While this kept your image from obstructing any other elements, it resulted in a fair bit of distortion.

2. By using a little math, you scaled down your image to a size while manually maintaining the aspect ratio. Because this might leave a blank space around the image, you can apply a black background. This is a useful technique to use when displaying large images in an application that has no control over the original image size. It allows for any image to comfortably fit in a given space, yet it maintains a visually appealing black background no matter the case.

Recipe 11-3: Manipulating Images with Filters

The Core Image framework, a group of classes that was introduced in iOS 5.0, allows you to creatively apply a great variety of "filters" to images. Although we won't be using any here, iOS 7 comes packed with many more available filters that can be implemented similarly, as we'll show here.

In this recipe, you'll apply two kinds of filters to an image, the Hue filter and the Straightening filter. The former changes the hue of the image, while the latter rotates an image to straighten it out.

You will build on the project you created in Recipes 11-1 and 11-2, adding functions to apply the filters.

Start by linking the CoreImage.framework library to your project (see Chapter 1 for a description of how to do this), and then import its API in the MasterViewController.h file. You also need a mutable array property to hold the filtered images you will display. Listing 11-20 shows the MasterViewController.h file with these changes marked in boldface.

Listing 11-20. Importing the Core Image framework and creating a property in the MasterViewController.h file

```
//
//  MasterViewController.h
//  Recipe 11-3 Manipulating Images with Filters
//

#import <UIKit/UIKit.h>
#import <CoreImage/CoreImage.h>
#import "DetailViewController.h"

@interface MasterViewController : UITableViewController <DetailViewControllerDelegateProtocol>
@property (strong, nonatomic) DetailViewController *detailViewController;
@property (strong, nonatomic) UIImage *mainImage;
@property (strong, nonatomic) NSMutableArray *filteredImages;

@end
```

Implement lazy initialization of the filteredImages property by adding the custom getter to MasterViewController.m, as shown in Listing 11-21.

Listing 11-21. Implementing the filteredImages property initializer

```
-(NSMutableArray *)filteredImages
{
    if (!_filteredImages)
    {
        _filteredImages = [[NSMutableArray alloc] initWithCapacity:3];
    }
    return _filteredImages;
}
```

Now, modify your detailViewController delegate methods again to include handling of this array. These changes are shown in Listing 11-22.

Listing 11-22. Modifying the detailViewController delegate methods to handle filtered images

```
- (void)detailViewController:(DetailViewController *)controller didSelectImage:(UIImage *)image
{
    self.mainImage = image;
    [self populateImageViewWithImage:image];
    [self.tableView reloadData];
}

- (void)detailViewControllerDidClearImage:(DetailViewController *)controller
{
    self.mainImage = nil;
    [self.filteredImages removeAllObjects];
    [self.tableView reloadData];
}
```

The populateFilteredImagesWithImage: method, which contains most of your Core Image framework code, is implemented as shown in Listing 11-23. This method, which creates a CIImage, requires the following steps:

1. Obtain a CIImage of the intended input image.

2. Create a filter using a specific name key. The name defines which filter will be applied as well as its various parameters that can be used.

3. Reset all parameters of the filter to defaults for good measure.

4. Set the input image to the filter using the inputImage key.

5. Set any additional values related to the filter to customize output.

6. Retrieve the output CIImage using the outputImage key.

7. Create a UIImage from the CIImage by use of a CIContext. Because the CIContext returns a CGImage, which memory is not managed by ARC, you also need to release it using CGImageRelease().

Listing 11-23. Implementing the populateImageViewWithImage: method

```
-(void)populateImageViewWithImage:(UIImage *)image
{
    CIImage *main = [[CIImage alloc] initWithImage:image];

    CIFilter *hueAdjust = [CIFilter filterWithName:@"CIHueAdjust"];
    [hueAdjust setDefaults];
    [hueAdjust setValue:main forKey:@"inputImage"];
    [hueAdjust setValue:[NSNumber numberWithFloat: 3.14/2.0f]
                 forKey:@"inputAngle"];
    CIImage *outputHueAdjust = [hueAdjust valueForKey:@"outputImage"];
    CIContext *context = [CIContext contextWithOptions:nil];
    CGImageRef cgImage1 = [context createCGImage:outputHueAdjust
        fromRect:outputHueAdjust.extent];
    UIImage *outputImage1 = [UIImage imageWithCGImage:cgImage1];
    CGImageRelease(cgImage1);
    [self.filteredImages addObject:outputImage1];
```

```
    CIFilter *strFilter = [CIFilter filterWithName:@"CIStraightenFilter"];
    [strFilter setDefaults];
    [strFilter setValue:main forKey:@"inputImage"];
    [strFilter setValue:[NSNumber numberWithFloat:3.14f] forKey:@"inputAngle"];
    CIImage *outputStr = [strFilter valueForKey:@"outputImage"];
    CGImageRef cgImage2 = [context createCGImage:outputStr fromRect:outputStr.extent];
    UIImage *outputImage2 = [UIImage imageWithCGImage:cgImage2];
    CGImageRelease(cgImage2);
    [self.filteredImages addObject:outputImage2];
}
```

> **Note** There are a large number of filters that can be applied to images, all with their own specific
> parameters and keys. To find details for a specific filter, see the Apple documentation at
> http://developer.apple.com/library/ios/#DOCUMENTATION/GraphicsImaging/
> Reference/CoreImageFilterReference/Reference/reference.html.

Next, add the filter functions to the table view. Start by making a small change to the
tableView:numberOfRowsInSection: delegate method, as shown in Listing 11-24.

Listing 11-24. Modifying the tableView:numberOfRowsInSection: method to account for new filters

```
- (NSInteger)tableView:(UITableView *)tableView numberOfRowsInSection:(NSInteger)section
{
    if (self.mainImage == nil)
        return 1;
    else
        return 5;
}
```

Also, update tableView:cellForRowAtIndexPath: to configure the cells for the new rows, as shown
in Listing 11-25.

Listing 11-25. Modifying the detailViewController delegate methods to handle filtered images

```
- (UITableViewCell *)tableView:(UITableView *)tableView cellForRowAtIndexPath:(NSIndexPath *)indexPath
{
    static NSString *CellIdentifier = @"Cell";

    UITableViewCell *cell =
        [tableView dequeueReusableCellWithIdentifier:CellIdentifier];
    if (cell == nil)
    {
        cell = [[UITableViewCell alloc] initWithStyle:UITableViewCellStyleDefault
            reuseIdentifier:CellIdentifier];
    }
```

```
    if (indexPath.row == 0)
        cell.textLabel.text = NSLocalizedString(@"Selected Image", @"Detail");
    else if (indexPath.row == 1)
        cell.textLabel.text = NSLocalizedString(@"Resized Image", @"Detail");
    else if (indexPath.row == 2)
        cell.textLabel.text = NSLocalizedString(@"Scaled Image", @"Detail");
    else if (indexPath.row == 3)
        cell.textLabel.text = NSLocalizedString(@"Hue Adjust", @"Detail");
    else if (indexPath.row == 4)
        cell.textLabel.text = NSLocalizedString(@"Straighten Filter", @"Detail");
    return cell;
}
```

Modify the `tableView:didSelectRowAtIndexPath:` method, as shown in Listing 11-26, to add the new filters.

Listing 11-26. Modifying the tableView:didSelectRowAtIndexPath: to add the new filters

```
- (void)tableView:(UITableView *)tableView didSelectRowAtIndexPath:(NSIndexPath *)indexPath
{
    if (self.mainImage != nil)
    {
        UIImage *image;
        NSString *label;
        BOOL showsButtons = NO;
        if (indexPath.row == 0)
        {
            image = self.mainImage;
            label = @"Select an Image to Display";
            showsButtons = YES;
        }
        else if (indexPath.row == 1)
        {
            image = [self scaleImage:self.mainImage
                toSize:self.detailViewController.imageView.frame.size];
            label = @"Chosen Image Resized";
        }
        else if (indexPath.row == 2)
        {
            image = [self aspectScaleImage:self.mainImage
                toSize:self.detailViewController.imageView.frame.size];
            label = @"Chosen Image Scaled";
        }
        else if (indexPath.row == 3)
        {
            image = [self.filteredImages objectAtIndex:0];
            image = [self aspectScaleImage:image toSize:self.detailViewController.imageView.frame.size];
            label = @"Hue Adjustment";
        }
```

```
    else if (indexPath.row == 4)
    {
        image = [self.filteredImages objectAtIndex:1];
        image = [self aspectScaleImage:image toSize:self.detailViewController.imageView.frame.size];
        label = @"Straightening Filter";
    }                       [self.detailViewController configureDetailsWithImage:image label:label
        showsButtons:showsButtons];
    }
}
```

As you can see in Listing 11-26, you're reusing the aspectScaleImage:toSize: method you created in the previous recipe to scale the filtered images so that they will fit nicely within the image view.

When running your application now, you can see the outputs of the two types of filters. Shown in Figure 11-9 is an example of the straightening filter. As you might remember from the code, it specified an angle of pi (3.14), which means a 180-degree rotation and an upside-down image.

Figure 11-9. The straightening filter has rotated an image 180 degrees

Combining Filters

It's easy to apply multiple filters to an image. You just combine them in a series by specifying the output image of one filter as the input image of another. As an example, you'll add a function that applies both the hue filter and the straightening filter to the selected image.

Add the code in 11-27 to the populateImagesWithImage: method to create a combination filter.

Listing 11-27. Modifying the populateImageViewWithImage: method to create a combination filter

```
-(void)populateImageViewWithImage:(UIImage *)image
{
    // ...

    CIFilter *seriesFilter = [CIFilter filterWithName:@"CIStraightenFilter"];
    [seriesFilter setDefaults];
    [seriesFilter setValue:outputHueAdjust forKey:@"inputImage"];
    [seriesFilter setValue:[NSNumber numberWithFloat:3.14/2.0f] forKey:@"inputAngle"];
    CIImage *outputSeries = [seriesFilter valueForKey:@"outputImage"];
    CGImageRef cgImage3 = [context createCGImage:outputSeries
        fromRect:outputSeries.extent];
    UIImage *outputImage3 = [UIImage imageWithCGImage:cgImage3];
    [self.filteredImages addObject:outputImage3];
}
```

Update the tableView:numberOfRowsInSection: method to show a sixth cell, as shown in Listing 11-28.

Listing 11-28. Updating the tableView:numberOfRowsInSection: method to create six table rows

```
- (NSInteger)tableView:(UITableView *)tableView numberOfRowsInSection:(NSInteger)section
{
    if (self.mainImage == nil)
        return 1;
    else
        return 6;
}
```

Likewise, add a sixth case to your tableView:cellForRowAtIndexPath: method to display the name of this sixth cell, as shown in Listing 11-29.

Listing 11-29. Modifying the tableView:cellForRowAtIndexPath: to set the sixth label title

```
- (UITableViewCell *)tableView:(UITableView *)tableView cellForRowAtIndexPath:(NSIndexPath *)indexPath
{
    // ...

    if (indexPath.row == 0)
        cell.textLabel.text = NSLocalizedString(@"Selected Image", @"Detail");
    else if (indexPath.row == 1)
        cell.textLabel.text = NSLocalizedString(@"Resized Image", @"Detail");
    else if (indexPath.row == 2)
        cell.textLabel.text = NSLocalizedString(@"Scaled Image", @"Detail");
```

```
    else if (indexPath.row == 3)
        cell.textLabel.text = NSLocalizedString(@"Hue Adjust", @"Detail");
    else if (indexPath.row == 4)
        cell.textLabel.text = NSLocalizedString(@"Straighten Filter", @"Detail");
    else if (indexPath.row == 5)
        cell.textLabel.text = NSLocalizedString(@"Series Filter", @"Detail");
    return cell;
}
```

Finally, add another case to the tableView:didSelectRowAtIndexPath: to initialize the detail view controller with the combined filter image, as shown in Listing 11-30.

Listing 11-30. Adding a new case to the tableView:didSelectRowAtIndexPath: method

```
- (void)tableView:(UITableView *)tableView didSelectRowAtIndexPath:(NSIndexPath *)indexPath
{
    if (self.mainImage != nil)
    {
        UIImage *image;
        NSString *label;
        BOOL showsButtons = NO;
        if (indexPath.row == 0)
        {
            image = self.mainImage;
            label = @"Select an Image to Display";
            showsButtons = YES;
        }

// ...

        else if (indexPath.row == 5)
        {
            image = [self.filteredImages objectAtIndex:2];
            image = [self aspectScaleImage:image toSize:self.detailViewController.imageView.frame.size];
            label = @"Series Filter";
        }
[self.detailViewController configureDetailsWithImage:image label:label showsButtons:showsButtons];
    }
}
```

When you test the application, your new double filter combines the effects of your previous two, resulting in a hue-adjusted and rotated image, this time with a 90-degree rotation, as shown in Figure 11-10.

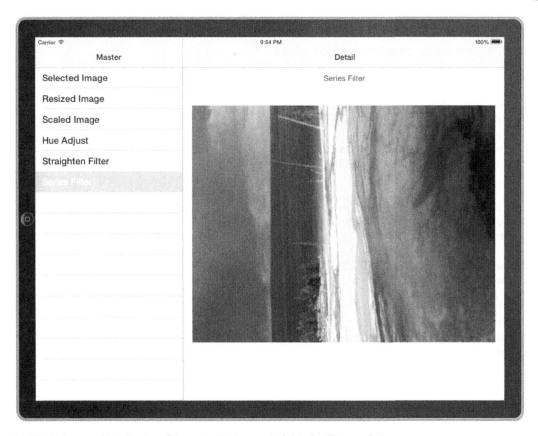

Figure 11-10. *An image with both a hue filter and a 90-degree straightening filter applied*

Note   The majority of the processing work, when dealing with the Core Image framework, comes from when the UIImage is created from the CIImage using the CIContext. The creation of a CIImage itself is a very fast operation. In this application, we have chosen to create all the filtered images at once to allow for quick navigation between each display. This is why, on selecting an image, your simulator may take a couple seconds to actually display the image and refresh. If you were building this application for release, you would want to convey in some way to the user that work is being done through a UIActivityIndicatorView or UIProgressView.

Creating Thumbnail Images for the Table View

As a final touch, we're going to return to the resizing topic of the previous recipe. You'll implement another aspect-scaling method that does what the Aspect Fill mode of an image view does; that is, it scales with maintained proportions but ensures that the entire area is being covered. This method is more suitable for the creation of thumbnail images, which you're now going to implement for the filter functions in the table view.

Start by adding the new scaling method shown in Listing 11-31 to the master view controller.

Listing 11-31. Implementing the aspectFillImage:toSize: method

```
-(UIImage *)aspectFillImage:(UIImage *)image toSize:(CGSize)size
{
    UIGraphicsBeginImageContext(size);
    if (image.size.height< image.size.width)
    {
        float ratio = size.height/image.size.height;
        [image drawInRect:CGRectMake(0, 0, image.size.width*ratio, size.height)];
    }
    else
    {
        float ratio = size.width/image.size.width;
        [image drawInRect:CGRectMake(0, 0, size.width, image.size.height*ratio)];
    }
    UIImage *aspectScaledImage = UIGraphicsGetImageFromCurrentImageContext();
    UIGraphicsEndImageContext();
    return aspectScaledImage;
}
```

Now you just need to modify the tableView:cellForRowAtIndexPath: again to include the selection of an image for the cell's imageView, as shown in Listing 11-32.

Listing 11-32. Adding a thumbnail to the cells in the tableView:cellForRowAtIndexPath: method

```
- (UITableViewCell *)tableView:(UITableView *)tableView cellForRowAtIndexPath:(NSIndexPath *)indexPath
{
    static NSString *CellIdentifier = @"Cell";

    UITableViewCell *cell =
        [tableView dequeueReusableCellWithIdentifier:CellIdentifier];
    if (cell == nil) {
        cell = [[UITableViewCell alloc] initWithStyle:UITableViewCellStyleDefault
            reuseIdentifier:CellIdentifier];
    }

    if (indexPath.row == 0)
        cell.textLabel.text = NSLocalizedString(@"Selected Image", @"Detail");
    else if (indexPath.row == 1)
        cell.textLabel.text = NSLocalizedString(@"Resized Image", @"Detail");
    else if (indexPath.row == 2)
        cell.textLabel.text = NSLocalizedString(@"Scaled Image", @"Detail");
    else if (indexPath.row == 3)
    {
        CGSize thumbnailSize = CGSizeMake(120, 75);
        UIImage *displayImage = [self.filteredImages objectAtIndex:0];
        UIImage *thumbnailImage = [self aspectFillImage:displayImage
            toSize:thumbnailSize];
        cell.imageView.image = thumbnailImage;
        cell.textLabel.text = NSLocalizedString(@"Hue Adjust", @"Detail");
    }
```

```
else if (indexPath.row == 4)
{
    CGSize thumbnailSize = CGSizeMake(120, 75);
    UIImage *displayImage = [self.filteredImages objectAtIndex:1];
    UIImage *thumbnailImage = [self aspectFillImage:displayImage
        toSize:thumbnailSize];
    cell.imageView.image = thumbnailImage;
    cell.textLabel.text = NSLocalizedString(@"Straighten Filter", @"Detail");
}
else if (indexPath.row == 5)
{
    CGSize thumbnailSize = CGSizeMake(120, 75);
    UIImage *displayImage = [self.filteredImages objectAtIndex:2];
    UIImage *thumbnailImage = [self aspectFillImage:displayImage
        toSize:thumbnailSize];
    cell.imageView.image = thumbnailImage;
    cell.textLabel.text = NSLocalizedString(@"Series Filter", @"Detail");
}
return cell;
}
```

When you test your application now, the cells for the hue, straightening, and series filters have a scaled thumbnail version of the larger image they refer to. Figure 11-11 shows an example of this.

Figure 11-11. An application with thumbnails in its table view

Recipe 11-4: Detecting Features

Along with the flexible use of filters, the Core Image framework has also brought the possibility of feature detection. With it, you can search images for key components such as faces.

In this recipe, you implement a facial detection application. Create a new single-view project for the iPhone device family. Once your project is created, add the Core Image framework to your project, just as in the preceding recipe.

Set the background color of the main view to black and add two image views and a button so that the user interface resembles Figure 11-12.

Figure 11-12. A simple user interface for face recognition

Create outlets for each of the three elements:

- mainImageView
- findFaceButton
- faceImageView

Also, create an action with the name "findFace" for the button.

Next, find an image to be displayed in your application and add it to your project. You can do this by dragging the file from the finder into the resources file of the project navigator. To properly test this application, try to find an image with an easily visible face.

Now you can build your viewDidLoad method to configure the image views as well as set the initial image to your main image view. Be sure to change the name of the image (testimage.jpg in the following code) to your own filename. These changes are shown in Listing 11-33.

Listing 11-33. Filling out the viewDidLoad method

```
- (void)viewDidLoad
{
    [super viewDidLoad];
    // Do any additional setup after loading the view, typically from a nib.
    self.mainImageView.contentMode = UIViewContentModeScaleAspectFit;
    self.faceImageView.contentMode = UIViewContentModeScaleAspectFit;

    UIImage *image = [UIImage imageNamed:@"testimage.jpg"];
    if (image != nil)
    {
        self.mainImageView.image = image;
    }
    else
    {
        [self.findFaceButton setTitle:@"No Image" forState:UIControlStateNormal];
        self.findFaceButton.enabled = NO;
        self.findFaceButton.alpha = 0.6;
    }
}
```

Now you can implement the findFace: action method to do the feature detection. You can use this method to determine the location of any faces in the given image, create a UIImage from the last face found, and then display it in the face image view.

Listing 11-34 uses the following steps to build the findFace implementation:

1. Acquire a CIImage object from your initial UIImage.

2. Create a CIContext with which to analyze images.

3. Create an instance of CIDetector with type and options parameters.

   The *type parameter* specifies the specific feature to identify. Currently, the only possible value for this is CIDetectorTypeFace, which allows you to specifically look for faces.

The *options parameter* allows you to specify the accuracy with which you want to look for features. Low accuracy will be faster, but high accuracy will be more precise.

4. Create an array of all the features found in your image. Because you specified the CIDetectorTypeFace type, these objects will all be instances of the CIFaceFeature class.

5. Create a CIImage using the imageByCroppingToRect: method with the original image as well as the bounds specified by the last CIFaceFeature found in the image. These bounds specify the CGRect in which the face exists.

6. Create a UIImage out of your CIImage (done exactly as in the previous recipe) and then display it in your UIImageView.

Listing 11-34. Full implementation of the findFace: action method

```
- (IBAction)findFace:(id)sender
{
    UIImage *image = self.mainImageView.image;
    CIImage *coreImage = [[CIImage alloc] initWithImage:image];
    CIContext *context = [CIContext contextWithOptions:nil];
    CIDetector *detector =
        [CIDetector detectorOfType:@"CIDetectorTypeFace"context:context
            options:[NSDictionary dictionaryWithObjectsAndKeys:
                @"CIDetectorAccuracyHigh", @"CIDetectorAccuracy", nil]];
    NSArray *features = [detector featuresInImage:coreImage];

    if ([features count] >0)
    {
        CIImage *faceImage =
            [coreImage imageByCroppingToRect:[[features lastObject] bounds]];
        UIImage *face = [UIImage imageWithCGImage:[context createCGImage:faceImage
            fromRect:faceImage.extent]];
        self.faceImageView.image = face;

        [self.findFaceButton setTitle:[NSString stringWithFormat:@"%i Face(s) Found",
            [features count]] forState:UIControlStateNormal];
        self.findFaceButton.enabled = NO;
        self.findFaceButton.alpha = 0.6;
    }
    else
    {
        [self.findFaceButton setTitle:@"No Faces Found"forState:UIControlStateNormal];
        self.findFaceButton.enabled = NO;
        self.findFaceButton.alpha = 0.6;
    }
}
```

When running your application, you can detect any faces inside your image, which will be displayed in your lower UIImageView, as in Figure 11-13.

Figure 11-13. An application detecting and cropping a face from an image

Summary

Images create our world. From the simplest of picture books that children love to read to the massive amounts of visual data transmitted around the Internet, pictures and images have become one of the key foundations of modern culture. iOS offers great tools to create, handle, manipulate, and display images in your applications. With these simple APIs, you can create more interesting and useful apps in less time.

In this chapter, you have learned how to draw use image views, resize images with maintained proportions, use filters to manipulate images, and detect faces in a photo. We hope this has given you the headstart you need to take full advantage of the powerful graphics features of iOS.

Graphics Recipes

In this chapter, we will explore UIKit, Quartz 2D, and Core Graphics. We've already used UIKit to create windows, buttons, and views. Quartz 2D is a rendering engine on which UIKit is built. Quartz 2D is part of the Core Graphics framework, and together they can help a developer create impressive views and interfaces. Any time you see an impressive custom interface such as Evernote, which looks completely different from the standard Apple interface, you can bet Core Graphics played a big part in making it happen. As a developer, you can use Core Graphics to customize virtually any aspect of your interface by subclassing existing Apple elements, such as buttons and table view cells.

While this chapter does not go deep into creating custom interfaces, we will provide you with a good foundation to build on. Throughout the next few recipes, we'll build a custom view that will include rectangles, ellipses, arcs, shadows, gradients, and custom text. We'll do this by creating a single view that will get more complex as the chapter progresses.

Recipe 12-1: Drawing Simple Shapes

Most artists start with simple shapes and build upon them until they have a completed work. In iOS, you also can start off with the basics of drawing simple shapes in a view and build upon them until you have a design.

In this recipe, we'll create a new view with a header bar and a circle. Start by creating a new single view application project. Before building the user interface, you will create a custom view that will implement some simple drawing code. Create a new subclass of UIView called "GraphicsRecipesView" and add the code in Listing 12-1 to its drawRect: method.

Listing 12-1. Implementing some drawing

```
//
//  GraphicsRecipesView.m
//  Recipe 12-1 Drawing Simple Shapes
//
```

```
#import "GraphicsRecipesView.h"

@implementation

// ...

// Only override drawRect: if you perform custom drawing.
// An empty implementation adversely affects performance during animation.
- (void)drawRect:(CGRect)rect
{

    CGContextRef context = UIGraphicsGetCurrentContext();

    //Set color of current context
    [[UIColor lightGrayColor] set];

    //Draw rectangle
    CGRect drawingRect = CGRectMake(0.0, 0.0f, 320.0f, 60.0f);
    CGContextFillRect(context, drawingRect);

    //Set color of current context
    [[UIColor whiteColor] set];

    //Draw ellipse <- I know we're drawing a circle, but a circle is just a special ellipse.
    CGRect ellipseRect = CGRectMake(60.0f, 150.0f, 200.0f, 200.0f);
    CGContextFillEllipseInRect(context, ellipseRect);
}
```

The following steps were added to the method in Listing 12-1 to draw basic shapes:

1. Obtain a reference to the current "context" represented by a CGContextRef.

2. Set the color of current context.

3. Define a CGRect in which to draw.

4. Fill in the current shape using the CGContextFillEllipseInRect function.

5. Repeat Steps 2 to 3 for each additional shape.

To display this in your preconfigured view, you must add an instance of this class to your user interface. This is done programmatically or through Interface Builder, the latter of which we demonstrate.

In the view controller found in the Main.storyboard file, drag out a UIView from the object library in the utilities pane into your view. Place the view in the window and drag it to fill the entire window, as shown in Figure 12-1. With the view selected, choose a different background from the attributes inspector. For this example, I used a light blue color.

Figure 12-1. Building your .xib file with a UIView

While your UIView is selected, go to the identity inspector in the right panel. Under the Custom Class section, change the Class field from "UIView" to "GraphicsRecipesView," as shown in Figure 12-2. This connects the view you added in Interface Builder with the custom class you created earlier.

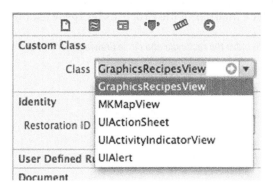

Figure 12-2. Connecting a custom class to a UIView

When running this application, you should see the output of your drawing commands converted into a visual display, resulting in the simulated view shown in Figure 12-3.

Figure 12-3. A custom view drawing a gray square at the top of screen as well as a white circle

Refactoring a Bit

Now we will clean up the code a bit and break each element into a separate function. That way we have the ability to reuse a function, and we can clean up our drawRect: method as well. The code we previously wrote in the drawRect method of the GraphicsRecipesView now looks like Listing 12-2.

Listing 12-2. Refactoring draw code to move the rectangle and circle drawings dedicated methods

```
- (void)drawRect:(CGRect)rect
{

    CGContextRef context = UIGraphicsGetCurrentContext();

    //Call function to draw rectangle
    [self drawRectangleAtTopOfScreen:context];

    //Call function to draw circle
    [self drawEllipse:context];

}
```

```objectivec
-(void)drawRectangleAtTopOfScreen:(CGContextRef)context
{

    CGContextSaveGState(context);
    //Set color of current context
    [[UIColor lightGrayColor] set];

    //Draw rectangle
    CGRect drawingRect = CGRectMake(0.0, 0.0f, 320.0f, 60.0f);
    CGContextFillRect(context, drawingRect);
    CGContextRestoreGState(context);

}

-(void)drawEllipse:(CGContextRef)context
{

    CGContextSaveGState(context);

    //Set color of current context
    [[UIColor whiteColor] set];

    //Draw ellipse <- I know we're drawing a circle, but a circle is just a special ellipse.
    CGRect ellipseRect = CGRectMake(60.0f, 150.0f, 200.0f, 200.0f);
    CGContextFillEllipseInRect(context, ellipseRect);
    CGContextRestoreGState(context);

}
```

In Listing 12-2, you'll see that we create two new functions and give an input parameter of type CGContextRef. This allows us to pass in the current context. Function calls CGContextSaveGState and CGContextRestoreGState have also been added. These will ensure that if we make a change inside these functions calls, such as by setting a color or shadow, it will apply only to this one function. Note that these functions save the state but *not* the current drawing. Restoring a state does not undo changes to a drawing, such as adding a rectangle or ellipse; it only restores values such as current fill color and shadowing properties.

Moving forward with the rest of these recipes, we'll be creating new functions and calling them from the drawRect: method.

Recipe 12-2: Drawing Paths

Thankfully, you are not limited to drawing only rectangles and ellipses. There are a few other functions. You can draw custom shapes by creating "paths" of points connected by lines or curves. To start, we'll draw a semi-transparent triangle that resembles a play button at the bottom of the screen below the white circle we created in Recipe 12-1. Create a new function titled "drawTriangle" and call that function from the drawRect: method, as shown in Listing 12-3.

Listing 12-3. Building your .xib file with a UIView

```
- (void)drawRect:(CGRect)rect
{

    CGContextRef context = UIGraphicsGetCurrentContext();

    //Call function to draw rectangle
    [self drawRectangleAtTopOfScreen:context];

    //Call function to draw circle
    [self drawEllipse:context];

    //Call function to draw triangle
    [self drawTriangle:context];

}

//...

-(void)drawTriangle:(CGContextRef)context
{

    CGContextSaveGState(context);

    //Set color of current context
    [[UIColor colorWithRed:0.80f
                     green:0.85f
                      blue:0.95f
                     alpha:1.0f] set];

    // Draw Triangle
    CGContextBeginPath(context);
    CGContextMoveToPoint(context, 140.0f, 380.0f);
    CGContextAddLineToPoint(context, 190.0f, 400.0f);
    CGContextAddLineToPoint(context, 140.0f, 420.0f);
    CGContextClosePath(context);
    CGContextSetGrayFillColor(context, 0.1f, 0.85f);
    CGContextSetGrayStrokeColor(context, 0.0, 0.0);
    CGContextFillPath(context);
    CGContextRestoreGState(context);
}
```

Listing 12-4 creates a shape by implementing the following steps:

1. Declare a new path inside the context.

2. Specify the starting point for the path.

3. Specify all points along the path.

4. Close the path.

5. Set the fill color and stroke color.

6. Fill the path.

> **Note**   We are using a different method of filling the path. We could have just as easily declared a new color by using [[UIColor colorWithRed:0.40f green:0.40f blue:0.40f alpha:0.85f] set]; at the beginning of the code segment and removing CGContextSetGrayFillColor. CGcontextSetGrayFillColor is a convenience function for using gray; we can use CGContextSetFillColor to choose any color we want.

Build and run the project and you should see a screen that resembles Figure 12-4 in the simulator.

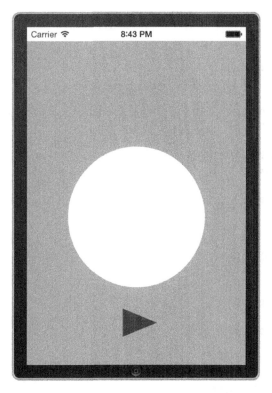

Figure 12-4. *A custom view with a path drawing of a triangle added*

Now let's take this one step further and draw an arc. This is a tad more complicated, but not too difficult. First we'll need to do a bit of math. Here is what you need to know to draw an arc using the CGContextAddArc function:

1. Determine the X and Y point coordinates of where the center of the arc is.

2. Decide on the radius of the arc.

3. Pick the start and end angles for the arc, both starting from the 3 o'clock position.

4. Determine whether the arc will sweep clockwise or counter clockwise.

Again, we'll create a new method to draw the arc and call it from within the drawRect: method, as shown in Listing 12-4.

Listing 12-4. Implementing a drawArc: method and calling it from the drawRect: method

```
- (void)drawRect:(CGRect)rect
{

    CGContextRef context = UIGraphicsGetCurrentContext();


    //Call function to draw rectangle
    [self drawRectangleAtTopOfScreen:context];

    //Call function to draw circle
    [self drawEllipse:context];

    //Call function to draw triangle
    [self drawTriangle:context];

    //Call function to draw arc
    [self drawArc:context];

}
-(void)drawArc:(CGContextRef)context
{

    CGContextSaveGState(context);

    //Set color of current context
    [[UIColor colorWithRed:0.30f
                     green:0.30f
                      blue:0.30f
                     alpha:1.0f] set];

    //Draw Arc
    CGContextAddArc(context, 160.0f, 250.0f, 70.0f, 0.0f, 3.14, 0);
    CGContextSetLineWidth(context, 50.0f);
    CGContextDrawPath(context, kCGPathStroke);
    CGContextRestoreGState(context);
}
```

In Listing 12-4 we're drawing an arc that is centered at X = 160 points and Y = 250 points. The radius is 70 points and the arc starts at 0 radians and ends at 3.14 (pi) radians, sweeping in a clockwise direction. To move in a counter-clockwise direction, replace 0 with 1. For this example, we set the line width for the arc to 50 points to give it a status-bar type of look.

If you build and run the project, you should now have a result that looks like Figure 12-5.

Figure 12-5. *A custom view with an arc drawn over the circle*

Recipe 12-3: Adding Fonts and Drawing Text

Current trends in design are putting more and more emphasis on typography and less emphasis on images, textures, and gradients. This is a consequence of having to deal with multitudes of screen sizes and having crisp displays that make text look much better. For this reason, making use of available iOS fonts as well as importing custom fonts is absolutely necessary for creating visually appealing applications.

Making Use of Available Fonts

There is a large list of system fonts installed with iOS 7, as Apple has put a lot more emphasis on typography for this iOS release. Apple has added literally hundreds of fonts since iOS 6.

> **Note**   In iOS 7, Apple also added the Text framework that allows even more control over fonts and gives you the ability to do everything from changing leading to creating custom font types. This type of customization is beyond the scope of this book, but you can learn more about it at `https://developer.apple.com/library/ios/documentation/StringsTextFonts/Conceptual/TextAndWebiPhoneOS/Introduction/Introduction.html#//apple_ref/doc/uid/TP40009542`.

To create a font object, you will need to make use of the `UIFont` class, which is built on the UIKit framework, the primary framework for displaying buttons, text, views, and the like. To declare a `UIFont` object you will need to know the name of the font family (such as Helvetica or Times New Roman) and the font face (such as Bold, Italic, and BoldItalic).

Declaring a `UIFont` object is easy once you know this information. The format should be as follows:

```
UIFont *fontObjectName = [UIFont fontWithName:@"fontFamily-fontFace" size:<#(CGFloat)#> ];
```

Thus, if you want to use the Helvetica family with the bold font face and a size of 12 points, the declaration would be the following:

```
UIFont *fontObjectName = [UIFont fontWithName: @"Helvetica-Bold" size: 12.0f];
```

Importing Your Own Fonts

First, you'll need a font to add to your project. Fortunately, you can find many open source fonts on the Google website at `http://www.google.com/fonts`. For this example, we downloaded the Oleo Script Swash Caps family with the bold face.

Now that we have a custom font, add it to your project by dragging and dropping it from the finder to the project navigator in Xcode. Once you are done, you should see it added to the project navigator, as shown in Figure 12-6.

Figure 12-6. Adding a font to the supporting files group

After you drag and drop the file, you will be presented with a dialog box. Make sure you select the check box "Copy items into destination group's folder (if needed)" and make sure you click the check box to add it to your target.

Next, from the project navigator expand the "Supporting Files" folder and open the GraphicsRecipes-Info.plist file.

Add a new key to the GraphicsRecipes-Info.plist file by selecting the "+" next to "Information Property List" and title it "Fonts provided by application." When you start typing in the field, it should come up as one of the selections. Make sure the Type is "Array."

Now create a new item under "Font provided by application" and give it a string value that matches the filename. Make sure you choose "String" for the Type.

Key	Type	Value
▼ Information Property List	Dictionary	(17 items)
▼ Fonts provided by application	Array	(1 item)
Item 0	String	OleoScriptSwashCaps-Bold.ttf
Get Info string	String	
Application Category	String	
Localization native development r...	String	en
Bundle display name	String	${PRODUCT_NAME}
Executable file	String	${EXECUTABLE_NAME}
Bundle identifier	String	NSCookbook.${PRODUCT_NAME:rfc1034identifier}
InfoDictionary version	String	6.0
Bundle name	String	${PRODUCT_NAME}

Figure 12-7. Adding a font to info.plist

Now you should be ready to use your font. Add a new method titled "drawTextAtTopOfScreen" to the GraphicsRecipesView file, as shown in Listing 12-5.

Listing 12-5. Implementing the drawTextAtTopOfScreen: method

```
-(void)drawTextAtTopOfScreen:(CGContextRef)context{

    CGContextSaveGState(context);

    //Create UIColor to pass into text attributes
    UIColor *textColor = [UIColor colorWithRed:0.80f
                     green:0.85f
                      blue:0.95f
                     alpha:1.0f];

    //Set font
    UIFont *customFont = [UIFont fontWithName:@"OleoScriptSwashCaps-Bold" size:40.0f ];
    //UIFont *customFont = [UIFont systemFontOfSize:20.0f];
    NSString *titleText = @"iOS Recipes!";

    [titleText drawAtPoint:CGPointMake(55,5) withAttributes:@{NSFontAttributeName:customFont,
                                                   NSForegroundColorAttributeName:textColor}];
    CGContextRestoreGState(context);
}
```

Of course, you'll need to call this from your drawRect: method, as shown in Listing 12-6.

Listing 12-6. Updating the drawRect method to include the drawTextAtTopOfScreen: method

```
- (void)drawRect:(CGRect)rect
{

    CGContextRef context = UIGraphicsGetCurrentContext();

    //Call function to draw rectangle
    [self drawRectangleAtTopOfScreen:context];


    //Call function to draw circle
    [self drawEllipse:context];


    //Call function to draw triangle
    [self drawTriangle:context];

    //Call function to draw arc
    [self drawArc:context];

    //Call function to draw text
    [self drawTextAtTopOfScreen:context];
    }
```

Build and run your project. You should see some new text with very nice typography, as shown in Figure 12-8.

Figure 12-8. *Custom view with custom font*

Recipe 12-4: Adding Shadows

Shadows can make graphical elements really pop. They provide a separation between graphics in a more stylish way than with a border or a stroke. In this recipe, we will add shadows to some of the components we've already created in the preceding recipes of this chapter.

Shadows are actually quite easy to implement because they can be drawn with one line of code. As you can see from the screen shot in Figure 12-9, we'll need to pass in a few parameters to get this done.

```
CGContextSetShadowWithColor( CGContextRef context , CGSize offset , CGFloat blur ,
    CGColorRef color )
```

Figure 12-9. *Setting a context shadow*

The first parameter should be familiar by now; in our example, this is simply the context we are currently working with. `CGSize` offset is the offset the shadow will have from the object. To set an offset, you can either pass in some `CGSizeMake` parameters, or if you want to have the shadow without an offset you can call a constant `CGSizeZero`, which effectively creates a `CGSizeMake(0, 0)`. To see the difference, following are a couple of screen shots (Figures 12-10 and 12-11), one with a zero offset and one with `CGSizeMake(10.0f, 15.0f)` applied to the circle in our example.

Figure 12-10. *Shadow with CGSizeZero*

Figure 12-11. Shadow with CGSizeMake(10.0f, 15.0f):

The other parameters needed are blur amount and color. By using the CGSizeZero option with this and changing the color to a light color, you can create a glow effect as well. In the following code, we modify two of our methods to apply a shadow to the text and a white circle, as shown in Listing 12-7.

Listing 12-7. Modifying the drawEllipse: and drawTextAtTopOfScreen: methods to include shadows

```
-(void)drawEllipse:(CGContextRef)context
{

    CGContextSaveGState(context);

    //Set color of current context
    [[UIColor whiteColor] set];

    //Set shadow and color of shadow
    CGContextSetShadowWithColor(context, CGSizeZero, 10.0f, [[UIColor blackColor] CGColor]);

    //Draw ellipse <- I know we're drawing a circle, but a circle is just a special ellipse.
    CGRect ellipseRect = CGRectMake(60.0f, 150.0f, 200.0f, 200.0f);
```

```
    CGContextFillEllipseInRect(context, ellipseRect);
    CGContextRestoreGState(context);

}

-(void)drawTextAtTopOfScreen:(CGContextRef)context
{

    CGContextSaveGState(context);

    //Set color of current context
    [[UIColor colorWithRed:0.80f
                     green:0.85f
                      blue:0.95f
                     alpha:1.0f] set];

    //Set shadow and color of shadow
    CGContextSetShadowWithColor(context, CGSizeZero, 10.0f, [[UIColor blackColor] CGColor]);

    //Set font
    UIFont *customFont = [UIFont fontWithName:@"OleoScriptSwashCaps-Bold" size:40.0f ];
    NSString *titleText = @"iOS Recipes!";

    //Draw text on screen
    [titleText drawAtPoint:CGPointMake(55,5)
                 withFont:customFont];
    CGContextRestoreGState(context);

}
```

That's it! Creating a simple shadow is actually pretty easy. We encourage you to vary the blur size and the colors. The view should look like Figure 12-12 when finished.

Figure 12-12. *Custom view with a shadow applied to circle and text*

Recipe 12-5: Creating Gradients

Gradients are another nice way to add good eye candy to an otherwise boring view. This recipe shows you what you need in order to create a gradient, which creates nice transitions from one color to the next.

Of all the graphical elements, gradients are a little tricky because they require quite a bit of input. You have to make several decisions, such as whether to make a gradient vertical or horizontal or whether to make a gradient circular or linear. In this recipe, we will focus on creating a vertical, linear gradient.

To create a gradient you'll need to perform the following steps:

1. Define start and end colors.

2. Set up a color space and a gradient space.

3. Define the gradient direction.

4. Create and draw the gradient.

Let's follow these steps to create yet another method to handle creating a gradient. Add the code in Listing 12-8 to your GraphicsRecipesView.m file.

Listing 12-8. Adding a drawGradient: method to the GraphicsRecipesView.m file

```
-(void)drawGradient:(CGContextRef)context{

    //Define start and end colors
    CGFloat colors [8] = {
        0.0, 0.0, 1.0, 1.0, // Blue
        0.0, 1.0, 0.0, 1.0 }; //Green

    //Setup a color space and gradient space
    CGColorSpaceRef baseSpace = CGColorSpaceCreateDeviceRGB();
    CGGradientRef gradient = CGGradientCreateWithColorComponents(baseSpace, colors, NULL, 2);

    //Define the gradient direction
    CGPoint startPoint = CGPointMake(160.0f,100.0f);
    CGPoint endPoint = CGPointMake(160.0f, 360.0f);

    //Create and Draw the gradient
    CGContextDrawLinearGradient(context, gradient, startPoint, endPoint, 0);
}
```

Now add the call for this method to the drawRect: method, as shown in Listing 12-9.

Listing 12-9. Adding the drawGradient: method call to the drawRect: method

```
- (void)drawRect:(CGRect)rect
{

    CGContextRef context = UIGraphicsGetCurrentContext();

    //Call function to draw rectangle
    [self drawRectangleAtTopOfScreen:context];

    /*
    //Set shadow and color of shadow
    CGContextSetShadowWithColor(context, CGSizeZero, 10.0f, [[UIColor blackColor] CGColor]);
     */

    //Call function to draw circle
    [self drawEllipse:context];

    //Call function to draw triangle
    [self drawTriangle:context];

    //Call function to draw arc
    [self drawArc:context];
```

```
//Call function to draw text
[self drawTextAtTopOfScreen:context];

//draw gradient
[self drawGradient:context];

}
```

Build and run the application. You should end up with the result in Figure 12-13.

Figure 12-13. *Custom view with a gradient applied*

Of course, this covers up all the other elements we added in the preceding recipes. Fear not, though, because we'll be addressing this in the next recipe.

Recipe 12-6: Clipping a Drawing to a Mask

At the end of the preceding recipe, we were left with the gradient covering the other drawings from the earlier recipes in this chapter. It would be better if we could clip the gradient to a small portion so we can see most of what is behind the gradient. Clipping to a mask is a lot like creating a window in which we can see a portion of what is drawn behind that window. The mask in this case is the shape of the window, which we will then clip everything around. We have the option of making the mask any shape we want, but in this example we'll create a small circle by creating a new method called `drawEllipseWithGradient` and calling it from our `drawRect:` method. This will give us a result where the gradient is completely contained within the circle.

Creating a mask from a drawing, or using a drawing to create a window, will require the following steps:

1. Create an Image context.

2. Create a new graphics context.

3. Translate and flip the context upside-down to compensate for Quartz's inverted coordinate system.

4. Draw the shapes we want to mask with.

5. Create a bitmap from our new image context drawing.

6. Use that bitmap to start masking.

7. Draw anything you want to mask, in this case a gradient.

We'll start first by created a new method, `drawEllipseWithGradient`, which takes a `CGContextRef` as an input and uses the steps we listed to create a circle with a gradient in it. Listing 12-10 shows the implementation of this method.

Listing 12-10 does exactly what we said we would do: we're creating a circle that is 100 points high by 100 points wide and is located at the center of the large white circle from Recipe 12-1. The reason we have to translate and scale the image is because Quartz uses a coordinate system that references the lower-left corner of the screen instead of the top left. This obviously causes problems when it comes to mixing coordinate systems. If the user switches from a 3.5" screen to a 4" screen, the vertical position of the circle would move downward. To fix this, we translate and scale so the coordinate systems match.

Listing 12-10. Implementation of the drawEllipseWithGradient: method

```
-(void)drawEllipseWithGradient:(CGContextRef)context{

    CGContextSaveGState(context);

    //UIGraphicsBeginImageContextWith(self.frame.size);
    UIGraphicsBeginImageContextWithOptions((self.frame.size), NO, 0.0);

    CGContextRef newContext = UIGraphicsGetCurrentContext();

    // Translate and scale image to compensate for Quartz's inverted coordinate system
    CGContextTranslateCTM(newContext,0.0,self.frame.size.height);
    CGContextScaleCTM(newContext, 1.0, -1.0);
```

```
    //Set color of current context
    [[UIColor blackColor] set];

    //Draw ellipse <- I know we're drawing a circle, but a circle is just a special ellipse.
    CGRect ellipseRect = CGRectMake(110.0f, 200.0f, 100.0f, 100.0f);
    CGContextFillEllipseInRect(newContext, ellipseRect);

    CGImageRef mask = CGBitmapContextCreateImage(UIGraphicsGetCurrentContext());
    UIGraphicsEndImageContext();

    CGContextClipToMask(context, self.bounds, mask);

    [self drawGradient:context];

    CGContextRestoreGState(context);

}
```

As usual, we want to call the new method created in Listing 12-10 from the drawRect: method, as shown in Listing 12-11. You might notice that we removed the previous method call to drawGradient and replaced it with the new function call drawEllipseWithGradient. This is because we are now calling the drawGradient: method from within the drawEllipseWithGradient method.

Listing 12-11. Removing the drawGradient: method call and replacing it with the drawEllipseWithGradient: call

```
- (void)drawRect:(CGRect)rect
{

    CGContextRef context = UIGraphicsGetCurrentContext();

    //Call function to draw rectangle
    [self drawRectangleAtTopOfScreen:context];

    //Call function to draw circle
    [self drawEllipse:context];

    //Call function to draw triangle
    [self drawTriangle:context];

    //Call function to draw arc
    [self drawArc:context];

    //Call function to draw text
    [self drawTextAtTopOfScreen:context];

    //Call function to draw ellipse filled with a gradient
    [self drawEllipseWithGradient:context];

}
```

If you build and run your application, you should be presented with a nice circular gradient in the middle of the larger circle.

Figure 12-14. *A completed custom view with a gradient circle*

Recipe 12-7: Programming Screen Shots

Just as you can put drawings and images into a graphics context, you also can easily take them out of a context. You can do this by making use of the UIGraphicsGetImageFromCurrentImageContext() function. This allows you to create a copy from the current collection of drawings and copy them into an image object. In Recipes 12-1 through 12-6, we created several drawings in the context. This recipe will make use of this collection of drawings.

We will build on the preceding recipes of this chapter and add a feature that takes a snapshot of the current view whenever the user shakes the device. The feature will display the snapshot in the lower-right corner of the screen, causing a nice, double-mirror effect on subsequent shakes.

Start by adding a property to the GraphicsRecipesView class to hold the latest snapshot. Open GraphicsRecipesView.h and add the declaration, as shown in Listing 12-12.

Listing 12-12. Creating a UIImage property in the GraphicsRecipesView.h file

```
//
//  GraphicsRecipesView.h
//  Recipe 12-7 Programming Screenshots
//

#import <UIKit/UIKit.h>
```

```
@interface GraphicsRecipesView : UIView
```

@property (strong, nonatomic)UIImage *image;

```
@end
```

Next, select the Main.storyboard file to edit the view controller using Interface Builder. Open the assistant editor and create an outlet for the custom view by Ctrl-dragging a blue line from it onto the ViewController.h file. Name the outlet "myView." For the outlet declaration to compile, you'll need to import GraphicsRecipesView.h, as shown in Listing 12-13.

Listing 12-13. Including the import statement in the ViewController.h file

```
//
//  ViewController.h
//  Recipe 12-7 Programming Screenshots
//

#import <UIKit/UIKit.h>
#import "GraphicsRecipesView.h"

@interface ViewController : UIViewController

@property (weak, nonatomic) IBOutlet GraphicsRecipesView *myView;

@end
```

Now, add the code that will draw the snapshot to the drawRect: method in GraphicsRecipesView.m, as shown in Listing 12-14.

Listing 12-14. Adding code to draw the snapshot in the drawRect: method

```
- (void)drawRect:(CGRect)rect
{
    // ...

    if (self.image)
    {
        CGFloat imageWidth = self.frame.size.width / 2;
        CGFloat imageHeight = self.frame.size.height / 2;
        CGRect imageRect = CGRectMake(imageWidth, imageHeight, imageWidth, imageHeight);
        [self.image drawInRect:imageRect];
    }
}

@end
```

As the next step, add the methods in Listing 12-15 to the view controller. These methods implement shake recognition that triggers the screen shot.

Listing 12-15. Adding methods to ViewController.m to handle shake recognition

```
//
//  ViewController.m
//  Recipe 12-7 Programming Screenshots
//

#import "ViewController.h"

@implementation ViewController

// ...

- (BOOL) canBecomeFirstResponder
{
    return YES;
}

- (void) viewWillAppear: (BOOL)animated
{
    [self.view becomeFirstResponder];
    [super viewWillAppear:animated];
}

- (void) viewWillDisappear: (BOOL)animated
{
    [self.view resignFirstResponder];
    [super viewWillDisappear:animated];
}

- (void) motionEnded: (UIEventSubtype)motion withEvent: (UIEvent *)event
{
    if (event.subtype == UIEventSubtypeMotionShake)
    {
        // Device was shaken

        // TODO: Take a screen shot
    }
}

@end
```

You will need to import the QuartzCore framework. Failing to do so causes a compiler error later when you access a layer on the view to draw the screen shot. So, open ViewController.h again and add the code shown in Listing 12-16.

Listing 12-16. Importing the QuartzCore framework

```
//
//  ViewController.h
//  Recipe 12-7 Programming Screenshots
//
```

```
#import <UIKit/UIKit.h>
#import <QuartzCore/QuartzCore.h>
#import "GraphicsRecipesView.h"

@interface ViewController : UIViewController

@property (weak, nonatomic) IBOutlet MyView *myView;

@end
```

Finally, implement the code for taking a snapshot and setting it to the image view, as shown in Listing 12-17. Take note that the setNeedsDisplay method in the UIView class instructs it to re-call its drawRect: method to incorporate any recent changes.

Listing 12-17. Implementing the motionEnded: withEvent: method

```
- (void) motionEnded: (UIEventSubtype)motion withEvent: (UIEvent *)event
{
    if (event.subtype == UIEventSubtypeMotionShake)
    {
        // Device was shaken

        // Acquire image of current layer
        UIGraphicsBeginImageContext(self.view.bounds.size);
        CGContextRef context = UIGraphicsGetCurrentContext();
        [self.view.layer renderInContext:context];
        UIImage *image = UIGraphicsGetImageFromCurrentImageContext();
        UIGraphicsEndImageContext();

        self.myView.image = image;
        [self.myView setNeedsDisplay];
    }
}
```

After testing the application again, you should see a screen similar to Figure 12-15 when you shake the device a couple of times.

Figure 12-15. *An application showing a screen shot of a screen that was displaying a screen shot already*

Note   If you run the app in the *iOS* simulator, you can simulate a shake by pressing Ctrl + Cmd + Z.

Summary

Throughout this chapter, you have learned most of the ways you can create shapes, gradients, and fonts using Core Graphics. It doesn't take a stretch of the imagination to see how these techniques could be useful when creating custom UI controls or to dynamically generate other types of feedback. In this chapter, we have only touched the surface of what is possible with Core Graphics. It's up to you as a developer to use this instruction as a foundation for creating awesome custom interfaces.

Chapter 13

Animation and Physics Recipes

On the iOS platform, animation plays an integral role in how users interact with devices. Sometimes animation can provide information, such as a spinning icon that lets users know when data is loading. At other times, animation is added for no other reason than to please the user.

Animation gives developers the ability to tell a story in a realistic and appealing way. With the new iOS 7 framework, UIKit Dynamics, you have a plethora of physics-influenced animation to choose from to make the story even more realistic. UIKit Dynamics allows you to add acceleration, spring behavior, and collision effects to view objects. Before this great new framework, developers had to use third-party libraries to achieve the same behavior. Using both UIView Animation and UIKit Dynamics, you can create a user experience that is immersive and captivating without using hundreds of lines of code.

Throughout this chapter, you will first learn the basics of animation where you will create animations of objects moving, rotating, and changing size. Then you will move into dynamic animations where you will learn how to add acceleration, force, collision, attachment, and spring behavior to your view objects.

Recipe 13-1. View Animation Using UIKit

In iOS you can animate using both the Core Animation framework and the UIKit Animation framework. The UIKit Animation framework is built on the Core Animation framework and gives you APIs that allow you to do high-level animations on view objects of all types. In this recipe, we will focus on the UIKit Animation framework and basic tasks such as moving, rotating, and scaling objects.

Start by creating a new single view application. To begin, you'll be creating a simple animation of a ball that goes from the top of the screen to the center of the screen. You can download the ball image (Ball.png) from the download page for this book at the Apress web site. Add the ball image to your project by dragging it into the resources folder from the Finder.

Create a new outlet in the ViewController.h file. You don't need to make any interface connections as you will be creating the ball image programmatically. Listing 13-1 shows the addition of this property.

Listing 13-1. Adding a UIImageView to the ViewController.h File

```
//
//  ViewController.h
//  Recipe 13-1 View Animation Using UIKit
//

#import <UIKit/UIKit.h>

@interface ViewController : UIViewController

@property (strong, nonatomic) UIImageView *blueBall;

@end
```

Now, move to the viewController.m file and modify the viewDidLoad method. The first bit of code, shown in bold in Listing 13-2, will be necessary for creating the ball image and defining the starting point.

Listing 13-2. Modifying the viewDidLoad Method, Initializing the Ball Image, and Setting Its Starting Point

```
- (void)viewDidLoad
{
    [super viewDidLoad];

    //Create ball image and add it to the view
    UIImage *blueBallImage = [[UIImage alloc] init];
    blueBallImage = [UIImage imageNamed:@"Ball"];
    self.blueBall = [[UIImageView alloc] initWithImage:blueBallImage];
    self.blueBall.frame = CGRectMake(self.view.frame.size.width/2-32.0f,
                                     20.0f,
                                     64.0f,
                                     64.0f);

    [self.view addSubview:self.blueBall];

}
```

At this point, you can run the application; you should see a ball at the top of the screen, as shown in Figure 13-1.

Figure 13-1. *The application with the blue ball image*

Here you see that you have created an image and set it in the top middle of the screen with a size of 64 x 64 points. Next, you need to create the animation. There are two ways to do this, but the best way is using the block approach. Back in iOS 4, Apple introduced the block approach, which you will see here. Before the block approach, each step of the animation was broken up into separate lines of code. The block approach is a much more concise way of doing animations because it uses much less code and it's easier to read. There is no need to learn the nonblock approach unless your application is targeted to iOS 3.2 and earlier.

To start with, you will be adding the `animateWithDuration` method call, as shown in bold in Listing 13-3. In this code, you set up an animation with a three-second duration. When the animation is completed, it will print "Animation Finished" to the console.

Listing 13-3. *Setting Up the animateWithDuration: Method Call*

```
- (void)viewDidLoad
{
    [super viewDidLoad];

    //Create ball image and add it to the view
    UIImage *blueBallImage = [[UIImage alloc] init];
    blueBallImage = [UIImage imageNamed:@"Ball"];
```

```
    self.blueBall = [[UIImageView alloc] initWithImage:blueBallImage];
    self.blueBall.frame = CGRectMake(self.view.frame.size.width/2-32.0f,
                                    20.0f,
                                    64.0f,
                                    64.0f);

    [self.view addSubview:self.blueBall];

[UIView animateWithDuration:3.0f
                 animations:^{
                     //start animations here
                 }
                 completion:^(BOOL finished) {
                     NSLog(@"Animation Finished");
                 }];

}
```

Next, you will complete the animation code. The code in bold in Listing 13-4 sets the new location of the ball directly in the middle of the screen once the animation has completed.

Listing 13-4. Modifying the viewDidLoad Method to Add the End Point for the Ball Animation

```
- (void)viewDidLoad
{
    [super viewDidLoad];
//...
    [UIView animateWithDuration:3.0f
                     animations:^{
                         self.blueBall.frame = CGRectMake(self.view.frame.size.width/2-32.0f,
                                                         self.view.frame.size.height/2 -32.0f,
                                                         64.0f,
                                                         64.0f);

                     }
                     completion:^(BOOL finished) {
                         NSLog(@"Animation Finished");
                     }];
//...
}
```

If you run the application, you will see the blue ball move from the top of the screen to the middle of the screen, as shown in Figure 13-2.

Figure 13-2. The app with the ball animation at its final destination

That's it for simple animation from one point to another! Now let's add to the complexity a bit by changing the size and alpha values of the ball image when it starts. Changing the alpha value will cause the animation to gradually become less transparent.

Changing Size and Transparency

Changing the size and alpha is easy when using UIKit Animation. In this section, you create an effect that will make the ball fade from nothing while gradually getting larger before it settles in the center of the view. To do this, modify the viewDidLoad method, as shown in Listing 13-5.

Listing 13-5. Modifying the viewDidLoad Method to Create the Growing, Fading Image Effect

```
- (void)viewDidLoad
{
    [super viewDidLoad];

    //Create ball image and add it to the view
    UIImage *blueBallImage = [[UIImage alloc] init];
    blueBallImage = [UIImage imageNamed:@"Ball"];
    self.blueBall = [[UIImageView alloc] initWithImage:blueBallImage];
```

```
        self.blueBall.frame = CGRectMake(self.view.frame.size.width/2-5,
                                         20.0f,
                                         10.0f,
                                         10.0f);
    self.blueBall.alpha = 0.0f;

    [self.view addSubview:self.blueBall];

    [UIView animateWithDuration:3.0f
                     animations:^{
                         self.blueBall.frame = CGRectMake(self.view.frame.size.width/2-32.0f,
                                                          self.view.frame.size.height/2 -32.0f,
                                                          64.0f,
                                                          64.0f);

                         self.blueBall.alpha = 1.0f;

                     }
                     completion:^(BOOL finished) {
                         NSLog(@"Animation Finished");
                     }];

}
```

Here you simply changed the size of the ball image by adjusting the frame. You also had to subtract 5 instead of 32 from half of the view so the ball would be centered at the top. Then you set the alpha value to 0 in the initial ball image position and back to 100 percent when the ball image reaches its destination.

If you run the application, you will see the image fade from the top of the screen to the middle of the screen while simultaneously getting larger.

Handling Rotation and Chaining Animation

Now that you have enabled movement, fading, and size, let's complete this recipe by adding rotation to the animation. You will want this new animation to occur once the first animation is complete. Once the first animation has completed and the ball goes to the center of the screen, you will then make the ball rotate 180 degrees.

Start by creating a new method in the ViewController.m file, as shown in Listing 13-6. You will use the animateWithDuration method as you did earlier.

Listing 13-6. Implementing the startRotationOfBall Method Without Adding the Animation

```
-(void)startRotationOfBall
{

    [UIView animateWithDuration:1.5f
                     animations:^{
                         //implement rotation code here
                     }
```

```
                    completion:^(BOOL finished) {
                        NSLog(@"Rotation Finished");
                    }];

}
```

Now let's add a rotation to the animation block. In Listing 13-7 you create a transform using the CGAffineTranformMakeRotation function. You might notice that you use the constant M_PI, which is 3.14 radians, or 180 degrees. You can change the rotation direction by making the M_PI value negative. A positive value will be counterclockwise, and a negative value will be clockwise.

Listing 13-7. Completing the Ball Rotation Animation Method

```
-(void)startRotationOfBall
{

    [UIView animateWithDuration:1.5f
                     animations:^{
                         self.blueBall.transform = CGAffineTransformMakeRotation(M_PI);
                     }
                     completion:^(BOOL finished) {
                         NSLog(@"Rotation Finished");
                     }];

}
```

The last thing to do is call this new method from the completion block of the first animation. This is a simple one-line call, as you can see in Listing 13-8.

Listing 13-8. Modifying the Completion Block of the First animateWithDuration: Method to Create the Rotation

```
- (void)viewDidLoad
{
//...

    [UIView animateWithDuration:3.0f
                     animations:^{
                         self.blueBall.frame = CGRectMake(self.view.frame.size.width/2-32.0f,
                                                          self.view.frame.size.height/2 -32.0f,
                                                          64.0f,
                                                          64.0f);
                         self.blueBall.alpha = 1.0f;

                     }
                     completion:^(BOOL finished) {
                         NSLog(@"Animation Finished");
                         [self startRotationOfBall];
                     }];

}
```

That's it! If you run your application, you will see the first animation finish, and then the ball will rotate 180 degrees counterclockwise. When the animations have completed, your application should look like Figure 13-3.

Figure 13-3. The completed app with rotation

In the next recipe, we'll create more realistic and interesting animations using UIKit Dynamics.

Recipe 13-2. Implementing UIKit Dynamics

UIKit Dynamics is a new framework in iOS 7 that gives developers the ability to add real-life movement to their animations. These movements include gravity, bouncing, collision, and even subtle effects such as friction.

In this recipe, we will show you many of the dynamic effects you can create Using UIKit dynamics as well as how to combine multiple effects. Near the end of this recipe, you will learn how to create a custom behavior class, which will allow you to bundle many custom behaviors and easily add effects to view components.

Using Gravity

To start, create a single view application and title it "Recipe 13-2 Implementing UIKit Dynamics." This time, fill in the class prefix with **Gravity**, as shown in Figure 13-4. For this recipe, you'll make somewhat extensive use of storyboards, so you might want to skim Chapter 2 to familiarize yourself. Not to worry, though, we'll be explaining all the steps necessary.

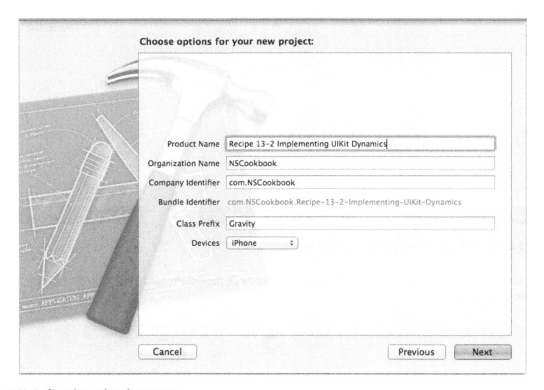

Figure 13-4. Choosing options for your app

Once the project is created, navigate to the Main.storyboard file and drag a new table view controller onto the storyboard. With the table view controller selected, choose Editor ➤ Embed In ➤ Navigation Controller from the Xcode file menu. Your storyboard should be arranged as shown in Figure 13-5.

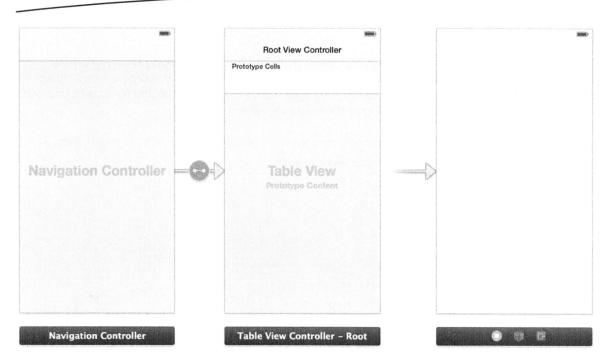

Figure 13-5. *The navigation controller without connections*

Next, select the table view and change the content from Dynamic Prototypes to Static Cells, as shown in Figure 13-6.

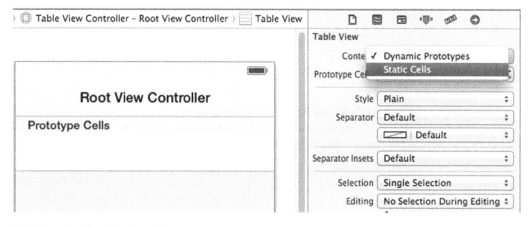

Figure 13-6. *Changing the table view cell type*

Once you change to static cells, the prototype cell will be replaced with three static cells. Control-click and drag from the first table view cell to the view controller, as shown in Figure 13-7. When the dialog box appears, choose Push under Selection Segue.

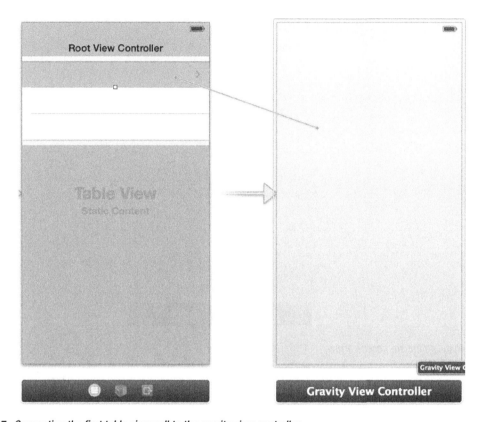

Figure 13-7. Connecting the first table view cell to the gravity view controller

Next, click and drag the arrow that is connected only to the gravity view controller and move it to the left side of the navigation controller, as shown in Figure 13-8.

Figure 13-8. Relocating the start scene arrow

Finally, drag an image view onto the gravity view controller and change its size to 64 x 64 points. As you did in Recipe 13-1, drag the Ball.png image file into the resources folder in the project navigator.

Next, set the image view image to Ball.png, as you did in Recipe 13-1. Also, change the title of the view controller to "Gravity" and the title of the table view controller to "Dynamics Playground." Your completed storyboard should look like Figure 13-9. You will also need to change the style of the table view cell from "custom" to "basic" from the attributes inspector with the cell selected. This will allow you to edit the title.

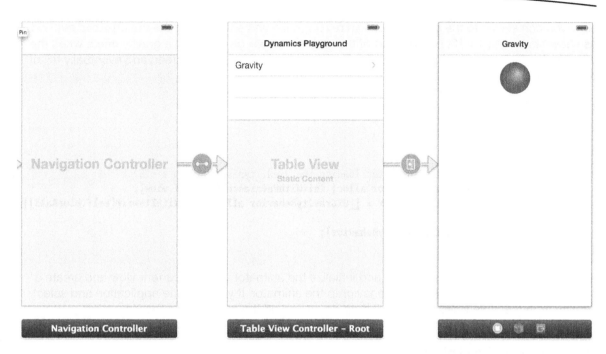

Figure 13-9. The complete interface

Now, if you run the application, you can tap the gravity table view cell, and it will take you to the gravity view controller with the ball. Of course, the ball will not do anything, but you are now set up with a good framework for the rest of this recipe.

Now we will implement the gravity behavior. Create an outlet from the blue ball to the GravityViewController.h file. Title the new outlet "blueBall." Also, add a new UIDynamicsAnimator property titled "animator" to the header file. When you are done, your GravityViewController.h file should have an outlet and a property, as shown in Listing 13-9.

Listing 13-9. The Start ViewController.h File

```
//
//  GravityViewController.h
//  Recipe 13-2 Implementing UIKit Dynamics
//
#import <UIKit/UIKit.h>

@interface GravityViewController : UIViewController

@property (weak, nonatomic) IBOutlet UIImageView *blueBall;
@property (nonatomic) UIDynamicAnimator *animator;

@end
```

Now you can switch to the `GravityViewController.m` file and start editing the `viewDidLoad` method, as shown in Listing 13-10. For this part of the recipe, you will give the ball a gravity effect when the view loads. This will make the ball accelerate toward the bottom of the screen and eventually fall off the screen.

Listing 13-10. Modifying the viewDidLoad Method to Create the Gravity Behavior

```
- (void)viewDidLoad
{
    [super viewDidLoad];
        // Do any additional setup after loading the view, typically from a nib.
    self.animator = [[UIDynamicAnimator alloc] initWithReferenceView:self.view];
    UIGravityBehavior *gravityBehavior = [[UIGravityBehavior alloc] initWithItems:@[self.blueBall]];

    [self.animator addBehavior:gravityBehavior];
}
```

In Listing 13-10, all you do is allocate and initialize the animator with the current view and create a gravity behavior. Then you add that behavior to the animator. If you load the application and select Gravity from the table view, the ball will drop down and off the screen once the view loads.

Gravity and Collision

Now you'll build on the previous example by making a collision with the view boundary. The steps to build this are as follows:

1. Drag a new view controller onto the storyboard.

2. As you did with the first view controller, Control-drag from the second table view cell to the new view controller and create a push selection segue.

3. Create a new image view that is 64 points x 64 points and set its image to "Ball.png."

4. Update the table view title with the value "Gravity with Collision" and give the same title to the new view controller.

When you are done with these steps, your storyboard scene should resemble Figure 13-10.

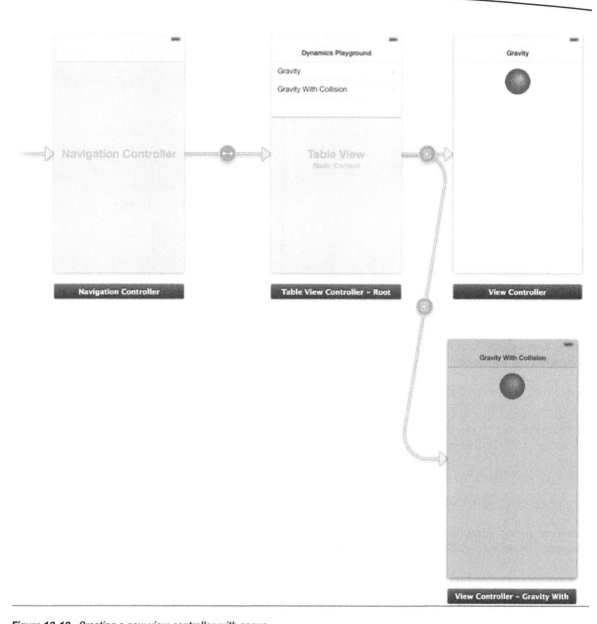

Figure 13-10. Creating a new view controller with segue

Because you created a new view controller on the storyboard, you will also need to create a new class with a UIViewController subclass. Title the new class GravityWithCollisionViewController and make sure the "With XIB for interface" check box is not selected.

Next, you will need to tie your new GravityWithCollisionViewController class to the new view controller. Do this by selecting the view and choosing the class from the identity inspector, as shown in Figure 13-11.

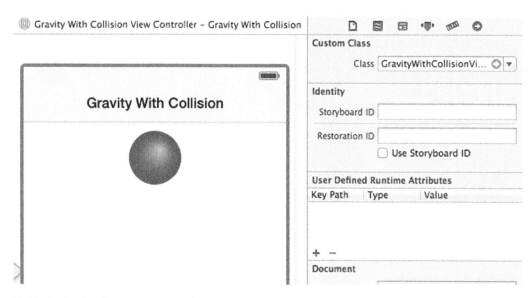

Figure 13-11. Setting the view controller class in a storyboard

Now you are ready to add some code. First, as you did in the GravityViewController class, create an outlet for the blue ball and a property for the animator. Listing 13-11 shows these changes.

Listing 13-11. The Finished GravityWithCollisionViewController.h File

```
//
//  GravityWithCollisionViewController.h
//  Recipe 13-2 Implementing UIKit Dynamics
//
#import <UIKit/UIKit.h>

@interface GravityWithCollisionViewController : UIViewController

@property (weak, nonatomic) IBOutlet UIImageView *blueBall;
@property (nonatomic) UIDynamicAnimator *animator;

@end
```

This time the viewDidLoad method will look a bit different. This code builds on the previous example and adds a new behavior. The viewDidLoad method should now look like Listing 13-12.

Listing 13-12. The Completed GravityWithCollisionViewController viewDidLoad Method

```
- (void)viewDidLoad
{
    [super viewDidLoad];
        // Do any additional setup after loading the view, typically from a nib.
    self.animator = [[UIDynamicAnimator alloc] initWithReferenceView:self.view];
    UIGravityBehavior *gravityBehavior = [[UIGravityBehavior alloc] initWithItems:@[self.blueBall]];
    UICollisionBehavior *collisionBehavior = [[UICollisionBehavior alloc]
initWithItems:@[self.blueBall]];
```

```
collisionBehavior.translatesReferenceBoundsIntoBoundary = YES;

[self.animator addBehavior:gravityBehavior];
[self.animator addBehavior:collisionBehavior];
```

}

In Listing 13-12 you are creating a new collision behavior. You do this by setting the translatesReferenceBoundsIntoBoundary property to "YES" so that the ball will collide with the bounds of the view. Finally, you add the new behavior to the animator.

If you run the application and select the Gravity with Collision table cell, the ball with fall and hit the bottom boundary and then bounce before it settles at the location, as shown in Figure 13-12.

Figure 13-12. Gravity with collision once the ball has settled

This is great, but what if you want to know when the ball began the collision or ended a collision? Fortunately, iOS 7 has some tools to handle this as well. For this example, you will modify the code so the ball will turn semi-transparent while bouncing. More specifically, the ball will hit the bottom of the frame and bounce. After the bounce, the ball will turn transparent every time it is not in contact with the bottom of the frame.

To do this, you'll need to declare the UICollisionBehaviorDelegate in the GravityWithCollisionViewController.h file, as shown in Listing 13-13.

Listing 13-13. Declaring the UICollisionBehaviorDelegate

```
//
//  GravityWithCollisionViewController.h
//  Recipe 13-2 Implementing UIKit Dynamics
//
#import <UIKit/UIKit.h>

@interface GravityWithCollisionViewController : UIViewController <UICollisionBehaviorDelegate>

@property (weak, nonatomic) IBOutlet UIImageView *blueBall;
@property (nonatomic) UIDynamicAnimator *animator;

@end
```

Next, you will need to set the collision delegate. To do this, modify the viewDidLoad method, as shown in Listing 13-14.

Listing 13-14. Setting the UICollisionBehaviorDelegate

```
- (void)viewDidLoad
{
    [super viewDidLoad];

    self.animator = [[UIDynamicAnimator alloc] initWithReferenceView:self.view];
    UIGravityBehavior *gravityBehavior = [[UIGravityBehavior alloc] initWithItems:@[self.blueBall]];
    UICollisionBehavior *collisionBehavior = [[UICollisionBehavior alloc]
initWithItems:@[self.blueBall]];

    collisionBehavior.translatesReferenceBoundsIntoBoundary = YES;
    collisionBehavior.collisionDelegate = self;

    [self.animator addBehavior:gravityBehavior];
    [self.animator addBehavior:collisionBehavior];

}
```

Listing 13-15 shows the necessary delegate methods that need to be added. The first method will set the alpha of the blue ball to 100 percent when the ball is in contact with the boundary. The second method will set the blue ball to an alpha value of 50 percent right after the collision has occurred. The resulting effect, as mentioned earlier, is that the ball will be semi-transparent any time it is not touching the boundary after the first bounce.

Listing 13-15. Implementing the Two collisionBehavior Delegates

```
-(void)collisionBehavior:(UICollisionBehavior *)behavior beganContactForItem:(id<UIDynamicItem>)item
withBoundaryIdentifier:(id<NSCopying>)identifier atPoint:(CGPoint)p
{
    [self.blueBall setAlpha:1.0f];
}
```

```
-(void)collisionBehavior:(UICollisionBehavior *)behavior endedContactForItem:(id<UIDynamicItem>)item
withBoundaryIdentifier:(id<NSCopying>)identifier
{
    [self.blueBall setAlpha:0.5f];
}
```

If you run the application now and select Gravity with Collision, you will see the ball fall from the top of the screen, bounce and turn semi-transparent, and then settle at the bottom without transparency.

Using Item Properties

Now you know how to add a gravity and collision behavior to a view, but what if you wanted to set how high the ball will bounce? To do this, you can add an elasticity property to the ball.

To create a new view controller, use the following steps:

1. Drag a new view controller onto the storyboard and connect it to the third table view cell with a push selection segue.

2. This time, add two balls to the new view and situate them as shown in Figure 13-13.

Figure 13-13. Setting up the item property view controller

3. As you did with GravityWithCollisionViewController, create a new
    UIViewController subclass and title it ItemPropertyViewController.

4. Create two new outlets for the balls. The ball on the left should have an outlet
    titled "ball1," and the ball on the right should be titled "ball2."

5. Create an animator property in the header file.

When you have finished these steps, your header file should resemble Listing 13-16.

Listing 13-16. The Final ItemPropertyViewController.h File

```
//
//  ItemPropertyViewController.h
//  Recipe 13-2 Implementing UIKit Dynamics
//
#import <UIKit/UIKit.h>

@interface ItemPropertyViewController : UIViewController

@property (weak, nonatomic) IBOutlet UIImageView *ball1;
@property (weak, nonatomic) IBOutlet UIImageView *ball2;
@property (nonatomic) UIDynamicAnimator *animator;

@end
```

Now you will edit your viewDidLoad method to include gravity and collision for both balls. This time
you will leave out the delegate for detecting collision and add the gravity and collision behaviors
necessary for both balls. These changes are shown in Listing 13-17.

Listing 13-17. Setting Up the viewDidLoad Method to Add Gravity and Collision Behaviors to the Balls

```
- (void)viewDidLoad
{
    [super viewDidLoad];

self.animator = [[UIDynamicAnimator alloc] initWithReferenceView:self.view];
    UIGravityBehavior *gravityBehavior = [[UIGravityBehavior alloc]
initWithItems:@[self.ball1,self.ball2]];
    UICollisionBehavior *collisionBehavior = [[UICollisionBehavior alloc]
initWithItems:@[self.ball1,self.ball2]];

    collisionBehavior.translatesReferenceBoundsIntoBoundary = YES;

    [self.animator addBehavior:gravityBehavior];
    [self.animator addBehavior:collisionBehavior];
}
```

Now comes the fun part. You are going to add a property to the second ball's behavior. There are actually quite a few properties to choose from. Here are all of the available properties:

- elasticity: A float value sets the collision elasticity; use 0 for nonelastic or 1 for very elastic.

- friction: A float value sets the friction of an object between others; use 0 for no friction.

- density: This is a float value for density; 1 is the default.

- resistance: A float value sets velocity damping; 0 is no velocity damping.

- angularResistance: This is a float value for angular velocity damping; 0 is no angular velocity damping.

- allowsRotation: A Boolean value sets whether an object will have locked rotation.

For this example, we will set the elasticity for the second ball image as shown in Listing 13-18, which will make it bounce higher when it collides with the boundary at the bottom.

Listing 13-18. Setting the Behavior Property on the Second Ball

```
- (void)viewDidLoad
//
//   ItemPropertyViewController.m
//   Recipe 13-2 Implementing UIKit Dynamics
//

{
    [super viewDidLoad];

    self.animator = [[UIDynamicAnimator alloc] initWithReferenceView:self.view];
    UIGravityBehavior *gravityBehavior = [[UIGravityBehavior alloc]
initWithItems:@[self.ball1,self.ball2]];
    UICollisionBehavior *collisionBehavior = [[UICollisionBehavior alloc]
initWithItems:@[self.ball1,self.ball2]];
    UIDynamicItemBehavior* propertiesBehavior = [[UIDynamicItemBehavior alloc]
initWithItems:@[self.ball2]];
    propertiesBehavior.elasticity = 0.75f;

    collisionBehavior.translatesReferenceBoundsIntoBoundary = YES;

    [self.animator addBehavior:propertiesBehavior];
    [self.animator addBehavior:gravityBehavior];
    [self.animator addBehavior:collisionBehavior];
}
```

If you run the app now, you will notice the two balls will fall and collide with the bottom of the view at the same time. The ball on the left will bounce once, but the ball on the right will bounce more than once and bounce much higher.

We encourage you to rearrange the balls in several ways and change the behaviors. For example, if you add resistance, the ball will resist gravity and accelerate more slowly.

Adding Snap

Now let's explore a behavior that will allow you to snap an object to a point on the view. The point in the view will be defined by a touch gesture, and the object in this case will be the ball. The snap behavior is kind of like a magnetic behavior. Wherever you touch the screen, the ball will shoot over to that location as if being attracted there by a magnetic force.

As usual, follow these steps to get started with a new view controller:

1. Drag a view controller onto the storyboard and give it an accompanying class titled `SnapViewController`.

2. Add one ball image view and an outlet for it titled "blueBall."

3. Add a `UIDynamicAnimator` property to the header file as you did before.

4. Because we have exceeded the number of table view cells provided, you will need to drag a new one onto the table view from the object library.

5. When the new cell is created, make a push selection segue connection between it and the new view controller.

By now your storyboard should look similar to the one in Figure 13-14.

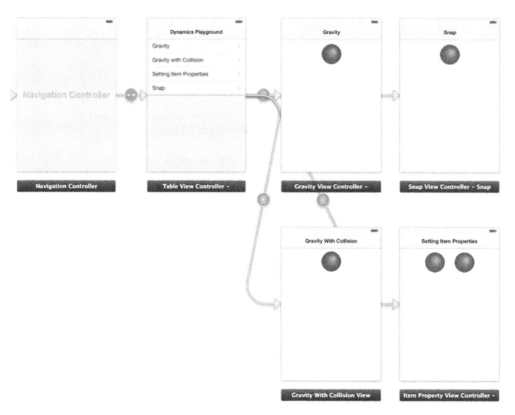

Figure 13-14. The full storyboard with the snap view controller added

Next, you will need to add a tap gesture recognizer, a property that recognizes a touch event, to the snap view controller. Do this by dragging a Tap Gesture Recognizer from the object library onto the new view controller in the storyboard. When you have done this correctly, you should see a gesture recognizer icon show up at the bottom of the view controller, as shown in Figure 13-15.

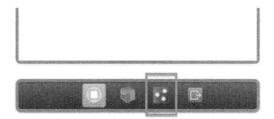

Figure 13-15. *Icon indicating added gesture recognizer*

Now you will need to make an action for the newly added gesture recognizer. To do this, Control-drag from the gesture icon shown in Figure 13-15 to the SnapViewController.h file shown in Figure 13-16. You can give this action a name of handleGestureRecognizer. Make sure you choose the type of action as UITapGestureRecognizer instead of id.

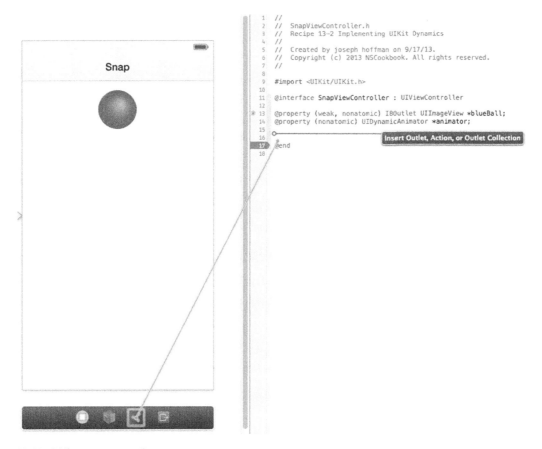

Figure 13-16. *Adding a gesture action*

Now your complete SnapViewController.h file should have two properties and a gesture action, as shown in Listing 13-19.

Listing 13-19. The Complete SnapViewController.h File

```
//
//  SnapViewController.h
//  Recipe 13-2 Implementing UIKit Dynamics
//

#import <UIKit/UIKit.h>

@interface SnapViewController : UIViewController

@property (weak, nonatomic) IBOutlet UIImageView *blueBall;
@property (nonatomic) UIDynamicAnimator *animator;

- (IBAction)handleGestureRecognizer:(UITapGestureRecognizer *)sender;

@end
```

Next, you will need to allocate and initialize the animator in the viewDidLoad method, as shown in Listing 13-20.

Listing 13-20. Initializing the Animator

```
- (void)viewDidLoad
{
    [super viewDidLoad];

    self.animator = [[UIDynamicAnimator alloc] initWithReferenceView:self.view];
}
```

Finally, you need to fill in the handleGestureRecognizer action method so that it creates the snap behavior when the user touches the screen. Listing 13-21 shows the implementation of this method.

Listing 13-21. Implementation of the handleGestureRecognizer: Action Method

```
- (IBAction)handleGestureRecognizer:(UITapGestureRecognizer *)sender
{
    CGPoint point = [sender locationInView:self.view];

    if([self.animator behaviors])
    {
        [self.animator removeAllBehaviors];

        UISnapBehavior* snapBehavior = [[UISnapBehavior alloc] initWithItem:self.blueBall
snapToPoint:point];
        [self.animator addBehavior:snapBehavior];

    }
```

```
    else
    {
        UISnapBehavior* snapBehavior = [[UISnapBehavior alloc] initWithItem:self.blueBall
snapToPoint:point];
        [self.animator addBehavior:snapBehavior];
    }
}
```

In Listing 13-21, you first set a CGPoint variable, which is a primitive data type that contains a screen coordinate. You set the CGPoint to the point in the view where the user touched. Then you check to see whether the animator already has a behavior. If there are behaviors, you remove them and add the new behavior. If this is the first touch, you just add the new behavior.

If you run the application and navigate to the snap view controller, you can touch anywhere in the view, and you will see the ball shoot over to where you touched. The behavior also adds a nice circle effect as the ball settles to the point.

Creating Push Behaviors

For this next view controller, you will be implementing both a continuous push behavior and an instantaneous push behavior. The continuous push will apply a magnitude to the view for the duration of the push. If you know anything about physics, this means it will accelerate because you are continuously adding more energy to the view. You can think of it like a car accelerating: the wheels are continuously pushing the car, so it accelerates. An instantaneous push, on the other hand, is more like velocity. This is similar to a pool cue hitting a cue ball. Once the ball has been hit by the cue, the ball will not speed up or slow down (much).

In this example, we will demonstrate these behaviors by applying each one of them to a separate ball image. As you will see, one ball will move along at a constant pace, while the other one will gradually pick up speed. Before we delve into the code, we'll provide brief explanations of the behavior properties.

Push behaviors need two properties in order to work:

- Magnitude: This is a float value defined by Apple as the "magnitude of the force vector for the push behavior." The default magnitude is nil, which means the object won't go anywhere. A magnitude of 1.0 will move a 100-point x 100-point view with a density of 1.0 at an acceleration of 100 points/second^2. So, after the first second, the view will have traveled 100 points; after the second, it will have traveled 300 points, and so on.

- Angle: This is a float value in radians. A positive value is clockwise, and a negative value is counterclockwise.

Now that you have a little background, follow these steps to get started:

1. Create a new view controller and tie it to the table view.

2. Create a new class titled PushViewController and connect it to the view controller.

3. Change the title of table view cell and the view controller to "Push." Create a new table view cell if needed.

4. Create a push selection segue between the table view cell and the view controller.

5. Add two 64-point x 64-point image views to the view controller with the image Ball.png, as shown in Figure 13-17.

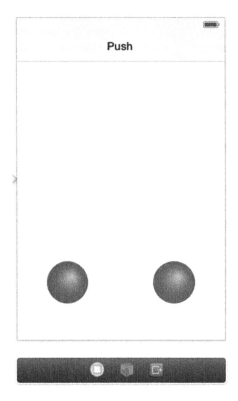

Figure 13-17. Push view controller layout

6. Add two outlets for the balls titled "ball1" and "ball2."

7. Add an animator property to the header file.

Once you are finished with these steps, your header file should look like Listing 13-22.

Listing 13-22. The Complete PushViewController.h File

```
//
//  PushViewController.h
//  Recipe 13-2 Implementing UIKit Dynamics
//
#import <UIKit/UIKit.h>

@interface PushViewController : UIViewController

@property (weak, nonatomic) IBOutlet UIImageView *ball1;
@property (weak, nonatomic) IBOutlet UIImageView *ball2;
@property (nonatomic) UIDynamicAnimator *animator;

@end
```

Now you will add the code to the viewDidLoad method to actually create the push behaviors.
Listing 13-23 shows the completed viewDidLoad method. In this code, you first create two types
of behaviors, one behavior for each ball. You set the angle and magnitude for each behavior. The
angle is negative because you want the balls to go upward, or 90 degrees in the counterclockwise
direction. Lastly, you add the behaviors to the animator.

Listing 13-23. The Complete viewDidLoad Method

```
- (void)viewDidLoad
{
    [super viewDidLoad];

    self.animator = [[UIDynamicAnimator alloc] initWithReferenceView:self.view];

    UIPushBehavior *instantPushBehavior = [[UIPushBehavior alloc] initWithItems:@[self.ball1]
mode:UIPushBehaviorModeInstantaneous];
    UIPushBehavior *continuousPushBehavior = [[UIPushBehavior alloc] initWithItems:@[self.ball2]
mode:UIPushBehaviorModeContinuous];

    instantPushBehavior.angle = -1.57;
    continuousPushBehavior.angle = -1.57;

    instantPushBehavior.magnitude = 0.5;
    continuousPushBehavior.magnitude = 0.5;

    [self.animator addBehavior:instantPushBehavior];
    [self.animator addBehavior:continuousPushBehavior];

}
```

Now if you build and select the Push from the table view, you will see the two balls take off at the same time. The left ball will have more velocity but will not speed up or slow down. The right ball will start off slow but quickly gain speed.

> **Note**   You might be wondering at this point how the ball can be accelerating without any density. By default, dynamic items all have a density of 1.

Spring and Attachment

The last pieces of the dynamics puzzle are springs and attachments. Using the attachment, you can attach two views with either a ridged attachment or a spring-like attachment. UIKit Dynamics gives us the power to choose anchor points to both arbitrary points or on the views themselves. Depending on how you attach these views, you can make some really cool effects using spring behavior.

For this section, you will attach a ball to an anchor point and then attach a star to the ball. The star will have an attachment a little left of center, which will cause the star to spin. The attachments will use the spring behavior, so they will bounce around. For added effect, you will also implement gravity and collision behaviors.

Once again, follow these steps to set up a new view controller:

1. Drag a new view controller onto the storyboard and connect it to a new table view cell.

2. Give the new view controller and table view cell a title of "Spring Attachment."

3. Create a push selection segue between the table view cell and the view controller.

4. Add a class titled `SpringAttachmentViewController` and connect it to the view controller.

5. Arrange the new view controller, as shown in Figure 13-18, with two 64-point x 64-point image views and set their images to `Ball.png` and `Star.png`. You can obtain the star from the Apress download page for this book.

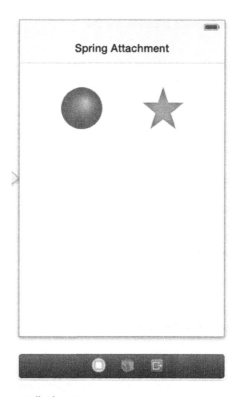

Figure 13-18. *Spring attachment view controller layout*

6.   Add outlets for the image views and name them "ball" and "star," respectively.

7.   Create an animator property.

The finished header file should look like Listing 13-24.

Listing 13-24. *The Complete SpringAttachmentViewController.h File*

```
//
//  SpringAttachmentViewController.h
//  Recipe 13-2 Implementing UIKit Dynamics
//
#import <UIKit/UIKit.h>

@interface SpringAttachmentViewController : UIViewController

@property (weak, nonatomic) IBOutlet UIImageView *ball;
@property (weak, nonatomic) IBOutlet UIImageView *star;
@property (nonatomic) UIDynamicAnimator *animator;
@end
```

First, you need to initialize the animator and add the gravity and collision behavior to it in the viewDidLoad method, as shown in Listing 13-25.

Listing 13-25. Adding Gravity and Collision Behaviors to the Ball and Star

```
//
//  SpringAttachmentViewController.m
//  Recipe 13-2 Implementing UIKit Dynamics
//

- (void)viewDidLoad
{
    [super viewDidLoad];

    self.animator = [[UIDynamicAnimator alloc] initWithReferenceView:self.view];

    UIGravityBehavior *gravityBehavior = [[UIGravityBehavior alloc]
initWithItems:@[self.ball,self.star]];
    UICollisionBehavior *collisionBehavior = [[UICollisionBehavior alloc]
initWithItems:@[self.ball,self.star]];

    collisionBehavior.translatesReferenceBoundsIntoBoundary = YES;

    [self.animator addBehavior:collisionBehavior];
    [self.animator addBehavior:gravityBehavior];
}
```

Next, you will create an anchor point. This anchor point is in the middle of the screen and 20 points down from the top of the screen. You will also create two attachment behaviors: one for the ball and one for the star. The ball is attached directly to the anchor point. The star is attached to the ball. The star also has an attachment offset 20 points left of center. As mentioned previously, this offset attachment will add a nice spinning effect. Each attachment will have a damping property and a frequency property. This is what gives you the spring effect. Feel free to adjust the values to see how it effects the animation later. Listing 13-26 shows this added behavior.

Listing 13-26. Adding Attachments and Spring Effects to the Ball and Star

```
- (void)viewDidLoad
{
    [super viewDidLoad];

    self.animator = [[UIDynamicAnimator alloc] initWithReferenceView:self.view];

    UIGravityBehavior *gravityBehavior = [[UIGravityBehavior alloc]
initWithItems:@[self.ball,self.star]];
    UICollisionBehavior *collisionBehavior = [[UICollisionBehavior alloc]
initWithItems:@[self.ball,self.star]];

    CGPoint anchorPoint = CGPointMake(self.view.frame.size.width/2, 20);

    UIAttachmentBehavior *ballAttachmentBehavior = [[UIAttachmentBehavior alloc]
initWithItem:self.ball attachedToAnchor:anchorPoint];
```

```
    UIAttachmentBehavior *starAttachmentBehavior = [[UIAttachmentBehavior alloc]
initWithItem:self.star offsetFromCenter:UIOffsetMake(-20.0, 0) attachedToItem:self.ball
offsetFromCenter:UIOffsetZero];

    collisionBehavior.translatesReferenceBoundsIntoBoundary = YES;

    [ballAttachmentBehavior setFrequency:1.0];
    [ballAttachmentBehavior setDamping:0.65];

    [starAttachmentBehavior setFrequency:1.0];
    [starAttachmentBehavior setDamping:0.65];

    [self.animator addBehavior:ballAttachmentBehavior];
    [self.animator addBehavior:starAttachmentBehavior];
    [self.animator addBehavior:collisionBehavior];
    [self.animator addBehavior:gravityBehavior];
}
```

After building the application, you will notice that the ball and star will drop and start bouncing around as if they are attached by a spring. The star will begin to erratically spin as it dangles from the ball. The star will hang below the ball when the animation settles, as shown in Figure 13-19.

Figure 13-19. *Ball and star bouncing and spinning about*

At this point, we have covered all the new dynamics behaviors. As you can see, there is a lot of power here at your disposal. Next, we will show you how to create a custom behavior class by subclassing the UIDynamicBehavior class. This will allow you to easily add custom behaviors to objects in the same way you add built-in behaviors.

Creating a Custom Behavior Class

Before we conclude this recipe, let's briefly discuss how to create a custom behavior class. When combining behaviors, it is a good practice to create a class to encompass all of them. The new class would typically have a descriptive title such as "BouncingCollisionBehavior" or something to that effect.

As an example, you will be combining the behaviors in SpringAttachmentViewController into a class. To start, create a new subclass of UIDynamicBehavior titled BouncingSpringBehavior.

Now open the header file for the new class and create a declaration for a custom initializer. The custom initializer will take an array of dynamic view items and a string that will store the anchor coordinate. Listing 13-27 shows this method declaration.

Listing 13-27. Declaring a Custom Initializer in the BouncingSpringBehavior Class

```
//
//  BouncingSpringBehavior.h
//  Recipe 13-2 Implementing UIKit Dynamics
//

#import <UIKit/UIKit.h>

@interface BouncingSpringBehavior : UIDynamicBehavior

-(instancetype)initWithItems:(NSArray *)items withAnchorPoint:(NSString *)anchorPointString;

@end
```

Now switch to the implementation file and fill out the custom initializer, as shown in Listing 13-28. The items that were changed from the previous example are now in bold.

Listing 13-28. The initWithItems:withAnchorPoint: Initializer Implementation

```
-(instancetype)initWithItems:(NSArray *)items withAnchorPoint:(NSString *)anchorPointString
{
    if(self=[super init])
    {
        CGPoint anchorPoint = CGPointFromString(anchorPointString);

        UIGravityBehavior *gravityBehavior = [[UIGravityBehavior alloc] initWithItems:items];
        UICollisionBehavior *collisionBehavior = [[UICollisionBehavior alloc] initWithItems:items];

        UIAttachmentBehavior *item1AttachmentBehavior = [[UIAttachmentBehavior alloc]
initWithItem:[items objectAtIndex:0] attachedToAnchor:anchorPoint];
```

```
        UIAttachmentBehavior *item2AttachmentBehavior = [[UIAttachmentBehavior alloc]
initWithItem:[items objectAtIndex:1] offsetFromCenter:UIOffsetMake(-20.0, 0) attachedToItem:[items
objectAtIndex:0] offsetFromCenter:UIOffsetZero];

        collisionBehavior.translatesReferenceBoundsIntoBoundary = YES;

        [item1AttachmentBehavior setFrequency:1.0];
        [item2AttachmentBehavior setDamping:0.65];

        [item1AttachmentBehavior setFrequency:1.0];
        [item2AttachmentBehavior setDamping:0.65];

        [self addChildBehavior:gravityBehavior];
        [self addChildBehavior:collisionBehavior];
        [self addChildBehavior:item1AttachmentBehavior];
        [self addChildBehavior:item2AttachmentBehavior];

    }

    return self;
}
```

The preceding code should look familiar. The difference is now it is inside an initializer of a different class. The initializer takes a string for the anchorPoint instead of a CGPoint. This is because CGPoint is a C struct and not an Objective-C object, which makes it difficult to pass as a parameter. To get around this, you'll use a nifty function to convert a string to a CGPoint. This CGPoint will be used to define the anchor point for the ball. When we create a behavior instance, we use a function to do the opposite.

As you have seen before, you will first create behaviors for gravity, collision, and the two attachments. Because the attachments are passed in as an array, the item at index 0 and index 1 are the ball and star, respectively. As you've done before, set the collision bound property to "YES." Then set frequency and damping behaviors for the spring effect. Lastly, add child behaviors to the BouncingSpringBehavior class and return an instance of itself.

The last thing left to do is change the SpringAttachmentViewController implementation file to take advantage of the class. Make the changes shown in Listing 13-29 in this file.

Listing 13-29. Setting the Newly Created UIDynamicBehavior Class

```
//
//  SpringAttachmentViewController.m
//  Recipe 13-2 Implementing UIKit Dynamics
//

#import "SpringAttachmentViewController.h"
#import "BouncingSpringBehavior.h"

@interface SpringAttachmentViewController ()

//...
```

```objc
- (void)viewDidLoad
{
    [super viewDidLoad];

    self.animator = [[UIDynamicAnimator alloc] initWithReferenceView:self.view];

    CGPoint anchorPoint = CGPointMake(self.view.frame.size.width/2, 20);
    NSString *anchorPointString = NSStringFromCGPoint(anchorPoint);

    BouncingSpringBehavior *bouncingSpringBehavior = [[BouncingSpringBehavior alloc]
initWithItems:@[self.ball,self.star] withAnchorPoint:anchorPointString];

    [self.animator addBehavior:bouncingSpringBehavior];

}
```

You can see from Listing 13-29 that you have significantly reduced the lines of code in the view controller from what it was previously. The implementation is now much easier to read. First, you create your animator and anchor point. Next, you convert that anchor point to a string and pass it into the new instance behavior initialization. Finally, you simply add that behavior to the animator.

That's it for this recipe. Even with everything shown here, we have only scratched the surface of what's possible with UIKit Dynamics. There are many ways properties and behaviors can be combined to create unique dynamic scenes.

Summary

In this chapter, you have learned the basics of using both UIView Animation and UIKit Dynamics. You now know how to create simple animations that vary in size, opacity, and rotation. You also know how to use UIKit Dynamics to create powerful effects replicating gravity, velocity, friction, spring motion, and countless combinations. These tools will give you the power to create amazing and interactive next-generation applications.

Chapter 14

User Data Recipes

No two people are alike, and in the same way no two iOS devices are alike. The information that one device stores depends on the person who uses it. We populate our devices with our lives, including our photos, calendars, notes, contacts, and music. As developers, it is important to be able to access all of this information regardless of the device so that we can incorporate it into our applications and provide a more unique, user-specific interface. In this chapter, we cover a variety of methods for dealing with user-based data. First we focus on the calendar, and then we focus on the address book.

Recipe 14-1. Working with NSCalendar and NSDate

Many different applications are used for time-based and date-based calculations. Examples include everything from converting calendars to sorting to-do lists to telling the user how much time remains before an alarm will go off. To use the more intricate, event-based user interface, you must have a solid understanding of the simpler NSDate-focused APIs.

In this recipe, you implement a simple application to illustrate the use of the NSDate, NSCalendar, and NSDateComponents classes by converting dates from the Gregorian calendar to the Hebrew calendar. The NSDate class is used to create dates and handle date operations such as comparing two dates. The NSCalendar class is used to keep track of NSDate objects and perform computations such as determining date ranges. The NSDateComponents class is used to pull out components of a date such as hours, minutes, and so on.

To begin, create a new single view application project. Switch to the Main.storyboard file and build a user interface that resembles Figure 14-1. Use the following components to create the interface:

- *Labels*: Month, Day, Year, Gregorian, Hebrew
- *Buttons*: To Hebrew, To Gregorian
- *Six text fields*: All with a placeholder value of 0

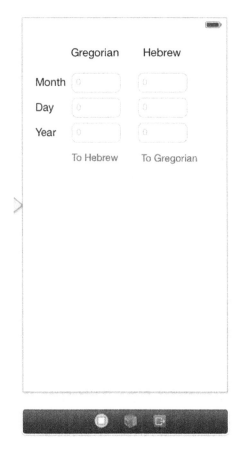

Figure 14-1. User interface for calendar conversion

You need to set up properties to represent each UITextField. The text fields will display conversions as well as take inputs. Create the following outlets:

- gMonthTextField
- gDayTextField
- gYearTextField
- hMonthTextField
- hDayTextField
- hYearTextField

Note   The *G* and *H* in these property names refer to whether the given UITextField is on the Gregorian or Hebrew side of the application.

You do not need outlets for the buttons, but create the following actions for when the user taps them:

- convertToHebrew

- convertToGregorian

To control the UITextFields programmatically, you need to make your view controller the delegate for them. First, add <UITextFieldDelegate> to your controller's header line so that it now looks like Listing 14-1.

Listing 14-1. The Complete ViewController.h File

```objc
//
//  ViewController.h
//  Recipe 14-1 Working With NSCalendar and NSDate
//

#import <UIKit/UIKit.h>

@interface ViewController : UIViewController<UITextFieldDelegate>

@property (weak, nonatomic) IBOutlet UITextField *gMonthTextField;
@property (weak, nonatomic) IBOutlet UITextField *gDayTextField;
@property (weak, nonatomic) IBOutlet UITextField *gYearTextField;
@property (weak, nonatomic) IBOutlet UITextField *hMonthTextField;
@property (weak, nonatomic) IBOutlet UITextField *hDayTextField;
@property (weak, nonatomic) IBOutlet UITextField *hYearTextField;

- (IBAction)convertToHebrew:(id)sender;
- (IBAction)convertToGregorian:(id)sender;

@end
```

Next, set all the UITextField delegates to your view controller by adding the code in Listing 14-2 to the viewDidLoad method of the implementation file.

Listing 14-2. Setting UITextField Delegates

```objc
- (void)viewDidLoad
{
    [super viewDidLoad];

    self.gMonthTextField.delegate = self;
    self.gDayTextField.delegate = self;
    self.gYearTextField.delegate = self;
    self.hMonthTextField.delegate = self;
    self.hDayTextField.delegate = self;
    self.hYearTextField.delegate = self;
}
```

Next, define the UITextFieldDelegate method textFieldShouldReturn: to properly dismiss the keyboard, as shown in Listing 14-3.

Listing 14-3. Implementation of the textFieldShouldReturn: Delegate Method

```
-(BOOL)textFieldShouldReturn:(UITextField *)textField
{
    [textField resignFirstResponder];
    return NO;
}
```

We briefly discussed the NSCalendar class earlier, but in this example this class is essentially used to set a standard for the dates you will later refer to. The NSCalendar method also allows you to perform several useful functions dealing with a calendar, such as changing which day that a week starts on or changing the time zone used. The NSCalendar class also acts as a bridge between the NSDate and NSDateComponents classes that you will see later.

You use two instances of the NSCalendar class to translate dates between the Gregorian calendar and the Hebrew calendar. Add these properties to your ViewController.h class:

```
@property (nonatomic, strong) NSCalendar *gregorianCalendar;
@property (nonatomic, strong) NSCalendar *hebrewCalendar;
```

Use lazy initialization for these properties. Lazy initialization basically allows us to forego initialization until these properties are needed. Add the custom getter implementations, as shown in Listing 14-4.

Listing 14-4. Creating Custom Getter Implementations for gregorianCalendar and hebrewCalendar Properties

```
-(NSCalendar *)gregorianCalendar
{
    if (!_gregorianCalendar)
    {
        _gregorianCalendar =
            [[NSCalendar alloc] initWithCalendarIdentifier:NSGregorianCalendar];
    }
    return _gregorianCalendar;
}

-(NSCalendar *)hebrewCalendar
{
    if (!_hebrewCalendar)
    {
        _hebrewCalendar =
            [[NSCalendar alloc] initWithCalendarIdentifier:NSHebrewCalendar];
    }
    return _hebrewCalendar;
}
```

These method overrides are necessary to make sure your calendars are initialized with their correct calendar types. Alternatively, you could simply initialize your calendars in the viewDidLoad method to be created when the app launches.

> **Note**   There are a large variety of different calendar types available for use with the NSCalendar class, including NSBuddhistCalendar, NSIslamicCalendar, and NSJapaneseCalendar.
>
> Given the immense multicultural nature of today's technological world, you might find it quite necessary to make use of some of these calendars! Consult the Apple documentation for a full list of possible calendar types.

Now that your setup is done, you can implement your conversion method, starting with the conversion from Gregorian to Hebrew, as shown in Listing 14-5.

Listing 14-5. Implementing the convertToGregorian: Method

```
- (IBAction)convertToGregorian:(id)sender
{
    NSDateComponents *hComponents = [[NSDateComponents alloc] init];
    [hComponents setDay:[self.hDayTextField.text integerValue]];
    [hComponents setMonth:[self.hMonthTextField.text integerValue]];
    [hComponents setYear:[self.hYearTextField.text integerValue]];

    NSDate *hebrewDate = [self.hebrewCalendar dateFromComponents:hComponents];

    NSUInteger unitFlags =
        NSDayCalendarUnit | NSMonthCalendarUnit | NSYearCalendarUnit;

    NSDateComponents *hebrewDateComponents =
        [self.gregorianCalendar components:unitFlags fromDate:hebrewDate];

    self.gDayTextField.text =
        [[NSNumber numberWithInteger:hebrewDateComponents.day] stringValue];
    self.gMonthTextField.text =
        [[NSNumber numberWithInteger:hebrewDateComponents.month] stringValue];
    self.gYearTextField.text =
        [[NSNumber numberWithInteger:hebrewDateComponents.year] stringValue];
}
```

As you can see from Listing 14-5, you are using a combination of NSDateComponents, NSDate, and NSCalendar to perform this conversion.

The NSDateComponents class, as mentioned earlier, is used to define the details that make up an NSDate, such as the day, month, year, time, and so on. Here, only the month, day, and year are being used.

As mentioned earlier, you use an instance of the NSCalendar to create an instance of NSDate out of the components you have defined.

One of the more confusing parts of the preceding method might be the use of the NSUInteger unitFlags, which is formatted quite unusually. Whenever you specify creating an instance of NSDateComponents out of an NSDate, you need to specify exactly which components to include from the date. You can specify these flags, called NSCalendarUnits, through the use of the NSUInteger, as shown.

Other types of NSCalendarUnits include the following, among many others:

- NSSecondCalendarUnit

- NSWeekOfYearCalendarUnit

- NSEraCalendarUnit

- NSTimeZoneCalendarUnit

As you can see, the specificity with which you can create instances of NSDate is highly customizable, allowing you to perform unique calculations and comparisons. For a full list of NSCalendarUnit values, refer to the NSCalendar class reference in Apple's developer API.

Because the values of NSDateComponents are of type NSInteger, you must first convert them to instances of NSNumber and then take their stringValue before you set them into your text fields.

Once you have defined your conversion from one calendar to the other, the reverse is simple, as you just need to change which text fields and calendar you use, as shown in Listing 14-6.

Listing 14-6. Implementing the convertToHebrew: Method

```
- (IBAction)convertToHebrew:(id)sender
{
    NSDateComponents *gComponents = [[NSDateComponents alloc] init];
    [gComponents setDay:[self.gDayTextField.text integerValue]];
    [gComponents setMonth:[self.gMonthTextField.text integerValue]];
    [gComponents setYear:[self.gYearTextField.text integerValue]];

    NSDate *gregorianDate = [self.gregorianCalendar dateFromComponents:gComponents];

    NSUInteger unitFlags =
        NSDayCalendarUnit | NSMonthCalendarUnit | NSYearCalendarUnit;

    NSDateComponents *hebrewDateComponents =
        [self.hebrewCalendar components:unitFlags fromDate:gregorianDate];

    self.hDayTextField.text =
        [[NSNumber numberWithInteger:hebrewDateComponents.day] stringValue];
    self.hMonthTextField.text =
        [[NSNumber numberWithInteger:hebrewDateComponents.month] stringValue];
    self.hYearTextField.text =
        [[NSNumber numberWithInteger:hebrewDateComponents.year] stringValue];
}
```

Your application can now correctly convert instances of NSDate between calendars, as shown in Figure 14-2. Try experimenting with different dates or even different calendars to see what kinds of powerful date conversions you can do.

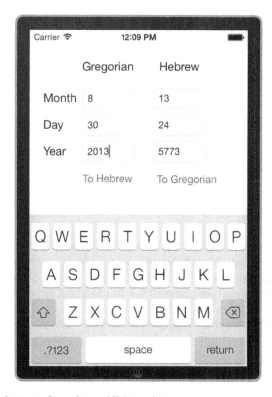

Figure 14-2. *An app that converts between Gregorian and Hebrew dates*

Recipe 14-2. Fetching Calendar Events

Now that we have covered how to deal with basic date conversions and calculations, we can go into details on dealing with events and calendars and interacting with the user's own events and schedule. The next few recipes combine to create a complete utilization of the Event Kit framework, which makes classes available for manipulating events and reminders.

First, create a new single view application project with the name "My Events App" or something similar. We'll be using this for the next few recipes. This time you use the Event Kit framework, so link EventKit.framework to your newly created project.

Because this app will access the device's calendars, you should provide a usage description in the project's Info.plist file. Add the "Privacy – Calendars Usage Description" key to the Information Property List and enter the text "Testing Calendar Events", as Figure 14-3 shows.

Key	Type	Value
▼ Information Property List	Dictionary	(15 items)
Privacy – Calendars Usage Descri...	String	Testing Calendar Events
Localization native development r...	String	en
Bundle display name	String	${PRODUCT_NAME}
Executable file	String	${EXECUTABLE_NAME}
Bundle identifier	String	NSCookbook.${PRODUCT_NAME:rfc1034identifier}
InfoDictionary version	String	6.0
Bundle name	String	${PRODUCT_NAME}
Bundle OS Type code	String	APPL
Bundle versions string, short	String	1.0
Bundle creator OS Type code	String	????
Bundle version	String	1.0
Application requires iPhone envir...	Boolean	YES

Figure 14-3. An app providing a calendar usage description in the Information Property List

Whenever you're dealing with the Event Kit framework, the main element you work with is an EKEventStore. This class allows you to access, delete, and save events in your calendars. An EKEventStore takes a relatively long time to initialize, so you should do it only once and store it in a property. Add the declarations shown in Listing 14-7 to the ViewController.h file.

Listing 14-7. Importing the Event Kit Framework and Adding an EKEventStore Property

```
//
//  ViewController.h
//  My Events App
//

#import <UIKit/UIKit.h>
#import <EventKit/EventKit.h>

@interface ViewController : UIViewController

@property (strong, nonatomic) EKEventStore *eventStore;

@end
```

The implementation for this first recipe is a simple logging of all calendar events within 48 hours from now. You're not going to build a user interface at this point; instead, all the relevant code will reside in the viewDidLoad method. We'll go through the steps first and then show you the complete implementation.

The first thing you need to do when you want to access the device's calendar entries is to ask the user for permission to do so. Do this using the requestAccessToEntityType:completion: method of EKEventStore, passing a code block that will be invoked when the asynchronous process is done (Listing 14-8).

Listing 14-8. Requesting Permission to Access Calendar Entries in the viewDidLoad Method

```
self.eventStore = [[EKEventStore alloc] init];

[self.eventStore requestAccessToEntityType:EKEntityTypeEvent
completion:^(BOOL granted, NSError *error)
```

```
{
    if (granted)
    {
        //...
    }
    else
    {
        NSLog(@"Access not granted: %@", error);
    }
}];
```

If access was indeed granted, you can go ahead and retrieve the information you want. In this case, you'll fetch all the calendar events from the current time and 48 hours from then. First create the two dates, as shown in Listing 14-9.

Listing 14-9. Creating Two Calendar Dates for the Current Time and Current Time + 48 Hours

```
NSDate *now = [NSDate date];

NSCalendar *calendar = [NSCalendar currentCalendar];
NSDateComponents *fortyEightHoursFromNowComponents = [[NSDateComponents alloc] init];
fortyEightHoursFromNowComponents.day = 2; // 48 hours forward
NSDate *fortyEightHoursFromNow =
    [calendar dateByAddingComponents:fortyEightHoursFromNowComponents toDate:now
        options:0];
```

> **Note**   As you can see, you use `NSCalendar` to help create the future date. This ensures a more accurate time than if you use `NSDate`'s method `dateWithTimeIntervalSinceNow:`. The reason it's more accurate is that `NSCalendar` takes into account the fact that not all days in a year are exactly 24 hours long. Although the difference in this case is insignificant, it's considered good practice to use the `dateByAddingComponents:toDate:` method to construct relative dates.

Now that you have the start date and the end date, you can create a search predicate for finding the events within that interval by using the `predicateForEventsWithStartDate:endDate:calendars:` method on the event store. By passing a value of `nil` to the `calendars` parameter of this method, you specify that you want your predicate to be applied to all calendars, as shown in Listing 14-10.

Listing 14-10. Creating an NSPredicate

```
NSPredicate *allEventsWithin48HoursPredicate =
    [self.eventStore predicateForEventsWithStartDate:now endDate:fortyEightHoursFromNow
        calendars:nil];
```

You then use the predicate to retrieve the actual events from the event store, as shown in Listing 14-11.

Listing 14-11. Retrieving Events from the Event Store

```
NSArray *events =
    [self.eventStore eventsMatchingPredicate:allEventsWithin48HoursPredicate];
```

Finally, you'll just iterate over the retrieved events and print their titles to the debug log, as shown in Listing 14-12.

Listing 14-12. Printing Event Titles

```
for (EKEvent *event in events)
{
    NSLog(@"%@", event.title);
}
```

Listing 14-13 shows the complete implementation of the viewDidLoad method.

Listing 14-13. The Complete viewDidLoad Implementation

```
- (void)viewDidLoad
{
    [super viewDidLoad];

    self.eventStore = [[EKEventStore alloc] init];

    [self.eventStore requestAccessToEntityType:EKEntityTypeEvent
     completion:^(BOOL granted, NSError *error)
     {
         if (granted)
         {
             NSDate *now = [NSDate date];

             NSCalendar *calendar = [NSCalendar currentCalendar];
             NSDateComponents *fortyEightHoursFromNowComponents =
                 [[NSDateComponents alloc] init];
             fortyEightHoursFromNowComponents.day = 2; // 48 hours forward
             NSDate *fortyEightHoursFromNow =
                 [calendar dateByAddingComponents:fortyEightHoursFromNowComponents
                     toDate:now options:0];

             NSPredicate *allEventsWithin48HoursPredicate =
                 [self.eventStore predicateForEventsWithStartDate:now
                     endDate:fortyEightHoursFromNow calendars:nil];
             NSArray *events = [self.eventStore
                 eventsMatchingPredicate:allEventsWithin48HoursPredicate];
             for (EKEvent *event in events)
             {
                 NSLog(@"%@", event.title);
             }
         }
     }
```

```
        else
        {
            NSLog(@"Access not granted: %@", error);
        }
    }];
}
```

Because the iOS simulator doesn't have calendar support, you need to test your app on a real device. Make sure the device has events scheduled to serve as your test data. Because the only output you are creating here is in the log, you also need to run the application from Xcode so as to capture the output. See Figure 14-4 for an example of such output.

```
2013-08-30 12:27:08.775 14-2 Fetching Calendar Events[2129:1803] Eat lunch
2013-08-30 12:27:08.776 14-2 Fetching Calendar Events[2129:1803] Go to the gym
2013-08-30 12:27:08.778 14-2 Fetching Calendar Events[2129:1803] Drink protein
2013-08-30 12:27:08.779 14-2 Fetching Calendar Events[2129:1803] Continue updating this book
2013-08-30 12:27:08.780 14-2 Fetching Calendar Events[2129:1803] Drink a homebrew
```

All Output ⬍   🗑 ▮ ▯

Figure 14-4. Output log for the application, showing the names of nearby events

The first time you run this app, you'll get an alert asking if your app should be allowed to access your calendar (see Figure 14-5). This is part of a privacy policy implemented in iOS 7. Because the calendar can contain private information that might be sensitive, apps must ask the user's explicit permission before accessing it.

Figure 14-5. An alert asking for the user's permission to access the calendar

The user is asked only once to grant an app access to the calendar. iOS remembers the user's answer on subsequent runs. If the user wants to change the current access setting, they can do that in the Settings app, under Privacy ➤ Calendars (see Figure 14-6).

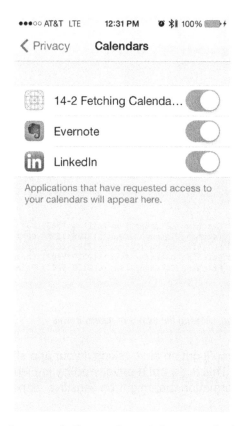

Figure 14-6. *The privacy settings showing an app that's currently granted access to the device's calendar*

Tip   Sometimes as a developer of these restricted features, you will want to reset the privacy settings to test the initial run scenario again. You can reset these settings in the Settings app, under General ➤ Reset using the Reset Location & Privacy option.

Recipe 14-3. Displaying Events in a Table View

Now that you can access your events, continue by creating a better interface with which to deal with them. In this recipe, you implement a grouped UITableView to display your events.

Start by turning the project into a navigation-based application. This will require a little bit of storyboarding. While we will try to explain all the steps well, it might be beneficial to read about storyboards in Chapter 2 before proceeding.

To begin, switch to the Main.storyboard file and select the view in the storyboard. With the view selected, choose Editor ➤ Embed In ➤ Navigation Controller from the main menu. Once this is done, a navigation controller will be created on the storyboard. You might want to drag the navigation controller off the view controller and arrange the two views, as shown in Figure 14-7.

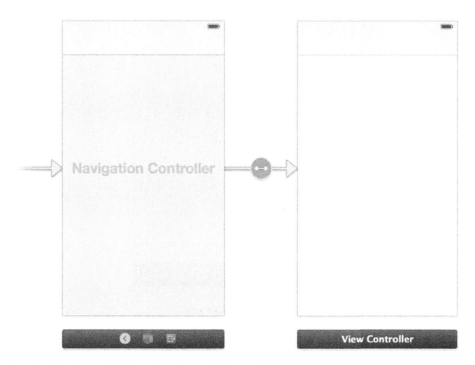

Figure 14-7. Arranging the view controller next to the navigation controller

Next, set up the user interface consisting of a UITableView. Select the View Controller from the Main.storyboard file in the project navigator.

Now you can add the table view from the object library and make it fill the available area. This will exclude the navigation bar. In the attributes inspector for the table view, make sure the Style attribute is set to Grouped. Your main view should now resemble Figure 14-8.

Figure 14-8. A user interface with a navigation bar and a grouped table view

Next, create an outlet for your UITableView. Name the outlet eventsTableView.

Before you switch to your implementation file, you will need to make some additional changes to the header file. First, add the UITableViewDelegate and UITableViewDataSource protocols to the class. Also define two new properties: an NSArray, which is used to hold references to all the calendars in the EKEventStore, and an NSMutableDictionary, which is used to store all your events based on which calendar they belong to. The ViewController.h file should now resemble the code in Listing 14-14.

Listing 14-14. The Complete ViewController.h File

```
//
//  ViewController.h
//  My Events App
//

#import <UIKit/UIKit.h>
#import <EventKit/EventKit.h>

@interface ViewController : UIViewController<UITableViewDelegate, UITableViewDataSource>
```

```
@property (strong, nonatomic) EKEventStore *eventStore;
@property (weak, nonatomic) IBOutlet UITableView *eventsTableView;
@property (nonatomic, strong) NSMutableDictionary *events;
@property (nonatomic, strong) NSArray *calendars;
```

@end

The next task you need to perform is to modify the viewDidLoad method. Specifically, you need to take these actions:

1. Set the title displayed in the navigation bar.

2. Add a Refresh button to the navigation bar.

3. Set up the table view's two delegate methods.

4. Populate the calendars array and the events dictionary.

To accomplish these things, make the changes shown in Listing 14-15 to the viewDidLoad method.

Listing 14-15. Modifying the viewDidLoad Method to Include a Bar Button Item and Set Delegates

```
- (void)viewDidLoad
{
    [super viewDidLoad];

    self.title = @"Events";

    UIBarButtonItem *refreshButton = [[UIBarButtonItem alloc]
        initWithBarButtonSystemItem:UIBarButtonSystemItemRefresh target:self
        action:@selector(refresh:)];
    self.navigationItem.leftBarButtonItem = refreshButton;

    self.eventsTableView.delegate = self;
    self.eventsTableView.dataSource = self;

    self.eventStore = [[EKEventStore alloc] init];

    [self.eventStore requestAccessToEntityType:EKEntityTypeEvent
     completion:^(BOOL granted, NSError *error)
     {
         if (granted)
         {
             self.calendars =
                 [self.eventStore calendarsForEntityType:EKEntityTypeEvent];
             [self fetchEvents];
         }
         else
         {
             NSLog(@"Access not granted: %@", error);
         }
     }];
}
```

The code in Listing 14-15 uses two methods that you haven't implemented yet. The first is the `refresh:` action method that will be invoked when the user taps the Refresh button on the navigation bar. Add the code in Listing 14-16 to the view controller class.

Listing 14-16. Implementing the refresh: Method

```
- (void)refresh:(id)sender
{
    [self fetchEvents];
    [self.eventsTableView reloadData];
}
```

The second unimplemented method is `fetchEvent`, which contains the code to actually query the `eventStore` for the events. Because you sort your events by the calendar they belong to, you perform a different query for each calendar, rather than just one for all events. This code is implemented in Listing 14-17.

Listing 14-17. Implementing the fetchEvents: Method

```
- (void)fetchEvents
{
    self.events = [[NSMutableDictionary alloc] initWithCapacity:[self.calendars count]];

    NSDate *now = [NSDate date];

    NSCalendar *calendar = [NSCalendar currentCalendar];
    NSDateComponents *fortyEightHoursFromNowComponents =
        [[NSDateComponents alloc] init];
    fortyEightHoursFromNowComponents.day = 2; // 48 hours forward
    NSDate *fortyEightHoursFromNow =
        [calendar dateByAddingComponents:fortyEightHoursFromNowComponents toDate:now
            options:0];

    for (EKCalendar *calendar in self.calendars)
    {
        NSPredicate *allEventsWithin48HoursPredicate =
            [self.eventStore predicateForEventsWithStartDate:now
                endDate:fortyEightHoursFromNow calendars:@[calendar]];
        NSArray *eventsInThisCalendar =
            [self.eventStore eventsMatchingPredicate:allEventsWithin48HoursPredicate];
        if (eventsInThisCalendar != nil)
        {
            [self.events setObject:eventsInThisCalendar forKey:calendar.title];
        }
    }

    dispatch_async(dispatch_get_main_queue(),^{
        [self.eventsTableView reloadData];
    });
}
```

You should recognize most of the preceding code from Recipe 14-2. The main difference is that you now perform a search for each calendar and store the results in the events dictionary using the respective calendar names as keys.

Also, when all the fetching is done, you're notifying the table view that its data has changed. However, because the fetchEvents method is invoked on an arbitrary thread and any user interface–related code must be run on the main thread, you need to dispatch that particular piece of code to make it run in the main thread.

With the data model in place, you can move your attention to the table view and its implementation. But before you do that, you'll add a few helper methods. These methods are quite small and simple in nature, but they help make the code you'll add in a minute easier to read. So, add the code in Listing 14-18 to the ViewController.m file.

Listing 14-18. Implementing Helper Methods in the ViewController.m File

```objc
- (EKCalendar *)calendarAtSection:(NSInteger)section
{
    return [self.calendars objectAtIndex:section];
}

- (EKEvent *)eventAtIndexPath:(NSIndexPath *)indexPath
{
    EKCalendar *calendar = [self calendarAtSection:indexPath.section];
    NSArray *calendarEvents = [self eventsForCalendar:calendar];
    return [calendarEvents objectAtIndex:indexPath.row];
}

- (NSArray *)eventsForCalendar:(EKCalendar *)calendar
{
    return [self.events objectForKey:calendar.title];
}
```

Now, implement a method to specify the number of sections it should display. You have one section per calendar, so this method is nice and easy (Listing 14-19).

Listing 14-19. Implementing the numberOfSectionsInTableView: Delegate Method

```objc
-(NSInteger)numberOfSectionsInTableView:(UITableView *)tableView
{
    return [self.calendars count];
}
```

You can also implement a method to specify your section titles, as shown in Listing 14-20.

Listing 14-20. Implementing the tableView:titleForHeaderInSection: Delegate Method

```
-(NSString *)tableView:(UITableView *)tableView titleForHeaderInSection:(NSInteger)section
{
    return [self calendarAtSection:section].title;
}
```

You also need to implement a method to determine the number of rows in each group, as given by the count of the array returned by your dictionary for a given section. Listing 14-21 shows this.

Listing 14-21. Implementing the tableView:numberOfRowsInSection: Delegate Method

```
-(NSInteger)tableView:(UITableView *)tableView numberOfRowsInSection:(NSInteger)section
{
    EKCalendar *calendar = [self calendarAtSection:section];
    return [self eventsForCalendar:calendar].count;
}
```

Finally, add the method that defines how your table's cells are created, as shown in Listing 14-22.

Listing 14-22. Implementing the tableView:cellForRowAtindexPath: Delegate Method

```
- (UITableViewCell *)tableView:(UITableView *)tableView cellForRowAtIndexPath:(NSIndexPath *)
indexPath
{
    static NSString *CellIdentifier = @"Cell";

    UITableViewCell *cell =
        [tableView dequeueReusableCellWithIdentifier:CellIdentifier];
    if (cell == nil)
    {
        cell = [[UITableViewCell alloc] initWithStyle:UITableViewCellStyleValue1
            reuseIdentifier:CellIdentifier];
    }

    cell.accessoryType = UITableViewCellAccessoryDetailDisclosureButton;
    cell.textLabel.backgroundColor = [UIColor clearColor];
    cell.textLabel.font = [UIFont systemFontOfSize:19.0];

    cell.textLabel.text = [self eventAtIndexPath:indexPath].title;

    return cell;
}
```

As Figure 14-9 shows, your application can now display all calendar events that occur within 48 hours.

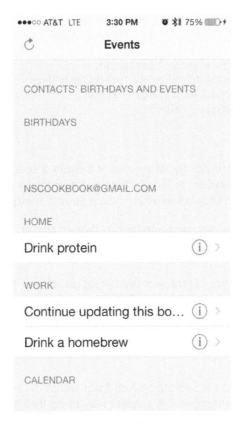

Figure 14-9. A simple app that displays calendar events within two days from now

Recipe 14-4. Viewing, Editing, and Deleting Events

The next step is to allow the user to view, edit, and delete events through predefined classes in the Event Kit UI framework.

You'll continue adding to the same project that you've been using since Recipe 14-2. This time you will use a couple of predefined user interfaces for viewing and editing calendar events. Specifically, you'll be utilizing the EKEventViewController and EKEventViewEditController classes. These are part of the Event Kit UI framework, so add EventKitUI.framework to the project.

You also need to import its API into the main view controller's header file, as shown in Listing 14-23.

Listing 14-23. Adding an Import Statement for the EventKitUI Framework to the ViewController.h File

```
//
//  ViewController.h
//  Calendar Events
//

#import <UIKit/UIKit.h>
#import <EventKit/EventKit.h>
#import <EventKitUI/EventKitUI.h>
```

```
@interface ViewController : UIViewController<UITableViewDelegate,
                                             UITableViewDataSource>

@property (strong, nonatomic) EKEventStore *eventStore;
@property (weak, nonatomic) IBOutlet UITableView *eventsTableView;
@property (nonatomic, strong) NSMutableDictionary *events;
@property (nonatomic, strong) NSArray *calendars;

@end
```

The next task is to implement behavior for when a user selects a specific row in your table view. You use an instance of the EKEventViewController to display information on the selected event. To do this, add the tableView:DidSelectRowAtIndexPath: data source method, as shown in Listing 14-24.

Listing 14-24. Implementing the tableView:didSelectRowAtIndexPath: Delegate Method

```
-(void)tableView:(UITableView *)tableView didSelectRowAtIndexPath:(NSIndexPath *)indexPath
{
    EKEventViewController *eventVC = [[EKEventViewController alloc] init];
    eventVC.event = [self eventAtIndexPath:indexPath];
    eventVC.allowsEditing = YES;
    [self.navigationController pushViewController:eventVC animated:YES];
    [tableView deselectRowAtIndexPath:indexPath animated:YES];
}
```

If the user has edited or removed the selected event from within the event view controller, you'll need to update the table view somehow. The easiest way to do this is to refresh it in the main view controller's viewWillLoad method, as shown in Listing 14-25.

Listing 14-25. Implementing the viewWillAppear Method to Refresh the Table View

```
- (void)viewWillAppear:(BOOL)animated
{
    [self refresh:self];
    [super viewWillAppear:animated];
}
```

For extra functionality, make your cell's detail disclosure buttons allow the user to proceed directly to editing mode through the use of the EKEventEditViewController. The EKEventEditViewController requires you to assign a delegate to handle its dismissal, so start by adding the EKEventEditViewDelegate protocol to the main view controller's class declaration, as shown in Listing 14-26.

Listing 14-26. Adding the EKEventEditViewDelegate to the ViewController.h File

```
//
//  ViewController.h
//  Calendar Events
//

#import <UIKit/UIKit.h>
#import <EventKit/EventKit.h>
#import <EventKitUI/EventKitUI.h>
```

```
@interface ViewController : UIViewController<UITableViewDelegate, UITableViewDataSource,
    EKEventEditViewDelegate>

@property (strong, nonatomic) EKEventStore *eventStore;
@property (weak, nonatomic) IBOutlet UITableView *eventsTableView;
@property (nonatomic, strong) NSMutableDictionary *events;
@property (nonatomic, strong) NSArray *calendars;

@end
```

Then, implement a method to handle the tapping of the disclosure buttons, as shown in Listing 14-27. As mentioned previously, this method will take you directly to editing mode.

Listing 14-27. Implementing the tableView:accessorButtonTappedForRowWithIndexpath: Delegate Method

```
-(void)tableView:(UITableView *)tableView accessoryButtonTappedForRowWithIndexPath:(NSIndexPath *)
indexPath
{
    EKEventEditViewController *eventEditVC = [[EKEventEditViewController alloc] init];
    eventEditVC.event = [self eventAtIndexPath:indexPath];
    eventEditVC.eventStore = self.eventStore;
    eventEditVC.editViewDelegate = self;
    [self presentViewController:eventEditVC animated:YES completion:nil];
}
```

Finally, implement the eventEditViewController:didCompleteWithAction: delegate method to dismiss the edit view controller, as shown in Listing 14-28.

Listing 14-28. Implementing the eventEditViewController:didCompleteWithAction: Delegate Method

```
-(void)eventEditViewController:(EKEventEditViewController *)controller
didCompleteWithAction:(EKEventEditViewAction)action
{
    [self dismissViewControllerAnimated:YES completion:nil];
}
```

Before you're done, you need to implement one last delegate method to specify the default calendar that will be used for the creation of new events. In the implementation shown in Listing 14-29, you simply return the default calendar of the device.

Listing 14-29. Implementing the eventEditViewControllerDefaultCalendarForNewEvents: Delegate Method

```
-(EKCalendar *)eventEditViewControllerDefaultCalendarForNewEvents:
(EKEventEditViewController *)controller
{
    return [self.eventStore defaultCalendarForNewEvents];
}
```

At this point, your application now allows the user to view and edit the details of an event in two different ways, through the use of either an EKEventViewController or an EKEventEditViewController. Figure 14-10 shows an example of the user interfaces of these view controllers.

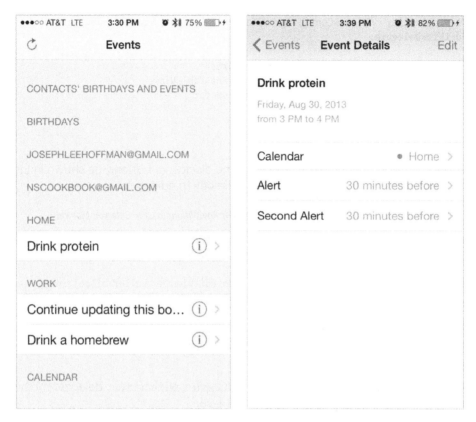

Figure 14-10. The user interfaces of an EKEventViewController and an EKEventEditViewController, respectively

Recipe 14-5. Creating Calendar Events

While it is fairly simple to allow users to create a calendar event by themselves, we, as developers, should always strive to simplify even the simple things. The less users have to do on their own, the happier they tend to be with the final product. To this end, it is important to be able to create and edit events programmatically, at the tap of a button.

Again, you'll continue adding to the project you created in Recipe 14-2. The first task is to add an Add button to the navigation bar. Go to the viewDidLoad method in ViewController.m and add the code in Listing 14-30.

Listing 14-30. Adding a UIBarButtonItem to the viewDidLoad Method

```
- (void)viewDidLoad
{
    [super viewDidLoad];

    self.title = @"Events";
```

```
UIBarButtonItem *refreshButton = [[UIBarButtonItem alloc]
    initWithBarButtonSystemItem:UIBarButtonSystemItemRefresh target:self
    action:@selector(refresh:)];
self.navigationItem.leftBarButtonItem = refreshButton;

UIBarButtonItem *addButton = [[UIBarButtonItem alloc]
    initWithBarButtonSystemItem:UIBarButtonSystemItemAdd target:self
    action:@selector(addEvent:)];
self.navigationItem.rightBarButtonItem = addButton;

// ...

}
```

When the user taps the Add button, the app will create a new event in the device's default calendar. To make things simple in this recipe, you ask the user to enter a title for the event using an alert view. To implement that, start by adding the UIAlertViewDelegate protocol to the main view controller's header declaration, as shown in Listing 14-31.

Listing 14-31. Declaring the UIAlertViewDelegate

```
@interface ViewController : UIViewController<UITableViewDelegate, UITableViewDataSource,
    EKEventEditViewDelegate, UIAlertViewDelegate>
```

Then add the action method that presents the alert view, as shown in Listing 14-32.

Listing 14-32. Implementing the addEvent: Action Method

```
- (void)addEvent:(id)sender
{
    UIAlertView * inputAlert = [[UIAlertView alloc] initWithTitle:@"New Event"
        message:@"Enter a title for the event" delegate:self cancelButtonTitle:@"Cancel"
        otherButtonTitles:@"OK", nil];
    inputAlert.alertViewStyle = UIAlertViewStylePlainTextInput;
    [inputAlert show];
}
```

Finally, add the delegate method that will be invoked when the user has tapped a button in the alert view, as shown in Listing 14-33.

Listing 14-33. Implementing the alertView:clickedButtonAtIndex: Delegate Method

```
- (void)alertView:(UIAlertView *)alertView clickedButtonAtIndex:(NSInteger)buttonIndex
{
    if (buttonIndex == 1)
    {
        // OK button tapped

        // Calculate the date exactly one day from now
        NSCalendar *calendar = [NSCalendar currentCalendar];
        NSDateComponents *aDayFromNowComponents = [[NSDateComponents alloc] init];
        aDayFromNowComponents.day = 1;
        NSDate *now = [NSDate date];
```

```
        NSDate *aDayFromNow = [calendar dateByAddingComponents:aDayFromNowComponents
            toDate:now options:0];

        // Create the event
        EKEvent *event = [EKEvent eventWithEventStore:self.eventStore];
        event.title = [alertView textFieldAtIndex:0].text;
        event.calendar = [self.eventStore defaultCalendarForNewEvents];
        event.startDate = aDayFromNow;
        event.endDate = [NSDate dateWithTimeInterval:60*60.0 sinceDate:event.startDate];

        // Save the event and update the table view
        [self.eventStore saveEvent:event span:EKSpanThisEvent error:nil];
        [self refresh:self];
    }
}
```

For the sake of demonstration, we have chosen a very simple method for creating these new events (see Figure 14-11). They are all set up a day in advance and last an hour. Most likely, in your application you would choose a more complex or user-input-based method for creating EKEvents.

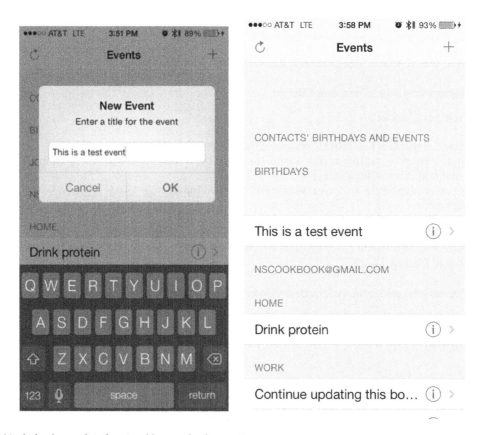

Figure 14-11. A simple user interface to add new calendar events

Creating Recurring Events

The Event Kit framework provides a powerful API for working with recurring events. To see how it works, you will change the event that this app creates and make it recur. Let's add the code first and look at how it works later. The code is shown in bold in Listing 14-34.

Listing 14-34. Modifying the alertView:clickedButtonAtIndex: Method to Add a Recurring Event

```
- (void)alertView:(UIAlertView *)alertView clickedButtonAtIndex:(NSInteger)buttonIndex
{
    if (buttonIndex == 1)
    {
        // OK button tapped

        // Calculate the date exactly one day from now
        NSCalendar *calendar = [NSCalendar currentCalendar];
        NSDateComponents *aDayFromNowComponents = [[NSDateComponents alloc] init];
        aDayFromNowComponents.day = 1;
        NSDate *now = [NSDate date];
        NSDate *aDayFromNow = [calendar dateByAddingComponents:aDayFromNowComponents
            toDate:now options:0];

        // Create the event
        EKEvent *event = [EKEvent eventWithEventStore:self.eventStore];
        event.title = [alertView textFieldAtIndex:0].text;
        event.calendar = [self.eventStore defaultCalendarForNewEvents];
        event.startDate = aDayFromNow;
        event.endDate = [NSDate dateWithTimeInterval:60*60.0 sinceDate:event.startDate];

        // Make it recur
        EKRecurrenceRule *repeatEverySecondWednesdayRecurrenceRule =
        [[EKRecurrenceRule alloc] initRecurrenceWithFrequency:EKRecurrenceFrequencyDaily
            interval:2
            daysOfTheWeek:@[[EKRecurrenceDayOfWeek dayOfWeek:4]]
            daysOfTheMonth:nil
            monthsOfTheYear:nil
            weeksOfTheYear:nil
            daysOfTheYear:nil
            setPositions:nil
            end:[EKRecurrenceEnd recurrenceEndWithOccurrenceCount:20]];

        event.recurrenceRules = @[repeatEverySecondWednesdayRecurrenceRule];

        // Save the event and update the table view
        [self.eventStore saveEvent:event span:EKSpanThisEvent error:nil];
        [self refresh:self];
    }
}
```

As you can see in Listing 14-34, you create an instance of the class EKRecurrenceRule to provide to your event. This class is an incredibly flexible method with which to programmatically implement recurrent events. With only one method, a developer can create nearly any combination of recurrences imaginable. The function of each parameter of this method is listed as follows. For any parameter, passing a value of nil indicates a lack of restriction.

- initRecurrenceWithFrequency: This specifies a basic level of how often the event repeats, whether on a daily, weekly, monthly, or annual basis.

- interval: This specifies the interval of repetition based on the frequency. A recurring event with a weekly frequency and an interval of three repeats every three weeks.

- daysOfTheWeek: This takes an NSArray of objects that must be accessed through the EKRecurrenceDayOfWeek dayOfWeek method, which takes an integer parameter representing the day of the week, starting with 1 referring to Sunday. By setting this parameter, a developer can create an event to repeat every few days, but only if the event falls on specified days of the week.

- daysOfTheMonth: This is similar to daysOfTheWeek. It specifies which days in a month to restrict a recurring event to. It is valid only for events with monthly frequency.

- monthsOfTheYear: This is similar to daysOfTheWeek and daysOfTheMonth; it's valid only for events with a yearly frequency.

- weeksOfTheYear: Just like monthsOfTheYear, this is restricted to events with an annual frequency, but with specific weeks to restrict instead of months.

- daysOfTheYear: Another parameter restricted to annually recurring events, this allows you to specify only certain days, counting from either the beginning or the end of the year, to filter a specific event to.

- setPositions: This parameter is the ultimate filter, allowing you to entirely restrict the event you have created to specific days of the year. In this way, an event that repeats daily could, for example, be restricted to occur only on the 28th, 102nd, and 364th days of the year, for whatever reason a developer might choose.

- end: This requires a class call to the EKRecurrenceEnd class and specifies when your event will no longer repeat. The two class methods to choose between are as follows:

  - recurrenceEndWithEndDate: Allows the developer to specify a date after which the event will no longer repeat

  - recurrenceEndWithOccurenceCount: Restricts an event's repetition to a limited number of occurrences

Based on all this, you can see that the recurring event you have created for demonstration will repeat every second Wednesday of each month up to a limit of 20 occurrences. Run the app, add an event, and check the calendar to see the changes.

This concludes the series of recipes that demonstrates the part of the Event Kit framework that handles calendar events. Next, we'll take a quick look at a related topic, namely, reminders.

Recipe 14-6. Creating Reminders

In iOS 6, Apple released an API that allows you to add entries to the Reminders app that was introduced in iOS 5. With this API, your apps can interact directly with this great utility and build features that automatically create reminders relevant to your users.

Setting Up the Application

In this recipe, you build a simple user interface that allows you to create reminders with two types of alarms: time-based and location-based. Start by creating a single view application project. You use both the Event Kit framework and the Core Location framework, so link the EventKit.framework and CoreLocation.framework binaries to the project.

This time you access two restricted services, Core Location and Reminders, which means you should provide usage descriptions for these in the project property list. Add the key "Privacy – Location Usage Description" with the text **Testing Location-Based Reminders** and the key "Privacy – Reminders Usage Description" with the text **Testing Reminders**, as shown in Figure 14-12.

Recipe 14-6 Creating Reminders 2 targets, iOS SDK 7.0	Key	Type	Value
▼ Recipe 14-6 Creating Reminders	▼ Information Property List	Dictionary	(16 items)
h AppDelegate.h	Privacy – Reminders Usage Descri...	String	Testing Reminders
m AppDelegate.m	Privacy – Location Usage Description	String	Testing Location – Based Reminders
Main.storyboard	Localization native development r...	String	en
h ViewController.h	Bundle display name	String	${PRODUCT_NAME}
m ViewController.m	Executable file	String	${EXECUTABLE_NAME}
Images.xcassets	Bundle identifier	String	NSCookbook.${PRODUCT_NAME:rfc1034identifier}
▼ Supporting Files	InfoDictionary version	String	6.0
Recipe 14-6 C...ders-Info.plist	Bundle name	String	${PRODUCT_NAME}
	Bundle OS Type code	String	APPL

Figure 14-12. *Setting usage descriptions for Location Services and Reminders*

Next, you'll build a user interface that resembles Figure 14-13, so go to the Main.storyboard file to edit the view controller. Drag in and position the two buttons and the activity indicator. To make the activity indicator appear only when active, set its "Hides When Stopped checkbox" property in the attributes inspector. This will make it initially hidden as well, which is what you want.

Figure 14-13. A user interface for creating two types of reminders

Create actions with the names addTimeBasedReminder and addLocationBasedReminder for the buttons and an outlet named activityIndicator for the activity indicator.

Next, go to ViewController.h, import the additional APIs you'll be utilizing, and declare the usual eventStore property, as shown in Listing 14-35.

Listing 14-35. Importing Frameworks and Adding an EKEventStore Property to the ViewController.h File

```
//
//  ViewController.h
//  Recipe 14-6 Creating Reminders
//

#import <UIKit/UIKit.h>
#import <EventKit/EventKit.h>
#import <CoreLocation/CoreLocation.h>

@interface ViewController : UIViewController<CLLocationManagerDelegate>
```

```
@property (weak, nonatomic) IBOutlet UIActivityIndicatorView *activityIndicator;
@property (strong, nonatomic)EKEventStore *eventStore;

- (IBAction)addTimeBasedReminder:(id)sender;
- (IBAction)addLocationBasedReminder:(id)sender;

@end
```

You'll use lazy initialization for the eventStore property, so go to ViewController.m and add the custom getter shown in Listing 14-36.

Listing 14-36. Implementing the eventStore Getter Method

```
- (EKEventStore *)eventStore
{
    if (_eventStore == nil)
    {
        _eventStore = [[EKEventStore alloc] init];
    }
    return _eventStore;
}
```

Requesting Access to Reminders

As with calendar events, access to Reminders is restricted and requires explicit acceptance from the user. In this recipe, you will implement a helper method that handles the requesting of Reminders access. Because this process is asynchronous, you will use the block technique to inject code to run in case access is granted.

Start by declaring a block type and the method signature in ViewController.h, as shown in Listing 14-37.

Listing 14-37. Declaring Block Types and Methods in ViewController.h

```
//
//  ViewController.h
//  Remind Me
//

#import <UIKit/UIKit.h>
#import <EventKit/EventKit.h>
#import <CoreLocation/CoreLocation.h>

typedef void(^RestrictedEventStoreActionHandler)();

@interface ViewController : UIViewController<CLLocationManagerDelegate>

@property (weak, nonatomic) IBOutlet UIActivityIndicatorView *activityIndicator;
@property (strong, nonatomic)EKEventStore *eventStore;
```

```
- (IBAction)addTimeBasedReminder:(id)sender;
- (IBAction)addLocationBasedReminder:(id)sender;
```

- (void)handleReminderAction:(RestrictedEventStoreActionHandler)block;

```
@end
```

The mission of the handleReminderAction: helper method is to request access to Reminders and invoke the provided block of code if granted. If access is denied, it simply displays an alert to inform the user. Listing 14-38 shows the implementation.

Listing 14-38. Implementing the handleReminderAction: Helper Method

```
- (void)handleReminderAction:(RestrictedEventStoreActionHandler)block
{
    [self.eventStore requestAccessToEntityType:EKEntityTypeReminder
                              completion:^(BOOL granted, NSError *error)
    {
        if (granted)
        {
            block();
        }
        else
        {
            UIAlertView *notGrantedAlert = [[UIAlertView alloc] initWithTitle:@"Access Denied"
                message:@"Access to device's reminders has been denied for this app."
                delegate:nil cancelButtonTitle:@"OK" otherButtonTitles:nil];

            dispatch_async(dispatch_get_main_queue(), ^{
                [notGrantedAlert show];
            });
        }
    }];
}
```

An important point to remember is that the completion block might be invoked on any arbitrary thread. So, if you want to perform an action that affects the user interface, for example displaying an alert view, you need to wrap it in a dispatch_async() function call to make it run on the main thread.

With the helper method in place, you can start implementing the action methods, starting with addTimeBasedReminder:. Listing 14-39 shows the general structure.

Listing 14-39. Implementing the addTimeBasedReminder: Method

```
- (IBAction)addTimeBasedReminder:(id)sender
{
    [self.activityIndicator startAnimating];

    [self handleReminderAction:^()
    {
        //TODO: Create and add Reminder
```

```
        dispatch_async(dispatch_get_main_queue(), ^{
            // TODO: Notify user if the reminder was successfully added or not
            [self.activityIndicator stopAnimating];
        });

    }];
}
```

Here you make use of the helper method you just created, providing a code block that will be invoked if access is granted by the user.

Now let's look at how to implement the first of the two TODOs in the preceding code.

Creating Time-Based Reminders

We'll show you the steps first and then the complete implementation of the addTimeBasedReminder: method later. The first thing you'll do when granted access is to create a new reminder object and set its title and the calendar (that is, Reminder List) in which it will be stored (Listing 14-40).

Listing 14-40. Creating an EKReminder Instance and Setting Properties

```
EKReminder *newReminder = [EKReminder reminderWithEventStore:self.eventStore];
newReminder.title = @"Simpsons is on";
newReminder.calendar = [self.eventStore defaultCalendarForNewReminders];
```

Next, you need to set a time for the reminder. In Listing 14-41, you set the actual time to tomorrow at 6 p.m. First, calculate the date for tomorrow by retrieving the current date and adding one day to it using NSDateComponents.

Listing 14-41. Setting the Time for the Reminder

```
NSCalendar *calendar = [NSCalendar currentCalendar];
NSDateComponents *oneDayComponents = [[NSDateComponents alloc] init];
oneDayComponents.day = 1;
NSDate *nextDay =
    [calendar dateByAddingComponents:oneDayComponents toDate:[NSDate date] options:0];
```

Then, to set the specific time to 6 p.m., extract the NSDateComponents object from nextDay, change its hour component to 18 (6 p.m. on a 24-hour clock), and create a new date from these adjusted components, as shown in Listing 14-42.

Listing 14-42. Setting the Specific Time

```
NSUInteger unitFlags = NSEraCalendarUnit | NSYearCalendarUnit | NSMonthCalendarUnit |
    NSDayCalendarUnit;
NSDateComponents *tomorrowAt6PMComponents =
    [calendar components:unitFlags fromDate:nextDay];
tomorrowAt6PMComponents.hour = 18;
tomorrowAt6PMComponents.minute = 0;
tomorrowAt6PMComponents.second = 0;
NSDate *nextDayAt6PM = [calendar dateFromComponents:tomorrowAt6PMComponents];
```

Next, create an EKAlarm with the time and add it to the reminder, as shown in Listing 14-43. It's recommended that you also set the dueDateComponents property of the reminder. This helps the Reminders app display more relevant information. Fortunately, you already constructed the required NSDateComponents object when you previously constructed the alarm date.

Listing 14-43. Creating an EKAlarm and Adding It to the Reminder

```
EKAlarm *alarm = [EKAlarm alarmWithAbsoluteDate:nextDayAt6PM];
[newReminder addAlarm:alarm];
newReminder.dueDateComponents = tomorrowAt6PMComponents;
```

Finally, save and commit the new reminder and inform the user whether the operation was successful. Because displaying a UIAlertView is affecting the user interface, this particular code needs to be run on the main thread, as shown in Listing 14-44.

Listing 14-44. Saving and Committing the New Reminder

```
// ...
NSString *alertTitle;
NSString *alertMessage;
NSString *alertButtonTitle;
NSError *error;
[self.eventStore saveReminder:newReminder commit:YES error:&error];
if (error == nil)
{
    alertTitle = @"Information";
    alertMessage = [NSString stringWithFormat:@"\"%@\" was added to Reminders",
        newReminder.title];
    alertButtonTitle = @"OK";
}
else
{
    alertTitle = @"Error";
    alertMessage = [NSString stringWithFormat:@"Unable to save reminder: %@", error];
    alertButtonTitle = @"Dismiss";
}

dispatch_async(dispatch_get_main_queue(), ^{
    UIAlertView *alertView = [[UIAlertView alloc]initWithTitle:alertTitle
        message:alertMessage delegate:nil cancelButtonTitle:alertButtonTitle
        otherButtonTitles:nil];
    [alertView show];
    [self.activityIndicator stopAnimating];
});
```

Listing 14-45 shows the complete implementation of the addTimeBasedReminder: action method.

Listing 14-45. The Complete addTimeBasedReminder: Implementation

```
- (IBAction)addTimeBasedReminder:(id)sender
{
    [self.activityIndicator startAnimating];

    [self handleReminderAction:^()
    {
        // Create Reminder
        EKReminder *newReminder = [EKReminder reminderWithEventStore:self.eventStore];
        newReminder.title = @"Simpsons is on";
        newReminder.calendar = [self.eventStore defaultCalendarForNewReminders];

        // Calculate the date exactly one day from now
        NSCalendar *calendar = [NSCalendar currentCalendar];
        NSDateComponents *oneDayComponents = [[NSDateComponents alloc] init];
        oneDayComponents.day = 1;
        NSDate *nextDay = [calendar dateByAddingComponents:oneDayComponents
            toDate:[NSDate date] options:0];

        NSUInteger unitFlags = NSEraCalendarUnit | NSYearCalendarUnit |
            NSMonthCalendarUnit | NSDayCalendarUnit;
        NSDateComponents *tomorrowAt6PMComponents = [calendar components:unitFlags
            fromDate:nextDay];
        tomorrowAt6PMComponents.hour = 18;
        tomorrowAt6PMComponents.minute = 0;
        tomorrowAt6PMComponents.second = 0;
        NSDate *nextDayAt6PM = [calendar dateFromComponents:tomorrowAt6PMComponents];

        // Create an Alarm
        EKAlarm *alarm = [EKAlarm alarmWithAbsoluteDate:nextDayAt6PM];
        [newReminder addAlarm:alarm];
        newReminder.dueDateComponents = tomorrowAt6PMComponents;

        // Save Reminder
        NSString *alertTitle;
        NSString *alertMessage;
        NSString *alertButtonTitle;
        NSError *error;
        [self.eventStore saveReminder:newReminder commit:YES error:&error];
        if (error == nil)
        {
            alertTitle = @"Information";
            alertMessage = [NSString stringWithFormat:@"\"%@\" was added to Reminders",
                newReminder.title];
            alertButtonTitle = @"OK";
        }
```

```
        else
        {
            alertTitle = @"Error";
            alertMessage = [NSString stringWithFormat:@"Unable to save reminder: %@",
                error];
            alertButtonTitle = @"Dismiss";
        }

        dispatch_async(dispatch_get_main_queue(), ^{
            UIAlertView *alertView = [[UIAlertView alloc]initWithTitle:alertTitle
                message:alertMessage delegate:nil cancelButtonTitle:alertButtonTitle
                otherButtonTitles:nil];
            [alertView show];
            [self.activityIndicator stopAnimating];
        });

    }];
}
```

You can now build and run the application and have it create a time-based reminder. The first time this app runs and you tap the button to create a time-based reminder, you'll be asked whether the app is allowed to access your reminders. Figure 14-14 shows an example of this alert.

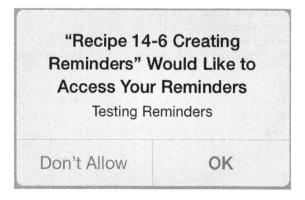

Figure 14-14. An app asking permission to access the user's reminders, giving "Testing Reminders" as a reason

Creating Location-Based Reminders

We're now going to raise the bar a little and create a location-based reminder. What you're going to do is to implement the addLocationBasedReminder: action method and make it create a new reminder with an alarm that's triggered when the user leaves the current location.

Again, you're going to use code blocks and make a helper method that handles the retrieving of the user's current location. As you'll soon realize, this will be a little more complicated because the API to get the device location is based on the delegate pattern and not on the usage of blocks. However, the complication will be hidden behind the nice little API that you'll set up to retrieve the location.

Add the bold code in Listing 14-46 to the ViewController.h file.

Listing 14-46. Modifying the ViewController.h File to Accommodate Location-Based Reminders

```
//
//  ViewController.h
//  Remind Me
//

#import <UIKit/UIKit.h>
#import <EventKit/EventKit.h>
#import <CoreLocation/CoreLocation.h>

typedef void(^RestrictedEventStoreActionHandler)();
typedef void(^RetrieveCurrentLocationHandler)(CLLocation *);

@interface ViewController : UIViewController<CLLocationManagerDelegate>
{
    @private
    CLLocationManager *_locationManager;
    RetrieveCurrentLocationHandler _retrieveCurrentLocationBlock;
    int _numberOfTries;
}

@property (weak, nonatomic) IBOutlet UIActivityIndicatorView *activityIndicator;
@property (strong, nonatomic)EKEventStore *eventStore;

- (IBAction)addTimeBasedReminder:(id)sender;
- (IBAction)addLocationBasedReminder:(id)sender;

- (void)handleReminderAction:(RestrictedEventStoreActionHandler)block;
- (void)retrieveCurrentLocation:(RetrieveCurrentLocationHandler)block;

@end
```

As you can see, the signature of the retrieveCurrentLocation: helper method resembles the handleReminderAction: you created in the previous section. The only difference is that its block argument has a CLLocation * parameter. You've also prepared the ViewController class to act as a Location Manager delegate by adding the CLLocationManagerDelegate protocol. Additionally, you've declared three private instance variables that you'll be using in the helper method later.

Now implement the retrieveCurrentLocation: helper method, as shown in Listing 14-47.

Listing 14-47. Implementing the retrieveCurrentLocation: Helper Method

```
- (void)retrieveCurrentLocation:(RetrieveCurrentLocationHandler)block
{
    if ([CLLocationManager locationServicesEnabled] == NO)
    {
        UIAlertView *locationServicesDisabledAlert = [[UIAlertView alloc]
            initWithTitle:@"Location Services Disabled" message:@"This feature requires
            location services. Enable it in the privacy settings on your device"
            delegate:nil cancelButtonTitle:@"Dismiss" otherButtonTitles:nil];
```

```
        [locationServicesDisabledAlert show];
        return;
    }

    if (_locationManager == nil)
    {
        _locationManager = [[CLLocationManager alloc] init];
        _locationManager.desiredAccuracy = kCLLocationAccuracyBest;
        _locationManager.distanceFilter = 1; // meter
        _locationManager.activityType = CLActivityTypeOther;
        _locationManager.delegate = self;
    }
    _numberOfTries = 0;
    _retrieveCurrentLocationBlock = block;
    [_locationManager startUpdatingLocation];
}
```

Refer to Chapter 5 for the details of this method. Note that you're initializing the _numberOfTries and _retrieveCurrentLocationBlock instance methods before starting the location updates.

Next, implement the delegate method for getting the location, as shown in Listing 14-48.

Listing 14-48.   Implementing the locationManager:didUpdateLocation: Delegate Method

```
- (void)locationManager:(CLLocationManager *)manager didUpdateLocations:(NSArray *)locations
{
    // Make sure this is a recent location event
    CLLocation *lastLocation = [locations lastObject];
    NSTimeInterval eventInterval = [lastLocation.timestamp timeIntervalSinceNow];
    if(abs(eventInterval) < 30.0)
    {
        // Make sure the event is accurate enough
        if (lastLocation.horizontalAccuracy >= 0 &&
            lastLocation.horizontalAccuracy < 20)
        {
            [_locationManager stopUpdatingLocation];
            _retrieveCurrentLocationBlock(lastLocation);
            return;
        }
    }
    if (_numberOfTries++ == 10)
    {
        [_locationManager stopUpdatingLocation];
        UIAlertView *unableToGetLocationAlert =
            [[UIAlertView alloc]initWithTitle:@"Error"
                message:@"Unable to get the current location." delegate:nil
                cancelButtonTitle:@"Dismiss" otherButtonTitles: nil];
        [unableToGetLocationAlert show];
    }
}
```

Again, refer to Chapter 5 for the details of retrieving locations. The important points to note with the preceding implementation are the following:

1. Invoke the code block that's stored in the _retrieveCurrentLocationBlock instance variable.

2. After ten tries, if you still not have obtained an accurate enough reading, abandon it and inform the user.

Finally, implement the addLocationBasedReminder: action method. It resembles a lot of the addTimeBasedReminder: method you implemented earlier, except it makes use of both helper methods and of course sets up a location-based reminder. Listing 14-49 shows the complete implementation with the differences to the addTimeBasedReminder: method marked in bold.

Listing 14-49. The Complete addLocationBasedreminder: Method Implementation

```
- (IBAction)addLocationBasedReminder:(id)sender
{
    [self.activityIndicator startAnimating];

    [self retrieveCurrentLocation:
     ^(CLLocation *currentLocation)
     {
         if (currentLocation != nil)
         {
             [self handleReminderAction:^()
              {
                  // Create Reminder
                  EKReminder *newReminder =
                      [EKReminder reminderWithEventStore:self.eventStore];
                  newReminder.title = @"Buy milk!";
                  newReminder.calendar =
                      [self.eventStore defaultCalendarForNewReminders];

                  // Create Location-based Alarm
                  EKStructuredLocation *currentStructuredLocation =
                      [EKStructuredLocation locationWithTitle:@"Current Location"];
                  currentStructuredLocation.geoLocation = currentLocation;

                  EKAlarm *alarm = [[EKAlarm alloc] init];
                  alarm.structuredLocation = currentStructuredLocation;
                  alarm.proximity = EKAlarmProximityLeave;

                  [newReminder addAlarm:alarm];

                  // Save Reminder
                  NSString *alertTitle;
                  NSString *alertMessage;
                  NSString *alertButtonTitle;
                  NSError *error;
                  [self.eventStore saveReminder:newReminder commit:YES error:&error];
                  if (error == nil)
```

```
                    {
                        alertTitle = @"Information";
                        alertMessage =
                            [NSString stringWithFormat:@"\"%@\" was added to Reminders",
                                newReminder.title];
                        alertButtonTitle = @"OK";
                    }
                    else
                    {
                        alertTitle = @"Error";
                        alertMessage =
                            [NSString stringWithFormat:@"Unable to save reminder: %@",
                                error];
                        alertButtonTitle = @"Dismiss";
                    }

                    dispatch_async(dispatch_get_main_queue(), ^{
                        UIAlertView *alertView =
                            [[UIAlertView alloc]initWithTitle:alertTitle
                                message:alertMessage delegate:nil
                                cancelButtonTitle:alertButtonTitle otherButtonTitles:nil];
                        [alertView show];
                        [self.activityIndicator stopAnimating];
                    });
                }];
            }
    }];
}
```

You can build and run the application again and this time create both a time-based and a location-based reminder. Figure 14-15 shows an example with the Reminders app displaying two different reminders created using this app.

Note   You might experience an error here if you do not have your reminders tied to your iCloud account. You can change this from the default reminders list found in Settings ➤ Reminders ➤ Default List. Location-based reminders will work only with an iCloud account. If you have another account, such as a Microsoft Exchange account, set to the Default List, this functionality will not work.

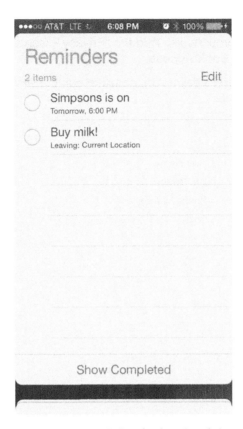

Figure 14-15. The Reminders app showing a time-based and a location-based reminder

Caution   Although working, this app has one serious flaw. Because the creation of reminders is running on a separate thread and might take a few seconds, the user can tap the buttons before the task has had a chance to finish. This starts a new process that, while accessing the same instance variables, might interfere with the ongoing task and cause unexpected behavior. The easy way to fix this issue is to disable the buttons while the creation of reminders is ongoing. We leave this implementation to you as an exercise.

Recipe 14-7. Accessing the Address Book

One of the most imperative functions of any modern device is storing contact information. As such, you should take care to develop applications that take advantage of this important data. In this recipe, we cover three basic functionalities for accessing and dealing with a device's contacts list.

First, create a single view application project called "My Pick Contact App."

For this recipe, you need to add two extra frameworks to your project: AddressBook.framework and AddressBookUI.framework.

Because the address book, like the calendar, is a restricted entity, you should provide a usage description in the application's property list. Add the "Privacy – Contacts Usage Description" key with the value **Testing Address Book Access**.

Next, switch to your view controller's Main.storyboard to edit the view, and create a view that resembles the one in Figure 14-16.

Figure 14-16. *User interface for accessing contact information*

Create these outlets to connect the elements to your code:

- firstNameLabel
- lastNameLabel
- phoneNumberLabel
- cityNameLabel

You do not need an outlet for the button, but create an action with the name pickContact for when the user taps it.

Now that your interface is set up, make some changes to the header file. First, add the following two import statements so you can access the Address Book and Address Book UI frameworks.

```
#import <AddressBook/AddressBook.h>
#import <AddressBookUI/AddressBookUI.h>
```

You use an instance of the class ABPeoplePickerNavigationController and set its peoplePickerDelegate property to your view controller, so you need to add the ABPeoplePickerNavigationControllerDelegate protocol implementation to your header file.

The header file, in its entirety, should now look like Listing 14-50.

Listing 14-50. The Complete ViewController.h File

```
//
//  ViewController.h
//  Recipe 14-7 Accessing the Address Book
//

#import <UIKit/UIKit.h>
#import <AddressBook/AddressBook.h>
#import <AddressBookUI/AddressBookUI.h>

@interface ViewController : UIViewController<ABPeoplePickerNavigationControllerDelegate>

@property (weak, nonatomic) IBOutlet UILabel *firstNameLabel;
@property (weak, nonatomic) IBOutlet UILabel *lastNameLabel;
@property (weak, nonatomic) IBOutlet UILabel *phoneNumberLabel;
@property (weak, nonatomic) IBOutlet UILabel *cityNameLabel;

- (IBAction)pickContact:(id)sender;

@end
```

Switch to the implementation file. There you will implement the pickContact: method to create an instance of ABPeoplePickerNavigationController, set its delegate, and then display it, as shown in Listing 14-51.

Listing 14-51. Implementing the pickContact: Action Method

```
- (IBAction)pickContact:(id)sender
{
    ABPeoplePickerNavigationController *picker =
        [[ABPeoplePickerNavigationController alloc] init];
    picker.peoplePickerDelegate = self;
    [self presentViewController:picker animated:YES completion:nil];
}
```

Now you just need to create your delegate methods, of which there are three you are required to implement. The first, and simplest, is for when the picker controller is canceled (Listing 14-52).

Listing 14-52. Implementing the peoplePickerNavigationControllerDidCancel: Delegate Method

```
-(void)peoplePickerNavigationControllerDidCancel:
(ABPeoplePickerNavigationController *)peoplePicker
{
    [self dismissViewControllerAnimated:YES completion:nil];
}
```

Next, define your main delegate method to handle the selection of a contact. The following is a step-by-step method implementation that demonstrates each part.

Your method header should look like Listing 14-53.

Listing 14-53. The Method Header

```
-(BOOL)peoplePickerNavigationController:
(ABPeoplePickerNavigationController *)peoplePicker
shouldContinueAfterSelectingPerson:(ABRecordRef)person
```

The first odd thing you might notice about this header is that the variable person is of type ABRecordRef, which does not have a * after it. This essentially means that person is not a pointer and thus will not be used to call methods. Instead, you will use predefined functions that utilize and access it. As you see, many parts of the Address Book framework use this "C-based" style.

Inside the method body, you first access the simplest properties, which are the first and last names of the chosen contact shown in Listing 14-54.

Listing 14-54. Setting the First and Last Name Properties

```
self.firstNameLabel.text =
    (__bridge_transfer NSString *)ABRecordCopyValue(person, kABPersonFirstNameProperty);
self.lastNameLabel.text =
    (__bridge_transfer NSString *)ABRecordCopyValue(person, kABPersonLastNameProperty);
```

The ABRecordCopyValue() function is your go-to call for any kind of accessing data in this section. It takes two parameters: the first is the ABRecordRef that you want to access, and the second is a predefined PropertyID that instructs the function on which piece of data to retrieve.

There are two types of values that can be dealt with by this function: single values and multivalues. For these first two calls, you are dealing only with single values, for which the ABRecordCopyValue() function returns a type of CFStringRef. You can cast this up to an NSString by adding the (__bridge_transfer NSString *) code in front of the value.

> **Note**   The __bridge_transfer command specifies that the memory management of the object is being transferred to ARC. You can find more information on this in Apple's documentation.

The next value you can access is the person's phone number, which is a multivalue. Multivalues are usually used for the properties of a person for which multiple entries can be given, such as address, phone number, or e-mail. When you copy this, you will receive a variable of type ABMultiValueRef, which you can then use to access a specific value, as shown in Listing 14-55.

Listing 14-55. Accessing the Phone Number

```
ABMultiValueRef phoneRecord = ABRecordCopyValue(person, kABPersonPhoneProperty);
CFStringRef phoneNumber = ABMultiValueCopyValueAtIndex(phoneRecord, 0);
self.phoneNumberLabel.text = (__bridge_transfer NSString *)phoneNumber;
CFRelease(phoneRecord);
```

By using the call ABMultiValueCopyValueAtIndex(phoneProperty, 0), you have specified that you want the first phone number stored for the given user. From there, you can set your label's text just as you did before.

The next multivalue you deal with is the main address of the chosen contact. When dealing with the address, an extra step is required, as an address is stored as a CFDictionary. You retrieve this dictionary using the ABMultiValueCopyValueAtIndex() function again and then query its values, as shown in Listing 14-56.

Listing 14-56. Querying CFDictionary for the Stores Values

```
ABMultiValueRef addressRecord = ABRecordCopyValue(person, kABPersonAddressProperty);
if (ABMultiValueGetCount(addressRecord) > 0)
{
    CFDictionaryRef addressDictionary = ABMultiValueCopyValueAtIndex(addressRecord, 0);
    self.cityNameLabel.text =
        [NSString stringWithString:
            (__bridge NSString *)CFDictionaryGetValue(addressDictionary,
                kABPersonAddressCityKey)];
    CFRelease(addressDictionary);
}
else
{
    self.cityNameLabel.text = @"...";
}
CFRelease(addressRecord);
```

You might be wondering about a couple of things with the code from Listing 14-56. First, why do you need to release, for example, addressDictionary and addressRecord, but not the first name and last name values that you retrieved earlier?

The reason is that, in those cases, you transferred the ownership of the value to the respective outlet by using the __bridge_transfer type specifier. But for the multivalue records, you didn't transfer ownership, so they must be released or their memory will be leaked.

The second thing you might be wondering is what the following piece of code is about:

```
self.cityNameLabel.text =
    [NSString stringWithString:
        (__bridge NSString *)CFDictionaryGetValue(addressDictionary,
            kABPersonAddressCityKey)];
```

Why are you suddenly using __bridge and not __bridge_transfer here? And why construct a new string using the stringWithString class method? Here too, the answer is ownership. The CFDictionaryGetValue() function, as opposed to ABMultiValueCopyValueAtIndex(), retains ownership of the value it returns. Because you want to store the string in your cityNameLabel.text property, you need to copy it first. And because you don't want to transfer ownership of the original string value (which would lead to a memory leak), you use a plain __bridge cast.

To finalize the implementation of the peoplePickerNavigationController:shouldContinueAfterSelectingPerson: delegate method, you dismiss the modal view controller and return NO. As a whole, your method should look like Listing 14-57.

Listing 14-57. The Complete peoplePickerNavigationController: Method

```
-(BOOL)peoplePickerNavigationController:
(ABPeoplePickerNavigationController *)peoplePicker
    shouldContinueAfterSelectingPerson:(ABRecordRef)person
{
    self.firstNameLabel.text =
        (__bridge_transfer NSString *)ABRecordCopyValue(person,
            kABPersonFirstNameProperty);

    self.lastNameLabel.text =
        (__bridge_transfer NSString *)ABRecordCopyValue(person,
            kABPersonLastNameProperty);

    ABMultiValueRef phoneRecord = ABRecordCopyValue(person, kABPersonPhoneProperty);
    CFStringRef phoneNumber = ABMultiValueCopyValueAtIndex(phoneRecord, 0);
    self.phoneNumberLabel.text = (__bridge_transfer NSString *)phoneNumber;
    CFRelease(phoneRecord);

    ABMultiValueRef addressRecord = ABRecordCopyValue(person, kABPersonAddressProperty);
    if (ABMultiValueGetCount(addressRecord) > 0)
    {
        CFDictionaryRef addressDictionary =
            ABMultiValueCopyValueAtIndex(addressRecord, 0);
        self.cityNameLabel.text =
            [NSString stringWithString:
                (__bridge NSString *)CFDictionaryGetValue(addressDictionary,
                    kABPersonAddressCityKey)];
        CFRelease(addressDictionary);
    }
```

```
    else
    {
        self.cityNameLabel.text = @"...";
    }
    CFRelease(addressRecord);

    [self dismissViewControllerAnimated:YES completion:nil];
    return NO;
}
```

There is a third delegate method you must implement in order to fully conform to the
ABPeoplePickerNavigationControllerDelegate protocol. It handles the selection of a specific
contact's property. However, because this recipe is simply returning after the selection of a contact,
this method will not actually be called. To get rid of the compiler warning, add the method in
Listing 14-58 with a simple implementation similar to your cancellation method.

Listing 14-58. Implementing the peoplePickerNavigationController:shouldContinueAfterSelectingPerson:identifier: Delegate Method

```
-(BOOL)peoplePickerNavigationController:(ABPeoplePickerNavigationController *)peoplePicker
shouldContinueAfterSelectingPerson:(ABRecordRef)person property:(ABPropertyID)property
identifier:(ABMultiValueIdentifier)identifier
{
    [self dismissViewControllerAnimated:YES completion:nil];
    return NO;
}
```

> **Caution**   Whenever you are copying values from an ABRecordRef, include a check to be sure that a value
> exists, as you did with the address. The previous code assumed that the first name, last name, and phone
> number exist, but an empty query can result in your application throwing an exception.

Your application can now access the address book, select a user, and display the information for
which you have queried. The first time the function is run, you're asked to grant the app access to
the device's Contacts app. Figure 14-17 shows examples of the app in different modes.

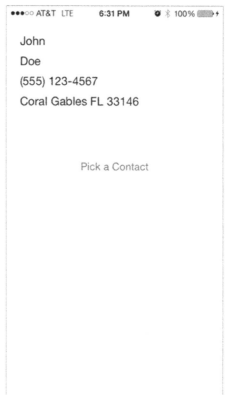

Figure 14-17. A request to access contact information is required, and contact information is retrieved from the address book and displayed in the app

While you have not included code to access all the possible values for an ABRecordRef, you should be able to use any combination of the utilized functions to access whichever ones you need.

Recipe 14-8. Setting Contact Information

Just as important as being able to access values is being able to set them. To this end, you will implement two different methods for creating and setting values of a contact and adding it to your device's address book.

First, create a new single view application project to which you link the Address Book and Address Book UI frameworks. Also, as you did in the previous recipe, you should provide a usage description in the application's property list. Add the "Privacy – Contacts Usage Description" key with the value **Testing Creating Contacts**.

Set up a simple user interface that allows users to create a new contact. In the Main.storyboard file, add a single UIButton titled "New Contact," as in Figure 14-18, to the view. Then create an action named addNewContact for when the user taps the button.

Figure 14-18. *Simple user interface setup for creating contacts*

Next, import your frameworks into your header file and configure your view controller's protocol to conform to. Conform your view controller to the ABNewPersonViewControllerDelegate protocol, and then add the usual two import statements.

```
#import <AddressBook/AddressBook.h>
#import <AddressBookUI/AddressBookUI.h>
```

Now, create a simple implementation, for which you have to define only two methods: the action to handle the selection of your button and the delegate method for an ABNewPersonViewControllerDelegate.

The action method looks like Listing 14-59.

Listing 14-59. Implementing the addNewContacts: Action Method

```
- (IBAction)addNewContact:(id)sender
{
    ABNewPersonViewController *view = [[ABNewPersonViewController alloc] init];
    view.newPersonViewDelegate = self;

    UINavigationController *newNavigationController =
        [[UINavigationController alloc] initWithRootViewController:view];
    [self presentViewController:newNavigationController animated:YES completion:nil];
}
```

The delegate method should look like Listing 14-60.

Listing 14-60. Implementing the newPersonViewController:didCompleteWithNewPerson: Method

```
-(void)newPersonViewController:(ABNewPersonViewController *)newPersonView
didCompleteWithNewPerson:(ABRecordRef)person
{
    if (person == NULL)
    {
        NSLog(@"User Cancelled Creation");
    }
    else
    {
        NSLog(@"Successfully Created New Person");
    }
    [self dismissViewControllerAnimated:YES completion:nil];
}
```

Unlike most modal view controllers that you deal with, the ABNewPersonViewController has only one delegate method that handles both success and cancellation, as opposed to others that have one method for each. As you can see, you differentiate between each result by checking to see whether the ABRecordRef person parameter is not NULL. Because this parameter is not a pointer, you compare it to the NULL value instead of nil.

At this point, you should be able to allow your user to create a new contact to be added to the address book, as the simulated app in Figure 14-19 shows.

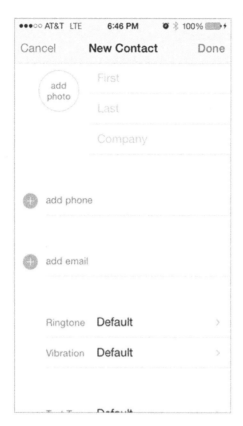

Figure 14-19. A blank ABNewPersonViewController

While you have provided users with a great deal of flexibility as to how they want their contacts to be set up, you have also provided them with a great deal of work to do, in that they have to type in every value they want. You will next see how to programmatically create records and set their values. For the purpose of demonstration, we will make it simple and provide the ABNewPersonViewController with preset values that are hard-coded.

You will populate the ABNewPersonViewController with preset values. Update the addNewContact: method, starting with adding hard-coded values, as shown in Listing 14-61.

Listing 14-61. Updating the addnewContact: Action Method with Preset Values

```
- (IBAction)addNewContact:(id)sender
{
    NSString *firstName = @"John";
    NSString *lastName = @"Doe";
    NSString *mobileNumber = @"555-123-4567";
    NSString *street = @"12345 Circle Wave Ave";
    NSString *city = @"Coral Gables";
    NSString *state = @"FL";
```

```
    NSString *zip = @"33146";
    NSString *country = @"United States";

    // ...
}
```

Next, create a new contact record and add values for the first name, last name, and phone contact information, as shown in Listing 14-62.

Listing 14-62. Creating the New Contact Record in the addNewContact: Action Method

```
- (IBAction)addNewContact:(id)sender
{
    // ...

    ABRecordRef contactRecord = ABPersonCreate();

    // Setup first and last name records
    ABRecordSetValue(contactRecord, kABPersonFirstNameProperty,
        (__bridge_retained CFStringRef)firstName, nil);
    ABRecordSetValue(contactRecord, kABPersonLastNameProperty,
        (__bridge_retained CFStringRef)lastName, nil);

    // Setup phone record
    ABMutableMultiValueRef phoneRecord =
        ABMultiValueCreateMutable(kABMultiStringPropertyType);
    ABMultiValueAddValueAndLabel(phoneRecord,
        (__bridge_retained CFStringRef)mobileNumber, kABPersonPhoneMobileLabel, NULL);
    ABRecordSetValue(contactRecord, kABPersonPhoneProperty, phoneRecord, nil);
    CFRelease(phoneRecord);

    // ...
}
```

The __bridge_retained type specifier indicates that you want to transfer ownership from an ARC-controlled object (NSString in this case) to a Core Foundation object (CFStringRef). This is necessary so these objects don't prematurely get released by ARC.

Now, the address record involves a bit more work to create the dictionary and add it to the contact record. This implementation is shown in Listing 14-63.

Listing 14-63. Adding the Address Record to the addNewContact: Action Method

```
- (IBAction)addNewContact:(id)sender
{
    // ...

    // Setup address record
    ABMutableMultiValueRef addressRecord =
        ABMultiValueCreateMutable(kABDictionaryPropertyType);
    CFStringRef dictionaryKeys[5];
    CFStringRef dictionaryValues[5];
```

```
        dictionaryKeys[0] = kABPersonAddressStreetKey;
        dictionaryKeys[1] = kABPersonAddressCityKey;
        dictionaryKeys[2] = kABPersonAddressStateKey;
        dictionaryKeys[3] = kABPersonAddressZIPKey;
        dictionaryKeys[4] = kABPersonAddressCountryKey;
        dictionaryValues[0] = (__bridge_retained CFStringRef)street;
        dictionaryValues[1] = (__bridge_retained CFStringRef)city;
        dictionaryValues[2] = (__bridge_retained CFStringRef)state;
        dictionaryValues[3] = (__bridge_retained CFStringRef)zip;
        dictionaryValues[4] = (__bridge_retained CFStringRef)country;

        CFDictionaryRef addressDictionary = CFDictionaryCreate(kCFAllocatorDefault,
            (void *)dictionaryKeys, (void *)dictionaryValues, 5,
            &kCFCopyStringDictionaryKeyCallBacks, &kCFTypeDictionaryValueCallBacks);
        ABMultiValueAddValueAndLabel(addressRecord, addressDictionary, kABHomeLabel, NULL);
        CFRelease(addressDictionary);

        ABRecordSetValue(contactRecord, kABPersonAddressProperty, addressRecord, nil);
        CFRelease(addressRecord);

        // ...
}
```

Finally, initialize and display the ABNewPersonerViewController with the new contact record, which you then release to avoid a memory leak, as shown in Listing 14-64.

Listing 14-64. Initializing and Displaying the ABnewPersonerViewController

```
- (IBAction)addNewContact:(id)sender
{
    // ...

    // Display View Controller
    ABNewPersonViewController *view = [[ABNewPersonViewController alloc] init];
    view.newPersonViewDelegate = self;
    view.displayedPerson = contactRecord;

    UINavigationController *newNavigationController =
        [[UINavigationController alloc] initWithRootViewController:view];
    [self presentViewController:newNavigationController animated:YES completion:nil];

    CFRelease(contactRecord);
}
```

If you build and run your application now, you should have the ABNewPersonViewController populated with the preset values, as shown in Figure 14-20.

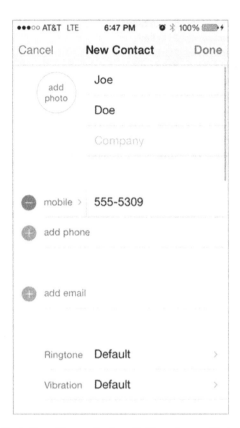

Figure 14-20. The ABNewPersonViewController with preset values that have been added programmatically

Summary

As you can see, there are many methods and functionalities for interacting with any specific user's personal data. From recurring events to multiple calendars to the vast number of contacts and phone numbers that most users have—all this information can be used to personalize an application for each user. In terms of user experience, being able to access, display, and edit this information allows us as developers to create more powerful, unique, and useful applications.

Chapter 15

Data Storage Recipes

When working in iOS, one of the most important concepts to understand is the implementation of persistence. This means having information saved and retrieved, or *persisted*, through the closing or restarting of an application. Just as pages from books can be read and re-read, even after closing and re-opening them, you can make use of certain key concepts in iOS to allow your information—from the simplest values to the most complex data structures—to stay stored in your device for indefinite periods of time.

In this chapter, we cover many data persistence methods that will allow you to save data for offline use including user defaults, documents, databases, and even iCloud. We will show you the different advantages, disadvantages, general uses, and complexities of each method so you can develop a full understanding of the best method of storage for any given situation.

Recipe 15-1. Persisting Data with NSUserDefaults

When developing applications, you often run into situations where you want to store simple values, such as user settings or some part of an app's state. While there are a variety of ways to store data, the easiest of these is the NSUserDefaults class, built specifically for such simple situations.

The NSUserDefaults class uses simple APIs to store basic values, such as instances of NSString, NSNumber, BOOL, and so on. It can also be used to store more complex data structures, such as NSArray or NSDictionary, as long as they do not contain massive amounts of data; for example, images should not be stored with NSUserDefaults.

In this recipe, you build a simple app that has a state that will persist using NSUserDefaults. Start by creating a new single view application and name it whatever you want. We've titled ours "Recipe 15-1 Persisting Data with NSUserDefaults."

Set up the user interface of this app. Select the Main.storyboard file to start editing the main view. Add two text fields, a switch and an activity indicator, and set them up so the user interface resembles Figure 15-1.

Figure 15-1. A user interface whose state will be persisted

As you can probably guess, the switch starts and stops the activity indicator. You also write code that persists the state of the switch along with the text you've entered in the text fields.

First, you need a way to reference the controls from your code, so create the following outlets:

- firstNameTextField
- lastNameTextField
- activitySwitch
- activityIndicator

You also need to intercept when the user taps the switch, so create an action named toggleActivity for its Value Changed event.

In the ViewController.h file, add the UITextFieldDelegate protocol to the ViewController class. You need this to control the keyboard later. The ViewController.h file should now resemble Listing 15-1.

Listing 15-1. The Complete ViewController.h File

```
//
//  ViewController.h
//  Recipe 15-1 Persisting Data with NSUserDefaults
//

#import <UIKit/UIKit.h>

@interface ViewController : UIViewController<UITextFieldDelegate>

@property (weak, nonatomic) IBOutlet UITextField *firstNameTextField;
@property (weak, nonatomic) IBOutlet UITextField *lastNameTextField;
@property (weak, nonatomic) IBOutlet UISwitch *activitySwitch;
@property (weak, nonatomic) IBOutlet UIActivityIndicatorView *activityIndicator;

- (IBAction)toggleActivity:(id)sender;

@end
```

Now start implementing the basic functionality of the controls, starting with the text fields. Open the ViewController.m file and add the code in Listing 15-2 to the viewDidLoad method.

Listing 15-2. Setting the Text Field Delegates

```
- (void)viewDidLoad
{
    [super viewDidLoad];

    self.firstNameTextField.delegate = self;
    self.lastNameTextField.delegate = self;
}
```

Next, add the delegate method shown in Listing 15-3 to the implementation file. It makes sure the keyboard gets removed if the user taps the Return button.

Listing 15-3. Implementing the textFieldShouldReturn: Delegate Method

```
-(BOOL)textFieldShouldReturn:(UITextField *)textField
{
    [textField resignFirstResponder];
    return NO;
}
```

Now it's time to implement the behavior of the switch. Listing 15-4 shows the implementation of the toggleActivity: action method.

Listing 15-4. Implementing the toggleActivity: Action Method

```
- (IBAction)toggleActivity:(id)sender
{
    if (self.activitySwitch.on)
    {
        [self.activityIndicator startAnimating];
    }
    else
    {
        [self.activityIndicator stopAnimating];
    }
}
```

The simple user interface is now fully functioning, and you should take it on a test spin. You should be able to enter text in the text fields and start and stop the activity indicator animation by tapping the switch. However, if you shut down the app and rerun it, the text will be gone and the switch will be back to its OFF state again. Let's implement some persistency, shall we?

As you know, you need to do two things to persist data: you need to save it, and you need to restore it—at appropriate times. There are basically two strategies for when to save persisted data. You can either store the data whenever it's changed or save it right before the app terminates. In this recipe, you implement the second strategy and have the state saved when the app enters the background.

Note   Normally, an app that's suspended is not terminated but put to sleep and can be reactivated and brought back to the same state without the need for persisting its data. However, in the case of low-memory conditions, an app can be terminated without warning. Because there is no way to know whether your app is being terminated, you should always be sure your persisted data is saved when the app enters the background.

To know when the app enters the background mode, you can use the notification center, which provides us with a lightweight custom delegation behavior, and register an observer of UIApplicationDidEnterBackgroundNotification. A good place to do this is when the view is loaded, so add the code in Listing 15-5 to viewDidLoad.

Listing 15-5. Registering an NSNotificationCenter Observer

```
- (void)viewDidLoad
{
    [super viewDidLoad];
        // Do any additional setup after loading the view, typically from a nib.
    self.firstNameTextField.delegate = self;
    self.lastNameTextField.delegate = self;

    [[NSNotificationCenter defaultCenter] addObserver:self
        selector:@selector(savePersistentData:)
        name:UIApplicationDidEnterBackgroundNotification object:nil];
}
```

Now you can implement in the savePersistentData: method the actual storing of the persistent data, as shown in Listing 15-6.

Listing 15-6. Implementation of the savePersistentData: Method

```
- (void)savePersistentData:(id)sender
{
    NSUserDefaults *userDefaults = [NSUserDefaults standardUserDefaults];

    //Set Objects/Values to Persist
    [userDefaults setObject:self.firstNameTextField.text forKey:@"firstName"];
    [userDefaults setObject:self.lastNameTextField.text forKey:@"lastName"];
    [userDefaults setBool:self.activitySwitch.on forKey:@"activityOn"];

    //Save Changes
    [userDefaults synchronize];
}
```

> **Tip** You can use NSUserDefault's resetStandardUserDefaults method to clear all data that's been previously stored. This can be a good way to reset your app to its standard settings.

What's left now is to load the data when the app launches. Start by adding a method to perform the loading, as shown in Listing 15-7.

Listing 15-7. Implementing the loadPersistentData: Method

```
- (void)loadPersistentData:(id)sender
{
    NSUserDefaults *userDefaults = [NSUserDefaults standardUserDefaults];

    self.firstNameTextField.text = [userDefaults objectForKey:@"firstName"];
    self.lastNameTextField.text = [userDefaults objectForKey:@"lastName"];
    [self.activitySwitch setOn:[userDefaults boolForKey:@"activityOn"] animated:NO];

    if (self.activitySwitch.on)
    {
        [self.activityIndicator startAnimating];
    }
}
```

Finally, call the loadPersistentData: method from the viewDidLoad method, as shown in Listing 15-8.

Listing 15-8. Calling the loadPersistentData: Method from Within the viewDidLoad Method

```
- (void)viewDidLoad
{
    [super viewDidLoad];
        // Do any additional setup after loading the view, typically from a nib.
    self.firstNameTextField.delegate = self;
    self.lastNameTextField.delegate = self;
```

```
[self loadPersistentData:self];

[[NSNotificationCenter defaultCenter] addObserver:self
    selector:@selector(savePersistentData:)
    name:UIApplicationDidEnterBackgroundNotification object:nil];
}
```

You're now done implementing the persistency of the app's state. Open the app, enter some text in the text fields, and turn the activity switch to ON. Now press the Home button on the device to make the app enter the background mode. The data should now be saved to NSUserDefault, but to truly test whether that really happened, you need to terminate the app before relaunching it. To do that, you can either stop the app's execution from Xcode or double-press the Home button and locate the "stubborn" app in the list of suspended apps; if you flick the app preview upward, it will shoot off the screen and close the app.

Now if you rerun the app, you'll see that it appears just as you left it. Figure 15-2 shows an example of this app right after it has been relaunched.

Figure 15-2. An app that has restored its state from the previous run, using NSUserDefaults

Although you did not use a great variety of values to store with NSUserDefaults in this short recipe, there are in fact methods to store almost any type of lightweight value, including BOOL, Float, Integer, Double, and URL. For any kind of more complex object, such as an NSString, NSArray, or NSDictionary, use the general setObject:forKey: method.

Remember, though, NSUserDefaults is meant for relatively small amounts of data. In the next recipe, we'll show you how you can store somewhat bigger chunks using files.

Recipe 15-2. Persisting Data Using Files

While the NSUserDefaults class is especially useful for doing quick persistence of light data, it is not nearly as efficient for dealing with large objects, such as documents, videos, music, or images. For these more complex items, you can use the iOS file management system.

In this recipe, you'll create a simple app that allows you to enter a long text and save it to a file. Start by creating a new single view application project. You can name it "Recipe 15-2 Persisting Data Using Files."

Next, build a user interface that resembles Figure 15-3. You'll need a label, a text field, a text view, and three buttons.

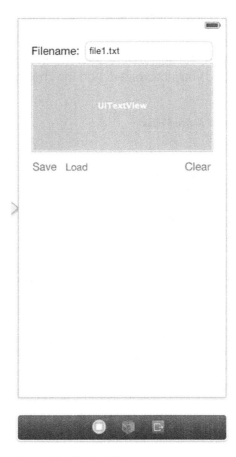

Figure 15-3. A simple app for editing, saving, and loading text files

Create the following outlets and actions for the respective components:

- *Outlets*: filenameTextField and contentTextView
- *Actions*: saveContent, loadContent, and clearContent

With the user interface in place, you can start implementing its functionality. But first create a helper method that transforms the relative file name into an absolute file path within the Documents directory of the device by adding the method shown in Listing 15-9 to the ViewController.m file.

Listing 15-9. Implementing the currentContentFilePath Method

```
- (NSString *)currentContentFilePath
{
    NSArray *documentDirectories =
        NSSearchPathForDirectoriesInDomains(NSDocumentDirectory, NSUserDomainMask, YES);
    NSString *documentsDirectory = [documentDirectories objectAtIndex:0];

    return [documentsDirectory
        stringByAppendingPathComponent:self.filenameTextField.text];
}
```

When the user taps the Save button, the app will need to save the content of the text view to the file path provided by the helper method you just created. Add the implementation shown in Listing 15-10 to the saveContent: action method.

Listing 15-10. Implementing the saveContent: Action Method

```
- (IBAction)saveContent:(id)sender
{
    NSString *filePath = [self currentContentFilePath];
    NSString *content = self.contentTextView.text;
    NSError *error;
    BOOL success = [content writeToFile:filePath atomically:YES
        encoding:NSUnicodeStringEncoding error:&error];
    if (!success)
    {
        NSLog(@"Unable to save file: %@\nError: %@", filePath, error);
    }
}
```

Conversely, when the user taps the Load button, the app will load the content from the file and update the text view. Listing 15-11 shows the implementation of the loadContent: action method.

Listing 15-11. Implementing the loadContent: Method

```
- (IBAction)loadContent:(id)sender
{
    NSString *filePath = [self currentContentFilePath];
    NSError *error;
    NSString *content = [NSString stringWithContentsOfFile:filePath
        encoding:NSUnicodeStringEncoding error:&error];
    if (error)
    {
        NSLog(@"Unable to load file: %@\nError: %@", filePath, error);
    }
    self.contentTextView.text = content;
}
```

Finally, the Clear button simply clears the text view using the action method shown in Listing 15-12.

Listing 15-12. Implementation of the clearContent: Action Method

```
- (IBAction)clearContent:(id)sender
{
    self.contentTextView.text = nil;
}
```

You now have a very rudimentary text file editor, so try it. Build and run the app. Enter some text in the text view, enter a file name in the Filename text input, and click the Save button. The app will create a file in the Documents directory on the device (or on your disk if you're running the app in the iOS simulator). To verify that it has been correctly saved, you can tap Clear to reset the text view and then Load. The text you just wrote should now reappear in the text view. You can also try to create different files by changing the contents of the Filename text field.

Although this app works, it has one serious problem that we'd like to address before leaving this recipe. If you save the content to an existing file, the app will silently overwrite its content, which might or might not be what the user wants. To make sure you catch the user's intention, you're going to check whether the file exists and ask for permissions to replace it if it does. Do this by changing the implementation of the saveContent: method. Start by extracting the actual saving into a helper method called saveContentToFile, as shown in Listing 15-13.

Listing 15-13. Implementation of the saveContentToFile: Method

```
- (void)saveContentToFile:(NSString *)filePath
{
    NSString *content = self.contentTextView.text;
    NSError *error;
    BOOL success = [content writeToFile:filePath atomically:YES
        encoding:NSUnicodeStringEncoding error:&error];
    if (!success)
    {
        NSLog(@"Unable to save file: %@\nError: %@", filePath, error);
    }
}
```

Make changes, as shown in bold in Listing 15-14, to the saveContent: method.

Listing 15-14. Updating the saveContent: Method to Alert the User Before Saving

```
- (IBAction)saveContent:(id)sender
{
    NSString *filePath = [self currentContentFilePath];
    NSFileManager *fileManager = [NSFileManager defaultManager];
    if ([fileManager fileExistsAtPath:filePath])
```

```
    {
        UIAlertView *overwriteAlert = [[UIAlertView alloc] initWithTitle:@"File Exists"
            message:@"Do you want to replace the file?" delegate:self
            cancelButtonTitle:@"No" otherButtonTitles:@"Yes", nil];
        [overwriteAlert show];
    }
    else
        [self saveContentToFile:filePath];
}
```

Add the UIAlertViewDelegate protocol to the ViewController.h file so the view controller can act as the alert view's delegate and intercept when the user taps its buttons. Listing 15-15 shows this change.

Listing 15-15. Declaring the UIAlertViewDelegate Protocol in the ViewController.h File

```
//
//  ViewController.h
//  Recipe 15-2 Persisting Data Using Files
//

#import <UIKit/UIKit.h>

@interface ViewController : UIViewController<UIAlertViewDelegate>

@property (weak, nonatomic) IBOutlet UITextField *filenameTextField;
@property (weak, nonatomic) IBOutlet UITextView *contentTextView;

- (IBAction)saveContent:(id)sender;
- (IBAction)loadContent:(id)sender;
- (IBAction)clearContent:(id)sender;

@end
```

Finally, back in ViewController.m, add the delegate method shown in Listing 15-16 for when the user taps one of the alert view's buttons.

Listing 15-16. Implementing the alertView:clickedButtonAtIndex: Delegate Method

```
- (void)alertView:(UIAlertView *)alertView clickedButtonAtIndex:(NSInteger)buttonIndex
{
    if (buttonIndex == 1)
    {
        // User tapped Yes button, overwrite the file
        NSString *filePath = [self currentContentFilePath];
        [self saveContentToFile:filePath];
    }
}
```

Now you're done and can run the app again. This time, if you try to save a file that already exists, you'll be asked if you want to replace it (see Figure 15-4).

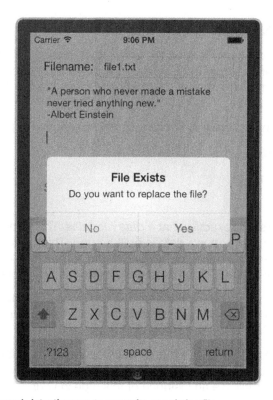

Figure 15-4. An app asking if the user's intention was to overwrite an existing file

In this demo app, you've worked only with text data. However, other types of data are equally simple. NSImage, for example, has methods for saving and loading from files, as have most other common data types. And even if what you want to save doesn't have direct file support, you can always convert it to an NSData object, which does.

While files are great for storing documents and isolated pieces of data, they are not very handy when it comes to persisting multiple objects with internal relationships, which is the natural data model of many apps. For these applications, a better alternative is to use the Core Data framework, the topic of the next recipe.

Recipe 15-3. Using Core Data

So far you have dealt with the quick implementation of NSUserDefaults for lightweight values as well as the file management system for larger amounts of data. While using the file management system is incredibly powerful for storing data, it can easily become quite cumbersome when dealing with complex data models of intertwined classes. For such cases, the best option becomes Core Data.

In this recipe, you build a simple word list app that persists its data using Core Data. But before you start, let's quickly go through the basics of this framework.

Understanding Core Data

The Core Data framework is designed around the concept of relational data. However, it's not a relational database but rather a layer of abstraction on top of a storage entity, usually SQLite. With Core Data you can focus on the structure of your data and leave the low-level relational database details for the framework to handle.

Put simply, Core Data, in conjunction with Xcode, allows a developer to perform three main tasks:

1. Create a data model

2. Persist information

3. Access data

First, it is important to understand exactly what a *data model* is. This term applies essentially to whatever structure any given application's data is built around. This could be something as simple as an `NSString` or an `NSArray` in a simple application, all the way up to a complex, interconnected system of object types, each with their own properties, methods, and pointers to other objects.

Core Data is one of the most powerful frameworks in iOS. Despite this, its API is surprisingly small, consisting of only a handful of classes for you to handle. Here are some brief descriptions of the few main classes that make up Core Data:

- `NSManagedObjectModel`: This object is how iOS refers to your data model, but you will have little to do with this class yourself. When you create your project for the first recipe, you will see an instance of this type in your application delegate, and you will see it used in some pregenerated methods. Aside from that, you will have no reason to deal with this class programmatically.

- `NSPersistentStoreCoordinator`: This class, too, is one that you rarely will need to deal with. It works mostly in the background of an application to "coordinate" between your application and the underlying database or "persistent store," but you will not need to send any actions to it. The most important part of this class that you need to know about is the type of persistent store that is being used. There are four types of persistent stores.

  - `NSSQLiteStoreType`: A database store built on SQLite

  - `NSBinaryStoreType`: A binary store type

  - `NSInMemoryStoreType`: An in-memory store

  - `NSXMLStoreType`: A store type using XML

The default value is `NSSQLiteStoreType`, specifying that you are using a persistent store built around the SQLite foundation. You will continue to use this type for the purpose of the Core Data recipes in this chapter.

- `NSManagedObjectContext`: This class, unlike the preceding two, is one you will be dealing with often. In the simplest terms, this class acts as a sort of workspace for your information. Any time you need to retrieve or store information, you will need a pointer to this class to perform the action. For this reason, a common practice in Core Data–based applications is to "pass around" a pointer to this class between each part of the application by giving each view controller an NSManagedObjectContext property.

- NSManagedObject: This class represents an instance of actual data in the data model.

- NSFetchedResultsController: This is the primary class for "fetching" results through the NSManagedObjectContext. It is not only very powerful but also very easy to use, especially in conjunction with UITableView. You will see plenty of examples of using this class in the recipes to come.

Now, let's start building the word list app.

Setting Up Core Data

The easiest way to set up Core Data for your app is to let Xcode generate the necessary code when you create the project. Create a new project called "Recipe 15-3 Using Core Data" using the Empty Application template, as shown in Figure 15-5.

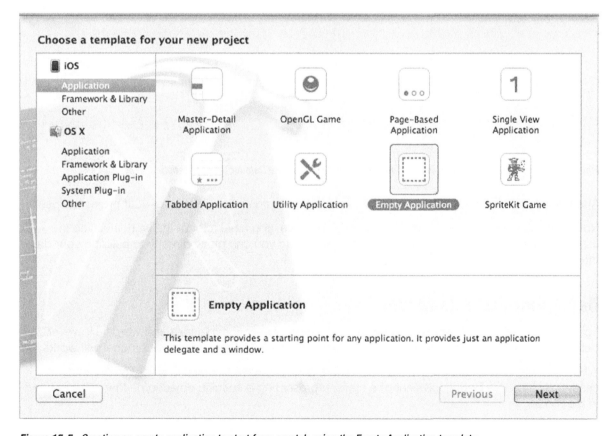

Figure 15-5. Creating an empty application to start from scratch using the Empty Application template

On the next screen, where you enter the project name, be sure to select the Use Core Data check box (see Figure 15-6).

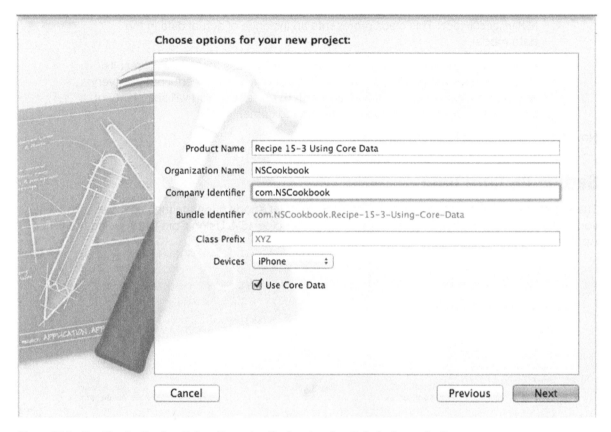

Figure 15-6. Checking the Use Core Data option makes Xcode set up Core Data for the application

After clicking Next, click Create on the next dialog box to finish the creation of your project as usual.

Now that you have set up your project to use Core Data, you have a lot of the work involved in using the Core Data framework already done for you, so you can move directly to building your data model.

Designing the Data Model

For this app, you build a simple data model consisting of only vocabularies and words. However, before you proceed to do anything in Xcode, you need to plan exactly how your model will work.

When working with a data model, the first kind of item you have to make is an *entity*. An entity is essentially the Core Data equivalent of a class, representing a specific object type that will be stored in the model.

In the same way that objects (or NSObjects in Objective-C) have properties, entities have *attributes*. These are the simpler pieces of data associated with any given entity, such as a name, age, or birthday, that do not require a pointer to any other entity.

Whenever you want one entity to have a pointer to another, you use a *relationship*. A relationship can be either to-one or to-many, referring to whether an entity has a pointer to one instance of another entity or multiple ones.

When dealing with the to-many relationship, you will notice that the entity has a pointer to a set of multiple other entities. Entities can easily have relationships that point to themselves, which might be the case of a Person entity having a relationship to another Person, in the form of a spouse. You can also set up *inverse relationships*, which act as paths back and forth between entities. For example, a Teacher entity might have a to-many relationship to a Student entity called "students," and the Student's relationship to the Teacher, called "teachers," will be the inverse of this. Figure 15-7 shows a diagram of this two-way relationship.

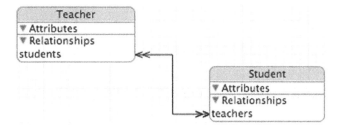

***Figure 15-7.** Two entities with a to-many relationship pointing to one another*

So for your data model, you have two entities with their respective attributes and relationships, as defined in Table 15-1.

***Table 15-1.** The Data Model of the My Vocabularies App*

Entity	Attributes	Relationships
Vocabulary	name	words
Word	word, translation	vocabulary

Note By convention, pluralized relationship names indicate a to-many relationship, while singular names are used for to-one relationships.

Now that you have the data model planned out, you can build this in Xcode. Switch to view your data model file, which is named Recipe_15_3_Using_Core_Data.xcdatamodeld, in your project. Your view should now resemble Figure 15-8.

Figure 15-8. *The Data Model Editor with an empty data model*

Now add the two entities of your data model. You can do this either by using the Editor menu or by using the Add Entity button located in the bottom-center area of the Xcode window. When you add an entity, you will need to click the entity, rename it "Vocabulary," and then click Return. Repeat the process for the Word entity.

> **Note**   It's easier to create all your entities first before trying to configure them; otherwise, you won't be able to set up the relationships.

After you've added the two entities, the list of entities should resemble Figure 15-9.

Figure 15-9. *The two entities of the My Vocabulary app data model*

Start by configuring the Vocabulary entity, so be sure the "Vocabulary" text is selected in the Entities section. By using the + button in the Attributes section, add an attribute called name with the type String selected in the Type drop-down menu, as shown in Figure 15-10.

Figure 15-10. An entity, Vocabulary, with a single attribute, name

Now you define the relationship of the Vocabulary entity. Under the Relationships area, add a relationship using the + button in that section. Name the relationship "words." As the relationship's destination, assign the Word entity. Until you create the relationship in the other entity, you cannot set up the inverse relationship, so leave it at No Inverse. The relationships set up for the Vocabulary entity should at this point be as in Figure 15-11.

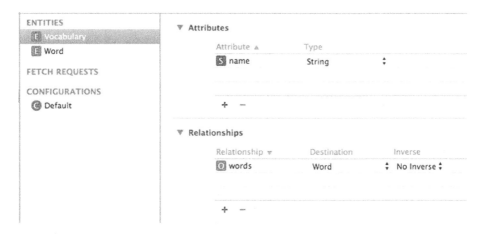

Figure 15-11. Configuring the Vocabulary entity's relationships

Now you will define this relationship as a to-many relationship. Do that by selecting one of the relationships and check the To-Many relationship option in the Data Model Inspector (which corresponds to the attributes inspector for view elements), as shown in Figure 15-12.

Figure 15-12. Defining a to-many relationship in the Data Model inspector

While you most likely will not need to worry about most of the other values in this inspector (at least for the purposes of this recipe), one of the values of higher importance is the Delete Rule drop-down menu. This value specifies exactly how this relationship is handled when an instance of the given entity is deleted from the NSManagedObjectContext. It has four possible values:

- *No Action*: This is probably the most dangerous value, as it simply allows related objects to continue to attempt to access the deleted object.

- *Nullify*: The default value, this specifies that the relationship will be nullified upon deletion and will thus return a nil value.

- *Cascade*: This value can be slightly dangerous to use, as it specifies that if one object is deleted, all the objects it is related to via this Delete Rule setting will also be deleted, so as to avoid having nil values. If you're not careful with this, you can delete unexpectedly large amounts of data, though it can also be very good for keeping your data clean. You might use this, for example, in the case of a "folder" with multiple objects. When a folder is deleted, you should delete all the contained objects as well.

- *Deny*: This prevents the object from being deleted as long as the relationship does not point to nil.

Change the Delete Rule to Cascade for this recipe so that if we delete a vocabulary, the words that pertain to it are deleted as well.

Now the time has come to configure the Word entity. In the same way you did for the Vocabulary entity, select the "Word" text in the Entities section; then move to the Attributes section and add two attributes this time, named word and translation. Use the type "String" for both of these attributes as well.

Also, add a relationship named vocabulary with the Destination set to Vocabulary. You can now also set the inverse relationship to words, as shown in Figure 15-13. This automatically sets up the inverse relationship for the words relationship as well (to vocabulary).

Figure 15-13. Configuring a relationship with an inverse

Note   Inverse relationships are not always required, though they tend to make the organization and flow of your application a little bit better, allowing you to more easily access any piece of data you need from any other piece of data.

Because the vocabulary relationship is a to-one relationship (a Word can belong only to one Vocabulary), you should not select the to-many option as you did with the words relationship.

As the final step in the process of creating the data model, create Objective-C classes that map to the respective entity. Make sure the Vocabulary entity is selected, go to the Editor menu and choose Create NSManagedObject Subclass. Then select both the Vocabulary entity and the Word entity, click the Next button, and then click the Create button. This adds new classes to the project named Vocabulary and Word, respectively.

This is all you need to do to create your data model. To get a graphic overview of the data model, change Editor Style to Graph in the lower-right corner of the Data Model Editor. The Graph Editor Style uses a UML notation to display the entities, their attributes, and their relationships, where a single arrow represents a to-one relationship and a double arrow represents a to-many relationship. The blocks might initially appear all stacked on top of each other, but if you drag them apart, your display should resemble Figure 15-14.

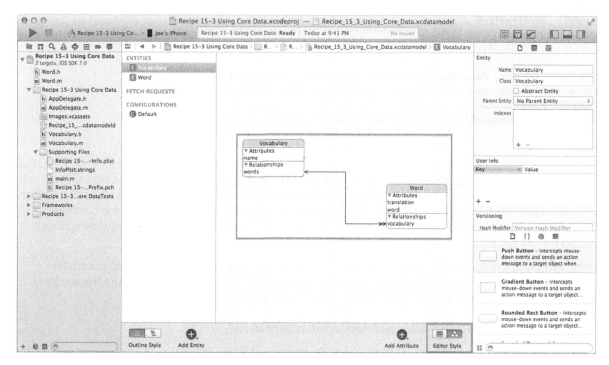

Figure 15-14. *A data model shown in the Graph Editor Style mode*

Now that you have your data model set up, you can start to build the user interface to display its data.

Setting Up the Vocabularies Table View

Next, you will set up a navigation-based app with a main table view displaying a list of vocabularies.

To start implementing this, add a new class to the project. Name the class VocabulariesViewController and make it a subclass of UITableViewController. You do not need a .xib file, so leave that option unchecked.

> **Note**   The `UITableViewController` class automatically sets up a table view and hooks up the necessary delegate properties. It's a convenient way to quickly set up a table view controller in an application.

Now make the changes to the `VocabulariesViewController.h` file, as shown in Listing 15-17.

Listing 15-17. Implementing the alertView:clickedButtonAtIndex: Delegate Method

```
//
//  VocabulariesViewController.h
//  Recipe 15-3 Using Core Data
//

#import <UIKit/UIKit.h>
#import "Vocabulary.h"

@interface VocabulariesViewController : UITableViewController<UIAlertViewDelegate>

@property (strong, nonatomic)NSManagedObjectContext *managedObjectContext;
@property (strong, nonatomic)NSFetchedResultsController *fetchedResultsController;

- (id)initWithManagedObjectContext:(NSManagedObjectContext *)context;

@end
```

What's worth mentioning about the code in Listing 15-16 is that the `fetchedResultsController` property keeps track of the fetched data and the `managedObjectContext` property allows you to make any necessary requests for data. You might also be wondering why you make the view controller conform to the `UIAlertViewDelegate` protocol. The reason is that you use an alert view as an input dialog for the vocabulary name later.

Now, switch to the `VocabulariesViewController.m` file to start implementing the view controller. Begin with the implementation for the custom initializer method. You'll want to replace the existing `initWithStyle` method, as shown with the initializer in Listing 15-18.

Listing 15-18. Implementing the initWithManagedObjectContext: Initializer Method

```
- (id)initWithManagedObjectContext:(NSManagedObjectContext *)context
{
    self = [super initWithStyle:UITableViewStylePlain];
    if (self)
    {
        self.managedObjectContext = context;
    }
    return self;
}
```

Next, add the helper method in Listing 15-19, which fetches all vocabularies in the data model and stores them in the `fetchedResultsController` property.

Listing 15-19. Implementing the fetchVocabularies Method

```
-(void)fetchVocabularies
{
    NSFetchRequest *fetchRequest =
        [NSFetchRequest fetchRequestWithEntityName:@"Vocabulary"];
    NSString *cacheName = [@"Vocabulary" stringByAppendingString:@"Cache"];

    NSSortDescriptor *sortDescriptor =
        [NSSortDescriptor sortDescriptorWithKey:@"name" ascending:YES];
    [fetchRequest setSortDescriptors:@[sortDescriptor]];

    self.fetchedResultsController = [[NSFetchedResultsController alloc]
        initWithFetchRequest:fetchRequest managedObjectContext:self.managedObjectContext
        sectionNameKeyPath:nil cacheName:cacheName];
    NSError *error;
    if (![self.fetchedResultsController performFetch:&error])
    {
        NSLog(@"Fetch failed: %@", error);
    }
}
```

In detail, the method in Listing 15-19 does the following:

1. The first thing you need for fetching data is an instance of the NSFetchRequest class. Here, you have used a designated initializer to specify an NSEntityDescription, though you can also add it later using the -setEntity: method.

2. While not required, you have set up a "cache name" to be used with your fetch request, with a different cache for each entity. This allows you to slightly improve the speed of your application if you are making frequent fetch requests, as a local cache is first checked to see whether the request has already been performed.

3. Every instance of NSFetchRequest is required to have at least one NSSortDescriptor associated with it. Here, you have specified a simple alphabetic sort of the name property for each of your entities. After all your NSSortDescriptors have been created, they must be attached to the NSFetchRequest using the setSortDescriptors: method.

4. After the NSFetchRequest is fully configured, you can initialize the NSFetchedResultsController using the NSFetchRequest and the NSManagedObjectContext. The last two parameters are both optional, though you have specified a cacheName for optimization. You can set both of these to nil if you want to ignore them.

5. Finally, you must use the performFetch: method to complete the fetch request and retrieve the stored data. With this method, you can pass a pointer to an NSError, as shown previously, to keep track of and log any errors that occur with a fetch.

In the `viewDidLoad` method, you initialize the view controller by setting its title and loading the vocabularies, as shown in Listing 15-20.

Listing 15-20. Modifying the viewDidLoad Method

```
- (void)viewDidLoad
{
    [super viewDidLoad];

    self.title = @"Vocabularies";

    [self fetchVocabularies];
}
```

To avoid presenting an empty list the first time the app is run, you'll preload the data model with a "Spanish" vocabulary, but only if no vocabularies exist. To do this, add the code shown in bold in Listing 15-21 to the `viewDidLoad` method.

Listing 15-21. Modifying the viewDidLoad Method to Preload with Vocabulary

```
- (void)viewDidLoad
{
    [super viewDidLoad];

    self.title = @"Vocabularies";

    [self fetchVocabularies];
    // Preload with a "Spanish" Vocabulary if empty
    if (self.fetchedResultsController.fetchedObjects.count == 0)
    {
        NSEntityDescription *vocabularyEntityDescription =
            [NSEntityDescription entityForName:@"Vocabulary"
                inManagedObjectContext:self.managedObjectContext];
        Vocabulary *spanishVocabulary = (Vocabulary *)[[NSManagedObject alloc]
            initWithEntity:vocabularyEntityDescription
            insertIntoManagedObjectContext:self.managedObjectContext];
        spanishVocabulary.name = @"Spanish";
        NSError *error;
        if (![self.managedObjectContext save:&error])
        {
            NSLog(@"Error saving context: %@", error);
        }
        [self fetchVocabularies];
    }
}
```

Next, you need to implement the required delegate and data source methods for the table view. First, implement the methods to specify the number of sections and rows shown in Listing 15-22.

Listing 15-22. Implementing the numberOfSectionsInTableView: and tableView:numberOfRowsInSection: Delegate Methods

```
- (NSInteger)numberOfSectionsInTableView:(UITableView *)tableView
{
    return 1;
}


- (NSInteger)tableView:(UITableView *)tableView numberOfRowsInSection:(NSInteger)section
{
    return self.fetchedResultsController.fetchedObjects.count;
}
```

As shown in Listing 15-22, the NSFetchedResultsController class contains a method fetchedObjects, which returns an NSArray of the objects that were queried for.

Listing 15-23 shows the method to configure the cells of the table view.

Listing 15-23. Implementing the tableView:cellForRowAtIndexPath: Delegate Method

```
- (UITableViewCell *)tableView:(UITableView *)tableView cellForRowAtIndexPath:(NSIndexPath
*)indexPath
{
    static NSString *CellIdentifier = @"VocabularyCell";

    UITableViewCell *cell =
        [tableView dequeueReusableCellWithIdentifier:CellIdentifier];
    if (cell == nil)
    {
        cell = [[UITableViewCell alloc] initWithStyle:UITableViewCellStyleValue1
            reuseIdentifier:CellIdentifier];
        cell.accessoryType = UITableViewCellAccessoryDisclosureIndicator;
    }

    Vocabulary *vocabulary = (Vocabulary *)[self.fetchedResultsController
        objectAtIndexPath:indexPath];
    cell.textLabel.text = vocabulary.name;
    cell.detailTextLabel.text =
        [NSString stringWithFormat:@"(%d)", vocabulary.words.count];

    return cell;
}
```

The basic setup of the main view controller is now finished, and the time has come to make it work, so go to the AppDelegate.h file and add the declarations shown in Listing 15-24.

Listing 15-24. Adding Declarations to the appDelegate

```
//
//  AppDelegate.h
//  My Vocabularies
//
```

```
#import <UIKit/UIKit.h>
#import "VocabulariesViewController.h"

@interface AppDelegate : UIResponder <UIApplicationDelegate>

@property (strong, nonatomic) UIWindow *window;

@property (readonly, strong, nonatomic) NSManagedObjectContext *managedObjectContext;
@property (readonly, strong, nonatomic) NSManagedObjectModel *managedObjectModel;
@property (readonly, strong, nonatomic) NSPersistentStoreCoordinator
    *persistentStoreCoordinator;
@property (strong, nonatomic) UINavigationController *navigationController;
@property (strong, nonatomic) VocabulariesViewController *vocabulariesViewController;

- (void)saveContext;
- (NSURL *)applicationDocumentsDirectory;

@end
```

As you can see from the code in Listing 15-24, the appDelegate is the place where Core Data has been set up for you. All you need to do is distribute the managed object context to the parts of your app that deal with the data.

In the application:didFinishLaunchingWithOptions: method in AppDelegate.m, add the code in Listing 15-25 to create and display the view controller in a navigation controller.

Listing 15-25. Creating and Displaying Both the View and Navigation Controllers

```
- (BOOL)application:(UIApplication *)application didFinishLaunchingWithOptions:(NSDictionary
*)launchOptions
{
    self.window = [[UIWindow alloc] initWithFrame:[[UIScreen mainScreen] bounds]];
    self.window.backgroundColor = [UIColor whiteColor];

    self.vocabulariesViewController = [[VocabulariesViewController alloc]
        initWithManagedObjectContext:self.managedObjectContext];
    self.navigationController = [[UINavigationController alloc]
        initWithRootViewController:self.vocabulariesViewController];
    self.window.rootViewController = self.navigationController;

    [self.window makeKeyAndVisible];
    return YES;
}
```

Now is a good time to build and run the app to make sure everything is set up correctly. If things go right, you should see a screen resembling Figure 15-15.

Figure 15-15. *A word list app with a single vocabulary*

To allow the user to add some data in the form of new vocabularies, put an "Add" button on the Navigation bar. Go back to the viewDidLoad method in VocabulariesViewController.m and add the code shown in Listing 15-26.

Listing 15-26. *Adding an "Add" Button to the Navigation Bar*

```
- (void)viewDidLoad
{
    [super viewDidLoad];

    self.title = @"Vocabularies";

    UIBarButtonItem *addButton =
        [[UIBarButtonItem alloc] initWithBarButtonSystemItem:UIBarButtonSystemItemAdd
            target:self action:@selector(add)];
    self.navigationItem.rightBarButtonItem = addButton;

    [self fetchVocabularies];

    // ...
}
```

Now implement the add action method, as shown in Listing 15-27. It brings up an alert view for the user to input a name of a new vocabulary.

Listing 15-27. Implementing the Add Action Method

```
- (void)add
{
    UIAlertView * inputAlert = [[UIAlertView alloc] initWithTitle:@"New Vocabulary"
        message:@"Enter a name for the new vocabulary" delegate:self
        cancelButtonTitle:@"Cancel" otherButtonTitles:@"OK", nil];
    inputAlert.alertViewStyle = UIAlertViewStylePlainTextInput;
    [inputAlert show];
}
```

Finally, implement the `alertView:clickedButtonAtIndex:` delegate method to create the new vocabulary if the user taps the OK button. Listing 15-28 shows this implementation.

Listing 15-28. Implementing the alertView:clickedButtonAtIndex: Delegate Method

```
- (void)alertView:(UIAlertView *)alertView clickedButtonAtIndex:(NSInteger)buttonIndex
{
    if (buttonIndex == 1)
    {
        NSEntityDescription *vocabularyEntityDescription =
            [NSEntityDescription entityForName:@"Vocabulary"
                inManagedObjectContext:self.managedObjectContext];
        Vocabulary *newVocabulary = (Vocabulary *)[[NSManagedObject alloc]
            initWithEntity:vocabularyEntityDescription
            insertIntoManagedObjectContext:self.managedObjectContext];
        newVocabulary.name = [alertView textFieldAtIndex:0].text;
        NSError *error;
        if (![self.managedObjectContext save:&error])
        {
            NSLog(@"Error saving context: %@", error);
        }
        [self fetchVocabularies];
        [self.tableView reloadData];
    }
}
```

If you build and run the app again, you now can add new vocabularies, as shown in Figure 15-16.

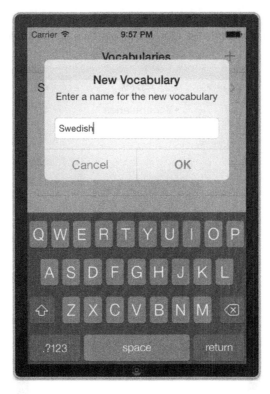

Figure 15-16. Adding a new vocabulary

As a final feature of the Vocabularies view controller, implement the ability to delete items. Do that by implementing the tableView:commitEditingStyle:forRowAtIndexPath: delegate method, as shown in Listing 15-29.

Listing 15-29. Implementing the tableView:commitEditingStyle:forRowAtIndexPath: Delegate Method

```
-(void)tableView:(UITableView *)tableView commitEditingStyle:(UITableViewCellEditingStyle)
editingStyle forRowAtIndexPath:(NSIndexPath *)indexPath
{
    if (editingStyle == UITableViewCellEditingStyleDelete)
    {
        NSManagedObject *deleted =
            [self.fetchedResultsController objectAtIndexPath:indexPath];
        [self.managedObjectContext deleteObject:deleted];
        NSError *error;
        BOOL success = [self.managedObjectContext save:&error];
        if (!success)
        {
            NSLog(@"Error saving context: %@", error);
        }
        [self fetchVocabularies];
        [self.tableView deleteRowsAtIndexPaths:@[indexPath]
            withRowAnimation:UITableViewRowAnimationRight];
    }
}
```

To test this feature, run the app again and swipe an item in the list. A red button should appear that allows you to delete the item in question. Figure 15-17 shows an example of this.

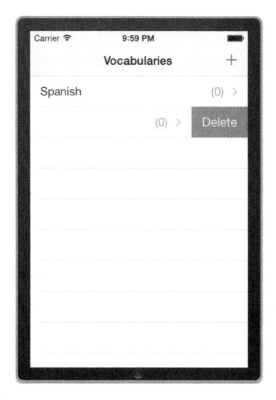

Figure 15-17. *Deleting a vocabulary*

With the Vocabularies view all set up, it's time to create the view that handles the words.

Implementing the Words View Controller

When the user selects a cell in the Vocabularies table view, another table view is presented displaying the words of that vocabulary.

Create a new UITableViewController subclass named WordsViewController, again without selecting the With XIB option.

You will initialize the Words view controller with a vocabulary, so you need a property and a custom initializer for that. You also need to import the Vocabulary and Word classes. Go to WordsViewController.h and add the declarations shown in Listing 15-30.

Listing 15-30. Updating the WordsViewController.h file for Words Implementation

```
//
//  WordsViewController.h
//  Recipe 15-3 Using Core Data
//
```

```
#import <UIKit/UIKit.h>
#import "Vocabulary.h"
#import "Word.h"

@interface WordsViewController : UITableViewController

@property (strong, nonatomic)Vocabulary *vocabulary;

- (id)initWithVocabulary:(Vocabulary *)vocabulary;

@end
```

Now switch to the WordsViewController.m file. The initializer method simply assigns the vocabulary property and is pretty straightforward. Listing 15-31 show the implementation.

Listing 15-31. Implementing the initWithVocabulary: Initializer Method

```
- (id)initWithVocabulary:(Vocabulary *)vocabulary
{
    self = [super initWithStyle:UITableViewStylePlain];
    if (self)
    {
        self.vocabulary = vocabulary;
    }
    return self;
}
```

The viewDidLoad method is more simple (at this point), setting only the view controller's title, as shown in Listing 15-32.

Listing 15-32. Setting the Title in the viewDidLoad Method

```
- (void)viewDidLoad
{
    [super viewDidLoad];

    self.title = self.vocabulary.name;
}
```

Listing 15-33 shows the required data source delegate methods.

Listing 15-33. Implementing Required Delegate Methods for the Number of Rows and Sections in the Table View

```
- (NSInteger)numberOfSectionsInTableView:(UITableView *)tableView
{
    return 1;
}

- (NSInteger)tableView:(UITableView *)tableView numberOfRowsInSection:(NSInteger)section
{
    return self.vocabulary.words.count;
}
```

Notice in Listing 15-33 how you use the corresponding property of the Vocabulary entity's words relationship to get the number of words. This is where the power of Core Data starts to show; you can handle the data as normal objects and ignore the fact that it's actually stored in a database.

Next, you'll design the table view cells to display both the word and its translation (as a subtitle). Do that by adding the implementation of the tableView:cellForRowAtIndexPath: delegate method shown in Listing 15-34.

Listing 15-34. Implementing the tableView:cellForRowAtIndexPath: Delegate Method

```
- (UITableViewCell *)tableView:(UITableView *)tableView cellForRowAtIndexPath:(NSIndexPath
*)indexPath
{
    static NSString *CellIdentifier = @"WordCell";

    UITableViewCell *cell =
        [tableView dequeueReusableCellWithIdentifier:CellIdentifier];
    if (cell == nil)
    {
        cell = [[UITableViewCell alloc] initWithStyle:UITableViewCellStyleSubtitle
            reuseIdentifier:CellIdentifier];
        cell.accessoryType = UITableViewCellAccessoryDisclosureIndicator;
    }

    Word *word = [self.vocabulary.words.allObjects objectAtIndex:indexPath.row];
    cell.textLabel.text = word.word;
    cell.detailTextLabel.text = word.translation;

    return cell;
}
```

To connect the two view controllers with each other, go back to VocabulariesViewController.h and import the Words view controller header file, as shown in Listing 15-35.

Listing 15-35. Adding an Import Statement to the VocabulariesViewController.h File

```
//
//  VocabulariesViewController.h
//  Recipe 15-3 Using Core Data
//

#import <UIKit/UIKit.h>
#import "Vocabulary.h"
#import "WordsViewController.h"

@interface VocabulariesViewController : UITableViewController<UIAlertViewDelegate>

@property (strong, nonatomic)NSManagedObjectContext *managedObjectContext;
@property (strong, nonatomic) NSFetchedResultsController *fetchedResultsController;

- (id)initWithManagedObjectContext:(NSManagedObjectContext *)context;

@end
```

Finally, in the VocabulariesViewController.m file, add the delegate method shown in Listing 15-36.

Listing 15-36. Implementing the tableView:didSelectRowAtIndexPath: Delegate Method

```
- (void)tableView:(UITableView *)tableView didSelectRowAtIndexPath:(NSIndexPath *)indexPath
{
    Vocabulary *vocabulary = (Vocabulary *)[self.fetchedResultsController
        objectAtIndexPath:indexPath];

    WordsViewController *detailViewController =
        [[WordsViewController alloc] initWithVocabulary:vocabulary];
    [self.navigationController pushViewController:detailViewController animated:YES];
}
```

Now is a good time to build and run to be sure everything is working properly. You can select a vocabulary and see its word list view, although empty at this point, as in Figure 15-18.

Figure 15-18. A vocabulary with no words in it

The next step is to implement a way for the user to add words to the vocabulary, again in the form of an "Add" button on the navigation bar. But before you add that button, create the view controller that handles the editing of the new Word object.

Adding a Word Edit View

Create a new subclass of UIViewController (not UITableViewController as before) with the name EditWordViewController. You'll build a user interface for it, so make sure the "With XIB for user interface" option is selected this time.

Open the EditWordViewController.xib file and build a user interface like the one in Figure 15-19. Because we'll be using a navigation controller, add the opaque navigation bar to the view by selecting it from the top bar drop-down in the attributes inspector with the full view selected.

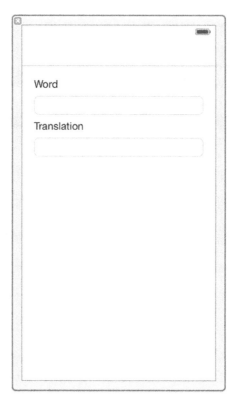

Figure 15-19. *A simple user interface for editing words*

As usual, create outlets for the text fields. Name them wordTextField and translationTextField, respectively.

With the user interface in place, you can move on to defining the programming interface of this view controller. You use Objective-C blocks to simplify the code on the calling side, which uses the class method shown in Listing 15-37 to present the edit view controller.

Listing 15-37. *Declaring the editWord: Class Method in the EditWordViewController.h File*

```
+ (void)editWord:(Word *)word
   inNavigationController:(UINavigationController *)navigationController
   completion:(EditWordViewControllerCompletionHandler)completionHandler;
```

The EditWordViewControllerCompletionHandler is a block type with two arguments, sender and canceled, as shown in Listing 15-38.

Listing 15-38. Creating the Block Type Declaration

```
typedef void (^EditWordViewControllerCompletionHandler)
    (EditWordViewController *sender, BOOL canceled);
```

To implement this API, you need a couple of instance variables and a custom initializer method. In all, add the bold code in Listing 15-39 to the EditWordViewController.h file.

Listing 15-39. The Complete EditWordViewController.h File

```
//
//  EditWordViewController.h
//  Recipe 15-3 Using Core Data
//

#import <UIKit/UIKit.h>
#import "Word.h"

@class EditWordViewController;

typedef void (^EditWordViewControllerCompletionHandler)(EditWordViewController *sender,
BOOL canceled);

@interface EditWordViewController : UIViewController
{
@private
    EditWordViewControllerCompletionHandler _completionHandler;
    Word *_word;
}

@property (weak, nonatomic) IBOutlet UITextField *wordTextField;
@property (weak, nonatomic) IBOutlet UITextField *translationTextField;

- (id)initWithWord:(Word *)word
    completion:(EditWordViewControllerCompletionHandler)completionHandler;

+ (void)editWord:(Word *)word
    inNavigationController:(UINavigationController *)navigationController
    completion:(EditWordViewControllerCompletionHandler)completionHandler;

@end
```

Now go to EditWordViewController.m and add the implementation in Listing 15-40 of the class method. It simply instantiates the edit view controller and adds it to the navigation controller stack.

Listing 15-40. Implementing the editWord: Class Method

```
+ (void)editWord:(Word *)word
    inNavigationController:(UINavigationController *)navigationController
    completion:(EditWordViewControllerCompletionHandler)completionHandler
{
    EditWordViewController *editViewController =
        [[EditWordViewController alloc] initWithWord:word completion:completionHandler];
    [navigationController pushViewController:editViewController animated:YES];
}
```

The initializer method stores away the word and the completion handler in the respective instance variable. Listing 15-41 shows this implementation.

Listing 15-41. Implementation of the initWithWord: Initializer Method

```
- (id)initWithWord:(Word *)word completion:(EditWordViewControllerCompletionHandler)
completionHandler
{
    self = [super initWithNibName:nil bundle:nil];
    if (self)
    {
        _completionHandler = completionHandler;
        _word = word;
    }
    return self;
}
```

When the edit view controller loads, it updates the two text fields with data from the provided Word object. It also adds two buttons, "Done" and "Cancel," to the navigation bar. To achieve that, add the code in Listing 15-42 to the viewDidLoad method.

Listing 15-42. Modifying the viewDidLoad Method to Set Text Fields and Add Buttons

```
- (void)viewDidLoad
{
    [super viewDidLoad];

    self.title = @"Edit Word";

    self.wordTextField.text = _word.word;
    self.translationTextField.text = _word.translation;

    self.navigationItem.rightBarButtonItem =
        [[UIBarButtonItem alloc] initWithBarButtonSystemItem:UIBarButtonSystemItemDone
            target:self action:@selector(done)];
    self.navigationItem.leftBarButtonItem =
        [[UIBarButtonItem alloc] initWithBarButtonSystemItem:UIBarButtonSystemItemCancel
            target:self action:@selector(cancel)];
}
```

As you can see from the code, two action methods have been hooked up to the buttons. Now you will need to implement them.

The first, done, updates the Word object with the data from the two text fields and then notifies the caller by invoking the completion handler block, sending "NO" for the cancel argument, as shown in Listing 15-43.

Listing 15-43. Implementing the Done Action Method

```
- (void)done
{
    _word.word = self.wordTextField.text;
    _word.translation = self.translationTextField.text;
    _completionHandler(self, NO);
}
```

The cancel action method is even simpler. It will notify the caller only if the user has canceled the edit, as shown in Listing 15-44.

Listing 15-44. Implementing the Cancel Action Method

```
- (void)cancel
{
    _completionHandler(self, YES);
}
```

You're now done with the edit view controller, so implement the code to display it. First, import the edit view controller in the WordsViewController.h file, as shown in Listing 15-45.

Listing 15-45. Importing the EditWordViewController.h File into the WordsViewController.h File

```
//
//  WordsViewController.h
//  Recipe 15-3 Using Core Data
//

#import <UIKit/UIKit.h>
#import "Vocabulary.h"
#import "Word.h"
#import "EditWordViewController.h"

@interface WordsViewController : UITableViewController

@property (strong, nonatomic)Vocabulary *vocabulary;

- (id)initWithVocabulary:(Vocabulary *)vocabulary;

@end
```

Next, add an "Add" button to the navigation bar of the words view controller class. Switch to the WordsViewController.m file and modify the viewDidLoad method, as shown in bold in Listing 15-46.

Listing 15-46. Creating an "Add" Button the WordsViewController Navigation Bar

```
- (void)viewDidLoad
{
    [super viewDidLoad];

    UIBarButtonItem *addButton =
        [[UIBarButtonItem alloc] initWithBarButtonSystemItem:UIBarButtonSystemItemAdd
            target:self action:@selector(add)];
    self.navigationItem.rightBarButtonItem = addButton;

    self.title = self.vocabulary.name;
}
```

Next, start implementing the action method of this button, as shown in Listing 15-47. It creates a new Word object, which it provides as an argument to the edit view controller.

Listing 15-47. The Starting Implementation of the Add Action Method

```
- (void)add
{
    NSEntityDescription *wordEntityDescription =
        [NSEntityDescription entityForName:@"Word"
            inManagedObjectContext:self.vocabulary.managedObjectContext];
    Word *newWord = (Word *)[[NSManagedObject alloc]
        initWithEntity:wordEntityDescription
        insertIntoManagedObjectContext:self.vocabulary.managedObjectContext];

    [EditWordViewController editWord:newWord
     inNavigationController:self.navigationController completion:
     ^(EditWordViewController *sender, BOOL canceled)
     {
         // TODO: Handle edit finished
     }];
}
```

When the edit view controller finishes, you either delete the new Word object if the user canceled or add it to the vocabulary and save it to the database. Either way, the edit view controller should be popped from the navigation controller. The complete implementation of the add action method should look like Listing 15-48.

Listing 15-48. The Complete Add Action Method Implementation

```
- (void)add
{
    NSEntityDescription *wordEntityDescription =
        [NSEntityDescription entityForName:@"Word"
            inManagedObjectContext:self.vocabulary.managedObjectContext];
    Word *newWord = (Word *)[[NSManagedObject alloc]
        initWithEntity:wordEntityDescription
        insertIntoManagedObjectContext:self.vocabulary.managedObjectContext];
    [EditWordViewController editWord:newWord
     inNavigationController:self.navigationController completion:
```

```
^(EditWordViewController *sender, BOOL canceled)
{
    if (canceled)
    {
        [self.vocabulary.managedObjectContext deleteObject:newWord];
    }
    else
    {
        [self.vocabulary addWordsObject:newWord];

        NSError *error;
        if (![self.vocabulary.managedObjectContext save:&error])
        {
            NSLog(@"Error saving context: %@", error);
        }
        [self.tableView reloadData];
    }

    [self.navigationController popViewControllerAnimated:YES];
}];
}
```

If you build and run now, you can add words to your vocabularies using the "Add" button in the respective Words view. Figure 15-20 shows an example of this.

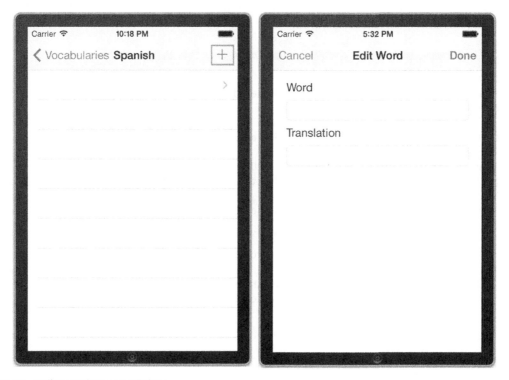

Figure 15-20. Adding words to a vocabulary

The user should of course be able to edit an existing word. You'll implement it so that when a user selects a cell, the edit view for that word is displayed. To do that, add the implementation shown in Listing 15-49 of the WordsViewController.m file to the tableView:didSelectRowAtIndexPath: delegate method.

Listing 15-49. Implementing the tableView:didSelectRowAtIndexPath: Method

```
- (void)tableView:(UITableView *)tableView didSelectRowAtIndexPath:(NSIndexPath *)indexPath
{
    Word *word = [self.vocabulary.words.allObjects objectAtIndex:indexPath.row];
    [EditWordViewController editWord:word
     inNavigationController:self.navigationController completion:
     ^(EditWordViewController *sender, BOOL canceled)
     {
         NSError *error;
         if (![self.vocabulary.managedObjectContext save:&error])
         {
             NSLog(@"Error saving context: %@", error);
         }

         [self.tableView reloadData];
         [self.navigationController popViewControllerAnimated:YES];
     }];
}
```

To allow the user to delete Words, add the tableView:commitEditingStyle:forRowAtIndexPath: delegate method, as shown in Listing 15-50.

Listing 15-50. Implementing the tableView:commitEditingstyle:forRowAtIndexPath: Delegate Method

```
-(void)tableView:(UITableView *)tableView
    commitEditingStyle:(UITableViewCellEditingStyle)editingStyle
    forRowAtIndexPath:(NSIndexPath *)indexPath
{
    if (editingStyle == UITableViewCellEditingStyleDelete)
    {
        Word *deleted = [self.vocabulary.words.allObjects objectAtIndex:indexPath.row];
        [self.vocabulary.managedObjectContext deleteObject:deleted];
        NSError *error;
        BOOL success = [self.vocabulary.managedObjectContext save:&error];
        if (!success)
        {
            NSLog(@"Error saving context: %@", error);
        }
        [self.tableView deleteRowsAtIndexPaths:@[indexPath]
            withRowAnimation:UITableViewRowAnimationRight];
    }
}
```

If you build and run now, you can delete words by sweeping your finger (or mouse pointer if you run in the iOS simulator), as shown in Figure 15-21.

Figure 15-21. Deleting a word in a Spanish vocabulary list

You're almost finished with this simple word list app, but there is one small issue that we'd like you to fix before we close this recipe. You've probably noticed that if you add words to a vocabulary and return to the main view, the item count for the vocabulary doesn't update. The easiest way to fix this is to reload the data whenever the view appears. To do that, add the method to the VocabulariesViewController.m file shown in Listing 15-51.

Listing 15-51. Implementing the viewWillAppear Override to Reload the Table

```
- (void)viewWillAppear:(BOOL)animated
{
    [self fetchVocabularies];
    [self.tableView reloadData];
}
```

Now if you try again, you'll see that the number within the parentheses updates to reflect the new number of items in the vocabulary (see Figure 15-22).

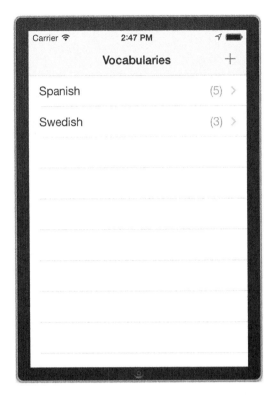

Figure 15-22. A word list app with two vocabularies containing five and three words, respectively

In this recipe, we have covered the basics of Core Data, one of the most integral parts of iOS development. You have seen a glimpse of its power and simplicity of use when it comes to data modeling, persistence, and access. However, we have by no means detailed every facet in the Core Data framework or even touched on many of the general subjects related to it. You can easily find entire books devoted to the subject of Core Data, and you probably should consult those sources to get a more complete view of exactly how much ability you have in controlling how your data is stored. The overview here has demonstrated a basic use of the framework and explained the key concepts needed to get started working with Core Data so that you can implement simple persistence in your applications without worrying about the more esoteric complexities. If you want to know more about this great framework, we recommend you start with Apple's documentation on this topic.

Persisting Data on iCloud

iCloud is Apple's data storage service for iOS and Mac devices. If iCloud is set up, iOS uses the service for tasks such as backups and synchronizing images between the user's different devices. iCloud comes with an extensive API so that your apps, too, can take advantage of its features, including persisting data and sharing state and files between all the user's devices. The other benefit is you can easily share information such as calendars between iOS and Mac devices. With the new Xcode 5 capabilities feature, which allows you to easily add capabilities such as iCloud and Game Center, it is now much less of a headache to set up iCloud services than with previous versions of Xcode.

Basically, iCloud comes with three kinds of storage:

- *Key-value storage*, which can be used to store preferences, settings, and other small-sized data

- *Document storage*, for file-based information such as images, text documents, files containing information about your app's state, and so on

- *Core Data storage*, which actually uses document storage to persist and synchronize your app's Core Data

In Recipe 15-4, we show you how you can implement key-value storage in your apps. Recipe 15-5 shows how you can create and store custom documents in iCloud. If you're interested in Core Data storage on iCloud, we recommend Apple's documentation.

> **Note**   The next recipe will require access to an iOS development program account as well as a physical iOS device. You can go to `http://developer.apple.com` to set up an account if you don't already have one.

Recipe 15-4. Storing Key-Value Data in iCloud

In this recipe, you set up an app for storing key-value data in iCloud. You use the key-value store to persist a simple user preference governing the font size of a displayed text. You start with the basic functionality of the app and then implement persisting to iCloud.

Create a new single view app project with the name "Testing iCloud." Select the `Main.storyboard` file and start building a user interface resembling the one in Figure 15-23.

Figure 15-23. A simple user interface with a text view and a segmented control

Create outlets for the controls and use the names fontSizeSegmentedControl and documentTextView, respectively. Also create an action named updateTextSize for the segmented control.

As you've probably guessed, the user can change the size of the text in the Text View using the segmented control. To implement that, go to ViewController.m and add the code in Listing 15-52 to the updateTextSize action method.

Listing 15-52. Implementing the updateTextSize: Action Method

```
- (IBAction)updateTextSize:(id)sender
{
    CGFloat newFontSize;
    switch (self.fontSizeSegmentedControl.selectedSegmentIndex)
    {
        case 1:
            newFontSize = 19;
            break;
        case 2:
            newFontSize = 24;
            break;
```

```
        default:
            newFontSize = 14;
            break;
    }
    self.documentTextView.font = [UIFont systemFontOfSize:newFontSize];
}
```

That's it! You can now run the app and change the text size from the segmented control, as shown in Figure 15-24.

Figure 15-24. Changing the text size with a segmented control

Notice that if you change the text size to, say, Large and terminate the app, the preference is not persisted and will be back to Small when you run the app again. You will implement persistence next, but instead of using NSUserDefaults, you'll use iCloud's key-value store. The advantage of using iCloud over local storage is that the preference can be persisted, not only between executions on your device but also shared by all your devices running this app. Additionally, if you remove and reinstall the app or log in and out of iCloud for some reason, the preferences will not be erased.

Let's go ahead and implement this feature, but first you need to do some configuring tasks to set up your app with iCloud.

Setting Up iCloud for an App

To set up iCloud, you must configure *entitlements*, which are special keys that allow you to use iCloud storage. Entitlements will be necessary to allow for iCloud and its key-value store. Navigate to the project's target settings and scroll and select the Capabilities tab. Select the switch to turn on iCloud and check Use Key-Value Store, as shown in Figure 15-25. Xcode then automatically generates an entitlements file with the correct settings.

Figure 15-25. Enabling entitlements to allow communication with iCloud

That is all that is needed to set up iCloud in iOS 7. Before iOS 7 and Xcode 5, setting up iCloud involved logging into the member center of the developer site and carrying out a few different steps. This was an annoying process to say the least. Now Xcode does everything for you behind the scenes.

Persisting Data in an iCloud Key-Value Store

You'll now move on to implement the storing of the text size preference in the iCloud key-value store. First, you'll need a property to store a reference to the key-value store. Go to ViewController.h and add the declaration shown in Listing 15-53.

Listing 15-53. Adding an NSUbiquitousKeyValueStore to the ViewController.h File

```
//
//  ViewController.h
//  Recipe 15-4 Storing Key-Value Data in iCloud
//

#import <UIKit/UIKit.h>

@interface ViewController : UIViewController

@property (weak, nonatomic) IBOutlet UISegmentedControl *fontSizeSegmentedControl;
@property (weak, nonatomic) IBOutlet UITextView *documentTextView;
@property (strong, nonatomic) NSUbiquitousKeyValueStore *iCloudKeyValueStore;

- (IBAction)updateTextSize:(id)sender;

@end
```

Now switch to ViewController.m and add the code in Listing 15-54 to the viewDidLoad method.

Listing 15-54. Setting Up iCloud in the viewDidLoad Method

```
- (void)viewDidLoad
{
    [super viewDidLoad];
    self.iCloudKeyValueStore = [NSUbiquitousKeyValueStore defaultStore];

    [[NSNotificationCenter defaultCenter] addObserver:self
        selector:@selector(handleStoreChange:)
        name:NSUbiquitousKeyValueStoreDidChangeExternallyNotification
        object:self.iCloudKeyValueStore];

    [self.iCloudKeyValueStore synchronize];
    [self updateUserInterfaceWithPreferences];
}
```

The code in Listing 15-54 does the following:

1. Gets a reference to the key-value store

2. Signs up for notifications when the data in the key-value store is changed by an external source (NSUbiquitousKeyValueStoreDidChangeExternallyNotification)

3. Makes sure the key-value store cache is up-to-date by calling synchronize

4. Updates the user interface with the values from the key-value store

> **Note**   Here, you're setting up the iCloud access directly in the main view controller, which is fine for the purpose of this recipe. However, in an app with several view controllers that access the key-value store, you should set it up in the app delegate instead and distribute the reference to whichever devices request it.

Next, implement the notification handler for when the iCloud data is changed by an external source, such as another device. For the sake of this recipe, you'll simply update the user interface with the new values shown in Listing 15-55.

Listing 15-55. Implementing the handleStoreChange: Method

```
- (void)handleStoreChange:(NSNotification *)notification
{
    [self updateUserInterfaceWithPreferences];
}
```

The updateUserInterfaceWithPreference helper method extracts the text size value from the key-value store and sets the selected index of the segmented control. This implementation is shown in Listing 15-56.

Listing 15-56. Implementing the updateUserInterfaceWithPreferences Method

```
- (void)updateUserInterfaceWithPreferences
{
    NSInteger selectedSize = [self.iCloudKeyValueStore doubleForKey:@"TextSize"];
    self.fontSizeSegmentedControl.selectedSegmentIndex = selectedSize;
    [self updateTextSize:self];
}
```

Finally, when the user changes the text size using the segmented control, you should write the new value to the key-value store for persistency in iCloud. Add the code to the updateTextSize: action method, as shown in Listing 15-57.

Listing 15-57. Updating the updateTextSize: Method to Write to the Key-Value Store

```
- (IBAction)updateTextSize:(id)sender
{
    CGFloat newFontSize;
    switch (self.fontSizeSegmentedControl.selectedSegmentIndex)
    {
        case 1:
            newFontSize = 19;
            break;
        case 2:
            newFontSize = 24;
            break;

        default:
            newFontSize = 14;
            break;
    }
    self.documentTextView.font = [UIFont systemFontOfSize:newFontSize];

    // Update Preferences
    NSInteger selectedSize = self.fontSizeSegmentedControl.selectedSegmentIndex;
    [self.iCloudKeyValueStore setDouble:selectedSize forKey:@"TextSize"];
}
```

> **Note** You're using the setDouble:forKey: method to store an Integer value here, but you can store any kind of key-value compliant data, such as NSStrings, BOOLs, NSData objects, or even NSArrays and NSDictionary objects.

That's all you need to do to store the preference value in iCloud. But before you can test your application, you must make sure your test device is properly configured to work with iCloud. In the Settings app on your device, navigate to the iCloud section. For this application to store data, your iCloud account must be properly configured and verified. This requires you to have verified your e-mail address and registered it as your Apple ID. The Documents & Data item should also be set to ON, as in Figure 15-26. You can, of course, easily configure this once your account is verified.

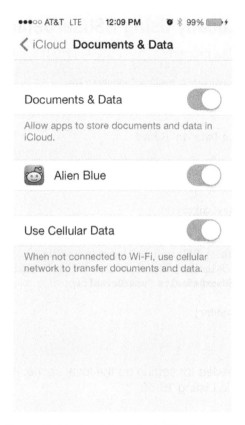

Figure 15-26. Documents & Data must be enabled to store information in iCloud

With iCloud set up on your device, you can build and run the app to test its new persistency feature. You should now be able to do the following:

- Set the text size preference to Medium or Large, terminate the app, and restart it; it should now automatically set the preference to the value you chose.

- Set the text size preference to Medium or Large, uninstall the app from the device, and then reinstall it; in a second or two, it should automatically set the preference to the value it had before uninstalling.

- Run the app on two different devices, change the preference on one device, and see it automatically reflected in the other (it might take some time before the change takes place).

This is all well and good; however, there is a problem with this implementation. It will not work if iCloud is turned off or unavailable. You can easily test this by running the app in the iOS simulator (which doesn't have support for iCloud). You'll see that the persistency doesn't work and the app is reset to the Small text size on every launch.

For these reasons, it's recommended that, in addition to the iCloud key-value store, you save the values in a local NSUserDefaults cache as well. This makes your app more robust and resilient to problems stemming from iCloud access problems. Fortunately, this is an easy fix, as the next section shows.

Caching iCloud Data Locally Using NSUserDefaults

Start by adding an NSUserDefaults property in the ViewController.h file, as shown in Listing 15-58.

Listing 15-58. Adding an NSUserDefaults Property to the ViewController.h File

```
//
//  ViewController.h
//  Recipe 15-4 Storing Key-Value Data in iCloud
//

#import <UIKit/UIKit.h>

@interface ViewController : UIViewController

@property (weak, nonatomic) IBOutlet UISegmentedControl *fontSizeSegmentedControl;
@property (weak, nonatomic) IBOutlet UITextView *documentTextView;
@property (strong, nonatomic) NSUbiquitousKeyValueStore *iCloudKeyValueStore;
@property (strong, nonatomic) NSUserDefaults *userDefaults;

- (IBAction)updateTextSize:(id)sender;

@end
```

There are only a few changes needed for setting up the local cache. First, in viewDidLoad you'll initialize the property, as shown in Listing 15-59.

Listing 15-59. Initializing the userDefaults Property from the viewDidLoad Method

```
- (void)viewDidLoad
{
    [super viewDidLoad];
    self.iCloudKeyValueStore = [NSUbiquitousKeyValueStore defaultStore];
    self.userDefaults = [NSUserDefaults standardUserDefaults];

    // ...
}
```

Next, when the preference value is written to iCloud, you'll write the same value to the NSUserDefaults. To do this, add the bold lines in Listing 15-60 to the updateTextSize: method.

Listing 15-60. Updating the updateTextSize Method Add Value to NSUserDefaults

```
- (IBAction)updateTextSize:(id)sender
{
    // ...

    // Update Preferences
    NSInteger selectedSize = self.sizeSegmentedControl.selectedSegmentIndex;
    [self.userDefaults setDouble:selectedSize forKey:@"TextSize"];
    [self.userDefaults synchronize];
    [self.iCloudKeyValueStore setDouble:selectedSize forKey:@"TextSize"];
}
```

Finally, when updating the user interface with the preferences, instead of just blindly taking the value from the iCloud key-value store, you'll first check and see whether it exists. If it doesn't, you'll use the value from the local cache instead. Listing 15-61 shows the new implementation of the updateUserInterfaceWithPreferences method.

Listing 15-61. The New Implementation of the updateUserInterfaceWithPreferences Method

```
- (void)updateUserInterfaceWithPreferences
{
    NSInteger selectedSize;

    if ([self.iCloudKeyValueStore objectForKey:@"TextSize"] != nil)
    {
        // iCloud value exists
        selectedSize = [self.iCloudKeyValueStore doubleForKey:@"TextSize"];
        // Make sure local cache is synced
        [self.userDefaults setDouble:selectedSize forKey:@"TextSize"];
        [self.userDefaults synchronize];
    }
    else
    {
        // iCloud unavailable, use value from local cache
        selectedSize = [self.userDefaults doubleForKey:@"TextSize"];
    }

    self. fontSizeSegmentedControl.selectedSegmentIndex = selectedSize;
    [self updateTextSize:self];
}
```

Now the app should work and persist its size text preference, both with iCloud and without it.

As you can see, working with iCloud key-value store is extremely simple. There's but one problem: you cannot store big chunks of data. There is a limit of 1 MB per application, and you can use no more than 1,024 keys to store the data. This makes it a poor candidate for application data model storage. For that, you can use the document store, which is what the next recipe is about.

Recipe 15-5. Storing UIDocuments in iCloud

Besides the key-value store, an iCloud account might consist of one or more *ubiquity* containers. A ubiquity container is like a file folder on your device that is automatically synced with a corresponding file folder in iCloud. Using the UIDocument API, you can create custom documents and store them in such a ubiquity container.

In this recipe, you'll build on the project from Recipe 15-4 and allow the user to store text as a document in iCloud. You might have noticed when we enabled iCloud that a ubiquity container was already created for you, as shown in Figure 15-27. In previous versions of Xcode, you would have had to add ubiquity containers; thankfully, you don't need to anymore.

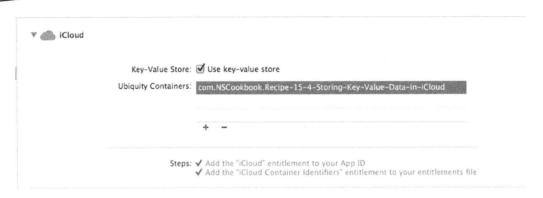

Figure 15-27. The ubiquity container we created in Recipe 15-4

To get started, make a small change to the user interface. Open the Main.storyboard file and add a button, as shown in Figure 15-28, to the view controller. Notice that we've decreased the height of the text view so that the "Save" button won't be concealed by the keyboard when the user enters text if using a non-4" screen.

Figure 15-28. The user interface with an added "Save" button for storing the text document in iCloud

Also, create an action with the name saveDocument for the Save button.

Next, you'll create a UIDocument subclass to handle the saving and loading of the text. Name the new class MyDocument.

The document has two properties, one for the text and one for a delegate used to notify the view controller that the remote text document has changed. Open MyDocument.h and add the code in Listing 15-62.

Listing 15-62. Adding a Protocol and Properties to the MyDocument.h File

```
//
//  MyDocument.h
//  Recipe 15-5 Storing UIDocuments in iCloud
//

#import <UIKit/UIKit.h>

@class MyDocument;

@protocol MyDocumentDelegate <NSObject>
- (void)documentDidChange:(MyDocument*)document;
@end

@interface MyDocument : UIDocument

@property (strong, nonatomic) NSString *text;
@property (weak, nonatomic) id<MyDocumentDelegate> delegate;

@end
```

The UIDocument class requires you to implement two methods. The first is contentsForType:error:, which is used to encode the data into its storing format. In this case, you save the string with an UTF8 encoding (Listing 15-63).

Listing 15-63. Implementing the contentsForType:error: Method

```
- (id)contentsForType:(NSString *)typeName error:(NSError *__autoreleasing *)outError
{
    if (!self.text)
        self.text = @"";
    return [self.text dataUsingEncoding:NSUTF8StringEncoding];
}
```

The other method, loadFromContents:ofType:error:, does the reverse, building an NSString out of raw data and setting it to your property. In the implementation shown in Listing 15-64, the method also invokes the delegate to notify the view controller of the content change.

Listing 15-64. Implementation of the loadFromContents:of Type: Method

```
-(BOOL) loadFromContents:(id)contents ofType:(NSString *)typeName
error:(NSError *__autoreleasing *)outError
{
    if ([contents length] > 0)
    {
        self.text = [[NSString alloc] initWithBytes:[contents bytes] length:[contents length]
encoding:NSUTF8StringEncoding];
    }
    else
    {
        self.text = @"";
    }

    [self.delegate documentDidChange:self];

    return YES;
}
```

Now that your data model is configured (yes, it is that simple!), you can move on to implement the persisting of the document. Go to the ViewController.h file and add two property declarations, one for referencing the document and one for the document's URL. Also, add the MyDocumentDelegate protocol to prepare the view controller for being the document's delegate. The ViewController.h file should now look like Listing 15-65.

Listing 15-65. The Complete ViewController.h File Implementation

```
//
//  ViewController.h
//  Recipe 15-5 Storing UIDocuments in iCloud
//

#import <UIKit/UIKit.h>
#import "MyDocument.h"

@interface ViewController : UIViewController<MyDocumentDelegate>

@property (weak, nonatomic) IBOutlet UISegmentedControl *fontSizeSegmentedControl;
@property (weak, nonatomic) IBOutlet UITextView *documentTextView;
@property (strong, nonatomic) NSUbiquitousKeyValueStore *iCloudKeyValueStore;
@property (strong, nonatomic) NSUserDefaults *userDefaults;
@property (strong, nonatomic) MyDocument *document;
@property (strong, nonatomic) NSURL *documentURL;

- (IBAction)updateTextSize:(id)sender;
- (IBAction)saveDocument:(id)sender;

@end
```

Next, go to the ViewController.m file. In the viewDidLoad method, add the bold line in Listing 15-66 to initiate an update of the Text View with the persisted text, if present.

Listing 15-66. Add a Method Call to Update the Document

```
- (void)viewDidLoad
{
    [super viewDidLoad];
    self.iCloudKeyValueStore = [NSUbiquitousKeyValueStore defaultStore];
    self.userDefaults = [NSUserDefaults standardUserDefaults];

    [[NSNotificationCenter defaultCenter] addObserver:self
        selector:@selector(handleStoreChange:)
        name:NSUbiquitousKeyValueStoreDidChangeExternallyNotification
        object:self.iCloudKeyValueStore];

    [self.iCloudKeyValueStore synchronize];
    [self updateUserInterfaceWithPreferences];

    [self updateDocument];
}
```

The updateDocument first checks to see whether iCloud is available, as shown in Listing 15-67.

Listing 15-67. Starting Implementation of the updateDocument Method

```
- (void)updateDocument
{
    NSFileManager *fileManager = [NSFileManager defaultManager];
    id iCloudToken = [fileManager ubiquityIdentityToken];
    if (iCloudToken)
    {
        // iCloud available

        // Register to notifications for changes in availability
        [[NSNotificationCenter defaultCenter] addObserver:self
            selector:@selector(handleICloudDidChangeIdentity:)
            name:NSUbiquityIdentityDidChangeNotification object:nil];

        //TODO: Open existing document or create new
    }
    else
    {
        // No iCloud access
        self.documentURL = nil;
        self.document = nil;
        self.documentTextView.text = @"<NO iCloud Access>";
    }
}
```

If iCloud is available, updateDocument will create an instance of MyDocument and either open it if it exists in the ubiquity container or save it to upload it. To avoid freezing the user interface during this time, it'll perform these actions on a different thread, as shown in Listing 15-68.

Listing 15-68. The Finished updateDocument Method

```
- (void)updateDocument
{
    NSFileManager *fileManager = [NSFileManager defaultManager];
    id iCloudToken = [fileManager ubiquityIdentityToken];
    if (iCloudToken)
    {
        // iCloud available

        // Register to notifications for changes in availability
        [[NSNotificationCenter defaultCenter] addObserver:self
            selector:@selector(handleICloudDidChangeIdentity:)
            name:NSUbiquityIdentityDidChangeNotification object:nil];

        dispatch_async(dispatch_get_global_queue(DISPATCH_QUEUE_PRIORITY_DEFAULT, 0),
        ^{
            NSURL *documentContainer = [[fileManager URLForUbiquityContainerIdentifier:nil]
                URLByAppendingPathComponent:@"Documents"];

            if (documentContainer != nil)
            {
                self.documentURL =
                    [documentContainer URLByAppendingPathComponent:@"mydocument.txt"];
                self.document =
                    [[MyDocument alloc] initWithFileURL:self.documentURL];
                self.document.delegate = self;
                // If the file exists, open it; otherwise, create it.
                if ([fileManager fileExistsAtPath:self.documentURL.path])
                    [self.document openWithCompletionHandler:nil];
                else
                    [self.document saveToURL:self.documentURL
                        forSaveOperation:UIDocumentSaveForCreating
                        completionHandler:nil];
            }
        });
    }
    else
    {
        // No iCloud access
        self.documentURL = nil;
        self.document = nil;
        self.documentTextView.text = @"<NO iCloud Access>";
    }
}
```

To handle whether the user logs out of iCloud or changes to a different account, add the implementation of the handleICloudDidChangeIdentity: notification method shown in Listing 15-69. It simply calls the updateDocument helper method.

Listing 15-69. Implementing the handleICloudDidChangeIdentity: Method

```
- (void)handleICloudDidChangeIdentity: (NSNotification *)notification
{
    NSLog(@"ID changed");
    [self updateDocument];
}
```

When the document content changes, the app should update the text view. This is done in the documentDidChange: delegate method. Because it might be called on an arbitrary thread, you need to make sure the updating is run on the main thread, as shown in Listing 15-70.

Listing 15-70. Implementing the documentDidChange: Method

```
- (void)documentDidChange:(MyDocument *)document
{
    dispatch_async(dispatch_get_main_queue(),
    ^{
        self.documentTextView.text = document.text;
    });
}
```

Finally, when the user taps the "Save" button, the document will be updated with the new text and saved to iCloud. To do that, add the implementation of the saveDocument: action method shown in Listing 15-71.

Listing 15-71. Implementing the saveDocument: Action Method

```
- (IBAction)saveDocument:(id)sender
{
    if (self.document)
    {
        self.document.text = self.documentTextView.text;
        [self.document saveToURL:self.documentURL
            forSaveOperation:UIDocumentSaveForOverwriting completionHandler:
         ^(BOOL success)
        {
            if (success)
            {
                NSLog(@"Written to iCloud");
            }
            else
            {
                NSLog(@"Error writing to iCloud");
            }
        }];
    }
}
```

That's it! Assuming your device is correctly configured, your simple application can store the document using the user's iCloud account, allowing you to easily persist data across multiple devices, application shutdowns, and even through system resets, as shown by Figure 15-29.

Figure 15-29. *Your application with text saved and loaded from iCloud*

Summary

Data persistence is one of the most important considerations in developing an application. Developers must consider the type of data they want to store, how much of it, how it connects, and whether their application might even stretch across multiple devices. From there, the choice must be made about which approach to use to store data, whether it is the simple NSUserDefaults method, the file management system, or the intricate Core Data framework. On top of this, the relatively new addition of the iCloud service has revolutionized the way that applications can store data, allowing persistence of data in near real time across devices running the same application. As memory, storage, and mobile applications continue to grow in size, importance, and relevance in the technological world, these topics will become significantly more relevant. By firmly understanding the most up-to-date concepts of data persistence in iOS, you can always keep your users updated with the fastest, most efficient, and most powerful methods of storing data possible.

Chapter 16

Data Transmission Recipes

As time has progressed and technology has developed, one of the clearest trends has been the growth in user-generated content. With the improvement of design technologies, Internet connection speeds, and network availability, the amount of data generated electronically per year has increased at a nearly unbelievable rate. The heart of this matter is based around the idea of allowing users to easily take in and redistribute information. While the social sharing tools Apple provides (see Chapter 8) are great for sharing content with multitudes of people or quickly generating email and text, sometimes you want a more personal experience, such as composing text messages and emails directly or even allowing the user to print something to keep. This chapter will cover these important features, which are often overlooked by other iOS reference sources.

In this chapter, you will need a physical device only to implement texting functionality, which you will build in your first recipe. All your other functionalities can be simulated.

Recipe 16-1: Composing Text Messages

Text messaging is still one of the most popular methods to transmit data between individuals. It's quick, easy, and powerful, and it's used across nearly all age groups. In iOS you can incorporate text messaging into your applications and provide the simple cross-application functionality that can so easily improve the overall quality of an application.

Start by creating a new project called "Recipe 16-1 Composing Text Messages," which you will use throughout this chapter. As usual, use the Single View Application template to create the project.

After clicking through to create your project, switch to the Main.storyboard file to begin editing the interface. Add a UITextView, with the default "Lorem Ipsum" text, to the top half of your view, as well as a UIButton—with the label "Text Message"—to the bottom. Connect these to your view controller as outlets with the property names inputTextView and textMessageButton. Set the background of the view controller to "Group Table View Background Color." Also, create an action named "textMessage" for the button.

Before you proceed, import the QuartzCore framework into the view controller's header file, as shown in Listing 16-1. This will allow you to add a corner radius to the text view, which will give it a nicer look.

Listing 16-1. Importing QuartzCore into the ViewController.h file

```
//
// ViewController.h
// Recipe 16-1 Composing Text Messages
//

#import <UIKit/UIKit.h>
#import <QuartzCore/QuartzCore.h>

@interface ViewController : UIViewController

@property (weak, nonatomic) IBOutlet UITextView *inputTextView;
@property (weak, nonatomic) IBOutlet UIButton *textMessageButton;

- (IBAction)textMessage:(id)sender;

@end
```

Now add the line shown in bold in Listing 16-2 to the viewDidLoad method. This will create the rounded corners on the text view.

Listing 16-2. Creating the text view rounded corners

```
- (void)viewDidLoad
{
    [super viewDidLoad];
    self.inputTextView.layer.cornerRadius = 15.0;
}
```

You can now test the app in the iPhone simulator. You won't need a physical device until you are ready to send a text message. Your view should now resemble the view simulated in Figure 16-1.

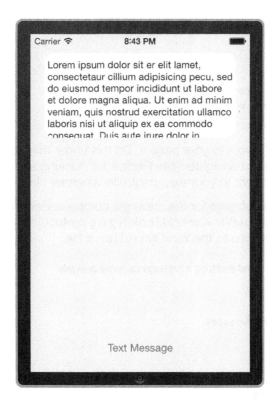

Figure 16-1. A simulated view of your user interface

To properly dismiss the keyboard, set the view controller as the delegate for your UITextView. Add the UITextViewDelegate protocol to the view controller's @interface declaration, as shown in Listing 16-3.

Listing 16-3. Setting the UITextViewDelegate protocol

```
//
// ViewController.h
// Recipe 16-1 Composing Text Messages
//

// ...

@interface ViewController : UIViewController<UITextViewDelegate>

// ...

@end
```

Now assign the text view's delegate property in the viewDidLoad method of the ViewController.m, as shown in Listing 16-4.

Listing 16-4. Setting the text view delegate property

```
- (void)viewDidLoad
{
    [super viewDidLoad];
    self.inputTextView.layer.cornerRadius = 15.0;
    self.inputTextView.delegate = self;
}
```

Next, add the MessageUI framework to your project. Do this under the General tab, with the root project selected, from the project navigator (see Recipe 1-2, Linking a Framework, for details). Also, add the required import statement to your view controller's header file.

Your view controller acts as a delegate for the message compose view controller that you'll create later, so add the MFMessageComposeViewControllerDelegate protocol to ViewController.h as well. Listing 16-5 shows these additions to the ViewController.h file.

Listing 16-5. Importing the framework and declaring a message compose delegate

```
//
//  ViewController.h
//  Recipe 16-1 Composing Text Messages
//

#import <UIKit/UIKit.h>
#import <QuartzCore/QuartzCore.h>
#import <MessageUI/MessageUI.h>

@interface ViewController : UIViewController<UITextViewDelegate,
    MFMessageComposeViewControllerDelegate>

// ...

@end
```

Now switch back to ViewController.m, where you will need to implement one of the UITextView's delegate methods, as shown in Listing 16-6. This will ensure that your keyboard is properly dismissed when the user taps the "Enter" key.

Listing 16-6. Implementing the textView:shouldChangeTextInRange:replacemetnText:Delegate method

```
- (BOOL)textView:(UITextView *)textView shouldChangeTextInRange:(NSRange)range
 replacementText:(NSString *)text
{
if ([text isEqualToString:@"\n"])
    {
        [textView resignFirstResponder];
        return NO;
    }
    return YES;
}
```

Now you can implement your `textMessage:` action method such that the text of your `UITextView` is transposed into a text message. For this example, simply set the recipient to a fake number. This implementation is shown in Listing 16-7.

Listing 16-7. Filling out the textMessage: action method

```
-(IBAction)textMessage:(id)sender
{
    if ([MFMessageComposeViewController canSendText])
    {
        MFMessageComposeViewController *messageVC =
            [[MFMessageComposeViewController alloc] init];
        messageVC.messageComposeDelegate = self;
        messageVC.recipients = @[@"3015555309"];
        messageVC.body = self.inputTextView.text;
        [self presentViewController:messageVC animated:YES completion:nil];
    }
    else
    {
        NSLog(@"Text Messaging Unavailable");
    }
}
```

The implementation of the `textMessage:` method should appear fairly straightforward. After using the `canSendText` method to check for texting availability, create an instance of the `MFMessageComposeViewController` class and then configure it with your fake recipient as well as the intended text. Finally, simply present the controller to allow your user to review the text message before sending it.

The `MFMessageComposeViewController` and its counterpart, the `MFMailComposeViewController`, which you will encounter later, are both classes that allow you to set their initial conditions and present them, but they do not allow you any control of the class once it has been shown. This is to ensure that the user has the final say in whether a message or mail sends, rather than any application sending it without informing the user.

You can implement your `MFMessageComposeViewController`'s `messageComposeDelegate` method to handle the completion of the message, as shown in Listing 16-8.

Listing 16-8. Implementing the messageComposeViewController:didFinishWithResult: delegate method

```
-(void)messageComposeViewController:(MFMessageComposeViewController *)controller
didFinishWithResult:(MessageComposeResult)result
{
    if (result == MessageComposeResultSent)
    {
        self.inputTextView.text = @"Message sent.";
    }
    else if (result == MessageComposeResultFailed)
    {
        NSLog(@"Failed to send message!");
    }
    [self dismissViewControllerAnimated:YES completion:nil];
}
```

Along with the two possible values of MessageComposeResults demonstrated in the preceding code, there is a third result, MessageComposeResultCancelled, which indicates that the user has cancelled the sending of the text message.

An added functionality in iOS 5.0 was the ability to receive notifications about the changing of the availability of text messaging. This functionality remains in iOS 7. You can register for such notifications by adding the following line to the viewDidLoad method in ViewController.m, as shown in Listing 16-9.

Listing 16-9. Registering an NSNotification for messaging availability

```
- (void)viewDidLoad
{
    [super viewDidLoad];
    self.inputTextView.layer.cornerRadius = 15.0;
    self.inputTextView.delegate = self;
    [[NSNotificationCenter defaultCenter] addObserver:self
        selector:@selector(textMessagingAvailabilityChanged:)
        name:MFMessageComposeViewControllerTextMessageAvailabilityDidChangeNotification
        object:nil];
}
```

The selector specified in Listing 16-9 can be defined so as to simply inform you of the change. In a full application, you might likely make use of a UIAlert to notify the user of this change as well, but we will avoid this process for demonstration purposes. Listing 16-10 shows the implementation of the method called in Listing 16-9.

Listing 16-10. Implementing the textMessagingAvailabilityChanged: method

```
-(void)textMessagingAvailabilityChanged:(id)sender
{
    if ([MFMessageComposeViewController canSendText])
    {
        NSLog(@"Text Messaging Available");
    }
    else
    {
        NSLog(@"Text Messaging Unavailable");
    }
}
```

Your app can now copy the body of your UITextView into a text message to be sent to your fake recipient. If you test this, however, keep in mind that the text messaging functionality will not be available on the iOS simulator. You have to test this on your physical device with cellular capabilities. Your simulation should appear as it does in Figure 16-2 once the "Text Message" button is clicked.

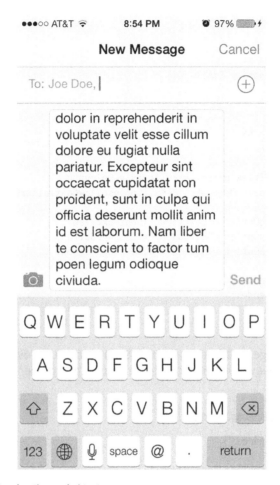

Figure 16-2. A simulated view showing the copied text

Recipe 16-2: Composing Email

Just as you could create and configure text messages to be sent from your application, you can also use the MessageUI framework to configure email messages using the counterpart to the MFMessageComposeViewController class, which is MFMailComposeViewController.

Building on the application from Recipe 16-1, add an option to email the message. Start by adding another button with the label "Mail Message." Create an outlet named "mailMessageButton" and an action called "mailMessage" for the button.

Similar to what you did in Recipe 16-1 with the MFMessageComposeViewController, you'll prepare the main view controller to be a delegate of MFMailComposeViewController. Your ViewController.h should now look like Listing 16-11.

Listing 16-11. The complete ViewController.h file

```
//
//  ViewController.h
//  Recipe 16-2 Composing Composing Email
//

#import <UIKit/UIKit.h>
#import <QuartzCore/QuartzCore.h>
#import <MessageUI/MessageUI.h>

@interface ViewController : UIViewController<UITextViewDelegate,
    MFMessageComposeViewControllerDelegate, MFMailComposeViewControllerDelegate>

@property (weak, nonatomic) IBOutlet UITextView *inputTextView;
@property (weak, nonatomic) IBOutlet UIButton *textMessageButton;
@property (weak, nonatomic) IBOutlet UIButton *mailMessageButton;

- (IBAction)textMessage:(id)sender;
- (IBAction)mailMessage:(id)sender;

@end
```

The setup for your mailMessage: method is also very similar to your previous textMessage: method. You create your composing view controller, configure it, and then present it. Listing 16-12 shows the implementation.

Listing 16-12. Implementing the mailMessage: method

```
- (IBAction)mailMessage:(id)sender
{
    if ([MFMailComposeViewController canSendMail])
    {
        MFMailComposeViewController *mailVC =
            [[MFMailComposeViewController alloc] init];
        [mailVC setSubject:@"Send It Out"];
        [mailVC setToRecipients:@[@"test@example.com"]];
        [mailVC setMessageBody:self.inputTextView.text isHTML:NO];
        mailVC.mailComposeDelegate = self;
        [self presentViewController:mailVC animated:YES completion:nil];
    }
    else
    {
        NSLog(@"E-mailing Unavailable");
    }
}
```

As you can see, the MFMailComposeViewController has a few different properties than the MFMessageComposeViewController that specifically configures a more complex email. These properties correlate to what you would expect from an email: a subject, recipients, and message body.

The MFMailComposeViewControllerDelegate protocol defines only one method, which you are required to implement to properly handle the completed use of the view controller by the user. Give this a simple implementation to log the result, as shown in Listing 16-13.

Listing 16-13. Implementing the mailComposeController:didFinishWithResult:error: method

```
-(void)mailComposeController:(MFMailComposeViewController *)controller
didFinishWithResult:(MFMailComposeResult)result error:(NSError *)error
{
    if (result == MFMailComposeResultSent)
        self.inputTextView.text = @"Mail sent.";
    else if (result == MFMailComposeResultCancelled)
        NSLog(@"Mail Cancelled");
    else if (result == MFMailComposeResultFailed)
        NSLog(@"Error, Mail Send Failed");
    else if (result == MFMailComposeResultSaved)
        NSLog(@"Mail Saved");
    [self dismissViewControllerAnimated:YES completion:nil];
}
```

Now your new application can present a view controller for sending email, as shown in Figure 16-3. Unlike the MFMessageViewController, however, you can actually test this functionality in the iOS simulator.

Figure 16-3. Composing an email using the MFMailMailComposeViewController

Quite conveniently, you can easily test all the functionalities of the MFMailComposeViewController using the simulator without any fear of sending multiple emails to any addresses, real or fake. The simulator does not actually send your test messages over the Internet, so you can easily test your mailComposeDelegate method's handling of the MailComposeResults.

Attaching Data to Mail

The MFMailComposeViewController includes functionality for you to attach data to your email from your application through the use of the addAttachmentData:mimeType:fileName: method. This method has three parameters:

- *attachment*: This parameter, an instance of NSData, refers to the actual data of the object that you want to send. This means for any object you want to attach, you will need to acquire the NSData for it.

- *mimeType*: This parameter is an NSString that the controller uses to define the data type of the attachment. These values are not specific to iOS, and so are not defined in the Apple documentation. They can, however, be easily found online. Wikipedia offers a very comprehensive article on possible values at http://en.wikipedia.org/wiki/Internet_media_type. The MIME type of a JPEG image, for example, is image/jpeg.

- *fileName*: This parameter is an NSString property to set the preferred name for the file sent in the email.

You will now add functionality to your application to access the user's image library, select an image, and then attach that image to your email.

Start by adding a UIImageView under your UITextView, along with a UIButton with the label "Get Image." To make the image view visible when no image is currently selected, change the Background Color attribute to white. Additionally, to avoid drawing outside the image view's frame, select its Clip Subviews attribute in the attributes inspector. Your view should now resemble Figure 16-4.

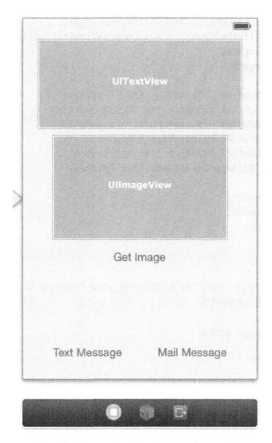

Figure 16-4. *Your new user interface with the ability to select an image*

Create outlets for the two elements and name them "imageView" and "getImageButton," respectively. Also, create the action "getImage" for the button.

Whenever you want to access the photo library of an iPhone, you need to use a UIImagePickerController set inside a view controller. Declare a UIImagePickerController property called "picker" in the main view controller's header file. You also need to instruct the view controller to conform to the UIImagePickerControllerDelegate and UINavigationControllerDelegate protocols. Overall your header file should now resemble Listing 16-14.

Listing 16-14. *The complete ViewController.h file*

```
//
//  ViewController.h
//  Recipe 16-2 Composing Email
//

#import <UIKit/UIKit.h>
#import <QuartzCore/QuartzCore.h>
#import <MessageUI/MessageUI.h>
```

```
@interface ViewController : UIViewController<UITextViewDelegate,
    MFMessageComposeViewControllerDelegate, MFMailComposeViewControllerDelegate,
    UIImagePickerControllerDelegate,
    UINavigationControllerDelegate>

@property (weak, nonatomic) IBOutlet UITextView *inputTextView;
@property (weak, nonatomic) IBOutlet UIButton *textMessageButton;
@property (weak, nonatomic) IBOutlet UIButton *mailMessageButton;
@property (weak, nonatomic) IBOutlet UIImageView *imageView;
@property (weak, nonatomic) IBOutlet UIButton *getImageButton;
@property (strong, nonatomic) UIImagePickerController *picker;

- (IBAction)textMessage:(id)sender;
- (IBAction)mailMessage:(id)sender;
- (IBAction)getImage:(id)sender;

@end
```

Now, you can write your getImage: method to present your popover controller with access to the photo library, as shown in Listing 16-15.

Listing 16-15. Implementing the getImage: method

```
- (IBAction)getImage:(id)sender
{
    self.picker = [[UIImagePickerController alloc] init];
    if ([UIImagePickerController
        isSourceTypeAvailable:UIImagePickerControllerSourceTypePhotoLibrary])
    {
        self.picker.sourceType = UIImagePickerControllerSourceTypePhotoLibrary;
        self.picker.delegate = self;

        [self presentViewController:self.picker animated:YES completion:nil];
    }
}
```

Now you just need to implement your UIImagePickerControllerDelegate protocol methods, as shown in Listing 16-16.

Listing 16-16. Implementing the UIImagePickerControllerDelegate protocol methods

```
-(void)imagePickerControllerDidCancel:(UIImagePickerController *)picker
{
    [self.picker dismissViewControllerAnimated:YES completion:nil];
}

-(void)imagePickerController:(UIImagePickerController *)picker
didFinishPickingMediaWithInfo:(NSDictionary *)info
```

```
{
    self.imageView.image = [info valueForKey:@"UIImagePickerControllerOriginalImage"];
    self.imageView.contentMode = UIViewContentModeScaleAspectFill;

    [self.picker dismissViewControllerAnimated:YES completion:nil];
}
```

As a final touch, to keep with the rounded corners theme, add a 15-point radius to the image view by setting the cornerRadius property in the viewDidLoad method, as shown in Listing 16-17.

Listing 16-17. Adding a cornerRadius property to the image view

```
- (void)viewDidLoad
{
    [super viewDidLoad];
        // Do any additional setup after loading the view, typically from a nib.
    self.inputTextView.layer.cornerRadius = 15.0;
    self.imageView.layer.cornerRadius = 15.0;
    self.inputTextView.delegate = self;

//...

}
```

At this point, if you run the application you can select an image and set it in your UIImageView. If you are testing this application in the simulator, you will need to acquire at least one image to put in your simulator's photo library. You can do this by dragging an image onto the iOS simulator window, which launches the Safari app. Click and hold the image to save it to the library. In Figure 16-5, the app is shown with an image already selected.

Figure 16-5. Running the app and tapping the "Get Image" button to attach an image to the email

Now you can continue to add the chosen image into your email. Modify your `mailPressed:` method to attach the image if one has been selected. Listing 16-18 shows this change.

Listing 16-18. Modifying the mailMessage: method to attach an image

```
- (IBAction)mailMessage:(id)sender
{
    if ([MFMailComposeViewController canSendMail])
    {
        MFMailComposeViewController *mailVC =
            [[MFMailComposeViewController alloc] init];
        [mailVC setSubject:@"Send It Out"];
        [mailVC setToRecipients:@[@"test@example.com"]];
        [mailVC setMessageBody:self.inputTextView.text isHTML:NO];
        mailVC.mailComposeDelegate = self;

        if (self.imageView.image != nil)
        {
            NSData *imageData = UIImageJPEGRepresentation(self.imageView.image, 1.0);
            [mailVC addAttachmentData:imageData mimeType:@"image/jpeg"
                fileName:@"SelectedImage"];
        }
```

```
        [self presentViewController:mailVC animated:YES completion:nil];
    }
    else
    {
        NSLog(@"Emailing Unavailable");
    }
}
```

Finally, you can modify your `MFMailComposeViewController`'s delegate method to reset the app once the email has been successfully sent (Listing 16-19).

Listing 16-19. Modifying the mailComposeController:didFinishWithResult:error: method

```
-(void)mailComposeController:(MFMailComposeViewController *)controller
didFinishWithResult:(MFMailComposeResult)result error:(NSError *)error
{
    if (result == MFMailComposeResultSent)
    {
        self.inputTextView.text = @"Mail sent.";
        self.imageView.image = nil;
    }
    else if (result == MFMailComposeResultCancelled)
        NSLog(@"Mail Cancelled");
    else if (result == MFMailComposeResultFailed)
        NSLog(@"Error, Mail Send Failed");
    else if (result == MFMailComposeResultSaved)
        NSLog(@"Mail Saved");
    [self dismissViewControllerAnimated:YES completion:nil];
}
```

If you test the application in the simulator now and attempt to send an email after selecting an image, you should see the chosen image inserted into your message, as in Figure 16-6.

Figure 16-6. Your application composing email with an attached image

Recipe 16-3: Printing an Image

Now that you have your application set up to handle both text and images, you can continue to enhance your functionality by adding the ability to print.

For this recipe we'll be building on the preceding recipe. Start by adding a new button titled "Print Image" and arrange it as shown in Figure 16-7. Add an action for the button titled "print" as well.

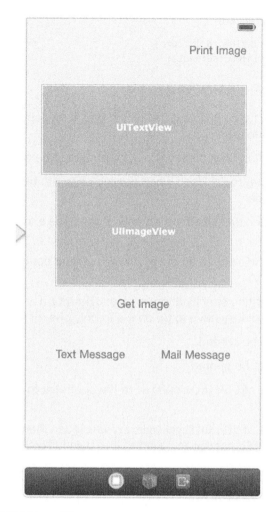

Figure 16-7. Interface with added "Print Image" button

Now you can add the print: action method to add your printing functionality, primarily through the use of the UIPrintInteractionController class. This class is your "hub" of activity when it comes to configuring print jobs. We will discuss the steps to set up this class individually before we look at the method as a whole.

Whenever you want to access an instance of a UIPrintInteractionController, you simply call for a reference to the shared instance through the sharedPrintController class method, as shown in Listing 16-20.

Listing 16-20. Creating a UIPrintInteractionController instance

```
UIPrintInteractionController *pic = [UIPrintInteractionController sharedPrintController];
```

Up next, you must configure the printInfo property of your controller, which specifies the settings for the print job. This is shown in Listing 16-21.

Listing 16-21. Configuring the printInfo property

```
UIPrintInfo *printInfo = [UIPrintInfo printInfo];
printInfo.outputType = UIPrintInfoOutputPhoto;
printInfo.jobName = self.title;
printInfo.duplex = UIPrintInfoDuplexLongEdge;
```

As you can see in Listing 16-21, you have set the outputType to specify an image. The three possible values for this property are as follows:

- *UIPrintInfoOutputPhoto*: Used specifically for photos to be printed

- *UIPrintInfoOutputGrayscale*: Used when dealing only with black text so as to improve performance

- *UIPrintInfoOutputGeneral*: Used for any mix of graphics and text, with or without color

You did not yet set this printInfo object as the printInfo of your controller because you will do a little more configuration shortly.

Next, you have to do an interesting specification for your UIPrintInteractionController. We say "interesting" because you absolutely have to do one, and only one, of four possible tasks:

- Set a single item to be printed.

- Set multiple items to be printed.

- Specify an instance of UIPrintFormatter to the controller to configure the layout of your page.

- Specify an instance of UIPrintPageRenderer, which can then have multiple instances of UIPrintFormatter assigned to it to gain full customization of your content layout over multiple pages.

Start off with the simplest option of setting a single item to be printed. To use these more simple options, this item must be either an image or a PDF file, so we'll simply print your selectedImage, as shown in Listing 16-22.

Listing 16-22. Setting an image for print

```
UIImage *image = self.imageView.image;
pic.printingItem = image;
```

Now that you know what you want to print, you can check the orientation of the image and configure your printInfo accordingly, as shown in Listing 16-23. You don't need to specify a portrait orientation as this is the default case.

Listing 16-23. Configuring the printInfo

```
if (!pic.printingItem && image.size.width > image.size.height)
    printInfo.orientation = UIPrintInfoOrientationLandscape;

pic.printInfo = printInfo;
pic.showsPageRange = YES;
```

Finally, present your UIPrintInteractionController. This class is equipped with three different methods for presenting itself, depending on your specific implementation:

- *presentFromBarButtonItem:animated:completionHandler::* If you are writing for an iPad, this method is designed for use when the application's "Print" button is placed in a toolbar.

- *presentFromRect:inView:animated:completionHandler::* This method is also only for use with the iPad, but allows you to present the controller from any part of the view. Usually, the rectangle specified will be the frame of your Print button, wherever it is located.

- *presentAnimated:completionHandler::* This method should be used whenever implementing printing on an iPhone due to the smaller screen. We'll be using this method in our project.

With this final method call, your print: method in its entirety will look like Listing 16-24.

Listing 16-24. The full print: method implementation

```
- (IBAction)print:(id)sender
{
    if ([UIPrintInteractionController isPrintingAvailable]
        && (self.imageView.image != nil))
    {
        UIPrintInteractionController *pic =
        [UIPrintInteractionController sharedPrintController];

        UIPrintInfo *printInfo = [UIPrintInfo printInfo];
        printInfo.outputType = UIPrintInfoOutputPhoto;
        printInfo.jobName = self.title;
        printInfo.duplex = UIPrintInfoDuplexLongEdge;

        UIImage *image = self.imageView.image;
        pic.printingItem = image;

        if (!pic.printingItem && image.size.width> image.size.height)
            printInfo.orientation = UIPrintInfoOrientationLandscape;

        pic.printInfo = printInfo;
        pic.showsPageRange = YES;

        [pic presentAnimated:YES completionHandler:
         ^(UIPrintInteractionController *printInteractionController, BOOL completed,
           NSError *error)
         {
            if (!completed && (error != nil))
            {
                NSLog(@"Error Printing: %@", error);
            }
```

```
        else
        {
            NSLog(@"Printing Completed");
        }
    }];
    }
}
```

Now when you run your application and select an image, you can print the image by tapping the "Print" button. This presents a view controller from which you can select a printer and further configure your specific print job. Unfortunately, if you're testing this in your simulator or don't have any wireless printers set up, such as printers compatible with the AirPrint technology that is built into the iOS operating system, you won't see any available printers to use, as shown in Figure 16-8.

Figure 16-8. *Your app with a new "Print" button, unable to find any AirPrint printers*

Luckily, Xcode comes with a fantastic application called Printer Simulator. With this program, you can fully simulate print jobs from your app. It even gives you a PDF file of your simulated output so you can see exactly how your image would have turned out without wasting any paper!

To run this program, Choose File ➤ Open Printer Simulator with the simulator open, as shown in Figure 16-9.

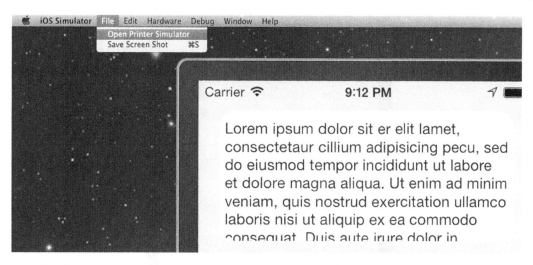

Figure 16-9. Showing the packaged content of the Xcode bundle

On running the Printer Simulator application, a variety of printer types are automatically registered for use. The simulator looks similar to Figure 16-10.

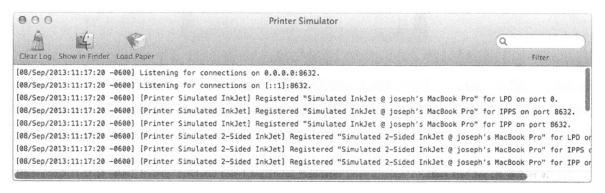

Figure 16-10. Printer Simulator registering multiple types of printers to simulate

On testing your application you should see different types of simulated printers with which to test your application. You can now choose one of the simulated printers from your app, as shown in Figure 16-11.

Figure 16-11. Selecting a simulated inkjet printer from your app

After you have selected a printer, you can print multiple copies as well as change the paper type before you print. After you tap the "Print" button, you should start seeing activity in your Printer Simulator, and shortly afterward, a PDF file opens with your final printout, resembling that shown in Figure 16-12.

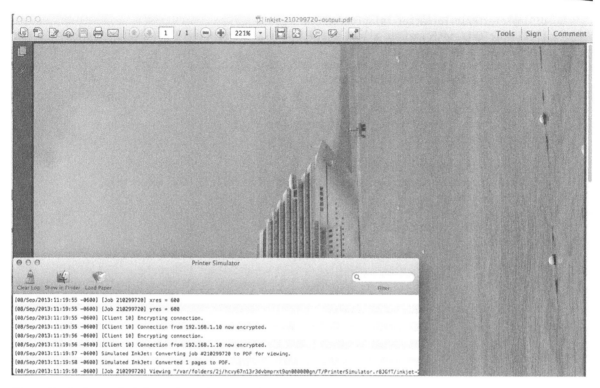

Figure 16-12. Output of printing an image from a simulated printer

Recipe 16-4: Printing Plain Text

Expanding on your previous recipe, you will add functionality to make use of a print formatter to allow you to print simple text.

First, add a new button titled "Print Text" and create an action for it titled "printText."

The new method for printing your text is then implemented, as shown in Listing 16-25.

Listing 16-25. Implementing the printText: method

```
- (IBAction)printText:(id)sender
{
    if ([UIPrintInteractionController isPrintingAvailable])
    {
        UIPrintInteractionController *pic =
        [UIPrintInteractionController sharedPrintController];

        UIPrintInfo *printInfo = [UIPrintInfo printInfo];
        printInfo.outputType = UIPrintInfoOutputGeneral;
        printInfo.jobName = self.title;
        printInfo.duplex = UIPrintInfoDuplexLongEdge;
        pic.printInfo = printInfo;
```

```
UISimpleTextPrintFormatter *simpleTextPF =
[[UISimpleTextPrintFormatter alloc] initWithText:self.inputTextView.text];
simpleTextPF.startPage = 0;
simpleTextPF.contentInsets = UIEdgeInsetsMake(72.0, 72.0, 72.0, 72.0);
simpleTextPF.maximumContentWidth = 6*72.0;

pic.printFormatter = simpleTextPF;

pic.showsPageRange = YES;

[pic presentAnimated:YES completionHandler:
 ^(UIPrintInteractionController *printInteractionController, BOOL completed,
   NSError *error)
 {
     if (!completed && (error != nil))
     {
         NSLog(@"Error Printing: %@", error);
     }
     else
     {
         NSLog(@"Printing Completed");
     }
 }];
    }
}
```

There are two main differences between this method and the print method shown in Listing 16-24 of the last recipe.

1. The `outputType` property in your `UIPrintInfo` is modified to the `UIPrintInfoOutputGeneral` value because you are no longer printing photos.

2. Instead of setting a `UIImage` to the `printingItem` property, you set an instance of `UISimpleTextPrintFormatter` to the `printFormatter` property. This object is initialized with the desired text and then configured through its properties.

   a. Values of 72.0 as insets translate to 1 inch, so you have given your output 1-inch insets and specified a 6-inch width for your content.

   b. The `startPage` property is used more at a later point, but allows you to specify the page in your job for your formatter to be applied to.

Tip When printing simple text, it is also quite easy to apply the preceding method to printing HTML-formatted text. To do this, simply make use of a `UIMarkupTextPrintFormatter` instead of a `UISimpleTextPrintFormatter`.

Just as before, by using the printer simulator you can generate your test output. Because you set your text view's text as the content of your print formatter, you simply get a document with some Lorem Ipsum text in it, as in Figure 16-13.

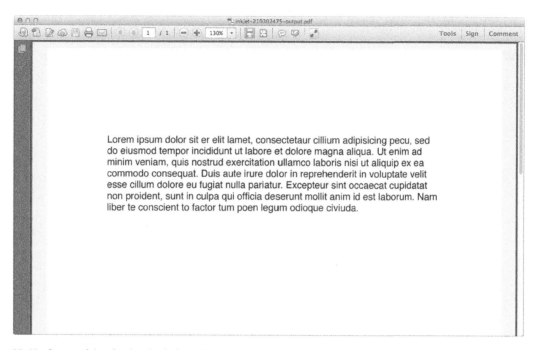

Figure 16-13. Output of the simulated printing of a simple text page

Recipe 16-5: Printing a View

This recipe builds on Recipe 16-4, except that this time, rather than printing plain text, we will print a text view.

Just as you can print text using a `UISimpleTextPrintFormatter`, you can print the contents of a view using another subclass of `UIPrintFormatter`—`UIViewPrintFormatter`.

Start by creating a new button titled "Print view" and create an action for it titled "printViewPressed."

Your newest printing method, `printView:`, closely resembles your preceding one, `printText:` from Recipe 16-4, with the key change of using a `UIViewPrintFormatter` instead. Listing 16-26 shows this implementation.

Listing 16-26. Implementing the printViewPressed: method

```
- (IBAction)printViewPressed:(id)sender
{
    if ([UIPrintInteractionController isPrintingAvailable])
    {
        UIPrintInteractionController *pic =
        [UIPrintInteractionController sharedPrintController];
```

```
    UIPrintInfo *printInfo = [UIPrintInfo printInfo];
    printInfo.outputType = UIPrintInfoOutputGeneral;
    printInfo.jobName = self.title;
    printInfo.duplex = UIPrintInfoDuplexLongEdge;
    printInfo.orientation = UIPrintInfoOrientationLandscape;
    pic.printInfo = printInfo;

    UIViewPrintFormatter *viewPF = [self.inputTextView viewPrintFormatter];

    pic.printFormatter = viewPF;
    pic.showsPageRange = YES;

    [pic presentAnimated:YES completionHandler:
     ^(UIPrintInteractionController *printInteractionController, BOOL completed,
       NSError *error)
    {
        if (!completed && (error != nil))
        {
            NSLog(@"Error Printing View: %@", error);
        }
        else
        {
            NSLog(@"Printing Completed");
        }
    }];
  }
}
```

Because your application makes use of only one of these, you simply have it print your UITextView's view, resulting in an output like that in Figure 16-14.

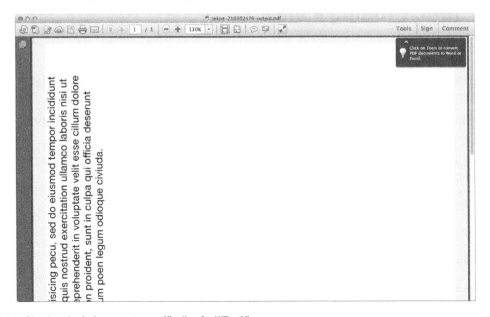

Figure 16-14. Simulated printing output, specifically of a UITextView

> **Note**   Although we're showing how to print a `UITextView`, the `UIViewPrintFormatter` class is capable of printing any `UIView` object.

That concludes this recipe. In the next recipe we'll cover a custom formatted print using page renderers.

Recipe 16-6: Formatted Printing with Page Renderers

A *page renderer* is essentially what allows you to fully customize the content of any print job. It allows you to not only format multiple pages with different print formatters, but also to draw custom content in the header, body, and footer of any page.

To use a page renderer, you must create a custom subclass of the `UIPrintPageRenderer` class from which you can override methods to customize the content of your printing job.

Create a new file using the Objective-C class template. When you enter your filename of `DTPageRenderer`, be sure that the file is a subclass of `UIPrintPageRenderer`, as shown in Figure 16-15.

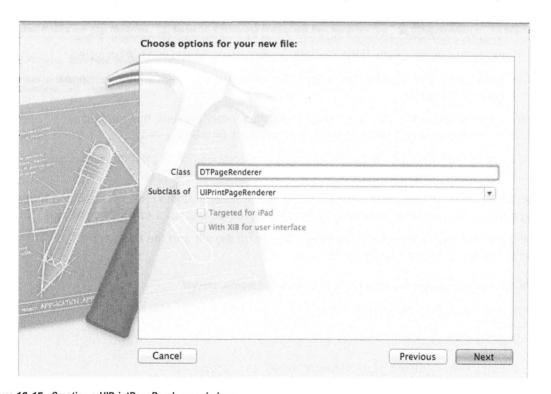

Figure 16-15. Creating a UIPrintPageRenderer subclass

Click through to create your new file.

Next, define two NSString properties, title and author, in the header of your renderer.

Listing 16-27. Adding properties to the DTPageRenderer.h file

```
//
// DTPageRenderer.h
// Recipe 16-6 Formatted Printing with Page Renderers
//

#import <UIKit/UIKit.h>

@interface SendItOutPageRenderer : UIPrintPageRenderer

@property (nonatomic, strong) NSString *title;
@property (nonatomic, strong) NSString *author;

@end
```

To customize the layout of your specific page renderer, you can override methods inherited from the UIPrintPageRenderer class. The way that this class is set up is that the drawPageAtIndex:inRect: method then calls four other methods:

- *drawHeaderForPageAtIndex:inRect:*: Used to specify header content; if the headerHeight property of the renderer is zero, this method will not be called.

- *drawContentForPageAtIndex:inRect:*: Draws custom content within the page's content rectangle.

- *drawFooterForPageAtIndex:inRect:*: Specifies footer content; this method will also not be called if the renderer's footerHeight property is zero.

- *drawPrintFormatter:forPageAtIndex:*: Uses a combination of print formatters and custom content to overlay or fill in a view.

You can override any of these five methods (including drawPageAtIndex:inRect:) to customize your printing content. In your case, you override the header, footer, and print-formatter methods.

You will have your header print the document's author on the left and the title on the right. The method to do this looks like Listing 16-28.

Listing 16-28. Implementing the drawHeaderForPageAtIndex:inRect: override method

```
- (void)drawHeaderForPageAtIndex:(NSInteger)pageIndex  inRect:(CGRect)headerRect
{
    if (pageIndex == 0)
    {
        UIFont *font = [UIFont fontWithName:@"Helvetica" size:12.0];
        CGSize titleSize = [self.title sizeWithAttributes:@{NSFontAttributeName:font}];

        CGFloat drawXTitle = CGRectGetMaxX(headerRect) - titleSize.width;
        CGFloat drawXAuthor = CGRectGetMinX(headerRect);
        CGFloat drawY = CGRectGetMinY(headerRect);
```

```
        CGPoint drawPointAuthor = CGPointMake(drawXAuthor, drawY);
        CGPoint drawPointTitle = CGPointMake(drawXTitle, drawY);

        [self.title drawAtPoint:drawPointTitle withAttributes:@{NSFontAttributeName:font}];
        [self.author drawAtPoint:drawPointAuthor withAttributes:@{NSFontAttributeName:font}];
    }
}
```

Your footer-implementation method looks similar and prints a centered page number. Because the page indexes start with 0, you must remember to increment all your values by 1. Listing 16-29 shows this implementation.

Listing 16-29. Implementing the drawFooterPageAtIndex:inRect: override method

```
- (void)drawFooterForPageAtIndex:(NSInteger)pageIndex inRect:(CGRect)footerRect
{
    UIFont *font = [UIFont fontWithName:@"Helvetica" size:12.0];
    NSString *pageNumber = [NSString stringWithFormat:@"%d.", pageIndex+1];

    CGSize pageNumSize = [pageNumber sizeWithAttributes:@{NSFontAttributeName:font}];
    CGFloat drawX = CGRectGetMaxX(footerRect)/2.0 - pageNumSize.width - 1.0;
    CGFloat drawY = CGRectGetMaxY(footerRect) - pageNumSize.height;
    CGPoint drawPoint = CGPointMake(drawX, drawY);
    [pageNumber drawAtPoint:drawPoint withAttributes:@{NSFontAttributeName:font}];
}
```

Finally, to deal with interlaced print formatters, implement the drawPrintFormatter:forPageAtInde x: method shown in Listing 16-30 to overlay a simple text over your view. This could easily be used to place some kind of "Proprietary Content" label over images or documents in a more targeted application.

Listing 16-30. Implementing the drawPrintFormatter:forPageAtIndex: override method

```
-(void)drawPrintFormatter:(UIPrintFormatter *)printFormatter forPageAtIndex:(NSInteger)pageIndex
{
    CGRect contentRect = CGRectMake(self.printableRect.origin.x,
                                    self.printableRect.origin.y+self.headerHeight, self.
printableRect.size.width,
                                    self.printableRect.size.height-self.headerHeight-self.
footerHeight);
    [printFormatter drawInRect:contentRect forPageAtIndex:pageIndex];

    NSString *overlayText = @"Overlay Text";
    UIFont *font = [UIFont fontWithName:@"Helvetica"size:26.0];
    CGSize overlaySize = [overlayText sizeWithAttributes:@{NSFontAttributeName:font}];

    CGFloat xCenter = CGRectGetMaxX(self.printableRect)/2.0 - overlaySize.width/2.0;
    CGFloat yCenter = CGRectGetMaxY(self.printableRect)/2.0 - overlaySize.height/2.0;
    CGPoint overlayPoint = CGPointMake(xCenter, yCenter);

    [overlayText drawAtPoint:overlayPoint withAttributes:@{NSFontAttributeName:font}];
}
```

In this method, it is important to note that you must draw the content of each printFormatter manually using its own drawInRect:forPageAtIndex: method. To avoid covering your header or footer, you specified a drawing area restricted by the headerHeight and footerHeight.

Now, back in your main view controller implementation file, be sure to import the newly created DTPageRenderer.h file:

```
#import "DTPageRenderer.h"
```

Add a new button to the layout titled "Print Custom" and give it an action titled "printCustom." As usual, you will need to implement the action method, which is shown in Listing 16-31.

Listing 16-31. Implementing the printCustom: method

```
- (IBAction)printCustom:(id)sender
{
    if ([UIPrintInteractionController isPrintingAvailable])
    {
        UIPrintInteractionController *pic =
        [UIPrintInteractionController sharedPrintController];

        UIPrintInfo *printInfo = [UIPrintInfo printInfo];
        printInfo.outputType = UIPrintInfoOutputGeneral;
        printInfo.jobName = self.title;
        printInfo.duplex = UIPrintInfoDuplexLongEdge;
        printInfo.orientation = UIPrintInfoOrientationPortrait;
        pic.printInfo = printInfo;

        UISimpleTextPrintFormatter *simplePF =
        [[UISimpleTextPrintFormatter alloc] initWithText:[self.inputTextView.text
                                                stringByAppendingString:@"iOS 7 Recipes"]];

        DTPageRenderer *sendPR = [[DTPageRenderer alloc] init];
        sendPR.title = @"My Print Job Title";
        sendPR.author = @"Document Author";
        sendPR.headerHeight = 72.0/2;
        sendPR.footerHeight = 72.0/2;

        [sendPR addPrintFormatter:simplePF startingAtPageAtIndex:0];

        pic.printPageRenderer = sendPR;

        pic.showsPageRange = YES;

        [pic presentAnimated:YES completionHandler:
         ^(UIPrintInteractionController *printInteractionController, BOOL completed,
           NSError *error)
         {
             if (!completed && (error != nil))
             {
                 NSLog(@"Error Printing: %@", error);
             }
```

```
        else
        {
            NSLog(@"Printing Completed");
        }
    }];
  }
}
```

This method includes the following extra steps from Recipe 16-5:

1. Create print formatters to be given to different pages. For this recipe, we have simply chosen to create one text view print formatter.

2. Create an instance of your DTRenderer class and configure it with a title, author, headerHeight, and footerHeight. If you did not specify the last two of these, your header and footer customization methods would not be called.

3. Add your print formatters to your page renderer and assign this renderer to your UIPrintInteractionController.

On testing this new functionality, your output will be a one-page text document, complete with simple headers, footers, and even a text overlay, as shown in Figure 16-16.

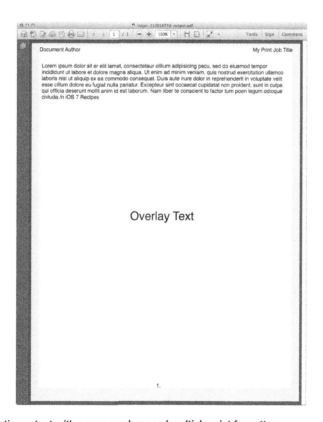

Figure 16-16. Simulated printing output with a page renderer and multiple print formatters

Due to the simplicity of your application, the screen shot in Figure 16-16 might not look like much, but considering your application of custom headers, footers, overlay content, and a page formatter, it actually gives a very good representation of the power of making use of a page renderer for printing when striving for ideal customizations.

Summary

When creating your applications, you should always have the user in mind. Every single aspect of your application should be designed to both allow and help the user accomplish a goal, and each aspect should then be optimized to expedite these goals. Functionalities to transmit data, such as sending text messages, constructing emails, or creating printouts, tend to be overlooked as unnecessary in this process, most often erroneously. Developers must always be careful to think from the user's standpoint and imagine what a user could do with any given feature. The simple possibility of printing content for later use or being able to easily email an interesting image to a friend could be the dividing line between what makes a customer buy your app over someone else's. By understanding and utilizing these "extra" functionalities, you can dramatically improve the functionality of your applications to better serve your end users.

Chapter 17

Game Kit Recipes

Game Center is an iOS service that increases the "replay factor" of your games. It provides a social hub-like interface into which your apps can integrate to allow a user to share scores, keep track of achievements, initiate turn-based matches, and even create multiplayer matches. The best part about Game Center is that it stores all this information on the Apple servers so you don't have to store it. With iOS 7, the user interface has been completely redesigned to provide a much cleaner interface.

In this chapter, we first cover some of the basics of the GameKit framework, which is what you use to make your games "Game Center aware." Next, we walk you through some practical examples, such as implementing leaderboards and achievements. Finally, we teach you how to create a simple, turn-based multiplayer game and integrate it with Game Center.

Recipe 17-1. Making Your App Game Center Aware

In this recipe, you create a simple game and connect it to Game Center. The game consists of four buttons. When the player taps a button, one of two things might happen: if the button is a "safe" button, the player's score is increased by one and the player is allowed to continue the game; if the button is a "killer" button, the game ends. Because the player has no way of knowing which button is which, there's no skill involved and thus not much of a game. However, it's easy to implement and therefore a good platform to show some of the basic features of Game Center.

> **Note** When creating a Game Center–aware game, it's always a good idea to implement the game first and be sure it works properly before involving Game Center.

Implementing the Game

Start by creating a new single view app project with the name "Lucky." We'll keep the same project name for the next few recipes because the bundle identifier, which is a unique app identifier, will be tied to the Game Center.

The game has three difficulty levels:

- *Easy game*: Only one of the four buttons is a "killer" button.

- *Normal game*: Two of the four buttons are "killer" buttons.

- *Hard game*: Three of the four buttons are "killer" buttons.

You will need to set up the main view of the app to be a menu page with options to start a game with one of those levels. You also need to use a navigation controller. To do so, select the view controller from the Main.storyboard file and choose Editor ➤ Embed In ➤ Navigation Controller from the Xcode file menu.

Next, add a label and three buttons to the root view controller from the object library and arrange everything to resemble the storyboard scene in Figure 17-1.

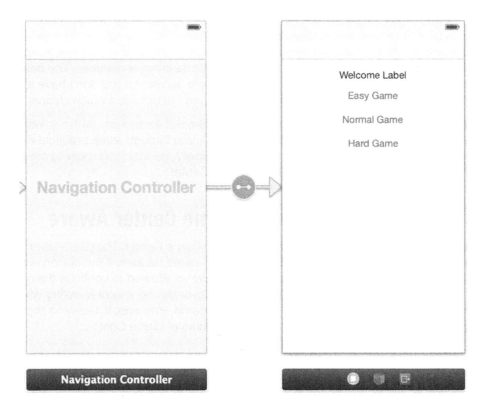

Figure 17-1. *The main menu view of the Lucky game*

Create an outlet named welcomeLabel for the label and actions named playEasyGame, playNormalGame, and playHardGame for when the user taps the respective button.

Next, set the title of the main view controller to "Lucky," and change the text of the Welcome label to "Welcome Anonymous Player." Do this by selecting the navigation bar and changing the title in the attributes inspector, as shown in Figure 17-2.

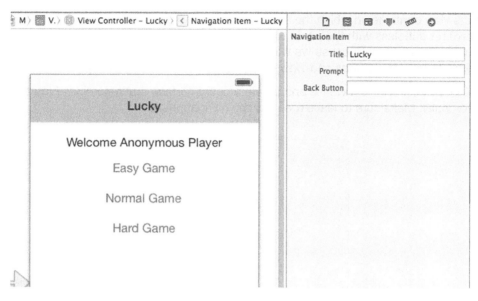

Figure 17-2. *Changing the root view controller title*

Build and run the app to make sure everything is working so far; you should see a screen resembling Figure 17-3.

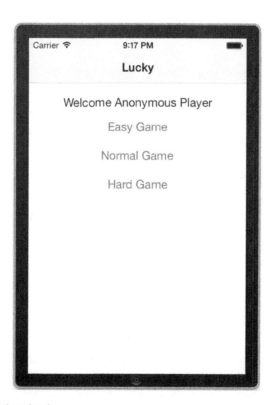

Figure 17-3. *The Lucky game has three levels*

Next, add the view controller in which the actual gameplay will take place. Create a new UIViewController subclass with the name GameViewController and make sure the "With XIB for user interface" option is selected. Because we will create a custom initializer in GameViewController, it makes sense to mix storyboards and .xib files in this instance for simplicity.

Select the GameViewController.xib file and create a user interface that resembles Figure 17-4 for the new view controller. Make sure to leave room for the navigation bar.

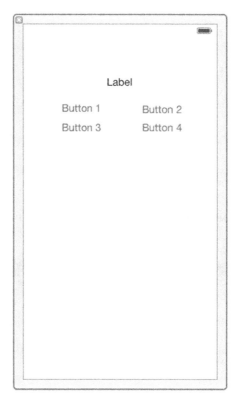

Figure 17-4. The user interface of the Lucky game

Create the following outlets for the added user interface elements in the GameViewController:

- scoreLabel
- button1
- button2
- button3
- button4

For the buttons, create an action that is shared by all the buttons and invoked when the user taps any one of them. To do that, start by creating an action named gameButtonSelected for Button 1. Be sure you use the specific type of UIButton for the method argument, as shown in Figure 17-5.

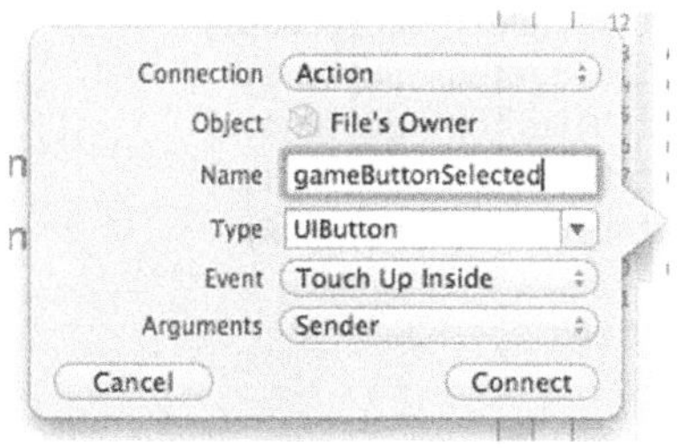

Figure 17-5. Creating an action with a specific type parameter

Now connect the remaining buttons to the same action you created for Button 1 by Ctrl-clicking the button to be connected and dragging the blue line onto the gameButtonSelected action declaration. When a Connect Action sign appears, as in Figure 17-6, you can release the mouse button and the action will become connected to the button.

Figure 17-6. Connecting a button to an existing IBAction

Be sure to connect all the remaining buttons to the gameButtonSelected action.

With the user interface elements properly connected to the code, you can move on to add some necessary declarations to the game view controller's header file. You need an initializer method and a couple of private instance variables. You also need the view controller to conform to the UIAlertViewDelegate protocol. So, go to GameViewController.h and add the code in Listing 17-1.

Listing 17-1. The Completed GameViewController.h File

```
//
//  GameViewController.h
//  Lucky
//

#import <UIKit/UIKit.h>
#import <GameKit/GameKit.h>

@interface GameViewController : UIViewController<UIAlertViewDelegate>
{
    @private
    int _score;
    int _level;
}
```

```
@property (weak, nonatomic) IBOutlet UILabel *scoreLabel;
@property (weak, nonatomic) IBOutlet UIButton *button1;
@property (weak, nonatomic) IBOutlet UIButton *button2;
@property (weak, nonatomic) IBOutlet UIButton *button3;
@property (weak, nonatomic) IBOutlet UIButton *button4;

- (IBAction)gameButtonSelected:(UIButton *)sender;

- (id)initWithLevel:(int)level;

@end
```

Now go to GameViewController.m to start implementing the initializing code. First, add the implementation of the initializer method shown in Listing 17-2.

Listing 17-2. Implementing the initWithLevel: initializer Method

```
- (id)initWithLevel:(int)level
{
    self = [super initWithNibName:nil bundle:nil];
    if (self)
    {
        _level = level;
        _score = 0;
    }
    return self;
}
```

Next, add the helper method shown in Listing 17-3 for updating the score label.

Listing 17-3. Implementing the updateScoreLabel

```
- (void)updateScoreLabel
{
    self.scoreLabel.text = [NSString stringWithFormat:@"Score: %i", _score];
}
```

Finally, add the code to the viewDidLoad method to set up the title and update the score label on game launch, as shown in Listing 17-4.

Listing 17-4. Adding Code to the ViewDidLoad Method to Set the Level and Update the Score

```
- (void)viewDidLoad
{
    [super viewDidLoad];

    switch (_level)
    {
        case 0:
            self.title = @"Easy Game";
            break;
```

```
        case 1:
            self.title = @"Normal Game";
            break;
        case 2:
            self.title = @"Hard Game";
            break;

        default:
            break;
    }

    [self updateScoreLabel];
}
```

Now pause the implementation of the game controller and go back to the main menu controller to connect the two view controllers. Start by adding the import statement to the ViewController.h file, as shown in Listing 17-5.

Listing 17-5. Importing the GameViewController.h File into the ViewController.h File

```
//
//  ViewController.h
//  Lucky
//

#import <UIKit/UIKit.h>
#import "GameViewController.h"

@interface ViewController : UIViewController

@property (weak, nonatomic) IBOutlet UILabel *welcomeLabel;

- (IBAction)playEasyGame:(id)sender;
- (IBAction)playNormalGame:(id)sender;
- (IBAction)playHardGame:(id)sender;

@end
```

Now switch to ViewController.m. To avoid some code duplication, add the helper method shown in Listing 17-6 that will take a level argument and instantiate and display a game view controller.

Listing 17-6. Implementing the playGameWithLevel: helper Method

```
- (void)playGameWithLevel:(int)level
{
    GameViewController *gameViewController =
        [[GameViewController alloc] initWithLevel:level];
    [self.navigationController pushViewController:gameViewController animated:YES];
}
```

You can now use this helper method to invoke a game of the respective level from the three action methods shown in Listing 17-7.

Listing 17-7. Implementing Methods to Start Each Game Type

```
- (IBAction)playEasyGame:(id)sender
{
    [self playGameWithLevel:0];
}

- (IBAction)playNormalGame:(id)sender
{
    [self playGameWithLevel:1];
}

- (IBAction)playHardGame:(id)sender
{
    [self playGameWithLevel:2];
}
```

Now is a good time to again build and run your app. If you've followed the steps correctly, you should be able to tap any of the three buttons in the menu view and have the game view presented, as in Figure 17-7.

Figure 17-7. The screen of an easy level of the Lucky game

With the main architecture of the app all set up, you can move on to implement the gameplay functionality. Start by initializing the buttons to be either "killer" or "safe" buttons. Go back to GameViewController.m and add the line in Listing 17-8 to the viewDidLoad method.

Listing 17-8. Adding a setupButtons Call to the viewDidLoad Method

```
- (void)viewDidLoad
{
    [super viewDidLoad];

    // ...

    [self updateScoreLabel];
    [self setupButtons];
}
```

Note that you implement this piece of code top-down, meaning you add code that invokes helper methods that do not yet exist. Don't worry about the compiler errors because they clear out as you add the missing methods. Now implement the setupButtons helper method. It simply delegates the job to three specific methods, one for each level, as shown in Listing 17-9.

Listing 17-9. Implementing the setupButtons Method

```
- (void)setupButtons
{
    switch (_level) {
        case 0:
            [self setupButtonsForEasyGame];
            break;
        case 1:
            [self setupButtonsForNormalGame];
            break;
        case 2:
            [self setupButtonsForHardGame];
            break;

        default:
            break;
    }
}
```

Next, implement the setup method for an Easy level game. An easy game sets up only one of the four buttons to be a "killer." To indicate a "killer" button, use the tag property; a zero (0) means "safe," while a one (1) indicates "killer." Listing 17-10 shows the implementation.

Listing 17-10. The setupButtonsForEasyGame Method Implementation

```
- (void)setupButtonsForEasyGame
{
    [self resetButtonTags];
    int killerButtonIndex = rand() % 4;
    [self buttonForIndex:killerButtonIndex].tag = 1;
}
```

As you can see, this method resets the button's tag property and picks a random button to make a "killer." It makes use of two helper methods that have not yet been created, resetButtonTags and buttonForIndex:. Let's start with resetButtonTags. It iterates over the four buttons and sets their tag property to 0, as shown in Listing 17-11.

Listing 17-11. Implementing the resetButtonTags Method

```
- (void)resetButtonTags
{
    for (int i = 0; i < 4; i++)
    {
        UIButton *button = [self buttonForIndex:i];
        button.tag = 0;
    }
}
```

The method in Listing 7-11 also makes use of the buttonForIndex: helper method. So go ahead and add it, as shown in Listing 17-12.

Listing 17-12. Implementing the buttonForIndex: Method

```
- (UIButton *)buttonForIndex:(int)index
{
    switch (index)
    {
        case 0:
            return self.button1;
        case 1:
            return self.button2;
        case 2:
            return self.button3;
        case 3:
            return self.button4;
        default:
            return nil;
    }
}
```

Now let's turn to setting up a Normal game. It's like an Easy game except it selects two "killer" buttons instead of one; Listing 17-13 shows the implementation.

Listing 17-13. Implementing the setupButtonsForNormalGame

```
- (void)setupButtonsForNormalGame
{
    [self resetButtonTags];
    int killerButtonIndex1 = rand() % 4;
    int killerButtonIndex2;
    do {
        killerButtonIndex2 = rand() % 4;
    } while (killerButtonIndex1 == killerButtonIndex2);
```

```
    [self buttonForIndex:killerButtonIndex1].tag = 1;
    [self buttonForIndex:killerButtonIndex2].tag = 1;
}
```

Finally, implement the setup method for a Hard game, where all but one button are "killers," as shown in Listing 17-14.

Listing 17-14. Implementing the setupButtonsForHardGame

```
- (void)setupButtonsForHardGame
{
    int safeButtonIndex = rand() % 4;
    for (int i=0; i < 4; i++) {
        if (i == safeButtonIndex) {
            [self buttonForIndex:i].tag = 0;
        }
        else
        {
            [self buttonForIndex:i].tag = 1;
        }
    }
}
```

What's left now is to implement the gameButtonSelected: action method. It checks the tag property of the sending button to see whether it is a "killer" or "safe" button. If it's "safe," the score will be increased and new "killers" will be picked. On the other hand, if it's a "killer," the game is finished, and an alert will be displayed showing the final score. Listing 17-15 shows the complete implementation.

Listing 17-15. Implementing the gameButtonSelected: Action Method

```
- (IBAction)gameButtonSelected:(UIButton *)sender
{
    if (sender.tag == 0)
    {
        // Safe, continue game
        _score += 1;
        [self updateScoreLabel];
        [self setupButtons];
    }
    else
    {
        // Game Over
        NSString *message = [NSString stringWithFormat:@"Your score was %i.", _score];
        UIAlertView *gameOverAlert = [[UIAlertView alloc] initWithTitle:@"Game Over"
            message:message delegate:self cancelButtonTitle:@"OK"
            otherButtonTitles:nil];
        [gameOverAlert show];
    }
}
```

The only task remaining now until the basics of the game are complete is to take the user back to the menu screen when the game is over and the user has dismissed the alert view. Do this by adding the delegate method shown in Listing 17-16.

Listing 17-16. Implementing the alterView:didDismissWithButtonIndex: Delegate Method

```
- (void)alertView:(UIAlertView *)alertView didDismissWithButtonIndex:(NSInteger)buttonIndex
{
    [self.navigationController popViewControllerAnimated:YES];
}
```

The game is now finished, so go ahead and test it. You should be able to choose between an Easy, Normal, and Hard game and play until you hit a "killer" button. Figure 17-8 shows a finished game for an Easy level.

Figure 17-8. A player has hit a "killer" button in a game of Lucky

With the game in place and working, you can turn your focus to making it Game Center aware.

Registering with iTunes Connect

Normally when you develop an iOS app, registering with iTunes Connect is the last step before publishing to the App Store. With Game Center–aware apps, this is a bit different. With a Game Center–aware app, you must register the app as soon as you are ready to start developing the Game

Center–specific functions. The reason you need to register the app with iTunes Connect is that Game Center needs to be aware of the app to test the functionality. Without registering, you will not be able to access the Game Center server, so nothing will work.

Once you've registered and marked the app as Game Center–aware, iTunes Connect sets up a *Game Center sandbox* for your app. The Game Center sandbox is a development area where you can test the Game Center integration without affecting production scores or achievements.

With iOS 7, you can easily enable Game Center if you have a developer account. With the root project selected, you can navigate to the Capabilities tab and turn on Game Center. When prompted for your team, select it and click Choose, as shown in Figure 17-9.

Figure 17-9. Configuring GameKit capabilities

Now that you have enabled the GameKit capability and chosen your provisioning profile, go to `http://itunesconnect.apple.com` and log in using your developer ID. Click the Manage Your Applications link, and then click the "Add New App" button. Follow the instructions, and when you reach the App Information page, enter the information shown in Figure 17-10 except for the app name, which needs to be unique and not used by any other developer. You could try using your initials as a prefix, as we did in the figure.

App Information

Enter the following information about your app.

Default Language	English
App Name	JHLucky
SKU Number	iOS7_Recipes_Lucky
Bundle ID	Xcode iOS App ID com NSCookbook Lucky – com.NSCookbo

You can register a new Bundle ID here.

Does your app have specific device requirements? Learn more

Cancel   Continue

Figure 17-10. Entering application information in iTunes Connect

Continue to fill out the required metadata information about your app. You also need to upload a screen shot and a large app icon. To save time, you can download the images from Source Code/Downloads from this book's page at www.apress.com. The required files are the following:

- Lucky Large App Icon.jpg
- Lucky Screenshot.png
- Lucky Screenshot (iPhone 5).png

When you're done filling out the required information, click Save. At this point you'll see a page resembling the one in Figure 17-11.

Figure 17-11. An app registered with iTunes Connect

Now, click the "Manage Game Center" button on the right side of the page. On the Enable Game Center page, click the "Enable for Single Game" button, as shown in Figure 17-12.

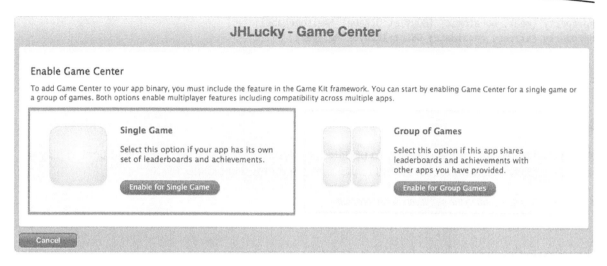

Figure 17-12. Enabling Game Center for an app in iTunes Connect

You're now done with the registration. Later, you will return to iTunes Connect to configure leaderboards and achievements, but for now go to your Xcode project to set up the basic Game Center support.

Authenticating a Local Player

With the Game Center sandbox enabled, you can go back to Xcode to implement Game Center support in the app. Your app checks whether Game Center is available and allows the user to sign in if that hasn't been done. Because we used the Capabilities tab to turn on Game Center, the info plist file and GameKit framework have already been set up for you. Now you can start jumping into some code.

Your users need to be logged in to Game Center to take advantage of its features. It's usually a good idea to authenticate the player at application launch so the player can start receiving challenges and other Game Center notifications right away. Go to ViewController.h, import the GameKit API, and add the property shown in Listing 17-17 to keep track of the logged-in player.

Listing 17-17. Adding a Property and Import Statement to the ViewController.h File

```
//
//  ViewController.h
//  Lucky
//

#import <UIKit/UIKit.h>
#import "GameViewController.h"
#import <GameKit/GameKit.h>

@interface ViewController : UIViewController
```

```
@property (weak, nonatomic) IBOutlet UILabel *welcomeLabel;
@property (strong, nonatomic) GKLocalPlayer *player;

- (IBAction)playEasyGame:(id)sender;
- (IBAction)playNormalGame:(id)sender;
- (IBAction)playHardGame:(id)sender;

@end
```

Add a custom setter for the property to update the "Welcome" label when the authenticated player changes. Go to ViewController.m and implement the method in Listing 17-18.

Listing 17-18. Implementing the setPlayer: Setter Method

```
- (void)setPlayer:(GKLocalPlayer *)player
{
    _player = player;
    NSString *playerName;
    if (_player)
    {
        playerName = _player.alias;
    }
    else
    {
        playerName = @"Anonymous Player";
    }
    self.welcomeLabel.text = [NSString stringWithFormat:@"Welcome %@", playerName];
}
```

The GameKit framework handles the authentication process for you. All you have to do is provide an authentication handler block to the localPlayer shared instance. Add a helper method, which assigns such a block, as shown in Listing 17-19.

Listing 17-19. Implementing the authenticatePlayer Method

```
- (void)authenticatePlayer
{
    __weak GKLocalPlayer *localPlayer = [GKLocalPlayer localPlayer];
    localPlayer.authenticateHandler =
    ^(UIViewController *authenticateViewController, NSError *error)
    {
        if (authenticateViewController != nil)
        {
            [self presentViewController:authenticateViewController animated:YES
                completion:nil];
        }
        else if (localPlayer.isAuthenticated)
        {
            self.player = localPlayer;
        }
```

```
        else
        {
            // Disable Game Center
            self.player = nil;
        }
    };
}
```

After an authentication handler is assigned, GameKit tries to authenticate the local player. The outcome can be one of three possible scenarios:

- If the user is not signed into Game Center, the authentication handler will be invoked with a login view controller provided by GameKit. All your app needs to do then is to present the view controller at an appropriate time. Whether the user signs in or cancels the view controller, your authentication handler will be invoked again with the new state.

- If the user is currently signed in, no view controller is provided, and the isAuthenticated property of localPlayer returns YES. Your app can then enable its Game Center features. In this case, that means assigning the player property.

- If the user is not signed in and Game Center is unavailable for some reason, no view controller is provided, and the isAuthenticated property returns NO. Your app should then disable its Game Center features or stop the execution, whichever makes the most sense. In this case, because you allow anonymous playing, you simply set the player property to nil.

Finally, to start the authentication process after the main view has finished loading, change the viewDidLoad method, as shown in Listing 17-20.

Listing 17-20. Updating the viewDidLoad Method to Make the authenticatePlayer Method Call

```
- (void)viewDidLoad
{
    [super viewDidLoad];

    self.player = nil;
    [self authenticatePlayer];
}
```

That's pretty much all there is to authenticating a user. When you run your app, it will prompt you to log in or create a new account, as in Figure 17-13. Once a user logs in, the user can access any app in Game Center, so if you or a user has authenticated to Game Center in another app, this can be passed to your app without prompting you to log in again.

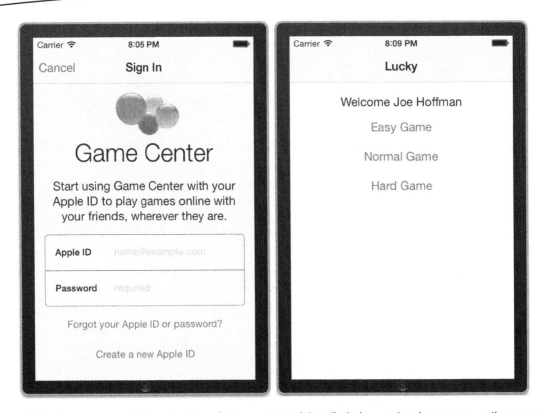

Figure 17-13. The Lucky app prompting for a Game Center account and then displaying a welcoming message on the menu screen

As a final touch before moving on to implement Game Center features, you add a button to the menu screen allowing the user to go to Game Center without leaving your app.

Displaying Game Center from Your App

Open the Main.storyboard file again and add a "Visit Game Center" button to the view controller so that the user interface resembles Figure 17-14.

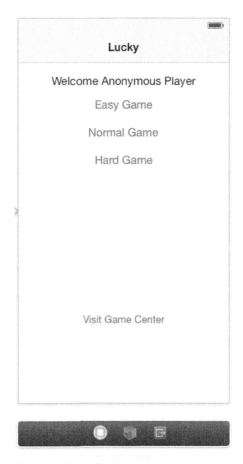

Figure 17-14. The menu screen with a "Visit Game Center" button

Create an action with the name showGameCenter for when the user taps the new button.

Next, go to ViewController.h and add the GKGameCenterControllerDelegate protocol, as shown in Listing 17-21.

Listing 17-21. Adding the GKGameCenterControllerDelegate to the ViewController.h File

```
//
//  ViewController.h
//  Recipe 17-1 Making Your App Game Center Aware
//

#import <UIKit/UIKit.h>
#import "GameViewController.h"
#import <GameKit/GameKit.h>

@interface ViewController : UIViewController<GKGameCenterControllerDelegate>

@property (weak, nonatomic) IBOutlet UILabel *welcomeLabel;
@property (strong, nonatomic) GKLocalPlayer *player;
```

```
- (IBAction)playEasyGame:(id)sender;
- (IBAction)playNormalGame:(id)sender;
- (IBAction)playHardGame:(id)sender;
- (IBAction)showGameCenter:(id)sender;
```

@end

Now, go to ViewController.m and add the implementation to the showGameCenter: action method shown in Listing 17-22.

Listing 17-22. Implementing the showGameCenter: Action Method

```
- (IBAction)showGameCenter:(id)sender
{
    GKGameCenterViewController *gameCenterController =
        [[GKGameCenterViewController alloc] init];
    if (gameCenterController != nil)
    {
        gameCenterController.gameCenterDelegate = self;
        [self presentViewController:gameCenterController animated:YES completion:nil];
    }
}
```

Finally, add the delegate method to dismiss the Game Center view controller when the user is finished with it, as shown in Listing 17-23.

Listing 17-23. Implementing the gameCenterViewControllerDidFinish: Delegate Method

```
- (void)gameCenterViewControllerDidFinish:(GKGameCenterViewController *)gameCenterViewController
{
    [self dismissViewControllerAnimated:YES completion:nil];
}
```

Now that you have a basic Game Center–aware app all set up, it's time to start implementing some of the Game Center features, starting with leaderboards.

Recipe 17-2. Implementing Leaderboards

Competing against others is an essential ingredient in gaming. The possibility for players to compare high scores and compete is an effective way to increase the replay factor of any game. With Game Center, this feature is easily implemented using leaderboards. In this recipe, you build on the project from Recipe 17-1 and implement leaderboard support. Leaderboards allow users to post the score to Game Center, which will in turn list the top-scoring players.

The first thing you need to do is to define in iTunes Connect the leaderboards you'll be using.

Defining the Leaderboards

Set up three different leaderboards for your app, one for each difficulty level.

Log in to http://itunesconnect.apple.com and click the Manage Your Applications link. Select the Lucky app you registered in Recipe 17-1, and then click the "Manage Game Center" button.

In the Leaderboards section, click the Add Leaderboard button. In the Add Leaderboard page (see Figure 17-15), choose to create a single leaderboard.

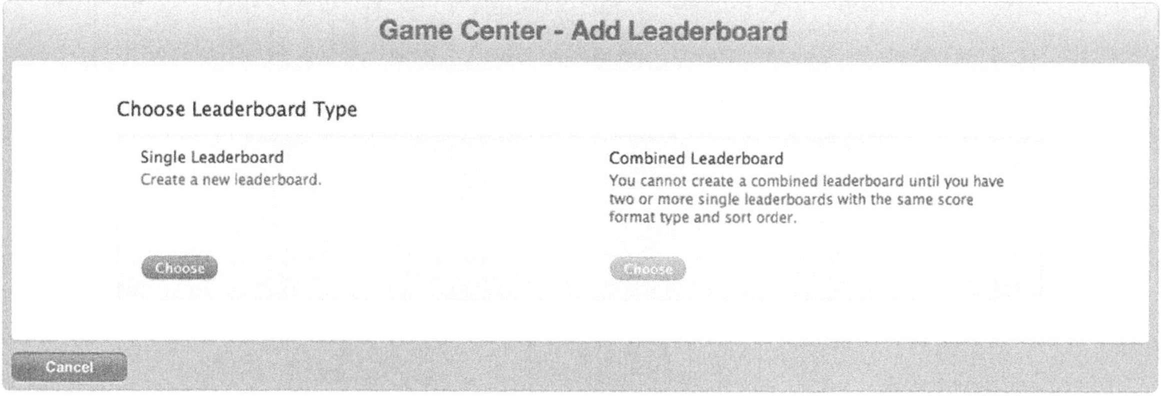

Figure 17-15. *Creating a single leaderboard*

> **Note**   Once a leaderboard has gone live for an app, it cannot be deleted, so create leaderboards with some thought. You can have up to 25 leaderboards per app. This allows you to create multiple leaderboards for different difficulties or even one for each level of your game, whatever makes the most sense.

Fill in a name and an identifier for the leaderboard. The name is an internal name for tracking purposes and will not be displayed to the player. (The display name is configured in the next step when adding a language.) Now select the score format type; in this case, you will use a simple integer, but you also can use time-based, floats, and currency. Select the sort order for your leaderboard and the score submission type. If you want high scores at the top (typical), then sort High to Low; if you want low scores at the top (for example, in a golf game), then sort Low to High.

You also need to set up at least one language for the leaderboard. To do that, click the "Add Language" button. Select the language and then enter a display name for the leaderboard; this is the name that is visible to the player in the game. You can set the formatting of the score and what unit to call them (singular and plural); in this case, they are Point and Points.

Figure 17-16 shows the configurations you'll be using for this leaderboard.

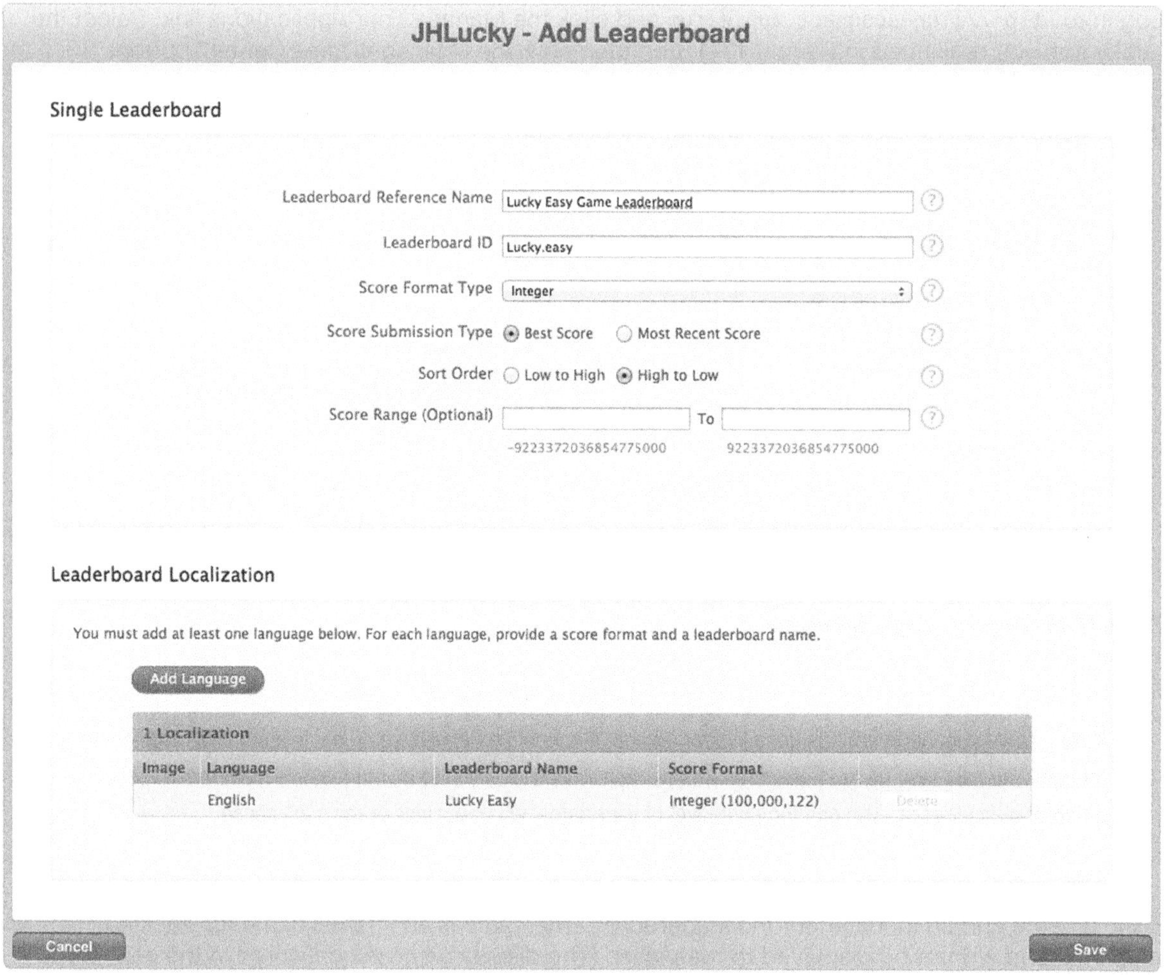

Figure 17-16. *Configuring a leaderboard for Lucky's Easy game high scores*

Once complete, click Save to store the leaderboard.

Repeat the process for the remaining two leaderboards, this time using Lucky.normal and Lucky. hard as leaderboard IDs. The resulting Leaderboards section should now resemble Figure 17-17.

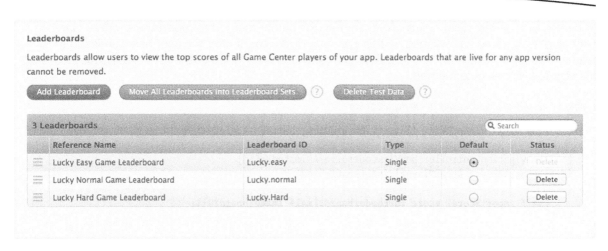

Figure 17-17. *Three leaderboards registered for the Lucky game in iTunes Connect*

Now, let's dive in to some code.

Reporting Scores to Game Center

To report a score to Game Center, use the GKScore class. Go to the GameViewController.m file and add the helper method shown in Listing 17-24. The method creates and initiates a new GKScore object, which it then reports to Game Center, providing a completion handler.

Listing 17-24. *Implementing the reportScore:forLeaderboard: Helper Method*

```
- (void)reportScore:(int64_t)score forLeaderboard: (NSString*)leaderboardID
{
    GKScore *gameCenterScore = [[GKScore alloc] initWithLeaderboardIdentifier:leaderboardID];
    gameCenterScore.value = score;
    gameCenterScore.context = 0;

    NSArray *scoresArray = [[NSArray alloc] initWithObjects:gameCenterScore, nil];

    [GKScore reportScores:scoresArray withCompletionHandler:^(NSError *error)
    {
        if (error)
        {
            NSLog(@"Error reporting score: %@", error);
        }
    }];
}
```

> **Note** If a score cannot be reported because of connection problems, GameKit stores the request and tries to resend the score later, making any kind of retry handling unnecessary in the preceding completion handler.

You can now use the reportScore:forLeaderboard: helper method to report the score to Game Center when a game has finished. In this app, you do this right after the user has dismissed the Game Over alert view. Add the code shown in bold in Listing 17-25 to the alertView:didDismissWit hButtonIndex: delegate method.

Listing 17-25. Adding Functionality to the Report Score

```
- (void)alertView:(UIAlertView *)alertView didDismissWithButtonIndex:(NSInteger)buttonIndex
{
    [self.navigationController popViewControllerAnimated:YES];
    if ([GKLocalPlayer localPlayer].isAuthenticated)
    {
        [self reportScore:_score forLeaderboard:[self leaderboardID]];
    }
}
```

The leaderboardID helper method returns the ID that corresponds to the current game level. Listing 17-26 shows this implementation.

Listing 17-26. Implementing the leaderboardID Method

```
- (NSString *)leaderboardID
{
    switch (_level) {
        case 0:
            return @"Lucky.easy";
        case 1:
            return @"Lucky.normal";
        case 2:
            return @"Lucky.hard";
        default:
            return @"";
    }
}
```

You can now build and run the app and play a game. Your score is automatically reported to Game Center. You can use the "Visit Game Center" button to view the resulting leaderboard, as shown in Figure 17-18.

Figure 17-18. A Game Center leaderboard with one score

Recipe 17-3. Implementing Achievements

Achievements in games are similar to badges and other accomplishable goals in most games. Using Game Center achievements, you can provide your players with a notification when they reach certain milestones. Achievements make most sense in games with natural milestones, such as beating a race course record in a racing game. However, to show you how they work, you'll set up one for the Lucky game project you built in Recipes 17-1 and 17-2.

Specifically, you reward the player with an achievement if she has managed to use all four buttons in a game. As with leaderboards, you'll start by registering the achievements in iTunes Connect.

Defining Achievements in iTunes Connect

Again, log in to http://itunesconnect.apple.com. Click Manage Your Applications, click the app you have set up for Game Center, and then click the "Manage Game Center" button.

You'll define three achievements, one for each level of difficulty. Start by clicking the Add Achievement button in the Manage Game Center page. Enter a name, ID, and point value, as shown in Figure 17-19. Also, set the Hidden and Achievable More Than Once options to No. In your own applications, you can set Hidden to Yes to surprise the users with achievements they didn't know existed. For this app, though, we'll make the user aware of all possible achievements.

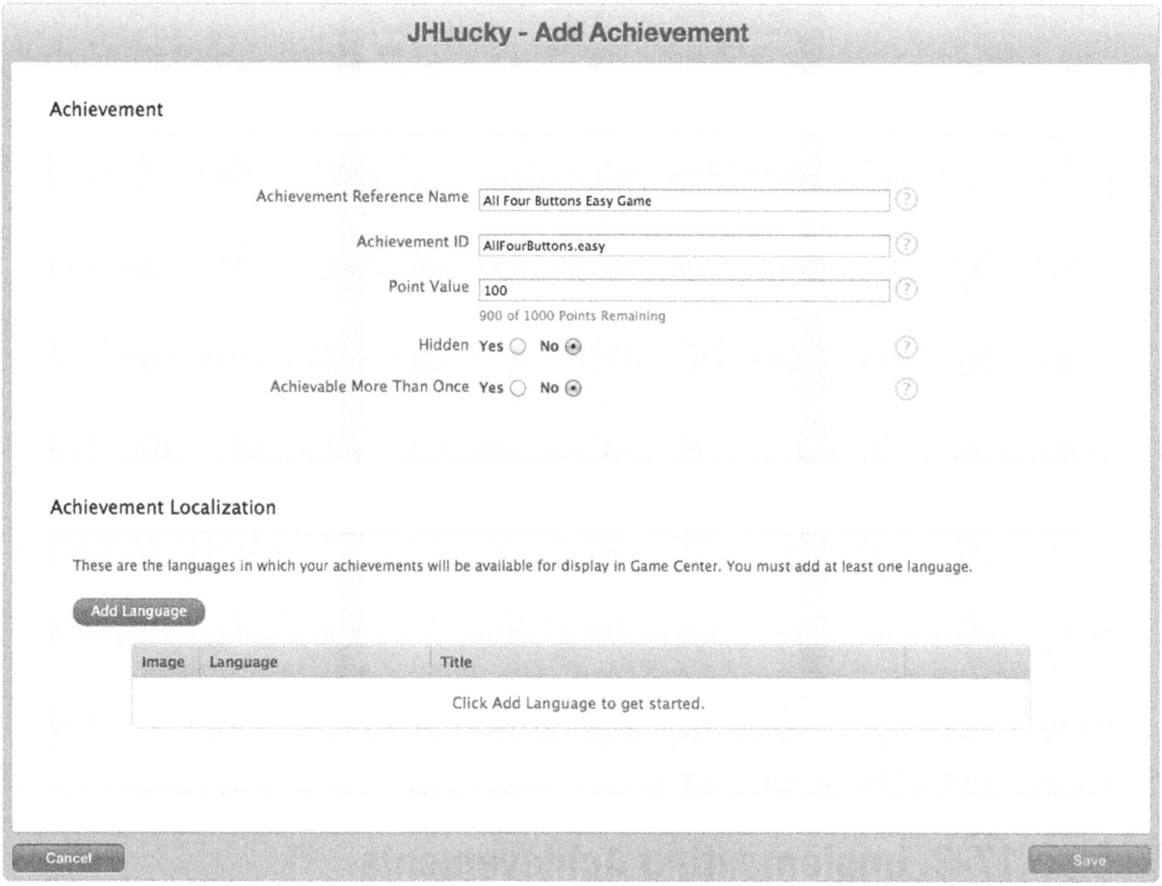

Figure 17-19. *Configuring a Game Center achievement in iTunes Connect*

Each game can have up to 1,000 achievement points. These points can be assigned to different achievements as you see fit, but each achievement can have a max of only 100 achievement points, which is what you used here.

As with leaderboards, you can't save an achievement until you add at least one language to it. To do that, click the "Add Language" button. The resulting view should resemble Figure 14–20 (after filling out the fields). Here, you can set the achievement title as well as the "pre-earned" description. The pre-earned description should detail how the achievement is earned. There is also an earned description, which is the description shown after the achievement is earned.

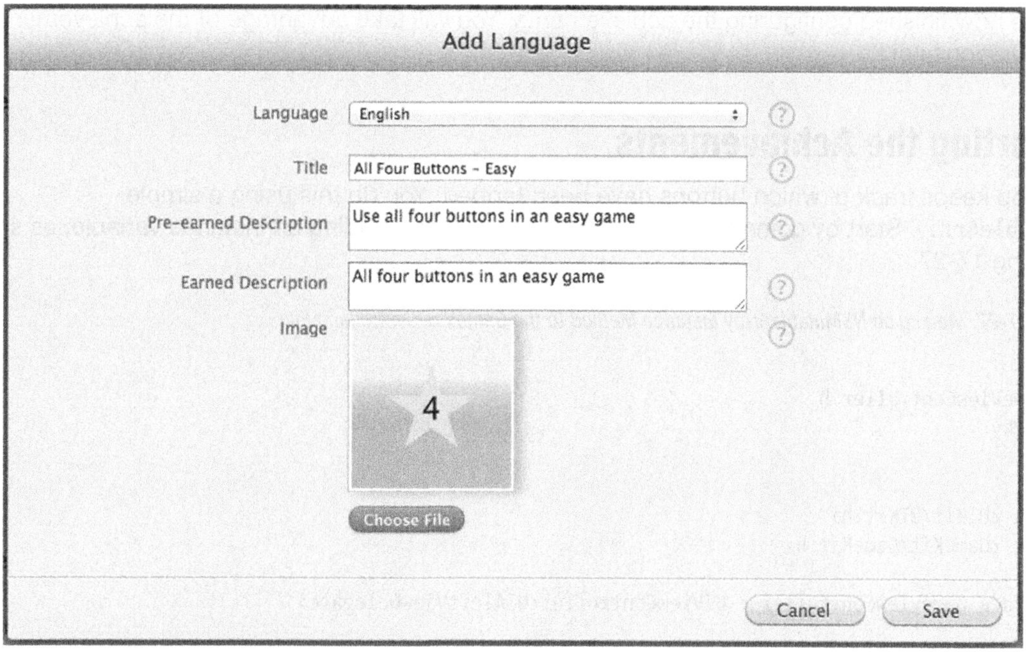
Add Language
Language
English
Title
All Four Buttons - Easy
Pre-earned Description
Use all four buttons in an easy game
Earned Description
All four buttons in an easy game
Image
4
Choose File
Cancel
Save

Figure 17-20. ***Configuring a language for a Game Center achievement***

Note that you need an image to depict the achievement in the Game Center app. You can download pre-made images for the three achievements from the web page of this book:

- `All Four Buttons Achievement Easy.png`
- `All Four Buttons Achievement Normal.png`
- `All Four Buttons Achievement Hard.png`

Save the language and then the achievement. You can now repeat the process for the other two achievements, using the IDs `AllFourButtons.normal` and `AllFourButtons.hard`, respectively.

Your list of achievements should now resemble Figure 17-21.

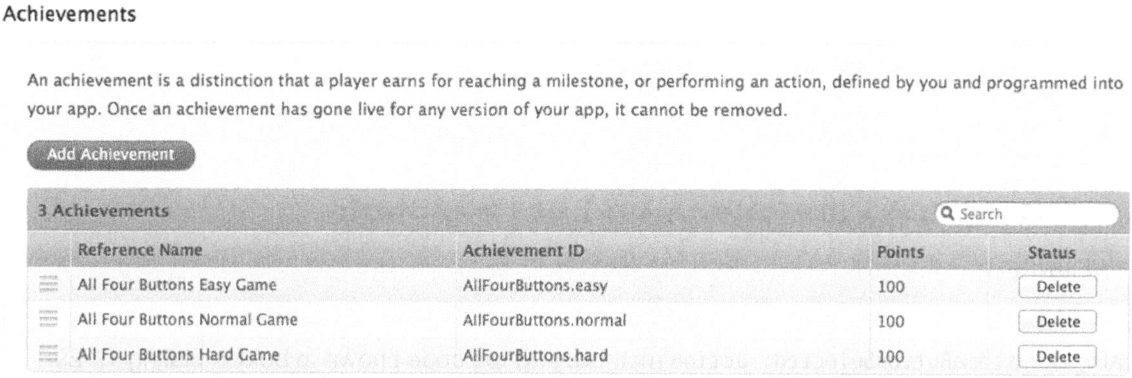
Achievements
An achievement is a distinction that a player earns for reaching a milestone, or performing an action, defined by you and programmed into your app. Once an achievement has gone live for any version of your app, it cannot be removed.
Add Achievement
3 Achievements
Search
Reference Name
Achievement ID
Points
Status
All Four Buttons Easy Game
AllFourButtons.easy
100
Delete
All Four Buttons Normal Game
AllFourButtons.normal
100
Delete
All Four Buttons Hard Game
AllFourButtons.hard
100
Delete

Figure 17-21. ***Three achievements defined in iTunes Connect***

You are now finished configuring the achievements. You will take advantage of the achievement configurations next.

Reporting the Achievements

This app keeps track of which buttons have been tapped. You do this using a simple NSMutableArray. Start by going to GameViewController.h and adding an instance variable, as shown in Listing 17-27.

Listing 17-27. Adding an NSMutableArray Instance Method to the GameVewController.h File

```
//
//  GameViewController.h
//  Lucky
//

#import <UIKit/UIKit.h>
#import <GameKit/GameKit.h>

@interface GameViewController : UIViewController<UIAlertViewDelegate>
{
    @private
    int _score;
    int _level;
    NSMutableArray *_selectedButtons;
}

// ...

@end
```

Next, go to ViewController.m and add code to instantiate the array in the initWithLevel: method, as shown in Listing 17-28.

Listing 17-28. Instantiating the Buttons Array in the initWithLevel: Method

```
- (id)initWithLevel:(int)level
{
    self = [super initWithNibName:nil bundle:nil];
    if (self)
    {
        _level = level;
        _score = 0;
        _selectedButtons = [[NSMutableArray alloc] initWithCapacity:4];
    }
    return self;
}
```

Finally, in the gameButtonSelected: action method, add the code shown in bold in Listing 17-29. The code adds the selected button to the array if it hasn't already been added. Then, if all four buttons have been tapped, it reports the achievement to Game Center using the helper method you implement next.

Listing 17-29. Modifying the gameButtonSelected: Method to Report the Achievement

```objc
- (IBAction)gameButtonSelected:(UIButton *)sender
{
    if (sender.tag == 0)
    {
        // Safe, continue game
        _score += 1;
        [self updateScoreLabel];
        [self setupButtons];
        if (![_selectedButtons containsObject:sender])
        {
            [_selectedButtons addObject:sender];
            if (_selectedButtons.count == 4)
            {
                [self reportAllFourButtonsAchievementCompleted];
            }
        }
    }
    else
    {
        // Game Over
        // ...
    }
}
```

Reporting an achievement is similar to the way you report leaderboard scores, except you use the class GKAchievement instead of GKScore. Listing 17-30 shows the implementation of the reportAllFourButtonsAchievementCompleted helper method.

Listing 17-30. Implementing the reportAllFourButtonsAchievementCompleted Method

```objc
- (void)reportAllFourButtonsAchievementCompleted
{
    NSString *achievementID = [self achievementID];
    GKAchievement *achievement = [[GKAchievement alloc] initWithIdentifier:achievementID];
    if (achievement != nil)
    {
        achievement.percentComplete = 100;
        achievement.showsCompletionBanner = NO;
        NSArray *achievementArray = [[NSArray alloc] initWithObjects:achievement, nil];

        [GKAchievement reportAchievements:achievementArray withCompletionHandler:^(NSError *error)
        {
            if (error != nil)
            {
                NSLog(@"Error when reporting achievement: %@", error);
            }
```

```
        else
        {
            [GKNotificationBanner showBannerWithTitle:@"Achievement Completed"
                                        message:@"You have used all four buttons and
earned 100 points!"
                                        completionHandler:nil];
        }
    }];    }
}
```

> **Note** For achievements that have a way to track submilestones, you can use the `percentComplete` property to report partial progress. For the purpose of this recipe, you directly set the `percentComplete` property to 100, which means the achievement is fully completed.

Finally, implement the `achievementID` helper method, which returns the achievement ID based on the current game level, as shown in Listing 17-31.

Listing 17-31. Implementing the achievementID Method

```
- (NSString *)achievementID
{
    switch (_level) {
        case 0:
            return @"AllFourButtons.easy";
        case 1:
            return @"AllFourButtons.normal";
        case 2:
            return @"AllFourButtons.hard";
        default:
            return @"";
    }
}
```

You can now build and run the app again. Start a game and try to use all four buttons. If you're lucky and don't hit a "killer," you'll be awarded an achievement. Figure 17-22 shows the Game Center view controller displaying a player who has been awarded all three available achievements.

Figure 17-22. A player who has completed three achievements in the game

With the current implementation, an achievement will be reported even though the player has previously completed it. Let's fix that. What you'll do is cache the achievements of the current player so that you can check whether an achievement has been completed previously before reporting it to Game Center. That way, you don't make any unnecessary server calls.

Start by adding an NSMutableDictionary property to hold the achievements. Go to ViewController.h and add the declaration shown in Listing 17-32.

Listing 17-32. Adding the MSMutableDictionary for Achievements to the ViewController.h File

```
//
//  ViewController.h
//  Lucky
//

#import <UIKit/UIKit.h>
#import "GameViewController.h"
#import <GameKit/GameKit.h>

@interface ViewController : UIViewController<GKGameCenterControllerDelegate>
```

```
@property (weak, nonatomic) IBOutlet UILabel *welcomeLabel;
@property (strong, nonatomic) GKLocalPlayer *player;
@property (strong, nonatomic) NSMutableDictionary *achievements;

// ...

@end
```

Next, go to ViewController.m and add the bold line shown in Listing 17-33 to the viewDidLoad method.

Listing 17-33. Initializing the Achievements Array in the viewDidLoad Method

```
- (void)viewDidLoad
{
    [super viewDidLoad];

    self.achievements = [[NSMutableDictionary alloc] init];
    self.player = nil;
    [self authenticatePlayer];
}
```

In the setter method of the player property, add the bold lines in Listing 17-34 to initiate the achievements dictionary. This basically removes all achievements when setting a new player and loads the achievements for those players using the loadAchievements helper method, which we'll implement shortly.

Listing 17-34. Modifying the setPlayer Setter Method to Load Achievements

```
- (void)setPlayer:(GKLocalPlayer *)player
{
    if (_player == player)
        return;
    [self.achievements removeAllObjects];

    _player = player;

    NSString *playerName;
    if (_player)
    {
        playerName = _player.alias;
        [self loadAchievements];
    }
    else
    {
        playerName = @"Anonymous Player";
    }
    self.welcomeLabel.text = [NSString stringWithFormat:@"Welcome %@", playerName];
}
```

The loadAchievements helper method loads the achievements for the current player and populates the dictionary, as shown in Listing 17-35.

Listing 17-35.　Implementing the loadAchievements Method

```
- (void)loadAchievements
{
    [GKAchievement loadAchievementsWithCompletionHandler:
    ^(NSArray *achievements, NSError *error)
     {
         if (error == nil)
         {
             for (GKAchievement* achievement in achievements)
                 [self.achievements setObject: achievement
                     forKey: achievement.identifier];
         }
         else
         {
             NSLog(@"Error loading achievements: %@", error);
         }
     }];
}
```

Next, update the `playGameWithLevel:` method to include the achievements in the initializer, as shown in Listing 17-36.

Listing 17-36.　Updating the playGameWithLevel: Method to Include Achievements

```
- (void)playGameWithLevel:(int)level
{
    GameViewController *gameViewController =
    [[GameViewController alloc] initWithLevel:level achievements:self.achievements];
    [self.navigationController pushViewController:gameViewController animated:YES];
}
```

Now initiate the game view controller with the achievements dictionary. First, go to `GameViewController.h` and make the changes shown in Listing 17-37.

Listing 17-37.　Modifying the GameViewController.h File to Accommodate Achievements Caching

```
//
//  GameViewController.h
//  Lucky
//

#import <UIKit/UIKit.h>
#import <GameKit/GameKit.h>

@interface GameViewController : UIViewController<UIAlertViewDelegate>
{
    @private
    int _score;
    int _level;
    NSMutableArray *_selectedButtons;
}
```

```
@property (weak, nonatomic) IBOutlet UILabel *scoreLabel;
@property (weak, nonatomic) IBOutlet UIButton *button1;
@property (weak, nonatomic) IBOutlet UIButton *button2;
@property (weak, nonatomic) IBOutlet UIButton *button3;
@property (weak, nonatomic) IBOutlet UIButton *button4;
@property (strong, nonatomic) NSMutableDictionary *achievements;

- (IBAction)gameButtonSelected:(UIButton *)sender;

- (id)initWithLevel:(int)level achievements:(NSMutableDictionary *)achievements;

@end
```

In GameViewController.m, make the corresponding changes to the initWithLevel: method, as shown in Listing 17-38.

Listing 17-38. Modifying the initWithLevel: Method to Add an Achievements Array

```
- (id)initWithLevel:(int)level achievements:(NSMutableDictionary *)achievements
{
    self = [super initWithNibName:nil bundle:nil];
    if (self)
    {
        _level = level;
        _score = 0;
        _selectedButtons = [[NSMutableArray alloc] initWithCapacity:4];
        self.achievements = achievements;
    }
    return self;
}
```

Next, define a helper method to get the current achievement by fetching it from the cache or create a new GKAchievement object if it doesn't exist, as shown in Listing 17-39.

Listing 17-39. Implementing the getAchievement Method

```
- (GKAchievement *)getAchievement
{
    NSString *achievementID = [self achievementID];
    GKAchievement *achievement = [self.achievements objectForKey:achievementID];
    if (achievement == nil)
    {
        achievement = [[GKAchievement alloc] initWithIdentifier:achievementID];
        [self.achievements setObject:achievement forKey:achievement.identifier];
    }
    return achievement;
}
```

Finally, change the reportAllFourButtonsAchievement method to use the new helper method, as shown in Listing 17-40.

Listing 17-40. Modifying the reportAllFourButtonsAchievementCompleted Method to Account for Cached Achievements

```
- (void)reportAllFourButtonsAchievementCompleted
{
    GKAchievement *achievement = [self getAchievement];
    if (achievement != nil && !achievement.completed)
    {
        achievement.percentComplete = 100;
        achievement.showsCompletionBanner = NO;
        NSArray *achievementArray = [[NSArray alloc] initWithObjects:achievement, nil];

        [GKAchievement reportAchievements:achievementArray withCompletionHandler:^(NSError *error)
        {
            if (error != nil)
            {
                NSLog(@"Error when reporting achievement: %@", error);
            }
            else
            {
                [GKNotificationBanner showBannerWithTitle:@"Achievement Completed"
                                          message:@"You have used all four buttons and
earned 100 points!"
                                          completionHandler:nil];
            }
        }];
    }
}
```

That's it. The app now only reports real progress and therefore does not unnecessarily use up network activity for reports that don't change the state of the Game Center.

Recipe 17-4. Creating a Simple Turn-Based Multiplayer Game

Gaming at its essence is a social activity. While playing against a computer can be fun, playing with or against other humans gives a new dimension to the gaming experience. Game Kit has great support for multiplayer games, both real-time and turn-based. This means two players can play a game and take turns on two different devices with nearly the same speed as if they were playing together on one device.

In this chapter, you'll build a simple turn-based tic-tac-toe multiplayer game that uses Game Center for matchmaking and the low-level network implementation. The Game Center matchmaking tools are helpful because they allow you to invite players to a game without writing a lot of extra code.

As usual when building a Game Center–aware app, start with the basic game functionality before adding any Game Center support.

Building the Tic Tac Toe Game

Create a new single view project called "Tic Tac Toe."

Start by building the basic user interface of the game. Open the Main.storyboard file to start editing the interface. Add a label and nine buttons with backgrounds to the view so it resembles Figure 17-23. For this example, we used a light gray background color. Also, add one more button in the upper-right corner to initiate gameplay.

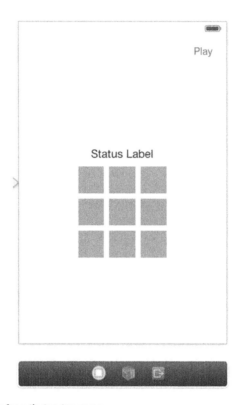

Figure 17-23. A simple user interface for a tic-tac-toe game

Create outlets with the following names for the respective elements:

- statusLabel
- row1Col1Button, row1Col2Button, row1Col3Button
- row2Col1Button, row2Col2Button, row2Col3Button
- row3Col1Button, row3Col2Button, row3Col3Button

Also, create an action with the name selectButton with the parameter type UIButton. Connect all the nine buttons to that action. Create another action for the play button called playGame. Next, go to ViewController.h and add the private instance variable shown in Listing 17-41.

Listing 17-41. The Complete ViewController.h File

```
//
//  ViewController.h
//  Tic Tac Toe
//

#import <UIKit/UIKit.h>

@interface ViewController : UIViewController
{
    @private
    NSString *_currentMark;
}

@property (weak, nonatomic) IBOutlet UILabel *statusLabel;
@property (weak, nonatomic) IBOutlet UIButton *row1Col1Button;
@property (weak, nonatomic) IBOutlet UIButton *row1Col2Button;
@property (weak, nonatomic) IBOutlet UIButton *row1Col3Button;
@property (weak, nonatomic) IBOutlet UIButton *row2Col1Button;
@property (weak, nonatomic) IBOutlet UIButton *row2Col2Button;
@property (weak, nonatomic) IBOutlet UIButton *row2Col3Button;
@property (weak, nonatomic) IBOutlet UIButton *row3Col1Button;
@property (weak, nonatomic) IBOutlet UIButton *row3Col2Button;
@property (weak, nonatomic) IBOutlet UIButton *row3Col3Button;

- (IBAction)selectButton:(UIButton *)sender;
- (IBAction)playGame:(id)sender;

@end
```

Because it's not an essential part of this recipe, we skip the details of the basic game implementation and instead ask that you go to the web page of this book (at www.apress.com), download the file ViewController.m, and add it to your project. However, make sure you go through the code carefully so that you understand how it works before moving on.

If you've added the code correctly, you should be able to run the app now and play a game of Tic Tac Toe against yourself. Figure 17-24 shows an example of a game that's halfway complete.

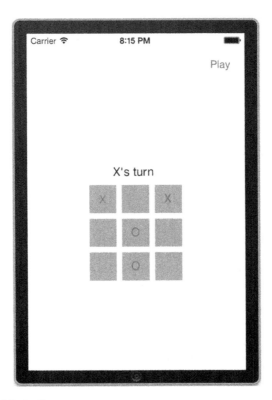

Figure 17-24. *An ongoing game of Tic Tac Toe*

With the basic game functionality in place, you can move on to implement Game Center support. As you know from earlier in this chapter, that starts with registering your app.

Preparing the Game for Game Center

First, you need to enable Game Center from the Capabilities tab and select a provisioning profile as we did in Recipe 17-1.

After you have enabled Game Center, the next step is to register your app with iTunes Connect. Again, refer to Recipe 17-1 for details. To save time, use the following art files from this book's web page for the Large App Icon and iPhone Screenshot files that you must upload as part of the registration.

- Tic Tac Toe Large App Icon.png
- Tic Tac Toe Screenshot.png
- Tic Tac Toe Screenshot (iPhone 5).png

Also, don't forget to enable Game Center (for Single Game) in the Manage Game Center page. Enabling Game Center is all you need to do for the sake of this recipe; there's no need to define any leaderboards or achievements for the Tic Tac Toe game.

After you've registered the app with iTunes Connect, you can start preparing it for Game Center. Go back to Xcode and link the GameKit framework to your project. Then open ViewController.h and add the property declaration to hold a reference to the local player. Your ViewController.h heading file should now look like Listing 17-42.

Listing 17-42. The Complete ViewController.h File

```
//
//  ViewController.h
//  Tic Tac Toe
//

#import <UIKit/UIKit.h>
#import <GameKit/GameKit.h>

@interface ViewController : UIViewController
{
@private
    NSString *_currentMark;
}

@property (weak, nonatomic) IBOutlet UILabel *statusLabel;
@property (weak, nonatomic) IBOutlet UIButton *row1Col1Button;
@property (weak, nonatomic) IBOutlet UIButton *row1Col2Button;
@property (weak, nonatomic) IBOutlet UIButton *row1Col3Button;
@property (weak, nonatomic) IBOutlet UIButton *row2Col1Button;
@property (weak, nonatomic) IBOutlet UIButton *row2Col2Button;
@property (weak, nonatomic) IBOutlet UIButton *row2Col3Button;
@property (weak, nonatomic) IBOutlet UIButton *row3Col1Button;
@property (weak, nonatomic) IBOutlet UIButton *row3Col2Button;
@property (weak, nonatomic) IBOutlet UIButton *row3Col3Button;

@property (strong, nonatomic) GKLocalPlayer *localPlayer;

- (IBAction)selectButton:(UIButton *)sender;

@end
```

The method to authenticate the local player is identical to what you did in Recipe 17-1. Go to ViewController.m and add the authenticateLocalPlayer helper method shown in Listing 17-43.

Listing 17-43. Implementing the authenticateLocalPlayer Method

```
- (void)authenticateLocalPlayer
{
    __weak GKLocalPlayer *localPlayer = [GKLocalPlayer localPlayer];
    localPlayer.authenticateHandler =
    ^(UIViewController *authenticateViewController, NSError *error)
    {
        if (authenticateViewController != nil)
        {
            [self presentViewController:authenticateViewController animated:YES
                completion:nil];
        }
```

```
        else if (localPlayer.isAuthenticated)
        {
            self.localPlayer = localPlayer;
        }
        else
        {
            // Disable Game Center
            self.localPlayer = nil;
        }
    };
}
```

As in Recipe 17-1, try to authenticate the local player directly on app launch. Add the bold line in Listing 17-44 to the viewDidLoad method.

Listing 17-44. Adding an authenticateLocalPlayer Method Call to the viewDidLoad Method

```
- (void)viewDidLoad
{
    [super viewDidLoad];

    [self enableSquareButtons:NO];
    self.statusLabel.text = @"Press Play to start a game";
    [self authenticateLocalPlayer];
}
```

Finally, add a couple of elements to the user interface for displaying the two Game Center players currently participating in the match. Add four labels and arrange them so that the view controller user interface resembles Figure 17-25. Note that "Playing X:" and "<Player 1 Label>" as well as "Playing O:" and "<Player 2 Label>" are separate labels.

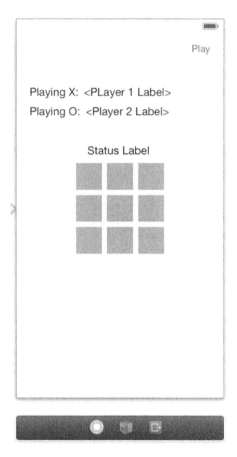

Figure 17-25. *A simple Tic Tac Toe user interface with labels showing the participating players*

Create outlets called player1Label and player2Label for the corresponding labels.

Now that you have the basic Game Center authentication in place, you can implement the next step, which is the matchmaking feature.

Implementing Matchmaking

For this recipe, you use the standard view controller provided by the GameKit framework to allow the user to find other players to play your Tic Tac Toe game with and to keep track of the games the player is currently involved in. Using the standard view controller saves you a lot of trouble implementing these matchmaking features.

Specifically, you will use the GKTurnBasedMatchmakerViewController to handle the matchmaking. Start by making the main view controller conform to the GKTurnBasedMatchmakerViewControllerDelegate protocol. You also need to hold a reference to a GKTurnBasedMatch object as well as two GKPlayer instances. So, go to ViewController.h and add the bold lines shown in Listing 17-45.

Listing 17-45. Updating ViewController.h to Include New Properties

```
//
//  ViewController.h
//  Tic Tac Toe
//

// ...

@interface ViewController : UIViewController<GKTurnBasedMatchmakerViewControllerDelegate>

// ...

@property (strong, nonatomic) GKLocalPlayer *localPlayer;
@property (strong, nonatomic) GKTurnBasedMatch *match;
@property (strong, nonatomic) GKPlayer *player1;
@property (strong, nonatomic) GKPlayer *player2;

- (IBAction)selectButton:(UIButton *)sender;

@end
```

Now, return to ViewController.m and replace the current implementation of the playGame: action method with the code shown in Listing 17-46. This code checks whether the user has signed in with Game Center. If not, an error message is displayed; otherwise, the method proceeds to create a match request and present a matchmaker view controller.

Listing 17-46. Replacing the Code in the playGame: Action Method

```
- (void)playGame:(id)sender
{
    if (self.localPlayer.isAuthenticated)
    {
        GKMatchRequest *request = [[GKMatchRequest alloc] init];
        request.minPlayers = 2;
        request.maxPlayers = 2;

        GKTurnBasedMatchmakerViewController *matchMakerViewController =
            [[GKTurnBasedMatchmakerViewController alloc] initWithMatchRequest:request];
        matchMakerViewController.turnBasedMatchmakerDelegate = self;
        [self presentViewController:matchMakerViewController animated:YES
            completion:nil];
    }
    else
    {
        UIAlertView *notLoggedInAlert = [[UIAlertView alloc] initWithTitle:@"Error"
            message:@"You must be logged into Game Center to play this game!"
            delegate:nil cancelButtonTitle:@"Dismiss" otherButtonTitles:nil];
        [notLoggedInAlert show];
    }
}
```

The matchmaker view controller requires you to implement a few delegate methods to handle the result of the user's decisions. The first is if the user cancels the dialog box, in which case you should simply dismiss the matchmaker view controller. This is shown in Listing 17-47.

Listing 17-47. Implementing the turnBasedMatchmakerViewControllerWasCancelled: Delegate Method

```
- (void)turnBasedMatchmakerViewControllerWasCancelled:
(GKTurnBasedMatchmakerViewController *)viewController
{
    [self dismissViewControllerAnimated:YES completion:nil];
}
```

The next scenario is if the view controller fails for some reason. Apart from dismissing the view, you also log the error, as shown in Listing 17-48.

Listing 17-48. Implementing the turnBasedMatchmakerViewController:didFailWithError: Method

```
- (void)turnBasedMatchmakerViewController:
(GKTurnBasedMatchmakerViewController *)viewController didFailWithError:(NSError *)error
{
    [self dismissViewControllerAnimated:YES completion:nil];
    NSLog(@"Error while matchmaking: %@", error);
}
```

Finally, if the matchmaker produced a match, the viewController:didFindMatch: delegate method is invoked with a GKTurnBasedMatch object. For now, simply store a reference to the match object, as shown in Listing 17-49.

Listing 17-49. Implementing the turnBasedMatchmakerViewController:didFindMatch: Delegate Method

```
- (void)turnBasedMatchmakerViewController:
(GKTurnBasedMatchmakerViewController *)viewController didFindMatch:(GKTurnBasedMatch *)match
{
    [self dismissViewControllerAnimated:YES completion:nil];

    self.match = match;
}
```

Receiving the match object from Game Center is a key event when implementing a turn-based game. At that point, the app should load the game data and set up the user interface to reflect the current state of the game.

To handle these things, add a custom setter method for the match property, as shown in Listing 17-50. It loads the participating players and the match data using two currently nonexistent helper methods that you'll implement soon.

Listing 17-50. Implementing the setMatch Custom Setter Method

```
- (void)setMatch:(GKTurnBasedMatch *)match
{
    _match = match;

    [self loadPlayers];
    [self loadMatchData];
}
```

Let's start with the loadPlayers method. Basically, you need to identify the players participating in the match and load information about them from the Game Center. The match object contains an array of GKTurnBasedParticipant objects, which you can use to get the playerIDs you need to load the information. Because you know that a game of Tic Tac Toe contains exactly two players, which is what you defined in the matchmaking request earlier, you can extract the participant objects, as shown in Listing 17-51.

Listing 17-51. Implementing the partial loadPlayers Helper Method

```
- (void)loadPlayers
{
    GKTurnBasedParticipant *participant1 = [self.match.participants objectAtIndex:0];
    GKTurnBasedParticipant *participant2 = [self.match.participants objectAtIndex:1];

    // TODO: Load player info
}
```

> **Note**   The participants array of the match object is arranged in the order of how the players take turns.
> You can therefore assume that the first object is player 1 and the second object is player 2 of the game.

A turn-based match can start without all seats being filled. This way, a player who starts a new match can make the first move without having to wait for the other player. Because of this, the playerID of the opponent's participant object might be nil at this point. For that reason, you need to design your code with care so that you don't send undefined playerIDs to the loadPlayersForId entifiers:withCompletionHandler: method. Add the bold code in Listing 17-52 to the loadPlayers method to handle that.

Listing 17-52. Adding Code to Account for Missing Players

```
- (void)loadPlayers
{
    GKTurnBasedParticipant *participant1 = [self.match.participants objectAtIndex:0];
    GKTurnBasedParticipant *participant2 = [self.match.participants objectAtIndex:1];

    NSMutableArray *playerIDs = [[NSMutableArray alloc] initWithCapacity:2];
    if (participant1.playerID &&
        ![participant1.playerID isEqualToString:self.player1.playerID])
```

```
    {
        [playerIDs addObject:participant1.playerID];
    }
    if (participant2.playerID &&
        ![participant2.playerID isEqualToString:self.player2.playerID])
    {
        [playerIDs addObject:participant2.playerID];
    }

    if (playerIDs.count == 0)
        return; // No players to load

    [GKPlayer loadPlayersForIdentifiers:playerIDs withCompletionHandler:
     ^(NSArray *players, NSError *error)
     {
         // TODO: Handle Result
     }];
}
```

Finally, when the players' objects have been loaded, you need to figure out which is which by checking their playerIDs. Listing 17-53 shows the entire loadPlayers method with recent changes in bold.

Listing 17-53. The Complete loadPlayers Method Implementation

```
- (void)loadPlayers
{
    GKTurnBasedParticipant *participant1 = [self.match.participants objectAtIndex:0];
    GKTurnBasedParticipant *participant2 = [self.match.participants objectAtIndex:1];

    NSMutableArray *playerIDs = [[NSMutableArray alloc] initWithCapacity:2];
    if (participant1.playerID && ![participant1.playerID isEqualToString:self.player1.playerID])
    {
        [playerIDs addObject:participant1.playerID];
    }
    if (participant2.playerID  && ![participant2.playerID isEqualToString:self.player2.playerID])
    {
        [playerIDs addObject:participant2.playerID];
    }

    if (playerIDs.count == 0)
        return; // No players to load

    [GKPlayer loadPlayersForIdentifiers:playerIDs withCompletionHandler:^(NSArray *players,
NSError *error)
    {
        if (players)
        {
            GKPlayer *player1;
            GKPlayer *player2;
            for (GKPlayer *player in players)
```

```
            {
                if ([player.playerID isEqualToString:participant1.playerID])
                {
                    player1 = player;
                }
                else if ([player.playerID isEqualToString:participant2.playerID])
                {
                    player2 = player;
                }
            }
            dispatch_async(dispatch_get_main_queue(),^{
                self.player1 = player1;
                self.player2 = player2;
            });
        }
        if (error)
        {
            NSLog(@"Error loading players: %@", error);
        }
    }];
}
```

The reason you wrap the assigning of the player1 and player2 properties within a dispatch_async call in the preceding code is because these assignments trigger an update of the user interface, so that piece of code needs to run on the main thread.

When the player1 and player2 properties are set, the respective label should be updated. To accomplish this, add the custom setter methods shown in Listing 17-54.

Listing 17-54. Implementing Custom Setter Methods for player1 and player2

```
- (void)setPlayer1:(GKPlayer *)player1
{
    _player1 = player1;
    if (_player1)
    {
        self.player1Label.text = _player1.displayName;
    }
    else
    {
        self.player1Label.text = @"<vacant>";
    }
}

- (void)setPlayer2:(GKPlayer *)player2
{
    _player2 = player2;
    if (_player2)
    {
        self.player2Label.text = _player2.displayName;
    }
```

```
    else
    {
        self.player2Label.text = @"<vacant>";
    }
}
```

Now, to initiate the player labels on app launch, you simply need to set the `player1` and `player2` properties to `nil` in `viewDidLoad`, as shown in Listing 17-55.

Listing 17-55. Setting the Players to nil to Initialize Them in the viewDidLoad Method

```
- (void)viewDidLoad
{
    [super viewDidLoad];

    [self enableSquareButtons:NO];

    self.statusLabel.text = @"Press Play to start a game";

    self.player1 = nil;
    self.player2 = nil;
    [self authenticateLocalPlayer];
}
```

Next, you'll turn your focus to the `loadMatchData` helper method. But before you start implementing that, let's add a couple of helper methods to encode and decode such data.

Encoding and Decoding Match Data

It's completely up to you how to choose to encode and decode the data you need to store the state of the game in Game Center. The only restrictions are that it is of type `NSData` and that you keep the size of the data within 64 KB. For the sake of this recipe, keep it simple and store the current state in a simple array, which you then transform into an `NSData` object using the `NSKeyedArchiver` class. Listing 17-56 shows the implementation.

Listing 17-56. Implementing the encodeMatchData Method

```
- (NSData *)encodeMatchData
{
    NSArray *stateArray = @[@1 /* version */,
    self.row1Col1Button.currentTitle, self.row1Col2Button.currentTitle,
        self.row1Col3Button.currentTitle,
    self.row2Col1Button.currentTitle, self.row2Col2Button.currentTitle,
        self.row2Col3Button.currentTitle,
    self.row3Col1Button.currentTitle, self.row3Col2Button.currentTitle,
        self.row3Col3Button.currentTitle
    ];
    return [NSKeyedArchiver archivedDataWithRootObject:stateArray];
}
```

It's generally a good idea to store a version number with the data in case you need to change the storage format in future upgrades of your app. This is why we added a number (1) as the first object of the array.

The corresponding decode helper method does the reverse and extracts the current state from the provided NSData object, as shown in Listing 17-57.

Listing 17-57. Implementing the decodeMatchData Method

```
- (void)decodeMatchData:(NSData *)matchData
{
    NSArray *stateArray = [NSKeyedUnarchiver unarchiveObjectWithData:matchData];

    [self.row1Col1Button setTitle:[stateArray objectAtIndex:1]
        forState:UIControlStateNormal];
    [self.row1Col2Button setTitle:[stateArray objectAtIndex:2]
        forState:UIControlStateNormal];
    [self.row1Col3Button setTitle:[stateArray objectAtIndex:3]
        forState:UIControlStateNormal];
    [self.row2Col1Button setTitle:[stateArray objectAtIndex:4]
        forState:UIControlStateNormal];
    [self.row2Col2Button setTitle:[stateArray objectAtIndex:5]
        forState:UIControlStateNormal];
    [self.row2Col3Button setTitle:[stateArray objectAtIndex:6]
        forState:UIControlStateNormal];
    [self.row3Col1Button setTitle:[stateArray objectAtIndex:7]
        forState:UIControlStateNormal];
    [self.row3Col2Button setTitle:[stateArray objectAtIndex:8]
        forState:UIControlStateNormal];
    [self.row3Col3Button setTitle:[stateArray objectAtIndex:9]
        forState:UIControlStateNormal];
}
```

The loadMatchData method shown in Listing 17-58 retrieves the stored data from Game Center and decodes it using the decodeMatchData method you just added. However, if the match contains no data yet, the method will instead reset the user interface to set the state for a new game.

Listing 17-58. Implementing the loadMatchData Method

```
- (void)loadMatchData
{
    [_match loadMatchDataWithCompletionHandler:^(NSData *matchData, NSError *error)
    {
        dispatch_async(dispatch_get_main_queue(),^{
            if (matchData.length > 0)
            {
                [self decodeMatchData:matchData];
            }
            else
            {
                [self resetButtonTitles];
            }
```

```
            NSString *currentMark;
            if ([self localPlayerIsCurrentPlayer])
            {
                [self enableSquareButtons:YES];
                currentMark = [self localPlayerMark];
            }
            else
            {
                [self enableSquareButtons:NO];
                currentMark = [self opponentMark];
            }
            self.statusLabel.text =
                [NSString stringWithFormat:@"%@'s turn", currentMark];
        });
    }];
}
```

The code in Listing 17-58 makes use of three helper methods that you've not yet defined. The localPlayerIsCurrentPlayer method shown in Listing 17-59 checks the currentParticipant property of the match object and compares it with the identity of the local player.

Listing 17-59. Implementing the localPlayerIsCurrentPlayer Method

```
- (BOOL)localPlayerIsCurrentPlayer
{
    return [self.localPlayer.playerID
        isEqualToString:self.match.currentParticipant.playerID];
}
```

The localPlayerMark method shown in Listing 17-60 returns *X* or *O* depending on whether the local player is player 1 or player 2.

Listing 17-60. Implementing the localPlayerMark Method

```
- (NSString *)localPlayerMark
{
    if ([self.localPlayer.playerID isEqualToString:self.player1.playerID])
    {
        return @"X";
    }
    else
    {
        return @"O";
    }
}
```

The opponentMark shown in Listing 17-61 simply returns the opposite of localPlayerMark.

Listing 17-61. Implementing the opponentMark Method

```
- (NSString *)opponentMark
{
    if ([[self localPlayerMark] isEqualToString:@"X"])
    {
        return @"O";
    }
    else
    {
        return @"X";
    }
}
```

Now that you have code to load match data all set up, let's look at the methods where your app saves the data. One place where you're expected to store an updated state to Game Center is when the local player has made a move and hands over the turn to the opponent.

However, before we update the advanceTurn method, let's make a necessary change to the selectButton: action method. You no longer rely on the _currentMark instance variable when setting the mark of a selected square button. In fact, when you've finished implementing the Game Center support, you can completely remove the _currentMark instance variable. Instead, you can safely assume that it's the local player who is making the moves (which is right because the opponent makes her moves remotely from another instance of the app). So, make the change shown in Listing 17-62 to the existing code.

Listing 17-62. Updating the selectbutton and Replacing the _currentMark Instance

```
- (IBAction)selectButton:(UIButton *)sender
{
    if (sender.currentTitle.length != 0)
    {
        UIAlertView *squareOccupiedAlert =
            [[UIAlertView alloc] initWithTitle:@"Invalid Move"
                message:@"You can only pick empty squares" delegate:nil
                cancelButtonTitle:@"OK" otherButtonTitles:nil];
        [squareOccupiedAlert show];
        return;
    }

    [sender setTitle:[self localPlayerMark] forState:UIControlStateNormal];
    [self checkCurrentState];
}
```

Make sure you also remove _currentMark from both the gameEndedWithWinner and gameEndedInTie methods.

Now the new implementation of the advanceTurn method saves the current state to Game Center, disables the square buttons, and hands over the turn to the opponent. Listing 17-63 shows the new code doing this.

Listing 17-63. Replacing the Code in the advanceTurn Method

```
- (void)advanceTurn
{
    [self enableSquareButtons:NO];
    self.statusLabel.text =
        [NSString stringWithFormat:@"%@'s turn", [self opponentMark]];
    self.match.message = self.statusLabel.text;
    NSData *matchData = [self encodeMatchData];
    [self.match endTurnWithNextParticipants:@[[self opponentParticipant]]
        turnTimeout:GKTurnTimeoutDefault matchData:matchData completionHandler:
    ^(NSError *error)
    {
        if (error)
        {
            NSLog(@"Error advancing turn: %@", error);
        }
    }];
}
```

The code in Listing 17-63 hands over the turn using a helper method to identify the opponent's participant object. Listing 17-64 shows the implementation for that method.

Listing 17-64. Implementing the opponentParticipant Method

```
- (GKTurnBasedParticipant *)opponentParticipant
{
    GKTurnBasedParticipant *candidate = [self.match.participants objectAtIndex:0];
    if ([self.localPlayer.playerID isEqualToString:candidate.playerID])
    {
        return [self.match.participants objectAtIndex:1];
    }
    else
    {
        return candidate;
    }
}
```

Another place you should store the game state is when the game has ended. There are two reasons why this is necessary. First, this is how the opponent will know the final state of the game. Second, the players can open a game that's ended to view the final state again.

In addition to saving the final state, when a game ends, your app needs to set the matchOutcome property of the participant objects. To do these things, make the changes shown in Listing 17-65 to the gameEndedWithWinner: method.

Listing 17-65. Setting the matchOutcome Property

```
- (void)gameEndedWithWinner:(NSString *)mark
{
    NSString *message = [NSString stringWithFormat:@"%@ won!", mark];
    UIAlertView *gameOverAlert = [[UIAlertView alloc] initWithTitle:@"Game Over"
```

```
        message:message delegate:nil cancelButtonTitle:@"OK" otherButtonTitles:nil];
    [gameOverAlert show];

    self.statusLabel.text = message;
    self.match.message = self.statusLabel.text;

    GKTurnBasedParticipant *participant1 = [self.match.participants objectAtIndex:0];
    GKTurnBasedParticipant *participant2 = [self.match.participants objectAtIndex:1];
    participant1.matchOutcome = GKTurnBasedMatchOutcomeTied;
    participant2.matchOutcome = GKTurnBasedMatchOutcomeTied;

    if ([participant1.playerID isEqualToString:self.localPlayer.playerID])
    {
        participant1.matchOutcome = GKTurnBasedMatchOutcomeWon;
        participant2.matchOutcome = GKTurnBasedMatchOutcomeLost;
    }
    else
    {
        participant2.matchOutcome = GKTurnBasedMatchOutcomeWon;
        participant1.matchOutcome = GKTurnBasedMatchOutcomeLost;
    }

    NSData *matchData = [self encodeMatchData];
    [self.match endMatchInTurnWithMatchData:matchData completionHandler:
    ^(NSError *error)
    {
        if (error)
        {
            NSLog(@"Error ending match: %@", error);
        }
        //
    }];

    [self enableSquareButtons:NO];
}
```

The corresponding change to the gameEndedInTie method is shown in Listing 17-66.

Listing 17-66. Updating the gameEndedInTie Method

```
- (void)gameEndedInTie
{
    NSString *message = @"Game ended in a tie!";
    UIAlertView *gameOverAlert = [[UIAlertView alloc] initWithTitle:@"Game Over"
        message:message delegate:nil cancelButtonTitle:@"OK" otherButtonTitles:nil];
    [gameOverAlert show];

    self.statusLabel.text = message;
    self.match.message = self.statusLabel.text;
    NSData *matchData = [self encodeMatchData];
    GKTurnBasedParticipant *participant1 = [self.match.participants objectAtIndex:0];
    GKTurnBasedParticipant *participant2 = [self.match.participants objectAtIndex:1];
```

```
        participant1.matchOutcome = GKTurnBasedMatchOutcomeTied;
        participant2.matchOutcome = GKTurnBasedMatchOutcomeTied;
        [self.match endMatchInTurnWithMatchData:matchData completionHandler:
        ^(NSError *error)
        {
            if (error)
            {
                NSLog(@"Error ending match: %@", error);
            }
            //
        }];
        [self enableSquareButtons:NO];
}
```

If the opponent quits the game prematurely, which can be done from the matchmaking view controller, the app needs to respond to this and declare the local player as the winner. Add the delegate method to deal with that scenario, as shown in Listing 17-67.

Listing 17-67. Implementing the turnBasedMatchmakerViewController:playerQuitForMatch: Delegate Method

```
- (void)turnBasedMatchmakerViewController:(GKTurnBasedMatchmakerViewController *)viewController
playerQuitForMatch:(GKTurnBasedMatch *)match
{
    if ([self.match.matchID isEqualToString:match.matchID])
    {
        [self gameEndedWithWinner:[self localPlayerMark]];
    }
}
```

You're nearly finished with this rather extensive recipe. The only task that's left is to handle the events triggered by the actions of the opponent.

Handling Turn-Based Events

To respond to the actions from the remote players, your app needs to assign a turn-based event handler. The first step is to conform to the GKLocalPlayerListener protocol. Go to ViewController.h and add it to the list of protocols, as shown in Listing 17-68.

Listing 17-68. Declaring the GKLocalPlayerListener Protocol in the ViewController.h File

```
//
//  ViewController.h
//  Testing Turn-Based Game
//

// ...
```

```
@interface ViewController : UIViewController<GKTurnBasedMatchmakerViewControllerDelegate,
    GKLocalPlayerListener>

// ...

@end
```

A good time to assign the event handler is right after the local player has been authenticated. Therefore, add the following custom setter for the localPlayer property, as shown in Listing 17-69.

Listing 17-69.   Creating a custom localPlayer property setter

```
- (void)setLocalPlayer:(GKLocalPlayer *)localPlayer
{
    _localPlayer = localPlayer;
    if (_localPlayer)
    {
[[GKLocalPlayer localPlayer] registerListener:self];
    }
    else
    {
[[GKLocalPlayer localPlayer] unregisterListener:self];
    }
}
```

There are two turn-based events that you need to handle. The first is when the turn has returned to the local player. Thanks to the code we've written, the only thing you need to do is assign the match property. This sets up the game with the new state and with the local player's turn to act. Implement this delegate method, as shown in Listing 17-70.

Listing 17-70.   Implementing the player:receivedTurnEventForMatch:didBecomeActive: Method

```
-(void)player:(GKPlayer *)player receivedTurnEventForMatch:(GKTurnBasedMatch *)match
didBecomeActive:(BOOL)didBecomeActive
{

    self.match = match;

}
```

The second event is when a match has ended remotely. In this case, you need to load the match data using your decodeMatchData: helper method. This, too, puts the game in a correct state, as shown in Listing 17-71.

Listing 17-71.   Implementing the handleMatchEnded: Delegate Method

```
- (void)handleMatchEnded:(GKTurnBasedMatch *)match
{
    if ([self.match.matchID isEqualToString:match.matchID])
    {
        [self.match loadMatchDataWithCompletionHandler:
         ^(NSData *matchData, NSError *error)
```

```
        {
            dispatch_async(dispatch_get_main_queue(),^{
                if (matchData.length > 0)
                {
                    [self decodeMatchData:matchData];
                }
                self.statusLabel.text = match.message;
            });
        }];
    }
}
```

You're done! To test this app, you need two or more Game Center accounts. It's recommended that you don't use your own account when testing Game Center features, so be sure to register a couple of test accounts.

You also need two devices to run the app simultaneously and get the real multiplayer feeling. You can, however, test it in the iOS simulator, but then you need to sign out the current player and sign in the opponent between the moves.

Figure 17-26 shows the turn-based matchmaking view controller and an ongoing multiplayer game of Tic Tac Toe. If you are using the simulator, you might have issues receiving turns if your firewall is enabled.

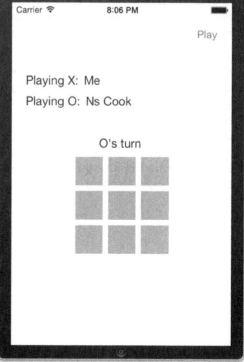

Figure 17-26. *A Game Center turn-based game of Tic Tac Toe*

> **Note**   At the time of this writing, the Game Center sandbox would not consistently notify the app that the other player had taken a turn. To fix this problem, you can create a button, which calls the `loadMatchData` method we already created. This will pull the match data again, and should update the current game state.
>
> ```
> (IBAction)reloadMatch:(id)sender
> {
>     [self loadMatchData];
> }
> ```

Although this recipe was quite long, there is still more to learn with multiplayer, turn-based games. You also have tools available to you that will allow more than two players and even allow you to take turns out of sequence. For more information on GameKit, see the Game Center programming guide at `https://developer.apple.com/library/ios/documentation/NetworkingInternet/Conceptual/GameKit_Guide/Introduction/Introduction.html`.

Summary

In this chapter, you've learned how to extend your game with Game Center and GameKit. You can include high scores in your games to encourage competition among players and establish bragging rights. You also can implement achievements that give your players a feeling of accomplishment during long levels or even easily provide mini-games within a game. Finally, you implemented basic multiplayer functionality in the form of a turn-based game to encourage even more social gameplay against live opponents.

Developing iOS applications is a multifarious process, a combination of visual design and programmatic functionality that requires a versatile skill set as well as significant dedication. Thankfully, Apple provides an excellent development tool set and programming language to work with, both of which are constantly updated and improved upon. With such a flexible language, tasks ranging from organizing massive data stores to complex web requests to image filtering can be simplified, designed, and implemented for some of the most widely used and powerful devices of our generation. Whether you use this book as a simple reference or a full guide, we hope you will use these recipes to build stronger applications to help improve and contribute to the world of iOS technology.

Index

I

J, K

▪ V, W, X, Y, Z

Get the eBook for only $10!

Now you can take the weightless companion with you anywhere, anytime. Your purchase of this book entitles you to 3 electronic versions for only $10.

This Apress title will prove so indispensible that you'll want to carry it with you everywhere, which is why we are offering the eBook in 3 formats for only $10 if you have already purchased the print book.

Convenient and fully searchable, the PDF version enables you to easily find and copy code—or perform examples by quickly toggling between instructions and applications. The MOBI format is ideal for your Kindle, while the ePUB can be utilized on a variety of mobile devices.

Go to www.apress.com/promo/tendollars to purchase your companion eBook.

CPSIA information can be obtained at www.ICGtesting.com
Printed in the USA
LVOW02s2050140314

377473LV00006B/117/P

9 781430 259596